LAWS AND RULES IN INDO-EUROPEAN

LAWS AND RULES IN INDO-EUROPEAN

Edited by
Philomen Probert and
Andreas Willi

CLARENDON · PRESS

OXFORD
UNIVERSITY PRESS

Great Clarendon Street, Oxford OX2 6DP

Oxford University Press is a department of the University of Oxford.
It furthers the University's objective of excellence in research, scholarship,
and education by publishing worldwide in

Oxford New York

Auckland Cape Town Dar es Salaam Hong Kong Karachi
Kuala Lumpur Madrid Melbourne Mexico City Nairobi
New Delhi Shanghai Taipei Toronto

With offices in

Argentina Austria Brazil Chile Czech Republic France Greece
Guatemala Hungary Italy Japan Poland Portugal Singapore
South Korea Switzerland Thailand Turkey Ukraine Vietnam

Oxford is a registered trade mark of Oxford University Press
in the UK and in certain other countries

Published in the United States
by Oxford University Press Inc., New York

First published 2012

British Library Cataloguing in Publication Data
Data available

Library of Congress Cataloging in Publication Data
Data available

Typeset by SPI Publisher Services, India
Printed on acid-free paper

ISBN 978–0–19–960992–5

In honour of John Penney

Contents

Preface x
Acknowledgements xii
Notes on contributors xiii
Abbreviations xvi
List of Figures xxi
List of Tables xxii

1. Introduction 1
Philomen Probert and Andreas Willi

Part I: Linguistic 'laws' in pre-modern thought

2. *Fern do frestol na .u. consaine*: perceptions of sound laws, sound change, and linguistic borrowing among the medieval Irish 17
Paul Russell

Part II: Rules of language change and linguistic methodology

3. Cladistic principles and linguistic reality: the case of West Germanic 33
Don Ringe

4. Older Runic evidence for North-West Germanic *a*-umlaut of *u* (and 'the converse of Polivanov's Law') 43
Patrick Stiles

5. A law unto themselves? An acoustic phonetic study of 'tonal' consonants in British Panjabi 61
Jane Stuart-Smith and Mario Cortina-Borja

6. Kuryłowicz's first 'law of analogy' and the development of passive periphrases in Latin 83
Wolfgang de Melo

7. Phonetic laws, language diffusion, and drift: the loss of sibilants in the Greek dialects of the first millennium BC 102
Anna Morpurgo Davies

Part III: Segmental sound laws: new proposals and reassessments

8. A rule of deaspiration in ancient Greek 125
Paul Elbourne

9. Regular sound change and word-initial */i̯/- in Armenian 134
Daniel Kölligan

10. Schrijver's rules for British and Proto-Celtic *-*ou̯*- and *-*uu̯*- before a vowel 147
Nicholas Zair

Part IV: Origins and evolutions

11. Origins of the Greek law of limitation 163
Philomen Probert

12. Re-examining Lindeman's Law 182
Peter Barber

13. Exon's Law and the Latin syncopes 205
Ranjan Sen

Part V: Systemic consequences

14. Brugmann's Law: the problem of Indo-Iranian thematic nouns and adjectives 229
Elizabeth Tucker

15. Kiparsky's Rule, thematic nasal presents, and athematic *verba vocalia* in Greek 260
Andreas Willi

Part VI: Synchronic laws and rules in syntax and sociolinguistics

16. *praetor urbanus – urbanus praetor*: some aspects of attributive adjective placement in Latin 279
David Langslow

Preface

Laws are a matter of great concern to the comparative linguist. To the Indo-Europeanist their significance is even twofold. Firstly, some of the earliest texts in a number of Indo-European languages—including, in fact, some that may be the earliest extant texts of the language family as a whole—are legal in nature: starting from the Hittites' worries over knocked-out teeth and merchants killed in Luwiya, and featuring other highlights such as the Old Latin *lex sacra* on the Forum cippus (aptly numbered 1 in *CIL* 1^2, despite not being the very oldest inscription in Latin), the constitutional and inheritance laws of Dreros and Gortyn in archaic Crete, the eighth-century *Críth Gablách* which lays down the divisions of rank in medieval Ireland, or the Old Icelandic *Grágás* corpus originating with the *alþingi*'s decision of AD 1117 to collect the new country's laws in a book, our field is literally strewn with relevant material, a source of equal joy and puzzlement to those who try to understand it.

Secondly, whatever contribution Indo-European linguistics has to offer to the endeavour of illuminating these and other ancient texts—by dissecting obscure forms, untangling syntactic relationships, or explaining fundamental meanings—it would be of little if any value if it were not rooted in the recognition of a rather different kind of laws: the 'laws' (or rules, or principles) followed by language in its natural evolution over time. It is this second type of 'Indo-European laws' that provides the thematic thread through the contributions to the present volume.

They, and the volume itself, are however dedicated to a man whose interests and competences easily encompass both, the 'philological' and 'historical' as much as the 'linguistic' side of Indo-European. John's publications bear witness to this, ranging from ancient anthropology (Penney 1988*a*) and the history of Mediterranean languages and writing systems (Penney 1988*b*, 2009, 2006) via Latin syntax and stylistics (Penney 1999, 2005) to Sabellic pronouns, Old Irish verbs, and Tocharian historical grammar (Penney 2002 1977 1976/7, 1989, 2004); but those who know John will also know that he, a modern-day Socrates, usually prefers the living word of lectures, seminars, and tutorials as a means to communicate, and pass on, his love for the subject.

Born in 1945 and educated at Radley College, John read Classics at Oxford from 1963 to 1967, followed by an MA also in Classics at Pennsylvania (1969);

he then took a Diploma in Comparative Philology back in Oxford (1971), where he completed his doctoral thesis on Greek and Indo-European ablaut in 1977. Five years earlier, in 1972, he had already become a University Lecturer in Classical Philology at Oxford, the position from which he now retires after 40 years that saw many changes, but none in his commitment to his students and the wider academic community. During this time, all the contributors to this volume, and generations of students and colleagues with them, have been impressed and inspired by John's breadth of knowledge, his inquisitiveness, and his critical acumen, which, thanks to their natural union with *elegantia* and *urbanitas*, never intimidates, but always challenges. There is no better way of testing a novel idea than presenting it to John: he will at once see its potentials and shortcomings, know if someone had it before, and point out where it may lead. Exceptionally, though naturally, little of what is printed on the following pages has benefitted from such advice before becoming ἀμετακίνητον. In gratitude we put it before John now, acknowledging him as a true incarnation of the highest non-royal grade in *Críth Gablách*: may he remain for years to come our *aire forgill*, or 'nobleman of conclusive testimony'.

Acknowledgements

The editors would like to thank not only all the contributors for the efficiency with which they supported the editorial process, and in particular Anna Morpurgo Davies for much valuable advice given at various stages, but also the Linguistics editor of Oxford University Press, John Davey, for the interest he personally took in the project; John Lowe and Alessandro Vatri, for generously taking on the preparation of subject index and word index respectively; Anthony Mercer, for his good-humoured and meticulous copy-editing; Lesley Rhodes, for help with proofreading; and Jenny Lunsford, for making sure that everything turned into a book in the end. They are also grateful for financial support received, in the form of a lecturing buy-out, from the John Fell Oxford University Press Research Fund.

Notes on contributors

Peter Barber studied Classics and Comparative Philology at Oxford, where he is now a Research Fellow at Wolfson College. His interests include Indo-European, Greek, and Indo-Iranian phonology, Greek verbal semantics, and contemporary syntactic theory. A book based on his dissertation 'Evidence for Sievers' Law in ancient Greek' will be published by Oxford University Press. His current research is on analogy in ancient Greek.

Mario Cortina-Borja is a Senior Lecturer in Statistics at the UCL Institute of Child Health. His research interests include infectious disease epidemiology, seasonality, epistasis, record linkage, and discrete probability distributions. In linguistics, he has published papers on Uto-Aztecan and Indo-European languages, stylometrics, and the Generalized Hermite and Gegenbauer probability distributions.

Wolfgang de Melo is Professor of Latin Linguistics at Ghent University. He was educated in Eichstätt, Oxford, and London; in Oxford, both his M.Phil. and D.Phil. were supervised by John Penney. He is the author of *The early Latin verb system* (2007) and is currently editing Plautus for the Loeb Classical Library.

Eleanor Dickey is Associate Professor of Classics at the University of Exeter. Her publications include *Greek forms of address* (1996), *Latin forms of address* (2002), and *Ancient Greek scholarship* (2007). Her research concerns the history and development of the Latin and Greek languages, language teaching and the study of language in antiquity, sociolinguistics, and the interaction and influence between Latin and Greek.

Paul Elbourne is Reader in Semantics at Queen Mary, University of London. He is the author of *Situations and individuals* (2005) and various articles in linguistics and philosophy journals.

Daniel Kölligan is Akademischer Rat in the Department of Linguistics at the University of Cologne. He studied Comparative Philology, Philosophy, and Greek Philology at Cologne, and wrote a doctoral thesis on verbal defectivity and suppletion in Greek (*Suppletion und Defektivität im griechischen Verbum*, 2007). From 2005 to 2008 he was research assistant in Comparative Philology at Oxford. Currently he is working on the historical morphosyntax of the verb in Classical Armenian.

David Langslow studied and subsequently taught Classical and Comparative Philology and Historical Linguistics in Oxford. Since 1999, he has been Professor of Classics at the University of Manchester and an Emeritus Fellow of Wolfson College, Oxford.

His publications have centred on the classical languages in general and medical Latin in particular, and include *Medical Latin in the Roman Empire* (2000), *The Latin Alexander Trallianus* (2006), and an annotated English edition of Jacob Wackernagel's *Lectures on syntax* (2009).

Anna Morpurgo Davies is Diebold Professor Emeritus of Comparative Philology at Oxford. She was educated in Italy but made her career in Oxford with frequent visits to the United States (Pennsylvania, Yale, Berkeley). She has worked on Indo-European linguistics, especially on Mycenaean, Ancient Greek, and Anatolian, and on the history of nineteenth-century linguistics. Among her publications are *Nineteenth-century linguistics* (1998) and *A companion to Linear B* I–II (2008–11, ed. with Y. Duhoux).

Philomen Probert is University Lecturer in Classical Philology and Linguistics at the University of Oxford and a Fellow of Wolfson College. She has written *A new short guide to the accentuation of Ancient Greek* (2003) and *Ancient Greek accentuation: synchronic patterns, frequency effects, and prehistory* (2006).

Don Ringe earned his PhD in Linguistics at Yale in 1984. He taught Classics at Bard College from 1983 to 1985; since 1985 he has been on the faculty in Linguistics at the University of Pennsylvania, where he has been a Full Professor since 1996. He is the author of numerous articles and three books (*On calculating the factor of chance in language comparison*, 1992; *On the chronology of sound changes in Tocharian*, 1996; *From Proto-Indo-European to Proto-Germanic*, 2006).

Paul Russell is Reader in Celtic in the Department of Anglo-Saxon, Norse, and Celtic in Cambridge. He studied at Oxford for his undergraduate degree in Classics and subsequently for the M.Phil. in General Linguistics and Comparative Philology and a D.Phil. in Celtic. His research interests include Celtic philology and linguistics (*Celtic word-formation: the velar suffixes*, 1990; *An introduction to the Celtic languages*, 1995), early Irish glossaries, early Welsh orthography, Middle Welsh translation texts, and medieval Welsh law.

Ranjan Sen is a Lecturer in Linguistics at the University of Sheffield. He studied Classics, Comparative Philology, and Phonetics at the University of Oxford, where he completed his D.Phil. entitled 'Syllable and segment in Latin' in 2009; a monograph based on this work is due to appear with Oxford University Press.

Patrick Stiles read English at Oxford for his first degree, concentrating on Old Germanic philology. He then took the Diploma in Comparative Philology (Germanic and Greek), which led to a doctorate ('Studies in the Germanic *r*-stems'). His subsequent publications have all been in the field of Germanic. His chief interest is historical and comparative linguistics, principally Indo-European, in particular Germanic and Balto-Slavic. He is an honorary research fellow at University College London.

Jane Stuart-Smith is a Reader in English Language at the University of Glasgow. She has written on variation and change in Glaswegian accent, the impact of the broadcast media on language change, the sociophonetics of British Asian accents, the phonetics and phonology of British varieties of Panjabi, the acquisition of literacy in Panjabi/English bilingual children, historical linguistics, and sound change. She is author of *Phonetics and philology: sound change in Italic* (2004).

Elizabeth Tucker read Classics followed by Oriental Studies at St Hugh's College, Oxford. Her doctoral thesis, which was on the Greek verb, was published in 1990 entitled *The creation of morphological regularity.* Subsequently her research and publications have focused on Indo-Iranian. Since 1976 she has taught Avestan, Old Persian, and Vedic for the Faculty of Oriental Studies at Oxford. At present she is Jill Hart Senior Research Fellow in Indo-Iranian Philology and a Fellow of Wolfson College, Oxford.

Andreas Willi is Diebold Professor of Comparative Philology at the University of Oxford and a Fellow of Worcester College. He has written *The languages of Aristophanes* (2003) and *Sikelismos: Sprache, Literatur und Gesellschaft im griechischen Sizilien* (2008) and edited *The language of Greek comedy* (2002). His research interests include historical sociolinguistics, Greek dialectology, the language/literature interface in the ancient world, and Greek, Latin, and Indo-European comparative grammar.

Nicholas Zair is a Research Fellow in Classics at Peterhouse, Cambridge. He studied Classics followed by Philology and Linguistics at Oxford. His doctoral thesis was on the reflexes of the Proto-Indo-European laryngeals in Celtic, and recent publications have dealt with further issues in the historical phonology and morphology of Celtic. He is currently working on the historical phonology of the Sabellic languages.

Abbreviations

1. Reference works

CEG	Hansen, P. A. (1983–9). *Carmina Epigraphica Graeca* (2 vols). Berlin: de Gruyter.
CIIC	Macalister, R. A. S. (1945–9). *Corpus Inscriptionum Insularum Celticarum* (2 vols). Dublin: Stationery Office.
CIL	*Corpus Inscriptionum Latinarum*. Berlin: Reimer/de Gruyter, 1853–.
DGE	Schwyzer, E. (1923). *Dialectorum Graecarum exempla epigraphica potiora*. Leipzig: Hirzel.
ECMW	Nash-Williams, V. E. (1950). *The early Christian monuments of Wales*. Cardiff: University of Wales Press.
GL	Keil, H. (ed.) (1855–80). *Grammatici Latini* (8 vols). Leipzig: Teubner.
GPC	Thomas, R. J., et al. (eds) (1950–2002). *Geiriadur Prifysgol Cymru. A dictionary of the Welsh language*. Cardiff: Gwasg Prifysgol Cymru.
ICS	Masson, O. (1983). *Les inscriptions chypriotes syllabiques* (2nd edn). Paris: de Boccard.
IEW	Pokorny, J. (1959). *Indogermanisches Etymologisches Wörterbuch*. Berne and Munich: Francke.
IG	*Inscriptiones Graecae*. Berlin: Reimer/de Gruyter, 1873–.
IvO	Dittenberger, W., and Purgold, K. (1896). *Die Ausgrabungen von Olympia*, v. *Die Inschriften von Olympia*. Berlin: Asher.
LIV	Rix, H., and Kümmel, M. (eds) (2001). *Lexikon der indogermanischen Verben: Die Wurzeln und ihre Primärstammbildungen* (2nd edn). Wiesbaden: Reichert.
LMP	*The other languages of England: linguistic minorities project*. London: Routledge and Kegan Paul, 1985.
LSAG	Jeffery, L. H. (1990). *The local scripts of Archaic Greece* (2nd edn, with supplements by A. W. Johnston). Oxford: Oxford University Press.
LSJ	Liddell, H. G., Scott, R., and Jones, H. S. (1940). *A Greek-English Lexicon* (9th edn). Oxford: Clarendon Press.
NK	Mitford, T. B. (1980). *The nymphaeum of Kafizin: the inscribed pottery*. Berlin and New York: de Gruyter.
OCD	Hornblower, S., and Spawforth, A. (eds) (1996). *The Oxford Classical Dictionary* (3rd edn). Oxford: Oxford University Press.

OLD	Glare, P. G. W. (ed.) (1996). *Oxford Latin Dictionary.* Oxford: Oxford University Press.
SEG	*Supplementum epigraphicum Graecum.* Alphen aan den Rijn and Germantown, Md./Amsterdam/Leiden: Sijthoff and Noordhoff/Gieben/Brill, 1923–.

2. Ancient authors and texts

Greek and Latin authors and texts are abbreviated according to *OCD* or, if not listed there, according to LSJ and *OLD* respectively.

AV	*Atharvaveda*
AVP	*Atharvaveda, Paippalāda* recension
AVŚ	*Atharvaveda, Śaunaka* recension
BĀU	*Bṛhadāraṇyaka-Upaniṣad*
DB	Dareios, Bīsutūn
ŁP‘	Łazar P‘arpec‘i
MS	*Maitrāyaṇi-Saṁhitā*
RV	*Ṛgveda*
ŚB	*Śatapatha-Brāhmaṇa*

3. Languages

Aeol.	Aeolic Greek
Alb.	Albanian
Arm.	Armenian
Att.	Attic Greek
Av.	Avestan
Balt.	Baltic
Cypr.	Cypriot Greek
Dor.	Doric Greek
Engl.	English
Fr.	French
Gaul.	Gaulish
Germ.	German
Goth.	Gothic
Gr.	Greek
Hitt.	Hittite
Hom.	Homeric Greek
IIran.	Indo-Iranian

Ion.	Ionic Greek
It.	Italian
Lac.	Laconian Greek
Lat.	Latin
Latv.	Latvian
LCorn.	Late Cornish
Lith.	Lithuanian
Luw.	Luwian
MBret.	Middle Breton
MCorn.	Middle Cornish
MIran.	Middle Iranian
ModBret.	Modern Breton
ModEA	Modern Eastern Armenian
ModGr.	Modern Greek
ModW	Modern Welsh
MP	Middle Persian
MW	Middle Welsh
Myc.	Mycenaean Greek
NP	Neo-Persian
OAv.	Old Avestan
OBret.	Old Breton
OCorn.	Old Cornish
OCS	Old Church Slavonic
OE	Old English
OF	Old Frisian
OHG	Old High German
OIA	Old Indo-Aryan
OIc.	Old Icelandic
OIr.	Old Irish
OIran.	Old Iranian
ON	Old Norse
OP	Old Persian
OPr.	Old Prussian
OS	Old Saxon
OW	Old Welsh
PGmc	Proto-Germanic
Phoen.	Phoenician

PIE	Proto-Indo-European
PItal.	Proto-Italic
PNWGmc	Proto-North-West Germanic
PWGmc	Proto-West Germanic
Russ.	Russian
RussCSl.	Russian Church Slavonic
Serb.	Serbian
Skt	Sanskrit
Span.	Spanish
Toch.	Tocharian
Vann.	Vannetais Breton
Ved.	Vedic
YAv.	Young Avestan

4. Grammatical terminology

acc.	accusative
act.	active
adj.	adjective
aor.	aorist
cas. obl.	*casus obliquus*
cas. rect.	*casus rectus*
dat.	dative
du.	dual
fem./f.	feminine
fut.	future
gen.	genitive
impf.	imperfect
ind.	indicative
inf.	infinitive
instr.	instrumental
ipv.	imperative
loc.	locative
masc./m.	masculine
mid.	middle
NAct	*nomen actionis*
NAg	*nomen agentis*
nom.	nominative

ntr./n.	neuter
obl.	oblique
opt.	optative
ptcpl.	participle
pl.	plural
pres.	present
sg.	singular
subj.	subjunctive
voc.	vocative
1pl., 2pl., 3pl.	first/second/third person plural
1sg., 2sg., 3sg.	first/second/third person singular

Additional subject-specific conventions are explained in chapters 2, 5, 13, and 16.

List of Figures

5.1a An example of a raw and smoothed pitch curve 69

5.1b The derivative of the smoothed pitch curve, from which the measures of 'pitch index' and 'pitch slope' were calculated 69

5.2 First two principal components for prevocalic Mid-tone (1) and High-tone (2) words for speaker 1 72

5.3 Relative vowel means for vowels 1 and 2 for intervocalic Mid-tone words for all speakers; relative vowel means for vowels 1 and 2 for words with High tone 74

12.1 R̥gvedic trimeter lines 185

12.2 *duvā́, duvé*, and *duvaú* (represented together as *duvV̄*) 194

12.3 *dvā́* and *dvé* (represented together as *dvV̄*) 194

13.1 *komfakioː → (kóm).fa.ki.{oː}* (> *coːnficioː*) 212

13.2 *dokitos → (dók).{tos}* (> *doctus*) 215

13.3 *konkitaːriː → (kónk).(tàː).{riː}* (> *cunctaːriː*) 216

13.4 *formokapeːs → (fórm).ka.{peːs}* (> *forcipeːs*) 218

13.5 *Falesinos → (Fá.les).{nos}* (> *Falernus*) 222

13.6 *pueritia → pu.(é.ri.ti).{a}* 223

13.7 *opitumus → (óp).tu.{mus}* (> *optimus*) 223

13.8 *pueritia → pu.(ér).ti.{a}* 224

13.9 *veteraːnus → ve.(tráː).{nus}* 226

List of Tables

4.1 Distribution of allophones of the four short accented vowels in North-West Germanic 45

5.1 Averages for pitch and consonantal measures for each speaker for Low- and Mid-tone (non-tonal) words, in prevocalic position, with *p*-values 71

5.2 Averages for pitch and consonantal measures for each speaker for High- and Mid-tone (non-tonal) words, in intervocalic position, with *p*-values 73

5.3 Averages for pitch and consonantal measures for each speaker for High- and Mid-tone (non-tonal) words, in final position, with *p*-values 75

5.4 Summary of results for pitch and consonantal measures for Low and High tones 76

6.1 An active paradigm 84

6.2 A passive paradigm 85

6.3 A very late passive paradigm 85

6.4 A first count 91

6.5 The relative frequency of double marking (passives) 92

6.6 The relative frequency of double marking (deponents) 93

6.7 A first count of simple and double forms in Hyginus and Vitruvius 95

6.8 A revised count of simple and double forms in Hyginus and Vitruvius 98

6.9 The passive in the *Peregrinatio Egeriae* 99

9.1 Influence of 2sg. on 2pl. pronominal forms in Armenian 140

9.2 Šatax and Muš evidence for Classical Armenian forms with /y/ 145

11.1 Early Greek paradigm of *ϝοῖκος* 'house' (cf. Skt *véśa-* 'house') 168

11.2 Early present and aorist active and middle finite forms and infinitives of *τρέπω* 'turn', shown with root accentuation 169

11.3 Early present and imperfect indicative forms of *ἵστημι* 'set up', shown with accent on the reduplication 171

11.4 Words with accentually 'long' or 'short' final *-οι/-αι* 180

11.5 Disyllabic words with initial consonant, light first syllable, and accentually 'long' or 'short' final *-οι/-αι* 181

12.1 The distribution of *purā́* in Ṛgvedic verse 189

15.1 Distribution of singular forms of δίδωμι and τίθημι in Herodotus 265
15.2 Stages in the development of thematic 3sg. *-*eti* in Greek 267
16.1 The placement of attributive *urbanus* in the corpus, by head noun, author, and number of occurrences 281
16.2 Placement of attributive *urbanus* by author 283
16.3 Attributive *urbanus* postposed: without focus, in the neighbourhood of focus, and bearing focus 290
16.4 Patterns of multiple modifiers including *urbanus* 302

1

Introduction

PHILOMEN PROBERT AND ANDREAS WILLI

In a widespread joke about linguists,[1] a linguist claims to have discovered a law that all odd numbers are prime:

–'Three is prime; five is prime; seven is prime.'
–'But nine isn't.'
–'Well, it's not a law, but it's a very strong tendency.'

Various things are parodied here, but one of these is that linguists like to discover laws, and like to state things as laws (or, we might add, rules). But linguists are not the only people who like laws: variants of the joke exist for many other fields. Lawyers, for example, argue from precedent that nine should be considered prime; physicists dismiss the number nine as an experimental error. The terms 'law' and 'rule' have different meanings for different people and in different contexts. In their most everyday uses, the terms refer to prescriptive ordinances—things one must (or must not) do—with laws made by governments and rules by lesser authorities. By extension[2] from universally binding ordinances, prototypical scientific or natural laws describe universally applicable principles. For example, although different planets have different orbits, if a line is drawn between the centre of any planet and the centre of its star, this line sweeps out equal areas in equal times (Kepler's second law of planetary motion).

[1] Many thanks to Darya Kavitskaya for this version of the joke.

[2] Zilsel (1942) shows that the modern use of terms such as 'natural law' essentially appeared in the seventeenth century (though there are forerunners from antiquity onwards), and was facilitated by the idea of prescriptive laws divinely imposed on nature. Thomas Huxley apparently felt that the term 'laws of Nature' still suggested divine ordinance when he called the metaphor an 'unhappy' one (1866: 636).

It is clear—by definition—that the laws of descriptive linguistics are not prescriptive ordinances.[3] Are they universal principles in the same sense as Kepler's law? The late nineteenth century saw fierce debate on this point. At the centre of the debate were sound laws,[4] such as the law that */s/ becomes /r/ between vowels in Latin. What would make this a natural law? Perhaps it would need to be exceptionless, in which case it would appear that we do not have a natural law because e.g. *rosa* 'rose' seems to have an unchanged intervocalic /s/. But what if we can explain the exceptions as due to the interference of analogy, borrowing, or further sound changes? Furthermore, what if we take it as axiomatic that sound laws are exceptionless, so that if a sound law has apparent exceptions, either it has been incorrectly formulated or the apparent exceptions are based on incorrect etymologies or are due to analogy, borrowing, or further sound changes—even if we cannot show which of these explanations is correct?

The extent to which sound changes are exceptionless was of course itself a focus of fierce debate.[5] But it soon came to be agreed that sound laws were in any case not comparable to the laws of the natural sciences, because they did not hold for all times and places.[6] Kepler's law holds for any planet in any solar system (and for other systems in which one body orbits another), but it is not true at all times and places that any [s] a language may have will become [r] intervocalically.[7] (If there were such a law, it would be difficult to see how any language could have intervocalic [s] at all.)

The nature of scientific laws and the structure of scientific explanation have themselves been the subject of considerable discussion over the last century, together with further discussion of the relationship between laws in science and laws in traditionally unruly disciplines, such as history.[8] One point to emerge from this discussion is the need to distinguish, in all disciplines, between different kinds of laws and different levels of explanation. Kepler's second law, for example, is now known to be derivable from Newton's second law of motion combined with his principle of universal gravitation—laws that account for a wider range of phenomena without invalidating Kepler's second law as

[3] Cf. Tobler (1879: 41–2).

[4] Cf. Tobler (1879: 43).

[5] See Schneider (1973: esp. 1–147), Morpurgo Davies (1998: 251–5).

[6] For an influential article in this debate, see Tobler (1879: esp. 44); for recent discussion, see Amsterdamska (1987: 112–20, esp. 118–20), Morpurgo Davies (1998: 252).

[7] Cf. Hempel and Oppenheim (1948: 153–7), on the reasons why a true sentence of the type 'Every apple in basket *b* at time *t* is red' does not qualify as a scientific law.

[8] See e.g. Schrödinger (1929), Zilsel (1941), Hempel (1942), Hempel and Oppenheim (1948); comparison between linguistic laws in particular with laws of other disciplines in Kovács (1971); for an instructive comparison drawn from linguistics, see also Hempel and Oppenheim (1948: 141).

a lower-level generalization.[9] In what follows we offer some reflections on different kinds of linguistic laws (or 'Gesetze', etc.) and rules (or 'Regeln', etc.).

1.1 Laws as observations of some sort of order

Both in linguistics and in the natural sciences, modern debates over the proper definition of terms such as 'law' and 'rule' arose once these terms were being applied, in practice, to cases in which facts were observed to occur in accordance with some sort of order. But order was observed in historical linguistic data long before terms such as 'sound law' were applied. Russell (chapter 2) opens our volume with an investigation of medieval Irish observations of what we might now call sound laws, and the relationship between these and similar observations in Priscian's *Institutiones Grammaticae*. It is, however, in the nineteenth century that clear distinctions start to be drawn between different kinds of regularity in historical linguistics.

1.2 Laws of language change

As we have noted, sound laws such as '*/s/ > /r/ between vowels in Latin' are limited in time and apply to specific languages or dialects. While they may be motivated by general principles of articulation, acoustics, and social interaction, they are not themselves even derivable from more general known principles—in part because we do not know enough about the initial conditions (such as irrecoverable social factors) in any given case.[10]

Sometimes the term 'law', or alternatively 'principle', is, however, used in linguistics for a higher-level claim about the nature of language change, to be understood as universal across times, places, languages, and dialects. For example, the 'regularity principle' itself is a claim about the way in which sound change operates, in any (spoken) language at any time. Stated in a banal way (one that sidesteps the vexed questions of definition surrounding both 'sound change' and 'regular'), the regularity principle states that 'sound change is regular'. Kuryłowicz famously posited a series of 'laws'[11] of analogy, or universal characteristics of analogical change (Kuryłowicz 1947). Kuryłowicz takes care to point out that his generalizations do not allow one to predict when

[9] See Huxley (1887: 215), Hempel and Oppenheim (1948: 146–7).

[10] On the need for known initial conditions, not only known laws, before scientific prediction is possible, cf. Zilsel (1941: 567–8).

[11] On Kuryłowicz's original wording, see section 1.9.

analogical change will occur, or its extent; but when analogical change does occur, its operation will be consistent with his generalizations, just as rainwater will take known paths once we know it is raining (especially Kuryłowicz 1947: 37).[12] A similar point could be made about most other such generalizations about language change: they describe what changes are possible, and the characteristics of particular types of change when they occur. They do not predict whether particular types of change will happen at all.

Validity across times and places may also be claimed in a more moderate way. Mańczak responded to Kuryłowicz's 'laws' of analogy by positing instead a series of 'tendencies' of analogy: characteristics claimed to be present more often than not. Although Mańczak only claimed the status of tendencies for his generalizations about analogical change, we should expect to find the effects of these tendencies across times and places unlike, say, the effects of a specific sound change such as ancient Greek [t^h] > modern Greek [θ].

What we know about general characteristics of language change—what types of language change occur, and how particular types of change proceed—crucially underpins comparative and internal linguistic reconstruction and our attempts to elucidate the details and pathways of documented historical changes. It is therefore essential that historical linguists remain alert for new evidence and insights into language change.

Part II of this book, *Rules of language change and linguistic methodology*, concentrates on such new evidence and insights into language change, and their methodological implications. Ringe (chapter 3) demonstrates that there were significant dialect differences within Proto-West Germanic well before the West Germanic languages ceased to undergo significant common innovations; he reflects on the impact which these findings should have for our view of West Germanic as a valid clade, and on the appropriate impact which findings of this kind should have for linguistic cladistics. Stiles (chapter 4) shows that the North-West Germanic split of /u/ into the allophones [o] and [u] by *a*-umlaut was phonologized (gave rise to separate phonemes /o/ and /u/) in the Older Runic language even before the loss of the conditioning environment; the principle known as Polivanov's Law, that there is 'no split without a merger' (see Collinge 1985: 253–4), is contradicted. Stiles argues that speakers first became aware of the phonetic difference between [o] and [u] and then, crucially, created analogical forms in which one allophone was substituted for another—a process which has sometimes been claimed not to occur. Widening the

[12] Winters (1997: 368, 379) claims (against the implication of Hock 1991: 214) that even once we know analogy is taking place, Kuryłowicz's 'laws' are intended as tendencies only. But the passage Winters cites in support of this claim (Kuryłowicz 1947: 23, the opening of his discussion of his second 'law') supports, if anything, the opposite view.

discussion, Stiles proposes a new classification of ways in which new phonemes come into existence. Stuart-Smith and Cortina-Borja (chapter 5) re-evaluate the Panjabi merger of the Indo-European voiced aspirates with unaspirated stops (either voiceless or voiced, depending on the environment), with tonal developments on adjacent vowels. They find that for some British Panjabi speakers, and in some positions, the stops that continue the voiced aspirates are different, at the fine phonetic level, from those that do not. Their findings offer support for the principle of 'near merger' identified by Labov (1994: 20) and suggest that this new principle needs to be considered when a sequence of changes is reconstructed. De Melo (chapter 6) examines the development from the Latin passive system (in which some passives are synthetic) to the Romance passive system (in which all passives are periphrastic, and tense is marked more clearly than in Latin). At first sight, these developments represent a rather straightforward application of Kuryłowicz's first law of analogy: in Hock's (1991: 212) reformulation, 'forms which are more "clearly" or "overtly" marked tend to be preferred in analogical change'. De Melo shows, however, that the internal complexity of developments taking place over many centuries needs to be appreciated before Kuryłowicz's first law can be assigned its proper role. Furthermore, he shows that 'clear' and 'overt' marking should not be lumped together; in the development of the Romance passive, clarity and the avoidance of ambiguity are consistently more important factors than overt marking. Morpurgo Davies (chapter 7) considers the likelihood of historical connections between instances of a change */s/ > /h/ or */s/ > /Ø/ occurring at different periods and in different dialects of ancient Greek. She suggests that where the same, or similar, changes occur in closely related languages or dialects, we need to consider not only the possibility of diffusion and of independent innovation but also the possibility of 'drift', in one of the senses discussed by Trudgill et al. (2000): change occurs independently, but variant forms of the same language share structural characteristics predisposing them to the same change.

1.3 Laws as regularities, with or without exceptions

Many laws and rules of historical linguistics describe sound changes, limited to particular periods and linguistic varieties. On one conception, these are laws if they hold absolutely, or at least, if there are no unexplained exceptions. One reason for historical linguists to like sound laws is that many are indeed statable (in ways that are non-trivial, i.e. do not simply amount to lists of examples) so that there are no unexplained exceptions. For example, for all classical Greek words with direct modern Greek descendants, if the classical word begins with /h/, the modern descendant has instead /Ø/.

Non-trivial generalizations that hold without unexplained exceptions are, at the very least, rather pleasing in themselves. More seriously, they are valuable because they help to constrain our reconstructions and etymologies. Famously, the suspicion that classical Greek /t^heós/ 'god' is cognate with Latin /deus/ 'god' is ruled out by our knowledge that classical Greek /t^h/ corresponds to Latin /f/ word-initially, not to Latin /d/. The discovery of a new sound law may also open up the possibility of new etymologies, and it may or may not require revisions to our reconstructions.

Part III, *Segmental sound laws: new proposals and reassessments*, begins with a proposal that, as formulated, has no unexplained exceptions. Elbourne (chapter 8) adduces further arguments in support of his proposed prehistoric Greek sound law */t^h/ > /t/ after */s, n, r, l/ (Elbourne 1998). Although he originally proposed this law while arguing that a series of voiceless aspirated stops needed to be reconstructed for Proto-Indo-European, he argues here that there is reason to posit his law, in some form, whether or not one reconstructs voiceless aspirates for Proto-Indo-European.

Elbourne's law, as stated, has no unexplained exceptions. But some regularities have been called 'laws' and 'rules' in spite of having apparent exceptions of which their authors are well aware. In some of these cases, the term 'law' or 'rule' may simply be used loosely, or used to signal a rather high degree of conformity (a regularity that holds 90% of the time, say, rather than only 60% of the time). For some linguists, the term 'law' (and especially 'sound law') simply refers to a change that can be observed in a series of different examples.

There are, however, two stronger senses in which a partial regularity—one with exceptions—may nevertheless be conceived as a 'law' or 'rule' or (particularly for the second sense we shall discuss) a 'principle'.

1.4 Laws as regularities that ought to hold absolutely

In the first of these senses, the terms 'law' and 'rule' are used because the nature of a linguistic change is such that the author views it as one that *ought* to be exceptionless. For example, a particular linguistic change is entirely phonologically motivated, and on this basis it is called a 'law' with the expectation that the apparent exceptions will, sooner or later, turn out to be based on incorrect etymologies, or to be due to analogy or borrowing, or to be rule-governed themselves, just as the nineteenth century saw Verner's discovery that apparent exceptions to Grimm's Law had their own regularities.

Part III continues with two sound laws considered in this spirit. Although Proto-Indo-European word-initial */i̯/ has four apparent outcomes in Armenian, Meillet (1903*b*: 29) proposed that the regular development—what we might call the 'sound law'—was Proto-Indo-European *#/i̯/ > Armenian #/dž/. Kölligan (chapter 9) finds further evidence in favour of Meillet's view, showing that the apparent examples of other outcomes are based on less convincing correspondences or incur the suspicion of being due to analogical remodelling or the interference of further sound changes. Conversely, Zair (chapter 10) argues that a merger long assumed for Proto-Celtic (**-ou̯-*, **-uu̯-* > **-ou̯-* / _V) should be abandoned, along with the search for a principled account of the British Celtic treatments of the alleged outcome **-ou̯-*. Instead, he argues that a better account—one involving fewer unexplained irregularities—of the British Celtic treatments of Proto-Celtic **-ou̯-* and **-uu̯-* presupposes the separate survival of these sequences into British Celtic.

1.5 Laws as heuristic principles

A related sense in which a regularity, especially a higher-level claim about the nature of language change, might be called a 'law' or 'rule'—and this time often a 'principle'—although its validity is not absolute, is that it is regarded as a useful heuristic tool, for example in reconstruction. An example we have already mentioned is the 'regularity principle'. The expectation illustrated in the previous section, that apparent exceptions to sound changes will sooner or later turn out to be rule-governed, is only sensible if sound changes can, in fact, be expected to be regular. The regularity principle states just this. Yet we now know that (even if we look beyond the special 'sporadic' types of sound change admitted by the neogrammarians) sound changes are not all exceptionless, even when they have run their course, but may leave a small number of exceptions, known as 'residue'. Nevertheless, it is often claimed that unless we assume that sound changes are regular, we will not be able to reconstruct proto-languages at all—that the regularity principle should be retained as a heuristic tool.[13]

This notion of a useful heuristic tool is worth examining in a bit more detail. Why should we bother to reconstruct proto-languages if we can do so only on the basis of assumptions we now know to be incorrect? If the regularity principle has any value as a heuristic tool it ought to be because we achieve

[13] For the methodological necessity to assume that sound changes are regular, see e.g. Leskien (1876: xxviii); for an attack on this notion, cf. Schuchardt (1885: 29–30). See further Hoenigswald (1978: 24).

more accurate results by assuming the regularity of sound change than by any alternative assumptions we can actually use as a basis for reconstructing.[14] But do we indeed achieve more accurate results like this? Intuitively, it would seem that the answer here is yes: we know that sound changes may leave residue, but in the absence of methods to identify likely examples of residue, the most accurate method of reconstruction available relies on the approximation that sound change is regular.[15] More accurate methods may become available, however, if historical linguists can develop not only more accurate models but ways of incorporating them in reconstruction.[16]

More generally, reconstruction and the explanation of linguistic change have to rely on the closest model of reality we can not only achieve but actually make methodological use of. Historical linguists therefore need not only to remain alert for new evidence and insights into language change, but also to consider what methods of reconstruction and explanation current knowledge about language change allows, and what principles or approximations these should be based on.

The use and discussion of heuristic principles appears at a number of points in this volume. Kölligan (chapter 9) and Zair (chapter 10) make use of the regularity principle *qua* heuristic principle. Stiles (chapter 4), although he argues that new phonemes may be created without a concomitant merger, in defiance of Polivanov's Law that there is 'no split without a merger', reflects (section 4.5.2) that methodologically such exceptional paths to phoneme formation should only be assumed if it is impossible to explain a new phoneme as the result of merger elsewhere in the system. In other words, Polivanov's Law should be assumed where possible; although some incorrect accounts of particular changes may result, current knowledge suggests that Polivanov's Law applies most of the time, so that we achieve more accurate results by assuming the law's validity where the data allow this possibility. Morpurgo Davies makes just this use of Polivanov's Law as a heuristic principle in arguing that Mycenaean Greek, which reflects a change of intervocalic *[s] to [h] but also has examples of analogically restored intervocalic [s], did not restore intervocalic [s] by analogy until [s] and [h] had ceased to be in complementary distribution (p. 115).

[14] An analogy might be the way in which the distribution of certain types of random variable is modelled in statistics by a mathematical formula which approximates the real distribution rather than replicating it exactly, but is amenable to mathematical manipulation so that the probability of a particular result can be calculated.

[15] Compare Hock (1991: 660), Clackson (2007: 32–3).

[16] In practice, the comparative method has long been supplemented by a suspicious attitude to correspondence sets comprising few correspondences, and towards reconstructions based on such correspondence sets (for example, the Proto-Indo-European 'pure velar' series); this suspicious attitude already constitutes a rudimentary way of flagging possible examples of residue.

1.6 Origins, development, and systemic consequences

When diachronic changes are formulated as laws or rules, they typically take a form such as 'A becomes B under conditions C, for linguistic variety D, during time period E'. However, this way of stating a diachronic change does not explain how and why it began, or identify stages through which it passed. Furthermore, careful attention to chronological layers in the analysis of primary material may either weaken or strengthen the evidence for a rule. In Part IV, *Origins and evolutions*, Probert (chapter 11) considers the factors triggering the Greek 'law of limitation', the Greek innovation restricting the distance from the end of the word where the accent can fall; she argues that reanalysis of forms whose prehistoric accentuation already 'conformed' to the (not yet existing) law played a crucial role. Barber (chapter 12) examines the distribution of Lindeman's Law alternants such as *dyaús/diyaús* 'heaven' in the *Ṛgveda*, arguing that the disyllabic forms are strongly associated with formulaic contexts where they are likely to represent an archaic survival. He concludes that the restriction of such alternants to potentially monosyllabic words cannot be used to draw substantial conclusions about the phonology of Vedic or Proto-Indo-European: this restriction may well be a by-product of the circumstances under which such archaic forms survived. Sen (chapter 13) shows how attention to chronology can clarify the conditions for Latin syncope; he argues that six different stages of Latin syncope, with their own synchronic motivations and phonetic environments, can be discerned up to classical Latin.

As well as being chronologically layered in their development, laws and rules may also have systemic consequences whose relationship to the original law or rule is not necessarily straightforward. An understanding of these systemic consequences may be necessary before the evidence for the original law or rule can be clearly seen—and yet systemic consequences are, of course, difficult to work out if the conditions for the original law or rule are less than fully understood. Part V, *Systemic consequences*, is devoted to laws and their systemic consequences, and the impact of the interplay between the two on our understanding.

Tucker (chapter 14) examines the effects of Brugmann's Law (apophonic **o* > Indo-Iranian *ā* in medial open syllables, with further conditions subject to debate) on several categories of Indo-Iranian thematic nouns ultimately related to Indo-European formations such as **bhóro-* or **-bhoró-*, showing how both short and long root vocalism spread analogically at particular periods and in particular categories, and the contrast between *-a-* and *-ā-* could be refunctionalized (e.g. to distinguish between *nomina agentis* and *nomina actionis*). Tucker's study also highlights that, when these systemic consequences are taken into account, some categories still provide irreducible evidence for

Kuryłowicz's (1927) restriction of Brugmann's Law to syllables not closed by an inherited laryngeal. Willi (chapter 15) argues that Kiparsky's rule for Greek, *-*Vti#*> *-*Vit*, caused (a) the third person singular of nasal-infix presents to *h_1-final roots to fall together with the third person singular of thematic presents, and (b), in some dialects, the third person singular of *-*ei̯e/o*- and *-*āi̯e/o*- presents to fall together with the third person singular of athematic presents in -ημι and -ᾱμι. These mergers then triggered (a) the thematization of nasal-infix presents to *h_1-final roots, and (b), in the relevant dialects, the athematic inflection of *-*ei̯e/o*- and *-*āi̯e/o*- presents. Conversely, the rule's ability to explain these awkward phenomena provides support for Kiparsky's rule itself, in a form close, but not identical, to its original formulation.

1.7 Synchronic laws and rules

The most obvious laws and rules of historical linguistics are diachronic ones, yet historical and comparative linguistics has to be based on adequate synchronic analyses of attested linguistic varieties. This point becomes especially clear where the necessary synchronic analyses are difficult to achieve, as often in syntax, pragmatics, or sociolinguistics. For example, attempts to reconstruct the syntax of Indo-European come up against (among other things) the limits of our syntactic understanding of early attested Indo-European languages; attempts to describe the early syntactic development of the Romance languages are plagued by the deficiencies of our syntactic understanding of Latin.

But there may be another reason why synchronic analysis is crucial for diachronic work. For several models of language change (e.g. reanalysis and extension, parameter resetting, or constraint reranking), the emergence of a new synchronic regularity is not merely a consequence of linguistic change. In an important sense, the emergence of the new synchronic state *is* the crucial linguistic change, since surface change only occurs once speakers have already started to operate with the new synchronic grammar. If some of these models capture any reality, even some of the time, historical linguists simply cannot ignore the synchronic laws and rules that come and go as languages change.

Moreover, not all synchronic rules come and go. On the synchronic as much as on the diachronic plane, a distinction needs to be made between generalizations specific to a particular linguistic variety at a particular period, and higher-level claims about the nature of synchronic linguistic systems—in other words, synchronic linguistic universals. An example of the latter is the law first posited by Kruszewski (1885: 263), that sound systems have a certain 'harmony' (or symmetry or pattern congruity): thus, if a language has a voiceless and a voiced stop series, the same places of articulation are likely to appear in both series. Many alleged linguistic universals are in fact tendencies rather than laws with absolute validity, but even so they are tendencies whose validity is not limited to a particular linguistic variety at a particular time: in order for any sort of universality to be a sensible claim, the alleged universal must at least be a fairly widespread synchronic phenomenon. Synchronic universals and tendencies are important for historical linguistics in so far as they (or rather their causes, whether or not these are known to us) may constrain language change.[17]

Part VI, *Synchronic laws and rules in syntax and sociolinguistics*, is devoted to synchronic laws of interest to historical linguists. Langslow (chapter 16) tests proposed rules for the placement of attributive adjectives in Latin against an analysis of the placement of attributive *urbanus* in a corpus of Latin prose works from Varro to Suetonius. Dickey (chapter 17) examines polite request formulae in Cicero's letters in the light of several different theories of linguistic politeness, three of these being theories for which some universality has been claimed, and the fourth having been developed specifically for Latin. She finds that, when combined with a careful examination of the Latin evidence, different theories help us to arrive at a better understanding of different request formulae. We do not yet have the laws and rules of Latin politeness (let alone language-universal politeness rules), but it seems that to understand Latin politeness fully we will need to identify and reconcile what is right about several different current theories.

1.8 Prescriptive rules

We have said that the laws of descriptive linguistics are not prescriptive ordinances, but this is not to deny that there are prescriptive rules for linguists to follow. One of these, hinted at by Collinge in his *The laws of Indo-European* (1985: 1), is that different laws should not be given the same name. In this connection we must confess that we have given this book a somewhat similar title to Collinge's. And yet there are differences; for example, the definite article of Collinge's title is lacking here. This book will not replace Collinge's masterly guide to the main named laws of Indo-European; it is exploratory rather than definitive. Yet Collinge's guide provides a context that makes it feasible to treat Indo-European laws and rules as a field in which much is clear, but specific problems can be taken up and new avenues explored. We hope that the near-minimal-pair titles will be seen as complementary.

[17] For informative debate on the relationship between language change and linguistic universals, both synchronic and diachronic, see the papers in Good (2008).

1.9 Laws, rules, principles, and tendencies: a case of partial terminological overlap

We have spoken so far of laws and rules, and sometimes of principles and tendencies, without attempting to draw clear boundaries between the meanings of these terms. In practice, the terms 'law' and 'rule' are often used interchangeably, in historical linguistics as in many other fields.[18] But some distinctions may be observed.

The term 'rule' is often (but not always) used for something with an input and an output: either a historical change (e.g. ancient Greek [t^h] became modern Greek [θ]) or the sort of replacement operation that models a synchronic alternation in generative grammar and much traditional grammar (e.g. voiced stops become voiceless word-finally in standard German).

The term 'law' may also be used for a historical change with an input and an output. So the historical change of ancient Greek [t^h] to modern Greek [θ] may be described either as a sound law or as a sound rule. The term 'law' is not, however, normally used for a replacement operation in a synchronic grammatical description. It is clear, for example, in Paul's (1909: 68) discussion of synchronic and diachronic operations that the term *Lautgesetz* is appropriate for the early Greek change, in historical terms, of a dental stop to /s/ before another dental stop. But when one says, in synchronic terms, that a Greek dental stop changes to /s/ before another dental stop (so that the root of e.g. πείθ-ω 'I persuade' turns its final /t^h/ into /s/ in the aorist passive infinitive πεισθῆναι 'to be persuaded'), this replacement operation is a *Regel*.

The term 'law' may, however, be used for a synchronic regularity conceived as a constraint rather than an operation with input and output. Thus, Wackernagel's Law describes the regular placement, in many languages, of unstressed elements in second position in the clause, without any implication (in its original formulation) that these elements move to second position from some other place.

Higher-level claims about language change, meant to be valid across time and across languages, may be called laws (as in Kuryłowicz's laws of analogy), or principles (as in the regularity principle); they are not normally called rules.

In a usage that cuts across these distinctions, however, some authors oppose the term 'law', for regularities that hold absolutely, to 'rule' or especially 'tendency', for regularities that hold less than absolutely.[19] Hence Kuryłowicz's

[18] Cf. Tobler (1879: 45). On other disciplines, cf. Huxley (1887: 213–14).

[19] Cf. the first sentence of chapter 16 (Langslow, p. 279): 'My purpose here is to present a case study against the background of attempts to explain with reference to rules (or regularities, or strong tendencies), if not laws, the placement of the attributive adjectival modifier of the noun in Latin.' Notice that (at least when stated in a theory-neutral way) the 'rules' of adjective placement

generalizations about analogical change, claimed to be valid whenever analogical change occurs, have come to be referred to as 'laws', while Mańczak's have been dubbed 'tendencies'.

Some of the distinctions just drawn between 'laws' and 'rules' make 'laws' the grander cousins of rules. If a regularity is valid across languages it is likely to merit the term 'law' (or 'principle'); if it is exceptionless, then even if it is specific to a particular period and linguistic variety it may also merit the term 'law'. More generally, the term 'rule' has slightly less grand connotations and is often used of a regularity whose significance is relatively local, or one named by an unpretentious person.[20] It is no accident that the joke we began with makes use of the grander term 'law'.

However, usage varies. We have mentioned Kuryłowicz's 'laws' of analogy and Mańczak's 'tendencies', but in Kuryłowicz's own presentation of his generalizations the term 'loi' is less prominent than 'formule'.[21] Mańczak in 1958 calls his own generalizations 'tendances générales',[22] but in 1978 (e.g. p. 54) he prominently calls them 'lois', although it is quite clear that he still means these to be statements about what happens more often than not. The rules of usage we have observed are not laws, but they are definite tendencies.

---

do not obviously have an input and an output: the sense of the term 'rules' as 'regularities with less absolute validity than laws' here trumps the idea that 'rules' have an input and an output. For similar usage in other fields, cf. Tobler (1879: 37–8, 40).

[20] For rules in the natural sciences as regularities whose importance is (in various ways) lower than that of laws, cf. Tobler (1879: 37–8, 40). In one such conception, laws are the inner causes of regularities, while rules are only the outer observable regularities themselves; Kovács (1971: 367–8, 378) advocates essentially the same conception for linguistics.

[21] 'Loi' at Kuryłowicz (1947: 20, 21, 25, 27); cf. Winters (1997: 368). Winters appears to consider this point to support her contention that Kuryłowicz did not mean his 'laws' as generalizations that hold absolutely. Given the usages we have discussed, Kuryłowicz's choice of terminology is certainly not irrelevant, but his views cannot simply be deduced either from his use of the term 'loi' or from his overall preference for 'formule'. Although Kuryłowicz's style is never easy, the reading of Hock (1991: 210–29) and others, that Kuryłowicz's laws are meant to hold whenever analogy takes place, is also supported by the use Kuryłowicz made of his laws in subsequent work, such as Kuryłowicz (1952*a*). Cf. Mańczak (1958: 417).

[22] See especially the discussion at Mańczak (1958: 417), in which Kuryłowicz's view is characterized as one in which there are 'lois absolues' in analogy, and is opposed to Mańczak's view that there are only 'tendances'; 'tendances' are then rephrased as 'règles' that hold for the larger part of the evidence.

Part I

Linguistic 'laws' in pre-modern thought

2

Fern do frestol na .u. consaine: perceptions of sound laws, sound change, and linguistic borrowing among the medieval Irish

PAUL RUSSELL

The following two entries are preserved in the early Irish glossary known as *Sanas Cormaic* [*SC*] 'Cormac's Glossary', attributed to Cormac mac Cuilennáin, king and bishop of Cashel who died in 908. They contain a statement which comes closest to a rule of linguistic relationship in medieval Irish sources:[1]

Fíne .i. ón fínemuin, ab eo quod est uinea, ar is gnáth ind ú consain lasin Laitneóir is fern frisindle lasin Gaoidel, ut est uir .i. fer, uita .i. fit, uirtus .i. firt, *quamuis hoc non per singula currat*.

Fíne .i. ón fínemuin] *interlinear* K; .i. ón fínemuin] *om.* BM; uinea] uinia H^{1ab}K; ú consain] consamhla M; frisindle] frisindleastar Y; fer] uisio .i. fiss *add.* BM; uita] uitua H^{1a}; hoc] *om.* Y.

[1] For discussion of *SC* and its relation to the other glossaries, see Russell (1988, 1996). The editions are based on the text of Y which is printed in K. Meyer (1912: 47, §576, and 49–50, §606, respectively) with significant variants provided from the other manuscript versions of *SC*; for the sigla used, see the list of abbreviations on p. 30. For discussion of the date of *SC*, see Russell (1988: 10–11, 1996: 161–5). In what follows, all translations are my own unless otherwise indicated. I am grateful for comments and suggested improvements from the editors, and also from Pádraic Moran and Deborah Hayden.

'*Fíne* (vine), i.e. from the word *fínemain* (vine, vineyard), from *uinea*, for it is usual that the consonant *u* in Latin corresponds to *f* in Irish, that is, *uir*, i.e. *fer* (man), *uita*, i.e. *fit* (life), *uirtus*, i.e. *firt* (courage), *although this may not operate in every single case*.'

Fé ab eo quod est uae. Ar is gnáth fernd do frestol na .u. consaine la Goídelae *ut predximus. Aliter...*

uae] ue .i. uae B, nae M; fernd] .f. BMH^{1a}; frestol] resdul M; na] *om.* B; .u.] no tarese na .u. *gloss in* B, uau M; Goídelae] Goedelu BM; ut prediximus *om.* YH^{1ab}K.

'*Fé* (woe!) from *uae*. For it is usual that Irish *f* corresponds to the consonant *u, as we have already said. Alternatively,... [an alternative explanation follows]*.'[2]

As it stands it looks like a statement of correspondence between Irish *f* and Latin *u*, although all the examples suggest that it refers to those consonants in initial position. Like all non-trivial statements of correspondence it also acknowledges that there might be exceptions to its generalization: *quamuis hoc non per singula currat*; even so, no exceptions are explicitly provided within the framework of this entry or the related ones. Although some of the following entries provide examples of Irish words beginning in *f-* which are derived from Latin words beginning with a consonant other than *u-/v-*, there is no gathering of the counterexamples.[3] Since such statements of correspondence require comparison between languages, it is hardly surprising that they are very rare in medieval sources. On the other hand, since the medieval Irish show themselves to be in many respects more linguistically aware than most, it is perhaps surprising that there is not more comment of this kind in Irish.

In addition to the group of glossaries to which *SC* belongs, other medieval Irish texts have a specifically linguistic starting point. For example, *Auraicept na n-Éces*, the 'Scholars' Primer', the core of which has been dated to the seventh century but which has acquired a vast amount of surrounding later commentary, takes as its premise the startling linguistic fact that, after the fall of the Tower of Babel, Irish was created by extracting all the best bits of other languages.[4] It goes on to make the implicit claim that, just like the other three sacred languages, Latin, Greek, and Hebrew, Irish has its own grammar similar to Priscian and Donatus for Latin. In addition, one of three great collections of Old Irish glosses is found in a ninth-century manuscript of Priscian's

[2] The alternative explains *fé* as a rod with which the undertaker measures the length of a corpse so as to dig the right size grave.

[3] Cf., for example, *SC* Y 613 *fiacail* 'tooth', Y 614 *fige* 'fixing' : both from parts of Latin *figo*; Y 617 *fidh* '?wood, letter' : Latin *fidus*; Y 623 *fascud* 'pressing' : Latin *fasces*; Y 634 *fell* 'deceit' : Latin *fello*; Y 640 *fedan* 'band of people' : Latin *foedus*; Y 644 *fuil* : (*quasi fluib*) Latin *fluuium*.

[4] Calder (1917: 1–2), Ahlqvist (1982: 47–8); for discussion, see Russell (2005*b*: 405–6).

Institutiones Grammaticae (St Gall, Stiftsbibliothek, MS 904) copied at Bangor or Nendrum in *c.* 851.[5]

But perhaps the richest collection of linguistic materials is gathered in the early Irish glossaries mentioned above, of which the versions of *SC* are developmentally the most sophisticated; for example, they often contain longer versions of entries or have edited together material which forms separate entries in other glossaries.[6] They all combine an interest in meaning with a concern for the origin of words and offer important evidence for how their Irish compilers thought about language and indeed languages—not only Irish, but also Latin, Greek, Hebrew, and other languages closer to home, such as British, Norse, Old English, and even Pictish.[7] Many entries simply supply a meaning for the lemma, in the form 'A .i. B' 'A means B' (often expanded by means of explanation, quotation, or a longer narrative), e.g. Y 207 *cobthach .i. búadach* '. . . i.e. victorious'. Others, however, display an interest in origins and etymology. This can take two basic forms: first, a native analysis where the lemma (always an Irish word) is broken down into smaller meaningful (in Irish) units, the sum of which provides a plausible explanation of the meaning of the lemma—e.g. Y 233 *conair .i. cen fér, cen ar* '*conair* (path), [*cen* 'without' + *fér* 'grass', or *cen* 'without' + *ar* 'ploughing'] i.e. without grass, without ploughing'.[8] This mode of analysis, though probably deriving from patristic exegesis and perhaps reaching Ireland via texts such as Isidore's *Etymologiae* and Jerome's *Hebrew Names*, was so embedded in Irish that it acquired its own name, *bélrae* (or *bérla*) *etarscarthae* 'separated (or segmented) language'.[9] It is widespread not only in the glossaries but also in the commentaries of law texts and other learned texts, notably the onomastic compilations such as *Cóir Anmann* (a compilation explaining personal names) and the *Dindshenchas Érenn* (place names).[10]

[5] For the date of the St Gall Old Irish glosses, see Ó Néill (2000: 178). The Old Irish glosses are printed and translated in Stokes and Strachan (1901–3: ii. 49–230), but without a complete Latin text; both the Old Irish and the Latin glosses are edited and translated in Hofman (1996), but only for the first five books of Priscian. The complete text of Priscian was edited by Martin Hertz and printed in *GL* ii. 1–iii. 384 Keil. An online edition of the St Gall Priscian has now been published by Pádraic Moran on the basis of work by Rijklof Hofman: http://www.stgallpriscian.ie.

[6] For details, see Russell (1988).

[7] On the British words in the glossaries, see Russell (1995); cf. also now discussion of some of the entries by Rodway (2009).

[8] The text within [. . .] shows the etymological breakdown of the entry. Note that the etymology of *conair* depends on the initial *f-* being lenited to /Ø/ after the preposition *cen*.

[9] Calder (1917: 100–3, ll. 1302–23); for discussion, see Russell (2008: 5–6).

[10] On *Cóir Anmann*, see Arbuthnot (2005–7); for the *Dindshenchas*, see Stokes (1892, 1893, 1894–5), Gwynn (1900, 1903–35).

The other mode of analysis was to derive the lemma from a word in another language, typically from one of the *tres linguae sacrae* of Latin, Greek, and Hebrew. In many cases, if the match is clear, the derivation is unproblematic and perspicuous; however, it is not always clear whether we are to think of the match as phonetic, phonological, or orthographical. Matters can be further complicated by cases where the match is not as close and some degree of formal manipulation is required for the derivation to be plausible. In such instances, it is often the case that a 'bridge' form marked by *quasi* is deployed to get us over the difficulty—e.g. Y 742 *imbliu quasi umbliu ab umbilico* '*imbliu* (navel), as if *umbliu*, from *umbilicus*', where *umbliu* has no other existence than to fill the developmental gap between the headword and Latin *umbilicus*. I have argued elsewhere (Russell 2005*a*) that such 'bridge' forms are probably not to be imagined as having any attested reality, but rather as marking a stage through which the form was thought to have passed—similar to the way in which an intermediate unattested 'starred' form might be used. Interestingly, the shifts associated with, and marked by, *quasi* are sometimes also described as 'corruption', Irish *trúaillned*: the source word is seen as having changed its forms to the extent that it might be regarded as somehow 'corrupted'. However, 'corruption' of this type does not seem to imply an inferior status. Forms of the verb, *trúaillnid* 'corrupt', occur eleven times in the analytical terminology of *SC*.[11] In all instances there is significant modification of the lemma going on which would require, at the very least, that the entry be marked with *quasi*. The majority of the instances involve a non-Latinate and non-Irish etymology—in six cases the etymology is from Welsh, or at least British, and two are from Greek, but it is not clear whether 'corruption' is invoked because the etymologies are somehow more distant;[12] it probably has to do more with the amount of formal manipulation which is required. A comparison with Isidore's *Etymologiae* (Lindsay 1911) suggests that *corrupte* is used to characterize single, apparently random, changes often involving simplification and implying some form of non-standard usage; thus at 9. 2. 20 *Philistim... nos modo corrupte Palaestinos uocamus* 'the Philistines... [whom] we now call, corruptly, Palestinians'; 17. 7. 66 *pausia, quam corrupte rustici pusiam uocant* 'the *pausia* olive, which country people corruptly call *pusia*'; 19. 29. 6 *gubellum corrupte a globo dictum per*

[11] *SC* Y: 111, 239, 327, 675, 684, 850, 852, 853, 888, 1011, 1212.

[12] Cf. Russell (1995: 169–70); apart from Y 111, 684, 850, 888, the remainder (Y 239, 327, 675, 684, 850, 853, 1011, 1212) involve a non-Latinate and non-Irish etymology.

diminutiuum quasi globellum '*Gubellum* is said corruptly as a diminutive of ball (*globus*) as if the word were *globellum*', etc.[13]

The upshot of this mode of analysis was that all similarity between languages was to be explained through borrowing, and thus it was possible, in theory, for regular correspondences to be noted. The question that arises with regard to Irish may therefore be why such correspondence is not noted more often. The regular correspondence between Latin *u/v* and Irish *f* is not unique; for example, it is possible to observe that Irish *c* often corresponded to Latin *p*, as in Irish *cáisc* 'Easter' : Latin *pascha* (Y 266), Irish *secht* 'seven' : Latin *septem* (Y 1143), Irish *fescer* 'evening, vespers' : Latin *uesper* (Y 593), and beyond *SC* Irish *corcur* 'purple' : Latin *purpura*, Irish *caille* 'veil' : Latin *pallium*, etc., but no generalization is made (Russell 1995: 170).

One important consequence of the type of etymological derivation described above—both the analytical segmentation and the cross-language etymologies (together with the inbuilt vagueness of the use of *quasi*)—is that we are able to gain a sense of the parameters of Irish 'native' phonology, that is, how the medieval Irish compilers of these glossaries (and behind them the compilers of the entries themselves) understood the relationship between the sounds of Irish. While straightforward 'dictionary'-style entries of the 'A .i. B' form do not give us much to work with, entries using *quasi* or some of the analytical 'splitting'-style of etymologies can allow us to work out what was an acceptable range of sound change, both within early Irish itself and in relation to the corresponding words in other languages. I have discussed this elsewhere in relation to entries containing *quasi*, but it may be useful to summarize those findings here (Russell 2005*a*: 56):

> The biggest category involves alternation between homorganic consonants differentiated by voice: *p/b* (Y 163, 529, 1065, 1076(ii), 1071), *c/g* (Y 344, 671, 675, 695, 705, 712, 719), *f/v* (Y 279, 457, 593, 621, 636, 639); or stop vs. fricative: *f/p* (Y 619, 630, 1062), *b/f* (Y 170, 596, 643, 1085), *t/th* (Y 852, 854), *g/gh* (Y 664). There is also some alternation involving the presence or absence of a consonant: *p/Ø* (Y 29), *b/Ø* (Y 151), *f/Ø* (Y 597, 771, 987, 1020), *g/Ø* (Y 1171), *s/Ø* (Y 286); between *s* or *ss* and clusters containing *s*: *s/ps* (Y 89), *s/x* (Y 214, 466), *sc/x* (Y 980), *ss/sp* (Y 593); alternation in nasal clusters: *nd/nn* (Y 355, 856), *ln/ll* (Y 389), *m(m)/mp* (Y 231).

[13] The translations are based on Barney et al. (2006: 193, 347, 389 respectively) but render *corrupte* as 'corruptly' in all these three examples; Barney et al. translate it either as 'corruptly' or as 'incorrectly'; cf. also 4. 7. 13 (Greek βράγχος : *brancias*), 9. 2. 123 (*Massyli* : *Massulos*), 15. 1. 5 (*Hierusalem* : *Hierosolyma* : *Solyma*), 15. 2. 42 (*propina* : *popina*), 16. 25. 18 (*Sicel* : *Siclus*), 17. 7. 29 (*xyliglycon* : *siliquam*), 17. 7. 54 (*rhododendron* : *lorandrum*), 17. 9. 65 (*citocacia* : *citociam*), 19. 1. 17 (*phaselus* : *baselus*), 20. 16. 5 (*sagma* : *salma*).

Alternation was also found between an initial consonant and its lenited variant, e.g. Y 619 *fled* 'feast' *quasi ple 7 ed . . .*, Y 630 *fec* 'spade' *quasi pec . . .*, Y 1062 *pait* 'skin-bottle' *quasi fu áit*, etc., or the presence or absence of an initial consonant, e.g. Y 597 *fothrucad* 'washing' *quasi othrucad . . .*, Y 771 *id* 'with' *quasi fid*, Y 1020 *odar* 'dun-coloured' *quasi fodor . . .*, Y 1286 *usqa* 'water' *quasi susge . . .* Note that all the above instances involve *quasi*, but they do therefore have the advantage of marking out forms which might be regarded as being on the edge of acceptability. Many other entries simply state the relationship without using *quasi*. To a large extent, the more systematic patterns mirror the consonant variation visible elsewhere in Old and Middle Irish, and especially in relation to the initial consonantal mutations, thus *f/Ø, s/Ø, t/th, d/dh, c/ch*, etc.[14] We may also note in these etymologies that the vowel alternations tend to be more fuzzy and unpredictable, and I have suggested that this too mirrors the late Old Irish and Middle Irish phonological developments whereby all unaccented vowels gradually fell together as /ə/, with only accented vowels (usually in initial syllables) retaining their distinctive quality (Russell 2005*a*: 58). It is also noteworthy that the glossaries make use of two technical terms, *cendfocrus* 'changing the initial consonant', e.g. Y 609 . . . *fol quasi sol, id est ab eo quod est solus Latine .i. fol cendfocrus .i. .f. pro .s.* '*fol* (?) as if *sol*, i.e. from Latin *solus*, i.e. the initial consonant of *sol* has changed, i.e. *f* for *s*'; and *díchned* 'loss of the initial consonant' (lit. 'beheading'), e.g. Y 151 *bec quasi ec Ebraice paruus interpretatur .i. dechned tosaig fil and* '*bec* (small) as if Hebrew *ec* which means "small", i.e. there is loss of the initial consonant', where the 'decapitation' of the word allows a better fit with a proposed Hebrew etymology.[15] Both are used to refer to the kind of changes to the beginnings of words which occur in mutating contexts in Irish (and also in other Celtic languages), as in, for example, *siur* 'sister' : *a fiur* 'his sister'.

So what, then, was so special about the correspondence between Irish *f-* and Latin *u-/v-* that it gave rise to this generalization, not just once but twice, within *SC*? The high number of examples may have something to do with it. In addition to the examples of *fer* 'man', *fit* 'life', *firt* 'courage', and *fé* 'alas' quoted within the two entries where the generalization is made (Y 576 and 606), it is striking that three other examples are presented in subsequent entries in the *F*-letter block of the short version of *SC*:

[14] Strictly speaking, the alternation of *s* and *Ø* is between /s/ and /h/, but /h/ is treated as /Ø/ in this type of analysis.

[15] Both terms figure in *Auraicept na n-Éces* where the former, *cendfocrus*, can also be used to refer to the change of a final consonant (e.g. Calder 1917: 138–9, l. 1795).

Y 577 *Fín ab eo quod est uinum* '*fín* (wine) from *uinum*'
Y 593 *Fescer .i. quasi uesper i.e. uesperum* '*fescer* (evening, vespers), i.e. as if *uesper*, i.e. *uesperum*'
Y 595 *Fis a uisione* '*fís* (vision) from *uisio*'.

In addition, in YAdd (the extra material added to each letter block in the longer Y group versions of *SC*), another six examples are presented which perhaps in a further redaction might have been edited together into a single entry on the correspondence of Irish *f*- and Latin *u*-/*v*-:

Y 621 *Focal quasi uocabulum .i. guthán* '*focal* (word) as if *uocabulum*, i.e. little voice'[16]
Y 622 *Fér a uere .i. ón errach* '*fér* (grass) from *uer*, i.e. spring'
Y 624 *Figell a uigilia .i. frithaire* '*figell* (vigil) from *uigilia*, i.e. keeping watch'
Y 625 *Faigin a uaigina .i. ón trúaill* '*faigen* (sheath) from *uagina*, i.e. from sheath'
Y 626 *Félet a uerbo uelo .i. fíalaigim* '*félet* (?) from the verb *uelo*, i.e. I cover over'
Y 639 *Fír quasi uír, a uero Latine* '*fír* (true) as if *uír*, from Latin *uerus*'.[17]

Thus, in the shorter versions of *SC* there are seven examples, and thirteen overall in the longer versions. But quantity may not be the only factor. Another factor is what the correspondence was thought to involve, that is, what its phonetic or phonological reality was. The question is worth exploring since, if the glossators thought that it was a correspondence between Irish /f/- and Latin /v/-, it does not seem to be that different from the correspondences noted above between an unvoiced and a voiced consonant; if so, there is no particular reason why it should have been worthy of note. If, on the other hand, it was felt to be a correspondence between Irish /f/- and Latin /w/-, then that might be a different matter; for the nature of that correspondence is rather different from the other types noted above which tend to be concentrated on the homorganic consonants.

At this point, some anachronistic modern philology might be in order. Two points are worth making: first, from a modern linguistic perspective the above list of correspondences contains some genuine instances of a borrowing from Latin, e.g. *fín* 'wine' < Latin *uinum*, *figell* < Latin *uigilia*, *fescer* < Latin *uesper*, and some which are in modern terms correspondents, e.g. *fír* 'true' and Latin *uerus* 'true', and some which are historically unrelated, e.g. *fér* 'grass' and Latin *uer* 'spring'. But a medieval, pre-neo-grammarian, linguist might be forgiven for

[16] To judge from the *-án* suffix on the gloss *guthán*, the *-ulum* of *uocabulum* was being treated as a diminutive suffix.

[17] Note the greater degree of formal manipulation required in those cases where *quasi* is used; thus, two changes have to be made to *uesper* (Y 593) to reach *fescer*, and in *uocabulum* (Y 621) we have to allow for the loss, or perhaps elision, of the syllable *-bu-* (perhaps understood as representing something like -/vu/-).

making the connections. Secondly, it seems to be the case that borrowings into British from Latin (many of which travelled on into Old Irish), and borrowings directly into Irish from Latin, indicate that Latin initial *u-* was still being pronounced as /w/-: Welsh reflexes show initial /gw/- velarized from /w/- and Irish reflexes have /f/-, suggesting that Latin /w/- fell together with native /w/- which developed to Old Irish /f/-.[18] In other words, it seems likely that we should treat the correspondence in phonological terms as between Irish /f/- and Latin /w/-.

However, none of this yet explains why this particular correspondence attracted the generalization. It might be helpful to begin by moving beyond the glossaries themselves and exploring other early Irish texts concerned with language to see whether they contain any similar material. Two texts mentioned above are worth exploring: *Auraicept na n-Éces*, the so-called 'Scholars' Primer', and the Old Irish glosses on the St Gall Priscian (both noted above). Neither should give us cause for great hope. The early core of the *Auraicept* is generally not concerned with the origins of specific words, nor the relationship between forms in Irish and those in another language; although the commentaries are often interested in the origin of terms and incorporate some etymological analysis, there is little that is relevant to our current concern. It has only one passage of potential interest in relation to the notion of correspondence, and that is ll. 1059–1101 (Calder 1917: 80–3); Ahlqvist (1982: 48, §1.15) treats the key point as part of the core text, and so the idea at any rate, if not all of the text, may well be quite early. However, this passage deals with the lexical rather than phonological correspondence (and uses the terms *frecra, fris-gair* 'correspond' as against the *frestol, fris-indlea* of *SC*) and reflects the view noted above that Irish cut out the best bits of the other languages, and *leithiu didiu in Gaedel i foclaibh 7 i litribh desin anda in Laitneoir* 'hence then, the Gael is wider in words and letters than the Latinist' (Calder 1917: 82–3, ll. 1094–5). Although letters are mentioned, the thrust of the argument is that Irish simply has more words for things than Latin, and in particular that Latin has no words corresponding to *grus* 'curds', *cloch* 'stone', and *linn* 'pool'.

Even though the argument here is not directly relevant to our discussion, it is striking that, although Irish has been cut out from the best of the other languages, and the implicit comparison is between Irish and all the rest of the languages, the explicit claim is that it is better and more lexically nuanced than

[18] For the debate over the apparently 'posh, upper-class' pronunciation of *u* as [w], rather than as [v], in British Latin, see Jackson (1953: 88–90), Gratwick (1982: 17–36), and most recently Adams (2007: 626–80). One difficulty is what would have happened to a reflex of a Latin /v/ anyway; would it have been treated as a lenited version of /b/ or /m/, or would it have fallen together with /w/? Cf. Russell (1985: 21–4).

Latin. The relationship between Irish and Latin is also, of course, an aspect of the Old Irish glosses on Priscian. But, when we turn to these, again the cupboard is relatively bare, not least because the glossators were usually not interested in generalization, but more in simply explaining what is in front of them on the page; indeed, so little are they concerned with generalizing that the same gloss (or variations on it) frequently reappears over and again, even within the range of a few pages. Moreover, as Hofman (1993) has demonstrated, they never seem concerned to make comparisons between Latin and Irish. On the other hand, while the glosses on Priscian do not seem to have much to offer, the text of Priscian's *Institutiones Grammaticae* itself may have more of significance (*GL* ii. 1–iii. 384 Keil).

While the main text of Priscian itself is not concerned with Irish, it is interested in correspondences between Latin and Greek, and so we might expect that the language of correspondence might at least surface. At various points in the section *De litera* (*GL* ii. 6–37 Keil) Priscian lists correspondences between Greek and Latin words and, although many of the correspondences are presented in a relatively vague manner, there are occasional instances of a more rigorous mode of presentation: thus, with reference to the correspondence between Greek initial /h/- and Latin /s/-:

> [S...] saepe pro aspiratione ponitur in his dictionibus, quas a Graecis sumpsimus, ut semis, sex, septem, se, sal: nam ἥμισυ, ἕξ, ἑπτά, ἕ, ἅλς apud illos aspirationem habent in principio (Priscian, *GL* ii. 32. 19–33. 1 Keil)[19]

> 'often [s] is put in these words which we have taken from Greek, instead of aspiration, such as *semis, sex, septem, se, sal*: for ἥμισυ, ἕξ, ἑπτά, ἕ, ἅλς have initial aspiration in Greek'

A list of correspondences (that is, rather than just one example), together with the use of a generalizing *saepe*, points to the proposal of some kind of a rule which goes beyond a simple observation; *saepe*, furthermore, also allows for the possibility of exceptions—i.e. it is often the case, but not always. We might also note that, as with the Irish examples with which we began, such correspondences are seen in terms of borrowing (*quas a Graecis sumpsimus*). An instance which comes significantly closer to what we see in Irish involves an extended comparison between the Aeolic Greek *digamma* and the use of Latin *u*:

> sciendum tamen, quod hoc ipsum Aeolis quidem ubique loco aspirationis ponebant effugientes spiritus asperitatem, nos autem in multis quidem, non tamen in omnibus illos sequimur, ut cum dicimus uespera, uis, uestis. hiatus quoque causa solebant illi interponere Ϝ, quod ostendunt et poetae Aeolide usi (Ἀλκμάν· 'καὶ χεῖμα πῦρ τε δάϜιον'): et

[19] For another version of this, cf. Priscian, *GL* iii. 16. 18–20 Keil.

epigrammata, quae egomet legi in tripode uetustissimo Apollinis, qui stat in Xerolopho Byzantii, sic scripta: Δημοφαϝων Λαϝοκοϝων. nos quoque hiatus causa interponimus u loco ϝ, ut Dauus, Argiuus, pauo, ouum, ouis, bouis. hoc tamen etiam per alias quasdam consonantes hiatus uel euphoniae causa solet fieri, ut prodest, comburo, sicubi, nuncubi, quod Graeci quoque solent facere: μηκέτι, οὐκέτι. sed tamen hoc attendendum est, quod praeualuit in hac litera [id est in u loco digamma posita] potestas simplicis consonantis apud omnium poetarum doctissimos. in b etiam solet apud Aeolis transire ϝ digamma, quotiens ab ρ incipit dictio, quae solet aspirari, ut ῥήτωρ βρήτωρ dicunt, quod digamma nisi uocali praeponi et in principio syllabae non potest. ideo autem locum quoque transmutauit, quia b uel digamma post ρ in eadem syllaba pronuntiari non potest. apud nos quoque est inuenire, quod pro u consonante b ponitur, ut caelebs, caelestium uitam ducens, per b scribitur, quod u consonans ante consonantem poni non potest. sed etiam Bruges et Belena antiquissimi dicebant teste Quintiliano, qui hoc ostendit in primo institutionum oratoriarum: nec mirum, cum b quoque in u euphoniae causa conuerti inuenimus, ut aufero pro abfero. (Priscian, *GL* ii. 17. 6–18. 14 Keil)[20]

'Note that, where the Aeolians used to put this (*sc.* a *digamma*) in place of aspiration avoiding the roughness of the breathing, we too follow them in many instances, but not however in all, such as when we say *uespera*, *uis*, *uestis*.[21] They also usually inserted ϝ to avoid hiatus, a usage which the Aeolic poets also show (Alcman: 'καὶ χεῖμα πῦρ τε δάϝιον'): and the epigrams, which I myself have read on the ancient tripod of Apollo which stands in the Xerolophon in Byzantium, written thus Δημοφαϝων Λαϝοκοϝων. We too insert *u* instead of ϝ to avoid hiatus, as in *Dauus, Argiuus, pauo, ouum, ouis, bouis*. This often happens also with some other consonants to avoid hiatus or for the sake of euphony, as in *prodest, comburo, sicubi, nuncubi*; the Greeks also often do this: μηκέτι 'no longer', οὐκέτι 'no longer'.[22] Even so, it is to be noted that the force of a single consonant prevails in this letter [i.e. in the use of *u* instead of the *digamma*] among the most learned of all the poets. The *digamma* ϝ usually turns into *b* among the Aeolians, whenever the word begins with ρ which is usually aspirated, thus for ῥήτωρ they say βρήτωρ because a *digamma* cannot be put in front of anything but a vowel and cannot be at the beginning of a syllable. Furthermore, it has also changed its position, because *b* or a *digamma* after ρ cannot be pronounced in the same syllable. With us too it is possible to find that *u* is replaced by *b*; thus, *caelebs*, 'leading the life of the heavenly ones', is written with *b*, because the consonant *u* cannot be put in front of a consonant.[23] But the ancients also used to say *Bruges* and *Belena* according to Quintilian, who shows this in

[20] On the *digamma*, see further Priscian, *GL* ii. 11. 5–12. 2 Keil; in the section *De litera*, Priscian *inter alia* also discusses *v* (*GL* ii. 15. 1–18. 4 Keil) and *f* (*GL* ii. 35. 13–21 Keil).

[21] This is one of a number of instances in Priscian where he sees Latin as following Aeolic Greek (often phrased as *in quo Aeolis sequimur*); cf. also Priscian, *GL* ii. 15. 2, ii. 26. 19, ii. 27. 25, ii. 28. 14, ii. 35. 15, ii. 38. 5, ii. 39. 21, ii. 40. 11, ii. 253. 17–18, iii. 16. 19, iii. 27. 6 Keil. For a recent discussion of the history of this idea and the definition of 'Aeolic' in Priscian (broadly 'any Greek dialect not Attic, Ionic or Doric'), see Maltby (2009: 242–4).

[22] On the concept of euphony, see below, p. 29.

[23] This statement seems to imply a pronunciation of the final syllable as -/eus/ or -/evs/.

the first book of his *Institutiones Oratoriae* (1. 4. 15); this is not surprising, since we find *b* turned into *u* for the sake of euphony, as in *aufero* for *abfero*.'

This passage presents striking similarities with the Irish passages cited at the beginning of this paper. First, there is the formal similarity of the *digamma* and *f*. Secondly, the correspondence between the use of the *digamma* in Aeolic Greek and the use of *u* in Latin seems to be expressed in a very similar way to the correspondence between Irish *f* and Latin *u*. Furthermore, the assertion that the correspondence has some exceptions (*nos autem in multis quidem, non tamen in omnibus illos sequimur*) seems to be echoed in the *quamuis hoc non per singula currat* of the Irish glossary. The links are tantalizing, but the obvious objection is that Priscian is discussing a correspondence between letters in Latin and Aeolic Greek, and that this has nothing to do with Irish.

We know, however, that this passage was known within the Irish glossarial tradition, and that the Aeolic connection was explicitly acknowledged. As Moran (2007: 84, 196 (and n. 34)) has pointed out, O'Mulconry's Glossary [O'M], a glossary which is notable for its proportionally higher density of Greek, Latin, and Hebrew explanations than the other glossaries, and which contains some of the linguistically earliest entries in the Irish glossarial tradition, contains the following entry: *briathor insce apud Eoles* (Stokes 1900: 241, §160) '*briathor* means word among the Aeolians'.[24] Almost certainly this has to reflect knowledge of the latter part of the passage quoted above which refers to the change of *digamma* to *β* before *ρ*. The headword *briathor*, probably derived from an earlier *brethor* (reflecting the early Old Irish change of /eː/ to /ia/ and perhaps also lenition of intervocalic /t/ to /θ/), surely represents a hibernicized version of the Aeolic form quoted above, *βρήτωρ*.

The Aeolic link with O'M is even more solidly based; in the programmatic statement with which the glossary begins, attention is drawn to its continental and classical content:[25]

Incipit discreptio (*sic*) de origine Scoticae linguae quam congregaverunt religiosi viri, adiunctis nominibus ex Hebraeicano Hironimi et tractationibus, i.e. Ambrosi, et Cassiani et Augustini et Eisidori, Virgili, Prisciani, Commiani, Ciceronis, necnon per literas

[24] Cf. also Moran (2011 and forthcoming). The previous entry in the glossary, §159, reads *brí 7 rethor .i. breuis 7 arathor*, to which the editor, Stokes, prefixed *[briathor .i.]*, and looks like an attempt to provide an Isidorian form of etymology to the same word; it is possible, in fact, that Stokes's textual addition (which is designed to provide it with a headword) is unnecessary, and that §159 was in origin part of §160, and by a scribal misreading was separated out into a separate entry. The St Gall glossators have no comment to make on these forms (Hofman 1996: i. 126, ii. 43).

[25] For discussion of this passage, see Russell (1988: 5–6), Jaski (2003: 11–12).

Graecorum, i.e. Atticae, Doricae, Eolicae lingae, quia Scoti de Graecis originem duxerunt, sic et lingam (*sic*).

'Here begins an account of the origin of the Irish language compiled by religious men by joining together names/nouns from the Hebrew etymologies of Jerome and from the biblical commentaries, namely those of Ambrosius, Cassianus, Augustine, Isidore, Virgil, Priscian, Cummean, and Cicero, and particularly from Greek literature, i.e. the Attic, Doric, and Aeolic dialects, since the Irish derive their origin from the Greeks, and thus too their language.'

While the Latin and Hebrew sources are characterized by reference to the names of various authors, Jerome, Virgil, Isidore, Priscian, et al., the Greek sources are strikingly described in terms of literature in various dialects, Attic, Doric, and Aeolic, followed by the explanation that it is from the Greeks that the Irish derive their origin and so also their language (*Scoti de Graecis originem duxerunt, sic et lingam*). Now it is noteworthy that most references to Aeolic Greek in Priscian and the other grammarians refer to one of two things, either to metrical matters (which is not our concern here) or to the section *De litera*, and especially to discussion of the digamma which is regularly characterized as the *digamma Aeolicum* (e.g. *GL* ii. 11. 5 Keil).[26] The section on the *digamma* linking it to the use of *u* in Latin is a standard feature in most of the grammarians and may well have been known in Ireland;[27] notably it occurs usually in a shorter form in commentaries to Donatus which are usually ascribed to Irishmen; for example, Murethach's *In Donati Artem Maiorem* contains the following passage (**bold** indicates the main text of Donatus):

Hvic item digammon adscribi solet id est adsignari uel dari **cvm sibi ipsa praeponitvr vt servvs vvlgvs.** Digammon dicitur duo gamma tali modo composita F. Obtinet enim eandem uim apud Graecos quam aspiratio apud Latinos, uidelicet addita pinguem reddit sonum, abstracta uero non minuit sensum. Et illa figura dicitur digamma; potestas autem eius uau dicitur. Sicut nos dicimus Helena, ita Greci Felena (Holtz 1977: 12–13, ll. 78–85).[28]

'To this is usually ascribed the *digamma*, i.e. assigned or given, **when it is placed in front of itself, such as *seruus, uulgus*.** The *digamma* is said to be made up of two *gamma*s, thus *F*. For it has the same force in Greek as aspiration in Latin, namely when it is added it gives a rich sound, but when it is removed it does not reduce the sense. And that form

[26] For a few exceptions, see Maltby (2009: 243–4).

[27] Cf., for example, *Cledonii Ars, GL* v. 27. 18–21 Keil; Diomedes, *GL* i. 422 Keil; Donatus, *Ars Maior, GL* iv. 368 Keil = Holtz (1981: 604); Pompeius, *in artem Donati, GL* v. 105 Keil; Sergius, *de littera, GL* iv. 476 Keil; *[Sergii] explanationes in artes Donati, GL* iv. 521 Keil; Servius, *in Donati artem maiorem, GL* iv. 422 Keil; *Marii Victorini ars, GL* vi. 14. 23–15. 14 Keil = Mariotti (1967: 87–8).

[28] More or less identical is the *Ars Laureshamensis* (Löfstedt 1977: 154. 97–155. 8).

is called a *digamma*; for its force is called *waw*. Just as we say *Helena*, the Greeks say /welena/.'

Thus, it would not be immediately obvious that Priscian must be the source for the discussion of the *digamma* were it not for the fact that the example of Aeolic *βρήτωρ* found in O'M is only found in Priscian (*GL* ii. 18. 6 and ii. 19. 20 Keil), and so we must assume a link with that grammar at least.

Another point of connection between this passage in Priscian and the Irish glossaries concerns the question of euphony: an entry in *SC* on *gabar* 'goat' makes a distinction between this word and its near homonym *gobar* 'horse', the latter of which it argues is derived from a British form *goor*.[29] Towards the end of the entry it claims that *rotuill in fili Gaidhelach .b. fris ar thucait mbindessa* 'the Irish poet added *b* to it for the sake of euphony'. Given that the 'euphonic' consonant is *b* and given the striking parallel between *ar thucait mbindessa* and *euphoniae causa* in Priscian, it is highly likely that this represents another link between these passages.

The entry, then, in *SC*, with which we began and which purports to offer a generalized statement about the correspondence between Irish /f/ and Latin /w/, appears to be modelled on the discussion in Priscian about the correspondence between the Aeolic Greek *digamma* and Latin *u*. The circumstantial and precise detail of the formal similarity between *f* and the *digamma*, the presence of a word in O'M from precisely this passage of Priscian, and the perceived connections between Aeolic Greek and Irish together lead us to suppose that the mode of thinking about linguistic relationships encapsulated in *fern do frestol na .u. consaine* is dependent on Priscian; not least it explains why it is this precise correspondence which is uniquely subject to a generalization in the Irish glossaries. We should, therefore, be very circumspect before using this evidence to say anything useful about how the medieval Irish saw the correspondences between Irish and Latin, or whether and how they might derive any linguistic rules from their observations. On the other hand, the early Irish glossaries with their preoccupations with etymology, phonology, and borrowing have much to offer those interested in the medieval phases of linguistic thought.[30]

[29] *SCY* 675 *gabar*; for further discussion and an edition and translation of the entry, see Russell (1995: 178–9). I suggested then that, since it seemed to be connected with white- or bright-colouring on horses, a connection with Welsh *gwawr* 'dawn' might be plausible; more recently Kelly (1997: 52) has proposed a connection with Welsh *gawr* 'grey'. The same example is quoted in *Auraicept na n-Éces* (Calder 1917: 46–9, ll. 628–38) as one of the four subdivisions of artificiality; for discussion, see Hayden (forthcoming).

[30] This paper, which in the writing turned into an exercise in scepticism, is offered in gratitude to John Penney who taught many of us to be sceptical and to question everything.

Abbreviations for glossaries cited above

B	(*SC*) *Leabhar Breac* (Dublin, Royal Irish Academy (RIA) MS, 23 P 16), pp. 263–72; see Stokes (1862: 1–44), O'Donovan and Stokes (1868) [reference by page and line number of Stokes's edition].
H^{1a}	(*SC*) Dublin, Trinity College (TCD) MS, 1317 (H. 2. 15b), pp. 13–37 (version C in Stokes 1862).
H^{1b}	(*SC*) TCD MS, 1317 (H. 2. 15b), pp. 77–102 (version C in Stokes 1862).
K	(*SC*) Dublin, University College, Franciscan (Killiney) MS A 12, pp. 1–40.
M	(*SC*) *The Book of Uí Maine* (RIA MS, D. ii. 1), pp. 177–184a (incomplete; only up to Y 1224); see K. Meyer (1919) [reference by the numbering according to Y].
O'M	(O'Mulconry's Glossary) *The Yellow Book of Lecan* (TCD MS, 1318 (H. 2. 16)), cols 88–122; see Stokes (1900) [references by the numbering of items].
SC	*Sanas Cormaic*
Y	(*SC*) *The Yellow Book of Lecan* (TCD MS, 1318 (H. 2. 16)), pp. 255a–283a; see K. Meyer (1912), O'Donovan and Stokes (1868) [reference by the numbering of items].
YAdd	The additional material in Y, H^{1ab}, and K, not found in the other versions of the glossary [reference by the numbering of items in K. Meyer (1912)].

Part II

Rules of language change and linguistic methodology

3

Cladistic principles and linguistic reality: the case of West Germanic

DON RINGE

A basic principle of cladistics is that only shared innovations which are unlikely to have occurred independently can prove shared history. Linguistic cladists therefore use a straightforward rule of thumb: languages can be assigned to the same clade only if they can be shown to share a respectably large number of significant innovations. By that criterion the West Germanic languages do constitute a valid clade; it is clear that Proto-West Germanic (PWGmc) was a single language (by some reasonable definition) for generations. However, we can also demonstrate that there were significant dialect differences within Proto-West Germanic well before it lost its linguistic unity.

A complete survey of the innovations shared by West Germanic languages is beyond the scope of a short article, but it is not necessary to assemble all the available evidence to show that Proto-West Germanic must have been a single language for some generations. We merely need to demonstrate that the attested West Germanic languages share one or more sets of significant innovations whose relative chronology can be recovered. The chronology of changes serves two purposes. On the one hand, languages are much less likely to have undergone innovations *in the same order* independently by chance. On the other hand, a sequence of changes should require more time to go to completion than a similar set of unrelated changes, thus ensuring that the period of linguistic unity demonstrated by the shared changes continued for a significant period of time.

The attested West Germanic languages share at least two series of crucially ordered changes, which I will call series A and series B. Series A is simple and relatively short. The earliest of its changes was discovered by Stiles (1985–6, 6: 89–94):

A1. Proto-Germanic (PGmc) intervocalic **dw*, **zw* > PWGmc **ww* (at least after short vowels).

The examples are few but clinching:

- PGmc **fedwōr* 'four' (Goth. *fidwor*) > PWGmc **fewwar* > OE *fēower*, OF *fiuwer*, OS *fiuwar* (OHG *fior* has been backformed to *fiordo* 'fourth', etc.; Stiles 1985–6, 6: 91–2).
- PGmc **izwiz* 'you (dat. pl.)' (Goth. *izwis*) > PWGmc **iwwi* > OE *īow*, OF, OS, OHG *iu*.
- PGmc **izweraz* 'your (pl.)' (Goth. *izwar*) > PWGmc **iwwar* > OE *īower*, OHG *iuwerēr*.

This sound change makes phonetic sense only if */d/ was still fricative *[ð] when preceded by a vowel. That enables us to order it before:

A2. PGmc */d/ = *[d ~ ð] > PWGmc */d/ = *[d]

that is, */d/ became a stop in all positions. Of course this is not a result of the comparative method, which yields only phonemic contrasts; we can be sure of it only because in the earliest stages of all West Germanic languages the outcome of PWGmc **d* is always a stop. That development must have preceded a morphologically conditioned innovation:

A3. PGmc **i* > Ø between root-final **t* or **d* and the **d* of the past-tense suffix (see Campbell 1962: 331), for example:

- OE (Northumbrian) *ġesætte*, OS *satta* 3sg. 'set' < PWGmc **sattē* < PGmc **satidē* (Goth. *satida*; cf. Runic Norse 1sg. *satido*); umlaut levelled into OE *sette*, OS *gisetta*; OHG **sattē* > **sazza* → *sazta* with regularized suffix.
- OS *latta* 3sg. 'became exhausted' < PWGmc **lattē* 'hindered' < PGmc **latidē*; umlaut levelled into OS *lettun* 'they hindered', OE *lette*; OHG *lazta* as above.
- OHG *tratta* 3sg. 'frequented' < PWGmc **traddē* < **tradidē* (cf. ON *traddi* 'caused to walk on', identical in shape but causative rather than intensive); umlaut levelled into OE *tredde* 'investigated'.
- So also OHG (3sg.) *quatta* 'called', *brutta* 'frightened', *scutta* 'shook' (beside regularized *scutita*), etc.

This change makes much better phonetic sense if intervocalic **d* was already a stop, and that is the basis for ordering it after A2.

Series B is more involved, and it begins with a sound change whose existence can only be inferred from the results of later changes. There is considerable evidence that the sound system of Proto-Germanic included labiovelar consonants (Ringe 2006*a*: 90–3). In Proto-West Germanic they were reanalysed as sequences of velar + **w*:

B1. **K^{w} > *Kw.*

Of course there is no direct evidence for such a subtle change; we can reconstruct it only from its interaction with the next three changes. The first of those was sweeping in its effects:

B2. Proto-Germanic short low vowels were lost word-finally (and before **-z*, if the latter had not already been lost)[1] when unstressed (i.e. except in monosyllables).

Every nominative and accusative singular of an *a*-stem noun in every West Germanic language exemplifies this change. Either as part of the same historical process or as a consequence of it, postconsonantal word-final semivowels became syllabic:

B3. **j, *w > *i, *u* / C__#.

This change provides part of our evidence for the resolution of labiovelars; consider the development of the adjective meaning 'alive':

- PGmc **k^{w}ik^{w}az* 'alive' (ON *kvikr*; cf. Ringe 2006*a*: 69, 91) > **kwikwaz, *kwikwa-* > PWGmc **kwiku, *kwik(k)wa-* (see below) >→ OE *cwicu/cwic*, OS *quik*, OHG *quek/queh* (with various levellings).

There are other straightforward examples with **w* and with **j*, such as:

- PGmc **gelwaz* 'yellow' (cf. Lat. *heluos* 'bay (horse)') > PWGmc **gelu, *gelwa-* > OE *ġeolu, ġeolw-*, OHG *gelo, gelaw-*.
- PGmc **harjaz* 'army' (Goth. *harjis*, ON *herr*) > PWGmc **hari, *harja-* > OE *here, herġ-*, OS, OHG *heri, heri-*.

Most *ja*-stem nom.-acc. sg. forms have been levelled away in favour of the oblique stems with gemination (see below). However, occasional Old High

[1] Of course this change would be easier to state if word-final **-z* in unstressed syllables had already been lost, and it clearly was lost early in the separate development of Proto-West Germanic; but, strictly speaking, we cannot prove the relative chronology of the two changes in question, and for that reason I take no account of it here.

German spellings like *beti* 'bed' preserve the effects of this sound change (Dal 1971: 68–9); in addition, Old English byforms of *i*-stems such as *mettas* 'foods', with *tt* < **tj*, point to the same conclusion. That is, because the paradigm of masculine *i*-stems had developed as:

- PGmc **matiz* 'food' (Goth. *mats*), acc. **matį*, gen. **matīz*, etc. > PWGmc **mati*, **mati*, **matī*, etc.

and the paradigm of masculine *ja*-stems had developed as:

- PGmc **sagjaz* 'retainer' (cf. Lat. *socius* 'ally'), acc. **sagją*, gen. **sagjas*, etc. > PWGmc **sagi*, **sagi*, **sagjas*, etc.

the nom.-acc. forms were ambiguous, leading language learners to transfer stems from one class to the other.

As the preceding discussion shows, all these developments must have preceded

B4. Gemination: clusters **Cj* became phonetically *[C^jC^j], i.e. palatalized geminates, unless **C* was **r* or **z*;[2] gemination of stops also occurred under unknown conditions before **w*, **l*, and **r*.

The West Germanic gemination before **j* is too well known to require exemplification here; the discussions of *ja*-stem nouns and class I weak verbs in any grammar of Old English or Old High German will provide numerous examples. Of particular interest to us is the fact that the **kw* which resulted from the resolution of PGmc **k^w^* (see above) sometimes underwent gemination to **kkw*, which proves that the **w* was a separate segment; for instance, of the Old High German forms of 'alive' cited above, *queh* reflects (**kwikwa-* >) **kwika-*, but *quek* must reflect (**kwikkwa-* >) **kwikka-* because of its unshifted *k*. Occasionally, all the attested forms reflect gemination, for example:

- pre-PGmc **tegus*, fem. **tegwī* 'thick' (cf. OIr. *tiug*) > PGmc **þekuz*, **þik^{w}ī* (cf. Heidermanns 1993: 617–18, Ringe 2006*a*: 90–1, 282–3) > **þekuz*, **þikkwī* (cf. ON *þjokkr/þykkr*)[3] >→ PWGmc **þikkwī* (masc. *ja*-stem, fem. *jō*-stem) > OE *þicce*, OS *thikki*, OHG *dick(i)*; cf. also OF *thiukke* 'extent', and see further below.

[2] Of course the change is easier to state if we posit merger of **r* and **z* before gemination. But the failure of **j* to geminate these consonants was probably a result of their phonetics, plausibly a retroflex place of articulation, and it is very likely that **z* had become a retroflex fricative before its merger with **r*; therefore we cannot reconstruct the relative chronology of the merger and gemination with any confidence.

[3] Velars were regularly geminated in Old Norse by a following **j* or **w*, but only when a short vowel preceded. The Old Norse change was almost certainly independent of the West Germanic gemination because of the relative chronologies of the changes in both languages.

Eventually **w* was lost after non-word-initial velars throughout the West Germanic area, but there are clear indications that that occurred after the daughter languages had parted company. For one thing, **kk* was not palatalized in OE *þicce* even though it appears to have been between high front vowels (Luick 1914–40: I.ii.840); the only convincing explanation for that outcome is that the following **w* still existed at the time of palatalization, since that would have been sufficient to block the palatalization of the voiceless stop, geminate or single (Brunner 1965: 168–9). But palatalization followed many Old English changes of low vowels, since it affected the initial consonants of *ġeat* 'gate', *ċeare* (obl. cases) 'worry' < **gæt, *kærǣ* < PWGmc **gat, *karā*, but not those of *gatu* 'gates', *caru* (nom. sg.) 'worry' < **gætu, *kæru* < PWGmc **gatu, *karu*. Those changes included not only the early ones shared (more or less) with Old Frisian, but also the specifically Old English changes of diphthongs, breaking, and the 'restoration' of **a* before syllables containing back vowels (see especially the chronology of Campbell 1962: 109). Thus Old English must have been significantly different from its neighbours by the time those **w* were lost. Secondly, in Old Frisian the loss of post-velar **w* was either preceded or accompanied by transfer of the rounding to the **i* of a preceding syllable; in addition to *thiukke* 'extent' (cited above), cf. for example:

- PGmc **sing^{w}aną* 'to sing' (Goth. *siggwan*, ON *syngva*) > PWGmc **singwan* > OE, OS, OHG *singan*, but OF *siunga*.

It seems clear that the loss of **w* was a parallel change, not a historically shared change. But that still leaves a sequence of four historically shared changes in series B.

The sequences of changes considered so far are enough to establish that West Germanic was in some sense a speech community for at least a few generations. However, there is a third sequence of changes which shows that there was some diversity within West Germanic well before changes stopped spreading through the whole community. This sequence involves a disputed point of morphology, namely the origin of the **ō* that is more or less pervasive in Old High German weak past inflection. I begin with a summary of that problem.

The indicative singular forms of the weak past can be reconstructed without difficulty from Gothic and Norse, including Runic Norse:

PGmc 1sg. **-dǭ* > Goth. *-da*, Runic Norse *-do*, ON *-ða*
PGmc 2sg. **-dēz* > Goth. *-des*, ON *-ðir*
PGmc 3sg. **-dē* > Goth. *-da*, Runic Norse *-de*,[4] ON *-ði*.

[4] On Runic Norse *talgidai*, see Hill (2004: 287 n. 84) and Ringe (2006*b*: 191–2), both with references. All other Runic Norse examples end in *-de*, including an example of *tawide* of about the same date as *talgidai*; the balance of evidence is therefore that *-dai* is either a reverse spelling or an error.

OE 1sg., 3sg. *-de* and 2sg. *-des* (recharacterized with a voiceless ending, since **-z* had been lost) can reflect the same preforms. The Old High German situation is very different.[5] 1sg. *-ta* can reflect PGmc **-dǭ*, but 3sg. *-ta* probably cannot reflect PGmc **-dē*; the only regular sources for its vowel are PGmc **-ǭ* and **-ōz*, both of which are morphologically impossible. Moreover, though the Old High German *Isidor* does occasionally exhibit a 2sg. *-dēs* (comparable to the Old English form), other dialects have *-tus*, and most have *-tōs* (Hill 2004: 287 with references). Further, while most Old High German dialects exhibit *-u-* in the plural indicative endings of the weak past, in agreement with all other Germanic languages, the Alemannic dialects (including that of *Isidor*) exhibit *-ō-* instead. Hill (2004: 291–3) proposes to project pl. **-ō-* back into Proto-Germanic; but such a solution should be avoided unless there are no feasible alternatives, because it requires independent levelling of strong past endings (certainly with **-u-*) into the weak past in all other Germanic dialects.[6] It is preferable to seek a purely Old High German solution to this purely Old High German anomaly.

The key to such a solution was suggested by Hollifield (1980: 151); what follows is an elaboration of Hollifield's solution in the context of the third sequence of changes. We do not know when word-final **-z* in unstressed syllables was lost in the development of Proto-West Germanic, but its loss can have been very early, since no other Proto-West Germanic sound change must have occurred before it. I therefore propose that sound change as:

C1a. **z* > Ø / [–stress] __#.

(The nom. sg. of every non-neuter *a*-, *i*-, and *u*-stem noun is an example of this change.) Another change that can have occurred indefinitely early is the loss of nasalization of word-final vowels (for the Proto-Germanic situation cf. Ringe 2006*a*: 85–6, 141–2). In most cases the result was loss of a contrast between non-nasalized and nasalized vowels, but since PGmc **-ō* had already become **-u* in the North-West Germanic period (cf. e.g. Campbell 1962: 139), this sound change:

C1b. **V* > [–nas] / __#,

[5] There is so much variation in the Old Saxon endings that it seems inadvisable to base any conclusions on them; for the facts, see e.g. Gallée (1910: 249–50).

[6] Independent levelling at least in Gothic and North-West Germanic is required, with extensive spread of the innovation through a North-West Germanic dialect continuum; possibly independent levelling in Gothic, Old Norse, and (non-Alemannic) West Germanic is required.

created new examples of word-final non-nasalized *-ō. By these two sound changes the paradigm of the weak past indicative in the singular must have become the following:

1sg. *-*dō* (by C1b)
2sg. *-*dē* (by C1a)
3sg. *-*dē* (no change).

The pattern of this paradigm, in which 2sg. = 3sg., conflicted with the pattern long established in the strong past, where 1sg. = 3sg.; we might therefore expect native learners to make errors in acquiring the weak past paradigm that could lead to remodelling. One plausible remodelling would be the spread of *-*dē* to the 1sg., so that 1sg. = 3sg. even at the cost of eliminating person-marking in the weak past indicative singular. The northern West Germanic dialects (ancestral to Old English and Old Frisian) might have done that; we cannot tell for certain, because pre-PWGmc *-ō and *-*ē* eventually merged in those dialects in any case (see below). The other plausible 'repair' of this paradigm would be the spread of 1sg. *-*dō* to the 3sg., creating a pattern identical to that of the strong past indicative singular: 1sg. = 3sg., but a distinctive 2sg. Apparently the southern dialects (ancestral to Old High German) adopted that solution. I therefore posit:

C2. 3sg. *-*dē* → *-*dō* = 1sg. *-*dō* (southern dialects only).

By this change the pivotal member of the paradigm, the 3sg. (unmarked for person and number), acquired a suffix vowel *ō. From there it could easily have spread through the rest of the paradigm by two further changes:

C3a. 2sg. *-*dē* → *-*dōs* (some southern dialects only) and
C3b. pl. *-*u*- → *-ō- (Alemannic dialects only).

But—crucially—all three of these changes could only have occurred *before* a further change which was shared by all West Germanic dialects:

C4. *ō > *ā / __(r)#

that is, *ō was unrounded to **ā* in final syllables if it was in absolute word-final position or was followed by **r*. Examples are fairly numerous, and they include the 1sg. and 3sg. endings under discussion:

- PGmc **fedwōr* 'four' (Goth. *fidwor*) > **fewwār* > PWGmc **fewwar* > OE *fēower*, OF *fiuwer*, OS *fiuwar*.
- PGmc **watōr* nom.-acc. sg. 'water' (cf. Goth. *wato* with *n*-stem inflection generalized) > **watār* > PWGmc **watar* > OE *wæter*, OF *weter*, OS *watar*, OHG *waʒʒar*.

- PGmc **gebōz* gen. sg. 'of a gift' (Goth. *gibos*, ON *gjafar*) > PWGmc **gebā* > OE *ġiefe*, OS *geƀa*, OHG *geba*.
- PGmc **gebǭ* acc. sg. 'gift' (Goth. *giba*) > PWGmc **gebā* > OE *ġiefe*, OS *geƀa*, OHG *geba*.
- PGmc **þanǭ* acc. sg. masc. 'that', **hʷanǭ* 'whom?' (Goth. *þana, ƕana*; cf. *ƕano-h* 'each') > PWGmc **þanā, *hwanā* > OE *þone, hwone*, OF *thene, hwane*, OS *thana*, cf. also *hwena* from the alternative interrogative stem.
- PGmc weak past ind. 1sg. **-dǭ* (cf. Goth. *-da*, Runic Norse *-do*) > PWGmc **-dā* > OE, OF *-de*, OS *-da* (?), OHG *-ta*; so also OS *-da* (?), OHG 3sg. *-ta*.
- PNWGmc nom. sg. **tungǭ* 'tongue', **hertǭ* 'heart' (ON *tunga, hjarta*; Goth. *tuggo, haírto* have a different, but probably also analogical, ending, cf. Ringe 2006*a*: 274–5) > PWGmc **tungā, *hertā* > OE *tunge, heorte*, OS *tunga, herta*, OHG *zunga, herza*.

After this change had occurred the southern weak past indicative 3sg. no longer ended in **-ō*; it follows that the spread of **-ō-* in the Old High German weak past must have occurred earlier. Nor was this unrounding the last change in the series shared by all West Germanic dialects; as in 'four' and 'water' above, it was followed by the shortening of vowels before word-final **r*:

C5. *V* > [–long] / __r#.

This is demonstrated by the fact that those Old High German documents that indicate vowel length in final syllables—the only West Germanic documents that do so—always have short vowels before word-final *-r* (Stiles 1985–6, 6: 88); thus we also find, for example:

- PGmc, PNWGmc **fadēr* 'father' (ON *faðir*; cf. Gr. πατήρ /patɛ́:r/) > PWGmc **fader* > OE *fæder*, OF *feder*, OS *fader, -ar*, OHG *fater*.

This sequence of changes establishes that there was dialect diversity in Proto-West Germanic well before it ceased to be a coherent speech community in the larger sense.[7]

What impact should these findings have on our assessment of West Germanic as a valid clade, and what more general impact should findings like these have on linguistic cladistics? There are several important points to be made in answering those questions.

[7] There are some other patterns of change that might also demonstrate this; the split of inherited **u* into **u* and **o* (somewhat differently in different West Germanic dialects), and the southern lowering of **i* before non-coronal consonants followed by non-high vocalics, are promising candidates.

There seems to be a widespread belief that *any* evidence of dialectal divergence followed by shared development invalidates a clade; colleagues who hold that extreme view insist, in effect, that every node in a *Stammbaum* must represent a completely uniform dialect. So far as I can see, such a demand infringes the uniformitarian principle because it is unrealistic: it ignores everything that we have learned in the past half-century about speech communities, linguistic variation within speech communities, and the progress of linguistic changes through speech communities (summarized and exemplified in Labov (1994) and (2001), for example). Absolutely uniform dialects are, at best, rare, and are usually spoken by speech communities so small that they are statistically unlikely to propagate and diversify into language families. It is therefore not surprising that colleagues who demand unitary protolanguages believe that *Stammbäume* are of no use.

Reality is more nuanced, and a realistic (i.e. uniformitarian) view must be more subtle. It is true that, if the support for a clade is weak, the kind of evidence represented by changes C2, C3a, and C3b can call the very existence of the clade into question. But the West Germanic clade is strongly supported. To the sound changes adduced above in its support, one can add some striking morphological changes, including the replacement of the strong past indicative 2sg. by the corresponding subjunctive form (e.g. **warst* 'you became' → **wurdī*) and the remodelling of the class I weak present suffix of verbs with heavy root-syllables (Cowgill 1959: 8). There are more than enough shared innovations to show that Proto-West Germanic was a *unified*, but not necessarily *uniform*, speech community for a significant period of linguistic history. Under the circumstances, the Old High German innovations in weak verb inflection add to our knowledge of variation within the Proto-West Germanic speech community without calling the existence of such a speech community into serious question.

The consequences for our understanding of linguistic cladistics in general are very similar. Recognizing West Germanic as a valid clade on the grounds of many shared innovations, in spite of a few divergences sandwiched in among them chronologically, is not in any sense a falsification; on the contrary, the evidence practically forces us to conclude that Proto-West Germanic was a language (with some dialect diversity) spoken by a speech community *sensu lato* (composed of smaller speech communities *sensu stricto*) for a considerable period of time. We merely need to recognize that a cladistic tree cannot include all the details that we can recover about the internal history and diversification of Proto-West Germanic. In the memorable words of Ross (1997: 213), a cladistic tree is often 'isomorphic enough with a wide-angle view of linguistic prehistory', though such trees 'are unavoidably unsubtle' (Ross 1997: 215).[8] To put it bluntly, we simply must not make unrealistic demands on our models of linguistic diversification, nor interpret them in non-uniformitarian ways.

[8] The alternative representation of 'lectal linkages' (i.e. dialects sharing innovations in overlapping patterns) developed in Ross (1997), and exemplified in Ross (1998), could usefully be applied to West Germanic. However, as Ross (1997: 215) points out, such diagrams are not well adapted to presenting chronological sequences of changes. In simple cases a *Stammbaum* can do that; but in a case like West Germanic, in which most early changes are in fact shared by all the attested daughters, nothing short of a chronological diagram of changes can present all the information available.

4

Older Runic evidence for North-West Germanic *a*-umlaut of *u* (and 'the converse of Polivanov's Law')

PATRICK STILES

4.1 Details of the change and its main structural effect

4.1.1 Introductory

North-West Germanic *a*-umlaut has been much discussed, yet it seems to me that some of the most interesting and fundamental problems have not received due attention. These are posed by the evidence of Older Runic inscriptions.

North-West Germanic is an intermediate proto-language, ancestor of both the North Germanic (Scandinavian) and West Germanic languages, which are attested in manuscripts from about 1150 and shortly before 700 AD, respectively, and which both have earlier runic traditions. They constitute two of the three branches of Germanic, the third being East Germanic, in effect Bishop Wulfila's Bible translation from the fourth century AD, which is attested in manuscripts written two centuries later. Older Runic is used to designate the (early North Germanic) language of runic inscriptions written in the Older Futhark alphabet, from the earliest examples, *c.* (1)50, up to *c.* 500 AD.[1]

[1] The question as to when the attestation starts depends on whether one thinks the inscriptions on the Meldorf fibula (dated to the first half of the first century AD) and the Osterrönfeld

This article is not intended as a contribution to linguistic theory, but to understanding how *a*-umlaut might have been phonologized. I lay no claims to originality in my analysis. Most of what I shall present lies buried in the secondary literature in the context of other topics, and I have done little more than disinter it. The ideas are hardly revolutionary; they have just not been applied to the specific problem of *a*-umlaut and are not reflected in our handbooks of Germanic. I have kept references to a minimum and concentrated on earlier work (cf. n. 3).

4.1.1.1 Mechanism

The term '*a*-umlaut' is used here—faute de mieux—as an inaccurate but convenient label to refer to a set of early assimilatory changes in North-West Germanic affecting the high and mid short vowels in accented syllables.[2] The Proto-Germanic inventory had four members: /i/, /e/, /a/, /u/ (cf. Benediktsson 1967). The change involved the lowering and raising of short *i* and *e* and the lowering of short *u*, depending on the one hand whether a high or low vowel followed in the next syllable and on the other whether a nasal-initial consonant cluster immediately followed. (The vowel *a* was unaffected by these changes.) The diphthong /eu/ was also subject to *a*-umlaut, but will not be of concern here.

4.1.1.2 Environments

The relevant environments are three in number: those that conditioned a high vowel, a low vowel, or were neutral. They are constituted as follows:

(a) High vowel: before *i*, *ī*, (*iu*) and *j* in the following syllable, and when the intervening consonantism starts with a nasal, regardless of the vocalism of the following syllable. (The sequence **-eww-* also became **-iggw-*

pot-sherd (dated to the first century AD) use runic, 'proto-runic', or Latin characters; cf. in the first instance Düwel (2008: 3, 23–4, 178–9). The rough cut-off date of *c.* 500 AD excludes 'transitional' inscriptions that still use the older alphabet but show linguistic innovations; cf. Grønvik (1998: 16–26). Older Runic is remarkably stable linguistically.

[2] The term '*a*-umlaut' could be justified on the basis that it is generally considered that the loss of this vowel in final syllables triggered phonologization of the change (cf. 4.2.2), but it will turn out that this is in fact not the case. Campbell (1962: §111) refers to 'a tendency to harmonize *e*, *i*, and *u* to the vowel which follows in the next syllable'. One could dub it the 'North-West Germanic short vowel shuffle', but the term might not catch on. See especially Benediktsson (1970: 100–5). The phonologized change of *a*-umlaut is exclusively a North-West Germanic phenomenon. Any phonemic distinctions between the short vowels /i/ and /e/, and /u/ and /o/ in Bible Gothic (cf. Braune and Heidermanns 2004: §§20, 24) are of independent origin, the result of separate Bible Gothic developments (cf. Bennett 1952, with references). It may be noted that so-called Crimean Gothic is to be classed as a North-West Germanic dialect, as it attests *a*-umlaut; note especially *Schuos* [for *Schnos**]: *Sponsa* 'fiancée' in the list of words not recognized by Busbecq ('cum nostra lingua non satis congruentia'). See Stearns (1978: 151–2), Grønvik (1983: 27).

regardless of the following vowel: see Heidermanns 1986: 297–9, Rasmussen 1989*a*; cf. Kock 1910: 98. Similarly, only the sequence *-ugg(w)-* occurs; cf. Kock 1898: 517.)

Examples: **gibid* 'gives' (beside *geban* 'to give'), **hringaz* 'ring' (< **hrengaz*, cf. Finnish *rengas*), **hundaz* 'dog'.

(b) Low vowel: before short *a*, long *ō* (and long *ā*, in so far as it existed). (Proto-Germanic absolute final bimoric long **-ō#* had already shortened to **-u* in North-West Germanic by the time of *a*-umlaut.)

Examples: **weraz* 'man' (< **wiraz*, cf. Lat. *vir*), **snozō-* 'daughter in law' (< **snuzō-*), **golþa* 'gold' (beside **gulþīn-* 'golden'), **korna* 'corn' (< **kurna*), **worhtō* 'I worked, made' (beside **wurhtē* 3sg.).

(c) Neutral: before *u*, *ū*, and *ē* (also short *e*, if it existed in unaccented syllables). Also when nothing followed (in monosyllables).

Examples: **siduz* 'custom', **meduz* 'mead', **wig* ipv. 'kill!', **weg* ipv. 'carry!', **sehs* 'six', **snuzu* nom. sg. 'daughter in law', **duhtēr* nom. sg. 'daughter'.

As can be seen, in environment (c) the vowel was unaffected and the etymological value was retained. This means that although /i/ and /e/ were to a large extent in complementary distribution (cf. 4.1.1.3), they did not fully merge as phonemes (cf. for example Beeler 1966, Benediktsson 1967: 190–4; already Luick 1914–40: 1.i. §71 A2).

4.1.1.3 Distribution of allophones

The distribution of allophones of the four short accented vowels in the various environments can be summarized as in Table 4.1.

Table 4.1 Distribution of allophones of the four short accented vowels in North-West Germanic

	High vowel	Low vowel	Neutral
/i/	[i]	[e]	[i]
/e/	[i]	[e]	[e]
/u/	[u]	[o]	[u]
/a/	[a]	[a]	[a]

This schema implies a stage in the development of the North-West Germanic languages when there were automatic positional allophones [i] and [e] of /i/ and /e/, and [u] and [o] of /u/ in the raising and lowering environments just specified. (By contrast, *a* occurred in all environments.) During this 'phonetic period', there were sub-phonemic variations within a paradigm, for example nom. sg. [duhte:r], but gen. pl. [dohtro:].

4.1.1.4 Creation of short /o/

The main structural effect of *a*-umlaut is the creation of the phoneme short /o/, split from Proto-Germanic /u/. (As concerns /i/ and /e/, the upshot is chiefly changes in the incidence of pre-existent phonemes.) Exploring the means whereby the single phoneme PGmc short /u/ came to be replaced by two phonemes, North and West Germanic /u/ and /o/, is the concern of this article.

4.2 The structuralist account and its inadequacies

4.2.1 *The change as 'secondary split'*

As the development of /u/ and /o/ from PGmc short */u/ entailed adding a new term to the phonemic inventory, the change is classified by structuralist theory as an example of secondary split (as opposed to primary split, where the 'splitting' allophones join pre-existing phonemes and the overall inventory is unaffected).[3] It is an axiom, known as Polivanov's Law,[4] that in a phonological system, there is 'no split without a merger'. That is to say: any split always involves a simultaneous merger of some kind. In primary split, the splitting-off allophone is the one that does the merging (and the process can also be styled 'partial merger'). In the case of secondary split, the merger takes place elsewhere, as the creation of the new phoneme is triggered by merger (including with zero) among the conditioning factors; loss of contrast there transfers the distinctive function to the conditioned phones.

4.2.2 *The classic interpretation*

The classic structuralist interpretation is that *a*-umlaut was phonologized by the loss (merger with zero) of one of the conditioning factors, short *a*, from final

[3] I focus on structuralist theory because I consider it the best-fitted to diachronic work, especially the kind of problem under consideration (cf. also Issatschenko 1973: 5). A sociolinguistic approach, by contrast, is not ideally suited for poorly documented or prehistoric stages, although see Ringe (2006*b*) for an inspired example. If they discuss these issues at all, other 'schools' differ largely in using their own terminology and notation. (I allude to some recent work by way of references to Joseph and Janda 2003.) As Jean Rostand observed: 'Le biologiste passe; la grenouille reste'.

[4] The 'law' is named after its framer, the Russian linguist and orientalist Yevgenij Dmitrievich Polivanov, who promulgated it in an article of 1928 (38 = 1974: 77). See especially Jakobson (1931: section IX); also Hoenigswald (1960: 77–8, 1999: 202–4).

syllables: thus, for example, nom. sg. /hurna/ [horna] > /horn/ 'horn'. That is, the allophones were in complementary distribution until they were phonemicized by the loss of final *-a* (generally regarded as the vowel that was lost earliest from final syllables).[5]

This view is epitomized by Moulton (1961*a*: 14–15):

Die komplementäre Verteilung von urgerm. *[i] und *[e], *[u] und *[o], *[iu] und *[eo] war von dem Weiterbestehen der unbetonten Vokale der folgenden Silben (**i*, **u*, bzw. **a*) völlig abhängig. Solange diese unbetonten Vokale fortlebten, wurde die komplementäre Verteilung der Allophone aufrechterhalten. Sobald die unbetonten Vokale aber zusammenfielen (welches jedenfalls theoretisch hätte vorkommen können) oder schwanden (welches tatsächlich eintrat), war die komplementäre Verteilung der betonten Vokale durchbrochen.

... um die phonetischen Oppositionen *[i e], *[u o], *[iu eo] zu phonologisieren, genügte es, daß die komplementäre Verteilung der Allophone in je einer Lautumgebung aufgehoben wurde. Der Verlust dieser unbetonten Vokale und damit die Phonologisierung der Allophone der betonten Vokale ist eine Erscheinung, die allen nord- und westgerm. Sprachen gemeinsam war.

(Moulton erroneously assumes complementary distribution; cf. 4.1.1.2–3.)

4.2.3 *Older Runic counter-evidence*

This account would be exemplary and unobjectionable, were it not for the existence of certain forms in the Older Runic language.[6] I cite as examples forms for which both reading and interpretation are fairly certain: **horna** 'horn' acc. sg. (Gallehus), **worahto** 'I made' [= *wor*^{a}*hto*] (Tune), **holtijaR** 'of Holt' (Gallehus), **dohtriR** 'daughters' nom. pl. (Tune).[7]

The first two examples have <**o**> (presumably *o*) correctly conditioned; the second two examples have <**o**> (presumably *o*) analogically transferred from a 'forme de fondation' to a 'forme fondée' and present an environment that 'ought' to have <**u**> (*u*).

[5] In my usage, a sound change is 'phonologized' and a specific allophone is 'phonemicized' (achieves phonemic status).

[6] Runes are transliterated into bold letters, while italics are used for transcriptions, which necessarily involve some degree of interpretation. R represents a rune written for etymological *z*, which had acquired some *r*-like features and eventually merged with original *r*. Runic forms are followed in brackets by the name of the monument on which they are found. The standard edition remains Krause and Jankuhn (1966).

[7] Note also **gudija** 'priest', ON *goði* (Nordhuglo), **wurte** '(s)he made', -**kurne** 'corn' dat. sg. (Tjurkö), without the conditions for lowering.

These forms confront the classic structuralist view with two problems:

(1) Short *-a* has clearly not been lost—indeed its retention after heavy and light syllables both medially and finally is one of the defining characteristics of the Older Runic linguistic stage, cf. Grønvik (1998: 15)—so we would not expect the allophones to be graphically represented. We should have only <**u**>-spellings in all these instances, representing /u/, and the rune <**o**> should denote solely the long vowel /o:/.[8] The fact that the allophones are graphically represented indicates that the sound change of *a*-umlaut, paradoxically and 'prematurely', has somehow been phonologized *before* the loss of its conditioning factors. In addition, and in apparent contradiction of Polivanov's Law (cf. 4.2.1), we appear to have an instance of split without merger. If it is not the loss of the conditioning factors, what has phonemicized the allophone [o] of the phoneme */u/?

(2) The distribution of allophones is patently *not* complementary, which again indicates that the sound change has been phonologized.

As scholars almost invariably remark, the forms **holtijaR**, nom. sg. of a derived adjective, and **dohtriR**, nom. pl., presuppose base-forms /holta-/* and /dohtar-/*.[9] But, although this statement is evidently correct, it cannot be said to be particularly illuminating for our purposes; the nub of the matter is how we are to account for such forms as /holta/* and /dohte:r/*. These forms, and /horna/ and /worhto:/, constitute the core of the problem that Older Runic poses for the classic structuralist view of *a*-umlaut; **holtijaR** and **dohtriR** are merely an epiphenomenon.

It is admittedly a very small corpus of four items—extendable to six if the base-forms just discussed are included—but adequate in the circumstances, I believe. That is, having more data would not necessarily tell us much more about the language. The two inscriptions come from south-east Norway (Tune) and south Jutland in Denmark (Gallehus), which involves a reasonable geographic spread.

4.2.4 *Distribution of reflexes*

There has been quite some discussion of the second problem mentioned in 4.2.3, that of the distribution of the reflexes, largely in the context of the question of '*i* and *e*, two phonemes or one?' (a non-issue as they were clearly two, cf. 4.1.1.2–3), and the problem of 'failure of *a*-umlaut of *i*'.[10] However, the focus here is on the phonologization of *o*.

[8] There is no evidence to lead us to believe that <**o**> is in fact a spelling for /u/ in these examples.

[9] *Dohtēr* has apparently been relexicalized, which is further evidence of phonologization of *a*-umlaut.

[10] One of the peculiarities of *a*-umlaut is that, whereas before following *i* and *j* only *i* generally occurs as a reflex, both *e* and *i* are tolerated as reflexes before *a* and *ō* (see the examples in the next

Of the West Germanic languages, High German is usually considered to have carried through the change of *u* to *o* most consistently, cf. OHG *wolf*, OE *wulf* 'wolf'. Yet, even here, by-forms—e.g. OHG *snora, snur(a)*, Germ. *Schnur* 'daughter in law', etc.—indicate that later repartitions are the result of analogy. In some instances, where there were both semantic and phonological variants, the products could be lexicalized, cf. OHG *stehhal(a)* 'drinking vessel' and *stihhil(a)* 'prick, sting (Germ. *Stachel*)', cognate with Goth. *stikls* 'drinking vessel'.

It should be noted that in North Germanic reflexes of the lowering of *u* to *o* show a dialectal distribution. There is a cline from west to east, with *o*-reflexes much more established in the west—in Icelandic, Faroese, Norwegian, and Danish west of the Great Belt (Jutlandic and on Funen)—than in Danish east of the Great Belt, Scanian (the dialect of Skåne), Swedish, and Old Gutnish (the language of the island of Gotland), where *u*-reflexes predominate. See Bandle (1973: 24–8), with important earlier references; compare also the discussion in Benediktsson (1967: 184–6). It is clear that the repartition is largely the result of secondary developments (cf. Kock 1910: esp. 138–9). Thus, even in Old Gutnish, which has one of the highest proportions of *u*-outcomes, the word for 'daughter' has preserved a reflex of **o* in certain forms of the paradigm, for example the accusative singular: *dōtur* (< **dohtaru*); while elsewhere showing a reflex of *u* levelled from case-forms providing a high-vowel environment: dat. pl. *dȳtrum* (see 4.1.1.2–3). This is no doubt because the *-*h*- was lost and the preceding vowel lengthened, fossilizing the alternation.[11]

Because of the nature of the evidence, the remainder of this article relates to Older Runic rather than the rest of North-West Germanic. However, the discussion is mainly about interpreting the evidence rather than the evidence itself.

4.2.5 *The problem of phonologization*

Relatively little attention seems to have been paid to the first problem mentioned in 4.2.3—how /o/ came to be phonemicized—except by some Scandinavian scholars whose response is to deny that there was any such thing as *a*-umlaut in the sense used here. (Part of the difficulty stems from a literalistic interpretation of *a*-umlaut to mean lowering before a following short *a* and nothing else, cf. n. 2.) These scholars operate instead with a lowering before certain consonants.

paragraph). Compare the treatment of Benediktsson (1967: 183–4). See Hock (1973) for a discussion of the issues and a summary of earlier work.

[11] Interestingly, some of the early material is in conformity with the later distribution: Gallehus **holtijaʀ** and **horna** are both from Jutland, Tune **worahto** and **dohtriʀ** from Norway, and Tjurkö **wurte** and **-kurne** from Sweden. Nordhuglo **gudija** comes from western Norway, however.

Thus Harry Andersen (1960: 406) speaks of '*o*-forms such as **holtijaR** (which presupposes **holta* not **hulta*) **worahto** and **dohtriR**, which can have nothing whatsoever to do with a presumed *a*-umlaut' and concludes that the 'shift of *u* to *o* must be extremely old in the Germanic languages (compare Gothic) and it must have been independent of a following *a*'.[12] He and others posit a Proto-Germanic lowering of *u* to *o* before certain consonants, notably *r, h*—as in Gothic—(and to a lesser extent *l*).[13]

This claim does not stand up to scrutiny. In the first place, it is directly refuted by such West Germanic forms as OE, OHG *burg* '(fortified) town', OHG *suht* 'illness', *zuht* 'nourishment, breeding, offspring'; as well as Old Gutnish *dȳtrum* dat. pl. 'daughter', cited in 4.2.4.

Secondly, the fact that Proto-Germanic had no /o/-phoneme means that if there was a lowering of /u/ before certain consonants, it must have been sub-phonemic. Yet, proponents of the lowering view offer no account of how a short [o]-allophone was phonemicized. (I would not deny the possibility that a lowering influence of *h*—and *r* and *l*—may have worked in such a way as to favour the generalization of *o*-variants, once the phoneme /o/ existed. Consonantal environments apparently played a role in determining lexicalized forms of words; cf. Bandle 1973: 25–7, with references.)

These scholars are right to have raised objections, for, as we have seen, there *are* problems the 'standard view' ignores. Grønvik (1998: 86) notes that 'diese Allophone [wurden] phonemisiert, ohne daß dieser Vorgang bisher völlig geklärt wäre. Diese Phonemisierung ist jedoch schon für die älteste Runensprache ... sicher nachzuweisen.' The problem should at least be addressed, even if it cannot be satisfactorily answered.

4.3 Ways in which allophones achieve phonemic status

4.3.1 The standard view

Conveniently for the present purposes, in a couple of articles Dobson explicitly considered the question of how it is that allophones come to be phonemicized (1962: 141–4, essentially repeated in 1969: 43–8). Two of the ways he gives in which 'a contextual variant, an allophone, comes to be regarded as a distinct

[12] '*o*-former som **holtijaR** (der forudsætter **holta* og ikke **hulta*), **worahto** og **dohtriR** der intet som helst kan have at gøre med en formodet *a*-omlyd'. 'Overgangen af *u* til *o* må være overordentlig gammel i de germanske sprog (sml. gotisk), og den må have været uafhængig af et følgende *a*'.

[13] As well as Harry Andersen, a vocal opponent of *a*-umlaut was Erik Harding; cf. Harding (1937–49: esp. items 22, 32, 45, 49, 65, 86 ('det obegripliga [incomprehensible] *a*-omljudet'), 97). Compare also Andersen (1986).

sound in its own right, a phoneme separate from the one from which it arose' (1962: 141) are of relevance to changes that add a phoneme to the inventory (cf. 4.2.1). These are (cf. 1969: 43):

(1) destruction, by some independent sound change, of the environment in which the allophone arose, so that it ceases to be tied to an existing phonetic context

(2) an allophone of one phoneme developed in one context or set of contexts may become phonetically identical with an allophone of a different phoneme developed in a different context or set of contexts, in such a way that the merged allophones are neither referable to a single source nor identifiable as occurring in limited and recognizable contexts.

The first method is prototypical secondary split; the second could result in merger with an existing third phoneme (and thus be a kind of 'partial merger') or it could lead to creation of a new phoneme (for example, in a given language, rounding of /e/ and fronting of /o/ could coincide and produce a previously non-existent /ö/; in those circumstances, the split would also be the product of a merger, although not among the conditioning factors). What is clear, however, is that neither of these routes can account for the phonologization of *a*-umlaut (cf. 4.2.3).

Dobson goes so far as to exclude a further way in which an allophone could become a phoneme (perhaps because he conceives of this as a general process that comes about 'when the variant ceases to be recognizably dependent on the context or contexts in which it originally developed', 1962: 141). In his later article (1969: 44), he writes:

analogical processes, as when a variant developed in one inflexional form is transferred to another, must always take place after a distinction has become phonemic;[3] the possibility of transference depends on observation and choice, and the lack of an automatic link with the context. Thus in primitive OE there must already have been a phonemic distinction between *æ* and *a* before **færiþ* could be remodelled as **fariþ* (to become *færþ*); it is the business of the phonologist to ask by what means it had become phonemic, for it certainly does not depend on the mere physical difference between the sounds, which is slight.

[3]Explanations which assume the analogical substitution of one allophone for another are contrary to principle...

(Cf. Dobson 1962: 143–4 n. 1.) Trnka ([1936 =] 1982: 30) seems to have been the first expressly to deny the possibility of analogical transference of allophones (also with reference to the Old English *a* ≠ *æ* opposition).

4.3.2 *Phonemicization by levelling*

However, Bazell, for one, had already dissented from this position, claiming that an allophone can indeed achieve phonemic status by 'levelling' (1952: 37):

The analogical transference of an allophone is by definition impossible, since the 'allophone' would then have phonemic status. Occasionally (although this is not a very productive source of new phonemes, and is even denied entirely by some scholars) new phonemic distinctions arise in this way. Thus the Old English short vowels *a* (before back vowels of the following syllable, including the combination *-ia-*) and *æ* (elsewhere) appear to have been variants before analogical forms (*fare* subj. pres. after infin. *faran* etc., as against *fære* dat. sing. of *fær*) arose.

Cf. also the discussion in Hoenigswald (1944: 82–3).

Bazell, I think, must be correct (probably also specifically for the *a* ≠ *æ* opposition in West Saxon Old English; similarly Samuels 1972: 35). Yet this observation still begs the question of how it can be that speakers should start shuffling around a supposedly automatic alternation.

4.3.3 *Alternations can cease to be automatic*

On this topic, C. A. Ladd (1964: 656) offers an interesting insight that adds detail and clarification to Bazell's statement. In brief, the alternation must cease to be wholly automatic—if by 'automatic' we mean that speakers are unaware of it. After a lapse of time, the allophonic rule that gave rise to the alternation is no longer 'live' and

a new generation of speakers hears the allophones as two sounds rather than one. We cannot suppose that children have to wait for a minimal pair before they decide whether two sounds form two separate phonemes or not; what matters is that they can interchange them freely... children learning the language... imitate the sounds in the distribution in which they heard them, a distribution which depends on phonetic criteria. At the same time, however, the way is now open for analogical interchange which will disturb the phonetic pattern. It is in fact the possibility of disturbance which indicates that the change has reached the phonemic level; the two things go hand in hand. Frequently, it is the appearance of analogical forms which leads to the recognition that the sound-change has occurred...

4.3.4 *The role of 'system balance'*

Some remarks of Kuryłowicz regarding the phonologization of '*a*-umlaut' are of relevance to how speakers might have become aware of the previously automatic alternation in this instance (1952*b*: 54):[14]

[14] The following quotation is taken out of context and some clarifying words are added in square brackets in order to help emphasize the desired point. The format is also altered and I silently emend one misprint and change the symbolization to make clear what are (allo)phones (also in square brackets) and what are phonemes (between slashes).

The rise of long *ā* . . . from *ē*₁ . . . severs the quantitative bond between [short] /a/ and [long] /o:/, the latter becoming the long grade of [o]. The vocalic timbres [o] and [u], up to now variants of a single phoneme /u/, become INDIRECTLY autonomous owing to the phonological distinction between the respective long vowels /o:/ and /u:/ . . .

Kuryłowicz incisively draws attention to the relevance of the North-West Germanic rise of a new long /a:/ phoneme (by shift). This had the effect of changing the correlations between short and long members of the phonological space. Linking the development of the short vowels to the shift of long /e:/ to /a:/ (except in final syllables) certainly correlates with the fact that *a*-umlaut is a non-Gothic North-West Germanic feature (cf. n. 2).

Elmer H. Antonsen developed Kuryłowicz's thought and interpreted it as demonstrating how [u] and [o] were phonemicized by what Antonsen came to call 'system balance' (e.g. 1965: 27, 1972: 138, 2002: 25). In his 1965 article, he noted that /o/ filled the 'hole in the pattern' of short vowels (compare also Benediktsson 1967: 177, 1970: 102). Introduction of a phoneme as a result of the re-evaluation of allophones in terms of the oppositions in the phonological system has been discussed several times by Moulton (his study 1961*b* offers an interesting analogue to the case of *a*-umlaut).[15]

Awareness of the distinction between the allophones is the necessary precondition, but levelling (which may itself have been 'unconscious') was the decisive step that gave phonological status to the variants by disrupting the complementary distribution.

4.4 Diachronic considerations and the question of reversion

4.4.1 *The transmission problem*

The factors outlined in 4.3.2–4 help explain how *a*-umlaut came to be phonologized before its conditioning factors were lost, in defiance of Polivanov's Law. Dobson—and, of course, many others; I am only using him as the representative of a viewpoint—had a too rigidly synchronic concept of the phoneme, and (as a corollary) an almost a-chronistic approach to its application to historical phonology (cf. 4.3.1). Language may be a system 'où tout se tient', as de Saussure maintained (see Koerner 1999), but it is rather a loose system and 'all grammars

[15] In the specific context of the creation of a short /o/ phoneme, we may also note that Haas (1978: 246–8) has observed that the quality of a short mid-back vowel in a given phonological system is often tied closely to the quality of the corresponding long mid-back vowel (a point at least anticipated by Moulton, e.g. 1960: 163, 1961b: 236–7, 1970: 23). Similarly, in the case of North-West Germanic, it could be argued that the influence of the long-vowel contrast /i:/ ≠ /e:/ helped preserve that between the short vowels /i/ and /e/ (cf. 4.1.1.2 end).

leak' (Sapir 1921: 38), even synchronic ones. If this were not so and they were 'watertight', there would be no redundancy and the loss of a phoneme, indeed any real change, would be impossible (cf. Hockett 1965: 203). The reality is continuous change and, even in a synchronic analysis, we are trying to hit a moving target.

The simplistic transfer of methods of synchronic analysis on to the diachronic plane is reminiscent of Zeno's paradoxes (cf. Coseriu 1958: 10–12 = 1974: 12–14). One of these is taken up memorably by Tolstoj, in the opening section of *War and Peace*, Book Three, Part Three: operating with discrete units of motion instead of continuous motion has the result that—'logically'—Achilles can never overtake the tortoise, who has been given a start, although we all know in reality that he can. Likewise—puristically—the *i*-mutation of short *o* is 'impossible', because, according to the rules of *a*-umlaut (cf. 4.1.1.2), only *u* could stand before an *i*-mutation factor. Yet, of course, the *i*-mutation of *o* is well attested, being reflected, for example, in OIc. *dǿtr* 'daughters' (nom. pl.). Janda and others have fallen into the same 'logical' trap (cf. Joseph and Janda 2003: 409–10 with references) in assuming that the loss of conditioning factors 'ought' in every case to result in reversion of allophones; cf. 4.4.2–3. This is a diachrony that is strangely devoid of history.

Even granting the correctness of the dogma that all speakers are totally unaware of subphonemic alternations, this could only really be so synchronically; it ignores the transmission of language from generation to generation (as noted by Ladd, cf. 4.3.3)—recognizing, of course, that generations form a continuum within the community, cf. Weinreich et al. (1968: 114) (already Saussure, *Cours de linguistique générale* I.2. §1 = 1955: 106).

4.4.2 *'Significant allophones'*

I think a point C. A. Ladd makes about Old English palatalization earlier in the article cited previously is a crucial one (1964: 655):

> what happens when a subphonemic variation becomes phonemic . . . is a vital stage in the process which has received curiously little attention . . . In the case of conditioned sound-change the result will eventually be a phonemic split of some sort. Now, it is surely not sufficient to say that in such cases a subphonemic variation becomes phonemic as the result, for instance, of a loss of conditioning sounds. In the case of the split between back and front *c* and *g* in Old English there is little question that other consonants than *c* and *g* originally had fronted allophones, as the same sounds which produced fronting of *c* and *g* also produced front mutation of the vowel of the preceding syllable, no matter what the intervening consonant. But only in the case of *c* and *g* had the variation between the two allophones reached such a degree that they could stand on

their own without the support of the conditioning sounds. In other words, even before the loss of the conditioning sounds, the two allophones must have been potentially phonemic...

It is probable that these reconstructable 'significant allophones', which hindsight reveals to have been 'potential phonemes', correspond synchronically to what may usefully be termed 'perceived allophones'.[16] Instead of an absolute divide between the phonemic and subphonemic, there is rather a cline from unconscious 'universal phonetic' accommodations, through unnoticed automatic alternations to perceived allophones (the dividing line between these two probably varying somewhat from speaker to speaker), and on to actual phonemic contrasts (the acid test being that they are actually exploited functionally). Here, there is also a range, from 'marginal phonemes', with minimal, to 'full phonemes', with maximal functional load.[17]

As C. A. Ladd has pointed out, minute changes in pronunciation cannot spread consistently through a speech community 'unless they spread by

[16] 'Perceived allophones', which must be based on a degree of phonetic *dis*-similarity, complement the 'phonetic similarity' criterion for phoneme identification. Others have come to similar conclusions; compare the discussion by Janda in Joseph and Janda (2003: 412–13).

[17] Compare the discussion of Janda in Joseph and Janda (2003: 415). The idea of the cline and problems of indeterminacy can be illustrated by the oft-discussed situation with [æ] in several varieties of contemporary 'standard English'. The speech-sound occurs in citation forms with three degrees of length: (i) short [æ] is found before voiceless consonants; while both (ii) slightly longer [æˑ] and (iii) fully long [æː] precede voiced segments. Examples are *bat*; *bade* (also pronounced [beid]); and *bad*. The first two sounds count as short and are automatic positional variants that sound 'the same' to naïve native speakers. The third is perceptibly different. While some words regularly have (iii), e.g. *mad, bad, sad*, there are no rules that predict whether certain other words will have (ii) or (iii). Thus I pronounce *cadge* [æˑ], but *badge* [æː], *mag* [æˑ] (short for *magazine*), but *bag* [æː]. In addition, the lexical incidence of the perceived long allophone varies from speaker to speaker. In my own speech, *brandy* and *shandy* are both pronounced with the long variant, whereas for some speakers they are conveniently distinguished, with *brandy*, a short drink, having variant (ii), while *shandy*, a long drink, has variant (iii); cf. Fudge (1977: 57, 64; to judge by his article, our distribution of (ii) and (iii) differs significantly). There are some potential minimal pairs, for example *candid* [kæˑndid] 'frank' vs. *candied* [kæːndid] 'covered with candy', although, again, I use the long phone (iii) for both (as does Fudge 1977: 58). Granted the existence of a noun *badger* 'someone who puts badges on things' (iii), derived from the verb *to badge*, it would contrast with the animal *badger* (ii) in my speech. There are thus some potential minimal pairs and, on some criteria, (iii) might count as a separate phoneme for some speakers, although not for others. However, the distribution and collocations of the words in question mean that there is no serious functional contrast. Wells (1982: 288) calls it 'marginally contrastive'. Compare the varying views on this issue—which is only raised here to make a general point—of Hoenigswald (1944: 82–3), Bazell (1952: 34; he deems it 'marginal', saying: 'It is neither quite true nor quite false to say that there is an opposition æ/æː in Standard British pronunciation'), C. A. Ladd (1964: 656), Fudge (1977), Lass (1984: 34–6). A classic example of perceived allophones are the German *Ich-* and *Ach-Laute*; native speakers have no difficulty in hearing the difference between the two sounds, while linguists debate whether they should be considered contrastive and thus different (albeit marginal) phonemes—supposed minimal pairs involve dubious lexemes, diminutive suffixes, or compounds (cf. Issatschenko 1973).

imitation'; further, 'to be imitable, variations in pronunciation must be perceptible' (1965: 100–1; cf. also Weinreich, Labov, and Herzog 1968: 130–1). If this were not so, mimicry (the imitation of someone else's speech idiosyncracies), let alone code-switching, would be impossible.

4.4.3 *Allophone formation and reversion*

Reversion, a subject that Ladd raises in the quotation given in 4.4.2, is a genuine issue. In many cases where split would be possible, the presumed allophonic variation effectively vanishes and no phonemicization takes place when the 'conditioning factors' are lost (cf. Hoenigswald 1999: 204). Polivanov had already observed that 'split can only take place when there is sufficient physical difference between the diverging variants' (1928: 38 = 1974: 77). Similarly, Hoenigswald added a caveat concerning secondary split: 'allophones become phonemes when part or all of their determining environments fall together without at the same time canceling the phonetic difference between the allophones in question' (1960: 94, also 77 'if the phones remain distinct'; cf. 1999: 204). Compare also the discussion of Janda (in Joseph and Janda 2003: 409–10, with references). Van Wijk, in the early days of Prague structuralism, explicitly recognized that whether phonologization takes place in a given instance is largely a matter of phonetics and thus subject to chance (e.g. 1939: 304–5).[18] Much the same point has been made by Ohala (e.g. in Joseph and Janda 2003: 683–5; perhaps it is not surprising that those who consider these issues reach similar conclusions). This underlines the fact that our knowledge is imperfect and little more is open to us than post-hoc rationalization.

Another factor to bear in mind when considering the apparent reversion of allophones that one might have expected to be phonemicized is the process of allophone formation. A prime example, which is scarcely mentioned by the handbooks, concerns the phonologization of *i*-umlaut in Old High German—or rather the non-phonologization of *i*-umlaut at the time of the loss of short *-i* after heavy syllables. This is certainly different from the situation in Old English: compare OE *giest, giestas* 'guest, guests' and *mann, menn* 'man, men', beside OHG *gast, gesti* and *man, man*. In view of the outcome of 'primary umlaut' (as in *gesti*), it is hard to see why supposed umlaut allophones (of *a*, at least) should have reverted before lost *-i*. Rather than positing wholesale reversion—shortly to be followed by phonemicization of other apparently 'identical'

[18] As Gould (2001: 228) remarks: 'Unpredictable contingency, not lawlike order, rules the pathways of history'.

conditioned variants—it seems more plausible to suppose that 'significant' *i*-umlaut allophones had not yet formed when short *-i* was lost after heavy syllables, but developed later, and were phonemicized by the loss of **-(i)j-* (including *-ja-* > *-e-*), which causes *i*-umlaut in both English and German, e.g. *to drench : tränken; to hear : hören*. (On the subject of allophone formation, we may further note that Russian shows no sign of developing an allophone [ŋ] in words such as *bank* 'bank': [bank], not †[baŋk].)

4.4.4 *Citation forms and the spoken chain*

It is also worth recalling that sound change originates not in citation forms but in the spoken chain. The allegro forms of connected speech are characterized by special allophones conditioned by their environment in the utterance, and varying degrees of reduction (utterances are often distinguished by distinctive features that do not play any part in the composition of the 'paradigmatic' phoneme inventory). In 'decoding speech', the listener evaluates them against the template of the lento citation forms (which conventionally serve as the basis of phonemic analysis).

At certain stages, when the divergence gets too big for 'comfort' (ease of comprehension), some sort of accommodation takes place in (sections of) the speech community. Either (somewhat more rarely, I should guess), speakers adjust their 'contextual forms' so as to bring them more into line with the citation form ('don't speak in such a slovenly fashion, dear'), or (the most usual strategy), the citation form is restructured to bring it more into line with the contextual form—a fact to which Polivanov already drew attention (1928: 39–40 = 1974: 77–8; cf. also Hockett 1965: 203). This must be what happens in the case of such 'radical' changes as *i*-umlaut, when a whole new class of (front rounded) phonemes enters the language and, for a period, the new forms that contain them compete with the 'original' forms.

This is one way in which sound change can take place within purely chronological 'space' (cf. C. A. Ladd 1964: 656, quoted in 4.3.3), even where there is little relevant geographical or sociological variation in a given speech community (e.g. a remote island containing a single village of egalitarians). Greater geographical dispersal and social stratification of a single speech community will certainly lead to widespread 'dialect borrowing' and a greatly increased rate of change, which again can be somewhat offset by literacy, standard languages, and so forth.

I have been concerned with some aspects of the 'generation of innovations' rather than the 'propagation of change' in all its sociolinguistic aspects, something we cannot reach in reconstructive work.

4.5 Main conclusions

4.5.1 *Review of how a phoneme can be introduced into the inventory*

To round off the discussion, I rehearse the various ways in which a new phoneme can be introduced into the inventory:

I. As the result of 'regular sound change', which is to say by secondary split, to which Polivanov's Law applies (cf. 4.2.1, 4.2.3(1)).

II. As the result of some kind of 'analogy' ('split without merger'), where—because it is not strictly a sound-change process—Polivanov's Law does not apply:

(a) The redistribution of perceived allophones by levelling within a paradigm and/or between a base and a (synchronic) derivative. This is the process I have invoked for NWGmc *a*-umlaut, where the allophones had come to be perceived through 'system balance' (4.3.4). Levelling of this kind is often tacitly adduced in historical work, but it is unclear to what extent it is explicitly acknowledged in historical linguists' theory of what they do. As in conventional secondary split (I), the variants must have been phonetically conditioned and phonemicization results from disruption of complementary distribution. This does not hold for the remaining two analogical types.

(b) 'Morphophonemic analogy'—the redistribution of allophones by pressure of an existing morphophonological alternation. Such a development was first suggested by Jakobson (1949: 17 = 1971: 114), with the example of Byelorussian palatalized consonants. The existence of the alternations /rv-ú/ 'I tear' /rv'-oš/ 'you tear', /vr-ú/ 'I tell lies' /vr'-oš/ 'you tell lies' calls into being the pair /tk-ú/ 'I weave' /tk'-oš/ 'you weave' (replacing /tk-oš/) and creates the phoneme palatalized /k'/, which up until then had been a positional variant of /k/ in other contexts.

(c) 'Morphophonemic genesis'—the recombining of existing distinctive features so as to fill out the pattern of a productive morphophonological alternation. A phoneme is created *de novo*, without there having been a pre-existing (phonetically conditioned) allophone awaiting phonemicization. This process was proposed by Moulton (1961*b*: esp. 243–6), with an example from Swiss German dialects, where the regularly developed umlaut alternation /ɔ/~/ö/ (alongside the regularly developed umlaut alternation /o/ ~ /ö/) was replaced by the alternation /ɔ/~/ɔ̈/, featuring the wholly new phoneme /ɔ̈/. See also Moulton (1967: 1402–5), where he introduced the term and added some analogous Dutch data.

III. Via 'foreign loans'—the result of borrowing of words containing the new phoneme (from another dialect or language). An example is the introduction of French loans with initial *v*- into Middle English dialects that lacked initial fricative voicing, which made the sound phonemic. In Modern Engish, /ž/ occurs in French loans such as *prestige*, and has brought within its orbit the medial sound of words such as *vision* (with [-ž-] from [-zj-]), beside *visible* (with [z]) and *visual*, which varies.

Whereas types I and II rely on factors internal to the phonological system, type III relates to external factors and, as a result, does not necessarily present a particularly interesting development structurally (although it may result in hole-filling).

4.5.2 *Methodological rider*

From a methodological perspective, I suggest one of the 'analogical' explanations (type II) should be adduced only if it does not prove possible to account for the phonologization as the result of a merger elsewhere in the system (type I).[19]

4.6 Summary of the process of *a*-umlaut

By way of summary, I supply a set of diagrams illustrating my scenario of the phonologization of North-Germanic *a*-umlaut, alongside the development of the vowel system (excluding diphthongs) and illustrated by key forms.

(i) Proto-Germanic (pre-allophone formation)

	i:	i	u	u:
	e:	e	a (å)	o: (å:)

*/duhtar(-)/	*/hultaz/
*/duhtariz/	*/hultijaz/

(ii) North-West Germanic ('insignificant allophones')

The shift of $\bar{e}_1$ to $\bar{a}$ (except in final syllables) triggers potential new correlations between short and long vowels and the likelihood of an allophone [o] of short /u/:

	i:	i		u	u:
$\bar{e}_2$ >	e:	e		[o]	o:
			a		
			a:		

*/duhtar(-)/ [dohtar(-)]	*/hultaz/ [holtaz]
*/duhtariz/	*/hultijaz/

[19] In the case of NWGmc *a*-umlaut, a sound change elsewhere may yet be found to have triggered phonologization.

(iii) North Germanic I ('significant allophones')

In terms of phoneme inventory, this is the same as North-West Germanic. However, a later generation, aided and abetted by the long-short vowel correlations, 'perceives' the [o] allophone of /u/ and levels it within paradigms and between bases and their derivatives. (The sound change has *ipso facto* ceased to be a 'live rule' by this stage, so the complementary distribution can be disrupted.)

*/duhtar(-)/ [dohtar(-)]	*/hultaz/ [holtaz]
*[doht(a)riz][20] ←	*[holtijaz] ←

(iv) North Germanic II (phonemes)

i:	i		u	u:
e:	e		o	o:
		a		
		a:		

/dohtar(-)/*	/holtaz/*
dohtriR	holtijaR

As both *u* and *o* occur in all positions, the way is open to their extensive shuffling, leading to the observed oddities of their distribution. (This is especially true of *i* and *e*, with the proviso that *e* generally does not occur before following *i* etc., in which case it falls in with /i/.) Redistributed *o* before following *i* etc., instead of reverting to *u*—an option not now open to it, as the allophonic rule is no longer live—persists, later developing the 'front mutation allophone' [ö] in this position (cf. 4.4.1).[21]

[20] If we recognize a sound change of PIE **-er(-)* to **-ar(-)* in Proto-Germanic unaccented syllables, the North-West Germanic paradigm of 'daughter' is seen to have lowering environments in the following case-forms: voc. sg. *-ar*, acc. sg. *-ar*, nom. pl. *-ar(z)*, gen. pl. *-rō*. This is a much stronger base—four endings out of nine—from which to generalize *o*-vocalism (cf. the doubts about *a*-umlaut in this form assembled by Andersen 1986: 118–19).

[21] An earlier version of this paper was presented at the Second International Symposium on Runes and Runic Inscriptions in Sigtuna, Sweden, in September 1985. I would like to thank a number of scholars who have been kind enough to read various drafts or discuss these issues over the years: Michael Benskin, Paul Bibire, N. E. Collinge, Martin Durrell, †Henry M. Hoenigswald, †David McLintock, †William G. Moulton, Lena Peterson.

5

A law unto themselves? An acoustic phonetic study of 'tonal' consonants in British Panjabi

JANE STUART-SMITH AND
MARIO CORTINA-BORJA

5.1 Introduction

In the introduction to the first volume of *Principles of linguistic change*, Labov (1994) discusses the importance of studying contemporary language for developing our understanding of the rule-governed nature of language change. He argues that in some instances 'the relevance of new data depends upon a new principle that was not evident to earlier investigators' (Labov 1994: 19–20). One such contribution relates to the notion of phonological merger, whereby sound change results in a loss of contrast. Labov provides evidence from a number of studies of sound change in progress where merger may be apparent, but where for some individuals a contrast may be maintained at the fine phonetic level (Labov 1994: 349–70). Such evidence motivates the proposal of an additional rule or principle, in this case 'the new principle of "near merger"' (Labov 1994: 20).

In this paper we present an acoustic phonetic study of lexical tone and stop contrasts in British Panjabi. Many instances of lexical tone derive historically from voiced aspirate stops in earlier forms of Old Indo-Aryan, which themselves continue the reconstructed Proto-Indo-European voiced aspirate series: the traditional account is that during the history of Indo-Aryan the voiced aspirates merged with voiceless or voiced plosives followed or preceded by tonal developments on adjacent vowels, the exact outcome depending on phonological environment (e.g. Bhatia 1993: xxv–xxvii).

Despite the interesting position of Panjabi as one of the few Modern Indo-Aryan languages to show lexical tone (cf. Baart 2003), there has been little phonetic investigation into the phenomenon (see e.g. Wells and Roach 1980), or consideration of the synchronic phonological contrasts which largely result from the consonant mergers specified by the sound law.[1] At the same time, varieties of Panjabi spoken by communities of South Asian heritage resident in Britain are informally reported to be undergoing further changes, including loss of lexical tone. This claim has also not received empirical attention. Our results both confirm the presence of tone in terms of pitch movement as expected, and suggest some attrition. They also indicate some fine phonetic differences in plosives which phonologically are assumed to be 'the same'. This suggests that we may also need to re-evaluate this Indo-European sound law as an instance of 'near merger'.

5.2 Tone in Panjabi

While the Proto-Indo-European voiced aspirate series, $*b^h$, $*d^h$, etc. are thought to have developed by the regular operation of sound laws into phonetically different series of reflexes in the Indo-European languages (e.g. voiceless aspirates in Greek, voiced plosives in Germanic and Celtic, and so on), they were maintained in Old Indo-Aryan, and are still realized today in most Modern Indo-Aryan languages as breathy-voiced stops (e.g. Stuart-Smith 2004). However, in the history of Panjabi the voiced aspirates underwent a further rule-governed set of changes involving tonogenesis whose outcome is usually formulated as: before a stressed syllable there is a merger with voiceless plosives and the stressed vowel carries a Low tone; after a stressed syllable the merger is with the voiced plosives, and the stressed vowel carries a High tone (cf. Bhatia 1993: xxv–xxvii).[2]

The resulting synchronic phonology of Panjabi is taken to show three stop series, plain voiceless /k/, plain voiced /g/, and voiceless aspirate /kh/, and three

[1] Other tonal developments unrelated to the development of the voiced aspirates also assume that tones occur in conjunction with voiced and/or voiceless plosives.

[2] These changes also affected Old Indo-Aryan *h*; we restrict the following discussion to the reflexes of the voiced aspirates.

lexical tones, Low, High, and Mid (e.g. Gill and Gleason 1963, Bhatia 1993: 331, 343–5). An example would be:

(1) Low /kàl/ 'work, labour' Mid /kal/ 'time' High /kál/ 'lazy'

Panjabi also shows phonemic stress, which for Mid-tone words is realized phonetically as longer vowel duration and increased pitch (e.g. Bhatia 1993: 343). The interaction of tone and stress is disputed. Tones are assumed to occur on stressed syllables in standard Panjabi by e.g. Bahl (1957*a*), Bhardwaj (1995), Sadanand and Vijayakrishnan (1995).

Tones are the property of the word, not the syllable, and as such Panjabi tone is more like pitch distinctions found in languages such as Swedish or Serbo-Croatian than those of African or Far Eastern languages (Cruttenden 1997: 11). There has been little acoustic phonetic investigation of Panjabi tone; most statements, such as those in Gill and Gleason (1963) on the standard dialect of Panjabi, Majhi, or in Joshi's study of tone in the Doabi dialect (e.g. Joshi 1973), are based on auditory impressions. Sampat's (1964) work is, however, based on instrumental observations of pitch (albeit for nonsense sequences in Majhi), as is that of Sandhu (e.g. 1968), who also looked at cues to the perception of tones in Majhi. A brief summary of this work is given in Wells and Roach (1980), who themselves report qualitative results of pitch contours (from electrolaryngographic data) for a set of minimal pairs/triplets for the Patiali dialect.

Phonetically, tones are realized as a pitch contour extending over the whole word (Sampat 1964, Sandhu 1968, Wells and Roach 1980). A particular phonation type, which involves a tenser, or 'constricted' phonation, has also been noted in the production of Low tone (cf. e.g. Joshi 1973: 53–5, Wells and Roach 1980: 89). The pitch contours associated with the tones are described differently by different linguists, but Low tone is generally given as 'low rising' and High tone as 'high falling', although it is also noted that the Doabi dialect, and certain varieties of Majhi, are said to show Low as 'high falling' and High as 'low rising' (see Joshi 1973, and also discussion in Bhatia 1975: 23–4). Mid tone is not reported to show specific pitch levels or movements.

In most cases Panjabi tones have developed diachronically from earlier voiced aspirate stops and /h/, which are continued in neighbouring New Indo-Aryan languages, such as Hindi. Sequences of stop and adjacent tone-bearing vowel are represented in Panjabi orthography (Gurmukhi script) with the signs used for the earlier voiced aspirates. The actual development is complex and not fully understood (see Bhatia 1975), although the development to Low tone at least may be due to inherent pitch lowering found in breathy-voiced stops (see Hombert, Ohala, and Ewan 1976). Tones are commonly taken to be synchronically fully independent of the stops from which they developed (e.g. Bhatia 1993: 344–5, 1975).[3] The distribution of Low and High tones in Panjabi is limited, and usually predictable, particularly for Low tone. There are also many more instances of Mid tone than either High or Low tone, which, along with the phonetic implementation of Mid tone, means that we can regard the lexicon as being split into 'non-tonal' (Mid-tone) and 'tonal' (Low- or High-tone) words.

5.2.1 Tone in British Panjabi

Panjabi is now widely spoken in a number of countries outside the Indian subcontinent. In Britain, speakers of Panjabi form one of the largest linguistic minorities (*LMP* 1985), although assessing the actual proportion of Panjabi speakers is notoriously difficult (Alladina 1993, Mahandru 1991, Verma 1995). Panjabi is spoken by immigrants originating ultimately from the now Indian states of Panjab and Haryana, and mainly from west Panjab and Mirpur District in Pakistan. Panjabi of the Indian subcontinent has a number of different regional dialects (e.g. Bhatia 1993: xxix–xxxi). Best represented in the UK are: Doabi—the dialect from the region around and south of the city of Jallunder; Majhi—the standard variety of Lahore and Amritsar; and what is commonly called 'Mirpuri'—the variety of the mainly rural area south of the city of Islamabad in Pakistan (Saifullah Khan 1977; cf. Ballard 1994).[4]

As in other transplanted languages (cf. Siegel 1988), variation and change in British varieties of Panjabi, including processes of koineization of features from the heritage dialects, is to be expected (see e.g. the work on overseas Hindi: Barz and Siegel 1988, Bhatia 1988). But while there has been research into the lexical, semantic, and syntactic characteristics of Panjabi spoken in Britain, particularly with reference to Panjabi/English code-switching (e.g. Romaine 1995, Reynolds 1998, Pert and Letts 2006), there is very little systematic research into phonetics and phonology despite informal reports from community members that the pronunciation of Panjabi in Britain is becoming distinct from that of family and friends in the Indian subcontinent.

[3] One of Bhatia's (1993: 344–5) main arguments for the morphologized nature of tones (the other is the independence of tone from stress in certain lexical items), that roots with Mid tone have developed High tone in certain grammatical categories (imperative, subjunctive, and future), does not appear to hold for British Panjabi.

[4] This largely oral, rural dialect is not usually included in discussions of Panjabi dialects (e.g. Bhatia 1993: xxix–xxxi).

Lexical tone is one phonological contrast which is informally reported as undergoing change, perhaps even loss, in British varieties of Panjabi (another is the dental/retroflex contrast; see Heselwood and McChrystal 1999). This was also suspected by the first author from her auditory impressions of lexical tone as she was taught Panjabi (General Certificate of Secondary Education) at night school. There has been no systematic study to investigate this claim. Indeed, tone in Panjabi has been relatively neglected in current phonetic and phonological literature (though see Sadanand and Vijayakrishnan 1995).

In this paper we present the results of a small-scale experimental phonetic investigation into tone in British Panjabi spoken in Oxfordshire. The focus of the experimental investigation was on tones adjacent to stop consonants. We had two main research questions:

(1) What is the nature of lexical tone in British Panjabi?
Are tones characterized by pitch movement, and if so, what is this like? Is there evidence to support informal reports and impressions that lexical tone is being lost? Are specific tones associated with particular phonatory characteristics?

(2) What is the nature of stops adjacent to tone-bearing vowels in British Panjabi?
It is usually claimed that tones from voiced aspirates are now fully independent of the stops from which they developed. In word-initial (prevocalic) position, voiced aspirates became voiceless stops, and in intervocalic and final position, voiced aspirates became voiced stops, leaving three series of stops and tones on the adjacent vowels. If the tones are indeed now synchronically independent from the stops, we would expect prevocalic /k/ and intervocalic/final /g/ adjacent to High and Low tones to be the same as /k/ and /g/ adjacent to Mid-, or non-tonal, vowels.

5.3 Method

5.3.1 Materials

In order to investigate the nature of tones in British Panjabi, and the nature of the stops with which they are associated, a set of words was selected which show tonal contrasts in three phonetic environments: *prevocalic*, also word-initial; *intervocalic*, which in this study refers to a sequence -VN_V-, since no truly intervocalic items were found; and *final* (pre-pausal word-final). The tonal contrast adjacent to velar stops was selected as generally representative. Labial stops could not be used because of additional fricative variants [v] and [f] for /b/ and /ph/. Retroflex stops were also rejected on the grounds that retroflexion itself may alter pitch, and because the dental/retroflex contrast in British Panjabi is undergoing change. Of velar and dental places of articulation, the velars showed more possible minimal pairs. The words chosen were either monosyllabic (prevocalic and final) or disyllabic (intervocalic), in order to minimize the other possible effects of consonants and vowels in longer sequences.

A dictionary search using the Punjabi-English dictionary published by Patiala University (Joshi and Gill 1994) identified twenty-three possible minimal pairs/triplets with prevocalic stops, six with intervocalic stops, and nine with final stops. For the prevocalic items the set of minimal pairs was reduced to three, with three different following vowel qualities, front /i/, back /u/, and low /a/:

(2) Prevocalic minimal pairs

Mid tone	*Low tone*
/kal/ 'time'	/kàl/ 'work'
/ki/ 'what(?)'	/kì/ 'ghee; clarified butter'
/kuk/ 'fast'	/kùk/ 'shriek'

In intervocalic position, there were considerably fewer items. Three minimal pairs were selected which were acceptable to the five speakers:

(3) Intervocalic minimal pairs

Mid tone	*High tone*
/ˈdʒəngi/ 'warlike'	/ˈdʒə́ngi/ 'plough handle'
/ˈsənga/ 'shyness'	/ˈsə́nga/ 'throat'
/ˈsəngi/ 'friend'	/ˈsə́ngi/ 'neck'

The situation was similar for the final minimal pairs, where even fewer minimal pairs were found; two possible sets were identified:

(4) Final minimal pairs

Mid tone	*High tone*
/bag/ 'garden'	/bág/ 'tiger'
/sing/ 'horn'	/síng/ 'lion'

Here the tonal contrast was always one of High or Low tone vs. Mid tone/no tone. In the prevocalic items this was Low vs. Mid tone; in the intervocalic and final, it was High vs. Mid tone. It was impossible to find meaningful canonical triplets for our informants.

5.3.2 *Informants*

We recorded five female adult speakers, whose average age was 45 years. All five are bilingual in English and Panjabi, and belong to a close-knit community in Oxfordshire, where all speakers have been resident for at least eighteen years. All originally migrated from areas which are now in the Indian states of Panjab and Haryana. These speakers together represent three dialects of Panjabi: Doabi, spoken in the Jallunder district (speakers 2 and 3), Powadhi, from around Chandigarh (speaker 5), and the standard dialect, Majhi, from Amritsar (speakers 1 and 4).

All speakers were linguistically naïve to the extent that when each was asked about lexical tone after the recording, none showed any awareness of the contrast between the words being one of pitch or tone, but could only talk about the words in terms of semantic contrasts.

5.3.3 *Procedure*

The recordings were made in the sound-proofed recording studio in the Oxford University Phonetics Laboratory. The words were written on cards in Panjabi orthography, put together with a number of other distractors, and shuffled. All informants read out the words in four different random orders. Audio and electrolaryngographic (Lx) waveforms were obtained for the readings from each speaker; some difficulty was encountered with obtaining a satisfactory Lx signal for speakers 1 and 3, and these data are not presented here.

5.3.4 *Measures*

We took a number of measures to examine the pitch and phonatory characteristics of tones and adjacent stops. Vowel quality and vowel duration were not considered, given the inconclusive results of Wells and Roach (1980).

5.3.4.1 Pitch measures

Time series of pitch points in Hz every 5 milliseconds (ms) were extracted from the vowel for prevocalic and final, and from both first and second vowels for intervocalic tokens. The pitch tracks were extracted from 25 ms after voicing onset to two-thirds of the duration of the vowel (prevocalic), from 25 ms after voicing onset to two-thirds of the vowel (final), and from 25 ms after voicing onset to two-thirds of the first vowel, and from 25 ms after voicing onset to the end of second vowel (intervocalic). 25 ms were added to voicing onset to eliminate the possible effects of consonant perturbations caused by the velar consonants, which from visual inspection of the pitch tracks were not seen to extend beyond 25 ms of release. Similarly, an arbitrary cut-off of two-thirds of the vowel length was made to counteract any possible influences from the following consonant. The words, as citation forms, tended to be quite long, and so two-thirds of the vowel duration gave a sufficient number of points for the pitch track to be useful. Three measures were derived from the pitch tracks: pitch mean, pitch index, and pitch slope.

pitch mean: To reflect the overall pitch of vowels we calculated the average in Hz of each pitch track extracted. The mean values of vowels 1 and 2 of the intervocalic tokens were also compared, to see if there was an overall pitch movement across the whole word (as has been noted in e.g. Wells and Roach 1980).

However, since pitch movement is often observed for Panjabi tones, two further pitch measures were taken to reflect the degree of pitch movement and the direction and extent of pitch movement, calculated from smoothed pitch tracks (Fig. 5.1a). We used cubic B-splines (Hastie and Tibshirani 1990) to smooth the observed pitch tracks. In order to have a comparable amount of smoothing for each data set we used spline smoothers with four degrees of freedom.[5] We needed to smooth the pitch tracks because the next step of our analysis required finding a global maximum (or minimum) in the pitch curve, and this could be affected by local random variation in the tracks. After obtaining the smoothed pitch curve we evaluated its first derivative (Fig. 5.1b) and obtained two measures:

pitch index: To allow us to study the rate of change of the pitch with respect to time, we calculated an index that measures this characteristic in terms of the variance with respect to zero of the values of the derivative. This number reflects the magnitude of the pitch movement, so, for example, the larger it is, the larger the frequency range spanned by the pitch curve.

pitch slope: To allow us to consider the relative velocity of the pitch movement in the first part of the curve, we calculated an index of 'pitch slope', which is the slope of a linear regression model fitted to the points of the pitch curve observed before its maximum or minimum time point.[6] If the index is negative, the pitch movement is falling, if positive, it is rising.

[5] This value was chosen for empirical reasons: larger numbers of this smoothing parameter tended to oversmooth the estimate, while smaller values often gave significantly biased estimates of the pitch curves. Four degrees of freedom provided an adequate compromise between bias and variance of the curve estimate for all the pitch curves.

[6] If the smoothed pitch curve was monotonically increasing or decreasing, then the linear model was fitted over all the observed time range.

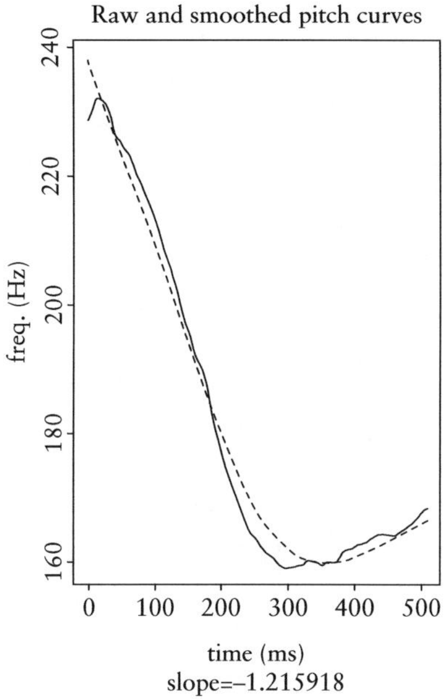

Fig. 5.1a An example of a raw and smoothed pitch curve

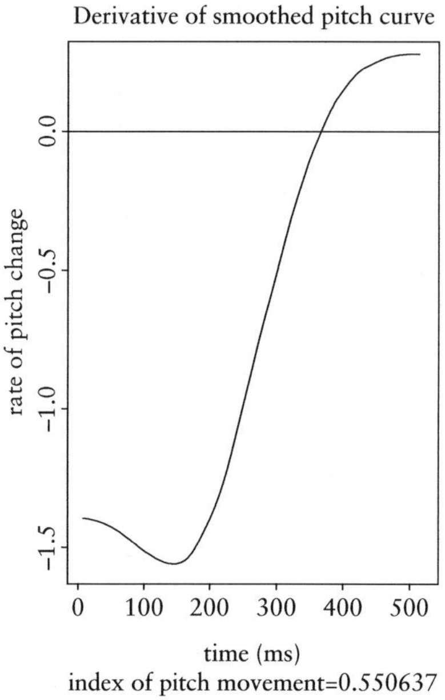

Fig. 5.1b The derivative of the smoothed pitch curve, from which the measures of 'pitch index' and 'pitch slope' were calculated

5.3.4.2 Consonantal measures

In order to examine the stops adjacent to tones, we took two measures to capture timing of onset of voicing with respect to articulatory release.

voice onset time (VOT): For the prevocalic stops we measured VOT from the acoustic waveform—from the burst to the first clear departure from the zero crossing—reflecting the first acoustic consequences of glottal pulsing.

noise offset: Visual inspection of acoustic waveforms and spectrograms indicated that intervocalic and final stops were always fully voiced during closure period, and final stops were often followed by a short vocalic offset. Given that VOT cannot be measured for these stops, and that one speaker showed a breathy-voiced release, we measured noise offset as the time between the burst and the onset of the vowel, defined as the full attainment of the second formant (see Davis 1994, who used this measure to distinguish Hindi stops).

5.3.5 *Statistical analysis*

The measures were analysed statistically using univariate and multivariate analysis, and all calculations were performed in S-PLUS 2000. We analysed the differences in the individual measures between tonal and Mid-tone/non-tonal words within each speaker using paired and independent *t*-tests and Wilcoxon-Mann-Whitney tests (Venables and Ripley 1992). Whenever there was reason to doubt the assumption of homogeneity of variances we used Welch's correction for the *t*-test. If there was evidence of non-normality, we used the nonparametric analogue.

Looking at the results of individual measures separately requires us to infer the patterning of phonetic characteristics being used to mark the contrast between tonal and Mid-tone/non-tonal words. The multivariate technique of principal component analysis (PCA) (Chatfield and Collins 1980, Krzanowski 1988) allows us to study directly the correlation structure of the data, and so how the measures together contribute to separate the two categories for each speaker at each position. PCA transforms the original data into orthogonal linear combinations of the variables (measures) which are ordered by the amount of variance which they concentrate.[7] It is then possible to characterize each principal component in terms of the original measures which contribute to them. The projections of observations into the space generated by the first two principal components are powerful exploratory tools for examining

[7] The projections obtained with PCA are linear, and sometimes a more complicated space is required to explore the data structure fully. We also applied a non-linear mapping technique due to Sammon (1969) and took advantage of its implementation in S-PLUS by Venables and Ripley (1992). The results from both linear and non-linear PCA were similar, and so we here present only the results from the linear PCA in section 5.4.

the multivariate structure of the data. In this way we can identify the extent to which our two assumed categories (tonal vs. Mid-/non-tonal) are actually reflected in the measures when considered together, and which measures are responsible for their separation.

5.4 Results

5.4.1 *Low vs. Mid (prevocalic)*

The contrast between Low- and Mid-tone words was realized differently in different speakers (see Table 5.1). While four of the speakers maintain the contrast through pitch patterns, one did not, but showed instead differences in VOT.

Table 5.1 Averages for pitch and consonantal measures for each speaker for Low- and Mid-tone (non-tonal) words, in prevocalic position, with *p*-values

Measure		Speaker				
		1	2	3	4	5
pitch mean (Hz)	Mid	258	193	207	220	169
	Low	205	180	203	209	172
	p-value	**0**	**0.03**	0.33	0.08	0.43
pitch index	Mid	0.35	0.02	0.16	0.19	0.04
	Low	1.6	1.33	0.2	0.38	0.14
	p-value	**0.02**	**0**	0.85	0.3	0.06
pitch slope	Mid	0.36	0.05	−0.14	−0.08	−0.09
	Low	−1.8	−1.77	−1.05	−0.45	−0.75
	p-value	**0.001**	**0**	**0**	0.2	**0**
voice onset time (ms)	Mid	41.4	24.7	34.6	64.1	31.3
	Low	27	30.8	30.7	42.9	27.6
	p-value	**0.004**	0.26	0.14	**0.04**	0.41

Note: Statistical significance is indicated in bold font for $p < 0.05$; $n = 120$.

Words with Low tone generally show a falling pitch movement, which sometimes rose again slightly. There was considerable variation in the degree of movement within and across speakers. Mid-tone words showed no such movement. These qualitative differences in pitch were reflected in significantly falling pitch slope measures for four speakers (1, 2, 3, 5). Two speakers (1, 2) also showed significantly higher values of pitch index for the tonal words than the non-tonal words, and significantly lower pitch means for the tonal vowel.

The prevocalic stops generally showed no vocal fold vibration during and just after closure. Only one speaker occasionally showed voicing during stop closure in tonal words. These were restricted to three repetitions of the word /kì/ 'ghee' and may be the result of influence from the English version of this word, which is usually pronounced as [gi]. Low-tone words also showed some indications of a more creaky phonation for speaker 5, particularly towards the end of the vowel, as opposed to modal voice in Mid-tone words. In two speakers (1, 4), prevocalic stops preceding Low tone showed significantly shorter VOT than those adjacent to Mid tones.

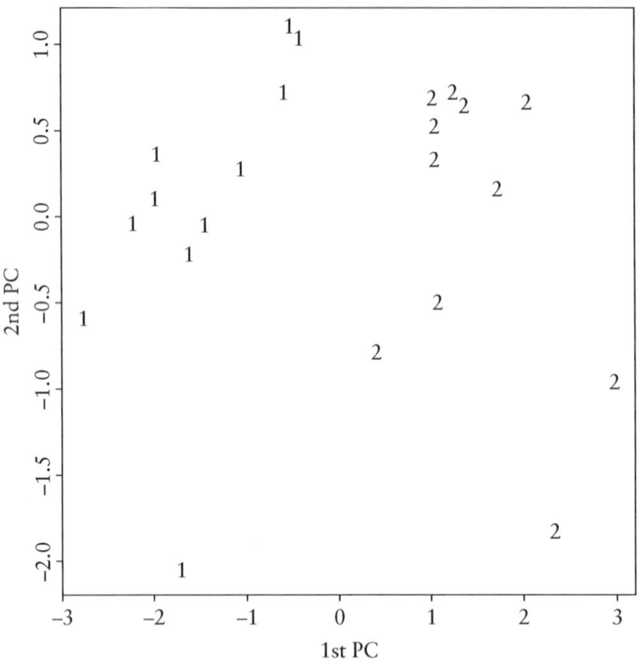

Fig. 5.2 First two principal components for prevocalic Mid-tone (1) and High-tone (2) words for speaker 1

The multivariate analysis showed clear separation between Low-tone and Mid-tone words for speaker 1 (Fig. 5.2), and relatively good separation was also found for speakers 2 and 3. For two of the speakers (1, 2) there was good explanation of variance through the first principal component (PC1) alone: for both, pitch slope emerged as the most important measure, but speaker 1 also showed VOT as an important measure in this contrast. For speakers 3, 4, and 5, the first two principal components together could account for a large amount of the variance in the data. For speaker 3, the main measures in PC1 were pitch slope, and then VOT, while in the second principal component (PC2) pitch mean and pitch index were most important. Speaker 4 showed pitch mean, and then pitch slope as the main contributors to PC1, and pitch slope and VOT for PC2. Pitch slope again emerged as important for speaker 5, as the main contributor to PC1, together with pitch index, while in PC2 the only measure of importance was VOT.

Of all the measures, pitch slope emerges from the PCA as consistently important, reflecting the importance of the presence (or absence) of falling pitch for marking the contrast in this phonetic environment. In the individual measures, VOT was found to be significant for two speakers (1, 4); in the PCA, VOT appears as an important contributor for four of the speakers. This suggests that the contrast phonetically is not only one of pitch differences, but also differences in stop adjacent to the tone-bearing vowel.

5.4.2 *High vs. Mid (intervocalic)*

The expected contrast would be a high or high-falling pitch for High tone in comparison with Mid tone. Again, the contrast was realized differently in different speakers (see Table 5.2), either through higher or rising pitch, or by breathy offset. Two speakers did not show the expected pitch pattern.

Table 5.2 Averages for pitch and consonantal measures for each speaker for High- and Mid-tone (non-tonal) words, in intervocalic position, with *p*-values

Measure		Speaker				
		1	2	3	4	5
pitch mean V1 (Hz)	Mid	220	192	195	207	177
	High	318	209	197	207	177
	p-value	**0**	0.11	0.64	0.85	0.11
pitch mean V2 (Hz)	Mid	245	194	215	216	170
	High	266	188	229	222	181
	p-value	0.405	0.29	0.09	0.55	0.05
pitch index V1	Mid	0.16	0.06	0.38	0.05	0.08
	High	1.54	0.11	0.63	0.03	0.07
	p-value	**0.005**	1	**0.02**	0.06	0.73
pitch index V2	Mid	0.16	0.84	0.22	0.26	0.3
	High	0.25	0.98	0.48	0.38	0.31
	p-value	0.123	0.95	0.34	0.52	0.79
pitch slope V1	Mid	−0.47	0.06	−0.7	−0.22	0.16
	High	1.78	0.26	−0.7	−0.13	0.2
	p-value	**0.001**	0.31	0.97	0.18	0.47
pitch slope V2	Mid	0.5	0.25	0.71	0.42	−0.08
	High	−0.96	0.67	0.5	0.88	−0.12
	p-value	**0.014**	0.2	0.2	0.34	0.91
noise offset (ms)	Mid	23.2	35.8	19.7	30.3	20.6
	High	30.1	142	22.4	34.1	20.9
	p-value	0.538	**0**	0.4	0.58	0.9

Note: Statistical significance is indicated in bold font for $p < 0.05$; V = vowel, $n = 120$.

Three speakers showed rising pitch movements or higher pitch. Speaker 1 showed a significantly rising pitch movement in the first vowel, accompanied by higher pitch mean in this vowel; the pitch then dropped sharply during the second vowel, although the pitch mean was still significantly higher than that of vowel 1 (line ○ in Fig. 5.3). Speakers 3 and 4, on the other hand, showed an overall rise in pitch across the whole word, reflected in a larger difference of pitch means in vowels 1 and 2 in High-tone than Mid-tone words; speaker 3 also showed more pitch movement in vowel 1 for High-tone words.

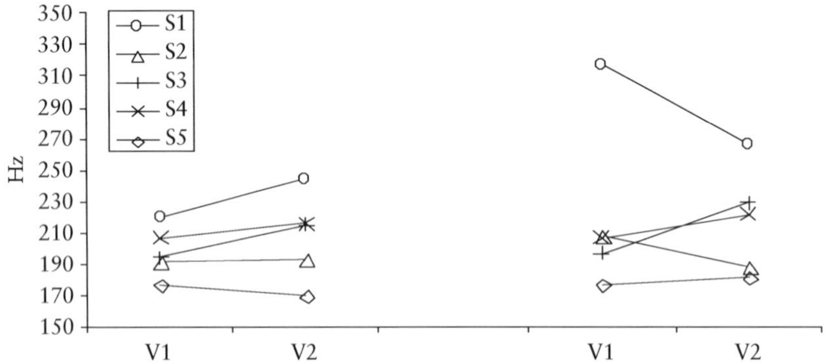

Fig. 5.3 (left) Relative vowel means for vowels 1 and 2 for intervocalic Mid-tone words for all speakers; (right) relative vowel means for vowels 1 and 2 for words with High tone

Two speakers did not show higher or rising pitch. Speaker 2 showed a clear period of breathy-voiced offset on release of the intervocalic stop in High-tone words, reflected in a significantly longer duration of noise offset. This speaker also shows a pitch drop in the second vowel, presumably relating to the breathy-voiced offset. But while a pitch drop is observed across the word, the pitch of the first vowel is not higher than that of the corresponding vowel in the Mid-tone word (line Δ in Fig. 5.3). The characteristics of High tone in speaker 5 are more difficult to identify; there is a marginally significant higher pitch mean in the second vowel in High-tone words, though no significant rise across the word (line ◊ in Fig. 5.3).

The multivariate analysis showed clear separation of High-tone and Mid-tone words only for speaker 1. The main finding is that the phonetic realization of the contrast inferred from the individual measures is most clearly reflected in the make-up of the first principal component, which usually accounts for about a third of the overall variance. Again, different speakers are using different patterns of measures. So, speaker 1 shows pitch measures from only the first vowel, speaker 2 shows measures relating to breathy offset affecting vowel 2, and speaker 3 shows the pitch means of vowels 1 and 2 reflecting the overall rise in pitch across the two vowels. Speaker 5, for whom no clear measures are identified, shows less structured grouping of measures; the picture is less clear for speaker 4.

5.4.3 High vs. Mid (final)

As for intervocalic position, the contrast between High tone and Mid tone was realized phonetically differently across the speakers (see Table 5.3), either through high or rising pitch, or through breathy-voiced offset to the voiced stop, or both, or neither.

Table 5.3 Averages for pitch and consonantal measures for each speaker for High- and Mid-tone (non-tonal) words, in final position, with *p*-values

Measure		Speaker				
		1	2	3	4	5
pitch mean (Hz)	Mid	171	192	218	206	190
	High	176	209	316	219	195
	p-value	0.318	0.11	**0**	0.97	0.63
pitch index	Mid	0.24	0.03	0.24	0.09	0.04
	High	2.26	0.09	0.54	0.09	0.2
	p-value	**0.008**	0.55	0.08	0.74	0.31
pitch slope	Mid	−0.03	−0.1	−0.33	−0.2	0.14
	High	0.89	0.32	−0.31	−0.02	0.44
	p-value	**0.008**	**0.01**	0.38	0.55	0.38
noise offset (ms)	Mid	25.9	37	38.5	25.8	53.6
	High	11.8	128	28.3	29.1	75.9
	p-value	**0.002**	**0.02**	0.67	0.62	0.26

Note: Statistical significance is indicated in bold font for $p < 0.05$; $n = 80$.

Speakers 1 and 2 showed clearly rising pitch in the vowel; speaker 3 also showed an overall higher pitch mean in the vowel. The findings for speaker 2 were somewhat surprising, since High tone was not only marked by rising pitch, but also by breathy-voiced offset to the final voiced stop, reflected in significantly longer duration of noise offset. All five speakers had fully voiced stop closures for the final stop consonant. Speakers 4 and 5 showed no observable differences in pitch or phonation between High-tone and Mid-tone words. The lexical contrast, which was apparently intact for each speaker, may be realized in another way, perhaps through vowel quality differences, although this is yet to be investigated.

The plotting of the first and second principal components from the multivariate analysis revealed relatively good separation for the two categories for four speakers (1, 2, 5 on PC1; 3 on PC2), but not for speaker 4. For three speakers the first principal component alone accounted for much of the variance, but for speakers 4 and 5 PC1 and PC2 were required for good explanation.

As might be expected, the first three speakers, who were all found to show significance in the individual pitch measures, also showed measures of pitch movement to be important contributors to PC1. Noise offset was important for speaker 2, as indicated by the individual measure analysis. Interestingly noise offset was also an important measure for the other two speakers in the PCA, and was the most important measure for speaker 3. Speakers 4 and 5, on the other hand, were not found to show significance in any of the measures identified. This is also reflected in the less clear picture in the PCA: in both cases the first two principal components were required to explain much of the variance, with all measures playing a role for both, indicating a more subtle contribution of these measures for this contrast.

5.4.4 *Summary*

The phonetic characteristics of tones and the stops adjacent to them for these five speakers of British Panjabi are summarized in Table 5.4. Pitch movement is often, but not always, associated with words where tone is expected, and less so for High tone than Low tone. The stops continuing the Old Indo-Aryan voiced aspirates are, for some speakers and in some positions, phonetically different from those which do not. There is variation across speakers to realize the same contrasts. There is also some evidence for the attrition of tone, if this is to be equated with pitch movement.

Table 5.4 Summary of results for pitch and consonantal measures for Low and High tones

Speaker		Low	High	
		prevocalic	intervocalic	final
1	pitch	low/falling	high/rising	high/rising
	stop	shorter VOT	–	–
2	pitch	low/falling	–	high/rising
	stop	–	breathy-voiced offset	breathy-voiced offset
3	pitch	falling	overall pitch rise	high
	stop	–	–	–
4	pitch	–	overall pitch rise	–
	stop	shorter VOT	–	–
5	pitch	falling	–	–
	stop	(slight creak)	–	–

Note: Mid tones showed an absence of the characteristics and so are not represented here.

5.5 Discussion

5.5.1 Pitch and tone in British Panjabi

Our key finding for pitch and lexical tone is that pitch movement is often, but not always, associated with words where tone is expected, and less so for High tone than Low tone. Our results are consistent with the expectation that rule-governed tonogenesis of the Old Indo-Aryan voiced aspirates did take place in Panjabi (Bhatia 1975). Previous phonetic investigations of Panjabi tone have also concentrated on the contribution of pitch to the tonal contrast (Wells and Roach 1980, Sampat 1964, Sandhu 1968). Wells and Roach reported pitch contours for each tone, which they identified as showing particular shapes in the first or second part of the word (whether mono- or disyllabic). In the first part of the word the Low-tone words showed a sharp drop in pitch, while Mid-tone and High-tone words showed relatively level pitch, although the High tone was at a relatively higher pitch than Mid. In the second part of the word, Low-tone and Mid-tone pitch contours are level, but that for High tone shows a steep fall. They also noted constriction of the larynx during the production of Low tone.

Four out of our five informants show Low tone generally characterized by falling pitch, with a roughly similar pattern to that described by Wells and Roach for Patiali. This was also the pattern found for Doabi by Bhardwaj (personal communication). We also found slightly creaky phonation in the production of Low tone in one speaker.

Our results for High tone show different patterns from those for the Patiali dialect in Wells and Roach (admittedly for different items), or for Doabi (Bhardwaj, personal communication). We found that the phonetic realization varied between intervocalic and final tokens and across speakers. Only speaker 1 showed the expected pitch pattern of a high or raised pitch followed by a subsequent fall. In intervocalic tokens two other speakers (3, 4) did show rising pitch, but across the whole word. Speaker 3 also showed raised pitch in her final words with High tone, but speaker 4 showed no evidence of pitch movement in this position. This lack of pitch contour for High tone was found generally for speaker 5. The findings for speaker 2 were more unexpected. In intervocalic position we found breathy-voiced offset to the voiced stops in the tonal words (with its own characteristic drop in pitch following the consonantal release). In final position we found both breathy-voiced offset and rising pitch. The contrast appears to be doubly marked for this speaker in this position.

Our data for words with Mid tone are entirely consistent with those of Wells and Roach, in that we found no evidence of pitch contours. These forms do indeed appear to be 'non-tonal'.

5.5.2 *Stops and tone in British Panjabi*

A less expected result was the discovery of differences in the phonetic realization of stops adjacent to tonal as opposed to non-tonal vowels, as reflected in voice onset time and noise offset measures. This suggests that the plosives continuing the voiced aspirates are, for some speakers and in some positions, phonetically different from those which do not, which in turn suggests that the outcome of the sound law was a near, rather than a complete, merger (cf. Labov 1994: 349–70).

We found that the voiceless stop in non-tonal words sometimes had a longer VOT than the voiceless stop in Low-tone/tonal words, suggesting that the contrast exists both in the realization of the stops and pitch contours. Moreover, non-tonal /k/, while showing longer VOT than tonal /k/, does not seem to fall within the category of the voiceless aspirate /kh/, which was not included in this experiment, but which appears to be characterized by relatively long VOT. Measurements of some additional distractor words included in the materials with /kh/ showed that speaker 1 had a mean VOT for /kh/ of 101 ms, as opposed to 41 ms for non-tonal /k/ and 27 ms for tonal /k/; speaker 4 had an average VOT of 100 ms for /kh/, but 64 ms for non-tonal /k/ and 43 ms for tonal /k/ (/g/ for both speakers is voiced with voicing lead). These observations would need to be substantiated by a full study of the four stop series (assuming that the stops adjacent to tones form an additional fourth series), but they may indicate that these speakers have four stop categories, in contrast to the standard assumption of three categories, where the word-initial voiceless stops before Low and Mid tones are phonologically and phonetically identical. The shorter VOT in tonal words may reflect the presence of constricted phonation on release of the stop consonant.

Speaker 2 typically showed stops with breathy-voiced offset in High-tone/tonal words, in contrast to plain voiced stops in non-tonal forms. Breathy voice is not otherwise reported as a possible realization of the tonal contrast of High vs. Mid in Panjabi (Majhi, Doabi, Patiali dialects).[8] In Panjabi orthography, the signs for the voiced aspirate stops are still retained, and are used to represent tonal words. The appearance of breathy-voiced stops could reflect either a spelling pronunciation, particularly by a speaker familiar with Hindi, or a pronunciation influenced by Hindi, which is regarded as a more socially prestigious language than Panjabi. However it is difficult to assume that breathy-voiced stops are simply a spelling pronunciation, because they are

[8] Western dialects of Panjabi, spoken in Pakistan, are reported as showing tones and voiced aspirates (see e.g. Bahl 1957*b*), but this is probably not relevant here, as none of the speakers come from areas now in Pakistan.

only found for High-tone words, but never for Low-tone words, whereas voiced aspirate graphemes are used for both tones. Again, if we assume that our speaker was using such a pronunciation as a result of Hindi influence, which is possible, we would have to note an odd asymmetry, with only High-tone words being affected.

5.5.3 Loss of lexical tone in British Panjabi

If lexical tone is assumed to refer to the realizations of Low-tone and High-tone words with particular pitch movements, our results partly align with these expectations. Two speakers show differences in pitch for tonal words in all phonetic environments; all speakers showed some evidence of pitch movements in at least one environment. At the same time, our findings are also consistent with the informal reports that a further sound change is in progress in British Panjabi, namely the loss of lexical tone probably as a result of language contact. Three speakers show pitch movements in only some phonetic environments, or no evidence for pitch movement at all. Thus there is some evidence for the loss of tone in British Panjabi, at least in terms of a reduction in the prevalence and distribution of pitch movements in High-tone and Low-tone words.

However, we have also found that the stops adjacent to tonal vowels can be phonetically different from those adjacent to non-tonal vowels: the contrast can be cued with pitch differences, pitch and consonantal differences, and consonantal differences alone. For most speakers in most phonetic environments, even if pitch movements are not used, the contrast is still being maintained. Only in two speakers and in one phonetic environment (High tone/final) does there appear to be no marking of the contrast at all. Overall we appear to be witnessing a change in progress in British Panjabi, which may ultimately result in the loss of the tonal contrast completely, but which at present is manifested in some reduction of the use of pitch patterns by some speakers.

The design of our experiment was informed by the assumption that characteristically 'British' varieties of Panjabi are currently developing which are different in certain respects from the original standard varieties spoken in India or Pakistan. This assumption seems intuitively likely, given both the geographical, cultural, and social separation of the British Panjabi communities from those of the Indian subcontinent, and also their social contacts within the UK. It is also supported by anecdotal observations from speakers themselves, who report that they have been regarded as speaking 'British' or 'English' Panjabi by friends and relatives from the subcontinent (and not just in the use of English lexical items).

The five speakers of this study together reflect three dialects recognized for the Indian subcontinent: Doabi (speakers 2 and 3), Powadhi (speaker 5), and the standard dialect, Majhi (speakers 1 and 4). Previous accounts of the phonetic realization of tones in these dialects note dialectal variation (e.g. Bhatia 1975 for Majhi; Joshi 1973 on Doabi). For example, for most varieties of Majhi, Low tone is described as a 'low rising' pitch movement, while for Doabi it is described as a 'high falling' pitch movement. However, despite the original dialect background of the speakers, all five speakers in our experiment showed the same type of pitch pattern for Low tone, in this case a falling pitch pattern. This suggests that despite different dialect origins, these speakers may now be converging on a particular realization characteristic of the emerging British variety spoken by the community to which they now belong. Thus these data also provide support at the phonetic level for the notion of 'British Panjabi'.

5.5.4 Tonal consonants in British Panjabi

The phonetic data suggest that the reflexes of the Old Indo-Aryan voiced aspirates may not have fully merged with voiceless and voiced stops after the historical processes of tonogenesis, since a fourth stop series still seems to persist for some speakers for some lexical contrasts. This, and the distributional observation that High and Low tone still appear to be strongly tied to the consonants with which they are historically associated, leads us to offer a phonological analysis which recognizes four stop series for British Panjabi: plain voiceless, plain voiced, voiceless aspirate, and a fourth category of tonal stops.

Within an autosegmental framework (e.g. R. Ladd 1996), we assume that the tonal consonants are lexically specified for High tone, which associates with the tonal consonant. Assuming a linguistic-phonetic interpretation of abstract phonological tone with respect to phonetic realization (Nolan 1998), the phonetic exponents of High tone are pitch movement and/or phonation differences, determined by the phonetic environment of the tonal consonant. Phonetic interpretation gives falling pitch movement in syllable onset (movement away from High), and rising pitch in coda (movement towards High). In disyllables stress plays a role in the parsing of the tonal consonant: in /ˈsə́ngi/ 'neck', where rising pitch is found, stress on the preceding syllable leads to the tonal consonant being treated as part of its coda. When stress falls on the following syllable, the tonal consonant is parsed as an onset, with falling pitch and constricted phonation, as in e.g. /nɪˈkàr/ 'decadence' (this word was not included in the experiment because it does not occur in a minimal pair, but this realization has been observed informally).

The phonatory characteristics of tonal consonants are predictable from the position of the tonal consonant in the syllable, and in the word. High tone is unspecified for values relating specifically to phonation type. If the tonal consonant is in coda position, whether intervocalic or final, we find voiced consonants, or breathy-voiced consonants for some speakers. If the tonal consonant is in onset position we find constricted or creaky phonation, with a voiceless consonant (sometimes with short VOT) in word-initial position, but a voiced consonant intervocalically. The phonetic specification for the phonation type during closure for tonal consonants in intervocalic position generally seems to involve voicing. The less usual association of phonation type and tone observed in this data, in particular Low tone with constricted or creaky phonation (and High tone with breathy phonation), makes it difficult to specify Panjabi tone in terms of standard feature systems which link tone and phonation (e.g. Halle and Stevens 1971).

Assuming a fourth series of tonal consonants helps account for the limited distribution of tone in British Panjabi. Mid tone can be dispensed with altogether (as indeed in certain traditional analyses, e.g. Bhardwaj 1995); we recall that in any case Mid-tone words far outnumber those with High and Low tone. Others have also argued for a single underlying tone for Panjabi. Sadanand and Vijayakrishnan (1995) have independently argued from impressionistic data that High tone adjacent to stops is derived synchronically from underlying phonological 'voiced aspirates' in the coda of the syllable. Baart (2003) also argues for a single underlying tone for Panjabi, but associating with the vowel and with the value Low. The assumption of tonal consonants also assumes a marginal phonological category which operates only for a small set of lexical contrasts.

5.6 Concluding remarks

In this paper we have presented the results of a small-scale acoustic phonetic investigation of lexical tone in a variety of Panjabi spoken in Oxfordshire. Lexical tone historically derives from a rule-governed development of the Old Indo-Aryan voiced aspirates, and these data confirm these expectations in the use of pitch differences for some speakers in certain phonetic environments. At the same time, we also find some evidence to support the assumption of a further ongoing sound change in progress in British Panjabi, gradual attrition of lexical tone.

But these data also reveal a less expected finding: the stops which continue the voiced aspirates, and are now adjacent to High and Low tones, are sometimes phonetically different from those which do not. This suggests that the sound law may not have resulted in a full merger of the reflexes of the voiced aspirates with the plain voiceless and voiced stops. This in turn provides more support for Labov's (1994) claim that new data may provoke the need for new principles, or laws to characterize language change; specifically, the British Panjabi data presented here are consistent with Labov's new principle of 'near merger'. The marginal stop category which seems to persist in this Indo-European language shows an interesting and apparently unusual array of phonetic correlates in terms of pitch, phonation, and consonantal offset. Until we have more information about lexical tone in this and other related varieties which show lexical tone (Baart 2003), we have to accept that the tonal consonants of Panjabi appear to be a law unto themselves.

6

Kuryłowicz's first 'law of analogy' and the development of passive periphrases in Latin

WOLFGANG DE MELO

Morphological and morphosyntactic change is far less amenable to laws and rules than phonological change. Nevertheless, a number of tendencies can be observed, which may not enable us to predict morphological change, but which can at least make sense of it. Some of these tendencies were called 'laws of analogy' by Kuryłowicz (1947). His first 'law' states that bipartite markers tend to replace isofunctional morphemes consisting of only one of these elements; or, in Hock's reformulation (1991: 211–12), that more clearly or overtly marked elements are preferred.

Kuryłowicz's first 'law' can help us to understand developments of passive periphrases in Latin. In early and classical Latin, the *infectum*-stem, which indicates simultaneity, forms synthetic passives; thus the present *amo* 'I love' and the imperfect *amabam* 'I loved' have *amor* 'I am loved' and *amabar* 'I was loved' as passive counterparts. The *perfectum*-stem, which indicates anteriority, cannot form synthetic passives. Instead, the *to*-participle is combined with the copula. Thus the perfect *amaui* 'I have loved' and the pluperfect *amaueram* 'I had loved' have *amatus sum* 'I have been loved' and *amatus eram* 'I had been loved' as passive counterparts. In the perfect and pluperfect passive the copula is in the present and imperfect, not in the perfect or pluperfect, because normally the participle itself already indicates anteriority.

The Romance passive is entirely periphrastic. In Italian, Latin *amor* is replaced by *sono amato*, from *amatus sum*, which has acquired present meaning; *amabar* is replaced by *ero amato*, from *amatus eram*, which has acquired imperfect meaning; and forms of the perfect/pluperfect type *amatus fui/fueram* also survive, for instance in *fui amato*.

The Romance passive obeys Kuryłowicz's first 'law': *amatus fueram* could be said to mark anteriority twice, on the participle and on the copula; or, since not all *to*-participles indicate anteriority, it at least marks the tense unambiguously. Among the new periphrases of *infectum* forms we cannot speak of double marking, but certainly of clearer marking. However, Kuryłowicz's law is only part of the story. In my contribution, I intend to examine texts from different periods and to show how this complex morphological change took place. I shall look at Plautus and Terence as representatives of early Latin; at Hyginus' *De astronomia* and Vitruvius' *De architectura* as specimens of Augustan prose; and, very briefly, at Caesarius of Arles, Gregory of Tours, and especially the *Peregrinatio Egeriae* as samples of late Latin.

6.1 Some paradigms

Before examining the morphological changes in detail, we must briefly go through a few paradigms. Table 6.1 presents the active forms of *amare* 'love'.

Table 6.1 An active paradigm

	Infectum	*Perfectum*
Infinitive	*amare*	*amauisse*
Indicative, past	*amabam*	*amaueram*
Indicative, present	*amo*	*amaui*
Indicative, future	*amabo*	*amauero*
Subjunctive, past	*amarem*	*amauissem*
Subjunctive, non-past	*amem*	*amauerim*

The *infectum*-stem indicates that the event expressed by the verb and its complements is simultaneous with another event. The *perfectum*-stem, by contrast, marks anteriority. Thus *amare* is simultaneous with the moment of speech and means 'to love', while *amauisse* is anterior to the moment of speech and means 'to have loved'. In the indicative, there are three tenses for each stem—past, present, and future. In the *infectum*, these three tenses mean 'I loved', 'I love', and 'I shall love'. In the *perfectum*, the meanings are 'I had loved', 'I have loved', and 'I shall have loved'. The subjunctive is similar, but does not distinguish between present and future.

Table 6.2 presents the passive forms of *amare*.

Table 6.2 A passive paradigm

	Infectum	*Perfectum*
Infinitive	*amari*	*amatus esse*
Indicative, past	*amabar*	*amatus eram*
Indicative, present	*amor*	*amatus sum*
Indicative, future	*amabor*	*amatus ero*
Subjunctive, past	*amarer*	*amatus essem*
Subjunctive, non-past	*amer*	*amatus sim*

Each active form is matched by a passive one. In the passive, the *infectum* is synthetic and contains the same *infectum*-stem as the active. The *perfectum* is analytic and contains the perfect passive participle and an *infectum* form of *esse*. The use of *infectum* forms of *esse* for the analytic passive of the *perfectum* is not as odd as it may seem. In *amatus sum* 'I have been loved', the perfect passive participle is marked for anteriority and passive voice, but since it cannot inflect for person, number, or the absolute tenses past, present, or future, it is combined with *esse* 'be'. As anteriority is already expressed through the participle, the non-anterior forms of *esse* can be used.

The Romance passive is essentially based on a Latin paradigm that has undergone extensive changes:

Table 6.3 A very late passive paradigm

	Infectum	*Perfectum*
Infinitive	*amatus esse*	*amatus fuisse*
Indicative, past	*amatus eram*	*amatus fueram*
Indicative, present	*amatus sum*	*amatus fui*
Indicative, future	*amatus ero*	*amatus fuero*
Subjunctive, past	*amatus essem*	*amatus fuissem*
Subjunctive, non-past	*amatus sim*	*amatus fuerim*

Naturally, not all Romance forms go back directly to this paradigm; for instance, both the synthetic future active and the analytic future passive were replaced by various types of periphrasis with *habere* 'have' (Italian, French, Spanish, Portuguese), *uelle* 'want' (Rumanian), or *debere* 'must' (Logudorese). For our purposes, however, the simplified paradigm of Table 6.3 will be sufficient. What we can see here is that after a phase of double marking of anteriority on participle and copula, the passive participle lost its meaning of anteriority; the absolute and relative tenses are exclusively expressed by the copula. It is important to note that some of these new forms already occur in early Latin. What did earlier scholars have to say about them?

6.2 Earlier research

Most of the earlier research on the subject falls into two categories: on the one hand there are scholars who examine individual authors in some detail and try to establish rules for them without considering diachronic developments; and on the other there are those who try to trace diachronic developments, without necessarily paying much attention to what individual authors can teach us.

Madvig (1842: 219) believes that there is always a clear semantic distinction between *amatus sum* and *amatus fui* in classical Latin. *Amatus sum* indicates either a past action or a present result, while *amatus fui* indicates a state that is past. On the other hand, Madvig also asserts (1842: 224) that *amatus fui* can be equivalent to *amatus sum*, but only in early Latin,[1] where the participle is more like an adjective, and in very late authors. Lebreton (1901: 203), looking exclusively at Cicero, essentially accepts Madvig's distinction, but argues that sometimes the two forms are equivalent. He also presents some interesting data concerning the distribution of forms in general and the frequency of the various combinations of tenses and moods in particular (1901: 207). The distribution of double forms in Cicero is not biased towards the letters, which indicates that the type is not colloquial. What is more, according to Lebreton the type *amatus fui* is not attested at all, even though the perfect indicative is the most frequent combination of tense and mood in the *perfectum*.[2] The types *amatus fuero/fuerim/fueram/fuissem/fuisse* are attested five, six, five, five, and two times, respectively. Riemann (1885: 215–26) thinks that *amatus fui* and *fuisse* always have special functions in Livy, essentially identical to those of the pluperfect, while *amatus fuero/fuerim/fueram/fuissem* sometimes have such special functions and sometimes not. He believes that the absence of special functions may be colloquial for these forms, but does not state why it is, then, that *amatus fui* and *fuisse* are not attested without such functions. Hoffmann (1997: 212–13) notes that in Ovid, the type *amatus fuissem* always functions as an unreal subjunctive. However, this is a finding that cannot be generalized. I have

[1] Lindsay (1907: 61–3) also regards the double forms as equivalent to the simple ones in Plautus.

[2] However, Menge, Burkard, and Schauer (2000: 191) cite *dispersa et dissipata . . . fuerunt* (Cic. *De or.* 1. 187), which I take as a double *perfectum.*

found tokens of the same type in Hyginus and Vitruvius which are purely temporal pluperfect subjunctives, without any unreal nuance. Hofmann and Szantyr (1965: 322) suggest that in any analysis of the double forms it would be important to distinguish between passives and deponents, and Stockert (1983: 217) claims that double forms are more frequent among the deponent verbs, without, however, presenting statistics.[3]

I shall at this point not discuss what other scholars have to say about individual late Latin authors. Instead, I shall turn my attention to those who describe diachronic developments. Muller (1924: 69–71) notes that passive future perfects and pluperfects with *fuero* and *fueram* are not particularly rare as early as the Augustan period, while the type *amatus fui* remains rare until late. He also argues that participles with *infectum* forms of the copula do not replace the synthetic passive of the *infectum* until late in the eighth century (1924: 78). The latter theory cannot be upheld, as *amatus sum* and *amatus sim* instead of *amor* and *amer* already occur in Palladius (fourth century), albeit rarely (Svennung 1935: 456–7). The first observation is correct, but Muller does not connect the rise of *amatus fueram* and other double *perfectum* forms with the rise of *amatus sum* instead of *amor*; in fact, he sees the two phenomena as independent. Salonius (1920: 291–2) also notes that *perfectum* forms of the copula replace the *infectum* forms before the type *amatus sum* instead of *amor* arises. He believes that the double *perfectum* forms came about because the participles were reanalysed as adjectives and that *amatus sum* instead of *amor* is so late because there was no need for it—after all, *amor* does not contain a participle which has turned into an adjective. This theory, which also implies that the rise of *amatus fueram* is independent of the rise of *amatus sum* instead of *amor*, makes me wonder why the vast majority of participles do not have comparative or superlative forms. Moreover, why did *amatus fueram* replace *amatus eram* before *amatus fui* replaced *amatus sum*? If we follow Salonius, there is no answer. Leumann (1921) believes that in later Latin the simple *perfectum* forms occurred in main clauses and the double *perfectum* forms in subordinate ones. He does not explain why this is. As noted above, the double-marked pluperfect and future perfect arose before the double-marked perfect. The reason why double-marked forms are more frequent in subordinate clauses is that subordinate clauses have more relative tenses (pluperfect, future perfect) than main clauses do.

[3] Useful statistics can be found in Blase (1896–8: 322), who looks at all periods of the language, but does not distinguish between deponents and passives, or between future perfects and perfect subjunctives.

Before embarking on a discussion of the early texts, we still have to look at some problems of disambiguation, as the boundaries between participles and other word classes are not always clear.

6.3 Problems of disambiguation

It is not always obvious what should count as a combination of past participle and copula, and where this is obvious, it can still be unclear whether such a combination should be classified as passive or deponent. This section outlines what kinds of difficulties exist and what general principles I apply in order to solve them.

The first and biggest problem is that the distinction between perfect passive participles and adjectives is often not clear-cut. Many transitive verbs have past participles which indicate that an entity is affected for some time or even on a permanent basis, and such participles often develop into adjectives. Thus the distinction between participles and adjectives inevitably gets blurred, and all classifications contain an element of arbitrariness. Compare:

(1) Ecquid beo te? (Ter. *Eun.* 279)
'Surely I'm making you happy?'

(2) Beatus eris si consudaueris. (Plaut. *Pseud.* 666)
'You'll be happy if you have sweated.'

(3) O quantum est hominum beatiorum,
quid me laetius est beatiusue? (Catull. 9. 10–11)
'O of all people happier than others, what is more cheerful or happy than me?'

In (1) *beo* is obviously a verb. (2) is ambiguous; *beatus eris* can be interpreted as a future perfect consisting of a participle with the copula ('you will have been made happy'), or it can be regarded as an adjective 'happy' in combination with the simple future of *esse*. In (3) the comparative forms *beatiorum* and *beatius* make it clear that we are dealing with adjectives.[4]

In my analysis, I have counted all comparative and superlative forms as adjectives, for instance *exclusissimus* 'most locked out' in Plaut. *Men.* 698,

[4] According to Priscian, *GL* ii. 550. 20–7 Keil, participles should be classified as adjectival if they are in the comparative or superlative, but as verbal if they select the same cases as finite verbs. Laughton (1964: 52) presents a problematic example from Cic. *De or.* 3. 31: *instructissimus a natura*, 'most instructed by Nature'. The superlative is typical of adjectives, but the agent expression is typical of verb forms.

and I have taken all forms negated by *in-* as adjectives as well, for instance *inuocatus* 'not invited' in Plaut. *Capt.* 70, even where the positive form plus copula counts as a regular passive.

From time to time it is also unclear if we are dealing with a participle or a noun. Again, some participles are never nominalized, but a few have been grammaticalized as nouns. In (4) *dictum* occurs twice, first as noun, then as participle:

(4) Nullumst iam dictum quod non dictum sit prius. (Ter. *Eun.* 41)
'There is no saying which has not been said before.'

The first *dictum* must be a noun because it is combined with *nullum*; if we were dealing with a participle, we would have *nihil iam dictumst* instead. The second *dictum* must be a participle because *dictum sit* has past meaning, as can be seen from *prius*. *Sit* in itself could not have past meaning.

Where we know that we are dealing with a participle rather than an adjective or a noun, we may still be uncertain whether the verb is in the passive or whether it is a deponent. *Vehere* and similar verbs have active meaning if the morphology is active ('drag'), but if the morphology is passive, they may either be genuine passives ('be dragged') or have a derived active meaning ('be dragged' → 'drive in a vehicle'). In the texts I looked at, the forms can always be interpreted as having the derived meaning, and therefore I have counted *uehi* and the like as deponents. Verbs such as *audere* and *lubere* are semi-deponents because they have active endings in the *infectum* and passive ones in the *perfectum*, even though there is no corresponding change of meaning. In the texts I examined, I only looked at periphrastic forms, so I have simply classified these verbs as deponents. I have counted all tokens of *factum esse* as passives of *facere*, even though some could also be analysed as suppletive forms of *fieri* 'happen', which does not always function as the passive of *facere* and which normally has active endings except in the infinitive.[5]

Now that I have looked at problems of classification, I can begin analysing the various types at different periods of the language.

6.4 Early Latin: Plautus and Terence

Double *perfectum* forms fully equivalent to their simple counterparts occur as early as Plautus. The fact that there is equivalence can be seen from the rules for

[5] But cf. passive *fitur* in Cato *orat.* 68 and active *fiere* in Enn. *Ann.* 354. A non-suppletive, periphrastic past *fitum est* is attested in Liv. Andron. *Od.* fr. 30.

the sequence of tenses and from coordination with, or parallelism to, 'regular' forms:

(5) Demaenetus: Vbi eris? Libanus: Vbiquomque lubitum erit animo meo. (Plaut. *Asin.* 110)
'Demaenetus: Where will you be? Libanus: Wherever the fancy will have taken me.'

(6) Si ego minam non ultus fuero probe quam lenoni dedi,
tum profecto me sibi habento scurrae ludificatui. (Plaut. *Poen.* 1280–1)
'If I shan't have taken revenge properly for the mina which I gave the pimp, then the city idlers shall make fun of me.'

In (5) the regular future perfect *lubitum erit* in a generalizing relative clause presumably indicates that Libanus must consider a place pleasant before going there. In (6) we get the double form *ultus fuero*. It stands in a conditional clause and is anterior to *habento*, and there is no reason why Plautus could not have written *ultus ero*, which would have been the expected form. In (7) and (8) we find a regular perfect indicative and a double form:

(7) Lassus sum hercle e naui, ut uectus huc sum: etiam nunc nauseo. (Plaut. *Amph.* 329)
'I'm tired from the ship, sailing as I have been here; even now I'm still seasick.'

(8) Vt uerba audio,
non equidem in Aegyptum hinc modo uectus fui,
sed etiam in terras solas orasque ultumas
sum circumuectus, ita ubi nunc sim nescio. (Plaut. *Mostell.* 993–6)
'To judge from his words, I have not only travelled to Egypt, but also to deserted lands, and I have travelled around the most distant shores, to such an extent am I at a loss as to where I am now.'

In (7) *uectus ... sum* is the normal narrative past tense. In (8) we find both *uectus fui* and *sum circumuectus*. The two clauses are coordinated by *non ... modo ... sed etiam* 'not only, but also', which points to temporal equivalence. Yet it is perhaps possible that relative chronology is marked here.

Interestingly, periphrastic forms instead of the synthetic passives of the *infectum*-stem are not yet attested in Plautus and Terence.

A first count of regular and double *perfectum* forms in Plautus and Terence can be found in Table 6.4. In this first count I do not distinguish between passives and deponents, nor do I take semantic considerations into account. I have not given figures for the pluperfect subjunctive because there are no double forms in these two authors and because the regular forms hardly ever have purely temporal meanings.

Table 6.4 A first count

	Regular forms	Double forms	Total	Double forms (%)
Perfect inf.	176	1	177	0.56
Pluperfect ind.	11	9	20	45
Perfect ind.	1383	25	1408	1.78
Future perfect	41	6	47	12.77
Perfect subj.	132	5	137	3.65

What Table 6.4 shows is that double forms are an important category in the pluperfect indicative, even though the absolute figures are low here, and in the future perfect. Elsewhere, such forms are rare.

However, what the table does not take into account is that not all double forms are semantically equivalent to their simple counterparts. Among the double pluperfects, there is one case where the double form has a special meaning:

(9) Quod, hic si pote fuisset exorarier
triduom hoc, promissum fuerat. (Ter. *Phorm.* 535–6)
'If he could have been persuaded to give me three days, the money had already been promised.'

By using the double form *promissum fuerat*, Terence shows that the promise was made before the other action; this other action, which was actually not realized, is in the pluperfect subjunctive (*pote fuisset exorarier*). In all other cases, however, the double pluperfect is equivalent to the regular form:

(10) Detineo te: fortasse tu profectus alio fueras. (Ter. *Eun.* 280)
'I'm keeping you; perhaps you had been on your way to some other place.'

Here the meaning is 'you had been on your way elsewhere when I started the conversation'; there is anteriority to an event which has not been stated explicitly. *Profectus eras* could have done the job as well. Note that we are dealing with a deponent here; but this temporal equivalence occurs with other types of verbs as well.

The double future perfect can express anteriority to a regular future perfect, but this happens only in Ter. *An.* 213, where *lubitum fuerit* 'the fancy will have taken him' is anterior to the normal future perfect *ceperit* 'he will have taken'. Elsewhere, the double forms are semantically equivalent to their simple counterparts. This equivalence of double forms and regular counterparts is perhaps not surprising in the pluperfect and the future perfect: anteriority to another pluperfect or another future perfect is not a grammatical category that can be expressed in the active.

The situation is different for the types *amatus fui* and *amatus fuerim*. While they can be equivalent to *amatus sum* and *amatus sim*, respectively, they can also function as pluperfect indicative and pluperfect subjunctive, almost as if the copula were in the imperfect indicative or subjunctive. These alternative pluperfect forms are actually not rare:

(11) Quod fui iuratus, feci. (Plaut. *Curc.* 566)
'I have done what I had sworn.'

(12) Periphanes: Quid erat induta? An regillam induculam an mendiculam?
Epidicus: Impluuiatam, ut istaec faciunt uestimentis nomina.
Periphanes: Vtin impluuium induta fuerit? (Plaut. *Epid.* 223–5)
'Periphanes: What was she wearing? A princess-tunic or a beggar-tunic? Epidicus: She was wearing a basin-tunic, as those people give names to their dresses. Periphanes: She wore a basin?'

In (11) *fui iuratus* is in a relative clause anterior to *feci* and hardly differs from *eram iuratus. Induor aliquid* means 'I am putting something on', and the perfect *indutus sum* means 'I have put something on, I am wearing something'. In (12) the question is not what the woman was putting on, but what she was wearing, so Periphanes uses the pluperfect *quid erat induta*, 'what was she wearing'. After Epidicus' reply, he is surprised and asks, again in the pluperfect, *utin impluuium induta fuerit?*, 'she wore a basin?'.

In order to see to what extent Plautus and Terence foreshadow the Romance system, we have to look at only those cases where the double forms are functionally equivalent to their regular counterparts. I do so in Table 6.5 for passives and in Table 6.6 for deponents, leaving out the infinitives because there is only one token with double marking, and that token has a specific function: *indutum fuisse* in Plaut. *Men.* 515 indicates the past state of having worn something as the result of the action of putting something on even further back in time.

Table 6.5 The relative frequency of double marking (passives)

	Regular forms	Double forms	Total	Double forms (%)
Pluperfect ind.	8	3	11	27.27
Perfect ind.	844	2	846	0.24
Future perfect	28	0	28	0
Perfect subj.	91	2	93	2.15
Total	971	7	978	0.72

Table 6.6 The relative frequency of double marking (deponents)

	Regular forms	Double forms	Total	Double forms (%)
Pluperfect ind.	3	5	8	62.5
Perfect ind.	539	9	548	1.64
Future perfect	13	4	17	23.53
Perfect subj.	41	1	42	2.38
Total	596	19	615	3.09

By comparing Table 6.4 with Tables 6.5 and 6.6, we can see a number of things. In early Latin, double *perfectum* forms sometimes have the function of indicating a further degree of anteriority, but sometimes no such function can be detected. The distribution of forms with and without this function is not random. Double perfects (indicative and subjunctive) have the function in around half of the cases and are, in effect, simply alternative pluperfects. Double pluperfects in the indicative and future perfects, on the other hand, mostly do not fulfil any special functions. If we only consider double *perfectum* forms without special anterior functions, only the double pluperfect indicatives and the future perfects are moderately frequent.

Among the deponents, double *perfectum* forms are more than four times as frequent as among the passives. Although the figures are low, the distribution pattern is so marked that it is significant. What is the reason for this? Originally the forms in *-to-*, which came to be used as participles in all Italic languages, were neutral with regard to voice and tense (Wackernagel 1926: 287–8). This can still be seen from forms like *cenatus*, which means 'someone who has eaten dinner' rather than 'someone who has been eaten for dinner', and *ueritus* 'someone who is afraid' rather than 'someone who was afraid'. The old indifference with regard to voice is easy to explain and can be dealt with swiftly here. Compare the following two English phrases:

(13) a stolen watch

(14) a drunken sailor

Participles in *-to-*, like their English equivalents in *-en* or *-ed*, used to indicate that an entity is affected by the action expressed through the verb. If the verb is transitive (*steal* in (13)), the object is affected and the participle is interpreted as passive. If the verb is intransitive or can at least be used intransitively (*drink* in (14)), the subject is affected and the participle is interpreted as active. Since participles in *-to-* are mostly formed from transitive verbs, they were eventually reanalysed as passive.

The indifference with regard to tense is more important here. Originally, deponents had present participles in **-mVnos* (compare Greek *hepomenos* 'following' < **sek^{w}omenos*), while other verbs had present active participles of the type *amans* and present passive participles in **-mVnos*. All present forms in **-mVnos* were lost, leaving only lexicalized traces like *alumnus* 'nursling' (< 'someone who is being raised') or *femina* 'woman' (< 'someone who is being sucked') (see Meiser 1998: 183 for details). This left non-deponent verbs with a present participle of the type *amans* and a neutral form in *-to-*, while deponents only retained the form in *-to-*. It is only natural, then, that the forms in *-to-* belonging to non-deponents became past forms more quickly because they were in opposition to present forms. Among deponents, present forms like *sequens* are relatively recent innovations[6] and the forms in *-to-* kept their non-past meaning for longer. This, then, may be the ultimate reason why deponents are more likely to be combined with *perfectum* forms of the copula than non-deponents.

While this explains why double *perfectum* forms predominate among the deponents, it does not help us with another question: why are the double forms more frequent in the pluperfect and the future perfect? There are two possible answers. When the participles in *-to-* acquired anterior meaning, forms like *amatus fui* became ambiguous between perfects and pluperfects and were thus avoided, but *amatus fueram* and *amatus fuero* retained pluperfect and future perfect meaning, simply because there is no separate category in the verb system which expresses a further degree of anteriority with respect to the pluperfect and the future perfect. The other explanation is that occasionally *amatus fueram* and *amatus fuero* can be used to make explicit anteriority to other pluperfects and future perfects, even though this is not a separate verb category as such. Since there is no such category, these double pluperfects and future perfects could then be reanalysed as normal pluperfects and future perfects and replace them; this is in agreement with the tendency stated by Hock that more overtly marked forms replace the less overtly marked ones.

I prefer this second explanation partly because it is in agreement with the gradual increase in double forms over time and partly because it also helps us to understand the absence of *amatus fuissem* in early Latin, which can hardly be accidental given the relatively large number of tokens of the type *amatus essem*. Pluperfect subjunctives can, like their indicative counterparts, express

[6] Note that there is no **rens* beside *ratus* in the whole of Latin literature. In early Latin, there is only non-past *ueritus*, while *uerens* is not attested before Nepos.

anteriority to past events if they are in temporal clauses, but many of them are modal forms used to mark the past irrealis. Thus *si tacuisses, philosophus mansisses* means 'if you had kept quiet, you would have remained a philosopher'. *Mansisses* is not anterior to anything else, and *tacuisses* is probably to be taken as simultaneous with *mansisses* rather than anterior to it. Both forms show that something could have happened in the past, but did not happen. Because of this predominantly modal rather than temporal function, there was no need to express a further degree of anteriority, and so no *amatus fuissem* was created in the early texts. But now it is time to look at what happened in the Augustan period.

6.5 The Augustan era: Hyginus and Vitruvius

Double *perfectum* forms are becoming more frequent in the Augustan period; however, there are no longer any significant differences between deponents and passives, and for this reason I shall no longer present their data separately in this section. Periphrases replacing passives of the *infectum* are still not attested. I have collected all the simple and double *perfectum* forms in two representatives of this period, Hyginus and Vitruvius. There are various ancient writers with the name Hyginus. I have looked at the author of the treatise *De astronomia*, which is nowadays generally assumed to have been written by a certain C. Iulius Hyginus between the last years of the first century BC and the first years of the first century AD (see Paniagua Aguilar 2006: 299–301). Marcus Vitruvius Pollio, the writer of *De architectura*, died around 25 BC.

Table 6.7 presents the simple and double *perfectum* forms in these two authors. In those boxes which contain three figures, the one to the left of the brackets is the sum of Hyginus and Vitruvius, and in the brackets the left figure gives the tokens in Hyginus and the right those in Vitruvius.

Table 6.7 A first count of simple and double forms in Hyginus and Vitruvius

	Simple forms	Double forms	Total	Double forms (%)
Perfect inf.	91 (44 + 47)	2 (2 + 0)	93	2.15
Pluperfect ind.	14 (3 + 11)	18 (5 + 13)	32	56.25
Perfect ind.	476 (104 + 372)	7 (1 + 6)	483	1.45
Future perfect	62 (1 + 61)	80 (8 + 72)	142	56.34
Pluperfect subj.	36 (11 + 25)	2 (0 + 2)	38	5.26
Perfect subj.	94 (36 + 58)	44 (2 + 42)	138	31.88

The figures for the two authors may look very different at first sight. However, most of the differences are due to the different sizes of the two works. Other differences are due to the fact that we are dealing with different text types. Vitruvius has disproportionately many future perfects, while future tenses in general are much rarer in Hyginus. This is because Vitruvius tells the reader how to do things; he gives instructions, and instructions are naturally future-oriented. Hyginus' work, on the other hand, is more descriptive; he informs readers about astronomical facts and presents the mythological background, which means that present and past tenses predominate in his writing.

What matters is the proportion of simple and double forms for each tense. These proportions are roughly the same for the two authors, with the exception of the future perfect and the perfect subjunctive. Hyginus has disproportionately many double future perfects and Vitruvius has disproportionately many double perfect subjunctives. Why should this be the case? In a prose text metre offers no help in distinguishing between the future perfect and the perfect subjunctive of the copula, so that they only look different in the first person singular. Syntactic criteria can help in some cases, but in many others it is impossible to distinguish between the two tenses, especially since there is also a semantic overlap. I have analysed the tokens in Hyginus myself, but for Vitruvius I have followed the analysis in the concordance by Callebat, Bouet, Fleury, and Zuinghedau (1984). To some extent, therefore, the differences are likely to be the result of different criteria for disambiguation. However, there is also a second reason, which should not be underestimated: many of the relevant forms in Vitruvius occur in subordinate clauses that are regularly in the indicative if they precede or follow other clauses; in Vitruvius, a large proportion of the subordinate clauses in question do not precede or follow other clauses, but rather are inside them, and since these other clauses are often in the subjunctive, the future perfect undergoes attraction of mood and is regularly turned into a perfect subjunctive.

Since the differences in the proportions of simple and double future perfects and perfect subjunctives can be explained in this way, we can look at the two authors together. What the first count reveals is that some tendencies seen in early Latin are continued: double forms now make up more than half of the future perfects and pluperfect indicatives. There is a marked increase in double perfect subjunctives, but double pluperfect subjunctives as well as double perfect indicatives and infinitives remain very rare.

As before, these figures are insufficient in themselves because some double forms have special functions, while others do not. (15) and (16) show double forms with special functions:

(15) Hercules missus ab Eurystheo ad Hesperidum mala nescius uiae deuenit ad Promethea, quem in Caucaso monte uinctum fuisse supra diximus. (Hyg. *Poet. astr.* 2. 15. 5)
'Hercules had been sent to the apples of the Hesperides by Eurystheus and, not knowing his way, came to Prometheus. We said above that he had been tied up in the Caucasus mountains.'

(16) Qui autem ratiocinationibus et litteris solis confisi fuerunt, umbram non rem persecuti uidentur. (Vitr. 1. 1. 2)
'But those who had put their trust in theory and literature alone can be seen to have followed a shadow rather than reality.'

In (15) *uinctum fuisse* is different from *uinctum esse*. The latter would mean that he was still bound at the time of speaking, while the former indicates that he had already been liberated. And in (16) *confisi fuerunt* functions as a pluperfect anterior to *persecuti uidentur.*

(17) and (18) demonstrate that not every double form has a special function:

(17) Quod si longior in sermone uisus fuero, non mea facunditate, sed rei necessitate factum existimato nec, si breuius aliquid dixero, minus idem ualere confidito quam si pluribus esset audiendum uerbis. (Hyg. *Poet. astr. praef.* 6)
'But if I shall have appeared rather prolix in my expression, believe that this happened not because of my garrulity, but because the subject matter forced me, and if I shall have said something rather briefly, trust that it is worth no less than if you had to hear it in more words.'

(18) Item Lacedaemone e quibusdam parietibus etiam picturae excisae intersectis lateribus inclusae sunt in ligneis formis et in comitium ad ornatum aedilitatis Varronis et Murenae fuerunt allatae. (Vitr. 2. 8. 9)
'In the same way at Sparta pictures, too, cut out from certain walls after the bricks had been cut through, were included in wooden frames and brought to the Comitium as an ornament for the aedileship of Varro and Murena.'

In (17) *uisus fuero* is anterior to *existimato*, not to a future perfect, and Cicero would probably have written *uisus ero*. In (18) *fuerunt allatae* would in the active be replaced by a perfect form, not a pluperfect one.

We can now leave out those double *perfectum* forms which have special functions and contrast the simple and double forms without such functions. The result can be seen in Table 6.8.

Table 6.8 A revised count of simple and double forms in Hyginus and Vitruvius

	Simple forms	Double forms	Total	Double forms (%)
Perfect inf.	91	0	91	0
Pluperfect ind.	14	17	31	54.84
Perfect ind.	476	2	478	0.42
Future perfect	62	70	132	53.03
Pluperfect subj.	36	2	38	5.26
Perfect subj.	94	41	135	30.37

The results are obvious. The double pluperfect indicatives and future perfects have increased greatly in number and constitute slightly more than half of all pluperfect indicatives and future perfects.[7] Double marking gains ground where no functional ambiguity can arise. Double perfect indicatives are still very rare, but double perfect subjunctives make up almost a third of all perfect subjunctives. The reason for this must be that when future perfects undergo modal attraction, they are turned into perfect subjunctives. Since there are now so many double future perfects, a large number of double perfect subjunctives are the natural result. Double pluperfect subjunctives are still very rare, and double perfect infinitives are only used where they fulfil special functions. But the trend towards double forms cannot be stopped, as I shall show in the next section.

6.6 Late Latin developments

Getting reliable linguistic information from late Latin texts is notoriously difficult because the milieu is diglossic. Practically all writers of the period aspire to write classical Latin, the language of education, but the spoken language of the time must have been very different. Authors like Boethius (*c.* 480–524) have a near-perfect mastery of classical Latin, which means that their value for learning about late Latin developments is minimal. Writers like Gregory of Tours (*c.* 538–94) are less educated and show linguistic changes more clearly. However, where they use classical constructions, one has to ask whether they are genuine survivals or whether they are learned ornaments of style. Yet when it comes to double *perfectum* forms, there is a very clear line of development from early Latin to late Latin, and there do not seem to be any

[7] The situation in Livy is essentially the same. For data on the two types of future perfect in Livy see Blase (1896–8: 322).

marked divergences from this line which could be explained by an author's learning. Thus we must conclude that the use of double *perfectum* forms was not influenced by prescriptive rules.

In the *Peregrinatio Egeriae*, written probably at the end of the fourth century, the passive paradigm looks as shown in Table 6.9 (Winters 1984: 447–50).

Table 6.9 The passive in the *Peregrinatio Egeriae*

	Simple forms	Double forms
Pluperfect ind.	--	*amatus fueram*
Perfect ind.	*amatus sum*	--
Imperfect ind.	*amabar*	*amatus eram* (rare)
Present ind.	*amor*	--
Pluperfect subj.	--	*amatus fuissem*
Perfect subj.	--	*amatus fuerim*
Imperfect subj.	*amarer*	*amatus essem* (rare)
Present subj.	*amer*	*amatus sim* (rare)

The present infinitive passive is regularly *amari*, while its perfect counterpart is either *amatus esse* or *amatus fuisse*.[8] Note that *amatus fueram* and the other forms with *fu-* no longer fulfil any special anterior functions. This is particularly obvious among the infinitives:

(19) Habebat autem ante se ipse fons quasi lacum, ubi parebat fuisse operatum sanctum Iohannem baptistam. (*Peregr. Eger.* 15. 2)
'But the fountain had in front of it something like a lake, where it appeared that St John the Baptist had worked.'

Here not only Plautus and Terence, but also Hyginus and Vitruvius, would have written *esse operatum*; they only use the type *amatus fuisse* for special functions. Note that Egeria does not employ *fuisse operatum* simply to indicate that the event took place long before her time. In 8. 3 she says *posita esse* when she is talking about a tree planted by the patriarchs, centuries before John the Baptist.

There are few periphrastic present passive subjunctives. The following token was considered a perfect subjunctive by Muller (1924: 83):

[8] Joffre's passive paradigm for Caesarius of Arles (died *c.* 542) is very similar: the future perfect, pluperfect indicative, and pluperfect subjunctive are consistently formed with *fuero*, *fueram*, and *fuissem*, the perfect subjunctive and perfect infinitive are formed either with *fuerim* and *fuisse* or with *sim* and *esse*, and the perfect indicative is formed with *sum* (1995: 314).

(20) Tantus rugitus et mugitus totius populi est cum fletu, ut forsitan porro ad ciuitatem gemitus populi omnis auditus sit. (*Peregr. Eger.* 36. 3)
'There is such an uproar and noise together with crying that the moaning of the entire people can be heard perhaps as far away as the city.'

I cannot see how *auditus sit* could be given a past interpretation.

Gregory of Tours (*c.* 538–94) lived more than a century after Egeria and shows practically the same paradigm (see Bonnet 1890: 641–3), but with the completion of a change still under way in Egeria: the past infinitive is now regularly *amatus fuisse*. Finally, in the Chronicle of Fredegar (seventh and eighth centuries) *amatus sum* loses ground to *amatus fui* (Haag 1898: 85–6).

6.7 Summary and conclusions

Double *perfectum* forms without special functions have a long history. In Plautus and Terence the double forms are considerably more frequent among the deponents, but the only tenses which have a fair number of them are the pluperfect (indicative) and the future perfect. The reason why deponents have more double forms is that here the participles in *-to-* remained unmarked for tense longer. Here the present participles are an innovation, so the forms in *-to-* had to mark simultaneity as well as anteriority. This is a crucial difference from the non-deponent verbs, which have old present participles. Double forms are more frequent in the pluperfect and the future perfect for a specific reason. *Amatus fueram* and *amatus fuero* could occasionally have been employed to indicate that events are anterior to other pluperfects and future perfects. But since anteriority to pluperfects and future perfects never became a linguistic category in its own right, these forms were reanalysed as simple pluperfects and future perfects. As pluperfect subjunctives are often unreal past subjunctives not expressing anteriority, there was not much need to maintain or create *amatus fuissem*, and this type is consequently not attested in Plautus and Terence. Kuryłowicz's first law does not create new forms, but helps to spread them.

In the Augustan period, double forms become more frequent. Hyginus and Vitruvius have double pluperfect indicatives, double future perfects, and double perfect subjunctives, all very frequent and all without special functions. Why did double perfect subjunctives, one of the rarest categories in early Latin, become so frequent, even though the perfect *amatus fui* and the double pluperfect subjunctives remained so rare? The reason seems to be that future perfects are now frequently formed by taking the passive participle in combination with the future perfect rather than the simple future of the copula. When a clause that would normally be in the future perfect is placed within a clause in the subjunctive, it is normal for this future perfect to be turned into a perfect subjunctive. If the future perfect is formed not with the simple future, but the future perfect of the copula, it is natural that the derived subjunctive should have the perfect subjunctive of the copula rather than the present subjunctive.

In Egeria, the double pluperfect subjunctive has become the norm. The form is easy to derive by analogy: *amaueram* : *amatus fueram* :: *amauissem* : *amatus fuissem*. The present and imperfect subjunctives show the first signs of being replaced by periphrastic forms, *amatus sim* and *amatus essem*; this change is the result of similar analogies. Since *amatus sim* and *amatus essem* are no longer interpreted as perfect and pluperfect subjunctives, respectively, this change is unproblematic. More overt marking wins out so long as no functional ambiguities can arise. *Amabar* is very slowly losing ground to *amatus eram*, which again cannot be interpreted as pluperfect any more. The perfect indicative with *sum*, being the most frequent past form, is still resisting change, and the present indicative can obviously not be replaced by *amatus sum* yet because that form is still a perfect. In Gregory of Tours, the perfect infinitive passive is now regularly formed with *fuisse*, and in the Chronicle of Fredegar, the perfect indicative is finally losing ground to the type *amatus fui*. When at last the present indicative passive becomes periphrastic, we have arrived at the Romance passive system.

Kuryłowicz's first 'law of analogy' did not give rise to the new forms, but helped to spread them, a spread that began with the pluperfect and future perfect. Once these new pluperfects and future perfects had become the norm, a chain shift had been triggered and other double-marked forms became more frequent. New periphrases, like the more overtly marked present tense *amatus sum* for *amor*, could only gain ground once the old perfect *amatus sum* had been replaced by *amatus fui*; avoidance of ambiguity and greater clarity are more important than more overt marking. Hock's reformulation of Kuryłowicz's law has the disadvantage that the expressions 'more clearly' and 'more overtly' are lumped together.

7

Phonetic laws, language diffusion, and drift: the loss of sibilants in the Greek dialects of the first millennium BC

ANNA MORPURGO DAVIES

7.1 Introduction: similar changes and their interpretation

It is not surprising that similar phonological changes occur in different languages, different periods, and different parts of the world. In all instances we must decide whether the changes are independent developments or are somehow linked. When the languages are related the problem is more pressing and we first need to ask whether the link is genetic. When we find that all Greek dialects have lost a word-final dental, as in ἔλυε from *ἔλυετ, the easiest hypothesis (which may of course be wrong) is that the change goes back to a common Greek period. On the other hand, when the same innovation occurs in Luwian, we pause because we do not want to postulate a Luwian-Greek subgroup. Alternatively the changes may be due to diffusion within a more or less continuous linguistic area or more generally to language contact (including substratum phenomena). Paul Kiparsky (1973*b*), for instance, argued that it was implausible that the dissimilation of aspirates (Grassmann's Law), which occurs in Indic and Greek, was due to independent innovations, and that there was enough evidence to attribute such a synchronic rule to a common

Greek-Indo-Iranian period. For another change, the $^*s > h/\emptyset$ change found e.g. in Greek, Iranian, Armenian, and Lycian A, scholars have asked whether it started in one of these areas and spread to the others. These questions are sometimes answered by exploiting what we know about absolute and relative chronology.

For the dissimilation of aspirates it is argued that it occurs in Greek *after* changes which are normally assumed to be exclusively Greek (such as $^*s > h$ between vowels or $^*d^h > t^h$). Kiparsky's views have not found favour among Indo-Europeanists, but an analysis of his arguments, which were based on a different view of both synchronic and diachronic phonology and a different concept of rule, obliges us to realize that much of our thinking about relative chronology, change, etc. depends on the theoretical framework that we adopt. From the point of view of the theory which Kiparsky accepted at the time, the chronology point made above does not constitute a serious objection to the whole argument, since he postulated an original dissimilation rule which yielded forms later lexicalized in Greek, and at a later stage partial rule reordering within Greek, with Grassmann's Law coming to follow rather than precede the devoicing of aspirates and the aspiration of /s/. This was challenged, however, on internal grounds and with regard to the validity of the etymologies on which it was based.[1]

For the $^*s > h/\emptyset$ change, which cannot be Indo-European since other Indo-European languages preserve the sibilant, it is pointed out that in Greece the change is earlier than our earliest Linear B texts (i.e. earlier than *c.* 1400 BC), while the Iranian change is likely to be much later. Though diffusion from Greek to the East cannot be entirely excluded, the time gap, as well as the geographical and cultural discontinuity in the relevant periods, make it difficult to make a case for it (Szemerényi 1968). In general it is very difficult to reconstruct with a degree of plausibility diffusion processes which belong to a prehistoric period. But what happens when the same or a similar change occurs in different ancient phases or different dialects of the same ancient language, at a time when we are able to assess the chronology and location of the changes? Here too things are not altogether clear. It is somewhat easier with morphology, syntax, or lexicon, but more difficult in the case of phonology. If in Greek Grassmann's Law is post-Mycenaean, we must explain why it is found in all dialects. Diffusion or independent development? I doubt that we have the evidence to decide. Similarly, we now assume that the development of the labiovelars into labials before a consonant or central vowel, including /o/, is

[1] But also on other more theoretical points; cf. e.g. Miller (1977). Currently the view begins to prevail that in Greek the dissimilation is post-Mycenaean, i.e. it occurred after changes which had not yet occurred in Mycenaean (such as the loss of intervocalic /h/), but the point is disputed and agreement has not been reached.

post-Mycenaean. But how do we account for this common outcome in a linguistic area which was heavily fragmented? We may think of diffusion during the so-called 'Dark Ages', since all the alphabetic evidence we have has already reached the labial stage. Alternatively we may think of independent developments which were in a sense prompted by their starting point. The shift from /k^{w}/ etc. to /p/ etc. is frequently found and perhaps no further explanation is needed. But we could also suppose, for instance, that in certain environments all inherited or even borrowed labiovelars at an early stage—perhaps pre-Mycenaean, perhaps Common Greek—had modified their original articulation moving, for instance, towards /p^{w}/ etc., and that the Mycenaean <*qa, qo*> signs indicated such sounds.[2] The shift to labial stop would then be even more trivial. In that case would we want to talk about diffusion or not? And if, as I believe, we cannot answer the question, is this because we do not have sufficient evidence? This change happened in the 'Dark Ages' and there is a sense in which the Dark Ages are not history but prehistory, since they do not provide us with direct written documentation.[3]

In a modern context linguistic diffusion can sometimes be documented, but here too the level of detailed information required to make a plausible case is forbidding.[4] If that is so, can we reasonably identify instances of phonological diffusion for the ancient world? I have already indicated that this is very difficult and perhaps impossible for prehistory, where it is mostly done on the basis of common sense (or lack of it) and of diffusion models established with the help of more promising modern data. But what about the historical period?

7.1.1 Loss of sibilants in first-millennium Greek

An example which Hellenists can consider in the context of the queries mentioned above is that of the *s* > *h* change which occurred in some Greek dialects in the first millennium BC, i.e. in the historical period and in a reasonably literate context. It bears an uncanny similarity to the prehistoric *s* > *h* change

[2] This would not oblige us, of course, to understand the <*qe, qi*> signs as also reflecting [p^{w}] etc.; we may attribute a so-called labiovelar to Mycenaean without at the same time committing ourselves to the view that it had the same phonetic features in all environments. It may be relevant that, in contrast with the traditional view, I believe, partly on morphological grounds, that in the dialects in which labiovelars developed into dental stops before front vowels this change followed, rather than preceded, the development into labial stops.

[3] For a wider discussion of related problems which impinge on language reconstruction and classification, see Garrett (1999, 2006).

[4] Trudgill (1983: 54–9) gives an impressive demonstration of how apparently detailed linguistic maps meant to show the diffusion of post-vocalic /r/ in Britain and uvular /r/ in Europe are not sufficient to give a true account of the facts.

which, as we have seen, characterizes Greek and other Indo-European languages and occurred before our first Mycenaean texts.

This paper will provide a brief summary of the first-millennium evidence, but its purpose is to highlight rather than to solve the problems raised by this change and to try to make explicit where the points of doubt are. After I had collected the data and written up my results I came to know, through the kindness of Professor Méndez Dosuna, an exhaustive and insightful unpublished dissertation (2008) by Dr Alonso Déniz, where all the evidence is discussed in detail; a recent article (2009) by the same author summarizes some of the dissertation's results. My factual conclusions, as I now see, largely overlap with those of Dr Alonso Déniz, which were reached on the basis of a more detailed analysis of the data, but once again my purpose is somewhat different. I was, and am, more interested in seeing where the advantages and pitfalls of this type of argumentation are than in reaching a definitive conclusion. However, Dr Alonso Déniz's work dispenses me from producing a long list of examples, which would simply replicate parts of his exhaustive lists. I ought to emphasize that when he and I differ I am far from certain that my views are preferable.

This paper would have been much better (and clearer) had I been able to discuss it with John Penney; I dedicate it to him in full awareness that neither this nor anything else will ever repay what I owe him.

7.2 Sibilants in Greek

Some background is necessary. In the shift from Proto-Indo-European to alphabetic Greek a sibilant was replaced by /h/ word-initially before a vowel and internally between vowels. In all likelihood the same change occurred in some pre-consonantal contexts which I choose to ignore here, but see Méndez Dosuna (1996: 100) and Alonso Déniz (2008: 12–15, 17–18). In all dialects (with the likely exception of Mycenaean in the second millennium BC) the new /h/ was lost internally between vowels; initial prevocalic /h/ was preserved in some dialects, such as Attic, but lost in others, such as Ionic and Elean. It seems likely that in a first (prehistoric) stage initial and intervocalic [h] was—partially at least—in complementary distribution with [s], which no longer occurred in those environments but had survived in word-final position and before and after certain consonants.[5] However, as early as the Mycenaean

[5] The question is complicated because in the Greek of the first millennium word-initial prevocalic /h/ also continued PIE *$\underset{\frown}{i}$, though the dating of this change is not altogether clear; we cannot be certain about the early fate of intervocalic *$\underset{\frown}{i}$, which in Greek eventually disappeared, possibly through an /h/ stage.

texts, we find both a sibilant and [h] in initial prevocalic position and internally between vowels. In these positions the Linear B texts have *<sV>* signs in words which either (i) are borrowed from non-Greek languages, or (ii) show analogical spreading of a sibilant, or (iii) have a sibilant from earlier clusters. Mycenaean words like *a_2-te-ro* /hateron/ (< **sm̥-tero-*) 'other' (cf. Gr. ἕτερος), *pa-we-a_2* /p^harweha/ (< **p^haru̯es-a*) 'cloths' (nom.-acc. ntr. pl., cf. Gr. φᾶρος), *me-zo-a_2* < **megi̯os-a* 'bigger, greater' (nom.-acc. ntr. pl., cf. Gr. μείζων), *we-te-i-we-te-i* /wetehi-wetehi/ 'every year' (loc. sg., cf. Gr. ἔτος) document the presence of initial and intervocalic /h/ from etymological **s*. It is not disputed that *<a_2>* indicates /ha/ and, though there are no signs **<he, hi, ho, hu>*, the *<-e-i>* spelling with hiatus points to the contemporary (or perhaps earlier?) occurrence of /h/ between the two vowels; an /ei/ diphthong would be written with a simple *<-e>*. We find initial prevocalic *<s>* and intervocalic *<s>*, e.g. in *se-ri-no* /selīnon/ 'celery' (cf. Gr. σέλινον), *sa-sa-ma* /sāsama/ 'sesame' (cf. Gr. σήσαμα), *ku-ru-so* 'gold' (cf. Gr. χρυσός), and *a-sa-mi-to* /asaminthos/ 'bath-tub' (cf. Gr. ἀσάμινθος), all words of non-Indo-European origin. With the exception of *su-qo-ta* /sug^{w}ōtāi/ 'swineherd' (dat. sg.) (cf. Gr. συβώτης), which has a problematic sibilant in alphabetic Greek too, there is no certain example of initial prevocalic *<sV->* from PIE **sV-*. On the other hand forms like *ka-ke-u-si* /k^halkeusi/ 'bronzesmiths' (dat. pl., cf. Gr. χαλκεύς), *e-re-u-te-ro-se* /eleut^{h}erōse/ 'freed' (3sg. aor., cf. Gr. ἐλευθερόω), etc. are written with an intervocalic *<-s->* which matches the **-s-* of the Indo-European locative plural and that of the Indo-European sigmatic aorist, though almost certainly the Mycenaean forms are due to analogical restoration.[6] Other forms like *pa-si* /p^hāsi/ (< **p^hāti*) 'says' (cf. Gr. φησί) or *to-so* /to(s)so-/ 'so much' (cf. Hom. τόσσος, Attic τόσος) *may* contain an intervocalic *-s-* from a dental before /i/ or from a *-ty-* cluster. In other words, though Mycenaean has initial and intervocalic [h] from **s*, it also seems to have a sibilant which occurs in the same positions in the word. Naturally enough, there is no proof that this also holds true for all contemporary forms of Greek, but there is no reason to think differently or to doubt that, perhaps in different periods, all Greek dialects went through the same phases.

[6] This may not be right for the aorist; if we start from a prehistoric **-s-m̥, *-s-e(t)* we would expect an **s* > *h* change followed by a later restoration of /s/. But the remodelling may have also started from the expected 2sg. and 3sg. athematic forms in **-s-s* > **-s* and **-s-t* > **-s*, with the addition of analogical vowels, in which case there need not have been an *-h-* stage.

7.2.1 *First-millennium evidence*

So much for the second millennium BC. The Mycenaean evidence is sufficient to show that the **s* > *h* change is earlier than our first Greek evidence and may be considerably earlier. In the first millennium, as we have seen, all dialects apparently lose intervocalic /h/ from **s* and may undergo as a result various forms of vocalic contraction or dissimilation. At the same time we find that the borrowed forms with initial and intervocalic /s/ which are attested in Mycenaean, as well as the restored forms of the /k^halkeusi/ and /eleut^{h}erōse/ type, are shared by all dialects. If we are right in reading the Mycenaean ending of dative/ locative plural *-o-i* as /-oihi/ (see below),[7] the -οισι ending of some dialects provides a post-Mycenaean example of analogical restoration of the sibilant. The dialects differ, however, in their treatment of consonant clusters or certain sequences of consonant and vowel. Thus the *-ti* > *-si* change found in the Mycenaean verbal endings such as *pa-si* /p^hāsi/ (quoted above) is widely attested in Arcado-Cypriot, Attic-Ionic, and Lesbian, but is not found in West Greek, Thessalian, and Boeotian, which preserve the more archaic *-ti*. Clusters like *-$t^{(h)}$i̯- and *-$k^{(h)}$i̯- may have different treatments, though it seems that *#$t^{(h)}$i̯V- > #*s*V- in all dialects. In the first millennium the number of intervocalic sibilants increases because of the simplification of some consonant clusters. When we find in Mycenaean *pa-sa* < **pant-i̯a* 'all' (fem.) (cf. Gr. πᾶσα) we do not know whether to read it /pansa/ or /pāsa/, though the former is more likely. In most Greek dialects we find πᾶσα (or παῖσα); similarly the simplification of *-ss-* or *-ds-* into *-s-* yields forms like Attic γένεσι (< *-εσ-σι) and ἐψήφισα (< *-ιδ-σα), etc., while in Mycenaean we cannot be certain whether to read *pa-we-si* 'cloths' (dat. pl.) as /p^harwessi/ or /p^harwesi/, etc.

The details could be multiplied but for e.g. Attic or Arcadian a simple statement would say that these dialects preserve initial /h/ from the second millennium while they have lost internal /h/; and that they have both initial and intervocalic /s/, with a distribution which is not drastically different from that of Mycenaean, though it seems likely that intervocalic /s/ is more frequent than in Mycenaean.

[7] This is now accepted in most Mycenological publications but is not undisputed. C. J. Ruijgh (e.g. 1967: 76–8) argued that *-o-i* was simply a spelling for /-ois/, though in the last years of his life he expressed some doubts orally, largely because of the presence in Arcadian of the two dat. pl. pronouns σφεις and σφεσιν in correspondence with Myc. *pe-i* /sp^{h}ehi/ (see Morpurgo Davies 1992: 428–30). A strong case against the traditional interpretation was made by Brixhe (1992)—cf. also Brixhe (2006: 51–3)—but has not found general acceptance.

7.3 Greek dialects with secondary loss of /s/

Some first-millennium dialects have <*h*> or <*Ø*> in correspondence with the intervocalic <*s*> which we find in e.g. Attic and Arcadian. They are Laconian, Western Argolic, Elean, and Cypriot; odd examples of loss of /s/ in other dialects have been quoted but they are all too doubtful to deserve consideration. Alonso Déniz (2008: 446–8, 2009: 14–15) has examined the possible additional evidence in detail and has rightly decided to dismiss it; here it seems superfluous to reconsider it since the rare examples are isolated and too uncertain.

A few examples of the basic change may be useful even if they are taken somewhat arbitrarily from much longer lists, for which I can again refer to Alonso Déniz (2008).[8]

Laconian: Amyclae *Ποhοιδᾶνος SEG* XI 692 (= *LSAG* p. 200, no. 34, cf. p. 448; late 6th century); Sparta *ἐποίεhε IG* V/1 696 (5th century); Gerenia (Messenia) *Ἀγεhίπολις IG* V/1 1338 (5th century); Sparta *Ποhοιδαῖα*, *Ἐλευhύνια*, *ἐνίκαhε*, etc., *IG* V/1 213 (date notoriously uncertain: early 4th century?); Sparta *Νικαhικλῆς IG* V/1 704 (4th century?); Sparta *νικάάς IvO* 171 (late 4th century); Tanaros *Ποhοιδᾶνι*, *Λύhιππον IG* V/1 1232 (4th century); Sparta *ἀπορρηhίαν SEG* XL 348 A 3–4 (3rd century); Sparta *βαἶλέος IG* V/1 885b (2nd century).

The examples range from the late sixth century BC[9] to the second century AD; they concern <*h*> or zero from intervocalic secondary /s/ of different origins (analogical restoration, *-ti-* clusters, pre-Greek names). All through this period we also find <*s*> writings, often for the same words and in the same inscriptions. (Full list of the epigraphic data in Alonso Déniz 2008: 28–117.)

Western Argolic: Argos (at Epidauros) *Νικαhαρίστα IG* IV/1^2 140 (5th century); Mycenae *Φραhιαρίδας IG* IV 492 (= *LSAG* p. 174, no.2; *c.* 500–480 BC?); Argos (at Olympia) *ἐποίϝεhε IvO* 631 (= *LSAG* p. 169, no. 19; *c.* 480–475 BC?); Argos (at Tylisos) *Κνοhίαν DGE* 84. 21–2 (but *Τυλισôι*; mid 5th century); Argos *Δ[μ]αἰππίδαι SEG* XXIX 361. 27 (*c.* 400 BC); Argos *περίσταἰν SEG* XVII 146. 8, *θηάυρόν SEG* XVII 146. 11, 21 (mid 4th century); Heraion *δαμόἰοι IG* IV 542

[8] I consider here only the epigraphic evidence; note that conventionally I write a rough breathing (*not* present in the inscription) where we would have expected <*s*> or <*h*>. For the literary evidence (mainly Laconian), the grammarians, and the glosses, see Alonso Déniz (2008: *passim*) with earlier references.

[9] Alonso Déniz (2008: 59–63) makes a strong case against deriving Lac. *Ϝορθαία* (attested in the late 7th century BC) from *Ϝορθασία*, as normally assumed. Given the uncertainty I have excluded *Ϝορθαία* from consideration and adopted Alonso Déniz's sixth-century dating for the start of the *s* > *h* change.

(cf. *DGE* 82 adn.; 3rd century?); Argos *Σωΐβιος τοῦ Σωίβίου* Vollgraff 1909, p. 176, no. 2, lines 7–8 (1st century).

The examples of <*h*> or zero from secondary /s/ range from the late fifth century to the first century BC. Earlier texts have only <*s*>, and through the whole period <*s*> alternates with <*h*> or zero. (Full list of the epigraphic data in Alonso Déniz 2008: 186–93; cf. also Alonso Déniz 2010.)

Elean: Olympia *φυγαδεύάντι, ἀδεαλτώhαιε* *DGE* 424. 6, 12 (= Minon 2007: i. 196–208, no. 30; 4th century); Alipheira *ἀ]ποτειάτω, καταχρααστω* *SEG* XXV 448 (= Minon 2007: i. 209–12, no. 31; *c.* 242 BC); Olympia *ποήάσσαι* (Att. *ποιήσασθαι*), *ποιήάται* (Att. *ποιήσηται*) *IvO* 39. 33, 36 (= *DGE* 425 and Minon 2007: i. 220–9, no. 34; early 2nd century).

The list above comprises the total of the evidence available for Elean (4th–2nd centuries only): six instances of aorists where presumably the lost /s/ was originally a restored /s/. For full discussion see Alonso Déniz (2008: 279–340) and Minon (2000 and 2007: ii. 344–5 and *passim*).

Cypriot: (From the seventh century, instances of word-final <*se*>, i.e. /-s/, missing. Idalion *ICS* 217 in the fifth century has instances of proclitics ending in /s/ which is not written before words which begin with a vowel: 217. 5 *ka-a-ti* /ka(h) a(n)ti/; *ka-u-ke-ro-ne* /ka(h) u-/; 217. 15 *ta-u-ke-ro-ne* /ta(h) u-/. The sequence 217. 19 *to-po-e-ko-me-no-ne* /to(n) po(h)ek^{h}omenon/ fits here.)

Amathus *o-na-i-ti-mo* (cf. *Ὀνασίτιμος*) *ICS* 195 (Eteocypriot, 4th century); Golgoi *e-pi-si-ta-i-se* /epista(h)is/, *po-ro-ne-o-i* /p^{h}roneō(h)i/, possibly *ku-me-re-na-i* if = /kumerna(h)i/ *ICS* 264 (4th century, metrical); Tamassos *a-la-si-o-ta-i* /Alasiōtāi/ vs. Phoen. *lhyts* *ICS* 215, 216 (4th century; cf. also ibid. the name *ma-na-se-se* vs. Phoen. *mnḥm*?); Kafizin (3rd century) *o-na-a-ko-ra-se* *NK* 132, 175 etc. (= *ICS* 229, × *c.* 8 in various states of preservation) vs. *o-na-sa-ko-ra-se* *NK* 117 etc. (×6) and alphabetic *Ὀνησαγόρας* (frequent)/ *Ὀνηαγόρας* (×1?). Ibid. *a-pa-i-re-i* /ap^{h}aire(h)i/ *NK* 266 (= *ICS* 231).[10]

This is the total evidence available for unwritten intervocalic /s/ (list and analysis in Morpurgo Davies 1988: 113–24; list for intervocalic /s/ in Alonso Déniz 2008: 409–11, for word-final /s/, 350–62).

[10] Interpretation disputed; cf. Alonso Déniz (2008: 421–3). Certainty is not possible but I prefer a dat. sg. /ap^{h}aire(h)i/ to the haplography of a possible dat. pl. /ap^{h}aire(h)i(h)i/.

7.3.1 *Summary of the evidence*

After some recent and not so recent work[11] the actual data are relatively well known. The evidence is mostly epigraphic.[12] All dialects in question have both writings with intervocalic <*s*> and writings with <*s*> replaced by <*h*> (Laconian, Argolic, Elean with one example) or with <*s*> simply absent, leaving a hiatus between the two vowels (Cypriot which has no signs for /h/, Elean and later phases of the other dialects). The sibilant which is being replaced may be an original restored sibilant as in the aorists, a sibilant derived from a cluster or an original dental as in *περίσταίν*, or a pre-Greek sibilant as in some ethnics or place names; in Elis where the examples are few and late the phenomenon is limited to aorist forms. In all these dialects the earliest texts have only *s*-writings and in the texts in koine <*s*> regularly appears. The chronology for the epigraphic data is best summarized by Alonso Déniz (2009: 17–19), who concludes that in Laconia we do not find <*h*> replacing <*s*> before the second half of the sixth century (earlier inscriptions from the late seventh century write <*s*>). In the western Argolid intervocalic <*h*> appears in the first half of the fifth century (in contrast with <*s*> in the sixth century), in Elis in the first half of the fourth century; on Cyprus intervocalic <*s*> may be missing from the fourth century but is present in the earlier syllabic texts. In other words the date of the first attestation differs in the various regions, and so does the distribution of the sibilants. Cyprus offers evidence for the aspiration or loss of word-final /s/, probably in specific environments, though we cannot define them with certainty;[13] this is at least two centuries earlier than the first instances of omitted intervocalic <*s*>. Glosses, which we cannot date, but may be still later, then reveal that word-initial /s/ could also be aspirated.[14]

In the three dialects of the Peloponnese, the first documented changes replace intervocalic <*s*> with <*h*> or <Ø>; we have no evidence for the aspiration of word-initial /s/. In Argolic word-final /s/ is preserved. In Elean we find word-final /s/ replaced by /r/ from the fifth century BC, conceivably in specific environments, though we can only speculate about them since the evidence is

[11] Cf. Alonso Déniz (2008, 2009) for all the evidence and above all for Laconian. Also Fernandez Alvarez (1981: 151–6) for Argolic; Minon (2007: ii. 343–52) for Elean; Morpurgo Davies (1988: 113–24) and Egetmeyer (2010: i. 160–83, especially 166–70) for Cypriot.

[12] For Laconian we also have some literary evidence; for the other dialects and above all Cypriot we have numerous glosses which, however, cannot be dated and are likely to be late.

[13] Alonso Déniz (2008: 375–403) discusses in detail the typology of the change and concludes on the basis of the data available that it started in unaccented words.

[14] See section 7.4.3 for a possible typological difference between Cypriot and the other dialects.

not sufficient. This so-called rhotacism is generalized in the later period but is never found in word-internal position; it is generally assumed that it is preceded by the voicing of the sibilant. In Laconian it looks as if word-final /s/ is preserved, but in the very late texts (second century of our era) we find rhotacism there too. In Elean, as we have seen, the evidence for the weakening of secondary /-s-/ is limited to the sigmatic aorist, and more precisely to aorists in which the sibilant apparently followed a long vowel (Minon 2007: ii. 344–5, 399–400).

Finally we must mention the Laconian spelling with <*s*> of original /t^h/, attested from the fourth century in inscriptions; this may have indicated a dental fricative, which may however have turned into a sibilant at some stage (Lazzeroni 1967: 66).

So much for the basic data. How do we interpret them?

7.4 Interpretation proposals

Past proposals, again summarized by Alonso Déniz (2008: 437–54, 2009), consider the possibility (a) of a continuous *s* > *h* change from prehistory to the mid first millennium and later, or (b) of substratum influence on the dialects involved with perhaps the exclusion of Elean (see Bechtel 1923: 320–2, 462–5, 838–9), or (c) of independent developments. Alonso Déniz himself rejects for the Peloponnesian dialects (a), (b), and (c), and argues for a diffusion process from Laconian to Argolic to eventually Elean. He does, however, think that Cypriot represents an independent development.

7.4.1 *The continuity hypothesis*

The first suggestion goes back to the start of Greek dialectology studies. According to Ahrens (1843: 74–9) there was some form of continuity, or at any rate a link, between the change of intervocalic Indo-European */s/ to /h/ in prehistoric Greek and the similar change in the later Greek dialects. Put in these terms (Ahrens 1843: 76 spoke of *sigma ejiciendi amor, quo omnes Graeci inclinarunt*) the suggestion is inoffensive but too vague to be tested. Going back to an early form of generative phonology we might be tempted to interpret the deletion or aspiration of the intervocalic sibilant as reflecting an abstract synchronic rule of fricative weakening or the like, which was part of the phonology of Greek both in the second and the first millennium.[15] However,

[15] For Attic, cf. e.g. Sommerstein (1973: 17 n. 22).

in the first-millennium dialects which we are discussing, the rule (a) would have to be differently formulated from that of the second millennium, since it does not apply to word-initial /s/,[16] and (b) would have had to undergo reordering if we assume for the second millennium BC the presence of surface forms like δαμόσιος (see δαμότης; Attic δημόσιος), with /t/ → /s/ before the /ios/ suffix, in contrast with Argolic δαμόϊος and perhaps δαμόhιος.[17] But if we remain within the limits of traditional historical phonology, which operates in terms of different surface outputs at different times, what does continuity mean? In our search for a claim that can be tested we might argue that in the dialects in question, if continuity existed, any new intervocalic /s/ introduced between, say, 1400 BC and the koine ought to have been aspirated and then lost. In that case, we would be entitled to argue that for some dialects the **s* > *h* change was not already concluded before the Mycenaean period.

7.4.1.1 Objections

The assumption has found no favour in the last century or so,[18] but until very recently little has been done to spell out why. Three points may speak against it:[19]

(i) It is difficult to dissociate the prehistoric change which aspirates /s/ between vowels from the change which aspirates /s/ word-initially before a vowel. In the first millennium, however (with the possible exception of Cypriot), initial /s/ is preserved.

(ii) We know that Mycenaean had already lost the intervocalic and prevocalic word-initial sibilant before our first documents and had created a new sibilant which seems stable through all of our Linear B documentation (see section 7.1); hence we must suppose that the original change had not only started but also been completed by 1400 BC or so (the presumed date of the first Mycenaean texts); otherwise some of the new sibilants would have turned into /h/.

[16] With the possible exception of Cypriot (see above).

[17] Evidence listed in Alonso Déniz (2009: 19). Mycenaean does not have /dāmosios/, but forms like *e-qe-si-jo* (vs. *e-qe-ta* 'follower') and *ra-wa-ke-si-jo* (vs. *ra-wa-ke-ta* 'people leader') show that it could have existed.

[18] I am not sure that I agree with the way in which Alonso Déniz (2008: 285, 450) interprets Brugmann and Thumb (1913: 144). In my view they are not arguing that the Elean aorists with no /s/ where we expect it are due to a continuation of the prehistoric process of /s/-loss; they are rather saying that those forms were inherited as such and never underwent the restoration of /s/.

[19] Note that for the likes of Kretschmer and Bechtel, who did not know the Mycenaean texts and did not have all our data, (ii) and (iii) below were not relevant, but they would have known that there was a time gap between the prehistoric *s* > *h* change and that which occurred in the Peloponnese and Cyprus in the first millennium.

(iii) With the increased evidence at our disposal we also know that some of the earliest first-millennium texts in the relevant dialects wrote <*s*> in sequences where later they wrote <*h*> or <Ø>; hence the change must be later than the earliest alphabetic texts in the Peloponnese, and this necessarily implies a gap between the pre-Mycenaean change and the first-millennium change.[20] This third point, when formulated at this level of generality, i.e. with reference to all the dialects in question, is relatively new and we owe its detailed documentation to Alonso Déniz (2008, 2009).

7.4.1.2 Counter-objections

It may be worthwhile to play the *advocatus diaboli* and ask whether the three points mentioned are decisive. The first may be indicative but by itself is not conclusive. A basic difficulty arises with reference to (ii) and (iii) above: how much can we trust the script(s), or rather our interpretation of the script(s)? We might start with Mycenaean. Let us suppose that after the change of intervocalic /s/ to /h/ had run its course there was no intervocalic /s/ left. At this stage, but still in the pre-Mycenaean period, we are told that new intervocalic sibilants were introduced thanks (*inter alia*) to the development of various sequences such as those in **didōti*, **toti̯o-*, **-id-si* (cf. the dat. pl. *pi-we-ri-si*), etc. (cf. Gr. δίδωσι, τόσ(σ)ος, etc.). In Mycenaean they came to be written with the <*sa, se, si, so, su*> signs, which were also used to indicate an etymological sibilant in pre- or post-consonantal position, as in e.g. *do-so-mo* /dosmos/ or *de-ka-sa-to* /deksato/. However, we cannot be certain that in intervocalic position the sounds in question were in fact [s] or even [z]; there may be reasons to suppose that some or even all of them were affricates or perhaps geminates.[21] Other words, like *sa-sa-ma* 'sesame', *ku-ru-so* 'gold', *a-sa-mi-to* 'bath-tub', do not continue an Indo-European sibilant, since they are borrowings from Semitic or from a pre-Greek language. No doubt they had some form of sibilant in their

[20] It is well known that the text of Alcman (7th century) preserves /s/ while Aristophanes' imitation of Laconian in the *Lysistrata* (5th century) has forms where <*s*> is not written between vowels (cf. Alcman Μῶσα vs. Aristophanes Μῶα), but the uncertainties about the textual tradition are such that not much can depend on this.

[21] Linear B, like the Cypriot syllabary, never indicated geminates in writing. The problem of the affricates is discussed by Bartoněk (1987: esp. 45; cf. also Bartoněk 2003: 143), who assumes that the <*s-*> signs may reflect both intervocalic /ts/ and intervocalic /s/. The original dimorphemic clusters of the **ti̯-* type, and some pre-Greek words (those which in the later dialects appear with either <σσ> or <ττ>), would still have /ts/ in Mycenaean (as in *a-pe-a-sa* /ap-e(h)atsa/ < **ap-esn̥t-i̯a* or *ku-pa-ri-so* /kuparitsos/), while monomorphemic **-ti̯-* as well as **-ts-/*-ds-*, **-ss-*, and some pre-Greek sibilants would have all yielded /s/, conceivably through a /ss/ stage (as in *to-so* < **toti̯os*, *pi-we-ri-si* < **-id-si*, *ze-u-ke-si* < *i̯eugessi*, and possibly *ko-no-so* /Knōs(s)os/). In fact, even if one accepts Bartoněk's reconstructions in full, it is not easy to decide whether his second type had /s/ or /ss/ at the time of the tablets.

original language, but presumably their pronunciation was adapted to whatever was available in the borrowing language, i.e. in the Greek of the time. If so, can we be certain that Mycenaean had intervocalic /s/? This skepticism may be excessive but the possibility must at least be considered that in Mycenaean intervocalic <*s-*> always represented an affricate or a geminate. The proposal that <*sa, se, si, so, su*> could also indicate affricates has been made by reputable authors for different purposes from our own. Note, however, that there is no reason to suppose that in word-initial position the *s*-signs indicated anything different from /s/ (/ss/ is probably excluded); if so, then in initial position at least there was a contrast between /s/ and /h/.

Let us now turn to the first-millennium data. Can we be certain that the earliest texts do not use traditional spellings, which would not reflect the real pronunciation? Take the case of Laconian. In a few early texts we have intervocalic <*s*> and no intervocalic <*h*>, and the sibilants mostly occur in proper names (personal names, place names, gods' names), which notoriously preserve traditional forms and spellings. There is little doubt that <*s*> is meant as a form of sibilant, but the problem is that we cannot be absolutely certain that it was pronounced as such in all environments. Traditional spellings are common and it is conceivable that the writing with sigma in intervocalic position conceals an [h] pronunciation which is not marked as such in writing until a later stage. Cypriot may offer some typological support for this hypothesis: in the fourth century we have at Tamassos two Cypriot-Phoenician bilingual inscriptions where we find the equivalences *ma-na-se-se : mnḥm* (*ICS* 215) and *a-la-si-o-ta-i : lhyts* (*ICS* 216), for the name Manasses and the ethnic Alasiotas. For the ethnic at least we are certain that Cypr. <*si*> corresponds to Phoen. <*hy*>; this makes it likely that <*-s-*> corresponded to an aspirated pronunciation.[22]

Let me summarize so far by saying that *if* (a) the Mycenaean sibilants in intervocalic position were in fact not (yet) simple sibilants but affricates or geminates, and consequently were not subject to aspiration, and *if* (b) the intervocalic sibilants written in the early documents of Laconian, Argolic, and perhaps Cypriot concealed under a traditional spelling an /h/, it would be legitimate to assume a form of continuity (defined as above) between the prehistoric **s* > *h* change and the later *s* > *h* change in these dialects. We would have in pre-Mycenaean times (i) a change from intervocalic /s/ to /h/; (ii) the creation (pan-Greek?) of a set of new affricates or geminates between vowels. Then (iii) in post-Mycenaean times the affricates or geminates (or

[22] On the other hand in the seventh century we find on Assyrian inscriptions *ú-na-sa-gu-su* for the name of King Onasagos (Egetmeyer 2010: i. 162), which speaks for an /s/ both written and pronounced.

some of them) would be replaced by simple sibilants, and (iv) in some dialects these would turn into /h/.

7.4.1.3 The evidence from morphology

Though this reconstruction may seem far-fetched (as indeed it is), it cannot be entirely excluded.[23] However, in my view there are some strong morphological objections which ought to be considered.

We find in Mycenaean examples of restored intervocalic sibilants in forms like *ti-ri-si*, Gr. τρισί, *qa-si-re-u-si*, Gr. βασιλεῦσι, *do-se*, Gr. δώσει, *e-re-u-te-ro-se*, Gr. ἠλευθέρωσε. These continue the Indo-European /s/ of the locative plural and of the future or the sigmatic aorist. There is reasonable agreement (but see n. 7) that in these forms the Mycenaean sibilants do not directly continue Indo-European /s/ but are due to analogical restoration, since we also have forms where restoration did not happen (*pe-i* /sp^{h}ehi/ 'to them'; *-o-i* /-oihi/, thematic dat.-loc. pl.). The restoration would have been modelled on those forms where the *s*-morphemes followed a consonant. But the restoration cannot have happened at a stage when the choice between [s] and [h] was automatic, i.e. when the two were in complementary distribution; it must have been later than that but still pre-Mycenaean. Does this speak against our imagined scenario which does not allow for a simple /s/ between vowels in Mycenaean? In a last-ditch defence we could argue that word-initial, postconsonantal, and preconsonantal /s/ alternated with intervocalic /ss/ (or /ts/?), i.e. that the contrast between /s/ and /ss/ (or /ts/?) was neutralized in certain positions. Perhaps it was /ss/ which was analogically introduced in the place of a weakening /h/. At a later stage this would have been simplified to /s/. In other words we could read the Mycenaean words above as /trissi/ (or /tritsi/?), /eleut^{h}erōsse/ (or /eleut^{h}erōtse/?), etc., and postulate that later on /ss/ or /ts/ were simplified into /s/. Is this plausible? It is not entirely impossible though it seems counterintuitive, and we can point out that the presence in later dialects of forms like τόσσος (rather than τόσος) and ἔσσονται next to dative plurals and aorists written with a single sigma[24] makes it difficult to reconstruct a plausible development.

[23] I am not convinced by Alonso Déniz's point (2008: 154–5 and 230–1, 2009: 17) that a clinching argument in favour of the late chronology of the *s* > *h* change in the first-millennium Peloponnese is that it happened after the dissimilation of the aspirates (Grassmann's Law), which in its turn is post-Mycenaean but earlier than our first inscriptions. The standard examples of Grassmann's Law concern adjacent syllables and there is no certain example where the dissimilating (as contrasted with the dissimilated) consonant is /h/; hence, while we expect **hek^{h}ōn* to yield ἔχων, we do not expect *Μναhίμαχος* and *Φραhιαρίδας* to dissimilate their /h/ and /p^{h}/ respectively. Also, I am not certain that Grassmann's Law is post-Mycenaean.

[24] This is the position of Laconian, though τόσσος occurs only in Alcman and ἔ]σσονται only in the fragmentary *IG* V/1 3. 7, which is in dialect but in the Ionic alphabet.

More significant, because presumably more recent, is the development of -οισι. Early Argolic has a few examples of dative plurals in -οισι (*SEG* XI 314), a form which is later replaced entirely by the standard -οις of the Doric dialects. If we can use the Mycenaean evidence to determine the linguistic state of the second millennium, we must assume that, in contrast with Myc. *-oi(h)i*, Argolic at some stage restored the sibilant on the model of the athematic inflection (Myc. /trisi/ etc.). This is likely to be a first-millennium restoration, and it would be somewhat perverse to assume that here too the restored form was /tsi/ or /ssi/. *Inter alia* the same sixth-century inscription where -οισι appears makes a distinction between <σ> and <σσ>, and in the datives only -σ- appears. Could we argue on the other hand that this is traditional spelling, with <*s*> written for an actually pronounced [h]? This too seems improbable. Argolic has a letter <*h*>, which is used in word-initial position (e.g. *hοιζ*, *hο* in *SEG* XI 314) and after digamma (ibid. Ϝhεδιέστας). If it had inherited a form /-oihi/ like that of Mycenaean and had not restored the sibilant it would have presumably written it with <*h*>. Traditional spelling in this case makes little sense and we should probably take <*s*> as representing a real sibilant. But, if so, we must accept that there was a period when not all intervocalic sibilants had turned into /h/. In other words, in terms of our definition of continuity, there is no continuity between the prehistoric *s* > *h* change and the historical *s* > *h* change.

If this is correct it seems likely that the conclusions reached for Argolic may legitimately be extended to the other relevant dialects. For Cypriot we have some independent evidence in the Assyrian spelling *ú-na-sa-gu-su* of Onasagos (cf. n. 22). The structure of the syllabary also points to an early intervocalic sibilant (Morpurgo Davies 1988: 118–19). It is possible of course that in some inscriptions <*s*> corresponds to an [h] pronunciation, but I feel inclined to follow my early conclusions, as well as Alonso Déniz's and Egetmeyer's more recent views, that in Cypriot the shift really happened at a later date.

7.4.2 *The substratum hypothesis*

Should we then accept one of the alternative hypotheses? Well before Bechtel other philologists had thought that the first-millennium change found in the Peloponnese and Cyprus was unlikely to be a Doric feature, and had wondered whether it could be due to the influence of the earliest Greek speakers in the eastern Peloponnese. In 1905 August Fick reacted against Meister's view that the loss of secondary /s/ was typical of Doric and argued that, since Argolic and Laconian shared this change with Cypriot, it was likely that the change originated in eastern 'Achaean'. He explained that he shared Hoffmann's view that Arcadian and Cypriot were a form of South 'Achaean' closely related to the

Northern Achaean Boeotian and Thessalian. This was a view largely accepted (cf. Solmsen 1907): Arcadian and Cypriot were Aeolic or rather Achaean dialects. After Kretschmer (1909) turned the discussion about the classification of Greek dialects into a historical account, the Achaeans were seen as the second of the three immigrant waves which had invaded the Peloponnese. In 1910 Kretschmer (1910: 153–4) argued again (somewhat tentatively) that the presence of the change in Cypriot as well as Laconian and Argolic could speak for a feature due to the Achaean linguistic layer, and suggested that the change was limited to the *altachäisch* dialect of the eastern and south-eastern Peloponnese, thus excluding Arcadia. Bechtel (1923: 320–2, 461–4) did in fact follow this line, excluding Elean from the discussion because he thought that the phenomenon was documented too late; he was followed by Thumb and Kieckers (1932: 85). The old discussions make clear that the crucial point is the desire to account in the same way for the change in Cypriot and in the two Peloponnesian dialects (or three if we include Elean). There was not, and at the time there could not be, any direct evidence for pre-Doric dialects in the area. Needless to say, after the decipherment of Linear B in the 1950s the position is different. We now know, rather than assume, that there were Greeks who did not speak a Doric dialect in the Peloponnese before the Doric speakers took over. So, there was a Greek substratum, but the existing Linear B documents offer no evidence for a difference between an eastern (Mycenae, Tiryns) and a western (Pylos) form of Mycenaean, though given the highly conventional character of Mycenaean literacy this is not surprising. They also offer no evidence for a change of secondary /s/ to /h/. This may of course have occurred without being indicated in writing. Unfortunately the point forcefully and usefully made by Alonso Déniz (2008: 438–46, 2009: 13–14), that the late appearance of the first-millennium *s* > *h* change in Cyprus (and indeed in the dialects of the Peloponnese) speaks against the assumption that in Cyprus the *h*-pronunciation was a feature imported from the mainland, cannot be conclusive. There may have been different social and/or ethnic strata, and one of these may have had [h] pronunciations from an earlier period, though that stratum came to the fore only later. However, the fact that in Cypriot the first evidence for an aspiration of /s/ concerns word-final position is significant, since it separates the change found in the Peloponnese from the Cypriot one.

The basic point is that while there is circumstantial, even if not conclusive, evidence against the substratum hypothesis, there is no positive evidence in its favour. Yet, unless we want to believe that all sound change is determined by substratum phenomena, this is a typical example of a suggestion which needs positive arguments to support it. If they are missing, as they are here, the hypothesis cannot be accepted.

7.4.3 Diffusion or independent developments?

We are then left with two possibilities: diffusion from one dialect to the other, presumably in the first millennium, or independent developments. All through the history of the question both possibilities have been considered. The most recent discussion, that of Alonso Déniz (2008, 2009), concludes that the Cypriot change is independent from that of the Peloponnesian dialects, while these probably share an innovation which may have started in Laconia—where the first examples of intervocalic <*h*> from /s/ are attested and the evidence is richer—and then spread to the western Argolid and later to Elis. The geographical distance may speak against a diffusion to Cyprus, as does the different development of /s/ aspiration (see above). In a widely-cited article of 1990 Ferguson argued for a major typological distinction in the diachrony of languages of a Spanish type and languages of a Greek type. The former weaken /s/ to /h/ starting with syllable-final position, first preconsonantally and word-internally, then word-finally, then in other positions. The latter weaken /s/ intervocalically and then word-initially, then word-internally before a consonant, and last, word-finally. From this point of view Cypriot would belong with the Spanish type and Laconian etc. with the Greek type, which would highlight the difference. However, Méndez Dosuna (1996) has made a good case for a somewhat less polarized description, pointing to prehistoric Greek changes like **nasu̯os* > **nahu̯os* > *nāwos* 'temple', or **$h_1$esmi* > **ehmi* > *ēmi* 'I am'. The problem is once again that there is no conclusive evidence. On balance the Cypriot changes seem to differ from the other changes, though I suspect that we do not know enough about the contacts between Cyprus and the Peloponnese in the first millennium to be certain that there were no possible channels of diffusion. But what about the Peloponnesian dialects? What tells us that the changes in the Peloponnese are not independent developments? Laconian and West Argolic are geographically close and the changes in question are close both in time and in nature, though relations between Laconia and Argolis were permanently hostile and it is not clear that wars are a good way of diffusing phonological change. The Elean evidence for change is later (fourth to second century) and is limited to one morphological category (the sigmatic aorist) and to a very few examples of that. Admittedly lexical diffusion works on limited word sets or categories, but is this a standard case? Minon (2000: 239, 2007: ii. 350–1) mentions the possibility (originally suggested by J.-L. García Ramón) that the change was limited to restored /s/ (as in the aorist), which at the time of the change could have been phonetically different from the secondary /s/ of words like πᾶσα 'all' (fem.). However, we have only six forms distributed over two centuries—not enough to judge.

7.4.3.1 Points of uncertainty

Let us briefly summarize the points of uncertainty for all our data.

(i) We are dealing with two different writing systems (three if we include Linear B): syllabic Cypriot and alphabetic Greek, and within alphabetic Greek with at least three different regional variants. We know that in Greece attitudes to the match between writing and phonology varied from region to region: indifference in Laconia, deep concern in Boeotia (Morpurgo Davies 1992). Yet we do not have sufficient data for Elis or Argolis and we cannot trust the graphic consistency of the Laconians, which means that, though the case made by Alonso Déniz for the relative dating of the change is the best one can make, we cannot reach certainty even on that point. Nor can we reconstruct with certainty the phonological systems of the dialects under consideration.[25]

(ii) If we want to think in terms of diffusion we lack data which allow us to follow the pattern of diffusion. Consider again the strictures delivered by Trudgill (1983; see n. 4) on the inadequacy of the standard dialect maps of Europe or Britain, which lack information about exact isoglosses, social details, age, distribution, etc. For ancient Greece we cannot hope to have this type of information.

(iii) The distinction between independent developments and diffusion is a perennial problem for all dialect geography (and of course for other disciplines such as archaeology and anthropology). In phonology we consider the possibility of diffusion when the languages or dialects in question are geographically close and/or on known communication routes (be they commercial or cultural), the chronology works, and, if we are lucky, more than one feature is spread. It is easier to make a case if the change considered is not a common change. If these conditions are met we then begin to look for sociolinguistic supporting evidence of the type indicated in (ii). In our case Lazzeroni (1967) has argued that Elean shares with Laconian both the *s* > *h* change and the assibilation of the dental aspirate (see n. 25). This may satisfy a requirement, though the second point is disputed, but is it enough, since we cannot proceed to the next step and since the aspiration of /s/ is found in a number of unrelated languages?

[25] In Laconian for instance we find at some stage that <σ> is used for the earlier <θ> letter. We debate whether <σ> represents [θ] or [s]. In Elean it is often, and possibly correctly, assumed that [t^h] had changed into [θ] or [s], but the evidence is very late except for a disputed infinitive ending in -σσαι where we expect -σθαι (Minon 2007: ii. 339). What should we conclude? And how relevant is this to the *s* > *h* change?

7.4.4 *Drift*

It looks as if we must reluctantly conclude that there is no evidence for continuity from the second millennium or for substratum influence, and that the data do not allow us to distinguish between diffusion and independent developments. We ought, however, to entertain a further possibility, which has recently been exploited in the analysis of so-called World English. I take two examples from recent work by Trudgill, which modify some of the standard views.

In contrast with Canadian and American English, which are predominantly rhotic, Australian and New Zealand English are predominantly non-rhotic, like most English and Welsh varieties, i.e. they have lost preconsonantal and word-final /r/ in words like *smart* or *car*, while retaining /r/ in other positions and word-finally before a word starting with a vowel. This was normally explained by pointing out that English was exported to America in the seventeenth century, before the loss of rhoticity in Britain, but to Australia and then New Zealand in the nineteenth century, when that loss had already happened in Britain. Yet recent discoveries have shown that in New Zealand (for which better evidence is available) and in Australia the language was originally rhotic and the loss of rhoticity is relatively recent. Trudgill et al. (2000: 120–4; cf. Trudgill and Gordon 2006: 244) argue that the new data make it likely that 'rhoticity was extremely common in 19th century Britain' and was brought from there to Australia and New Zealand. Later on it was lost in parallel in England, Australia, and New Zealand through a process of 'drift', to use Sapir's terminology. Similar conclusions are reached for other examples. I quote only one: the merger of the English vowels of e.g. *square* and *near* which is happening in New Zealand, where it is now practically complete; the same merger occurs for the majority of speakers in Norfolk in Britain and in the English of Newfoundland (Trudgill 2003). Diffusion is highly unlikely given the geographical distribution; the change has occurred independently in the various places but we cannot exclude a general predisposition to it in what are, after all, variant forms of the same language. Once again one may appeal to drift (cf. Trudgill et al. 2000, and see below).

Our Greek problem is different, but another possibility is now opened. In languages or dialects which have a common origin Trudgill et al. (2000) distinguish between a first form of drift which is in fact the continuation of an inherited change in progress, even if this is concealed by lack of evidence (as for the loss of rhoticity in New Zealand and Australia), and a second form of drift which is the result of a structural predisposition towards a certain change; this would be the case of the merger described above. The point is that our four dialects (including Cypriot) show similar, even if not identical, changes in regions which are not too remote from each other. It may be counterintuitive to treat them as independent phenomena but at the same time there is not enough evidence to attribute the whole set of changes to diffusion, and, as we have seen, Alonso Déniz excludes it for Cypriot. Drift may help, if taken in the second of the meanings discussed by Trudgill et al. (2000). Yet, if we do not want to return to nineteenth-century imagery and think of drift as a mysterious overpowering force which dominates the life of language, what would account for such a predisposition? Perhaps we may appeal to a suggestion by Méndez Dosuna (1996), who points out that in languages where consonantal length is phonologically relevant there is a tendency to maximize the distance between /s/ and /s:/ by shortening /s/ as much as possible. If this is applied to Greek, where phonologically long /s:/ occurs only between vowels, we can assume that this tendency to shorten intervocalic /s/ may eventually have led to a further form of weakening, i.e. aspiration. Of the dialects that we have been discussing, Laconian, Argolic, and Elean all provide evidence for <*ss*> between vowels; the Cypriot syllabic writing obviously cannot do so, though we may want to argue that Cypriot was like Arcadian, which does. Even so, it would still be difficult to understand why Cypriot lost its final sibilants before the intervocalic ones.

7.5 Conclusion

To conclude: whatever one says about this subject is to a large extent hypothetical and structural explanations are notoriously so. To make a case for diffusion and the like in the prehistoric period is almost impossible, but in the historical period too some linguistic developments may remain partially or totally impenetrable. In our case we do not have sufficient data to make a water-tight case for whatever account we choose to give. However, the starkness of the contrast between independent development and diffusion may be reduced if we introduce drift as a third possibility and assume that in languages or dialects which have the same origin there is often a structural predisposition to certain changes. It should be emphasized that 'such changes may, but need not occur' (Trudgill et al. 2000: 112). It is conceivable that appealing to this form of drift may help us to understand the weakening of secondary intervocalic /s/ in some Greek dialects of the first millennium BC. At the same time we should note that any change is subject to a number of different and perhaps contrasting sociolinguistic influences, some of which may act as catalysts. Diffusion is bound to be one of these. Drift and diffusion are not mutually exclusive and may conspire towards similar results. We cannot demonstrate it but this may be the solution to our problem.

Part III

Segmental sound laws: new proposals and reassessments

8

A rule of deaspiration in ancient Greek

PAUL ELBOURNE

8.1 Introduction

It is the purpose of this paper to revisit a sound law for ancient Greek that I postulated in earlier work (Elbourne 1998).[1] In the context of arguing for the existence of a phonemic series of voiceless aspirated stops in Proto-Indo-European, I proposed that early Greek had a sound law deaspirating inherited $*t^h$ when it came after */s, m, n, r, l/. In the present paper, I will discuss the formulation of the law and provide a fresh parallel for it. And I will argue that the question of whether the law actually formed part of the history of Greek is independent of the question of whether Proto-Indo-European had phonemic voiceless aspirates. There are good reasons, I maintain, to accept the existence of the postulated sound change, at least in some version, whether or not one believes in a series of voiceless aspirates for Proto-Indo-European.

[1] It is a great pleasure to contribute to a volume dedicated to John Penney, who was responsible for impressing upon me the idea that theories in linguistics could be questioned. When I was taking the Comparative Philology option in Classics Mods at Oxford, over twenty years ago now, I had the good fortune to attend John's lectures on Indo-European phonology. The picture of the proto-language that gradually emerged in those lectures seemed impregnable. But after teaching us the standard laryngeal theory (three laryngeals, no PIE **a*, everything very neat), John finished the last lecture of the term by saying, with the urbane good humour that is characteristic of him, 'So that's laryngeal theory. I, for one, don't believe a word of it.' The effect of seeing such a grand theoretical edifice treated with the suspicion that I did not know, at the time, that it deserved was electrifying for my undergraduate brain. I should add, however, that I do not know how much John approves of what I have written since, and partly as a result of, that experience. I have a terrible suspicion that he doesn't believe a word of it.

Before I explore these issues, however, I will give some more background on the original formulation of the rule.

8.2 The original formulation of the rule

In Elbourne (1998), I argued that we should return to the neogrammarian position and reconstruct four series of stops for Proto-Indo-European, distinguished by binary oppositions of voicing and aspiration, as in Sanskrit: $*t$, t^h, d, d^h, and similarly for other places of articulation. The suggested four-series system contrasts with a position that originates with Saussure, whereby voiceless aspirates should be viewed as secondary creations of the daughter languages, leaving $*t$, d, d^h, and so on, for Proto-Indo-European. As part of my case for reinstating voiceless aspirates, I assembled two sets of correspondences that suggest ancestral phonemes of this nature and which do not fit into the correspondences that would be posited by a three-series model. The members of the first set exemplify the following abbreviated schemas:

(1) PIE $*k^h$ > Sanskrit *kh* : Greek χ : Armenian *x*

(2) PIE $*k^{wh}$ > Sanskrit *kh* : Greek ϕ : Armenian *x*

(3) PIE $*p^h$ > Sanskrit *ph* : Greek ϕ : Armenian *p‘*

(4) PIE $*t^h$ > Sanskrit *th* : Greek θ : Armenian *t‘*

Among the correspondences that exemplify these schemas are the following (here shorn of philological detail):

(5) Sanskrit *śaṅkhá-* ‘conch shell’ : Greek *κόγχος* ‘mussel’

(6) Sanskrit *skhálate* ‘stumble, trip; make a mistake’ : Greek *σφάλλομαι* ‘stumble, trip; make a mistake’ : Armenian *sxalem, sxalim* ‘stumble, trip; make a mistake’

(7) Sanskrit *sphārá-* ‘large, great; loud’ : Greek *σφηλός* ‘strong’

Altogether, I assembled eighteen correspondences that fit these schemas. The most important for present purposes are those that involve a dental voiceless aspirate in Greek:

(8) Sanskrit *rátha-* ‘chariot’ : Greek *ἐπίρροθος* ‘helper’ (< ‘charioteer’)[2] : Latin *rota* ‘wheel’

[2] For details of the addition of *ἐπίρροθος* to this well-known correspondence, see Elbourne (2011).

(9) Greek **σκῆθος* 'harm' (in *ἀσκηθής* 'unscathed') : Gothic *skaþis* 'harm'

(10) Sanskrit *-tha* (2sg. perfect ending) : Greek *-θα* (2sg. perfect ending)

(11) Sanskrit *-thāḥ* (2sg. aorist middle ending) : Greek *-θης* (2sg. aorist passive ending)[3]

Alongside the eighteen correspondences that accord with the schemas in (1)–(4), however, are others, seven in number, in which corresponding to a Sanskrit voiceless aspirate there is a Greek plain voiceless stop:

(12) Sanskrit *panthāḥ* 'way, road' : Greek *πάτος* 'path', *πόντος* 'sea'

(13) Sanskrit *pṛthu-ka-* 'young of an animal' : Greek *πόρτις* 'calf' : Armenian *ortʻ* 'calf'

(14) Sanskrit *pṛthu-* 'wide' : Greek *πλατύς* 'wide'

(15) Sanskrit *asthi* 'bone' : Greek *ὀστέον* 'bone'

(16) Sanskrit *sthā-* 'stand' : Greek *ἵστημι* 'set up'

(17) Sanskrit *sthag-* 'cover' : Greek *στέγω* 'cover'

(18) Sanskrit *-iṣṭha-* (superlative suffix) : Greek *-ιστος* (superlative suffix)

Clearly, in order for the case for ancestral voiceless aspirates to hold water, it is necessary to explain the diverse reflexes they would have in Greek. Building on work by Zubatý (1892: 3), I attempted to do just this with my postulated rule for the early[4] history of Greek: *$^*t^h$* becomes *t* after */s, m, n, r, l/. It will be observed that all of the cases in (12)–(18) involve what would be, on my view, a dental voiceless aspirate following one of these five phonemes. (Assume that the sound change took place at a time when there was still a vocalic /n/ in *πάτος* and a vocalic /l/ in *πλατύς*.)

Furthermore the rule does not make any wrong predictions about the eighteen correspondences in the first set of data: the only apparent counterexample is *οἶσθα* 'you know', where the old perfect ending *-θα* comes after an /s/. But given the root in question this does not present a problem: the word might have been **woid-t^ha* or **woit-t^ha* when the rule took place, as we can tell by inspection of the Sanskrit cognate *vettha*. Alternatively, the aspiration might have been maintained in *οἶσθα* on the analogy of the pronunciation of the suffix

[3] For this equation, see Elbourne (1998: 18–21), with earlier literature.

[4] The inherited Proto-Indo-European voiced aspirates were not affected by the change and must have retained their voicing at the time of the rule's operation.

in other words where it occurred, assuming it was more widespread at the time than it was in archaic or classical Greek.

I still believe that this postulated sound law is on the right lines. However, I must admit to one infelicity in my original presentation of it. As well as describing it in the way I just did, by listing the phonemes that constituted the environment (*/s, m, n, r, l/), I also attempted to give a unified phonological description of the environment. To be precise, I suggested the following formulation:

(19) $*t^h > t / \begin{bmatrix} +\text{cons} \\ +\text{cont} \end{bmatrix}$ _____

The original dental voiceless aspirate lost its aspiration, in other words, after a consonant that was [+continuant]. In classifying nasals as [+continuant], I was guided largely by a passage in which Kenstowicz (1994: 27) says that the [continuant] value of nasals is not clear, since although they involve oral closure they still have air passing through the nasal cavity during their articulation and can be prolonged (by humming) like fricatives. But my impression is that the standard practice in the field is to classify as [+continuant] all and only those sounds that involve air passing through the oral cavity (cf. Halle 1992: 208, Clements and Hume 1995: 254–6 and 271–3, T. A. Hall 2007: 319). This would rule out the nasal stops. My presentation here has been quite justifiably criticized (in personal communications).

8.3 Reformulating the rule

What to do? I am agnostic between the following four options.

Firstly, it is worth pointing out that not all historically conditioned phonemic distributions are phonologically neat. The treatment of PIE $*d^h$ word-medially in Latin springs to mind: *b* after **u*, before or after **r*, and before **l*; and *d* elsewhere.[5] The *ruki* rule is another sound law whose environment cannot obviously be described in unified phonological terms.[6] Perhaps the current deaspiration rule is yet another messy rule.

Secondly, and relatedly, one could suggest (as Jan Henrik Holst has, personal communication) that the rule in question operated in two phases, one involving **s* and one involving the sonorants */m, n, r, l/. Both individual phases would then be phonologically neat.

[5] See Stuart-Smith (2004: 213–17) for discussion.

[6] See, for example, Hock (1991: 442) for this judgement. Suggestions for a unified phonological description of the *ruki* environment have included [+high] (Kiparsky 1973*a*) and [dorsal] (Clements and Hume 1995: 303–4).

Thirdly, it is possible that we should say that the deaspiration took place only after *coronals*. Inspection of the cases in (12)–(18) reveals that the only phonemes after which the rule can actually be seen to operate are /s, n, r, l/, which are all presumably [+coronal]. If we look at the cases involving $*t^h$ giving Greek /tʰ/, i.e. examples (8)–(11), we find that this does not create any problems there. Again, the only apparent counterexample is Greek οἶσθα, which could be circumvented by the analogical solution given above.

And fourthly, there is one more possibility for a phonologically neat formulation of the rule, which is that $*t^h$ became *t* after segments that were [+consonantal]. This feature is defined solely in terms of the severity of the constriction in the mid-sagittal region of the vocal tract (Chomsky and Halle 1968: 302, T. A. Hall 2007: 314), and so it is probable that the 'vocalic' (i.e. syllabic) */n/ in πάτος and the 'vocalic' */l/ in πλατύς would have qualified. Once more there are no counterexamples in (8)–(11). The persistence of aspiration in the verbal endings -θα and -θης would be explained by the occurrence of these suffixes on roots that ended in a vowel, such as θνᾱ- 'die' and στᾱ- 'stand'. The perfect ending -θα, of course, was once much more common than it is in attested Greek (Schwyzer 1939: 662, Chantraine 1961: 293, Rix 1992: 256).

I do not see how to choose between these four possibilities at the moment. For the sake of convenience, then, in the rest of this chapter I will revert to my former notation and simply list (or *snarl*) the phonemes that constitute the environment of the rule: */s, n, r, l/.

8.4 Parallels for the rule

Are there any parallels for a process of $*t^h$ becoming *t* after */s, n, r, l/? In Elbourne (1998) I cited partial parallels from later Greek: examples of -στ- for -σθ- in West Locrian, Phocian, and Elean (Bechtel 1923: 17, 107, 842, Lejeune 1972: 60) and examples of -ντ- for -νθ- in Argolis (Lejeune 1972: 60). These all involve deaspiration of a dental voiceless aspirate after phonemes from my list.

We should also compare the change of Indo-Iranian $*t^h$ to Iranian *t* after *s* and *n* (Bartholomae 1883: 47–8, Zubatý 1892: 1–3, Reichelt 1967: 41–2), a development that involved some of the very roots that are in play in the postulated Greek sound change: Avestan *stā-* vs. Sanskrit *sthā-* 'stand', Avestan *pantå* vs. Sanskrit *pánthāḥ* 'way', and so on.

But at the time of my earlier work on this topic I had not yet noticed what I now regard as the closest parallel, which is the wholescale recapitulation of the rule in almost every detail in Greek as spoken in Egypt in the Hellenistic period. Gignac (1970, 1976) conducted an extensive survey of spelling alternations in

Greek non-literary papyri from Egypt dating from the third century BC to the eighth century AD. He reports that there is frequent replacement of the letters *θ*, *φ*, and *χ* with *τ*, *π*, and *κ*, respectively, in restricted phonological environments. One environment, which is not relevant for current purposes, is when the originally aspirated stops came before another aspirated stop (Gignac 1970: 196). The other environments, strikingly, were when the originally aspirated stops came after /s, m, n, r, l/ (with occasional examples of deaspiration also occurring *before* liquids and nasals; Gignac 1970: 196). Here are some examples of apparent deaspiration after /s/ in the papyri:

(20) *τιθέστωι* (for *τιθέσθω*) *P Teb.* 72. 455, 456 (114 BC)

(21) *σκῶσιν* (for *σχῶσιν*) *P Oxy.* 1068. 20–21 (3rd century AD)

(22) *εἰσπορά* (for *εἰσφορά*) *P London* 1249. 6 (AD 345)

And here are some examples of deaspiration after liquids and nasals:

(23) *ἀπελτῖν* (for *ἀπελθεῖν*) *P Teb.* 575 (2nd century AD)

(24) *ἀπελτοῦσα* (for *ἀπελθοῦσα*) *BGU* 380. 3–4 (3rd century AD)

(25) *ξηραντῖσαν* (for *ξηρανθεῖσαν*) *P Oxy.* 53. 10 (AD 316)

(26) *ἀμπώτε(ραι)* (for *ἀμφότεραι*) *P Ryl.* 160b. 6 (AD 37)

As is evident, the change in question affected all the voiceless aspirates,[7] not just the dental one; but this is the only significant difference between the developments in Egyptian Greek and the rule I posit for a much earlier stage of Greek.

There is no satisfactory explanation of these alternations in terms of speakers of another language not perceiving aspiration in Greek in certain environments. Many of the papyri were of course written by native speakers of Greek. And in the Bohairic dialect of Coptic, spoken throughout the Delta, there was an opposition between aspirated and plain voiceless stops very like the one found historically in Greek (Gignac 1970: 198). It seems, then, that the spelling alternations are indicative of a sound change whereby voiceless aspirates in Egyptian Greek lose their aspiration after /s, m, n, r, l/ (Gignac 1970: 201, 1976: 86).

8.5 The necessity of the rule

In two subsequent publications (Elbourne 2000, 2001), I argued that the methods that have been used to explain away voiceless aspirates as secondary

[7] For the likelihood that <*θ*>, <*φ*>, and <*χ*> continued to represent voiceless aspirated stops (not fricatives) in Egypt as late as the early Byzantine period, see Gignac (1970: 199, 1976: 98–101), Teodorsson (1977: 238–241), and Horrocks (2010: 170).

creations of the Indo-European daughter languages (aspiration by laryngeal, and so on) are entirely unsuccessful and not adequate to explain the data adduced in Elbourne (1998). My position was, and remains, that reconstructing voiceless aspirates for Proto-Indo-European is the only principled option here. But I am aware—alas!—that this remains a minority view.[8] For the benefit of those who doubt this thesis, I now propose to argue a related point: even if one wishes to exclude voiceless aspirates from Proto-Indo-European, there is still good reason to posit a version of the sound change I have been discussing.

To start with, it is useful to review the two lists of correspondences under consideration: those where a dental voiceless aspirate in Sanskrit corresponds to a dental voiceless aspirate in Greek (examples (8)–(11)), and those where Greek cognates show plain dental voiceless stops (examples (12)–(18)). I have given extensive philological details about these correspondences in my previous work (Elbourne 1998, 2000, 2001, 2011). I submit that they are all perfectly solid. Any philologist should want to capture them, whether or not he or she believes in voiceless aspirates in Proto-Indo-European.

What options are open, then, to a theorist who wishes to capture these correspondences but who does not wish to posit phonemic voiceless aspirates in Proto-Indo-European? The first decision such a theorist will have to make, presumably, is whether to admit voiceless aspirates in at least some of the relevant words in a stage later than Proto-Indo-European but before the break-up of Greek and Indo-Iranian. Following West (2007: 6), I will call this hypothesized language *Graeco-Aryan*.[9] Suppose that there were voiceless aspirates in at least some of the relevant words in Graeco-Aryan. Then how should we explain the attested situation in the daughter languages, in which there are more inherited dental voiceless aspirates in Sanskrit than in Greek? The easiest way, it seems to me, would be to say that Sanskrit reflects the situation in Graeco-Aryan and that some dental voiceless aspirates were lost in Greek. But this, presumably, would entail that my sound law, or something like it, was operative in Greek.

What if one wishes to say that there were voiceless aspirates in Graeco-Aryan but that Sanskrit does not reflect the situation in Graeco-Aryan in this respect?

[8] In recent times, of course, Szemerényi advanced this position in various editions of his *Einführung in die vergleichende Sprachwissenschaft* (e.g. Szemerényi 1996). Holst (1998) has argued for it, Meier-Brügger (2002: 125) is not unsympathetic to it, and Barrack (2003) suggests that it be taken seriously.

[9] The Graeco-Aryan hypothesis goes back at least to Kretschmer (1896: 168–70). Further discussion of the idea can be found in Durante (1976), Euler (1979), and Clackson (1994).

The most obvious move here would be to say that Greek reflects the situation in Graeco-Aryan and that Indo-Iranian innovated[10] by introducing further voiceless aspirates. Let us think about what this entails. If the situation in Graeco-Aryan with respect to the relevant voiceless aspirates was like the situation in Greek, and if there were no voiceless aspirates in Proto-Indo-European, then Graeco-Aryan must have innovated voiceless aspirates. What the triggering environment may have been for this hypothetical change is uncertain, of course; but for the sake of argument let us assume that following laryngeals were responsible.[11] Given that some of the strongest evidence for laryngeals in the relevant words is to be found in cases where there is no aspirated stop in Greek (πόντος, πλατύς), we must suppose, if Graeco-Aryan was like Greek in this respect, that one of two things happened. One possibility is that Graeco-Aryan initially innovated a situation like that in Sanskrit and then underwent a *Rückverwandlung*, whereby the aspiration was lost in the relevant words that did not have aspiration in Greek. What would have been the triggering environment for the *Rückverwandlung*? Well, the Graeco-Aryan words without aspiration in the relevant places, on this view, are such that their dental stops come after */s, n, r, l/, whereas this is not the case with the Graeco-Aryan words that have aspiration on this view. So we would end up positing a version of my law for Graeco-Aryan. The second possibility is that in the innovation of aspiration in Graeco-Aryan, aspiration could be produced by laryngeals everywhere except in the presence of a certain further environment, an environment that would exempt the words in (12)–(18) from being aspirated. What do the plain voiceless dental stops in the words in (12)–(18) have in common, in terms of their environment, which is not to be found in the case of dental stops in the words in (8)–(11)? Why, they all occur after */s, n, r, l/. To be precise, the hypothetical theorist whom we are contemplating at the moment would need two laws, which could be formulated something like this:

(27) Aspiration of */p, k, k^w/ before HV

(28) Aspiration of */t/ before HV except after */s, n, r, l/

It can be seen that (28) is a kind of inverse version of the law I posit for Greek, which would be summarized as follows:

(29) Deaspiration of *t^h after */s, n, r, l/

[10] How? Perhaps by laryngeals or similar (see below) lingering on into Indo-Iranian and working their aspirating magic at last, centuries after the original innovation of aspiration in Graeco-Aryan.

[11] For arguments against attributing the innovation of voiceless aspirates to laryngeals, see Elbourne (2000).

The rule in (28) is more complicated than the one in (29), however, and might be dispreferred, other things being equal. (And of course the theorists in question need (27) as well.) But, if (28) is assumed, we have not exactly the law I posit for Greek but a kind of inverse version of it in the history of Graeco-Aryan.

So far I have been exploring the options open to a theorist entertaining the hypothesis that there were no voiceless aspirates in Proto-Indo-European but there were some in Graeco-Aryan. But what of theorists who do not want to admit voiceless aspirates either to Proto-Indo-European or to Graeco-Aryan? They must presumably say that Greek and Indo-Iranian innovated voiceless aspirates in separate secondary developments. We are now faced with a set of questions and responses analogous to the ones we just considered. How does it come about that Sanskrit displays more dental voiceless aspirates than Greek in the relevant words? Perhaps the simplest solution is to say that Greek innovated the Sanskrit situation (separately from Sanskrit, of course) and then underwent my law.

The obvious alternative is again analogous to one of the options that we have just considered on behalf of the other theorists. It might be maintained that laryngeals (say) induced aspiration in */p, k, k^w/ in the normal way; and that in the case of **t* they did so only following phonemes that did not belong to the group */s, n, r, l/. In other words, we would have the following two laws for Greek, precisely similar to the ones posited for Graeco-Aryan by the other theorists:

(30) Aspiration of */p, k, k^w/ before HV

(31) Aspiration of */t/ before HV except after */s, n, r, l/

This, then, would result in a kind of inverse version of my law being posited for Greek.

8.6 Conclusion

My position is still that Proto-Indo-European had a phonemic series of voiceless aspirates and that their development in Greek is to be explained by positing deaspiration of inherited *t^h after */s, n, r, l/. If we want to find a unified phonological description of this environment, it can more insightfully be described as deaspiration after segments that are [+coronal] or [+consonantal] than as deaspiration after continuants. Furthermore, I maintain that even those who do not reconstruct phonemic voiceless aspirates for Proto-Indo-European have reason to adopt some version of this law.

9

Regular sound change and word-initial */i̯/- in Armenian

DANIEL KÖLLIGAN

9.1 Presumable results of */i̯/- in Armenian

One of the well-known *cruces* in Armenian historical phonology is the question of the development of Proto-Indo-European */i̯/ in word-initial position, for which no fewer than four different outcomes seem to present themselves: /dz/ as in *jez* 'you (acc. pl.)' ~ Skt *yūyam*; /dž/ as in *ǰowr* 'water' ~ Lith. *jū́rės*; /Ø/ as in *nêr/ner* 'sister-in-law' < PIE **(H)i̯enh$_2$ter-*; and /l/ as in *lowc* 'yoke' ~ Skt *yugam*. Here, as in many other cases of Armenian historical phonology, the scantiness of the *comparanda* does not seem to admit any safe conclusions.[1] Nevertheless, the discussion of this subject that now spans more than a century may still be enriched by aspects both new and seemingly forgotten. After a short review of the history of research on this subject (section 9.2), the main arguments will be put forward that speak in favour of the sound law assumed by Meillet, viz. PIE *#/i̯/ > Arm. #/dž/ (section 9.3), followed by a discussion of apparent cases of PIE *#/i̯/ > Arm. /dz/ (section 9.4), and PIE *#/i̯/ > Arm. /Ø/ (section 9.5).

[1] Cf. e.g. Godel (1975: 81): 'The development of initial **y* is uncertain'; Clackson (1994: 52), Lamberterie (1988/9: 247).

9.2 History of research

While Hübschmann (1883: 66) compared the pronoun of the 2pl. Skt *yūyam*, Goth. *jus*, etc. with Arm. *jez* 'you (acc. pl.)' and tentatively assumed a development of PIE */i̯/ > Arm. /dz/, Meillet (1903*b*: 29) posited PIE *#/i̯/ > Arm. #/dž/ because of the assumed equation Lith. *jū́rės* 'sea' : Arm. *ǰowr* 'water'.[2] This position was taken over by most scholars and found its way into the handbooks;[3] still, trying to bolster up Hübschmann's position, Pedersen (1906: 405)[4] adduced Arm. *jow* 'egg', comparing this with NP *xāya* and 'Old Slavonic' *jaje*, which he interpreted as stemming from **i̯ōi̯o-* via assimilation from **ōi̯o-*. Minshall (1955) was the first to introduce laryngeals into the equation, assuming a development */Hi̯/- > /dž/, but he did not present any further evidence for this. Some scholars tried to see the treatment of */i̯/ as one of the many alleged parallels between Armenian and Greek; thus Pisani (1950: 180) posited both the outcomes /dž/ and /Ø/ for Armenian,[5] in parallel to the development of PIE */i̯/ to Gr. /d^z/ beside /h/.[6] This was accepted by Greppin (1972, 1978) with the further assumption that the outcome depended on the presence or absence of a preceding laryngeal, i.e. *#/Hi̯/ > /dž/ vs. */i̯/ > /Ø/, and by Morani (1981), who, like Greppin, viewed this double development as an Armeno-Greek parallel. The opposite development was assumed by Schmitt (1996: 23), viz. */Hi̯/ > */i̯/ > /Ø/ vs. */i̯/ > /dž/. Complete loss of word-initial *yod* has been assumed by Kortlandt in various publications,[7] since in his opinion the etymology Arm. *ǰowr* : Lith. *jū́rės* is wrong and loss of *yod* is seen in the relative pronoun *or* < **i̯o-ro-*; in the interrogative pronoun *o(v)* which, according to Kortlandt, took its anlaut **i̯o-* instead of expected **k^wo-* from the relative pronoun like Polish *jak* 'how' vs. Russ. *kak*; and in *nêr/ner* 'sister-in-law' ~ PIE **i̯enh$_2$ter-* (cf. section 9.5). Following this view, Martirosyan (2010) has put forward explanations of Arm. *ors* 'hunting; game' and *êg* 'female' implying loss of word-initial /i̯/ (cf. section 9.5).[8] Finally, a development of PIE */i̯/ >

[2] In Meillet (1936: 51–2) he added Gr. ζῆλος 'zeal' : Arm. *ǰanam* 'try, make an effort', and consequently changed his formulation from 'on ne possède aucun exemple pour le traitement de i.-e. **y* en arménien' (i.e. except *ǰowr*) to 'on ne possède que peu d'exemples pour le traitement de i.-e. **y* en arménien'.

[3] Among others Cuny (1943: 59), Solta (1963: 100), Schmitt (1981, 2007: 70, 77), J̌ahowkyan (1967: 221–2), J̌ahowkyan (1982: 40–1), Winter (1999).

[4] 'Idg. *i̯* ist im Armenischen niemals zu *ǰ* geworden.'

[5] *ǰowr* vs. the relative pronoun *or* < **i̯o-ro-*, and his etymology of *asem* 'say' : Skt *yaś-as* 'fame', both of which he tried to relate to PIE **i̯ak-*.

[6] The exact conditioning of this difference remains unclear; Pisani only speaks of an 'intensivizazzione'.

[7] E.g. Kortlandt (1997, 1998).

[8] Martirosyan (2010: 276, 544, 706).

Arm. /l/, such as seems to be indicated by Arm. *leard* 'liver' : PIE **i̯ekʷr̥t* and *lowc* 'yoke' : PIE **i̯ugom*, is usually discarded nowadays,[9] as for both words different explanations have been given: *lowc* may have taken /l/ under the influence of antonymic *lowcanem* 'loosen, untie' (: Skt *rujáti* 'breaks', OE *lūcan* 'weed'),[10] *leard* under that of **lei̯p-* 'fat', Gr. λιπαρός, or **lei̯s-* 'fat', cf. Hitt. *liššši-* 'fat'.[11]

9.3 Pro */i̯/- > /dž/

There are four Armenian words that seem to speak in favour of a development PIE */i̯/ > Arm. /dž/ in word-initial position: *ǰowr* 'water', *ǰanam* 'try, make an effort', *ǰov* 'sprout', and *ǰori* 'mule'.[12]

ǰowr 'water', if taken together with Lith. *jū́ra*, pl. *jū́ros, jū́rės* 'sea', Lith. *jáura* 'moor, bog', and OPr. acc. sg. *iūrin* 'sea', points to a PIE noun **i̯eu̯H-r-*.[13] Since Old Prussian also attests a form *wurs* 'lake, pond' (given as translation of Germ. 'Teich' (<Tych>) in the Elbing Vocabulary no. 61), which seems to be connected with Skt *vār, vāri* 'water', it has frequently been assumed that this is to be connected with Lith. *jū́ra* as well.[14] Against this, Petit (2004: 53–4) has argued for two different etyma reflected in Baltic.[15] Starting with the Baltic forms one could posit an *r*-stem **Heu̯H-r-*, **HuH-r-*, whose full-grade form would have given Balt. **jāur-* (> Lith. *jáura*), and whose zero-grade form Balt. **ūr-* (> OPr. *wurs* with secondary /w/ in anlaut) in Lithuanian would have taken /j/ from the full-grade variant, hence **jūr-* (Lith. *jū́ra*). Germanic and Italic forms such as ON *úr* 'drizzle, thin rain', OE *éar* 'sea', and Lat. *ūr-īna* 'urine' might belong here too. Apart from the assumption of some analogical

[9] Cf. Olsen (1999: 19), Martirosyan (2010: 316–17).

[10] For the influence of antonyms, cf. Engl. *female* [fiːmeɪl] (< fr. *femelle*) with [eɪ] after *male* [meɪl]. Cf. also Martirosyan (2010: 316).

[11] Cf. e.g. Benveniste (1935: 8–9 and 182, **li̯ēkʷ-r̥* from **lei̯kʷ-* 'organe laissé, abandonné (aux dieux)'), Schindler (1966, Hitt. *liššši-* 'the fat thing' > 'liver', Arm. *leard* < **lisr̥t* may be a rhyming formation to **i̯ekʷr̥t*, cf. also *neard* 'sinew' < **snēu̯r̥t* ~ Skt *snā́van-*, Gr. νεῦρον, etc.), J̌ahowkyan (1967: 221), Arbeitman (1980, **lipar i̯ekʷr̥t* 'fat liver' > **lipar*, with the obvious Romance and Greek parallels Lat. *(iecur) ficatum* 'liver stuffed with figs' > Span. *higado*, etc., Gr. (ἧπαρ) συκωτόν 'liver stuffed with figs' > ModGr. συκώτι), Olsen (1999: 191–2, **lisi i̯ekʷr̥t* contaminated to **lisr̥t (i̯ekʷr̥t)* > Arm. *leard*). Martirosyan (2010: 307) additionally considers analogical influence of *leɫi* 'gall, bile' (of unknown etymology) or *lanǰ* 'breast' < 'lung'; cf. also Martirosyan (2010: 707).

[12] For the following discussion, cf. also Greppin (1972: 76), Greppin (1978: 141 n. 2), J̌ahowkyan (1967: 221–2), and J̌ahowkyan (1982: 40).

[13] Not treated in Hübschmann (1897). For this reconstruction and further related forms, cf. Wodtko, Irslinger, and Schneider (2008: 404–5).

[14] Cf. Pedersen (1906: 405), Meillet (1920: 251), Mawet (1986: 85 n. 41), Kortlandt (1997: 7), Kortlandt (1998: 15), Beekes (2003: 162).

[15] Against this connection cf. also Olsen (1999: 50).

remodellings, this solution does not explain Arm. *ǰowr* and Skt *vār, vāri* 'water', for which one would have to assume *Schwebeablaut* **Hu̯eH-r-* vs. **Heu̯H-r-*.[16] The more economical solution is thus to start with two different roots: **i̯euH-r-/i̯uH-r-* (Lith. *jū́ra*, OPr. *iūrin*, Arm. *ǰowr*) and **u̯eH-r-/uH-r-* (full grade in Skt *vār*, Luw. *waršа-*, OIr. *fír* 'milk', which speaks in favour of **u̯eh*$_1$*-r-*; zero grade in OPr. *wurs*, ON *úr*, Lat. *ūr-īna*, Toch. A *wär*, B *war*).[17] Other attempts to explain the Armenian form without recourse to Lith. *jū́ra* etc. have proved fruitless.[18]

ǰanam 'to try, make an effort' has been connected with Gr. ζῆλος 'zeal' by Meillet (1936: 52). Under this root **i̯eh*$_2$- 'ask, strive for' one may subsume: Skt *yāmi* 'I ask', *īmahe* 'we ask' (**i̯i-i̯h*$_2$*-med*^{h}*h*$_2$), YAv. *yāsaiti* 'asks', Gr. δίζημαι 'search', Toch. B subj. *yāṣtär* 'will/shall beg', and nominal forms such as Skt *yātar-* prob. 'avenger', Gr. (Hesychius) Ζητήρ· Ζεὺς ἐν Κύπρῳ, and the denominal verb (derived from the participle *ζητός) ζητέω 'seek, desire'.[19] The plural forms of a nasal present of the type **C-ne-H-/C-n-H-* would have been **i̯-n̥h*$_2$*-més, -tés, -énti* and would have given Arm. *ǰana-mkʿ, -aykʿ, -an*, after which the singular may have been remodelled to *ǰanam, -as, -ay*. The corresponding noun *ǰan* (*i*-stem, instr. *ǰaniw*[20]) could either be a back-formation to *ǰanam*[21] or, as per Klingenschmitt (1982: 90), an independent formation in **-ni-*, i.e. **i̯eh*$_2$*ni-*, as in *ban* < **b*^{h}*eh*$_2$*ni-* (cf. ON *bøn* 'request, prayer'). *ǰanam* could either be derived from the latter or be an independent nasal present built on the root; cf. *ban* 'word, thing' : *banam* 'to open' (**b*^{h}*eh*$_2$*-ni-* : **b*^{h}*-n(e)-h*$_2$*-*^{ti}).

[16] As assumed, e.g., by Mažiulis (1988–: ii. 54–6, s.v. *iūrin*).

[17] Cf. also Wodtko, Irslinger, and Schneider (2008: 715–16).

[18] Patrubany *apud* Hübschmann (1899: 49) tried to connect *ǰowr* with Skt *kṣárati* 'flows', Gr. φθείρω, an etymology which found its way into *IEW* (487, s.v. **g*^{w}*hđer-*); Pedersen initially seems to have favoured this explanation as well (cf. Pedersen 1905*a*: 209, where he calls it 'enticing' ('verlockend')), but later assumed a connection with Skt *dháyati* 'sucks' and *dadhi-* n. 'sour milk' (**d*^{h}*e-d*^{h}*h*$_1$*-* from **d*^{h}*eh*$_1$*(i̯)-*), implying a sound change PIE **d*^{h}*i̯* > Arm. *ǰ* as in *mēǰ* 'middle' < **med*^{h}*i̯os*. As for the meaning, he compared Skt *páyas* 'milk, water'; cf. Pedersen (1906: 429) and Kortlandt (1998: 15). But *páyas* seems to mean only 'milk' and 'juice' in Indo-Iranian (cf. Mayrhofer 1986–2001: ii. 83), and it is unclear what the result of a preform **d*^{h}*h*$_1$*i̯Vr-* would be in Armenian (probably **dai̯Vr-* > **daVr-*). Similarly, it is unclear what the development of the preform underlying Skt *kṣárati* and Gr. φθείρω, PIE **g*^{w}*ĝ*^{h}*er-* (cf. *LIV* 213), would be in Armenian. Winter (1965*b*: 114) assumed that *ǰ-* in *ǰowr* developed in a syntagm with its antonym *howr* 'fire', i.e. *howr ǰowr*, with *Ri̯* > *Rǰ* between words as in word-final position in *sterǰ* 'infertile' < **steri̯a-*. However, there does not seem to be evidence for a more than occasional combination of these two words in Classical Armenian texts (e.g. Eznik 3 *ew howr ew ǰowr, tʿe ǰowr tʿe howr*, Agathangelos 174 *očʿ howr, očʿ ǰowr*).

[19] Cf. García Ramón (1999).

[20] Also attested in Agathangelos, Łazar Pʿarpecʿi, the 'Biwzandaran Patmowtʿiwnkʿ', Irenaeus, Movses Xorenacʿi, Yovhannes Drasxanakertcʿi. E.g. 2 Thessalonians 3. 8 *ǰaniw ew vastakov zcʿayg ew zcʿerek gorceakʿ* 'we worked with labour and toil night and day'.

[21] Cf. in this sense Olsen (1999: 90).

ǰov (gen. _-oy_ and _-ow_) 'sprout, twig, offspring'[22] has been connected with Gr. ζειαί 'spelt', Lith. _jãvas_, pl. _javaĩ_ 'corn', Skt _yáva-_ 'corn, barley, millet', _yávasa-_ 'grass, pasture', MP/NP _ǰaw_ 'barley', adj. NP _ǰawin_ 'of barley', etc., PIE _*i̯eu̯o-_.[23] The _o_-vocalism of the root could either be a morphological _o_-grade or the result of the development of _*eu̯_ > _ou̯_ as in _nor_ 'new' < _*nou̯oro-_ < _*neu̯oro-_, _č'ogay_ 'I went' < _*ki̯ou̯-a-_, and _ołaṙoganem_ 'to irrigate' ← _*srou̯e/o-_ < _*sreu̯-e/o-_,[24] i.e. _*i̯eu̯o-_ > _*i̯ou̯o-_ > _ǰov_. In the latter case the _o_-stem inflection could be justified by assuming a secondary derivation from the collective-feminine _ā_-stem _*i̯eu̯eh_$_2$ 'corn' → _*i̯eu̯-h_$_2$_-ó-_ 'having ears of corn', in the former a back-formation from the _o_-grade collective _*i̯ou̯eh_$_2$ (like Gr. ἀστήρ : ἄστρα : ἄστρον) or, again, a possessive formation _*i̯ou̯-h_$_2$_-ó-_. Since _ǰov_ can also inflect as a _u_-stem (cf. Awetik'ean, Siwrmêlean, and Awgerean 1836: ii. 675), the immediate preforms of Arm. _ǰov_ may have been _*i̯ou̯o-_ and/or _*i̯ou̯u-_, which could also go back to an _i_-stem _*i̯ou̯-i-_ (e.g. _*i̯eu̯-ih_$_2$), if one assumes a sound change _*-u̯i-_ > _*-u̯u-_.[25] The difference in meaning between the Armenian and the Persian forms makes it unlikely that the former were borrowed from the latter.[26]

Finally, one might tentatively suggest that Arm. _ǰori_, _-woy_ 'mule' (: Genesis 45. 23 _tasn ǰori_ : δέκα ἡμιόνους) belongs to the root PIE _*i̯eu̯-_ 'to yoke' (: Skt _yuváti_ 'yokes', _niyut-_ 'team'), and reconstruct a pre-Arm. form _*i̯e/ou̯o-ro-_ 'yoked animal' (> _*ǰou̯oro-_ > _ǰor-_, cf. _*neu̯oro-_ > _nor_ 'new') with the same suffix _-i_ as in _ayci_ 'goat', _mari_ 'female bird', _mak'i_ 'ewe', etc.;[27] cf. also Lith. _jáutis_ m. 'bull, ox' and (from PIE _*i̯eug-_ 'to yoke') Lat. _iūmentum_ 'mule, beast of burden' (_*i̯eug-s-mn̥-to-_).[28]

---

[22] Ačaṙyan (1971–9): _boysi cil kam ənjiwł_ 'bud, sprout', whence _ǰovanal_ 'to grow, bud'; Awetik'ean, Siwrmêlean, and Awgerean (1836): _stełn. ənjiwł. šaṙawił. t'aw ost. sałart' owṙčac'eal_ 'branch, shoot, fresh twig, leaf'.

[23] Cf. Ačaṙyan (1971–9: iv. 131); not treated in Hübschmann (1897), Meillet (1936), _IEW_, Solta (1960), Wodtko, Irslinger, and Schneider (2008). The etymology is rejected by Mawet (1986: 85 n. 41) because of the difference in meaning.

[24] Cf. Klingenschmitt (1982: 204), Olsen (1999: 31–2).

[25] Cf. the discussion in Olsen (1999: 788).

[26] Southern (2002[2006]) interprets _*i̯eu̯o-_ as _*h_$_2$_i̯eu̯o-_ and as a derivative of _*h_$_2$_ei̯-u-_ 'life(-force)'. In this case the assumption of a morphological _o_-grade in Armenian would be more likely, and the laryngeal would be lost regularly by the 'Hirt-Saussure effect', #HRo- > #Ro-, i.e. _*h_$_2$ _i̯ou̯o-_ > _*i̯ou̯o-_ > _ǰov_. It seems less likely that _*H_ remained unvocalized until after the development _*e.u̯_ > _*o.u̯_. If Hittite _eua(n)-_ '[a kind of] grain' belongs to this root, word-initial _*Hi̯-_ is less likely, though, as in that case one would expect Hitt. /i̯/ (cf. _i̯anzi_ 'they go' < _*h_$_1$_i̯-énti_; Kloekhorst 2008: 263–4).

[27] Cf. Martirosyan (2010: 559–60). Martirosyan's etymology rests among other things on the assumption of a not unproblematic sound change _*d_^{z}_i̯_ > _*dž_ (_*ĝ_^{h}_io-ter-i(h_$_2$_)os_ 'horse-like').

[28] For mules used for transport, cf. Agathangelos 803 _Ew hanēin zGrigor yoskiapat kaṙsn ark'ownakans, spitakajig ǰorwoc'n_ 'And they put Gregory in the royal carriage that was decorated with gold and drawn by white mules'.

9.4 Contra */i̯/- > /dž/

Apparent exceptions to the development assumed here are the oblique forms of the pronoun of the second person plural *jez*, *jer*, etc., and *jow* 'egg', as first adduced by Pedersen (1906: 405).

The connection between Arm. *je-* and Skt *yūyam*, Goth. *jus*, etc., is only an indirect one.[29] The suffix *-ĝ^h^i* that may have been at home in the oblique forms of the pronoun of the first person singular (dat. *inj* < *em-ĝ^h^i*, cf. Lat. *mi-hi*, Skt *ma-hy-am*) spread to the dat., acc., and loc. forms of the other personal pronouns, hence 2sg. **tu̯e-ĝ^h^i*, 1pl. **me-ĝ^h^i*. A similar development has taken place in OHG acc. 1pl. *uns-ih* 'us', 2pl. *iuw-ih* 'you' after acc. 1sg. *mih* 'me', acc. 2sg. *dih* 'you', and OE acc. 1sg. *mec* (beside *mē*) → acc. 1pl. *ūsic* (beside *ūs*), 2sg. *þec* (beside *þē*) → acc. 2pl. *ēowic* (beside *ēow*).[30] In intervocalic position */ĝʰ/ developed regularly to /z/, hence *k'ez* [kʰez], *mez* [mez] vs. *inj* [indᶻ]. The intermediate forms of *k'ez* and *mez* will thus have been **k'eji* /kʰedᶻi/ and **meji* /medᶻi/. Influence of the 2sg. on the 2pl. pronominal forms is seen in the nominative, where the expected form **ǰowk'*[31] was remodelled after the sg. *dow* to *dowk'*.[32] After the development of **tu̯* > *k'* in the oblique cases of the 2sg. (**tu̯eso* > *k'o*, etc.) the distinctive person marker was the word-initial consonant (2sg. *k'-ez* vs. 1pl. *m-ez*), a pattern which was extended to the 2pl., i.e. the stem **i̯ū-* was remade into **i̯-* (> **ǰ-*) after the model of the singular, while in the nominative *dowk'* was synchronically analysable as *dow* + plural ending *k'* (see Table 9.1).[33]

29 Cf. Hübschmann (1883: 66), Meillet (1920: 251), Olsen (1999: 54). Schmitt (1981: 117) remarks that the origin of this stem is unclear, Meillet (1936: 92) calls it 'assez obscur[s]', adding 'on sait que le pronom de 2me personne du pluriel a des formes divergentes dans les diverses langues'. Pedersen (1905*a*: 204): *je-* 'somehow' ('doch jedenfalls irgendwie') belongs to Skt *yūyam*. Kortlandt (1998) assumes a preform **i̯u̯e-*, but the development of such an anlaut-cluster in Armenian is unclear.

30 Cf. Ramat (1981: 92–3), Seebold (1984: 32).

31 Cf. Meillet (1936: 92).

32 It seems more plausible to assume a remodelling of the inherited form than a complete new formation based on the singular, as in that case one might expect a similar formation in the first person (*es* : †*esk'* like *dow* : *dowk'*). The remodelling may have been triggered by the phonetic similarity between *dow* and **ǰowk'*.

33 This seems more likely than to assume a form **i̯u̯eĝ^h^i*, as the development of the group /i̯u̯/ is unclear. Alleged cases with the inverse order /u̯i̯/ giving Arm. /dž/, such as *aṙaǰ* 'front' < **pr̥h₃u̯i̯o-* (Olsen 1999: 26, 811), need not prove anything for /i̯u̯/ and are better explained differently anyway (*aṙaǰ* 'front' < *aṙ aǰ* 'on the right', cf. Martirosyan 2010: 104; *olǰ* 'whole' < **(s)oli̯o-*, OIr. *uile*).

Table 9.1 Influence of 2sg. on 2pl. pronominal forms in Armenian

2sg.	2pl.
dow	**i̯ūs* > **ǰuk‘* → *dow-k‘*
**tu̯e-ĝʰi* > **k‘-eji*	→ **ǰ-eji* > **ǰ-ez*

Winter (1999: 318–19) assumed an assimilation **ǰez* > *jez* (from 'shibilant – sibilant' to 'sibilant – sibilant' as Winter calls it, i.e. from a palato-alveolar to an alveolar affricate), but in all other secure cases of assimilation the manner of articulation as either affricate or fricative is identical in the two segments; cf. *čanač‘em* < **canač‘em* vs. aor. *caneay*, and *žoyž* < **z-oyž* (cf. Meillet 1936: 29). It therefore seems less likely that the assimilation happened at the stage of a preform **ǰez*, which would rather lead to **zez* or, less likely, **žež*.[34] It seems more probable that the assimilation occurred at a time when the second consonant was still an affricate, i.e. remodelled **i̯eĝʰi* > **ǰeji* [d$^{\check{z}}$ed^{z}i], and with regressive assimilation (as in *čanač‘em* and *žoyž*) > **jeji* [d^{z}ed^{z}i],[35] and regular development of intervocalic [d^{z}] > [z], hence *jez* [d^{z}ez].[36]

Pedersen (1906: 404) compared Arm. *jow* 'egg' with Serb. *jaje* 'egg' and assumed a preform **i̯ōi̯o-* with 'expressive' and/or assimilated word-initial /i̯/,[37] while Bugge (1893: 16) put forward the explanation of an original compound **jow-ow* 'fish-egg', where **jow* would be an earlier form of *jowkn* 'fish'. But the existence of such a preform is doubtful, and it is unclear why 'fish-egg' should have developed into the general word for 'egg'. The explanation is clearly *ad hoc*. Besides discussing the probability of a geminate cluster /i̯i̯/ developing into /dž/, Olsen (1999: 54) proposes a preform **ĝʰutom*, i.e. a substantivized verbal adjective, comparing ON *gjóta hrǫgnum* 'spawn' and Lat. *fundere* in the meaning 'generate, produce'. If one follows Schindler's analysis (Schindler 1969) of PIE 'egg' as **ō-h_2u̯i-ó-* 'that which is at the bird', with **ō* being the preposition found in Skt *ā*, one might equally well assume a form **ĝʰo-h_2u̯i-o-* with the

[34] Note the regressive assimilation in *čanač‘em* and *žoyž*. *jez* is the only case in Winter's corpus with a combination of affricate *j* + fricative *z*; the inverse order does not occur.

[35] As proposed already by Meillet (1920: 251, 'au datif-accusatif plur. *jez* "vous", le *ǰ* aurait été remplacé par *j* sous l'influence du *j* intérieur; car *jez* repose sur un ancien **ǰeji* (cf. *inj* "à moi")') and Minshall (1955: 500, 'The original palatal affricate /ǰ/ became the dental affricate /j/ under the influence of the following dental affricate /j/ at a time before the latter became a voiced sibilant'). Greppin's negative assessment of a derivation of *jez* from a preform **ǰeji* (Greppin 1972: 76) seems to rely on a misquotation of Meillet, to whom he attributes a derivation from **ǰez*.

[36] Cf. also Martirosyan (2010: 243). The form **jej(i)* would thus have belonged to the most common case of combinations of identical sounds in Winter's corpus (e.g. *c* – *c* 16×, *c‘* – *c‘* 8×, *j* – *j* 8×, *s* – *s* 17×, etc.).

[37] Accepted by *IEW* (783–4, s.v. **ō(u̯)i̯om*); no proposal in Derksen (2008: 27).

preposition *$\hat{g}^h$*(o)-*,[38] which would have developed via **jōw* > **juw* > **jow* with regular loss of /u̯/ after /u/.[39] A different possibility that, as far as I know, has not been discussed so far,[40] is to assume that *jow* was influenced by *jag* 'chick, young; sparrow' (: *στρουθία* Luke 12. 6),[41] from which *jow* may have taken the initial /dz/.[42] Beside the semantic proximity,[43] the monosyllabicity of the regular result of inherited **ōu̯i̯om* > **ow* in Armenian may have given rise to its remodelling,[44] as happened also to Arm. *owstr* 'son': the regular Armenian outcome of what in Greek is *υἰύς* (later *υἱός*) and in Tocharian A *se*, B *soy*, PIE **su-i̯u-*, was **ow*, which was remodelled to *owstr* after *dowstr* 'daughter'.[45] *jow* 'egg' and *jag* 'young' are attested side by side in the Bible and in Łazar P'arpec'i [ŁP']:

Deuteronomy 22. 6 *Ew et'ē dipesc'is bownoy hawowc' aṙaǰi k'o i čanaparhi, et'ē i cáṙ ew et'ē i getni, jagowc' kam jowoc', ew mayrn ǰeṙeal nstc'i i veray jagowc'n kam jowoc'. mí aṙnowc'ows zmayrn handerj ordwovk'n*

Ἐὰν δὲ συναντήσῃς νοσσιᾷ ὀρνέων πρὸ προσώπου σου ἐν τῇ ὁδῷ ἢ ἐπὶ παντὶ δένδρει ἢ ἐπὶ τῆς γῆς, νεοσσοῖς ἢ ᾠοῖς, καὶ ἡ μήτηρ θάλπῃ ἐπὶ τῶν νεοσσῶν ἢ ἐπὶ τῶν ᾠῶν, οὐ λήμψῃ τὴν μητέρα μετὰ τῶν τέκνων

[38] Cf. OCS *za* < *$\hat{g}^h$*ō* and Arm. *z-* < **j-* before C (e.g. *z-na* 'him/her/it' < **j-na* as in *ozni* 'hedgehog' < **ojni*, Lith. *ežỹs*, OHG *igil)* < *$\hat{g}^h$*o/e-*; PIE *$\hat{g}^h$*-di̯es* 'on that day, yesterday', Skt *hyaḥ*, Gr. *χθές*, Lat. *heri*, etc.

[39] The most likely explanation of PIE 'egg', though, is that of a *vr̥ddhi*-formation **h₂ōu̯i̯o-* 'belonging to the bird'; cf. Martirosyan (2010: 439).

[40] Not mentioned in Martirosyan (2010: 439), who concludes that 'the initial *j-* remains unclear'.

[41] Cf. the translation given in Awetik'ean, Siwrmêlean, and Awgerean (1836): *νεοσσά, νοσσίον, pullus, noracin haw ew t'ṙč'own, kam ayl kendani* 'new-born chicken or bird or other animal'.

[42] On the etymology of *jag* (*u*-stem), cf. Hübschmann (1897: 185), who classified it as a Persian loanword; cf. NP *zāq*. Olsen (1999: 110–11) points out that usually MP *z* is represented in Arm. as *z*, hence *jag* may be an inherited word to be compared with Alb. *zog* '(young) bird', PIE *$\hat{g}^h ag^h$*u-* or, with Demiraj (1997: 430), *$\hat{g}^h$*u̯aG*$^{(w)}$-, a connection that G. Meyer (1892: 18) had already seen. Cf. also Orel (1998: 525), who speaks of an 'oriental *Wanderwort*'.

[43] As in Proto-Indo-European, where 'egg' is a derivative of 'bird', in Gr. *νεοσσός* 'chick' can also mean 'yolk' (Ar., Arist., Theophr., etc.); cf. also *νεοσσεύω* 'to brood' and ModEA *havkit'* 'egg' (with *hav* 'hen' as first member).

[44] Cf. Bugge (1893: 16, 'The reason why **u* was replaced by *ju* was the fact that **u* was of insufficient phonetic substance') and Solta (1960: 178, 'A form **u* would no longer be a word!'). There do not seem to be unambiguous examples for the development of the long diphthong **ōu̯* in Armenian (*kov* 'cow' might equally go back to the full grade *g^w*ou̯-*; cf. also *kogi* 'butter' < *g^w*ou̯i̯o-*).

[45] Note that there is no feminine prefix *d-* or the like; the process cannot therefore have happened in the opposite direction. A similar case is that of *tal* 'husband's sister' ← PIE **ĝelH-* (: Gr. *γάλως*, Lat. *glōs*, OCS *zъlъva*) influenced by *taygr* 'husband's brother' (cf. Martirosyan 2010: 595–6); in Middle Persian *pusar* 'son' beside *pus* 'son' acquired its ending *-ar* from *duxtar* (obl.) beside *duxt* (casus rectus) 'daughter' and probably *pidar* 'father'; cf. also NP, where beside *pus* and *pusar* there is a form *pisar* 'son' after *pidar* (cf. Nyberg 1974: 163, s.v. *pus*).

'If a bird's nest happens to be before you along the way, in any tree or on the ground, with young ones or eggs, with the mother sitting on the young or on the eggs, you shall not take the mother with the young.'[46]

ŁPʻ 1. 7 *jkowns i orsoy ew bazmazan vayreni hawowcʻ jags ew kam jows i kłzeacʻ getoyn bereal* 'they brought fish they had caught and the chicks of various wild birds and also eggs from the river islands'

9.5 Apparent cases with #/∅/

The Armenian relative and adjectival interrogative pronoun *or* would seem to be a clear example for PIE */i̯/ > Arm. /∅/ (if one assumes that it was remade from original **(H)i̯o-* into **(H)i̯o-ro- > or*). *or* cannot be explained without a look at the interrogative pronoun *o(v)*, though, which seems more problematic: the question here is whether PIE $*k^w$ was lost, hence $*k^w$*os* > *o(v)*, which seems to be counterevidenced by *kʻan* 'as', if it is the cognate of Lat. *quam* or goes back to a preform $*k^w eh_2$-*n̥t* (cf. also *kʻani* 'how much').[47] Kortlandt's[48] solution is to assume that the stem of the relative *o-* < **i̯o-* was taken over into the interrogative, as in Polish *jak* 'how' beside Russian *kak* 'how'. In a similar vein, if one does not want to assume */i̯/ > /∅/, one could hypothesize that the source for the relative and the interrogative was the demonstrative stem **so* > Arm. *o(v)*, which first replaced the relative stem **i̯o-* (as, e.g., in Germanic) and then the interrogative as well. Finally, it is possible that (as e.g. in Latin) the interrogative pronoun $*k^w$*o-* was used as a relative pronoun with loss of $*k^w$-.[49]

Arm. *nêr* (*ner*), gen. *niri*, has usually been connected with Lat. *ianitrices*, Gr. εἰνατέρες, Skt *yātar-*, and RussCSl. *jatry* 'sister-in-law', although the details of the phonetic development remain problematic. As no further cases for the context **i̯en-* or **Hi̯en-* have been adduced so far, it seems impossible to come to a definite conclusion, as is illustrated by the numerous attempts to

[46] Quoted by Eznik (§406): *ew očʻ zhaw i jowocʻ kam i jagowcʻ veray nsteal i miasin miangamayn ar̃nowl* 'et, une mère-oiseau, sur œufs ou poussins assise, ensemble avec eux il défend de la prendre' (Mariès and Mercier 1989: 678).

[47] Cf. Klingenschmitt (1982: 169).

[48] Cf. Kortlandt (1997, 1998).

[49] If one does not accept a sound-law $*\#k^w o > *\#o$-, one might assume that after a dissimilation $*k^w \dots k^w > \emptyset \dots k^w$ in the archaic-looking *inčʻ* 'something/what' < $*k^w imk^w id$ (: Skt *kim̥cid*) the new vocalic anlaut spread to *(z-)i* 'what' (< $*k^w id$) and to $*k^w o$- > **kʻo* → *o*; cf. Kölligan (2006). Alternatively, $*k^w imk^w id$ may have resulted in **čʻinčʻ* 'something', which was reanalysed as **čʻ-inčʻ* 'nothing'; cf. Pedersen (1906: 385) with reference to Bugge (1897: 58). The same might apply to *erb* 'when', if from $*k^w e\text{-}b^h rV$- (cf. *erbemn* 'sometimes', *erbêkʻ* 'sometimes, ever'), i.e. **čʻerb* 'when; sometimes, ever' → **čʻ-erb* 'never' → *erb*, if the form is to be equated with Gr. ὄφρα (**(H)i̯o-*b^h*r̥-tʔ*) and Toch. A *kupre(ne)*, B *kwri* < $*k^w i\text{-}b^h r\text{-}en[\text{-}en]$. Cf. Hackstein (2000: 180); doubts in Hübschmann (1897: 443).

derive the form, most of which apply some irregular and otherwise unattested sound change:[50] while Solta (1960: 193–4) remained sceptical about the relationship of *nêr* to its supposed cognates in other languages, Winter (1965*b*: 114) assumed a development **i̯en-* > *en-* > *in-*, without discussing further questions like ablaut, development of the word-internal laryngeal, etc. Similarly, Pisani (1966: 228–9) proposed a development **i̯* > *h* > Ø (: **i̯eneter* > **hinei̯r* > **hnēr* > *nêr*). Hamp (1966) assumed a metathesis of **in* > *ni̯* (: **i̯enh$_2$tēr* > **i̯enatēr* > **i̯inatēr* > **i̯nai̯r* > **ni̯ai̯r* > *nêr*, with **i̯ai̯* > *ê* as in **ti-ai̯r* 'lord' > *têr*, cf. *ti-kin* 'lady'), for which there are no other examples. The same goes for Klingenschmitt's assumption of a metathesis (*apud* Tremblay 2003: 158 n. 199) **i̯inai̯ir* > **nii̯ai̯ir*. Different solutions have been proposed for the development of the word-internal laryngeal as well: while Schmitt (1996), who posits *#*Hi̯-* > #*i̯-* vs. *#*i̯-* > #*dž-*,[51] assumes **Hi̯enh$_2$tēr* > **i̯enatēr*, followed by assimilation to **i̯eneter* > **i̯nei̯r* > **nei̯r* > *nêr*, Olsen (1999: 190–1) proposes loss of laryngeal in **Hi̯enh$_2$tēr* > **i̯entēr* > **i̯inēr* > **i̯nēr* > **nir*, from which a new nominative *nêr* was created (although a paradigm **nir*, gen. **nri*, would have been perfectly acceptable). In a similar manner, Ravnaes and Kortlandt start from an original non-nominative form: Ravnaes (1991: 4 and n. 1) *apud* Schmitt (1996) from an acc. sg. **i̯inai̯eran* > **i̯nēran* > *nêr*, Kortlandt (1997: 7–8), who assumes regular loss of *#/i̯/ in Armenian, from nom. sg. **i̯enh$_2$tēr* > **indir*, acc. sg. **i̯enh$_2$term̥* > **inderan*, gen. sg. **i̯n̥h$_2$tros* > **anau̯ro*, after which nom. sg. **inir*, acc. sg. **ineran*, gen. sg. **inau̯r*, and finally acc./nom. sg. **inei̯ir* > *nêr*.

Apart from these explanations there are further possibilities, if one wants to uphold the etymological relationship with *(H)i̯enh$_2$ter-*:

(a) analogical loss of /i̯/ in a preform **i̯inei̯r*, in which **i̯-* was reinterpreted as a non-phonemic glide before /i/ (cf. the case of *(y)ašt* < MIran. *yašt*, place name *(Y)aštišat*)

(b) resyllabification in the zero-grade **Hi̯n̥H-ter-* → **HinH-ter-* > **in(a)i̯er-* > **əner-*[52]

[50] Cf. the summarizing discussions in Olsen (1999: 190–1) and Tremblay (2003: 158 n. 199).

[51] Further examples for a development **Hi̯-* > *i̯-* are lacking, though. A case in point could be the relative pronoun **Hi̯o-(te)ro-* > *or*, which might be a derivative of the demonstrative stem **Hei/i-*; but *or* is more likely to go back to **k^{w}o-(te)ro-* (cf. above). The analysis with **H-* would be matched by Pinault's interpretation of the word as **h$_1$i̯-en-h$_2$-ter-* 'belonging to the group of those acquired by the household by means of exchange' (cf. **h$_1$ai̯-* 'take, acquire', cf. Pinault 2005 and 2007). Similarly Cuny (1943: 66) proposed a preform **i̯n(ə)er-* with loss of /i̯/.

[52] Cf. already J̌ahowkyan (1982: 214 n. 42, '**ineter* > **nei̯r* > *ner*').

(c) assimilation **i̯enHter-* > **nenHter-*, zero grade **nnHter-*, simplified to **nHter-*

(d) regular loss of /i̯/ before /i/ (: **i̯en-* > **i̯in-* > **in-* > **ən-* > **n-*).

Finally, one might come back to Solta's position and question whether *nêr* is actually related to Skt *yātar-*, etc. Again there are various possibilities, including forms starting with /p/ or /s/:

(a) **pen-tēr* > **(h)indir* > **ənir* > **nir* with analogical nom. sg. *nêr* (as in Olsen's scenario) or from the acc. **pentérm̥* > **hindéran* > **ənéra(n)* > *ner.* The etymon would be that of Lat. *penus, -oris* n., *penus, -ūs* m. 'food', *penes* 'belonging to, at, possessed by', *penitus* 'inside', *Penātes* 'house gods', etc., thus 'the one belonging to the house (by marriage)'

(b) **sen-tēr* or **sen-terā* 'the older one' > **hinir* > **ənir* > **nir* or **hinera* > **əner* > **ner*, which seems unlikely semantically

(c) connection with Ved. *nanā* 'mother', *nánāndar-* 'husband's sister, sister-in-law': a preform **nana* may have been remade into **na-tēr* after the model of the other kinship terms (and as probably in Proto-Indo-European in the case of 'mother', **mātēr*, if originally a *Lallwort*) and then developed via **nai̯ir* > **nai̯r* > *nêr*, or, starting from **ne(ne)-*, **ne-tēr* > **nei̯ir* > *nêr* (cf. Pashto *ndror* 'husband's sister' < **nanandar-*).[53]

ors 'hunt; hunted animal, game' has usually been connected either with Lat. *porcus* '(young) pig'[54] or Gr. πόρκος 'fish-trap' (Pl.+),[55] i.e. **pork̂o-*. Martirosyan (2010: 544) sees a better semantic fit in Gr. ζόρξ, δόρξ, δορκάς, etc. 'roe, deer' (: MW *iwrch* 'roe-deer') < **i̯ork̂o-*, which he assumes to have meant 'wild animal, game'. None of these proposals can do without the assumption of semantic specializations or generalizations, which are of course always possible. A further possibility is to connect *ors* with Gr. ἕρκος 'enclosure, fence, net, toils' (cf. Pind. *Nem.* 3. 51 κτείνοντ' ἐλάφους ἄνευ κυνῶν δολίων θ' ἑρκείων 'slaying deer without dogs or deceitful nets') and ἑρκοθηρικός 'hunting with the net' (Pl. *Soph.* 220c), ὁρκάνη 'fence', and probably ὅρκος m. 'oath' (*'binding word'?). **sork̂o-* would equally well yield Arm. *ors*, and may have meant either 'fencing in, enclosure', which developed via 'hunting ground' to 'hunt', or 'laying traps' *vel sim.*, whence 'hunt'.

[53] Cf. Tremblay (2003: 89–90). According to Morgenstierne (2003: 58) the Pashto form might be an early loan from Indic.

[54] Cf. Ačaṙyan (1971–9: iii. 588), Clackson (1994: 164).

[55] Solta (1960: 428), Olsen (1999: 13).

The etymology of *êg, igi* 'female' (*i-/a*-stem) (: Gr. θῆλυς 'female') has so far remained obscure; Olsen (1999: 946) classifies it as a loanword of unknown origin. Martirosyan (2010: 276) ventures a connection with Skt *yoṣā-* f. 'girl, young woman' and reconstructs a pre-Arm. form **i̯eu̯s-ih₂/i̯eh₂-* or **i̯eu̯s-it-* (: Skt *yoṣit-* 'girl, young woman'), which would have developed via **i̯eu̯(h)i-* > **ei̯u̯i-* > *êg*. Apart from the question of the loss of initial /i̯/, there do not seem to be further examples for *i*-epenthesis after /e/, as opposed to the well-known cases after /a/ (**h_2nēr* > **anir* > **ai̯nir* > *ayr* 'man'; **ali̯o-* 'other' > *ayl*, etc.) and probably after /o/ (*t'oyl* 'weak, sloppy' < **tolh₂i-*; *boyl* 'company, assembly' < **bʰoli-* ∼ *bolor* 'round; all'?),[56] except in connection with sibilants and affricates (*êš* 'donkey' < **eyš* < **h₁eḱu̯o-*; *mêǰ* 'middle' < **meyǰ* < **medʰi̯o-*). Another possibility might be to connect *êg* with the root **pei̯H-* 'to swell (with milk)', as in Gr. πίων, πίειρα, Skt m. *pīvan-*, f. *pīvarī-* 'fat', Skt *payas-* 'milk', Av. *paēman-* 'mother's milk', Lith. *pýti* 'to lactate', and probably OS *fēmea* 'woman', ON *feima* 'girl', OE *faemne* 'virgin, maid, woman'. A pre-Arm. **poi̯H-u̯-eh₂* would most probably develop via **poi̯u̯ā* (with regular loss of /H/ in the context /oRHC/) > **(h)êga* > *êg*.[57] The closest formal equivalent may be Gr. πόᾱ 'grass', Lith. *píeva*, Latv. *piẽva* 'meadow', which may be transferred epithets 'the fat (grass)'.[58]

9.6 Voiced and voiceless /h/ in Modern Armenian

Weitenberg (1986) has shown that a voiced /h/ that occurs in some modern Armenian dialects can be traced back to the glide /y/ in Classical Armenian; cf. the data from the dialects of Šatax and Muš (Table 9.2).[59]

Table 9.2 Šatax and Muš evidence for Classical Armenian forms with /y/

Classical	Šatax	Muš
owm 'to whom?'	–	*h'um*
owsti 'whence?'	*h'ust*	*h'ust*
owr 'where?'	*[dor]*	*h'ur*

56 Cf. Olsen (1999: 795–8).

57 This seems preferable, if /u̯/ > /g/ is regular only before /a, o/ (cf. Olsen 1999: 787), to a preform **poi̯H-u̯-ih₂*, which would immediately yield the Arm. *i*-stem (> **oi̯gi* > *êg*).

58 Skt *yoṣā-* could be an adj. 'young' < **(h₂)i̯eu̯-s-eh₂*, from an *s*-stem **(h₂)i̯eu̯-os/es-* (like *vatsá-* 'calf' from **u̯et-os/es-*) built on **h₂oi̯u-/h₂i̯eu̯-s*.

59 Cf. also Ačaṙyan (1909: 49).

This allows us to reconstruct early by-forms with initial /y/ to those attested in Classical Armenian without /y/ in cases where the modern dialects show voiced /h/, e.g. **y-aysôr* beside *aysôr* 'today'. As Weitenberg (1986: 97) points out, in the majority of these cases we may be dealing with the preposition *y-* which was prefixed to words with spatial and temporal meaning. It does not seem to be necessary to assume higher antiquity for these forms than Classical Armenian.[60]

9.7 Summary

The good etymologies seem to point to a development of PIE */i̯/ > Arm. /dž/ in word-initial position. The amount of analogical change and/or borrowings that have to be assumed under different assumptions seems to be much higher.[61] Arm. *nêr* could speak in favour of loss of /i̯/ before /i/, but as long as no further examples can be adduced, this must remain an open question.

[60] Weitenberg (1986: 99) considers the possibility of tracing these forms back to Proto-Indo-European, especially **i̯ur* and **i̯or*. The lack of these forms in the classical language and the ensuing necessity to explain the attested forms *owr*, *owm*, *owst* as secondary speak against this. Weitenberg (1986: 99) assumes a morphophonemic development as in *ašt* from *yašt*, where *y-* was reinterpreted as the preposition *i/y-*. But the lack of any variants with **y* in the case of *owm* etc. in the classical language, in contrast to the case of *(y)ašt*, makes this unlikely. In Weitenberg (1997: 48) the form Muš *h̯‘ur* 'where?' is explained as stemming from 'Class. *yur* (= *i ur*)'.

[61] E.g. *ǰan* 'effort, zeal' as an Iranian loanword (Martirosyan 2010: 556), although Av. and OP *yāna-* 'request, favour' differs in meaning; analogical influence of **i* on *inč‘*. *ǰowr* 'water' is not treated in Martirosyan (2010).

10

Schrijver's rules for British and Proto-Celtic *-*ou̯*- and *-*uu̯*- before a vowel

NICHOLAS ZAIR

10.1 Introduction[1]

It is commonly accepted that *-*ou̯*- (from *-*eu̯*- and *-*ou̯*-) and *-*uu̯*- fell together as *-*ou̯*- in Proto-Celtic before a vowel (thus Morris Jones 1913: 103, Cowgill 1985*b*: 20–2, McCone 1996: 55;[2] see Schrijver 1995: 326–8 for full bibliography). However, until recently the wide range of apparent reflexes of this *-*ou̯*- in Welsh was problematic: cf. **tou̯e* > MW *teu* 'yours', **lou̯ero*- > MW *llawer* 'large number, enough', **suu̯ano*- > MW *huan* 'sunlight'.

In a thorough and meticulous examination of the evidence Schrijver (1995: 326–45) argues that the different results in Welsh depend on the position of the Proto-British accent and the quality of the vowel following the *-*ou̯*-/-*uu̯*-

[1] This article is dedicated to John Penney, whose talk at an Oxford open day first inspired my interest in philology. I owe much to his teaching and advice. Peter Schrijver generously hosted me in Utrecht, discussed the present work with me at an early stage, and provided me with a pre-publication copy of his article on Old British. Paul Russell read an earlier draft and provided helpful comments and suggestions. I am most grateful to them both. They do not necessarily agree with my views, and remaining errors and infelicities are of course my own. The research was carried out while in receipt of a Scatcherd European Scholarship from the University of Oxford and the Sir John Rhŷs Studentship at Jesus College, Oxford.

[2] Except where followed by *-*i*-. See section 10.2.

cluster. Schrijver's discussion of the question is perceptive,[3] and the position of the Proto-British accent did indeed play a key role in the development of **-ou̯-* and **-uu̯-*. However, it will be argued below that the variation in Welsh is better explained as reflecting the preservation of original **-ou̯-* and **-uu̯-* separately into Proto-British.

The other Celtic languages provide very slim evidence for the reflexes of **-uu̯-* and **-ou̯-*. Surprisingly little can be taken from Irish, as noted by Uhlich (1995: 19–20). This is because even if **-uu̯-* had been preserved, **-uu̯a-* and **-uu̯o-* would both have given **-ou̯a-* by a rule which lowered high vowels when followed by **-a-* or **-o-* in the next syllable. Conversely, **-ou̯i-* and **-ou̯u-* would have given **-uu̯i-*, **-uu̯u-* by raising of **-o-* by high vowels in the following syllable (McCone 1996: 110–11). Only before **-e-* can **-ou̯-* and **-uu̯-* be distinguished. The sole good example is OIr. *oäc* 'young' < early OIr. *oëc* < **i̯ou̯enko-* < **i̯uu̯anko-* < **h_2i̯u-h_3n̥-k̂o-* (cf. Goth. *juggs*, Skt *yuvaśáḥ* 'young', Lat. *iuuencus* 'young, young man, young bull'). The raising of **-ank-* to **-enk-* is prior to lowering of **-u-* by **-a-* in the following syllable (McCone 1996: 74–5, 106–7; see Sims-Williams 2003: 296–301 for a chronology of Irish sound changes). Other examples mentioned by Uhlich (1995: 20 n. 52) are doubtful, such as McCone's (1991: 132) derivation of OIr. *boí* '(s)he was' from **buu̯et* (see Schumacher 2004: 251–4 for objections and an alternative derivation).

Irish therefore supports the hypothesis that **-ou̯-* and **-uu̯-* fell together as **-ou̯-*, but with the most slender evidence. Gaulish is problematic for different reasons, since it demonstrates three different reflexes of **-ou̯-* and **-uu̯-*; cf. *lugoues* 'Lugs' < **lug-eu̯-es*, *δρυίδης* 'druid' < **dru-u̯id-*, *Lauenus* (personal name) < **lou̯-eno-*. The Gaulish evidence is collected and discussed in the appendix, but it is too uncertain to be used. That of Celtiberian and Lepontic is too scanty and etymologically unclear and will not be considered here.

10.2 Schrijver's analysis of **-uu̯-* and **-ou̯-*

The British evidence is clearly crucial for deciding the question of the Celtic reflexes of **-ou̯-* and **-uu̯-*. Schrijver proposes that **-ou̯-* and **-uu̯-*, which had fallen together as **-ou̯-* in Proto-Celtic, regularly gave Middle Breton *-(a)ou-*, Modern Breton *-aou-*, Old Cornish *-ou-*, Middle Cornish *-ow-*. The usual reflexes of this **-ou̯-* in Welsh and the Vannetais dialect of Breton were OW

[3] For example, he observes that singulatives such as MW *cneuen* 'nut' beside *cneu* 'nuts' cannot be used as evidence because they carried over the vocalism from the base form; this point had not been noted by e.g. Jackson (1953: 370–2, 384–5).

-ou-, MW *-eu-*, ModW *-au-*, Vann. *-eu-*. For example, the nom. pl. ending **-eu̯es* > **-ou̯es* gave OW *-ou*, MW *-eu*, ModW *-au*, MBret. *-(a)ou*, ModBret. *-où*,[4] Vann. *-eu*, MCorn. *-ow; *duu̯o* gave OW *dou*, MW *deu*, ModW *dau*, OBret. *dou, dau*, MBret. *d(a)ou*, ModBret. *daou*, Vann. *deu*, MCorn. *dow, dew*[5] 'two' (cf. Lat. *duo*).

Other results of **-ou̯-* and **-uu̯-* > **-ou̯-* reflect conditioned reflexes in various environments. The earliest was final *i*-affection, as in **dru-u̯id-s* > MW *dryw* 'druid, seer', **luu̯ī* > MW *llyw* , OCorn. *leu*, LCorn. *lew* 'rudder', MBret. *leuyaff*, ModBret. *levian̄* 'to steer'. I follow Schrijver (1995: 338–40) in taking this development as an example of regular *i*-affection in British Celtic rather than the retention of **-uu̯-* before **-i-* in Proto-Celtic, as supposed by McCone.[6]

In Welsh and Vannetais, but not in Cornish or the other dialects of Breton, **-ou̯-/-uu̯-* > **-ou̯-* was subject to further conditioned changes. Before **-ă-* we find Welsh *-u-* and Vannetais *-o(h)-*: thus **suu̯ano-* > MW, ModW *huan* 'sun, sunlight; shining, bright, sunny'; **ku/ou̯annV-* > MW, ModW *cuan*, Vann. *kohann* 'owl'. OBret. *couann*, MBret. *couhenn*, *caoüen*, ModBret. *kaouenn* 'owl' of course show the same reflex as in other environments.

Before any other vowel, **-ou̯-/-uu̯-* > **-ou̯-* in the Proto-British antepenultimate syllable gave Welsh *-aw-: *lou̯eno-* > MW *llawen* 'joyful, happy, glad'; **ko/uu̯ot-* > MW *cawad* 'gust, shower' (this etymology is discussed at greater length in section 10.6 below). Vannetais shows two different results: **lou̯eno-* > Vann. *leùen* 'merry, jovial, happy' beside **ko/uu̯ot-* > *kohad* 'gust, attack, shower'. The Cornish and Breton cognates are MBret. *louen*, MCorn. *lowen* and OBret. *couatou*, MBret. *couhat*, ModBret. *kaouad*, OCorn. *couat*, MCorn. *cowas*.[7]

In some respects Schrijver's analysis is surely correct; in particular, the differing reflexes of **-ou̯-* and **-uu̯-* are indeed dependent on the position of the Proto-British accent. However, other parts of it are problematic: for

[4] The development of MBret. *-(a)ou* to ModBret. *-où* is regular in an unstressed syllable; the original Proto-British accent, which was word-final after apocope, was retracted to the new penultimate syllable in both South-West British and West British (Jackson 1967: 262).

[5] Expected *dow* is found only in composition (Schrijver 1995: 331 n. 1).

[6] Since, as we shall see, **-ou̯-* and **-uu̯-* did fall together as **-ou̯-* in the original British penultimate syllable, I assume that *i*-affection affected both in the same way. If Welsh *Cernyw*, Cornish *Kernow*, Breton *Kernev* 'Cornwall' come from **kornou̯(i̯)ī* (Schrijver 1995: 297), this is the only good evidence for *i*-affection of original **-ou̯-*. Lat. *Iouis* > MW *ieu*, ModW *Iau*, MBret. *iaou*, ModBret. *yaou*, MCorn. *yow* 'Thursday' shows the same reflex as **-ou̯-* before other vowels, rather than *i*-affection. However, as Schrijver (1995: 340 n. 1) points out, it is possible that *ieu* etc. really came from *Iouem* rather than *Iouis*.

[7] Some of the forms discussed here have Welsh alternative forms in which [u̯] is replaced by [v], e.g. *cafod*, *i(e)fanc*. On this variation, see Russell (2003: 41–3).

example, the development of **-ou̯-* in Welsh being dependent both on its position in the word and on the quality of the following vowel. Given the relatively small amount of evidence, it may just be a coincidence that all examples of Welsh *-u-* are followed by **-ā̆-*; if a single governing factor for the Welsh development can be discovered, that ought automatically to be preferred. But even if Schrijver were right about the Welsh environment, his rules do not completely explain the Vannetais developments, which show both *-eù-* and *-oh-* from **-ou̯-* in the penultimate syllable before a vowel other than **-ā̆-*. Again, it would be far preferable if there were a unitary explanation for both the Welsh and Vannetais developments, which otherwise appear too similar to be independent.

MW *cawad* etc. are even more difficult to explain. Schrijver derives them from a preform **ko/uu̯ot-* > **kou̯ot-*, but elsewhere (Schrijver 1995: 116–28) he demonstrates that lenited **-u̯o-* had already given **-u̯a-* in Proto-British (e.g. **k^{w}etu̯ores* > MW *pedwar*, MCorn. *peswar*, OBret. *petguar* 'four'; cf. Gr. τέτταρες, Lat. *quattuor*). As a Proto-British change, this ought to have already affected **kou̯ot-*, giving **kou̯at-* by the time Welsh underwent the changes to **-ou̯-*, whence Welsh †*cuad*. Schrijver (1995: 335) notices this problem, and suggests avoiding it by ordering **-u̯o-* > **-u̯a-* after **-ou̯a-* became **-ʉa-* > MW *-ua-*.[8] But Schrijver also states that **-ʉ-* arises in front of **-ə-*, which developed only in Welsh by epenthesis before **sT-* and from **-ɨ-* < **-i-* in pretonic syllables (Schrijver 2011: 15, 40). According to Schrijver's proposals, this means that the fronting of **-u-* to **-ʉ-* must postdate a purely Welsh development, and therefore cannot also precede the Proto-British change of **-u̯o-* to **-u̯a-*.

10.3 Pretonic **-uu̯-* and **-ou̯-*

The etymology of *cawad* etc. will be quite a complex question, and can be left aside while we take a second look at the Welsh and Vannetais evidence for **-ou̯-* and **-uu̯-*. The first noticeable thing is that one feature connects all the forms which give Welsh *-u-* and Vann. *-oua-* > *-oha-*.[9] The data in question are **suu̯ano-* > MW, ModW *huan* 'sunny', **su(u̯)-V-* > MW *hu-* 'good-', **kuu̯annV-* > MW, ModW *cuan*, Vann. *kohann* 'owl', and **iuu̯anko-* > Vann. *iouank* 'young' (Schrijver 1995: 326–45).

8 The symbols used in this article for British phonemes are those of Schrijver (2011): thus **-ʉ-* for the predecessor of MW *-u-* < **-oi̯-*, **-ou̯-*, and **-u-* before **-β-*, rather than **-ü-* as in Schrijver (1995). The symbol **-ü-* is instead used for the result of *i*-affected **-u-*.

9 The spelling *-oha-* represents a hiatus *-oä-*, after loss of *-u-* intervocalically.

The least reliable of these is **ku̯u̯annV-*, since its root is probably onomatopoeic and subject to continuing deformation (cf. Lith. *kóvas* 'jackdaw', Gr. *καύᾱξ* 'seagull'). However, the comparison with OHG *hūwo* 'owl', while not precisely superimposable on the Celtic form, makes **kuu̯annV-* a possible reconstruction.

The evidence of Vann. *iouank* 'young' < **iuu̯anko-* (cf. OIr. *oäc*, section 10.1 above) is not necessarily reliable, because the Welsh reflex is irregular by any formulation of the reflexes of **-ou̯-* and **-uu̯-*: **iuu̯anko-* > MW *ieuanc*.[10] But the Breton and Cornish forms are perfectly regular with regard to the first syllable (MBret. *youanc*, ModBret. *yaouank*, OCorn. *iouenc*, MCorn. *yowynk*), and the Vannetais reflex matches that of **kuu̯anno-* > *cohann* so is probably also regular.

MW *huan* < **suu̯ano-* reflects either **suh*$_2$*en-o-* or **suh*$_2$*on-o-*, perhaps derived from the original oblique stem of the Indo-European word for 'sun' (cf. Avestan gen. sg. *x*^{v}*əng* 'sun' < **suu̯enos*) via a metathesized secondary zero-grade **suh*$_2$*-* from **sh*$_2$*u-* (cf. OIr. *súil* 'eye' < **suh*$_2$*-l-i-* < **sh*$_2$*u-l-i-*, Gr. *ἠέλιος* 'sun' < **seh*$_2$*u̯-el-i̯o-*).[11]

MW *hu-* < **su-* < **h*$_1$*su-* (cf. Gr. *ἐΰ-*) is found only before vowels (unlike its allomorph *hy-*). As already mentioned, Schrijver states that **su-* develops to MW *hu-* only before a vowel that reflects British **-ă-* or Proto-Welsh **-ə-*. However, the only instance I have been able to find in *GPC* of **su-* before any other vowel which is attested in Middle or early Modern Welsh is MW *hyys* 'edible' < **su-issV-*. Here, *hy-* rather than *hu-* is probably due to *i*-affection. Contrary to Jackson (1953: 590–1, 664–81), internal *i*-affection was a British Celtic change, before the Welsh reduction of pretonic **-i-* and **-u-*, and therefore affected **-u-* in Welsh as in Cornish and Breton (Schrijver 1995: 162–4, 1998: 425–8). Consequently, **-u-* was fronted to **-ü-*, and was included in the Welsh reduction of pretonic **-ü-* > **-ɵ-* > **-ə-* (written *-y-* in Middle Welsh), whence *hyys* [*həɨs*] < **hü-ɨss* < **su-issV-*. When followed by a vowel other than **-i-*, **su-* > *hu-* did not undergo reduction, no doubt because **-u-* had already become **-ʉ-*. In *huynys* 'fine island' < **su-inissV- i*-affection of **-u-* would not be expected because **-i-* became **-ə-* in a pre-pretonic syllable in

[10] The preform **iuu̯anko-* should have given †*iuanc*. Schrijver (1995: 344–5) suggests that the sequence **i̯u-* was not acceptable in the sound system of Welsh. Another possibility is that *ieuanc* was created by analogy with the superlative. Superlative **ieu̯isamos* gave MW *ieuhaf* regularly through **iau̯haμ* with development of **-au̯-* to **-ou̯-* > MW *-eu-* in pretonic syllables (Schrijver 1995: 270–2, 345). Alternatively, initial **i̯-* may have caused dissimilatory lowering of **-ʉu̯-* to give *-eu-*.

[11] For **CIHC-* < **CHIC-* as a Proto-Indo-European rule, see Winter (1965*c*: 192), Mayrhofer (1986: 175). In this article C represents any consonant, T any voiceless stop, R any resonant, H any laryngeal, and I any high vowel.

British Celtic prior to internal _i_-affection (Schrijver 2011: 12).[12] Forms like _huyscein_ 'spreading' must be late formations since the development of a prothetic _*-ə-_ before _*sT-_ occurred only in Welsh. The spread of _hu-_ over _hy-_ is unsurprising since _hu-_ was the usual prevocalic allomorph, _hy-_ appearing mainly before consonants with the exception of the relic form _hyys_.

Turning to MW _-aw-_, Vann. _-eù-_, two preforms are possible for MW _llawen_, Vann. _leùen_ and MW _llawer_. For the former, _llawen_ and Gaulish _Lauenus_ (personal name) point to _*lau̯eno-_, while MCorn. _lowen_, MBret. _louen_ suggest _*lou̯eno-_. The same distinction is found between MW _llawer_ and MCorn. _lower_. Although Schrijver reconstructs _*lou̯eno-_ for _llawen_, _*lau̯eno-_ < _*lh_$_2$_u̯-eno-_ is, on the face of it, more plausible. The root is that of Gr. ἀπολαύω 'have enjoyment of, have benefit of, enjoy' < _*leh_$_2$_u̯-_ (_IEW_ 655, Schrijver 1991: 240–1). Schrijver argues for a remade Celtic root _*leu̯(h_$_2$_)-_ because of MW _golud_ 'riches' from _*u̯o-lou̯-to-_ < _*u̯o-leu̯(h_$_2$_)-to-_ rather than †_golawd_ < _*u̯o-lau̯-to-_ < _*u̯o-leh_$_2$_u-to-_. But _golud_ could reflect an o-grade _*u̯o-loh_$_2$_u-to-_, so Schrijver's reconstruction rests on very little.[13] However, he is right that MCorn. _lowen_, MBret. _louen_ cannot reflect anything other than _*lou̯eno-_, given forms like OCorn. _auhel_, MCorn. _awel_ 'weather, wind, breeze, gale', MBret. _auel, avel_, ModBret. _avel_ 'wind' < _*au̯elā_ (cf. Gr. ἄελλα 'stormy wind, whirlwind') and OBret. _cauel_, MBret. _cauell_, ModBret. _kavell_ 'cradle' < British Latin _*cauellus_. A South-West British rule _*lau̯V-_ > _*lou̯V-_ would be completely _ad hoc_. So, regardless of the precise details of its formation, _*lou̯eno-_ is the more likely reconstruction. This is backed up by MW _llawer_, MCorn. _lower_. Although _IEW_ (655) derives this from _*lau̯ero-_, from the same root as _llawen_, the existence of OIr. _roar, loor, lour_ 'enough, sufficient', _ro·fera_ 'is sufficient' strongly argues for _*ro-u̯er-o-_ > _*lou̯ero-_, with independent dissimilation of _*r . . . r_ to _*l . . . r_ in both British and Irish.

The forms with _-u-_ and _-aw-_ in Welsh show a very simple correlation: all the forms which give _-u-_ probably or possibly reflect earlier _*-uu̯-_. Apart from MW _cawad_, which is presently uncertain, both forms with _-aw-_ reflect earlier _*-ou̯-_. There is less Vannetais evidence, but again a distinction appears: _*lou̯eno-_ > Vann. _leùen_ beside _*kuu̯annV-_ > Vann. _kohann_ 'owl', _*iuu̯anko-_ > Vann. _iouank_.

[12] Original _*-u-_ was reduced to _*-ɵ-_ > _*-ə-_ in pre-pretonic syllables; if this also applied to _*-uu̯-_ we ought to find MW _*hy-ynys_ [_həənɨs_], and _hu-ynys_ must be a later replacement.

[13] And Isaac (2007) argues that tautosyllabic _*-ou̯-_ and _*-au̯-_ fell together, in which case it would not be possible to distinguish between them here.

10.4 Stressed _*-uu̯-_ and _*-ou̯-_

So far we have only examined _*-ou̯-_ > MW _-aw-_, Vann. _-eù-_ and _*-uu̯-_ > MW _-u-_, Vann. _-ou-/-oh-_ in the first syllable of originally trisyllabic words. This clear distinction is lost in originally disyllabic words, where _*-ou̯-_ and _*-uu̯-_ invariably give the same results. Taken from Schrijver (1995: 328–33), the most reliable evidence for (_*-eu̯-_ >) _*-ou̯-_ consists of the original _u_-stem plural ending _*-eu̯es_ > _*-ou̯es_ > OW _-ou_, MW _-eu_, ModW _-au_, MBret. _-ou_, _-aou_, ModBret. _-où_, Vann. _-eu_, MCorn. _-ow_ (cf. Gaul. _-oues_); _*k̂V-k̂lou̯e_ > MW _cigleu_ '(s)he heard' (cf. OIr. _-cúalae_); and _*teu̯e_ > _*tou̯e_ > MW _teu_, ModW _tau_ 'yours' (cf. OIr. _taí_, Skt _táva_). Good evidence for _*-uu̯-_ includes _*knuu̯V-_ > MW _kneu_, ModW _cnau_, OBret. _cnou_, MBret. _kanou_, _cnou_, ModBret. _kraoñ_, Haut Vann. _queneu_ 'nuts', LCorn. _knufan_ (singulative) 'nut' (cf. OIr. _cnú_, Lat. _nux_); _*kruu̯V-_ > MW _creu_, ModW _crau_, MCorn. _crow_ 'gore, blood, slaughter' (cf. OIr. _crú_); and _*duu̯o_ > OW _dou_, MW _deu_, ModW _dau_, OBret. _dou_, _dau_, MBret. _d(a)ou_, ModBret. _daou_, Vann. _deu_, MCorn. _dow_, _dew_ 'two' (cf. Lat. _duo_).

On the basis of this evidence we can conclude that in the Proto-British penultimate syllable _*-ou̯-_ and _*-uu̯-_ fell together. In the Proto-British antepenultimate syllable they remained distinct, giving MW _-aw-_, Vann. _-eù-_ and MW _-u-_, Vann. _-ou-/-oh-_ respectively; in the rest of Breton and in Cornish, the two sounds subsequently fell together, giving MBret. _-(a)ou-_, MCorn. _-ow-_ as in original penultimate syllables. MW _cawad_, Vann. _kohad_ 'gust' are still problematic, and will be discussed in section 10.6.

10.5 Latin loanwords as evidence for _*-uu̯-_ > MW _-aw-_?

Two Latin loan words also pertain to the question of the reflex of _*-uu̯-_: Lat. _construenda_ > ModW _cystrawen_ 'syntax' and Lat. _ruīna_ > ModW _rhewin_ 'ruin'. A third piece of evidence is found in the inscription from Cornwall IGENAVI MEMOR / INGENVI MEMORIA (_CIIC_ 466 = Okasha 1993: no. 23, the first line written in Ogam). According to Jackson (1953: 365–6), these forms reflect a characteristically British Latin development of _*-CuV-_ to _*-Cuu̯V-_ seen also in inscriptional PVVERI (_CIIC_ 327 = _ECMW_ 43), followed by a change of unstressed _*-uu̯-_ to _*-au̯-_.[14] The stress is determined by the Latin rather than the British accent; hence the lack of the change in PVVERI. However, Schrijver considers them to be Welsh words undergoing the change (_*-uu̯-_ >) _*-ou̯-_ > _*-au̯-_ in the

[14] ModW _rhewin_ does not directly attest _*rau̯īna_ rather than _*rou̯īna_, but it cannot come from _ruīna_, which would have given †_rhywin_.

British pretonic syllable. This is quite plausible, since *cystrawen* and *rhewin* are loanwords into Welsh and since 'British' IGENAVI is counterposed to Latin INGENVI which has preserved the Latin spelling.

However, more consideration is necessary before these words are included in our evidence. In Vulgar Latin unstressed **(-)CuV-* (and **(-)CoV-*) usually became **(-)Cu̯V-*; cf. Fr. *janvier* < Lat. *ianuārius*, It. *quagliare* < Lat. *coagulāre*, and '*uacua* non *uaqua*' at *Appendix Probi* 14.[15] After certain consonants, including *-r-*, this **-u̯-* was lost: Lat. *februārius* is found as *febrarias* in Pompeii (*CIL* 4. 4182, 4983, 8820), giving It. *febbraio*; the *Appendix Probi* 208 says '*Februarius*, non *Febrarius*' (Väänänen 1981: 46–7, Smith 1983: 904–5). In principle, therefore, we would probably expect to find *construenda* > †*constrenda* > ModW †*cystren*, *ruīna* > †*rīna* > ModW †*rhin*. Posttonic *-u-* was lost before *-o-* and *-u-*, e.g. *mortus* for *mortuus* at Pompeii (*CIL* 4. 3129, 5279, 5282); IGENVVS in an inscription from Cirencester (Hassall, Wilson, and Wright 1972: 352, Smith 1983: 922) shows the expected development. We might expect to find Latin INGENI in our inscription by analogy with the nominative singular. Alternatively, INGENVI could be a spelling for *ingenu̯ī*, but IGENAVI suggests otherwise.

However, in some other cases **(-)CuV-* did not develop to **(-)Cu̯V-*, e.g. Lat. *ruīna* > It. *rovina*, Old Span. *juvizio* < Lat. *iudicium* (Smith 1983: 917). These are probably learned borrowings from Latin, rather than direct descendants of Vulgar Latin; the same explanation may also apply to *cystrawen* and *rhewin* (the semantics of *cystrawen* certainly suggest a learned borrowing). IGENAVI also appears in a Latinizing environment, since it is accompanied in the inscription by its Latin equivalent; the genitive singular ending -I is certainly a Latinism because apocope has already occurred (MEMOR < MEMORIA).

The native evidence for a different reflex of **-ou̯-* and **-uu̯-* in inherited words in Welsh and Vannetais is quite clear. If the Latin evidence is part of the Welsh development, then (learned) Latin **-uu̯-* was evidently treated differently from inherited **-uu̯-*. This is easily explained if inherited **-uu̯-* had already given **-ʉu̯-* in Old West British before the Latin words were borrowed: in that case it is very likely that the Old West British pronunciation of Latin **-uu̯-* was nearer to **-ou̯-* than to **-ʉu̯-*, and consequently shared in the development of **-ou̯-* to **-au̯-*.[16]

[15] Using Powell's (2007) edition of the *Appendix*.

[16] A pronunciation of Latin **-uu̯-* as **-ou̯-* is already implicit in Schrijver's treatment of these words, since he supposes that original **-uu̯-* had fallen together with **-ou̯-* in Proto-Celtic, well before the Latin loanwords.

However, the possibility should not be ruled out that the development of Latin _*-uu̯-_ to _*-au̯-_ should be kept separate from the Welsh change. IGENAV- ought to go back to _*ingenúu̯us_ if stressed according to British rules, but the development to _*-au̯-_ only occurs in unstressed syllables. If, as supposed by Jackson, the British Latin development of _*-uu̯-_ to _*-au̯-_ is separate and relies on the Latin accent, the development of _*ingénuu̯us_ to IGENAV- would be expected. But this word is problematic more generally for other reasons: the inscription containing it comes from Cornwall rather than Wales, and the non-Latin part may in fact be Irish (cf. OIr. _mebuir_ < _memoria_; thus Jackson 1953: 141, Sims-Williams 2003: 221, 315). Although it may be that IGENAVI in this conceivably South-West British or Irish inscription reflects a West British pronunciation of an originally Latin name, this is by no means certain.

Whatever the explanation for the Latin loanwords which show a development of _*-uu̯-_ to _*-au̯-_, they do not provide a strong argument against the native evidence for the retention of the distinction between _*-ou̯-_ and _*-uu̯-_.

10.6 MW _cawad_ and the South-West British treatment of _*-au̯a-_

The correct reconstruction of MW _cawad_, Vann. _kohad_, MBret. _couhat_, MCorn. _cowas_ remains to be considered. Either _*kuu̯otV-_ or _*kou̯otV-_ would give the attested Breton and Cornish forms, but _*kuu̯otV-_ > _*kuu̯atV-_ would have given MW †_cuad_ (cf. _huan_ < _*suu̯ano-_), while _*kou̯otV-_ > _*kou̯atV-_ would have given Vann. †_keùad_ (cf. _leùen_ < _*lou̯eno-_). Indo-European cognates include Lat. _caurus_ 'north-west wind' < _*k̂h_$_1$_u̯-er-o-_, OCS _sěverъ_ 'north' < _*k̂eh_$_1$_u̯-er-o-_, perhaps OE _scūr_, Goth. _skūra_ 'shower, gust' < _*(s)k̂uh_$_1$_-rV-_ (_IEW_ 597, Schrijver 1995: 337, de Vaan 2008: 100).[17] There remains one reconstruction which might give the attested forms: I suggest that _cawad_ etc. come from _*k̂h_$_1$_u̯-otV-_ > _*kau̯otV-_ > _*kau̯atV-_.[18] This would obviously give MW _cawad_,

[17] Russell (2003: 43) takes the Welsh variant _cawod_ as original, reconstructing _*kom-pot-_, the root being the same as in ModW _odi_ 'fall'. But this is quite unlikely, for several reasons. Apart from a single Middle Welsh text which has _cafod_, all the earliest attestations of the word have _cawad_ (variously spelt): _GPC_ (443), Lloyd-Jones (1931–63: i. 117), and all the Brittonic languages attest to _*-a-_ in the second syllable. Formally, we would have to assume, _ad hoc_, that _*-mp-_ gave British _*-mu̯-_ (which would give _*-u̯-_ regularly).

[18] There was a general British change of _*-oRa-_ > _*-aRa-_ (cf. MW, ModBret. _taran_ 'thunder' < _*toranV-_; Schrijver 1995: 94–7). According to Schrijver (1995: 99–100), _*-ou̯a-_ did not take part in this change, but as will be seen directly below, his example of retention of _*-ou̯a-_ reflects dissimilated _*-ɔu̯a-_ < _*-au̯a-_ (and of course forms like MW _cuan_ never went through a stage †_kou̯annV-_). Therefore, depending on the relative chronology, it would also be possible to reconstruct _*kou̯h_$_1$_-ot-_ > _*kou̯at-_ > _*kau̯at-_.

but the development to Vann. _kohad_, MBret. _couhat_, MCorn. _cowas_ requires explanation. A dissimilation of the first vowel of _*-au̯a-_ > _*-ɔu̯a-_ to give Vann. _-o(h)a-_, MBret. _-ou(h)a-_, MCorn. _-owa-_ is phonetically plausible: it would be easy for the labiality of the _*-u̯-_ to be misanalysed as belonging to the preceding vowel, and this would be further reinforced by dissimilatory pressure. A similar spread of labiality in the other direction can be seen during the course of the history of Welsh, whence the variant _cawod_ (cf. _pedwor_, _pedwar_ 'four'; Morris Jones 1913: 38).

The use of the symbol -ɔ- here requires some explanation. Inherited _*-ā-_ > _*-ɔ̄-_ > _*-ɔ-_ in Proto-British normally gave MW _-aw-_, MBret. _-eu-_, MCorn. _-u-_, _-e-_, _-eu-_ (e.g. _*b^{h}rātēr_ > MW _brawd_, MBret. _breuzr_ 'brother', _*lāmā_ > MCorn. _luf_ etc. 'hand'). However, before _*-u̯-_ it did not undergo this development, or fall together with original _*-ou̯-_, instead giving OW _-ou_, MW _-o_, e.g. MW _clo_ 'lock, bolt' < _*klɔ̄u̯V-_ < Lat. _clāuus_ or _clāuis_. In Breton and Cornish it fell together with _*-ou̯-_, e.g. MBret. _clou_ (Schrijver 2011: 26). It is assumed here that in Vannetais, as in Welsh, it remained distinct from _*-ou̯-_.

The proposed dissimilation of _*-au̯a-_ > _*-ɔu̯a-_ in South-West British is not purely _ad hoc_. MBret. _louazr_, ModBret. _laouer_, Vann. _louer_ 'trough' are derived by Schrijver (1995: 99, 335) from _*lou̯atro-_ < _*lou̯h$_1$-tro-_. However, there is good reason to reconstruct _*leu̯h$_3$-tro-_ instead. Firstly, nouns formed with the instrument suffix _*-tro-_ had _e_-grade root (Olsen 1988: 4). Secondly, an Indo-European rule ('Saussure's effect') deleted laryngeals in the environment _*-oRH-_ (Rasmussen 1989_b_: 175–85, Nussbaum 1997). The root is actually _*leu̯h$_3$-_ (_LIV_ 418), so _*lou̯h$_3$-tro-_ would have given _*lou̯tro-_ > MBret. _†luzr_. Mycenaean Greek _re-wo-to-ro-_ = *λεϝοτρο- attests the original form _*leu̯h$_3$-tro-_; Homeric Greek λοετρόν 'bath' is the result of a metathesis of _*-eRo-_ to _*-oRe-_ also found in Gr. ἐστόρεσα 'I spread' < _*-sterosa_ < _*sterh$_3$-s-_ (Cowgill 1965: 158–9, Peters 1987: 289–90 n. 1).

A form _*leu̯h$_3$-tro-_> _*leu̯atro-_ would give _*lau̯atro-_ in Proto-Celtic by Joseph's Law, whereby _*-eRa-_ became _*-aRa-_ (Joseph 1982, Schrijver 1995: 73–93). ON _lauðr_, OE _lēaþor_ 'foam' from _*lou̯atro-_ or _*lau̯atro-_ probably reflect a loanword from Celtic at this stage (Cowgill 1965: 158–9). (Late) Gaul. _lautro_ gl. _balneo_ provides further evidence for a Celtic preform _*lau̯atro-_, but this is very unreliable because the reflexes of _*-Vu̯-_ clusters are so uncertain in Gaulish (and it is not clear how many of the words in the eighth-century Endlicher's Glossary are actually Gaulish). More reliable is the Old British place name _Lauatris_ (Rivet and Smith 1982: 384), but it is just possible that this is really a Latin word: it has Latin morphology and, although the usual Latin word for bath is _lauābrum_, Lat. _lātrīna_ 'washing-place' implies the existence of _*lauātrum_.

A similar dissimilation of *-*au̯a*- to that of South-West British also seems to have occurred in Irish. Thus OIr. *loäthar* > *lóthar* 'basin, trough' shows the expected reflex of **lou̯atro*- rather than **lau̯atro*-, which would give †*luäthar* > †*lúathar* (cf. gen. sg. **au̯etos* > **auu̯eθa* > **auu̯eθ* > **auëθ* > **uëth* > *úath* 'poetic inspiration'; Uhlich 1995: 17 n. 35). More evidence for the regular result of *-*au̯a*- comes from OIr. *coär* 'warrior',[19] which is cognate with MW *caur*, ModW *cawr* 'giant', Gaul. *Cauarius, Cauarillus*, Galatian *Καυαρος* (personal name), perhaps ModBret. *keur*-, *ker*- in *keur-eug* 'saumon coureur', *ker-luz* 'sea-loach' (cf. Skt *śávīra*- 'powerful'; Schrijver 1995: 98). Here the existence of original Proto-Celtic **kau̯aro*- < **keu̯aro*- < **k̂eu̯H-ro*- is demonstrated by the Welsh and Breton reflex of **kau̯ro*- < **kau̯aro*- by an early syncope (Schrijver 1995: 16–22, 87–101); the second *-*a*- (but not necessarily the first) is demonstrated by the Gaulish forms. A reconstruction **k̂ou̯H-ro*- is further ruled out by Saussure's effect, which would produce **k̂ou̯ro*-. Since the change in the first vowel of *-*au̯a*- is phonetically well founded, its occurrence independently in both South-West British and Irish is not too great a coincidence.

10.7 Conclusion

Schrijver's observation that the development of the reflexes of original *-*uu̯*- and *-*ou̯*- was dependent on the position of the Proto-British accent is crucially important to our understanding of the problem. However, his addition of following *-*ă̄*- as a further conditioning factor complicates the issue and fails coherently to explain the Vannetais reflexes. Furthermore, the etymology of MW *cawad* 'gust, shower' cannot be adequately reconstructed using his rules. A far better explanation can be provided if we accept that Proto-British had inherited the separate sequences *-*ou̯*- and *-*uu̯*-.

We can reconstruct the following chronological developments. In Proto-British, stressed *-*úu̯*- fell together with *-*óu̯*-. In West British, the vowel of pretonic *-*ou̯*- was lowered to *-*au̯*- > MW -*aw*- (MW *llawen*). Remaining stressed *-*óu̯*- developed to Old Welsh -*ou*, Middle Welsh -*eu*. The vowel of remaining pretonic *-*uu̯*- underwent dissimilation from following *-*u̯*- in both West and South-West British, being fronted in West British to *-*ʉu̯*- > MW -*u*- (MW *huan* < **suu̯ano*-). In South-West British *-*ou̯*- developed the same way in stressed and unstressed syllables, giving MBret. -*ou*-, MCorn. -*ow*-, Vann. -*eù*-

[19] On *coär* as the correct form, see Uhlich (1995: 23–4 nn. 66, 67).

(MBret. *louen*, Vann. *leùen*, MCorn. *lowen* < *loueno-*). The vowel of remaining pretonic *-uu̯- was lowered to *-ɔu̯-; the same vowel arose by dissimilation in *-au̯a- > *-ɔu̯a-. The sequence *-ɔu̯- fell together with *-ou̯- in most of Breton and in Cornish to give MBret. -ou-, MCorn. -ow- (MBret. *youanc*, MCorn. *yowynk* < *iu̯u̯anko-*), but avoided the fronting that occurred to *-ou̯- in Vannetais and gave Vann. -ou- > -oh- (*iouank*).

The different developments according to syllable position must be seen in light of the British accent, which before the time of the apocope of final syllables had come to fall on the penultimate syllable (Schrijver 1995: 16–22). Differing reflexes according to accentual position are common in the British languages (e.g. *-i̯- > *-d̯- after *-i- occurs only when preceding *-i- was stressed). It may seem counter-intuitive that lack of stress should be associated with the maintenance of the distinction between *-ou̯- and *-uu̯-, since it often leads to neutralization of vowel quality. However, lower vowels tend to be perceived as less rounded, and lack of stress is likely to further reduce rounding (for further discussion and references see Vine 2006: 229–30). Therefore, it is phonetically natural that the difference between *-uu̯- and *-ou̯- should be maintained in unstressed syllables, even when it is lost in stressed ones. It may even be maximized, as in the further lowering and unrounding of *-ou̯- to *-au̯- in Welsh, which has an exact parallel in Proto-Italic, where Thurneysen-Havet's Law caused *-ou̯- to become *-au̯- in unstressed position (Vine 2006). In South-West British, the subsequent loss of the distinction between *-ɔu̯- < *-uu̯- and *-ou̯- may be connected with the retraction of the accent onto the penultimate syllable (the old pre-apocope antepenult) in Breton and Cornish; in Vannetais, where final stress was maintained (Jackson 1967: 79), so was the distinction between *-ɔu̯- and *-ou̯-.

It has now been demonstrated that the British evidence can only be satisfactorily explained by accepting an inherited distinction between *-ou̯- and *-uu̯-. This clearly shows that *-ou̯- and *-uu̯- before a vowel must have remained separate in Proto-Celtic, and that in pretonic syllables this distinction was retained all the way into Welsh and Vannetais, although it was lost in Cornish and the other dialects of Breton. The very slim evidence of Old Irish suggests that *-uu̯- had become *-ou̯- in that language, at least in some environments (early OIr. *oëc* from *i̯ou̯enko- < *i̯u̯u̯anko-*): this must have been an innovation. The evidence of Gaulish is collected in an appendix below; although nothing firm can be said about its treatment of *-ou̯- and *-uu̯-, it may be that they had fallen together here too.

Appendix: Gaulish evidence for *-*ou̯*- and *-*uu̯*-

The Gaulish forms which are likely to reflect *-*ou̯*- are:[20]

- nom. pl. -*ou̯es* in *Lugoues*
- **Oui*- 'sheep' as a name element in forms like *Ouio-rix*, *Oi-menus* (cf. Lat. *ouis*)
- *Bouus*, *Bouo*-, *Bουι*- 'cow' as a name/name element (cf. Gr. *βοῦς*)
- *Lauenus* 'merry' as a name (cf. MW *llawen*).

Those likely to reflect *-*uu̯*- are:

- *Κνουιλλα* 'little nut' as a name (cf. MW *cneu*)
- Gallo-Gr. *δρυίδης*, Gallo-Lat. *druides* (nom. pl.) 'druid' (cf. MW *dryw*)
- *Iuuantus*, *Iouanti* (gen. sg.), *Iouantu*- 'youth', *Iouincus* 'young' as a name/name element (cf. MBret. *youanc*)
- *su*- 'good' before a vowel in names like *Su-agrus*, *Su-ausia* (cf. MW *hu*-)
- Gallo-Lat. *cauannum* (acc. sg.) 'owl', *Cauannus*, *Cauanos* as a name (cf. MW *cuan*).

There appear to be two possible reflexes of *-*ou̯*- (-*ou*- and -*au*-), and three of *-*uu̯*- (-*uu*-, -*ou*-, -*au*-), but several of these forms may be unreliable. *su*- could reflect the generalized pre-consonantal allomorph, as apparently occurred with MCorn. *he*-, *hy*-, ModBret. *he*- (Schrijver 1995: 333–4). Since *δρυίδης*, *druides* is only found in Latin and Greek, the consistent spelling with -*u*- need not tell us very much about the quality of the vowel (perhaps the spelling with -*u*- rather than -*o*- was conditioned by the following high vowel?). The vowel of *Bouus* may have been replaced by that of the athematic form *Bo*- (found as a name element) < *g^w*ou̯-s*.

On the other hand, although Schrijver suggests that *cauannum* reflects a Latin attempt to pronounce a sound foreign to Latin, it is spelled the same way when it appears as a Gaulish name, so is probably reliable. The spellings of *Iuuantus* vs. *Iouanti* may suggest that *-*uu̯*- and *-*ou̯*- had fallen together at least in some cases. The resulting sound was clearly closer to *-*ou̯*-, since the spelling *Iuu*- is attested only once, while *Iou*- is very often found.

It is tempting to see an accent-based explanation for the Gaulish developments, similar to that of the British forms, but subsequent to a falling together of *-*uu̯*- and *-*ou̯*-. For the assumption that Gaulish also had a penultimate accent see Schrijver (1995: 20–1). Thus we find *-*óu̯es* > -*oues*, **óu̯i*- > **oui*- (assuming that compound forms adopted the vocalism of the simplex). *Κνουιλλα* could have adopted the vocalism of the base form **knúu̯V*-. On the other hand, **lou̯éno*- > *Lauenus* and **kuu̯ánno*- >

[20] Not included here are Gaul. **bau̯a* > Fr. *boue* 'mud', the name *Louernios*, *Λουερνιος*, and *secoui*. Although Delamarre (2003: 69) reconstructs **bau̯a* < **bou̯ā*, MW *baw* 'dirt, filth, mud' shows that the preform is **bau̯ā*. *Louernios* probably comes from **loërno*- < **loperno*- with graphic -*u*- having developed as a hiatus filler rather than being inherited (Schrijver 1998). The meaning and etymology of *secoui* are too uncertain (Delamarre 2003: 268).

Cauanos would reflect the unstressed development. However, this account cannot explain *Iuuantus* < **i̯uuántu-*, *Iouincus* < **i̯uu̯ánko-*.

Postscript: Shortly before this chapter went to print, Anders Jørgensen (personal communication) kindly informed me that Vannetais *leùen* 'merry, jovial, happy', on which the case for a distinction between **-ou̯-* and **-uu̯-* in Vannetais relies, may be a lexicographical ghost word. It is only attested in the area of Plumergat, as *leùin*, where the *-i-* in the final syllable may be a feature of the local dialect, but may also reflect back-formation from *leùiné* 'joy', in which the first vowel is due to internal *i*-affection (cf. Breton *levenez*). However, the development proposed here for *leùen* does seem to have occurred in the derivatives *leùenan* 'wren' (cf. Breton *laouenan*), *leùénus* 'joyous' (which, however, is itself only known from an early dictionary). The argument for a distinction between **-ou̯-* and **-uu̯-* in Welsh is of course unaffected by questions about the Vannetais form.

Part IV

Origins and evolutions

11

Origins of the Greek law of limitation

PHILOMEN PROBERT

11.1 Introduction

This chapter proposes a historical account of the Greek 'law of limitation', the restrictions on the distance from the end of the word where the accent may fall.[1] At the same time, the chapter proposes an origin for the behaviour of some word-final diphthongs as 'short for accentuation' and others as 'long for accentuation'.

11.1.1 The law of limitation

Some languages have a word accent whose position is straightforwardly predictable: for example, the accent always falls on the word-initial syllable. In classical Latin, the position of the accent is likewise predictable, although it follows a more complex rule: the penultimate syllable is accented if this syllable is heavy, otherwise the antepenultimate; or, if the word is too short for these rules to apply 'normally', the initial syllable is accented. By contrast, the position of the ancient Greek accent is not predictable from the shape of a word alone, and yet there are some restrictions on its placement—some positions in the word where (with one limited group of exceptions) we can be sure not to find the accent. These restrictions are known collectively as the 'law of limitation', and may be stated as follows:

[1] It is a pleasure to offer John Penney a chapter that originated at the Oxford Comparative Philology Seminar, to which John has given so much over so many years. I am grateful for comments from participants in this seminar and its sister seminar in Cambridge; and to Eleanor Dickey and Andreas Willi, for discussion of the written version.

The accent does not fall further from the end of the word than the antepenultimate syllable, or the penultimate if the final syllable is heavy. For the purposes of this law, a single word-final consonant does not count towards syllable weight.

(An accent as far from the end of the word as the law of limitation allows is called 'recessive'. Further restrictions regulate the occurrence of acute and circumflex accents: we shall return to these shortly.)

The law of limitation is common to all Greek dialects for which we have evidence, except possibly Thessalian (which would, however, have innovated vis-à-vis the other Aeolic dialects).[2] The law may well have arisen before the main dialect divisions of historical times, although caution is necessary because accentual phenomena can spread. The law of limitation has a small number of exceptions apparently resulting from Attic-Ionic quantitative metathesis having occurred *after* the limitation of the accent: πόληος 'of the city' > πόλεως. Since there are metrically guaranteed examples of quantitative metathesis in Homer, the law of limitation predates the latest stages of the Homeric tradition, and may be considerably older still. It is clear that it is an innovation of Greek, not inherited from Indo-European.

11.1.2 The choice between acute and circumflex accent on a long vowel or diphthong

Accented long vowels and diphthongs were accented either on their first half (first 'mora'), or on their second; in the former case the accent is represented as a circumflex (σοφοῦ), in the second as an acute (σοφούς). Short vowels were simply accented or unaccented: an accent on a short vowel is represented as an acute (σοφός).[3]

On accented final syllables the choice between circumflex and acute is morphologically based: certain endings take a circumflex if accented at all (e.g. gen. pl. -ῶν), others an acute (e.g. acc. pl. -ούς). On non-final syllables the choice between circumflex and acute is phonologically determined: a long accented vowel or diphthong in the penultimate syllable takes a circumflex if the final syllable has a short vowel (σωτῆρα, πολυπῖδαξ); other accented long vowels in non-final syllables take an acute (σοφώτατος, ἀνθρώπους). But the scope of the rule prescribing a cirumflex in words of shape σωτῆρα (the 'σωτῆρα rule') appears to differ from one dialect to another: neither Doric nor Boeotian applied the rule to all instances to which it applied in Attic and *koiné*. Nevertheless, it has been argued persuasively that, in some form and at some period,

[2] See Probert (2006: 72–4), with literature.

[3] The grave accent, a sandhi variant of the acute, is not relevant here.

the σωτῆρα rule operated in these dialects too (for Boeotian, see Hermann 1918: 274–5; for Doric, Hinge 2006: 124–8).

I remain agnostic as to how acutes and circumflexes were distributed on non-final syllables at an early stage, such as when the law of limitation came into existence. The σωτῆρα rule may have existed in some form already, or it may be a later development. Alternatively, the σωτῆρα rule and law of limitation arose together. In what follows I shall attempt to account for the origins of the restrictions as to the number of syllables from the end of the word where the accent might fall (the law of limitation as defined under 11.1.1), leaving aside the origins of the σωτῆρα rule.

11.1.3 *Final diphthongs*

Diphthongs count as long vocalic nuclei for the purposes of poetic metre,[4] and in general they are treated as long vowels by the accentuation rules. But in absolute word-final position, in Attic and *koiné* (on Doric see section 11.4.1), the diphthongs -αι and -οι 'count as short' *for the purposes of the accentuation rules only* in indicatives, subjunctives, imperatives, infinitives, and nominatives plural. In optatives, locative adverbs, and some interjections, final -αι and -οι 'count as long'. Thus βούλομαι 'I want' (indicative), βούλωμαι 'I might want' (subjunctive), παίδευσαι 'educate!' (imperative), and ἄνθρωποι 'people' (nominative plural) allow an acute on the antepenultimate syllable. The forms παιδεῦσαι 'to educate' (aorist infinitive) and οἶκοι 'houses' (nominative plural) allow a circumflex on a long vowel in the penultimate syllable. By contrast, the acutes on the -ευ- of παιδεύοι 'may he educate' (present optative) and παιδεύσαι 'may he educate' (aorist optative) show that the final diphthong 'counts as long', as does the circumflex on the final diphthong of the locative adverb Μεγαροῖ 'at Megara' and the interjection αἰαῖ.

11.2 Historical accounts of the law of limitation

There have been many attempts to formulate the law of limitation, in synchronic terms, in such a way that it emerges naturally from some simple and plausible principle.[5] The problem is inherently tricky and there is still little or no agreement on the details of the phonological analysis from which the law

4 A complication not immediately relevant (but see the appendix) is that in Homer any word-final long vowel or diphthong may be treated as light before a word-initial vowel, and the diphthongs -αι and -οι especially favour this treatment, evidently because the -ι may be interpreted as consonantal between vowels. See Hartel (1874), Chantraine (1958: 88–9).

5 For discussion, see Probert (2006: 108–12, 120–3).

of limitation should follow. Considerably less attention has been devoted to uncovering the historical processes that might have given rise to the law of limitation, but the question has been approached especially by Lucidi (1950) and Kuryłowicz (1968: 86).

Among earlier suggestions, one might mention Hermann's view (1923: 88–9) that the law of limitation arose in two stages: first a restriction to the last three syllables (irrespective of any vowel quantities or syllable weights), then a second restriction to the last three vocalic morae in words with heavy final syllable.[6] While this account breaks the law of limitation down into two simpler innovations instead of one complex one, we are not told what motivated the initial restriction of the accent to the last three syllables, or the subsequent further restriction.

Like Hermann, Lucidi (1950) regards the law of limitation as arising in essentially two steps, but his first step (1950: 82) is the restriction of the accent to the last three vocalic morae (so *πόλεμος*, *πολέμου*, *ἀνθρώπου*, but **ἀνθρῶπος* not *ἄνθρωπος*, **λεγῆτον* not *λέγητον*). At this stage Lucidi assumes the continued existence of forms such as **δώρον*, with inherited acute accent on the penultimate. After this first step, he takes processes of compensatory lengthening to have given rise to forms such as *φέρουσα* (< **φέρονσα*), so that some words with a long vowel in the penultimate syllable now had the accent four vocalic morae from the end (1950: 84, 86).

Lucidi then posits a second step for Attic-Ionic and Aeolic (but not Doric): in every word with a short vowel in the final syllable and a long accented vowel in the penultimate, the accent was retracted by one vocalic mora. Thus, words such as **ἀνθρῶπος* and **λεγῆτον* became *ἄνθρωπος* and *λέγητον*, while **δώρον* became *δῶρον* (1950: 85–6). This second step thus produced both the law of limitation in its eventual form and the *σωτῆρα* rule. Aeolic, Doric, and Attic subsequently underwent further innovations, which need not concern us here.

Lucidi proposes several possible motivations for his second step. Firstly, he suggests that there was a tendency for the length of the vowel in a final syllable to be confused with the weight of the syllable, and that this confusion led to a wider reinterpretation of the restrictions on the accent as based on syllable weight rather than vowel quantity (1950: 83–4, 86). If so, forms like **ἀνθρῶπον* might have come to follow those like *λέγοντα* (with a heavy penultimate syllable providing no obstacle to an accent on the antepenultimate). Secondly, the appearance of forms such as *φέρουσα* would have contributed to the loss of the perception that a long vowel in the penultimate syllable prevented the accent falling on the antepenultimate (1950: 86). Thirdly, Lucidi (1950: 88 n. 1) allows the possibility of some substrate influence.

[6] A somewhat similar account already in Pedersen (1905*b*: 340–1).

Kuryłowicz (1968: 86) gives a different account, appealing to an idea that with the rise of the acute/circumflex distinction (which Kuryłowicz takes to be a Greek innovation) a syllabic sequence x ∪ had become equivalent to —. A trisyllabic word of the form x́ x ∪ (e.g. *λέγομεν*, *ἄνθρωπος*) might then be reanalysed as accented on the syllable immediately preceding the 'end-complex' x ∪ (equivalent to —). The idea that words were accented either on the end-complex or on the preceding syllable was then generalized from words of shape x x ∪.

Both Lucidi's account and Kuryłowicz's still suffer from somewhat inadequate motivation. As motivation for his initial three-mora rule, Lucidi (1950: 92) suggests that early Greek had a secondary accent on the antepenultimate vocalic mora, but independent evidence for this secondary accent is lacking. Kuryłowicz assumes that the law of limitation was due to reanalysis of words of shape x x ∪. But why should words of this shape have been so influential? In addition, Kuryłowicz's account requires an equivalence between the syllabic sequences x ∪ and —, for which the only evidence appears to be the details of the law of limitation (see Kuryłowicz 1968: 84).

Both Lucidi's account (in its second step) and Kuryłowicz's, however, appeal to the fact that some words 'obeyed' the law of limitation before this law came into effect. This point is worth taking seriously, since a promising model for many types of linguistic change is the reanalysis of existing forms, followed by the extension of a new regularity extracted from these forms.[7] The suggestion offered here retains and extends the point that some words already 'obeyed' the not yet existing law of limitation.

11.3 A new suggestion

We might expect early Greek to have had approximately the second-declension noun paradigm shown in Table 11.1, with an accent on the first syllable throughout.[8]

[7] Cf. (on syntactic change) Harris and Campbell (1995: 61–119).

[8] The stage represented is one in which the nom. pl. ending is already *-οι* (not **-ōs*), and Osthoff's Law has already taken place (hence dat./instr. pl. *-οις*, not **-ōis*). Different decisions on these points would not affect the argument much (but on the nom. pl. ending see section 11.4), and I do not mean to claim that the replacement of nom. pl. **-ōs* by *-οι*, or Osthoff's Law, can necessarily be brought into a relative chronology with the law of limitation. I do not attempt a reconstruction of the dual forms, the old ablative, the old instrumental singular, or the old dative plural; but such forms as one might reconstruct for these slots (e.g. abl. sg. *ϝοίκω*) would not affect the argument.

Table 11.1 Early Greek paradigm of *Ϝοῖκος* 'house' (cf. Skt *véśa-* 'house')

	Singular	Plural
Nom.	Ϝοῖκος	Ϝοῖκοι
Acc.	Ϝοῖκον	Ϝοίκους
Gen.	Ϝοίκοιο	Ϝοίκων
Dat./Instr.	Ϝοίκῳ	Ϝοίκοις
Loc.	Ϝοίκοι	Ϝοίκοισι

Note: In this paradigm and further paradigms below, the distribution of acutes and circumflexes shown is guided by the historically attested forms; no claim is made about any prehistoric distribution of acute and circumflex accents.

What is of interest here is not only that all these forms of a root-accented noun with fairly short stem already 'obey' the law of limitation. They do so in a non-trivial way. Most of the forms in the paradigm are disyllabic, but the trisyllabic forms (*Ϝοίκοιο* and *Ϝοίκοισι*) happen to have a light final syllable and therefore also 'obey' the law of limitation. If one reckons the position of the accent from the end of the word, the accent falls on the penultimate syllable in all forms with a heavy final syllable, and on the antepenultimate only in trisyllabic forms with a light final syllable.

In the verbal system, underived thematic verbs such as *τρέπω* behave remarkably similarly. It is normally assumed that finite verbs were unaccented in some syntactic positions in early Greek and accented in others, as in Vedic (see e.g. Sihler 1995: 238–9, Meier-Brügger 2002: 184; but cf. section 11.5 below). In accented positions, the present indicative active of *τρέπω* would have been accented on the non-ablauting *e*-grade root throughout, and would have 'obeyed' the law of limitation in the same non-trivial way as the forms of *Ϝοῖκος*: sg. 1. *τρέπω*, 2. *τρέπεις*, 3. *τρέπει*, du. 2. *τρέπετον*, 3. *τρέπετον*, pl. 1. *τρέπομεν*, 2. *τρέπετε*, 3. (early Greek) *τρέποντι*. Not only the present indicative active, but most of the originally root-accented finite forms and infinitives—those built on the thematic present stem *τρεπε/ο-* or the sigmatic aorist stem *τρεψ-*—would have behaved in the same way. These forms are shown in Table 11.2, approximately as they would have looked in accented position, with an accent on the root. An asterisk indicates that the relevant form does not have the accent in its historical position, i.e. does not already 'obey' the law of limitation. The singly and doubly underlined forms end in *-αι* or *-οι*, and will be discussed in due course. Unaugmented forms of the imperfect and aorist indicatives are shown, since I assume that the augment was an independent particle until relatively late in the prehistory of Greek, and was often absent at an early period.[9] The future optative is omitted, as this is not attested until the fifth century (Schwyzer and Debrunner 1950: 337).

[9] Cf. the total or almost total absence of the augment from Mycenaean, and the preponderance of unaugmented past indicatives in Homer (see Chantraine 1958: 483–4, with important caveats) and the *Ṛgveda* (Macdonell 1916: 122).

Table 11.2 Early present and aorist active and middle finite forms and infinitives of *τρέπω* 'turn', shown with root accentuation

(pres. ind. act.)			(fut. ind. act.)		
Sg.	Du.	Pl.	Sg.	Du.	Pl.
1. τρέπω		τρέπομεν	τρέψω		τρέψομεν
2. τρέπεις	τρέπετον	τρέπετε	τρέψεις	τρέψετον	τρέψετε
3. τρέπει	τρέπετον	τρέποντι	τρέψει	τρέψετον	τρέψοντι
(pres. subj. act.)			(pres. opt. act.)		
Sg.	Du.	Pl.	Sg.	Du.	Pl.
1. τρέπω		τρέπωμεν	τρέποιμι		τρέποιμεν
2. τρέπῃς	τρέπητον	τρέπητε	τρέποις	τρέποιτον	τρέποιτε
3. τρέπῃ	τρέπητον	τρέπωντι	τρέποι	*τρέποιτην	τρέποιεν
(aor. subj. act.)			(aor. opt. act.)		
Sg.	Du.	Pl.	Sg.	Du.	Pl.
1. τρέψω		τρέψωμεν	τρέψαιμι		τρέψαιμεν
2. τρέψῃς	τρέψητον	τρέψητε	τρέψαις/-ειας	τρέψαιτον	τρέψαιτε
3. τρέψῃ	τρέψητον	τρέψωντι	τρέψαι/-ειε	*τρέψαιτην	τρέψαιεν/-ειαν
(unaugmented impf. ind. act.)			(unaugmented aor. ind. act.)		
Sg.	Du.	Pl.	Sg.	Du.	Pl.
1. τρέπον		τρέπομεν	τρέψα		τρέψαμεν
2. τρέπες	τρέπετον	τρέπετε	τρέψας	τρέψατον	τρέψατε
3. τρέπε	*τρέπετην	τρέπον	τρέψε	*τρέψατην	τρέψαν
(pres. ind. mid.)			(fut. ind. mid.)		
Sg.	Du.	Pl.	Sg.	Du.	Pl.
1. τρέπομαι		*τρέπομεθα	τρέψομαι		*τρέψομεθα
2. τρέπεαι	τρέπεσθον	τρέπεσθε	τρέψεαι	τρέψεσθον	τρέψεσθε

(continued)

Table 11.2 Continued

3. τρέπεται	τρέπεσθον	τρέπονται	τρέψεται	τρέψεσθον	τρέψονται
(pres. subj. mid.)			(pres. opt. mid.)		
Sg.	Du.	Pl.	Sg.	Du.	Pl.
1. τρέπωμαι		*τρέπωμεθα	*τρέποιμην		*τρέποιμεθα
2. τρέπηαι	τρέπησθον	τρέπησθε	τρέποιο	τρέποισθον	τρέποισθε
3. τρέπηται	τρέπησθον	τρέπωνται	τρέποιτο	*τρέποισθην	τρέποιντο
(aor. subj. mid.)			(aor. opt. mid.)		
Sg.	Du.	Pl.	Sg.	Du.	Pl.
1. τρέψωμαι		*τρέψωμεθα	*τρέψαιμην		*τρέψαιμεθα
2. τρέψηαι	τρέψησθον	τρέψησθε	τρέψαιο	τρέψαισθον	τρέψαισθε
3. τρέψηται	τρέψησθον	τρέψωνται	τρέψαιτο	*τρέψαισθην	τρέψαιντο
(unaugmented impf. ind. mid.)			(unaugmented aor. ind. mid.)		
Sg.	Du.	Pl.	Sg.	Du.	Pl.
1. *τρέπομην		*τρέπομεθα	*τρέψαμην		*τρέψαμεθα
2. τρέπεο	τρέπεσθον	τρέπεσθε	τρέψαο	τρέψασθον	τρέψασθε
3. τρέπετο	*τρέπεσθην	τρέποντο	τρέψατο	*τρέψασθην	τρέψαντο
(pres. ipv. act.)			(aor. ipv. act.)		
Sg.	Du.	Pl.	Sg.	Du.	Pl.
2. τρέπε	τρέπετον	τρέπετε	τρέψον	τρέψατον	τρέψατε
3. *τρέπετω	*τρέπετων	*τρέποντων[a]	*τρέψατω	*τρέψατων	*τρέψαντων
(pres. ipv. mid.)			(aor. ipv. mid.)		
Sg.	Du.	Pl.	Sg.	Du.	Pl.
2. τρέπεο	τρέπεσθον	τρέπεσθε	τρέψαι	τρέψασθον	τρέψασθε
3. *τρέπεσθω	*τρέπεσθων	*τρέπεσθων	*τρέψασθω	*τρέψασθων	*τρέψασθων
(infinitives)					
τρέπειν, τρέψειν, τρέψαι, τρέπεσθαι, τρέψεσθαι, τρέψασθαι					

[a] The alternative classical form τρεπέτωσαν appears too late to be relevant (see Chantraine 1961: 270). Likewise the alternative 3pl. aor. ipv. act. τρεψάτωσαν, 3pl. pres. ipv. mid. τρεπέσθωσαν, and 3pl. aor. ipv. mid. τρεψάσθωσαν.

As the asterisks show, not all of these forms already 'obey' the law of limitation. But some of the exceptions are very rare in attested Greek and likely to have been rare at every period: third person dual optatives (*τρέποιτην, *τρέψαιτην, *τρέποισθην, *τρέψαισθην), third person dual imperfect and aorist indicatives (*τρέπετην, *τρέψατην, *τρέπεσθην, *τρέψασθην), and third person dual imperatives (*τρέπετων, *τρέψατων, *τρέπεσθων, *τρέψασθων). The remaining exceptions are first person plural middle forms (*τρέπομεθα (pres.), *τρέψομεθα, *τρέπωμεθα, *τρέποιμεθα, *τρέψωμεθα, *τρέψαιμεθα, *τρέπομεθα (impf.), *τρέψαμεθα), first person singular middle forms with secondary ending (*τρέποιμην, *τρέψαιμην, *τρέπομην, *τρέψαμην), and third person singular and plural imperatives (*τρέπετω, *τρέποντων, *τρέψατω, *τρέψαντων, *τρέπεσθω, *τρέπεσθων, *τρέψασθω, *τρέψασθων). Although the first person forms, in particular, will have been fairly frequent in certain kinds of discourse (such as first-person narrative), these forms are heavily outnumbered, at least in their paradigm, by forms that already 'obey' the law of limitation.

A similar point could be made about other common paradigms. If reduplicated presents were originally accented on the reduplication, as in Vedic (cf. Ringe 2006*a*: 37–8, 40), the present and imperfect indicative paradigms of ἵστημι 'set up' would have looked roughly as shown in Table 11.3.

Table 11.3 Early present and imperfect indicative forms of ἵστημι 'set up', shown with accent on the reduplication

(pres. ind. act.)			(unaugmented impf. ind. act.)		
Sg.	Du.	Pl.	Sg.	Du.	Pl.
1. ἵστᾱμι		ἵσταμεν	ἵστᾱν		ἵσταμεν
2. ἵστᾱς	ἵστατον	ἵστατε	ἵστᾱς	ἵστατον	ἵστατε
3. ἵστᾱτι	ἵστατον	ἵσταντι	ἵστᾱ	*ἵστατην	ἵσταν
(pres. ind. mid.)			(unaugmented impf. ind. mid.)		
Sg.	Du.	Pl.	Sg.	Du.	Pl.
1. ἵσταμαι		*ἵσταμεθα	*ἵσταμην		*ἵσταμεθα
2. ἵστασαι	ἵστασθον	ἵστασθε	ἵστασο	ἵστασθον	ἵστασθε
3. ἵσταται	ἵστασθον	ἵστανται	ἵστατο	*ἵστασθην	ἵσταντο

Apart from sigmatic aorists (accented on the root, as discussed), and some other root-accented (or 'Narten') paradigms, most other athematic verbal paradigms originally accented the syllable before the ending in singular active forms, otherwise the ending (see Ringe 2006*a*: 35–6, 40). The shape of Greek verbal endings ensures that most such forms will not even have been 'recessive' when accented,[10] let alone 'violated' the law of limitation (so e.g. 1sg. *δαμνâμι, 1pl. *δαμναμέν). The same is true for most suffixed thematic present forms, since most thematic suffixes were accented on the thematic vowel (see Ringe 2006*a*: 28–9, 39–40).[11]

In order to show that a high proportion of early Greek words 'obeyed' the law of limitation *avant la lettre*, however, we require not only that the majority of forms in some common nominal and verbal paradigms already 'obeyed' the law of limitation, but that the majority of forms in actual early Greek discourse did so. We do not, of course, have a wide variety of early Greek texts, and we cannot always reconstruct prehistoric accentuation, but we do have some early Greek, especially the Homeric poems, and internal or comparative evidence often shows where the attested accentuation is due to one of the main Greek accentual innovations: the law of limitation or the recessive accentuation of most finite (and some non-finite) verb forms. The following extract from the *Iliad* shows an attempt to reconstruct the pre-law-of-limitation accentuation, with particular attention to the forms whose attested accentuation is most likely to be innovated: forms attested with recessive accent, if the recessive accent does not fall on the word-initial syllable, and all recessive verb forms. Asterisks show where the reconstructed position for the accent is not the historically attested one. No attempt has been made to reconstruct unaccented verbs, since it is doubtful whether we really know their distribution in early Greek (cf. also section 11.5); the distribution found in Vedic would make *ἐᾶ́ (line 2), τρέπεν (line 3), τρέπεν (line 7), and ἐέλπετο (line 8) unaccented.

> *Ζεὺς δ' ἐπεὶ οὖν Τρῶάς τε καὶ Ἕκτορα νηυσὶ πέλασσεν*[12],
> *τοὺς μὲν *ἐὰ*[13] *παρὰ τῆισι πόνον τ' ἐχέμεν καὶ ὀϊζύν*
> *νωλεμέως*[14], *αὐτὸς δὲ πάλιν τρέπεν*[15] *ὄσσε φαεινώ*

[10] Except for active singular forms such as unaugmented 1sg. aor. στῆν < **steh₂-m*, which are technically recessive, but only because they are so short.

[11] Cf. the sample Indo-European verb, noun, and adjective paradigms laid out by Ringe (2006*a*: 35–40, 47–52), in which the majority of forms already 'obey' the law of limitation.

[12] An old *s*-aorist built on an *e*-grade root **pelh₂-* (see Chantraine 1968–80, s.v. πέλας); old root accentuation is expected.

[13] The etymology and history of ἐάω are unclear. The verb may originally have had an athematic present stem ἔᾰ- (cf. Chantraine 1958: 305, 1968–80, s.v. ἐάω), but the imperfect ἔᾱ (with long ᾱ) is most easily explained as contracted from thematic *ἐα(ι̯)έ. Since most **i̯e-/i̯o-* presents and imperfects were originally accented on the suffix **i̯e-/i̯o-*, the accentuation *ἐᾶ́ should tentatively be assumed here for early Greek.

[14] Cf. the related adverb νωλεμές (originally acc. sg. neuter of an *s*-stem adjective).

[15] An underived thematic present: root accentuation is expected. So also in line 7.

νόσφιν, ἐφ' ἱπποπόλων[16] Θρῃκῶν *καθορωμενὸς[17] αἶαν
Μυσῶν τ' ἀγχεμάχων[18] καὶ ἀγαυῶν Ἱππημολγῶν
γλακτοφάγων[19] *Ἄβιων[20] τε *δίκαιοτατων[21] *ἄνθρωπων[22].
ἐς Τροίην δ' οὐ πάμπαν ἔτι τρέπεν ὄσσε φαεινώ·
οὐ γὰρ ὅ γ' *ἄθανατων[23] τιν' ἐέλπετο[24] ὃν κατὰ θυμόν
ἐλθόντ' ἢ Τρώεσσιν ἀρηξέμεν ἢ Δαναοῖσιν. (*Iliad* 13. 1–9)

(The distribution of acutes and circumflexes is again guided by the historically attested forms and is not intended to be significant. No attempt has been made to reconstruct pre-law-of-limitation rules for the accentuation of words followed by enclitics; in the first line *Τρῶάς* is printed as attested, with a second accent due to *τε*, but no significance is to be ascribed to this accent.)

This extract contains 69 word tokens, or 46 if enclitics,[25] proclitics and monosyllabic pronoun forms,[26] and elided δ(ϵ) are excluded. Of these 46 full word tokens, only six have the accent somewhere other than its historical

[16] Accentuation on the second member of the compound is expected for a verbal governing compound in which the second member has active meaning. In Vedic, such compounds have the accent on the final syllable. In Greek, the accent appears on the penultimate syllable instead if this syllable is light. The divergence between Greek and Vedic is likely to be due to retraction of the accent in Greek, although the details have been disputed (see Probert 2006: 93–4). Thus the form *ἱπποπόλων* will have been preceded by an earlier **ἱπποπολῶν*. I do not claim to know which of these forms existed when the law of limitation came in, but the essential point is that neither would 'violate' the not yet existing law.

[17] Participles in *-μενο-* (IE *-mh$_1$no-) are likely to have inherited an accent on the last syllable, as found in Vedic perfect participles in *-āná-* (< *-mh$_1$nó-) and some Greek present and aorist participles lexicalized as nouns: *Σῳζομενός*, *'Ορχομενός*, *Στησαμενός*, *Τεισαμενός*, *Φαμενός*, *δεξαμενή* 'reservoir', and *εἱαμενή* 'meadow' (cf. Probert 2006: 92).

[18] In spite of the attested nom. sg. masc./fem. *ἀγχέμαχος* (for the accent see [Arcadius] 102. 5, 103. 15 Schmidt), inherited accentuation on the second member is expected for a verbal governing compound whose second member has active meaning; cf. n. 16. For the inconsistent accentuation of *-μαχος* compounds as attested, cf. Risch (1974: 207).

[19] An even older form will have been **γλακτοφαγῶν* (see n. 16).

[20] Historical *Ἀβίων* is due to the law of limitation; cf. nom. sg. *Ἄβιος*.

[21] It is difficult to reconstruct a pre-law-of-limitation position for the accent here, but the historical paradigm shows that the accent on the syllable *-τα-* is due to the law of limitation (cf. nom. sg. masc. *δικαιότατος*). Vedic superlatives in *-tama-* (the closest Vedic equivalents to the Greek superlatives in *-τατο-*) do not follow a simple accent rule, but are rarely accented on the suffix *-tama-* (see Macdonell 1916: 454).

[22] Historical *ἀνθρώπων* is due to the law of limitation; cf. nom. sg. *ἄνθρωπος*.

[23] Historical *ἀθανάτων* is due to the law of limitation (cf. nom. sg. masc./fem. *ἀθάνατος*); accentuation on the privative prefix is expected for a privative bahuvrīhi compound.

[24] Probably not an augmented form but an unaugmented thematic imperfect, with the same prothetic vowel as in the Homeric present *ἐέλπεται* (see Lejeune 1972: 174–5). If so, the accent should already have been on the root. If, however, *ἐέλπετο* is an augmented form, the accent should have been on the augment at an early stage (**ἔελπετο*).

[25] *τ(ϵ), γ', τιν'.*

[26] *ἐπεί, καί, τούς, παρά, ἐφ', ἐς, οὐ, ὅ, ὅν, κατά, ἤ.*

position. Of these, only four actually 'violate' the later law of limitation: *Ἄβιων, *δίκαιοτατων, *ἄνθρωπων, *ἄθανατων. The other two (*ἐά́ and *καθορωμενός) will acquire recessive accentuation when this is generalized to most finite and some non-finite verb forms, but the prehistoric accentuation is nearer to the end of the word and therefore compatible with the later law of limitation.

Such evidence as we have thus suggests that a sizeable proportion of early Greek word tokens already 'obeyed' the law of limitation. The law of limitation might, therefore, have originated with a reanalysis of the situation as one where the law of limitation actually existed as an operative part of the grammar. For this reanalysis to survive and for the resulting regularity to be extended across the vocabulary, the law of limitation needed to be synchronically plausible or at least possible. This chapter will not explore possible synchronic analyses, but it is clear from the very existence of the law of limitation that a viable synchronic analysis was available to speakers.

We have so far left the double accentual treatment of word-final -αι and -οι out of the discussion. The next section proposes a historical explanation for this double treatment that would, if correct, provide further support for our reanalysis-based account of the law of limitation.

11.4 Word-final -αι and -οι

In Table 11.2, the forms of τρέπω that end in -αι or (in one instance) -οι have all been underlined. All already 'obey' the law of limitation in its eventual form, but some (given double underlining) do so only by virtue of the fact that their final diphthong somehow 'counts short' for the purposes of accentuation: indicatives τρέπομαι, τρέπεαι, τρέπεται, τρέπονται, τρέψομαι, τρέψεαι, τρέψεται, τρέψονται; subjunctives τρέπωμαι, τρέπηαι, τρέπηται, τρέπωνται, τρέψωμαι, τρέψηαι, τρέψηται, τρέψωνται; and infinitives τρέπεσθαι, τρέψεσθαι, τρέψασθαι. Others (given single underlining) 'obey' the law of limitation just as if they ended in an ordinary long vowel or diphthong: optatives τρέποι, τρέψαι; aorist imperative middle τρέψαι; aorist infinitive active τρέψαι. What is striking here is that the words in the first list coincide almost entirely with the verbal forms whose final -αι counts as 'short' for the purposes of the accent. Of eight indicative, eight subjunctive, four infinitive forms and one imperative ending in -αι, all the indicative and subjunctive forms and three of the infinitives have the root as the antepenultimate syllable, so that the prehistoric root accentuation looks just like the historical recessive accentuation, with final -αι counting as 'short' for the purposes of the accent. The much shorter second list, by contrast, includes both the optatives ending in -αι or -οι, the forms whose final diphthongs we are accustomed to consider 'long' for accentual purposes.

Although the match between the two lists and the two kinds of final diphthongs is not perfect, the striking correlation suggests that the 'short' treatment of indicative and subjunctive -αι, and the 'long' treatment of optative -αι/-οι, may be due to the terminations that happen to occur in verbal paradigms. Indicative, subjunctive, and infinitive -αι occur in disyllabic terminations[27] (-ομαι, -εαι, -εται, -ονται, -ωμαι, -ηαι, -ηται, -ωνται, -εσθαι, -ασθαι) as well as in monosyllabic terminations (e.g. κεῖμαι 'I lie', κεῖται 'he lies', κεῖνται 'they lie', τρέψαι 'to turn') while optative -αι/-οι occurs only in monosyllabic terminations (-οι, -σαι). One might have expected the plethora of root-accented indicatives, subjunctives, and infinitives in -ομαι, -εαι, -εται, -ονται, -ωμαι, -ηαι, -ηται, -ωνται, -εσθαι, and -ασθαι to have prevented our reanalysis of early Greek accentuation. Instead, the reanalysis was tailored to fit the evidence: a feature common to all these forms, namely the final diphthong, was interpreted as counting 'short' for accentuation. (The potential for -οι and -αι, however pronounced, to be interpreted phonologically as -οι̯ and -αι̯ may well have facilitated this aspect of the reanalysis, by allowing some final -οι and -αι diphthongs to be treated as vowel-plus-consonant sequences at some level of synchronic representation.[28]) Optatives in -αι and -οι, on the other hand, offered no evidence that their final diphthongs counted as 'short', and accordingly their final diphthongs did not receive such a 'short' analysis.

The accentually 'long' treatment of final -οι in locative adverbs—i.e. old locative singulars—becomes explicable on the same basis. These old locatives add to the basic stem only the syllable -οι, so that if the citation form is disyllabic (as ϝοῖκος) the locative is disyllabic too (as ϝοίκοι), and so if the accent is on the root the locative is accented on the penultimate syllable, just like the optatives

[27] I use the word 'termination' here for the part of the verb following the root (regardless of whether this should be considered the synchronic 'ending').

[28] In recent work, the words with accentually 'short' final diphthongs are sometimes taken to have generalized prevocalic sandhi variants in *-oi̯* and *-ai̯*, accented as if they ended in a -VC sequence (e.g. **leík^{w}etoi̯*), while the words with accentually 'long' final diphthongs generalized preconsonantal variants in *-oi* and *-ai* (such as locative **woíkoi*) (so Olander 2009: 68–9; somewhat differently Nagy 1970: 137–8; differently again Bonfante 1986: 375–6). Alternatively, the variants with *-oi̯* and *-ai̯* were not themselves generalized at any stage, but the 'hyper-recessive' accentuation of forms such as prevocalic **léik^{w}etoi̯* was generalized to the preconsonantal variants (Jasanoff 2009: 56 n. 23). The suggestion I offer here does not allow for a stage at which the law of limitation was already in effect but the split (along morphological lines) between 'accentually short' and 'accentually long' final diphthongs had yet to be established. However, I find it very likely to be relevant that a high vowel as second element of a diphthong was phonologically interpretable as either consonantal or vocalic.

τρέποι and τρέψαι. In other words, the short *o*-stem nominals that provided evidence for the law of limitation did not provide any evidence against an ordinary 'long' treatment of the locative singular termination -οι.

This analysis does not explain the accentually 'short' treatment of nominative plural -οι/-αι, or of -αι in imperatives. We might note that *o*- and *ā*-stem nominative plural endings -οι and -αι are original only in pronominal forms, such as τοί and ταί—monosyllables for which it may be meaningless to ask whether the diphthongs counted as 'long' or 'short'. In *o*- and *ā*-stem nouns and adjectives the endings -οι and -αι are secondary (although pre-Mycenaean) replacements for inherited **-ōs* and **-ās*. Conceivably the law of limitation was in place by the time -οι and -αι spread to nouns and adjectives, and nominative plural -αι then followed the majority of word-final -αι diphthongs in being counted as 'short' for the purposes of the accent. Nominative plural -οι would have been the first example of word-final -οι, as opposed to -αι, counting 'short' for the accent, but in view of the parallelism that Greek developed between the *o*-stem and *ā*-stem declensions it would not be surprising if this *o*-stem ending copied the word-final -αι of the *ā*-stem nominative plural. Furthermore, nominative plural -οι and -αι were treated as accentually 'long' in Doric (see Hinge 2006: 127), perhaps also a sign that the accentual treatment of nominative plural -οι/-αι was determined at a late stage and on a dialect-specific basis.

The origins of the aorist middle imperative in -αι are unclear; the form may be identical in origin to the aorist infinitive active (τρέψαι), and if so this original identity may account for the 'short' treatment of the final diphthong in both forms. At some stage, the recessive accentuation that was generalized through the verbal system would affect the middle imperative (cf. trisyllabic βούλευσαι) but not the active infinitive (cf. βουλεῦσαι) (cf. Chantraine 1961: 272).

Some accounts of the accentual treatment of final -αι and -οι suggest that there was at some relevant stage some prosodic difference, beyond the rules of accentuation, between the accentually 'short' and 'long' final diphthongs.[29] Hermann (1923: 101) suggested that it was worth investigating the prevocalic metrical treatment of accentually 'short' and 'long' final -αι/-οι before vowels

[29] So recently Olander (2009: 68–9), envisaging a stage at which a generalized prevocalic sandhi variant *-ai̯#/-oi̯#* (giving the forms with 'accentually short' final diphthong) contrasted with the generalized preconsonantal variant *-ai#/-oi#* (giving the forms with 'accentually long' final diphthong). If such a stage existed in the prehistory of the Homeric poems, one might expect to find the 'accentually short' final diphthongs treated as light before a vowel more often in Homer than the 'accentually long' ones.

in Homer, but did not investigate this question himself.[30] A brief treatment of this question is provided in the appendix; on the basis of the evidence summarized there, Homer does not appear to provide evidence for a difference in length or weight between accentually 'short' and 'long' final -αι/-οι. While not proving that there was never any length or weight distinction, these Homeric data are certainly compatible with a morphological account such as is offered here.[31]

11.4.1 *Two questions*

Although no attempt is made here to account for the attested distribution of acute and circumflex accents, their eventual distribution raises two questions for the suggested origins of the double treatment of final -αι and -οι. These cannot be treated here in detail, but I sketch them briefly, with possible answers.

Firstly, why do nominatives plural with *accented* -αι or -οι (e.g. σοφαί, σοφοί) have an acute, while locatives singular with *accented* -οι (e.g. Μεγαροῖ) have a circumflex? Although some difference between two types of final diphthong might seem to be indicated, the accentuation of these endings is in line with that of other nominal endings: nominative and accusative endings with accented long vowels regularly have an acute accent (nom. sg. -ᾱ́, acc. sg. -ᾱ́ν, nom./acc. du. -ᾱ́, acc. pl. -ᾱ́ς; nom./acc. du. -ώ, acc. pl. -ούς), while endings of other cases with accented long vowels regularly have a circumflex (gen. sg. -ᾶς, dat. sg. -ᾷ, gen./dat. du. -αῖν, dat. pl. -αῖς, dat. sg. -ῷ, gen./dat. du. -οῖν, gen. pl. -ῶν, dat. pl.

[30] For the optative and nom. pl. endings Hartel (1874: 371) suggested that either no distinction, or even the opposite of the expected distinction (optative -οι/-αι less readily treated as heavy), was observable, but also did not investigate the matter in detail. Hermann (1923: 100) claims that among all *accented* final long vowels and diphthongs, those with a circumflex are treated as heavy more readily than those with an acute, but apparently fails to control e.g. for the disproportionate incidence of the long diphthongs -ῷ, -ῇ, -ᾷ (genuinely prone to heavy treatment: see Hartel 1874) among circumflexed final long vowels and diphthongs.

[31] A survey of attempts to account for the double accentual treatment of final -οι and -αι cannot be attempted here; for literature see Meier-Brügger (1992: 285–6) and Olander (2009: 66–9), and add Jasanoff (2009: 56 n. 23). It is, however, worth noting that the morphological facts crucial to the present account resemble some that have long been noticed. Thus, paradigmatic pressure has been held to account for the accentuation of κελεύοι like κελεύοις, but λείπεται like λείπει (see Risch 1975: 473, Jasanoff 2009: 56 n. 23; the possibility of λείπεται in the first place is sometimes motivated in terms of a prevocalic sandhi variant *$leik^{w}eto\underset{\frown}{i}$*, accented *$l\acute{e}ik^{w}eto\underset{\frown}{i}$*: see n. 29). For the account offered here the crucial point is rather the monosyllabic character of the termination -οι and the disyllabic character of -εται, combined with the overall tendency for Greek nominal and verbal terminations to be either (a) monosyllabic or (b) disyllabic with a light second syllable. But just these facts also give rise to paradigms in which κελεύοι stands beside κελεύοις, and λείπεται beside λείπει. A quite different account, due to Kiparsky (1967: 124–8), is summarized by Willi, this volume, p. 261.

-*οῖς*). Whatever the ultimate reasons for this distribution,[32] its application included endings consisting of the diphthongs -*αι* and -*οι*.

Secondly, whatever the antiquity of the *σωτῆρα* rule, why does it treat the same final diphthongs as 'short' as does the law of limitation, if there is nothing really 'short' about these final diphthongs? Here the answer may lie in the way in which the double accentual treatment of final diphthongs came to be interpreted synchronically. Even if 'accentually long' final -*αι* and -*οι* were never actually longer than their 'accentually short' counterparts, their different treatment by the law of limitation could have come to be interpreted in terms of an abstract length distinction, with the distribution of acute and circumflex accents coming to be tied to vowel length on this abstract level. Moreover, one of the main dialect divergences in the application of the *σωτῆρα* rule lies in the treatment of final diphthongs. In Doric, the only final diphthongs to have been treated as 'short' by the law of limitation were the middle endings -*ται*, -*σθαι*, etc., but these were treated as 'long' by the *σωτῆρα* rule (hence e.g. *μαρτύρεται* but *δραμείται* < **δραμέεται*: see Hinge 2006: 127). Conceivably both Attic-Ionic and Doric had, at one stage, (i) the law of limitation and (ii) a basic *σωτῆρα* rule tied to vowel lengths on the phonological surface. But then Attic-Ionic, but not Doric, adjusted the *σωτῆρα* rule to match the abstract vowel length distinction implied by the law of limitation.

11.5 A further suggestion: origins of recessive accentuation in the Greek finite verb

It was suggested in section 11.3 that most Greek verbal (as well as nominal) forms already 'obeyed' the law of limitation before this law was in force, either because they were already 'recessive' or because they were accented nearer to the end of the word than the position for 'recessive' accentuation. Furthermore, verb forms built on underived thematic present stems or sigmatic aorist stems were mostly 'recessive' already. From the earliest attested stages, thematic presents and sigmatic aorists are particularly well represented in Greek. One might, therefore, wonder whether the recessive accentuation of most finite verb forms arose as part of the same reanalysis of early Greek accentuation as the law of limitation itself.

[32] On this question, see Jasanoff (2004: 247–9 with 248 n. 2, 253 n. 15).

The standard explanation of recessive accentuation in the Greek finite verb is that old unaccented verb forms became recessive as a consequence of the law of limitation, with the law of limitation being interpreted as limiting the length of a word-final unaccented sequence (Wackernagel 1877). This explanation requires an Indo-European starting-point for the unaccented verb forms of Vedic. Recent work on Vedic, however, accounts increasingly for the distribution of accented and unaccented verbs in terms of Vedic itself (Klein 1992, Hock forthcoming), while retaining some element of Indo-European origin. The suggestion made here for Greek would, while not demonstrating either presence or absence of unaccented verbs for Indo-European, eliminate the Greek evidence for Indo-European unaccented verbs.[33]

11.6 Conclusion

The reconstructions of early Greek nominal and verbal morphology and accentuation presented here are, of course, subject to numerous uncertainties. If they are at least broadly correct, however, a large proportion, probably a majority, of early Greek word tokens 'obeyed' the law of limitation before this law was even in force. Not only did a large proportion of early Greek word tokens already 'obey' the law of limitation, but they did so in such a way that if the position of the accent was reckoned from the end of the word (perhaps because an accent affected primarily the pitch contour at the end of the word), the law of limitation was suggested especially strongly: the accent fell on the penultimate syllable in forms with a heavy final syllable, and on the antepenultimate in trisyllabic or longer forms with a light final syllable.

Appendix: Homeric treatment of final -αι and -οι before vowels

The data summarized in Table 11.4 would appear to show a slightly greater preference for light treatment of 'accentually short' *-οι* and *-αι*.

[33] Hock's (forthcoming) account of ancient Greek as well as Vedic verbal accentuation is economical in a different way. I have not been able to take this article fully into account, and I am currently agnostic as to whether Hock's account is preferable to the one offered here, or even ultimately compatible with it.

Table 11.4 Words with accentually 'long' or 'short' final -οι/-αι[a]

	Treated as light before vowel	Treated as heavy before vowel
With 'accentually long' diphthong:	78 (92%)	7 (8%)
Optatives in -οι/-σαι		
Locative οἴκοι 'at home'		
(Tokens from *Iliad* and *Odyssey*[b])		
With 'accentually short' diphthong:	468 (94%)	30 (6%)
Nom./voc. pl. forms in -οι/-αι		
Infinitives in -αι, -μεναι		
1sg., 2sg., 3sg., and 3pl. forms in -μαι, -αι, -ται, -νται		
Imperatives in -σαι		
(Tokens from *Iliad* 1–4 and *Odyssey* 1. 1–4. 549[c])		

[a] Tokens collected are those found before vowels, including aspirated vowels but not vowels preceded by etymological Ϝ. Forms other than those listed in the left-hand column (e.g. καί, πόποι) are excluded, as are all monosyllabic pronoun forms including οἱ, αἱ, τοί, ταί, οἵ, αἵ. Many of the excluded forms are proclitics, enclitics, interjections, and words whose final -αι or -οι cannot be securely identified as accentually 'short' or 'long'. Word tokens with elided final diphthong (which are very infrequent) are disregarded.

[b] Collected from Prendergast and Marzullo (1962) and Dunbar and Marzullo (1962), and checked against West (1998–2000) and Von der Muehll (1962).

[c] The proportion of Odyssean to Iliadic lines in this sample equals the proportion of lines in the *Odyssey* to that in the *Iliad*. Any differences in occurrence or treatment of final diphthongs between the *Iliad* and *Odyssey* should thus not affect comparison between the two rows of the table.

The discrepancy seen here is, however, not statistically significant.[34] Furthermore, it turns out that over half of our prevocalic word tokens with 'accentually short' final diphthongs are *only* usable in the hexameter if the final diphthong is treated as light (276 out of 498 prevocalic word tokens with 'accentually short' diphthongs, or *c.* 55%). By contrast, only 17 of the 85 prevocalic word tokens with 'accentually long' diphthongs (20%) require light treatment of the final diphthong. The difference here is due to the preponderance, among words with 'accentually short' final diphthongs only, of disyllabic terminations with light penultimate syllable, especially verbal -ομαι, -εαι, -εται, third person plural -αται, and Aeolic infinitive -μεναι. When these follow a heavy syllable, the word must be placed before a vowel, with the final syllable treated as light. This need to place many words with an 'accentually short' final diphthong before a vowel, with light treatment of the diphthong, in fact follows from precisely the tendency for words with 'accentually short' final diphthongs to be shaped differently from those with 'accentually long' final diphthongs.

[34] $X^2 = 0.60$; $p = 0.44$.

If the metrical treatment of 'accentually short' final diphthongs is genuinely to be compared with that of 'accentually long' final diphthongs, words of the same metrical shape need to be compared. Table 11.5 shows the treatment of disyllabic word tokens in our sample beginning with a consonant (not including *h*, but including etymological *ϝ*), and with light first syllable.

Table 11.5 Disyllabic words with initial consonant, light first syllable, and accentually 'long' or 'short' final *-οι/-αι*

	Treated as light before vowel	Treated as heavy before vowel
With 'accentually long' diphthong: Forms as in Table 11.4 (Tokens from *Iliad* and *Odyssey*)	37 (95%)	2 (5%)
With 'accentually short' diphthong: Forms as in Table 11.4 (Tokens from *Iliad* 1–4 and *Odyssey* 1. 1–4. 549)	26 (81%)	6 (19%)

This time the 'accentually long' final diphthongs appear to show a greater preference for 'light' treatment than the 'accentually short' final diphthongs: the opposite of the preference that might be expected if 'accentually long' final *-αι/-οι* were genuinely longer than 'accentually short' final *-αι/-οι*. There are too few tokens now in the right-hand column of the table for a chi-squared test of statistical significance to be valid. However, it is at least clear that on the basis of the evidence examined here, there is no indication that 'accentually long' final diphthongs are more prone to metrically heavy treatment in Homer than 'accentually short' ones.

12

Re-examining Lindeman's Law

PETER BARBER

12.1 Introduction

This is intended as a contribution to the study of Vedic and Indo-European phonology.[1] We will examine Vedic evidence for Lindeman's Law (Lindeman 1965) from a fresh perspective, considering the role of Vedic formulaic composition in the distribution and preservation of archaisms. I am honoured to be able to dedicate this to John Penney, who has been an inspirational teacher and a constant source of wise advice, help, and encouragement through the years.

According to Lindeman's Law, Indo-European monosyllabic words with an initial cluster of a consonant and a prevocalic non-syllabic resonant (e.g. **Ci̯V-*, **Cu̯V-*, etc.) could exhibit an alternative disyllabic form **Cii̯V-* or **Cuu̯V-*, with a syllabic resonant and an epenthetic glide.[2] The distribution of these alternative forms is often thought to be conditioned by the preceding phonological environment: the monosyllabic alternant being found after words ending in a short vowel, and the disyllabic alternant after words ending in a consonant or long vowel, or after a pause.

[1] I would like to thank Anna Morpurgo Davies, Elizabeth Tucker, Philomen Probert, and Don Ringe, who all read a version of this work in its very early stages and provided many useful comments. I would also like to thank the editors for their useful suggestions and corrections. All errors and omissions are, of course, my own responsibility.

[2] Lindeman (1965) followed Edgerton (1934, 1943, 1962) in supposing that monosyllables beginning with **CrV-*, **ClV-*, **CnV-*, or **CmV-* could exhibit disyllabic alternants **Cr̥rV-*, **Cl̥lV-*, **Cn̥nV-*, and **Cm̥mV-*. However, there is essentially no evidence for this in the *Ṛgveda*, as Sihler (2006: *passim*) has shown. Therefore, we will not explore this possibility.

The best evidence for this comes from the *Ṛgveda*. Even though postconsonantal prevocalic syllabic semivowels are almost always written with signs for non-syllabic semivowels, the existence of disyllabic variants such as *diyaús* beside *dyaús* 'sky' (nom. sg.) and *diyā́m* beside *dyā́m* (acc. sg.) is guaranteed by the frequent need to restore this missing syllable in verse, to conform to well-established constraints of metre.

I will argue that all frequently attested Ṛgvedic forms exhibiting such word-initial alternations have another feature in common, besides monosyllabicity: they exhibit unusual distributional restrictions above and beyond those imposed by metre. Moreover, in many cases these restrictions can be seen as an emergent property of the formulaic systems in which a number of the Lindeman's Law forms can be shown to be embedded. We will consider the implications which these formulaic contexts may have for our understanding of the circumstances under which these pairs of monosyllabic and disyllabic alternants were preserved, and the consequences for our ability to accurately formulate the conditions under which word-initial alternation originally took place.

12.2 The basis for Lindeman's Law

It has long been known that it is necessary to restore disyllabic *diyaús* beside *dyaús*, *diyā́m* beside *dyā́m*, etc. in the *Ṛgveda*. But it was Lindeman (1965) who first attached significance to the consistent absence of forms such as **diyúbhis* beside *dyúbhis* (instr. pl.), arguing that only forms which were potentially monosyllabic could exhibit these alternations.[3] This represented a break from the theories of Edgerton (1934, 1943, 1962), who argued that word-initial alternations were once prevalent in all words beginning *CRV-*.[4]

However, one persistent inheritance from Edgerton's approach is the notion that word-initial semivowel syllabicity was determined by the surrounding phonological environment in the *Ṛgveda* and in Indo-European. The inherent appeal of this idea lies in obvious parallels that can be drawn with well-supported and reasonably well-understood principles governing the syllabicity of Ṛgvedic semivowels *word-internally*. Eduard Sievers (1878: 129) showed that postconsonantal prevocalic syllabic semivowels were found after consecutive consonants (e.g. *márt-iya-* 'mortal'), or after a long vowel plus a consonant

[3] The few alternating polysyllables belong to paradigms containing Lindeman's Law monosyllables, or else are transparent compounds of such forms. Analogical spread seems likely.

[4] We should note that most of the metrical judgements on which Edgerton based this wider theory have been overturned; see Sihler (2006: *passim*).

(e.g. *vīr-íya-* 'heroism'), while non-syllabic semivowels were found after a short vowel followed by a single consonant (e.g. *áv-ya-* 'from sheep').[5]

Word-initial alternants seem to exhibit similar patterns. We restore disyllabic *duvā́-* 'two' on thirty-five occasions following a long vowel or a consonant, or line-initially, but seven out of nine occurrences of monosyllabic *dvā-* follow words ending in a short vowel. So, superficially, this looks like Sievers' Law operating across word boundaries. Indeed, Schindler (1977), in a very influential formulation, recast Sievers' Law in terms of Lindeman's Law, suggesting that all such syllabicity alternation was confined to the last syllable of the word; in monosyllables the last syllable and the first syllable are one and the same and so we see word-initial alternation between **i/*u* and **i̯/*u̯*.

However, involvement of the phonological environment has been thrown into serious doubt by the independent work of Sihler (1969, 1971, 2006) and Horowitz (1974). Sihler (1969) showed that the structure of R̥gvedic verse is such that *any word* with the same metrical shape as Lindeman-Edgerton variants tends to be distributed in accordance with the conditions of Sievers' Law. This effectively rules out the possibility of showing whether the distribution of Lindeman's Law forms was dependent on the weight of preceding sequences, even in principle.

These points notwithstanding, we can be certain that the alternations themselves are genuine and Lindeman's restriction to potential monosyllables remains valid. Even if the nature of R̥gvedic metre does not allow us to know how the variants were originally determined, we can at least see whether their metrical distribution tells us anything about their history.

12.3 Vedic metre and metrical freedom

Lindeman's Law variants have several unusual features. The main peculiarity is that even though they are metrically simple and easily accommodated, they exhibit highly restricted distributional patterns, with a strong tendency for the disyllabic member of each pair to occur line-initially. It is not unusual for R̥gvedic words to adopt favoured positions; what remains unexplained is the remarkably consistent behaviour of these forms.

We will restrict our attention to examples in trimeter verse, which comprises about two thirds of the *R̥gveda*. This is a metre with rich internal structure,

[5] For detailed discussion of the historical linguistic literature, see Seebold (1972: 25–175), Horowitz (1974: 11–38), and Collinge (1985: 159–74). For an overview of the Indo-European position, see Mayrhofer (1986: 164–7).

providing a consistent basis for describing the range of positions occupied by certain forms (not all structures in trimeter verse have analogues in dimeter verse). We will generally only discuss examples where both alternants occur in trimeter verse.

A large majority of trimeter lines can be divided into three parts, denoted schematically in Fig. 12.1 (see Arnold 1905: 188).

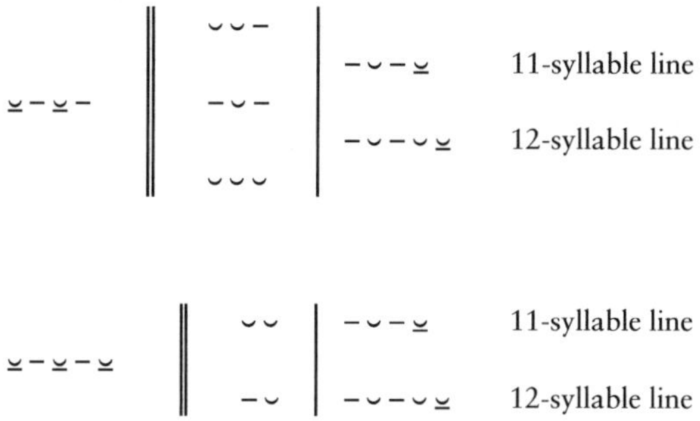

Fig. 12.1 Ṛgvedic trimeter lines

The most notable feature is the caesura, occurring after the fourth or fifth syllable in the vast majority of instances (the early and late caesura respectively). The four or five syllables between the beginning of the line and the caesura constitute the 'opening'. The three syllables following the early caesura or the two syllables following the late caesura are known as the 'break'. The metrically restrictive final portion of the line from the eighth syllable to the end of the line is the 'cadence'.

This metrical scheme can often successfully predict Ṛgvedic word distributions. Consider, for example, the distribution of non-alternating *dyúbhis*, which occurs in almost every metrical position which the above scheme would have predicted:

- syllables 1–2 (5×: *RV* 1. 112. 25a, 3. 31. 16d, 10. 7. 4d, 10. 7. 5a, 10. 59. 4c)
- syllables 3–4 (2×: *RV* 1. 53. 4a, 7. 18. 2b)
- syllables 5–6 in early-caesura lines (2×: *RV* 6. 5. 6c, 10. 3. 3c)
- syllables 6–7 in a late-caesura line (1×: *RV* 1. 34. 8d)
- syllables 11–12 (2×: *RV* 3. 3. 2c, 9. 86. 42b).

Importantly, these metrical patterns are not absolutely rigid. We also find *dyúbhis* in an unexpected position, making the fourth syllable light:

- syllables 4–5 of a late-caesura line (1×: *RV* 2. 1. 1a).

Other possibilities—metrically acceptable in theory—are not attested:

- syllables 6–7 of an early-caesura line
- syllables 7–8 of a late-caesura line
- syllables 9–10.

In spite of these gaps, which may be due to chance, we would not hesitate to characterize *dyúbhis* as metrically unrestricted or free. The distribution is very close to what we would expect within the limits imposed by the metre.

12.4 Lindeman's Law alternants

Among Lindeman's Law monosyllables, a rather different picture emerges. We expect monosyllabic *dyaúḥ* and *dyā́m* to favour the same positions as any other heavy monosyllable with an initial consonant cluster:

- syllables 1–5 in the opening
- immediately after the caesura
- syllable 8 in early-caesura lines
- syllable 11 in eleven-syllable lines.

We might also expect *diyaúḥ* and *diyā́m* to favour a fairly wide range of positions:

- syllables 1–2
- syllables 3–4
- syllables 6–7 in early-caesura lines
- syllables 7–8
- syllables 9–10
- syllables 11–12 in twelve-syllable lines.

However, our expectations are defeated in a rather striking fashion. There are twenty examples of *diyaúḥ* in trimeter verse (see Atkins 1968), occurring in a very limited range of metrical environments and strongly favouring the beginning of the line:

- syllables 1–2 (17×)[6]
- before the caesura (1×: *RV* 10. 45. 8d)
- line-finally (2×: *RV* 1. 89. 4b, 8. 20. 6a).

Similarly, *diyā́m* occurs only in two environments:

- syllables 1–2 (5×: *RV* 1. 52. 11d, 1. 141. 8b, 1. 174. 3b, 4. 22. 3d, 10. 16. 3b);
- before the caesura (1×: *RV* 7. 3. 3c).[7]

[6] *RV* 1. 52. 10a, 2. 4. 6d, 3. 6. 3a, 4. 1. 10d, 4. 21. 1d, 4. 22. 4b, 5. 41. 11d, 6. 36. 5b, 6. 50. 13d, 6. 51. 5a, 6. 68. 4d, 7. 7. 5c, 9. 86. 9b, 10. 36. 2a, 10. 44. 8b, 10. 59. 3b, 10. 132. 6b.

[7] This disyllabic form can be restored in two different ways. Sometimes it must be disyllabic even though the effect of the word-initial cluster is still felt, and *dyáam* is posited. Arnold (1905: 90) only posits *dyáam* where metrically necessary, in other instances preferring *diyā́m* wherever

By contrast, monosyllabic *dyaúḥ* exhibits almost the full range of possibilities, but with a distinct tendency to occur line-finally:

- line-initially (6×: *RV* 1. 164. 33a, 2. 2. 5d, 6. 20. 1a, 8. 100. 12b (*pace* Nooten and Holland 1994: 416, 645), 10. 29. 6b, 10. 74. 2d)
- at various places in the opening (6×: *RV* 4. 51. 11d, 6. 17. 9a, 6. 70. 6a , 10. 59. 7b, 10. 88. 8d, 10. 121. 5a)
- before the caesura (7×: *RV* 1. 57. 5c, 1. 131. 1a, 1. 133. 6b, 1. 89. 10a, 5. 59. 8a, 5. 54. 9b, 10. 63. 3b)
- at the beginning of the cadence (8×: *RV* 1. 71. 8b, 3. 54. 19c, 5. 57. 4d, 6. 58. 1b, 6. 72. 3b, 7. 87. 6a, 10. 88. 2c, 10. 92. 4a)
- line-finally (22×).[8]

Similarly, *dyā́m* occurs in a wide range of positions, but favours the cadence:

- line-initially (5×: *RV* 2. 12. 12d, 4. 36. 1d, 5. 63. 3d, 5. 63. 6d, 10. 65. 7c)
- within the opening (10×)[9]
- before the caesura (11×)[10]
- after the early caesura (2×: *RV* 2. 11. 5c, 2. 11. 15d)
- at the beginning of the cadence (22×)[11]
- line-finally (19×).[12]

Clearly, there are significant distributional tendencies. Disyllabic forms show a strong preference for the beginning of the line, but occur before a pause (i.e. before the caesura or line-finally) with disproportionately lower

disyllabic scansion is required. Sihler (2006: 80–2) reverses this tendency in the case of *RV* 7. 3. 3c, marginally preferring *dyáam* on the basis that *diyā́m* is otherwise restricted to verse-initial position. This is a sensible decision. However, insofar as the positional restrictions are precisely what we are interested in here, the reasoning on either account becomes circular and we probably cannot use the evidence of this line-internal form with any confidence. There are no instances in which we are required to scan disyllabic *dyaúḥ* in an analogous fashion.

[8] *RV* 1. 94. 16d = 9. 97. 58d, 1. 130. 10d, 3. 32. 11c, 4. 1. 17a, 4. 17. 1b, 4. 17. 2a, 4. 17. 4a, 4. 17. 13c, 5. 36. 5a, 5. 45. 2d, 5. 45. 3c, 5. 58. 6d, 6. 12. 2b, 6. 52. 2d, 7. 5. 4a, 7. 34. 23b, 7. 84. 2a, 10. 10. 5d, 10. 45. 4a, 10. 67. 5d, 10. 132. 4a.

[9] *RV* 6. 17. 7b, 9. 85. 9a, 7. 33. 5a, 10. 81. 2d, 4. 33. 1d, 6. 47. 5d, 9. 86. 29c, 10. 94. 12d, 2. 12. 2d, 10. 67. 10b.

[10] *RV* 1. 35. 7d, 1. 121. 2a, 2. 15. 2a, 2. 17. 2d, 3. 30. 9c, 5. 46. 3b, 5. 57. 3a, 7. 24. 5d, 8. 42. 1a, 10. 111. 5c, 10. 125. 7d.

[11] *RV* 1. 31. 4a, 1. 32. 4c, 1. 35. 9d (in a hybrid verse, see Arnold 1905: 15, 215), 1. 51. 9c, 1. 96. 2c, 1. 164. 11b, 1. 180. 10c, 2. 17. 5d, 3. 32. 8c = 10. 121. 1c, 3. 34. 8c, 6. 30. 5d, 6. 64. 2b, 9. 96. 3c, 10. 45. 7d, 10. 55. 1c, 10. 63. 10a, 10. 68. 11b, 10. 88. 3c, 10. 88. 9c, 10. 92. 1d, 10. 149. 1b.

[12] *RV* 1. 33. 14c, 1. 121. 3c, 1. 154. 4c, 1. 173. 6d, 3. 30. 11b, 3. 38. 2b, 3. 59. 1b, 4. 6. 2d, 4. 45. 5a, 5. 29. 6d, 5. 62. 3a, 5. 85. 4a, 6. 47. 29a, 6. 51. 8b, 9. 97. 13b, 10. 3. 5d, 10. 74. 2a, 10. 81. 6b, 10. 89. 4d.

frequency. Monosyllabic forms strongly favour positions before a pause. They can occur line-initially, but comparatively this is disfavoured. This pattern could represent the remnants of a complementary distribution.[13] There does not appear to be any clear metrical, syntactic, or phonological reason for these patterns.

A number of avenues for investigation suggest themselves. These restrictions might be due to chance or the common tendency of Ṛgvedic words to adopt favoured positions; as Sihler (2006: 42) points out, Ṛgvedic distributions are seldom truly random, and often exhibit marked positional preferences. For this reason, one would like to know whether the patterns found in *diyaús/dyaús* and *diyā́m/dyā́m* can be found in other Lindeman's Law forms. Equally, one wonders whether many 'ordinary' disyllabic forms could exhibit just such distributions for reasons which, if not directly driven by metrical necessity, were at least not peculiar to Lindeman's Law disyllables. If similar distributional tendencies are regularly found in non-Lindeman contexts, then they would be less likely to have significance for our understanding of Lindeman's Law.

These possibilities need to be explored before we can know whether to attach any significance to these patterns. Should the patterns prove significant, then a more interesting prospect altogether would be raised. If these restrictions could be construed as an indication that the *metrical properties* of *d(i)yaús* and *d(i)yā́m*, and possibly some other similar forms, were not sufficient on their own to explain their *distributional properties* in Ṛgvedic verse, then this might suggest that some other dependency was at work within the pāda, limiting the range of metrical possibilities for *d(i)yaús* and *d(i)yā́m* beyond our initial statistical expectations. In that case, an obvious approach would be to investigate whether the Lindeman's Law forms show any tendency to be involved in fixed or formulaic collocations which might cause them to be more readily confined to certain positions. If questions of formulaic language arise, then these factors may begin to have a more tangible bearing on our understanding of the history of Lindeman's Law.

12.5 The behaviour of 'ordinary' disyllabic forms

We know from the testimony of *dyúbhis* that a restricted distribution is not a general property of disyllables. However, *diyaús* and *diyā́m* are metrically quite different from *dyúbhis*. A true metrical equivalent would be *purā́* 'before', which consists of a light syllable with a single consonant in the onset followed by a heavy syllable. Sihler (1969: 261–2) used this form to illustrate a 'typical'

[13] This has not gone unnoticed (see Sihler 1971: 69 and Atkins 1968: 684), but thus far an explanation is lacking.

distribution for forms of this shape. We can use his collection of the evidence to illustrate that there is no *inherent* restriction on the distribution of disyllables with this metrical structure (Table 12.1).

Table 12.1 The distribution of *purā́* in Ṛgvedic verse

Position	*purā́* (adverb)	*purā́* (preposition)	Total
Initial	3	8	11
Last before break	8	2	10
Cadence	7 (non-final)	1	8
Final	2	0	2
Other	3	0	3

Unfortunately, it is impractical, for reasons of space, to give proper statistical controls which could rigorously assess the likelihood that any particular Lindeman's Law form would exhibit skewed distributions. However, these methodological limitations are mitigated by the fact that *diyaús* and *diyā́m* are not unique, but form part of a much larger set of parallel examples. Furthermore, we shall presently move beyond this reliance on the 'bulk' distributional properties of Lindeman's Law forms and consider directly the collocational characteristics which may lie behind these metrical properties.

12.6 Other disyllables alternating with monosyllables

Sihler (2006: 10) suggests that the pāda-initial tendency of *diyaús* might be part of a phenomenon which subsumes and goes beyond the Lindeman's Law monosyllables:

> This is the position, also, where virtually all of the reasonably certain examples of disyllabic *gā́m* acc. 'cow', *gā́s* aor. 'you go', *kṣā́m* 'earth' and other monosyllables scanning as disyllables are found. (Sihler 2006: 10)[14]
>
> ...one has to wonder if there is a common thread between all these disyllabic forms. If so, that thread cannot have anything to do with Sievers'-Lindeman's Law (Sihler 2006: 177)

The distribution of *kṣáam* beside *kṣā́m* etc. should indeed have nothing to do with Lindeman's Law. If correct, then this observation suggests that being

[14] This stance is a little inconsistent with his contention that line-internal examples of disyllabic *dyā́m* should be restored as *dyáam* (see above, n. 7).

restricted to a line-initial position is a general, if unusual, feature of all forms exhibiting monosyllable/disyllable pairs, regardless of their historical origin. In that case, we could not learn anything peculiar to Lindeman's Law forms from their distribution.

However, Sihler's claim does not seem to be borne out by the evidence. We find only 59% (20/34) of such disyllables verse-initially in trimeter pādas.[15] The remainder occur in various positions in the cadence (8×),[16] or the break (1×),[17] or before the caesura (5×).[18] These data suggest that the mere existence of monosyllabic and disyllabic variants is insufficient to explain the skewed distribution of Lindeman's Law disyllables.[19]

12.7 Further examples among Lindeman's Law forms

The unusual distributional tendencies of *diyaús/dyaús* and *diyā́m/dyā́m* are in fact pervasive among the Lindeman's Law monosyllables.

12.7.1 t(u)vā́m

Monosyllabic *tvā́m* 'you' (acc. sg.)[20] might be expected to occupy the same wide range of potential positions as *dyaús* and *dyā́m*. In fact *tvā́m* occupies every single expected position and no position which we would consider disfavoured. But in contrast to *dyaús* and *dyā́m*, there does not appear to be any strong bias towards one position:

- syllable 1 (7×: *RV* 2. 1. 13c, 6. 15. 8a, 6. 26. 2c, 7. 11. 2a, 10. 98. 9b, 10. 122. 5c, 10. 122. 7c)
- syllable 2 (3× in early-caesura lines: *RV* 3. 8. 11c, 4. 12. 1a, 7. 22. 2c)

[15] *RV* 6. 6. 4b, 1. 174. 7b (*kṣáam*); 5. 43. 6b (*gnáam* 'wife, divine female', acc. sg.), 5. 43. 13c, 6. 50. 15c, 6. 68. 4a (*gnáaḥ*, nom. pl.); 1. 151. 4d, 6. 46. 2c (*gáam*); 4. 1. 15b, 9. 87. 7d (*gáaḥ*, acc. pl.); 4. 19. 4b (*váaḥ* 'water'); 1. 189. 2c (*púuḥ* 'stronghold, rampart', nom. sg.); 4. 42. 5a, 4. 42. 5b, 10. 48. 1c, 10. 49. 2a, 10. 52. 4a (*máam* 'me'); 6. 19. 10d (*dháaḥ* 'put'); 4. 20. 4c (*páaḥ* 'drink'); 4. 55. 5c (*páat* 'protect').

[16] *RV* 10. 59. 10a (*gáam*); 1. 101. 5b (*gáaḥ*); 4. 42. 9a, 10. 167. 4c (*vaam* 'you'); 6. 15. 3a (*bhúuḥ* 'be'); 1. 173. 8c, 10. 23. 1c, 10. 48. 9a (*bhuut*).

[17] *RV* 4. 28. 5d (*kṣáaḥ*).

[18] *RV* 10. 31. 9a (*kṣáam*); 5. 46. 8a (*gnáaḥ*); 10. 49. 1a (*daam* 'gave'); 6. 63. 9c, 10. 80. 4a (*daat*).

[19] This conclusion is unaffected by including examples from dimeter verse; indeed the proportion of pāda-initial examples is lower: 47% (9/19 examples).

[20] We will not discuss nom. sg. *tvám/tuvám* < **tū* + particle **-óm* (see Sihler 1971: 67), since *tv-/tuv-* here results from an ongoing Vedic process of desyllabification in progress within the *Ṛgveda*. Accusative *tvā́m/tuvā́m* seems to derive from **tu̯e-* + **-om* and hence can potentially be regarded as containing the reflex of an Indo-European sequence **tu̯-/tuu̯-*.

- syllable 2 (3× in late-caesura lines: *RV* 3. 35. 9b, 5. 29. 11c, 8. 60. 1c)
- syllable 3 (5× in late-caesura lines: *RV* 2. 18. 3c, 3. 43. 4a, 7. 7. 7a = 7. 8. 7a (following Nooten and Holland's 1994: 290 scansion with pāda-initial *nū*), 10. 112. 7a)
- syllable 4 (6× in early-caesura lines: *RV* 1. 48. 14a, 1. 91. 21d, 2. 11. 1c, 3. 8. 1a, 4. 18. 12b, 5. 32. 12a)
- syllable 5 (5×: *RV* 7. 21. 8a, 8. 103. 13c, 10. 10. 13c, 10. 10. 14a, 10. 38. 5a)
- first syllable of the cadence (1×: *RV* 2. 17. 7b)
- line-finally (1×: *RV* 8. 36. 2a).

We might suppose *tuvā́m* could occupy the same positions theoretically available to *diyaús* and *diyā́m*. But not all potential positions are occupied despite ample attestation, and *tuvā́m* shows a highly skewed distribution favouring the beginning of a line for no clear metrical reason:

- syllables 1–2 (70×, out of seventy-six occurrences)[21]
- syllables 3–4 in early-caesura lines (2×: *RV* 2. 17. 8a, 4. 19. 1a)
- syllables 7–8 (1×: *RV* 10. 79. 6b)
- syllables 9–10 (2×: *RV* 1. 72. 3a, 7. 22. 6b)
- syllables 11–12 (1×: *RV* 8. 36. 3a).

This skew parallels that of *diyaús* and *diyā́m*, except that there does not seem to be evidence for a complementary distribution. The monosyllabic variant does not show any aversion to the line-initial position.

12.7.2 t(u)vát

We would expect disyllabic *tuvát*, the ablative of the second person singular pronoun, to occur in a wide range of positions:

- syllables 1–2
- syllables 3–4
- syllables 5–6 in early-caesura lines
- syllables 6–7
- syllables 7–8

[21] *RV* 1. 31. 11a, 1. 40. 2a, 1. 53. 11c, 1. 102. 9a, 1. 102. 10c, 2. 1. 8a, 2. 1. 8b, 2. 1. 9a, 2. 1. 9b, 2. 1. 13a, 2. 1. 13b, 2. 32. 3d, 3. 9. 7c, 3. 17. 4c, 3. 43. 1d, 4. 1. 1a, 4. 11. 5a, 4. 16. 18c, 5. 3. 8a, 5. 4. 1a, 5. 8. 1a, 5. 8. 2a, 5. 8. 3a, 5. 8. 4a, 5. 8. 6a, 5. 8. 7a, 5. 11. 5c, 5. 11. 6a, 5. 11. 6d, 6. 1. 5a, 6. 1. 5b, 6. 4. 7a, 6. 7. 4a, 6. 9. 7b, 6. 26. 2a, 6. 26. 2d, 6. 46. 1c, 6. 46. 6a, 7. 1. 3c, 7. 5. 5a, 7. 9. 6a, 7. 12. 3b, 7. 17. 6a, 7. 18. 4c, 7. 88. 6b, 8. 15. 8c, 8. 15. 9c, 8. 19. 29c, 8. 21. 2c, 8. 53. 8c, 8. 60. 5c, 8. 60. 10c, 8. 98. 12a, 9. 68. 7a, 9. 86. 24a, 9. 86. 24c, 9. 86. 30c, 9. 106. 8c, 9. 107. 24c, 10. 42. 4a, 10. 45. 11a, 10. 69. 10b, 10. 91. 9a, 10. 98. 9a, 10. 112. 9b, 10. 122. 5d, 10. 122. 7a, 10. 147. 2c, 10. 147. 2d, 10. 160. 2b.

- syllables 9–10
- syllables 11–12 in twelve-syllable lines.

In fact, *tuvát* has a strong tendency to appear line-initially:

- syllables 1–2 (15×)[22]
- syllables 3–4 (1× in an early-caesura line: *RV* 7. 11. 1b, following Arnold 1905: 308)
- syllables 9–10 (1× in a twelve-syllable line: *RV* 10. 18. 13a)
- syllables 11–12 (1× in a twelve-syllable line: *RV* 10. 91. 8d).

Monosyllabic *tvát* should also be capable of a wide distribution in theory:

- syllables 1–4 of the opening
- syllable 5 (as part of the opening or early-caesura break)
- syllable 6
- syllable 7 in late-caesura lines
- syllable 8 in early-caesura lines
- syllable 9
- syllable 11.

In fact, *tvát* favours the opening, which has fourteen out of seventeen examples. Interestingly, despite this skew, *tvát* never occurs line-initially (in contrast with *tuvát*):

- syllable 2 (5×: *RV* 1. 84. 19c, 3. 17. 5a, 5. 3. 5a, 6. 24. 6a, 6. 61. 14d)
- syllable 3 (7× in late-caesura lines: *RV* 1. 57. 4c, 2. 28. 6d, 3. 30. 1d, 5. 31. 2c, 6. 34. 1b, 7. 32. 19c, 8. 66. 13c)
- syllable 4 (2× in early-caesura lines: *RV* 4. 22. 6c, 10. 112. 9c)
- syllable 6 (1× in an early-caesura break: *RV* 10. 121. 10a)
- syllable 9 (2× as the second syllable of the cadence: *RV* 2. 33. 10d, 6. 21. 10d).

Again, we see a partial complementarity between monosyllabic and disyllabic alternants, which certainly seems to call for further investigation.

12.7.3 t(u)vé

We expect *tuvé*, the locative singular of the second person pronoun, to be able to occupy the same theoretical range of positions as *tuvā́m*, *diyaús*, and *diyā́m*, but once again we find a skewed distribution:

[22] *RV* 3. 14. 6a, 4. 11. 3a, 4. 11. 3b, 4. 11. 3c, 4. 11. 4a, 4. 11. 4c, 4. 11. 4d, 6. 7. 3a, 6. 7. 3b, 6. 13. 1a, 6. 31. 2a, 7. 5. 3a, 7. 21. 3c, 8. 97. 14c, 10. 98. 2b.

- syllables 1–2 (27×)[23]
- syllables 3–4 (2× in early-caesura lines: *RV* 4. 2. 9b, 7. 4. 4d)
- syllables 9–10 (2× in eleven-syllable lines: *RV* 1. 72. 6a, 10. 44. 4c[24])
- syllables 11–12 (2× in twelve-syllable lines: *RV* 1. 48. 10a, 8. 61. 6c).

We expect *tvé* to occupy the same wide range of positions theoretically available to *tvā́m*, *dyaús*, and *dyā́m*. Indeed, just as with *tvā́m*, we find the entire range of possible positions attested, without any particular preferences:

- syllable 1 (1× in a late-caesura line: *RV* 2. 1. 14a)
- syllable 2 (2×: *RV* 2. 9. 3d, 7. 1. 21c)
- syllable 3 (2× in late-caesura lines: *RV* 6. 34. 1a, 6. 47. 14a)
- syllable 4 (2× in early-caesura lines: *RV* 6. 12. 2a, 7. 8. 5a)
- syllable 5 (3× in late-caesura lines: *RV* 3. 19. 4a, 6. 1. 13c, 8. 66. 12a)
- syllable 6 (1× in a late-caesura line: *RV* 6. 11. 3a)
- syllable 8 (3×: *RV* 5. 33. 6a, 7. 18. 1c, 10. 142. 1a)
- syllable 11 (3× in eleven-syllable lines: *RV* 6. 1. 13d, 10. 98. 10a, 10. 105. 8c).

12.7.4 d(u)vá-

There may be evidence for a complementary distribution between monosyllabic and disyllabic case forms of *dvá-* 'two'. It is difficult to discern any pattern, since individual attestations are few. But if we are entitled to combine the data from metrically equivalent parts of the paradigm, an interesting result emerges.

In principle, *duvā́*, *duvé*, and *duvaú* should be able to occupy the same positions as *tuvā́m*, while *dvā́*, *dvé*, and *dvaú*[25] should be parallel to *tvā́m*. But this does not explain the actual distribution seen in Fig. 12.2 and Fig. 12.3.[26]

23 *RV* 1. 36. 5c, 1. 36. 6a, 1. 51. 7a, 1. 59. 1b, 1. 73. 7a, 1. 94. 3b, 1. 169. 5a, 2. 11. 12a, 2. 28. 8c, 3. 20. 3d, 5. 3. 1c, 6. 1. 3b, 6. 5. 2a, 7. 1. 17a, 7. 5. 6a, 7. 11. 3b, 7. 12. 3c, 7. 18. 1a, 7. 18. 1c, 8. 4. 16c, 8. 19. 8c, 8. 103. 5c, 9. 110. 7a, 10. 43. 2b, 10. 69. 8a, 10. 120. 3a, 10. 140. 3c.

24 On this cadence, see Arnold (1905: 319) and Nooten and Holland (1994: 654).

25 Note that while monosyllabic *dvaú* does exist, it is not attested in trimeter verse in the *Ṛgveda*.

26 The boxes in these diagrams represent positions in trimeter lines where forms appear or could have appeared, together with the number of attestations. Geometrical difficulties make it expedient to omit a box representing syllables 7–8 in the first diagram. No examples occupy this position.

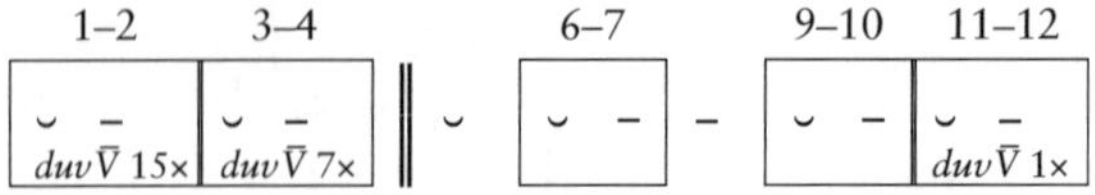

Fig. 12.2 *duvā́*, *duvé*, and *duvaú* (represented together as *duvV̄*)[a]

[a] Syllables 1–2: *duvā́* at *RV* 1. 162. 19b, 1. 164. 20a, 6. 67. 1d, 7. 18. 22b, 9. 86. 42c, 10. 27. 17c, 10. 27. 23d; *duvé* at *RV* 1. 95. 1a, 1. 155. 5a, 4. 58. 3b, 5. 47. 5c, 7. 18. 22a, 10. 27. 7c, 10. 88. 15a, 10. 88. 16a. Syllables 3–4: *duvā́* at *RV* 1. 144. 4a, 8. 29. 8a, 8. 29. 9a, 10. 48. 7b; *duvé* at *RV* 1. 185. 2a, 3. 30. 11a, 3. 56. 2d. Line-finally: *duvé* at *RV* 1. 161. 3c.

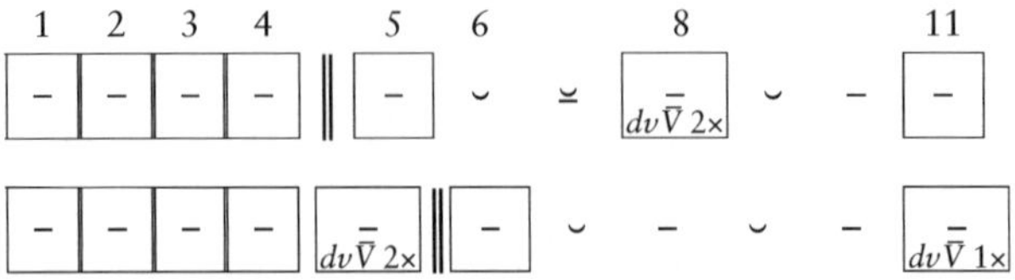

Fig. 12.3 *dvā́* and *dvé* (represented together as *dvV̄*)[a]

[a] Syllable 5: *dvā́* at *RV* 10. 17. 2d; *dvé* at *RV* 3. 2. 9d. Syllable 8: *dvā́* at *RV* 4. 33. 5a; *dvaú* at *RV* 1. 35. 6a. Line-finally: *dvaú* at *RV* 5. 62. 6d.

Twenty-two out of twenty-three disyllabic examples occur in positions 1–2 or 3–4, while the five monosyllabic examples occur in the fifth syllable of the line or later. This seems to represent a near-complementary distribution, though only if we accept the validity of combining the data in this way. Of course, the complementarity is not perfect, because there is a single line-final example of disyllabic *duvā́*.

12.7.5 s(i)yá-/t(i)yá-

The demonstrative pronoun *syá-/tyá-* 'this (one)' behaves slightly differently from the other Lindeman pairs discussed so far. The disyllabic forms *siyá, siyā́, tiyám, tiyát, tiyā́,* and *tiyé* are not well-attested individually. But when the data is combined, it is clear that examples outside the opening are very rare. This property does not emerge in any obvious way from metrical considerations:

- syllables 1–2 (6×: *RV* 1. 52. 1a, 5. 32. 4a, 5. 32. 5a, 5. 32. 6a, 5. 32. 8a, 10. 178. 1a)
- syllables 2–3 (1×: *RV* 1. 104. 2a)
- syllables 3–4 of late-caesura lines (5×: *RV* 1. 100. 17a, 5. 33. 10a, 6. 27. 4a, 6. 65. 1a, 10. 138. 6a)
- syllables 3–4 of early-caesura lines (6×: *RV* 1. 88. 5a, 6. 44. 16a, 7. 75. 3a, 7. 75. 4a, 7. 80. 2a, 9. 111. 2a)

- syllables 4–5 of late-caesura lines (2×: *RV* 7. 8. 2a, 7. 19. 2a)
- line-finally (1×: *RV* 10. 75. 6b).

The monosyllabic forms show a similarly restricted distribution:

- syllable 1 (2×: *RV* 1. 110. 3c, 2. 30. 8c)
- syllable 3 of late-caesura lines (34×)[27]
- syllable 3 of early-caesura lines (29×)[28]
- syllable 4 of early-caesura lines (17×)[29]
- syllable 5 of late-caesura lines (7×: *RV* 7. 23. 3c, 1. 61. 3a, 10. 41. 1a, 1. 61. 15a, 6. 18. 3a, 10. 35. 1a, 10. 124. 5a)
- syllable 6 (1×: *RV* 1. 161. 4b)
- syllable 9 (1×: *RV* 10. 68. 7a).

Both monosyllabic and disyllabic alternants show marked restrictions, but in this instance their distributions almost completely overlap. Both sets of forms are practically confined to the opening, in which eighty-nine out of ninety-one monosyllabic and twenty out of twenty-one disyllabic examples are found. Monosyllabic examples tend to avoid the beginning of the line, in contrast to the disyllabic alternant.

12.7.6 j(i)yók

It is usually supposed that *jyók* 'for a long time' is from the same root as *dyaús*, and that the initial cluster represents a contamination between the expected form **dyók* and the regular outcome of a Middle Indo-Aryan sound change *j(j)- < dy-*.[30] However, in that case we would need to suppose that disyllabic *jiyók* is a replacement for **diyók*, because otherwise we would have to accept the unlikely resolution of a Middle Indo-Aryan cluster.

[27] *RV* 2. 31. 4a, 2. 38. 1a, 4. 38. 7a, 4. 40. 4a, 4. 45. 1a, 5. 30. 1a, 5. 56. 7a, 6. 50. 13a, 6. 71. 1a, 6. 71. 4a, 7. 38. 1a, 7. 60. 2a, 7. 68. 9a, 9. 84. 4a, 9. 89. 1a, 9. 96. 15a, 5. 1. 7a, 6. 50. 6a, 7. 68. 7a, 8. 86. 4a, 9. 84. 5a, 10. 11. 4a, 1. 139. 2a, 3. 62. 1c, 6. 51. 1a, 6. 62. 3a, 6. 63. 1a, 7. 73. 4a, 2. 31. 5a, 4. 6. 9a, 9. 92. 4a, 10. 138. 1a, 8. 48. 11a, 1. 51. 1a.

[28] *RV* 2. 31. 3a, 2. 33. 7a, 2. 36. 5a, 7. 67. 7a, 7. 69. 5a, 8. 27. 12a, 9. 87. 4a, 9. 97. 46a, 10. 92. 12a, 1. 151. 2a, 5. 46. 5a, 7. 68. 6a, 10. 112. 4a, 1. 122. 4a, 3. 30. 3d, 6. 50. 10a, 10. 61. 15a, 4. 6. 10a, 5. 33. 8a, 5. 33. 9a, 5. 46. 6a, 7. 36. 7a, 1. 88. 6a, 1. 119. 9a, 1. 165. 6a, 1. 178. 1a, 1. 181. 8a, 7. 95. 4a, 1. 63. 8a.

[29] *RV* 6. 22. 6a, 10. 80. 3a, 1. 63. 4a, 1. 63. 7a, 4. 5. 9a, 4. 12. 6a, 4. 51. 1a, 6. 20. 13a, 6. 63. 2c, 8. 96. 16a, 8. 96. 17a, 8. 96. 18a, 10. 89. 8a, 7. 104. 20a, 1. 104. 5a, 1. 92. 1a, 7. 78. 3a.

[30] On such 'prakritisms' in the *Ṛgveda*, see Renou (1957: 7); on the sound change, Wackernagel (1896: 163) and Debrunner (1957: 87).

Atkins (1968: 709) notes that *j(i)yók* is almost always disyllabic (9/13 occurrences, monosyllabic twice).[31] He also observes that it is almost always line-initial, 'for which the reasons are unclear': 'One receives the impression that *diyaús* and *diyā́m* and *jiyók* are remnants from a very early stage of poetic composition' (Atkins 1968: 709). Unfortunately, Atkins does not elaborate on this thought. Nevertheless, his observations are more or less in keeping with the results obtained so far. The distribution of disyllabic forms is very limited:

- syllables 1–2 (6×: *RV* 1. 33. 15c, 1. 136. 6f, 2. 30. 10c, 4. 25. 4b, 6. 15. 1d, 10. 37. 7d);
- syllables 9–10 (1×: *RV* 7. 22. 6c).

Monosyllabic *jyók* only occurs line-initially (2×: *RV* 6. 28. 3d, 10. 124. 1d).

The monosyllabic form is more restricted than its disyllabic partner. However, given the small number of attestations, it is not clear that we can draw many conclusions regarding its original distribution. Disyllabic *jiyók* on the other hand can probably be said to show a restricted distribution given the number of instances and the range of positions theoretically available.

12.7.7 s(u)vā́t, s(u)vaíḥ, *and* s(u)vā́m

We only have a few examples of each case form of the possessive adjective *svá-/suvá-* 'own'. If it is legitimate to combine data from metrically equivalent forms, then forms with the shape *suvV̄C* (*suvā́t, suvaíḥ*, and *suvā́m*) tend to cluster around the line-initial position:

- syllables 1–2 (6×)[32]
- syllables 7–8 (1× *suvā́t* straddling the transition between an early-caesura break and the cadence: *RV* 5. 87. 4c)
- syllables 10–11 (1× *suvaíḥ* in an eleven-syllable line: *RV* 10. 74. 2d).

Monosyllabic forms of the shape *svV̄C* appear in a wider range of positions and show a preference for the end of the line:

- syllable 1 (1× *svaíḥ* in an early-caesura line: *RV* 8. 97. 3c)
- syllable 2 (1× *svā́m* in an early-caesura line: *RV* 1. 33. 13d)
- syllable 4 (2× *svā́m* in early-caesura lines: *RV* 10. 61. 7a, 10. 120. 9b)

[31] In *RV* 9. 91. 6d and 10. 59. 6c, we find *j(i)yók* and *sū́r(i)yam* 'sun'. One extra syllable is needed in each line and it is unclear whether to restore *jiyók* or *sū́riyam*. These instances will be left aside.

[32] Five examples in early-caesura lines: 1× *suvā́t* (*RV* 10. 124. 2d), 1× *suvaíḥ* (*RV* 3. 53. 8d), 3× *suvā́m* (*RV* 8. 11. 10c, 10. 56. 6c, 10. 56. 7c); and 1× *suvaíḥ* in a late-caesura line (*RV* 8. 18. 13c).

- syllable 5 (1× *svaíḥ* in a late-caesura line: *RV* 1. 68. 8b)
- syllable 11 (6×: *svā́t* at *RV* 6. 17. 5d; *svā́m* at *RV* 3. 53. 8b, 6. 11. 2d; *svaíḥ* at *RV* 1. 181. 4b, 6. 5. 4c, 6. 67. 1d).

However, caution is required, since even pooling this data does not produce a particularly decisive outcome and it does not seem wise to speculate too much on the basis of these examples. When dealing with small numbers of instances, there is always the danger that chance has played a role.

12.8 Inconclusive examples

Several disyllabic forms do not exhibit any obvious sign of distributional restrictions or skews. What these forms have in common is the very small number of attested instances. It could be that the lack of sufficient data prevents a more marked distribution from emerging, but this is simply speculation. The disyllabic examples alone are given here by way of illustration:

suváḥ 'own' (nom. sg.)	syllables 3–4 (1× in an early-caesura line: *RV* 10. 18. 1b)
suvám (acc. sg.)	syllables 2–3 (1× in an early-caesura line: *RV* 1. 58. 2a[33])
	syllables 6–7 (3×: *RV* 5. 58. 7b, 6. 41. 1c, 10. 56. 2d)
	syllables 7–8 (1×: *RV* 6. 28. 2b)
	syllables 10–11 (1× in an eleven-syllable line: *RV* 7. 82. 6b)
suvā́ (nom. sg. fem.)	syllables 1–2 (1× in an early-caesura line: *RV* 10. 83. 5d)
(acc. pl. ntr.)	syllables 9–10 (1×: *RV* 10. 23. 4a)
suvé (loc. sg.)	syllables 1–2 (1× in a late-caesura line: *RV* 4. 16. 10c)
	syllables 3–4 (2× in early-caesura lines: *RV* 6. 40. 5b, 10. 105. 10c)
	syllables 5–6 (1× in the break: *RV* 7. 36. 5b)
	syllables 9–10 (3×: *RV* 1. 94. 14a, 2. 2. 11d, 5. 48. 3c)
jiyā́- 'bow string'	syllables 1–2 (1×: *RV* 6. 75. 3d)
śvás 'tomorrow'	syllables 3–4 (1× in an early-caesura line: *RV* 1. 167. 10b)
duvís 'twice'	syllables 1–2 (2×: *RV* 6. 66. 2b, 10. 120. 3b)
	syllables 9–10 (1× in a twelve-syllable line: *RV* 1. 53. 9a)

We set aside examples where we cannot find both alternants in trimeter verse, since these provide no basis for comparison. We cannot use *hiyaḥ* 'yesterday', since it occurs only once in a trimeter line. Similarly, in trimeter verse we only find disyllabic optatives of 'to be' *siyā́m* (2× line-initially: *RV* 6. 50. 9c, 8. 19. 25b)

[33] However, cf. Oldenberg (1909–12: i. 58) for an alternative scansion.

and *siyā́t* (2× line-initially: *RV* 3. 1. 23c, 7. 34. 21b). There are syllabicity alternations in *śvan-/śuvan-* 'dog', but no relevant examples in trimeter verse.

12.9 Enclitic forms

Resolution of the enclitic pronouns *t(u)vā* 'you' and *t(u)va-* 'other, another' is very much dependent on the weight of the preceding syllable (see Arnold 1905: 95). Otherwise, their distribution seems free within the limits imposed by their enclitic status. Sihler's (1971: 67–8 and n. 76) view that enclitics could straightforwardly obey *Sievers'* Law, being in effect part of the preceding phonological word, seems completely plausible. From this perspective, we ought not to discuss these examples on the same basis as other Lindeman forms, and I leave them aside.

12.10 Explaining Lindeman's Law distributions

Our investigation shows that well-attested examples of Lindeman's Law forms share some rather peculiar distributional features. The positions adopted by disyllabic forms are more restrictive than might have been expected on metrical grounds alone, and there is a marked tendency for these forms to occur initially in the pāda. The widespread nature of the phenomenon argues strongly against the possibility of this being a chance occurrence, and the contrasting behaviour of other disyllables from non-Lindeman contexts further suggests that this pattern is noteworthy.

If we find a particular position consistently favoured without particularly good metrical reasons, then we are inclined to conclude that this is a *traditional* or *stylistic* feature. This impression is strengthened when considering the evidence for a partial complementary distribution of forms in *dyaús/diyaús*, *diyā́m/dyā́m*, *dvá-/duvá-*, and *perhaps* in *s(u)vā́*, *s(u)vaíḥ*, *s(u)vā́m*, albeit with very few examples. We also saw hints that certain monosyllabic forms avoid the most favoured position of the disyllabic form in other instances: *s(i)yá-/t(i)yá-* and *t(u)vát*. Such suggestions of complementary distributions are reminiscent of patterns seen in formulaic language, where a number of more or less fixed expressions, which have co-existed for a considerable time, ultimately come to occupy distinct metrical contexts.

One might object to these ideas on the grounds that one might have expected it would be the *cadence* of trimeter verses, with its fixed metrical patterns, that would be expected to preserve fossilized forms. However, there is at least one other instance where more examples of apparent archaisms survive in the opening than elsewhere. Disyllabic genitives in *-aam* (for *-ām*), which are often taken to preserve the hiatus from an intervocalic laryngeal, preferentially occur in the opening, or less often just after the caesura in trimeter verse (see Arnold 1905: 93).

We suggested earlier that, at least in some cases, the distribution of Lindeman's Law disyllables might be more explicable if they were particularly inclined to fall into a narrow range of traditional collocations, since the theoretical range of possible metrical positions would thereby be narrower than the one which would pertain to the same form in isolation.

12.10.1 d(i)yaús *reconsidered*

It is instructive to consider expressions for 'heaven and earth', which constitute a substantial proportion of the occurrences of nom./voc. *dyaús* and *diyaús*.[34] Disyllabic *diyaús* occurs in lines together with a word for 'earth' in twelve out of twenty examples in trimeter verse (60%).[35] By contrast, such expressions only account for twelve out of fifty examples of monosyllabic *dyaús* (24%).[36] At a minimum, this demonstrates that the monosyllabic and disyllabic variants do not have an identical function in the *Ṛgveda*, just as they do not have an identical metrical distribution. It seems a distinct possibility that the functional differences will ultimately account for the distributional differences.

In 40% of the instances of *diyaús* and 20% of the instances of *dyaús* we find *pṛthivī́* in the same line. Often *d(i)yaús* and *pṛthivī́* are conjoined with *ca* 'and' or *ca* ... *ca*, and usually the two terms are non-adjacent with *pṛthivī́* appearing after the caesura.[37]

In seven examples we find *diyaús* line-initially with *pṛthivī́* immediately after the caesura:

[34] It is much harder to draw meaningful comparisons between *diyā́m* (or perhaps *dyáam*) and *dyā́m*, as the disyllabic form has only six occurrences in trimeter verse.

[35] There are eight examples with *pṛthivī́*, three examples with *bhūmi-* or *bhūma-*, and one with *kṣā́ḥ*.

[36] There are ten examples with *pṛthivī́*, one with *bhūma-*, and one with *kṣā́ḥ*. Note that the examples of monosyllabic *dyaús* given in the analysis in section 12.4 only amount to forty-nine instances. The figure used here also takes into account *RV* 10. 132. 1a, which is an irregular line of unclear metrical structure, but which is nonetheless usable in this context, where we are interested primarily in the collocational characteristics of these forms.

[37] Discontinuous formulas with the second member at a metrical colon boundary are typologically quite common: cf. ἄνδρα ... πολύτροπον 'the versatile man' (Hom. *Od.* 1. 1), where ἄνδρα is line-initial and πολύτροπον comes after the trochaic caesura (see Watkins 1992: 408). For a comprehensive overview of collocations entered into by all morphological forms of *dyaús* and *pṛthivī́*, see Ditrich (2010), though she does not differentiate between monosyllabic and disyllabic forms of *dyaús*.

#diyaús ⏘ – ‖ *pṛthivī́* (5×: *RV* 3. 6. 3a, 6. 51. 5a, 6. 68. 4d, 7. 7. 5c, 10. 36. 2a)
#diyaús ⏘ – ⏘‖ *pṛthivī́* (2×: *RV* 6. 50. 13d, 9. 86. 9b)

Twice when paired with *pṛthivī́*, *diyaús* is qualified as *pítaḥ* 'father', and in one of these instances *pṛthivī́* is qualified as *mā́ta* 'mother', with the resulting expression occupying all but the last two syllables of the line:

#díyaus pítaḥ ‖ *pṛ́thivī mā́tar* (*RV* 6. 51. 5a)

In another instance, *diyaús* occurs line-finally and this pairing constitutes almost the whole of the break and cadence:

‖ *pṛthivī́ (tat) pitā́ diyaúḥ#* (*RV* 1. 89. 4b)

Monosyllabic *dyaús* also co-occurs with *pṛthivī́* after the caesura with considerable regularity. There are examples in the opening:

dyaús ⏑ ⏑ – ‖ *pṛthivī́* (1×: *RV* 10. 29. 6b)
– *dyaús ca* – – ‖ *pṛthivī́ ca* (1×: *RV* 4. 51. 11d)
– – *dyaús* – –‖ *pṛthivī́ ca* (1×: *RV* 10. 121. 5a)
– – – *dyaús ca* ‖ *pṛthivī́ ca* (1×: *RV* 6. 70. 6a)

In one instance, *pṛthivī́* does not immediately follow the caesura:

– *dyaús* – ⏑‖ – *pṛthivī́* (1×: *RV* 10. 88. 8d)

Interestingly, we never see *dyaús* in the last syllable of the opening adjacent to *pṛthivī́*. There is no obvious metrical reason for this. One possibility would be a blocking effect caused by the availability of the *dvandva* compound *dyā́vāpṛthivī́*. But without further investigation this remains mere speculation.

It is more common to find patterns in which *pṛthivī́* follows the caesura and monosyllabic *dyaús* occurs in the cadence:

‖ *pṛthivī́ utá dyaúḥ* (4×: *RV* 1. 94. 16d, 7. 5. 4a, 9. 97. 58d, 10. 10. 5d)
‖ *pṛthivī́ dyaús utā́paḥ* (2×: *RV* 3. 54. 19c, 10. 88. 2c)

So, the near-complementary distribution of *diyaús* and *dyaús* is also found in discontinuous collocations with *pṛthivī́*; the positions which *diyaús* occupies are disfavoured (though not completely avoided) by *dyaús* and vice versa. Furthermore, we only find *diyaús* in a few word order patterns, whereas *dyaús* is more flexible and appears to be the default syllabification.

It seems attractive to suppose that these formulas for 'heaven and earth' constitute at least a partial explanation for the distributional characteristics of *d(i)yaús*. Perhaps pāda templates in which the word signifying HEAVEN was required to be line-initial became particularly associated with the disyllabic alternant, while those where it was required to fall in the cadence and other positions became associated with monosyllabic *dyaús*. Such a functional split would be plausible, because mature formulaic systems do not tend to tolerate redundancy. The associations could have been completely arbitrary in the first instance; we would not need to suppose that this disposition of the available material represents vestiges of an inherited phonological distribution, though of course that possibility, though probably unprovable, does exist.

It might be objected that we could consistently assume that the causality runs in the opposite direction, in other words, that these formulaic instances of *d(i)yaús* merely *reflect* overall distributional properties of *d(i)yaús* and that the near-complementary distribution of word order patterns follows naturally enough from the near-complementary distribution of *diyaús* and *dyaús*. However, while it is obvious how distributional tendencies of a certain set of formulaic patterns might emerge in the overall statistical distribution of *d(i)yaús*, it is completely unclear how an overall statistical distribution could exist independently of the individual instances from which it is constituted.

The formulaic nature of these collocations seems to provide a basis, albeit preliminary and partial, for understanding the distribution of *d(i)yaús*. However, considerably more work is required to understand the pattern completely. For example, it remains an open question whether there are further significant formulaic elements among the other instances of *d(i)yaús*,[38] or whether the distribution of 'heaven and earth' formulas alone was sufficient to provide an historical basis for creating innovative verses with *dyaús* and *diyaús* in those particular traditional positions.

12.10.2 syá-/tyá- *reconsidered*

We might be able to explain restrictions on *s(i)yá-/t(i)yá-* in a similar fashion. Klein (1998) conducted a study of Ṛgvedic collocations entered into by *s(i)yá-/t(i)yá-*, though without making a distinction between monosyllabic and disyllabic variants. He pointed out that *s(i)yá-/t(i)yá-* already seems to constitute an archaism in the *Ṛgveda*, being morphologically restricted to nominative/accusative forms, with just four exceptions. He also noticed their restriction to the opening, usually in the first pāda in a stanza,[39] attributing this behaviour

[38] There might be hints from patterns like *#diyaúr ná bhū́miḥ* (*RV* 10. 132. 6b), *#diyaúr ná bhū́miṃ* (*RV* 10. 59. 3b), *#diyaúr ná bhū́ma* (*RV* 6. 36. 5b), etc.

[39] Klein (1998: 362) includes dimeter pādas and by his count 198 of the 204 occurrences are in the pāda opening with 188 instances in the first pāda of the stanza.

to the fact that *s(i)yá-/t(i)yá-* is only found in a few relatively fixed expressions in stylized openings.

Of the nine collocation types Klein identified for *s(i)yá-/t(i)yá-* more generally, only five are represented in the disyllabic alternants.[40] Furthermore, over three-quarters of the disyllabic examples belong to just two of those types. If the disyllabic alternants had reflected the properties of Ṛgvedic *s(i)yá-/t(i)yá-* taken as a whole, then we might have expected these two types to account for less than one-third of the examples.[41] Given the capacity of all of Klein's collocational types to accommodate extra particles and/or incorporate various metrically distinct elements, it would be very difficult to attribute this skew to any metrical necessity.

So it now seems that disyllabic alternants exhibit an even more restrictive distribution than their monosyllabic counterparts in formulaic terms, even if this was not immediately evident when looking at the positions in the line which both sets of forms occupy.

Unfortunately, it is not possible to explore here the collocations entered into by all the other Lindeman's Law alternants. But there are hints that such formulaic patterns might be more widespread. For example, very often *tuvā́m* is followed by a disyllabic god's name, usually Agni, but sometimes Indra in the vocative. It would be interesting to know the extent to which such expressions are conventionalized or stylized. There are certainly patterns here which would bear further investigation.

12.11 Lindeman's Law beyond the *Ṛgveda*

We have an important and unexpected confirmation of the notion that Lindeman's Law disyllables might survive in formulaic contexts, from the Brāhmaṇic period. Jamison (1986) notes that a considerable number of forms in Vedic prose have 'assigned syllable counts', i.e. an indication of the number of syllables. When forms contain a postconsonantal prevocalic semivowel, the assigned syllable counts in the Brāhmaṇas and Upaniṣads often reflect Vedic rules of distraction rather than the Classical Sanskrit pronunciation:

bhū́mir antárikṣaṃ dyaúr íti / aṣṭā́v akṣárāṇi (*BĀU* V. 14. 1 = *ŚB* XIV. 8. 15. 1)
'"Earth, atmosphere, heaven" is eight syllables'

[40] Klein's Types I (10×), IV (2×), V (6×), IIIB (1×), IIA (1×), and one uncategorized example.

[41] Overall, 64/204 Ṛgvedic instances belong to Types I and V.

Given that *bhū́mir antárikṣam* and *dyaúr* superficially have seven syllables collectively, this implies that the pronunciation *diyaús* was preserved in the Brāhmaṇic period, in the context of liturgical archaisms. Jamison (1986: 167–81) finds that *tvác* 'skin' must be read with two syllables at *MS* III. 3. 3 and *ŚB* X. 4. 1. 16–17, in a formulaic context, or, as Jamison also puts it, in a 'piece of patterned traditional lore'. This is very interesting, because disyllabic *tuvác* is not preserved in the *Ṛgveda*, which has only *tvác*, suggesting that this is an overlooked example of Lindeman's Law. From our perspective, this example can serve to demonstrate that the formulaic context in which many of the Ṛgvedic Lindeman's Law variants are found is probably not an incidental feature, but is likely to have been instrumental in the preservation and metrical disposition of these forms.

12.12 Some conclusions

Lindeman's Law monosyllable/disyllable alternations take place in a handful of archaic, largely inherited words. Practically all well-attested disyllabic examples exhibit highly restricted, and in some cases demonstrably formulaic, distributions in Vedic verse or prose. None of this is terribly surprising, if one starts from the assumption that this semivowel syllabicity alternation is ultimately inherited from Indo-European.

However, these findings do seem to speak against Sihler's (1971: 76–7 n. 25) suggestion that this Ṛgvedic variation can be explained, in some cases, as a product of the Middle Indo-Aryan desyllabification of prevocalic semivowels secondarily making its way into the *Ṛgveda* and appearing as an alternation. Nor do they seem consistent with Sihler's (2006: 184–5) suggestion that many individual analogical innovations within Indic are responsible.

The alternations seem to be ancient and embedded in formulaic language. However, this characteristic in itself raises an epistemological problem when it comes to Indo-European reconstruction. Insofar as Lindeman's monosyllabicity criterion was primarily based on a synchronic observation of what was preserved in the *Ṛgveda*, the circumstances of that preservation start to matter very much. The question becomes whether the Lindeman monosyllable/disyllable pairs necessarily constitute an accurate reflection of the prehistoric situation, if they were in some circumstances preserved in and mediated by formulaic language.

One could easily imagine a situation in which the circumstances of preservation could be biased towards preserving monosyllable/disyllable pairs but not, for example, disyllable/trisyllable pairs like **diyubhis* beside *dyúbhis*, or even

**diyā́vāpṛthivī́* beside *dyā́vāpṛthivī́* (assuming for one moment that such things could have existed). Factors such as this might be ascertainable through further study of the general properties of other established Ṛgvedic formulaic systems.

To pursue the example: there is no indication that *dyúbhis* enters into any habitual collocations or formulaic patterns in the *Ṛgveda*, nor is its distribution in any way restricted beyond the normal limits imposed by trimeter verse. If there is a potential contrast between the forms which preserve syllabicity alternations and those that do not, above and beyond Lindeman's criterion of monosyllabicity, then we have to wonder whether we are entitled to automatically build monosyllabicity into our description of word-initial semivowel syllabicity alternations.

These doubts are of course based on a rather preliminary examination of the Lindeman's Law material; there are many avenues for further enquiry. In no way does any of this entitle one to claim that this kind of word-initial alternation was any more widespread at some point further in the past. It simply counsels caution, until more can be established about the structure and formation of Ṛgvedic formulaic language.

Hence, the metrical peculiarities of these forms do not help us in deciding what to reconstruct for Indo-European; they simply suggest that we should exercise restraint before building on them too heavily. It is sobering to remember how slim the evidential basis really is and that other interpretations of the facts would be perfectly consistent. In general, therefore, it seems premature to project into Indo-European the monosyllabicity criterion on word-initial syllabicity alternations. It seems better to admit that we do not really know what the determining factors were.

13

Exon's Law and the Latin syncopes

RANJAN SEN

13.1 Introduction

Metrical structure was a conditioning factor in Latin syncope, but not in a rhythmic fashion.[1] Syncope neither helped bring about an alternating rhythm (e.g. **opifakiom* > *officium* 'service', not †*O.pi.FA.ki.{om}*, where capitals denote some stress),[2] nor did it target specific positions in a rhythmical structure, such as the second, 'weak' position of LL and HL feet (Jacobs 2004), or 'trapped' light syllables (Mester 1994). Rather, syncope was brought about by a combination of metrical factors: the pressure to parse syllables into feet,

[1] I owe a great debt of gratitude to John Penney both for his sage guidance over the years (there is only one voice I hear when I silently ask myself 'Do you really believe that?'), and for the inspiration to revisit these recalcitrant problems. I should also like to thank the editors for their valuable comments. All errors are of course my own.

[2] Notations used: (...) = foot, '.' = syllable boundary, * = reconstructed form (or OT markedness constraint), † = incorrect reconstruction/development, {...} = extrametrical syllable, ː = long vowel, ⟨ ⟩= syncopated syllable, L = light syllable, H = heavy syllable, σ = either heavy or light syllable, L+ = a light syllable that became heavy after syncope of the vowel of the following syllable, by attachment of the stranded onset consonant to its coda. The acute accent denotes primary stress and the grave secondary stress. Latin received orthography (with the addition of the length mark where appropriate) is used for attested Latin forms (e.g. *iuːnioːreːs*) and International Phonetic Alphabet (IPA) symbols for reconstructed forms (e.g. **juwenioːseːs*). For the purposes of this investigation, I shall recognize four periods in the history of Latin: (i) archaic Latin, from the earliest attestations in the 7th century BC to the beginning of the literary period in 240 BC, (ii) early Latin, from 240 BC to the beginning of Cicero's career in 81 BC, (iii) classical Latin, from 81 BC until the death of Augustus in AD 14, and (iv) imperial Latin, from AD 14 onwards.

the pressure for stress and weight to coincide, and most importantly, the pressure for feet to be as close to a word edge as possible.

Latin syncope has resisted formulation in terms of strict rules or sound changes for two reasons. Firstly, syncope was not a monolithic archaic Latin phenomenon, but continued to occur throughout Latin history, with different metrical, phonotactic, and morphological constraints in different time periods and registers. Secondly, the interaction of metrical factors is complex, so syncope is not restricted to certain fixed positions. Previous attempts at finding a metrical context offer useful insights, but do not provide a comprehensive account. Cowgill (1970) argued that syncope was to be expected in the second and fourth syllables, if light, in words of more than four syllables, thus **awida:kiter* > *auda:cter* 'boldly'. However, syncope also occurred in the second and third syllables (**pri:semokapem* > *pri:ncipem* 'chief'),[3] or just the third syllable (**u:surapa:re* > *u:surpa:re* 'to usurp'). Mester (1994) argues that syncope occurred where a light syllable was 'trapped' between two heavy syllables, or between a heavy syllable and the end of a word. The syllable was trapped as it could not be parsed using bimoraic feet (H and LL). However, many other contexts for syncope occur, as the above examples illustrate. Jacobs (2004) appeals to the 'uneven' trochaic foot (HL) to posit the context for syncope to be the weak position of disyllabic feet, hence the second syllable in (HL) and (LL). Again, this does not match the evidence, and Jacobs's (HL) foot will be evaluated later in this chapter. Sihler (1995: 70) states that 'in a PItal. tetrasyllable with two light medial syllables (schematically x$\breve{x}\breve{x}$x) the second vowel regularly syncopates' (**kʷi:nkʷedekem* > *qui:ndecim* 'fifteen'), but acknowledges counterexamples in which syncope is found in the third syllable, since 'a cross-current arises from the especial readiness of short vowels following *l* and *r* to syncopate' (**sepelitos* > *sepultus* 'buried'). Is this a 'cross-current', or is the syncopating syllable merely conditioned by phonotactic and morphological constraints when the metrical prerequisites for syncope were in place?

Sihler names his rule 'Exon's Law'. However, Charles Exon's original formulation (1906: 128) differs from Sihler's in a crucial fashion—the position of the syncopating vowel is not stipulated: 'In all words or word-groups of four or more syllables bearing the chief accent on a long syllable, a short unaccented medial vowel was necessarily syncopated, but might be restored by analogy'. Exon holds that this syncope occurred both in early Latin, probably in the third

[3] See section 13.6.2. As syncope is sensitive to word shape, this study will focus on oblique case forms of nouns and infinitive forms, showing the stem vowel, of verbs. Although nominative or singular present tense forms might have been analogical bases, the numerous forms using the stems employed here should at least give us reliable metrical shapes for many forms in the language.

century, in words in which stress lay on a stressed heavy penult/antepenult, and in archaic Latin, where the stressed heavy syllable was word-initial. This more general formulation is a promising attempt at finding order, but its very generality feels unsatisfactory. Can we be more specific?

13.2 The problems

A first problem is that counterexamples to Exon's Law abound, although it is clear that phonotactic constraints blocked syncope where word-shape requirements were met. Thus, HLHσ *ambula:re* 'to walk' did not syncopate to †*ambla:re*, as the sequence /bl/ was unacceptable (note early Latin anaptyxis in this sequence). Contrast the outcome of a later imperial syncope: *oculus non oclus* 'eye' in the *Appendix Probi* (*GL* iv. 198. 18; cf. Italian *occhio*).[4] Similarly, the selection of the syncopated vowel in HLLσ in archaic times was presumably also governed by phonotactics: **amp^h^orela* lost the second of its two internal light syllables (> *ampulla* 'flask') as deleting an inter-sonorant vowel was presumably preferable to creating the sequence /pr/ at that time. Note, however, the numerous Exon's Law examples which resulted in stop + /r/, such as *aperi:lis* > *apri:lis* 'April'. It is clear, therefore, that phonotactic constraints changed over the course of Latin history.

A second problem is that syncope was morphologically constrained. It usually respected the vowel in verbal roots and so failed to occur to these targets (Rix 1966). When the word shape and phonotactics were such to trigger syncope, there are occasionally indications that the vowel loss would have occurred were it not for morphological constraints. For example, **súb-rapuit* would regularly have given *surpuit* under Exon's archaic syncope (where the first syllable was stressed), and we do indeed find this form in Plautus (*Capt.* 760), and later in Lucretius (2. 314) and Horace (*Carm.* 4. 13. 20). However, the regular Latin form is *surripuit* with vowel reduction rather than syncope, maintaining a vowel in the root. Morphology also played a major role in syncope in the form of analogical and paradigmatic levelling, as Exon notes (1906: 133): 'The length and accentuation of Latin words varied so continually in inflexion and derivation (*ámo*, *amámus*, *amátio*, *amatiónis*) that we might confidently have predicted that any phenomenon which depended upon those two factors would be powerfully modified in the end by levelling'. However, appeals to levelling should always be made with caution, and we must ensure

[4] The *Appendix Probi* has been variously dated from the third to the eighth century AD. See Quirk (2005) for detailed bibliography.

that analogy is not merely invoked because a phonological pattern is not immediately forthcoming.

A third problem, the focus of this paper, resides in the fact that there are evidently non-Exon's Law metrical contexts for syncope, such as HLσ, LLσ, LLLσ, and LLLLσ. Exon (1906: 131) explains some of these forms through levelling within a paradigm (e.g. **aːridoːs* > *ardor* 'burning, fire' on **aːridoːris* > *ardoːris* (gen.)) or by analogy on a derived form (e.g. *caldus* 'warm' on *cal-daːrium* 'hot room'), and others by arguing for their clitic status. The single accentual unit brought about by combining a clitic with a content word, forming a 'word-group' (note the wording of his law), gave an Exon's Law configuration. The difference between the syncopated preposition *supraː* 'above' and the unsyncopated adjective *superus* can be attributed to the former's proclitic status in its prepositional use, so *superáːviam* > *supraːviam*. But it is difficult to see how particular nouns and verbs can be explained in this way, and it can only be that these forms present word shapes that are configurations for syncope.

Chronology is a final problem. It is notoriously difficult to pinpoint what structures underwent syncope at which times given that unsyncopated forms are often not attested but reconstructed. Rather infelicitously, the main development that would allow us to construct a relative chronology is the rhotacism of intervocalic */s/ > /r/, whose chronology is itself obscure, although the evidence seems to indicate a change in the fourth century BC. Whether syncopated forms show intervocalic rhotacism therefore indicates whether the surrounding vowels were present or lost by the fourth century. A second chronological indication is the position of the stress accent: if the syncopated vowel would have borne stress under the Penultimate Law of classical times, we can deduce that syncope occurred at an earlier stage, given the likely perceptual robustness of stressed-syllable vowels. Thus, **adtetuliː* > *attuliː* must have occurred when the initial syllable, and not the syllable /te/, was stressed.

13.3 Phonology

It has long been recognized that numerous Latin phenomena can be accurately analysed in terms of foot structure (Jakobson 1937, Allen 1973, Mester 1994). Within the typology of foot parameters found in the world's languages (see Hayes 1995), classical Latin can be analysed using moraic trochees (i.e. left-headed foot types (ĹL) and (H́)), final-syllable extrametricality (i.e. the final syllable is not parsed into a foot), right-to-left foot formation (i.e. unparsed material is restricted to the left edge of the word), and the head foot is the rightmost (i.e. the last foot in the word contains the primarily stressed syllable; other feet assign secondary stresses to their heads). The classical Latin Penultimate Law of stress assignment is easily analysed this way: stress falls on the penult if heavy (i.e. a bimoraic trochee, hence a well-formed foot on its own: *(cò:n).(féc).{tus}* 'completed'), and the antepenult if the penult is light (i.e. the head syllable of the final trochee: *(cò:n).(fí.ci).{o:}* 'I complete').

Iambic shortening in early Latin is a good example of what might occur when the different pressures towards foot formation conflict. Assuming that every word must contain a foot (the Strict Layer Hypothesis; Selkirk 1984), words of the shape LH (*amo:* 'I love') pose a problem: the parse (L)H observes extrametricality, but forms an ill-formed moraic trochee; L(H) violates extrametricality, but forms a well-formed foot; (LH) violates extrametricality and also forms an ill-formed foot. The early Latin solution is to shorten the long vowel in the second syllable (or to treat a doubly closed syllable as light, e.g. *legŭnt*), thus *amo*, allowing a parse (LL), breaking extrametricality, deleting a mora, but creating a well-formed foot, which parses all the syllables. Pressures towards applying metrical structure therefore include: forming bimoraic trochees, parsing syllables, preserving input material (here moras; in the case of syncope, vowels), respecting extrametricality, and aligning feet to the right edge of the word. We shall see that syncope is the outcome where a shortened form is deemed the best strategy to resolve these conflicts.

Conflict resolution is captured well by Optimality Theory (OT), and this framework has been used in recent analyses of Latin metrical phenomena (Jacobs 2000, 2003*a*, 2003*b*, 2004, Prince and Smolensky 2004). For ease of comparison with these works and metrical analyses of non-Latin phenomena, and since OT provides good theoretical machinery to analyse the typology of metrical phenomena, I shall adopt OT formalisms. The different pressures can be captured by the following constraint set, along the lines of Prince and Smolensky (2004):

(1) Constraint set

FtBin	Feet are bimoraic[5]
NonFinality (NonF)	A foot may not be final (i.e. final-syllable extrametricality)
Parse-σ	Parse syllables into feet

[5] Prince and Smolensky's formulation of FtBin is 'feet are binary at the level of the syllable or mora'. I have altered the constraint following Mester's (1994) observation that Latin feet seem to have been strictly bimoraic, as this seems to offer the best analysis for stress assignment, iambic/cretic shortening processes, and as demonstrated below, syncope.

Weight-to-Stress Principle (WSP)	Heavy syllables are stressed
Stress-to-Weight Principle (SWP)	Stressed syllables are heavy
Max-V	An underlying vowel must be parsed (i.e. no vowel-deletion)

The constraint Parse-σ is violated when there is a 'stray' syllable which cannot be incorporated into a well-formed foot, hence FtBin is the higher-ranked constraint, e.g. *fa.(cí.li).{us}* 'more easily' rather than *(fà).(cí.li).{us}* with an initial monomoraic foot. The location of the stray syllable was deemed to be evidence for directional foot formation in rule-based metrical theory. However, such accounts fail to deal straightforwardly with languages which show right-to-left parsing, but have an initial trochee (Garawa), and those which have left-to-right parsing, but a final trochee (Polish). Optimality Theory deals with directionality effects by means of a family of 'alignment' constraints, whereby one prosodic category edge aligns with another (McCarthy and Prince 1993). The requirement that the right edges of all members of the prosodic category 'foot' be aligned to the right edge of some member of the prosodic category 'prosodic word (PrWd)' results in all feet occurring as close to the end of the word as possible. If the specified edges are changed to the left, then all feet are constructed as close to the start of the word as possible.

(2) Alignment constraints on foot position

Align-Foot, R, PrWd, R (abbreviated as All-Ft-R)	The right edge of every foot coincides with the right edge of some prosodic word (one violation for each syllable between the right edge of any foot and the right edge of the word)
Align-Foot, L, PrWd, L (All-Ft-L)	The left edge of every foot coincides with the left edge of some prosodic word

These constraints are violated by every foot that is not final/initial in PrWd. Violations therefore occur in any word of more than one foot in a gradient fashion, each foot being judged by its distance in syllables from the specified word edge. However, as long as Parse-σ is higher ranked than the alignment constraint, feet will be formed in an apparently iterative directional manner. If, however, the alignment constraint is ranked above Parse-σ, non-iterative footing is the result, with only a single stress-assigning foot constructed. The expanded theory of 'Generalized Alignment' (McCarthy and Prince 1993) has been successful in accounting for several language phenomena ranging through stress-assignment, the alignment of morphemes with prosodic categories, infixation, and phenomena attributed to extrametricality and cyclicity.[6] As we shall see, Latin stress placement and syncope are sensitive to the principle of alignment. Regarding stress placement, the change from initial-syllable stress in archaic times to the Penultimate Law in classical times can be analysed by a change in the aligned edges from left to right, and the designation of the head foot (that bearing primary stress) as the rightmost rather than the leftmost (ALIGN-HD-FOOT, R, PRWD, R: 'The final foot is the head foot'). Such a change was plausibly brought about by input data which was ambiguous as to the aligned edge, e.g. *(gau).(de:).{re}* 'to rejoice', and a similarity in the perceptual correlates of primary and secondary stresses. With regard to syncope, if vowel-deletion in certain phonetic environments was permitted by the grammar (low-ranking MAX-V), then it might be used to reduce the number of syllables between a foot-edge and a word-edge, thus achieving a better satisfaction of the alignment constraint.

To recap, our reconstruction of the synchronic grammars of different periods of Latin should have the same metrical, phonotactic, and morphological pressures in each posited time period, with each grammar predicting the syncopes that we can ascribe to its period. This study will focus upon the metrical conditions for syncope, acknowledging the potential influences of phonotactics and morphology where relevant, but enumerating phonetic environments rather than analysing them. However, comparing the phonetic environments for each syncope that we hypothesize offers a good test to evaluate whether we are on the right track: if a diachronic re-ranking of constraints results in syncope in a number of different metrical configurations, we expect those syncopes to show identical phonotactic constraints (or in practice, a notable overlap). We have no such expectation regarding syncopes motivated by different changes in metrical constraints.

The data used in the study are taken from the standard handbooks of Latin (Lindsay 1894, Niedermann 1997 (1906), Sommer 1948, Allen 1973, Sommer and Pfister 1977, Leumann 1977, Sihler 1995, Meiser 1998), together with specific studies into the phenomena in question (e.g. Exon 1906), and further evidence where relevant to particular questions. The phonetic environments listed below are therefore not likely to be exhaustive, but the evidence discussed in the literature gives us a good basis from which to begin.

[6] The patterns seen in Garawa and Polish are achieved through the interaction of different alignment constraints obtaining between the edges of foot and PrWd, using additional constraints requiring that the edge of a PrWd is aligned to *some* foot (not that all feet are aligned to the edge of a PrWd): ALIGN-PRWD, L/R, FOOT, L/R. If these are higher ranked than ALL-FT-L/R, the result is the construction of a single foot at one word edge, then apparently directional footing from the other.

13.4 Early archaic Latin

The earliest examples of Latin syncope appear to date from the sixth to fifth centuries BC, occurring at the same time as vowel reduction in non-initial syllables. Both archaic phenomena have been attributed to the archaic 'strong' initial-syllable stress, which might have manifested itself through greater intensity and duration. The latter certainly appears to have been the case: undershoot-based reduction of the type seen in Latin occurs in languages with a significant durational asymmetry between stressed and unstressed syllables (Barnes 2006: 29), suggesting a notable prominence of the initial syllable. From a metrical perspective, archaic Latin words therefore uniformly began with a left-headed foot.

There is evidence to suggest, however, that this was the only foot constructed by the phonology of archaic Latin. Three pieces of evidence suggest that a sequence such as HLLσ was footed (H́)LLσ, with only the stressed syllable parsed, and not (H́)(L̀L)σ with more parsing, and secondary stress on the first light syllable: (1) syncope commonly targeted the first light syllable (**amb^{h}ik^{w}olos* > *anculus* 'manservant'), (2) vowel reduction in internal light syllables was insensitive to position within the word (**komfakio:* > *co:nficio:* 'I complete'), and (3) both light syllables were sometimes syncopated, suggesting no metrical structure beyond the stress-assigning foot (**deksiteros* > **dekstr̩s* > *dexter* 'right', **mrewisema* > **browisema* > *bru:ma* 'mid-winter'). As seen above, this is brought about by the ranking of ALL-FT-L above PARSE-σ (Fig. 13.1).

	/HLLσ/ *komfakio:*	ALL-FT-L	PARSE-σ
	(H́)(L̀L)σ	*!	*
☞	(H́)LLσ		***

Fig.13.1 *komfakio: → (kóm).fa.ki.{o:}* (> *co:nficio:*)

Internal light syllables were left unparsed, but can the same be said for internal heavy syllables? If the weight-to-stress principle (WSP) was higher ranked than the alignment constraint, then all internal heavy syllables would be parsed as well-formed bimoraic trochees in themselves, and attract a secondary stress, thus **(kóm).(fàk).{tos}* 'completed'. However, closed-syllable vowel reduction provides strong evidence that this was not the case. The resistance of closed syllables to the extreme reduction to /i/ seen in open syllables cannot be ascribed to a secondary stress, as closed syllables which would have fallen in the weak position of an initial stress-assigning foot (ĹH), hence would not have been secondarily stressed, show precisely the same pattern of reduction as other closed syllables, and do not undergo extreme reduction: **(jú.wen).ta:ts > iu.ven.ta:s* 'youth', not †*(jú.win).ta:s*.

Early archaic Latin words therefore only contained a single left-headed foot, placing stress on the initial syllable, with the rest of the word left unparsed. This foot need not even have been quantity-sensitive, in that there was no correlation between stress and syllable weight: both initial light and heavy syllables bore stress, and the evidence above suggests that no other syllable bore stress even if heavy. However, the introduction of quantity sensitivity (i.e. some correlation between stress and heavy syllables; see below) offers a clue as to why further parsing and ultimately syncope came to occur.

13.5 Archaic SWP syncope

The early archaic system whereby each word contained only a single, word-initial, quantity-insensitive foot came under threat when the stress of the initial syllable created a significant asymmetry in the duration and intensity of the initial and other syllables, such that vowel reduction resulted. The greater prominence of the initial syllable seems to have resulted in a pressure to reinforce the strong stress with syllable weight, a phenomenon formalized by the stress-to-weight principle (SWP), and seen in languages such as modern Italian, where every stressed syllable must be heavy. The raising of SWP above MAX-V resulted in second-syllable syncope in initial LL sequences, as the onset of the second syllable came to form a coda of the first. Words of the shape LLσ/LLLσ therefore syncopated to Hσ/HLσ, but only under tight phonotactic restrictions.

(3) Phonetic environments for archaic SWP syncope (LL-initial words)
- Between identical stops: **ré-kekidi:/-tetuli:/-peperi:/-pepuli: > reccidi:/rettuli:/repperi:/reppuli:* 'I fell back/brought back/discovered/repulsed'
- Dorsal + coronal stop: **dokitos > doctus* 'learned', **sekatos > sectus* 'cut'
- /nl/: **dwenelos > bellus* 'handsome'
- /sN/: **posinere > po:nere* 'to put', **susemere > su:mere* 'to take up'
- /lN/: **kolamenos > culminis* 'roof', **wolaneses > vulneris* 'wound'
- /wk/: **rawikos > raucus* 'hoarse'
- /wr/: **re-wersos > ru:rsus* 'again'
- /n-str, w-str/: **monestrom > mo:nstrum* 'portent', **jowestos > iu:stus* 'just'

Several features attest to the antiquity of this syncope. First, unsyncopated forms are not attested, with the exception of *columen*. In this case, it is likely that /lm/ was a marginal environment for syncope, resulting in variant forms surviving. The explanation of de Vaan (2008: 127) that *culmen* arose by analogy on the longer oblique case forms where syncope was expected (i.e. *columen*, *culminis*) is problematic in the absence of any other evidence for such variation, and given forms like *vulnus*, *-eris* with no trace of unsyncopated forms anywhere in the paradigm, presumably because /ln/ was a robust syncope environment. With regard to Gr. *balaneion* > *balineum* 'bath', we cannot be certain that it failed to show archaic syncope because of metrical or phonotactic constraints. As a loan from Greek, it is equally possible that it displayed resistance to syncope as a result of its loanword status, and it is indicative that the native word *vulnus* in precisely the same context did syncopate. Therefore, *balineum* underwent archaic vowel reduction, but failed to go so far as to syncopate. It did however undergo syncope much later, presumably when it was no longer constrained by the loanword phonology. Second, /sN/ was a pre-rhotacism environment for syncope.[7] Third, the change */o/ > /u/ before a coda dark-*l* took place after this syncope. Fourth, SWP-induced syncope can even occur in heavy syllables in LH-initial words to achieve a heavy initial, although only to yield /wr/ and notably between /n, w/ and the sequence /s/ + stop, thus in addition to the above, **fawestos* > *faustus* 'fortunate' (cf. *faventia* 'auspicious behaviour' at Acc. *trag.* 511), **awispeks* > *auspex* 'augur', *fenestram* > *fenstram* (Pl. *Cas.* 132) or *fe:stra* 'window', **awisdi:re* (cf. Gr. **awisthanomai* > *aisthanomai*) > **awzdi:re* > *audi:re* 'to hear', IOVESTOD (*CIL* 1^2. 1) > *iu:sto:* 'lawful (abl.)'. Finally, this last sequence */owe/ regularly yielded /u:/ as a result of this syncope, and not /o:/ as later. The plausibly early univerbated LH-initial **re-werd-tos* gives us **ro-wersos* > **rowrsos* > *ru:rsus*, unlike **mowetos* > *mo:tus* 'motion'.[8] The fact that no example of third-syllable syncope in words ending LLLσ shows any of these consonantal environments (e.g. *$\underline{\text{geme}}$*$\textit{nelos}$ 'twin') indicates why SWP did not result in second-syllable syncope to HLσ at an early stage in those words. Similarly, /pt, pf/ were not environments for archaic SWP-induced syncope, as shown by *opifex* 'artisan', and evidence that unsyncopated forms were still recognizable to an early Latin speaker (see section 13.7).

[7] **osVnos* > *ornus* 'kind of ash-tree' (de Vaan 2008: 435) remains problematic.

[8] We are still unable to decide between PItal. **aramos* and **armos* 'shoulder, upper arm' (de Vaan 2008: 55) on the basis of the environments found. However, *antae* 'square pilasters' seems more likely to derive from **anta:i* rather than **anata:i* (de Vaan 2008: 44) given non-syncopating *monitus* 'warned'.

The constraint ranking required for archaic SWP syncope is therefore: ALL-FT-L, SWP » MAX-V » PARSE-σ. MAX-V must be ranked above PARSE-σ as non-second-syllable syncope was not triggered at this stage, hence deletion could not occur simply to reduce the number of unparsed syllables (Fig. 13.2).

	/LLσ/ *dokitos*	ALL-FT-L	SWP	MAX-V	PARSE-σ
	(ĹL)σ		*!		*
☞	(Ĺ+)⟨L⟩σ			*	*

Fig.13.2 *dokitos → (dók).{tos}* (> *doctus*)

13.6 Exon's Law syncopes

13.6.1 Alignment syncope

Shortly after SWP syncope, and still in early archaic times, we find the first alignment-induced syncope. As stress coincided with weight, speakers came to associate weight with stress, so assigning a stress also to word-internal heavy syllables. This quantity-sensitive phenomenon is codified as the weight-to-stress principle (WSP); when ranked above ALL-FT-L, the result is that each internal heavy syllable was footed, thus **(kón)ki(ta:)ri:* (> *cuncta:ri:* 'to hesitate'). Any word shape with internal syllables containing a long vowel or closed syllable therefore incurred violations of ALL-FT-L, e.g. **(kón)ki(ta:)ri:* incurs two violations as a result of the internal foot starting two syllables into the word. A pressure to minimize such violations arose, and an obvious repair strategy was syncope, a result of low-ranking MAX-V, thus reducing the number of syllables between the internal foot and the left edge: *(cunc)(ta:)ri:*. The archaic strong prominence of the start of the word that motivates such changes can therefore be formalized as high-ranking ALL-FT-L, and I shall refer to this syncope as 'alignment syncope'. The constraint ranking must be WSP » ALL-FT-L » PARSE-σ, MAX-V (as SWP is not relevant for this syncope, we shall omit it). Note also that the word shapes affected all present metrical contexts for Exon's early syncope, which specifically required the presence of a penultimate/antepenultimate heavy syllable. Here, we posit that syncope in these words occurred under archaic initial stress (Fig. 13.3).

	/HLHσ/ _konkita:ri:_	WSP	ALL-FT-L	MAX-V	PARSE-σ
	(H́)LHσ	*!			***
☞	(H́)⟨L⟩(H̀)σ		*	*	*

Fig.13.3 _konkita:ri:_ → _(kónk).(tà:).{ri:}_ (> _cuncta:ri:_)

(4) Word shapes affected by alignment syncope
- HLHσ: *_konkita:ri:_ > _cuncta:ri:_ 'to hesitate'
- HLLHσ: *_u:surapa:re_ > _u:surpa:re_ 'to usurp'
- HLHLσ: *_posteri:die:_ > _postri:die:_ 'on the next day'
- LHLHσ: *_magistera:tus_ > _magistra:tus_ 'magistrate' (cf. LHLLσ _magisterium_ 'office of a president')
- LLHσ: *_aperi:lis_ > _apri:lis_ 'April'
- LLLHσ: *_juwenio:se:s_ > _iu:nio:re:s_ 'younger (pl.)'
- LLHLσ: *_awida:kiter_ > *_auda:kiter_[9] 'boldly'

The clitic groups identified by Exon also belong here, as the final heavy syllables of the clitics formed an internal foot. This underlies Pedersen's (1922) observation that syncope is expected in HLσ only where the final syllable contained a long vowel, not if it had a short vowel (syncope in HLσ forms with a short vowel in the final syllable comes under archaic parsing syncope, section 13.6.2). Furthermore, it is also plausible that the stem following the clitic bore an initial stress, hence formed an internal foot, again triggering left-alignment syncope once the clitic group formed a single PrWd.

(5) Alignment syncope in clitic groups
- HLH-: *_enfera:_ > _infra:_ 'under', *_entera:_ > _intra:_ 'within', *_ekstera:_ > _extra:_ 'outside', *_komtera:_ > _contra:_ 'against', *_ultera:_ > _ultra:_ 'beyond'
- LLH-: *_supera:_ > _supra:_ 'above', *_retero:d_ > _retro:_ 'behind', _kitera:_ > _citra:_ 'on this side', *_propeter_ > _propter_ 'near'

[9] (1) Alignment syncope does not motivate syncope of the fourth-syllable vowel in *_awida:kiter_. This is induced by archaic parsing syncope. (2) Forms resulting in secondary syllabic liquids and nasals are left aside in this discussion and require further investigation, e.g. HLσ *_po:klelom_, *_tignelom_ > HHσ _po:cillum_, LHσ _tigillum_; H/LLHσ *_sakrod_^{h}_o:tem_, *_faklita:tem_ > LHHσ _sacerdo:tem_, _faculta:tem_.

The phonetic environments for syncope in these groups are also strikingly homogeneous. Most notably, syncope occurred in stop + liquid (*TR*) sequences in this and no other syncope until pre-classical times.

(6) Phonetic environments for archaic alignment syncope

- *TR: *posteri:die:, *magistera:tus, *aperi:lis* above, **exterim-secus* > *extri:nsecus* 'to the outside', **diskapuli:na* > *discipli:na* 'instruction', **aperi:cus* > *apri:cus* 'sunny'; clitics, e.g. **supera:*
- /pt, kt/: **konkita:ri:* above
- /dt, dk, dn/: **kedate* > *cette* (clitic) 'give me', **praidiko:nem* > *praeco:nem* 'crier', **ordina:re* > *orna:re* 'to adorn'[10]
- /mt, mk/: **Pometi:nai* > *(palu:de:s) Pompti:nae* '(fens) of Pometia', **no:mokapa:re* > *nuncupa:re* 'to call'
- /nd/: **wi:node:mia* > *vinde:mia* 'vintage'
- /rp, rt/: **u:surapa:re* above, **wirotu:tem* > *virtu:tem* 'valour'
- /wd, wn, ws/: **awide:re* > *aude:re* (cf. *avidus*) 'to dare', **ga:wide:re* > *gaude:re* 'to rejoice', IOVESAT (*CIL* I^2. 4) > **iousat* > *iu:rat* 'swears (3sg.)'[11]

There are again several indications of the antiquity of this syncope. The change */o:/ > /u/ in closed syllables (**no:mokapa:re* > *nuncupa:re*) occurred after this syncope, as did consonantal epenthesis in **Pometi:nai* > **Pomti:nai* > *Pompti:nae*. We encountered a plausible morphological influence in clitic groups—the stem possibly had initial stress—and this might be extended to compounds which had not yet been completely univerbated. This could explain the instance of archaic */owe/ > /u:/ in **noweno-dinai* > *nu:ndinae* 'market day', beside later */owe/ > /o:/ in **nowenos* > *no:nus* 'ninth', if the former was footed *(nówe)no(dì)nai*, with a stress on the first syllable of the second element of the compound (as in any other PrWd), triggering alignment syncope. The later change to /o:/ was plausibly a context-free development, as also seen in */awV/ > /au/ (e.g. **kawitos* > *cautus* 'wary'; cf. still *cavitum* in the *Lex Agraria, CIL* I^2. 585. 6).

The non-rhythmic nature of this syncope is clear from HLLHσ words in which syncope occurred in either the second or the third syllable. There was no

[10] *Ordina:re* 'to place in rows' was analogically formed on *ordo:* 'row'.

[11] *Pro:vide:re* 'to foresee' is probably an analogical survival based on *vide:re* 'to see'. The semantically specialized **pro:videntem* > *pru:dentem* 'clever' reflects the regular development. *Aude:re*, *iu:ra:re*, and other originally LL-initial words might have come about through archaic SWP syncope, but as syncope yielding /w/ + /d, n, s/ seems to occur where the initial syllable was already heavy (**ga:wide:re*), alignment syncope is the better account. *Rursus* has no internal heavy syllable, so SWP syncope must be the explanation.

specific metrical position for syncope, but rather, the metrical profile of the word was optimized by the deletion of whichever vowel phonotactics and morphology permitted. Thus, in morphologically and metrically identical **u:surapa:re* and **no:mokapa:re*, we find third-syllable syncope in the first, and second-syllable syncope in the second: /sr/ and /kp/ were not syncope environments at this stage.

13.6.2 Archaic parsing syncope

The application of metrical structure word-internally motivated a greater pressure towards full parsing by an extension of the pattern of constructing non-initial feet in heavy syllables. This can be formalized as the raising of the constraint PARSE-σ. However, the step-wise raising of PARSE-σ has intriguing consequences: if it is raised above MAX-V but not above ALL-FT-L, a situation arises whereby the number of unparsed syllables is minimized by syncope, but internal light syllables are still not given metrical structure, owing to the higher ranking of the alignment constraint. Internal heavy syllables are still parsed due to undominated WSP. Therefore, a sequence HLLσ would still have a single initial foot, but the greater importance of minimizing unparsed syllables over the retention of underlying vowels results in syncope to (H)Lσ. I shall refer to this as archaic parsing syncope (Fig. 13.4).[12]

	/HLLσ/ *formokape:s*	WSP	ALL-FT-L	PARSE-σ	MAX-V
	(Ĥ)(L̀L)σ		*!	*	
	(Ĥ)LLσ			***!	
☞	(Ĥ)⟨L⟩Lσ			**	*

Fig.13.4 *formokape:s* → *(fórm).ka.{pe:s}* (> *forcipe:s*)

(7) Word shapes affected by archaic parsing syncope
- HLLσ: **formokape:s* > *forcipe:s* 'tongs'
- HLLLσ: **ambikaputem* > *ancipitem* 'two-faced'

[12] As there is no indication of SWP-induced syncope any longer, we can presume that the SWP was lower ranked than the above constraints by this stage. Plausibly, the introduction of secondary stresses and internal parsing reduced the prominence of the initial syllable, hence SWP was no longer transparent to the learner.

- LLLLσ: **pueropara* > *puerpera* 'woman delivered of a child', **opifakiom* > *officium* 'service' (cf. *opifex*)
- LHLσ: **koro:nela* > *coro:lla* 'small garland'
- LLLHσ: **opifaki:na* > *offici:na* 'workshop'
- HLσ, HHLσ, HLHLσ, LLHLσ: see below
- LLLσ: see next section

(8) Phonetic environments for archaic parsing syncope
- /pf/: **opifakiom*, **opifaki:na* above (see next section)
- /tp, dt/: **hostipotem* > *hospitem* 'guest', **ad-tetuli:* > *attuli:* 'I brought to'
- /(k)st/: **deksiteros* > *dexter* 'right'
- /(r)k^wn/: *k^w*erk*^{w}*ineos* > *querneus* 'of oak'
- /(n)k^wd, (m)bk/: *k^w*i:nk*^{w}*edekem* > *qui:ndecim* 'fifteen', **ambikaputem* above
- /mk/: **formokape:s* above[13]
- /nl/: **koro:nela* above
- /rp, rg, rl/: **subrapuit* > *surpuit* 'he stole', **pueropara* above, **per-/porregere* > *per-/porgere* 'to advance/extend', **amp*^{h}*orela* > *ampulla* 'flask'[14]
- /ln/: **po:pulinos* > *po:pulnus* 'derived from poplar'

The phonetic environments for alignment syncope and parsing syncope are clearly different, indicating their different motivations. Coronal + dorsal stop is no longer an environment (**praidiko:nem* vs. *participium* 'participle', *qua:rticipem* 'fourth in order'), nor is /pt/ (not **ambikaputem* > †*aŋkeptem*, beside clitic **propeter*), nor most notably *TR* (*magisterium* 'office of a president' beside *magistra:tus*, *in-/exterior* 'inner/outer' beside *intra:/extra:*, *ampulla* not †*amprela*). Again, we see syncope in whichever syllable is phonotactically best suited, hence second-syllable syncope in **hostipotem*, but in the third syllable of **amp*^{h}*orela*.

There are indications that this syncope occurred after rhotacism: **jousagiom* > *iu:rgium* 'quarrel'. However, HLLLσ **pri:semokapem* > *pri:ncipem* 'chief' suggests later rhotacism, as does HLLLσ **eksteresemos* > *extre:mus* 'utmost', LLLLσ **superesemos* > *supre:mus* 'highest', and HLσ **pri:semos* > *pri:mus* 'first'. These together all seem to indicate a context-free deletion of a vowel in

[13] *Mu:nicipium* 'community' suggests that a consonant had to precede the nasal for syncope to occur, thus **pri:smokapem* and **formokape:s*, but **mu:ni(a)-kapiom*.

[14] **subrapuit* and **per-/por-/sub-regere* offer the only examples of stem-initial syncope in prefixed verbs. This is a good indication that the forms syncopated well after the preverb and verb were felt to form a single prosodic unit. Cf. **u:surapa:re* > *u:surpa:re* in alignment syncope for an example of stem-initial syncope in nominal + verbal stems.

the sequence */sm/ at an early archaic stage, that is, it occurred regardless of metrical structure whenever the phonetic conditions were in place. Therefore, alignment syncope resulted in **ekster-/super-esmos* > *extre:mus/supre:mus*, and parsing syncope induced **pri:smokapem* > *pri:ncipem*. We would also expect alignment syncope to yield HLHσ **a:side:se* > *arde:re* 'to burn' and **jousaga:re* > *iu:riga:re* 'to quarrel', but the presence of a rhotacized consonant in these forms indicates that they occurred later. An analogical explanation on the basis of *iu:rgium* and *a:ridus* (later *ardus*) 'dry' seems most straightforward, as alignment syncope clearly occurred before rhotacism, and the attestations of unsyncopated HLHσ *iu:rigandum* (Pl. *Merc.* 119) and *obiu:rig-* 'reprove' (Pl. *Bacch.* 1020, *Merc.* 46, *Trin.* 68) seem to indicate that syncope in the verb was more recent than alignment syncope.[15]

The word shapes H$\underline{\text{L}}\sigma$, HH$\underline{\text{L}}\sigma$, HLH$\underline{\text{L}}\sigma$, LLH$\underline{\text{L}}\sigma$, LH$\underline{\text{L}}\sigma$ are all expected to undergo parsing syncope (where underlining indicates the relevant syllable). However, the formation of the 'uneven trochee' (HL) would permit these configurations to survive unsyncopated, as left-alignment would not be compromised, thus (HL)σ, (H)(HL)σ (one violation as in (H)(H)Lσ), (HL)(HL)σ, (LL)(HL)σ. Indeed, the diachronic raising of PARSE-σ would provide a good motivation for the introduction of (HL) into the foot inventory, as more parsing would be achieved with the same degree of left-alignment. However, the phonetic environments in which these forms syncopate seem little different from those above, and there is no further indication that syncope was later here. On the contrary, we find that the assimilation */nl/ > /ll/ is still in progress, and as above, we do not find syncope in *TR* (*exteri:*).

(9) Phonetic environments for archaic parsing syncope in possible (HL) words
- /kt/: **auda:kiter* > *auda:cter* 'boldly'
- /(r)k^{w}n/: **k^{w}erk^{w}inos* > *quernus* 'of oak' (analogical explanation on *querneus* also possible)
- /(n)kt/: **konkiti:* > *cuncti:* 'together'
- /nl/: **oinelos* > *u:llus* 'any', **wi:nelom* > *vi:llum* 'small quantity of wine'
- /ln/: **o:lena* > *ulna* 'forearm'

To conclude this section, we should note that HLσ and LLLLσ syncope also occurred in /rd/ and /rt/, but there are indications that these occurred at a later stage to which we now turn.

[15] De Vaan (2008: 53) states that *ardeo:* is derived from *a:r(i)dus*, and *ardor* 'burning, fire' from *ardeo:*.

13.7 *(LLL) and early SWP syncope

The ranking WSP » ALL-FT-L » PARSE-σ » MAX-V triggered archaic parsing syncope, but did not induce parsing of internal light syllables. We entertained the hypothesis that the pressure to parse while maintaining left-alignment might have induced the introduction of (HL) into the foot inventory, but rejected the position on the basis of the evidence. However, the early Latin stress pattern seen in *puéritia* 'boyhood' indicates that another foot form does seem to have been introduced into the inventory as a result of the above pressures: ternary branching (LLL) (see Halle and Vergnaud 1987, Levin 1988, Dresher and Lahiri 1991, Rice 1992). Second-syllable stress in *puéritia* is confirmed by the consistent ictus in this position in the early dramatists (Ter. *Haut.* 183). Using only bimoraic feet, left-alignment predicts †*(pú.e).ri.ti.{a}* and right-alignment †*pu.e.(rí.ti).{a}*. Full parsing also predicts stress on either the first or third syllable depending on the alignment of the head foot. The only analysis that predicts this pattern is a right-aligned ternary branching foot (ĹLL), thus *pu.(é.ri.ti).{a}*. Similarly, we can hypothesize that *balineum* 'bath' was fully parsed *(bá.li.ne).{um}*: words of the shape LLLσ were stressed on the first syllable in early Latin (Lindsay 1894: 173–4).[16]

Returning to archaic Latin, (LLL) feet allowed forms like **(o.pi.fa).(ki:).{na}*, **(o.pi.tu).{mus}*, *(ba.li.ne).{um}* to be fully parsed without compromising left-alignment. At this stage, right-alignment of feet (ALL-FT-R) began to arise partly from the paucity of cues for learning left-alignment in fully parsed words.[17] Note that even ternary feet could not protect LLLLσ (**pueropara*, **opifakiom*) and LLLHσ (**opifaki:na*) from archaic parsing syncope and alignment syncope respectively: syncope reduced the number of unparsed syllables in LLLLσ and improved the left-alignment of the heavy syllable in LLLHσ. Although *opifici:na* at Pl. *Mil.* 880 suggests that syncope was relatively recent,

[16] The correct theoretical analysis of the ternary pattern is still debated. See Elenbaas and Kager (1999), although their account (denying ternary feet and using the interaction of the LAPSE constraint with alignment and parsing constraints) still does not work for early Latin.

[17] There is insufficient space here to develop a full account of the change of stress position in Latin, which would probably involve a detailed consideration of derivational levels in the synchronic phonology of archaic Latin. The lexical (word-level) constraint ranking developed thus far predicts no parsing of internal LL sequences, but full parsing of the kind likely to have made edge-alignment ambiguous to the learner (e.g. *(im).(pe.ri).{um}*) might have arisen in the post-lexical phonology, where PARSE-σ was higher ranked. This is similar to Mester's (1994) 'subsidiary footing', i.e. foot-formation at a later derivational stage to stress assignment. Diachronic sound change has been interpreted as commonly arising in the post-lexical phonology; over time, its domain might shrink in successive synchronic phonologies to the word level, then stem level (morphologization), before affecting the underlying form (lexicalization) (e.g. Bermúdez-Otero 2006).

it must have occurred under initial stress, hence perhaps the connection with *opifex* 'artisan' (no syncope expected) could explain the extended survival of the longer form.

Syncope after rhotacism in LLL sequences indicates that the constraint *(LLL) was raised above Max-V in late archaic times. Feet were plausibly still left-aligned at this stage, and the phonetic environments and subsequent sound changes indicate a certain antiquity (Fig. 13.5).[18]

	/LLLσ/ *Falesinos*	All-Ft-L	Parse-σ	*(LLL)	Max-V
	(ĹL)Lσ		**!		
	(ĹLL)σ		*	*!	
☞	(ĹL+)⟨L⟩σ		*		*

Fig.13.5 *Falesinos* → *(Fá.ler).{nos}* (> *Falernus*)

(10) Phonetic environments for *(LLL) syncope
- /lt/: **sepelitos* > *sepultus* 'buried'
- /nl/: **gemenelos* > *gemellus* 'twin'
- /rn/: **Falesinos* > *Falernus* 'Falernian', **koselinos* > **korelinos* > **kolerinos* > *colurnus* 'made of hazel'

Deleting the second-syllable vowel in the above examples would have resulted in phonotactically dispreferred sequences (†*seplitos*, †*kolrinos*, †*Falrinos*).

The ranking Parse-σ » *(LLL) meant that where phonotactics prevented syncope, a ternary branching foot was still formed (*pueritia*). After the archaic period, the head foot moved from the leftmost to the rightmost, and All-Ft-L was ranked below All-Ft-R: *puéritia* can only be explained by a right-aligned ternary branching foot: *pu.(é.ri.ti).{a}*, not †*(pú.e.ri).ti.{a}*. We also see again the influence of the stress-to-weight principle (SWP): the constraint did not trigger syncope, but had the side-effect of preventing full parsing, even though it is certain that Parse-σ must have been raised above All-Ft-R by this stage to give metrical structure to internal LL (e.g. *(ìm).(pé.ri).{um}* 'command') (Fig. 13.6).

[18] The creation of an unstressed internal heavy syllable by syncope, violating WSP, again suggests derivational levels in the synchronic phonology. Stress was assigned using a ternary branching foot in the lexical phonology, but the higher ranking of *(LLL) in the post-lexical phonology triggered syncope, although stress position remained faithful to the lexical assignment. WSP was therefore lower ranked in the post-lexical phonology, and is therefore omitted here.

	/LLLL/σ *pueritia*	SWP	PARSE-σ	ALL-FT-R	*(LLL)	MAX-V
	(L̀L)(L̀L)σ	**!	*	****		
	LL(ĹL)σ	*	***!	*		
	(ĹL)LLσ	*	***!	***		
	L(ĹL)Lσ	*	***!	**		
	(ĹLL)Lσ	*	**	**!	*	
☞	L(ĹLL)σ	*	**	*	*	

Fig.13.6 *pueritia → pu.(é.ri.ti).{a}*

Syncope in *(ó.pi.tu).{mus}* > *(óp).ti.{mus}* 'best' occurred before Plautus. Inscriptional OPITVMA in the archaizing first-century BC inscription *CIL* 1^2. 1016 might indicate that /pt/ presented a syncope context in the not-too-distant past, although OPTVMO in the Scipio epitaph *CIL* 1^2. 32 from around 200 BC provides a *terminus ante quem*. *Optimus* performs more poorly on two constraints than the unsyncopated form: one syllable fewer is parsed than in *opitumus*, and the single foot is one syllable further from the right edge of PrWd. A higher-ranked constraint must have triggered syncope, and as *(LLL) must be ranked below PARSE-σ to achieve a ternary foot in *pueritia*, the triggering constraint must be SWP with /pt/ as a syncopating environment at this time. The survival of forms such as *capitis* 'head (gen.)' must then be explained by reinforcement by repetition in the paradigm (Fig. 13.7).

	/LLLσ/ *opitumus*	SWP	PARSE-σ	ALL-FT-R	*(LLL)	MAX-V
	L(ĹL)σ	*!	**	*		
	(ĹL)Lσ	*!	**	**		
	(ĹLL)σ	*!	*	*	*	
☞	(Ĺ+)⟨L⟩Lσ		**	**		*

Fig.13.7 *opitumus → (óp).tu.{mus}* (> *optimus*)

Syncopated *puértia* first appears at Hor. *Carm.* 1. 36. 8, indicating a similar chronology to that seen in LLLσ *bálineum* > *bálneum*, which also had stress on the first of three short syllables in early Latin, and was only syncopated post-

Plautus.[19] We do not find ternary branching feet in classical Latin, and LLL*σ* words that had not contained phonetic environments for syncope were stressed according to the Penultimate Law (e.g. *mu.(lí.e).{rem}* 'woman'). Note that the classical Penultimate Law would have placed the stress on the syncopating syllable in †*ba.(lí.ne).{um}* and †*(pù.e).(rí.ti).{a}*, so syncope must have occurred in early Latin, and *(LLL) raised further. Once /ln/ and /rt/ came to present syncopating environments, SWP and *(LLL) triggered syncope (whichever was higher ranked), with the other also being satisfied as a result. Perhaps the paucity of remaining words of the shape LLL*σ* resulted in the raising of *(LLL) (Fig. 13.8).

	/LLLLσ/ *pueritia*	*(LLL)	SWP	Parse-σ	All-Ft-R	Max-V
	(L̀L)(ĹL)σ		**!	*	****	
	LL(ĹL)σ		*!	***	*	
	(ĹL)LLσ		*!	***	***	
	L(ĹL)Lσ		*!	***	**	
	(ĹLL)Lσ	*!	*	**	**	
	L(ĹLL)σ	*!	*	**	*	
☞	L(Ĺ+)⟨L⟩Lσ			***	**	*

Fig.13.8 *pueritia* → *pu.(ér).ti.{a}*

Third-syllable syncope in LLL*σ* failed to make the initial stressed syllable heavy, but satisfied *(LLL): *(mí.se.ri).{tus}* > *(mí.ser).{tus}* 'pitied' (Val. Max. 7. 4. 3, 9. 3. 4, *Carmina Latina Epigraphica* 512. 5). The identical phonetic environment /rt/ is confirmation that the syncopes occurred in the same synchronic phonology.

High-ranking SWP also triggered syncope in (LL) feet, thus *(cá.li).{dus}* > *(cal).{dus}* 'hot', *(só.li).{dus}* > *(sól).{dus}* 'solid' (*CIL* 1^{2}. 593. 114, 115; 45 BC). Quintilian (1. 6. 19) reports that Augustus viewed the longer form *calidum* as *περίεργον* 'excessive', indicating well-established syncope by the late first century BC. The similarity between this phonetic environment and the above (liquid + coronal stop/nasal) again corroborates the view that the syncopes were contemporaneous.

[19] [Caper] prefers *balneum* (*GL* vii. 108. 7 Keil).

(11) Phonetic environments for *(LLL)/SWP syncope
- /rt, rd/: *pueritia*, *misertus*; *viridis* > *virdis* 'green' (Cato *Agr.* 145. 3, Lucil. 945(?))
- /ld/: *calidus*, *solidus*
- /ln/: *balineum*

13.8 Early/classical parsing syncope

To complete the picture, it seems that in early and classical Latin the pressure to parse resulted in the phonetic environments for syncope being relaxed further. HLσ *a:ridus* 'dry', with a 'trapped' L between H and the final syllable (Mester 1994), is attested in Plautus (*Rud.* 574), hence survived archaic parsing syncope. But Plautus also has Hσ *ardus* with full parsing (*Per.* 266), indicating that /rd/ could result from syncope only from early Latin.

(12) Word shapes affected by early/classical parsing syncope
- HLσ: *a:ridus* above, *la:ridum* > *lardum* 'bacon', *iu:gera* > IUGRA 'two-thirds of an acre of land (pl.)' (*CIL* 1^2. 585. 14, 25; 111 BC), *asperi:s* > *aspri:s* 'rough (abl. pl.)' (Verg. *Aen.* 2. 379)
- LHLσ: *magistera* > *magistra* 'female instructor', *sinistera* > *sinistra* 'left side'
- LLHσ: *vetera:nus* > *vetra:nus* 'veteran'
- LLHLσ: *stabula:rius* > *stabla:rius* 'of a stall'

(13) Phonetic environments affected by early/classical parsing syncope
- /rd/: *a:ridus*
- /spr, str/: *asperi:s*, *magistera*, *sinistera*
- /tr, gr/: *vetera:nus*, *iu:gera*
- /Tl/: *stabula:rius*

Strikingly, stop + liquid was an acceptable environment for avoiding trapped light syllables in early Latin. In developments such as *(ve.te).(ra:).{nus}* > *ve.(tra:).{nus}*, *(sta.bu).(la:).ri.{us}* > *sta.(bla:).ri.{us}*, the syncopated forms incur one more violation of PARSE-σ than the unsyncopated forms. However, the higher ranking SWP deems the syncopated forms with an unparsed light syllable preferable to forms with secondarily stressed light syllables (Fig. 13.9).

	/LLHσ/ *vetera:nus*	SWP	Parse-σ	All-Ft-R	Max-V
	(ÌL)(H́)σ	*!	*	***	
	LL(H́)σ		***!	*	
☞	L⟨L⟩(H́)σ		**	*	*

Fig.13.9 *vetera:nus* → *ve.(trá:).{nus}*

13.9 Conclusions

Syncope has presented numerous difficulties for the student of Latin linguistics. Resistance and reversal under analogical pressure have obscured the picture greatly, and the evidence taken together presents few patterns in either the phonetic environment or the metrical context for syncope. This account has demonstrated that a careful re-examination of the evidence, exercising extreme caution in categorizing the data according to phonetics, metrics, and chronology, can help find some order amid the chaos. Exon's first insight that any light internal syllable could be a target led us to reject the position that syncope in Latin was rhythmical in nature. No specific metrical position was targeted, neither Jacobs's 'weak position' nor Mester's 'trapped' syllables. However, Exon's second insight that the stressed syllable was often heavy pointed us to the fact that once internal heavy syllables were footed, their better alignment triggered syncope. We identified six syncopes at different periods of Latin, with their own synchronic motivations, and with different phonetic environments: (1) archaic SWP syncope, (2) alignment syncope, (3) archaic parsing syncope, (4) *(LLL) syncope, (5) early SWP/*(LLL) syncope, and (6) early/classical parsing syncope.

Establishing the reasons and environments for Latin syncope might greatly assist us in evaluating competing etymologies, where one or both invoke syncope at a certain period in a given phonetic environment. Etymologies live or die by the phonological developments they posit. Ultimately, it is hoped that these results will form the foundations of a comprehensive account of Latin metrical structure from archaic to classical times, incorporating the changes in the position of the accent, and shortening/lengthening processes such as iambic and cretic shortening. This has hitherto proved elusive, but would significantly add to our understanding of the development of Latin from its parent language.

Part V
Systemic consequences

14

Brugmann's Law: the problem of Indo-Iranian thematic nouns and adjectives

ELIZABETH TUCKER

14.1 Introduction

According to Brugmann's own presentation of the evidence for what is today called 'Brugmann's Law', Proto-Indo-European **o* which was in apophonic relationship with **e* developed to Indo-Iranian *ā* in medial open syllables but not in final syllables (Brugman 1876: 367–81). Morphological categories in Old Indo-Aryan which have been considered particularly significant for establishing the validity of Brugmann's Law include: the singular active forms of the perfect such as *cakā́ra* 'has made'; Class 10 presents that may continue Indo-European *o*-grade *-éye-/-éyo-* presents; inherited *u*-stem nouns such as *dā́ru-* 'wood' corresponding to Greek *δόρυ*; and thematic nominal stems such as *-kārá-* 'maker', which appear as the second element in nominal compounds, and which are usually considered to reflect the same Indo-European class as Greek *τομός* 'cutter'. Brugmann himself later retracted his 'law', and during the 20th century the exact conditions for a sound change PIE **o* > IIran. *ā* have been much debated (cf. Burrow 1975, Collinge 1985: 13–21, Volkart 1994). All the Indo-Iranian categories present exceptions to the rule, as do various more isolated formations, e.g. Skt *práti-*, OP *patiy* 'toward', cf. Gr. *πρός*, *ποτί*, etc. The most generally accepted modification is that of Kuryłowicz (1927), according to which apophonic *o in a syllable closed by an inherited laryngeal did not develop to IIran. *ā*. However, because, in particular, of the preponderance of early attested thematic nominal forms with unexpected short *-a-* in their root syllable (Vedic *bhára-/-bhará-* supposedly reflecting PIE *$*b^h$óro-/-b^horó-*, etc.) Kuryłowicz (1956: 325–35) later denied the validity of Brugmann's Law as a phonological rule and instead proposed a morphophonemic explanation for the occurrence of Indo-Iranian *ā* as a reflex of the Indo-European *o*-grade.

Thanks to detailed philological studies devoted to the Old Indo-Aryan or Indo-Iranian material, such as Jamison (1983) and Kümmel (2000), many of the problems relating to Brugmann's Law in the verbal categories have now been solved. However, in the case of the thematic nouns and adjectives, if the *τόμος*/ *-*τομός* pattern[1] is accepted as the starting point and the restriction to Brugmann's Law involving laryngeals is also accepted, the sheer untidiness of the Old Indo-Aryan data is enough to cause despair: root-accented *jána-* 'person' and *jā́na-* 'birth' from *jan^i-*, suffix-accented *-kará-* and *-kārá-* 'maker', *evāvadá-* 'speaking so' and *saṃvādá-* 'conversation', *saṃnayá-* and *nāyá-* both meaning 'leader', all in the *Ṛgveda* Family Books. Yet it is agreed that these vocalic quantities are difficult to explain without Brugmann's Law since in the *Ṛgveda* forms with lengthened vocalism are confined to thematic verbal nouns and adjectives from *CVC- or *CVCH- roots. The category was discussed in Lubotsky (1988: 60–72) and then by Hajnal (1994) and, although both these studies make important observations about the Indo-Iranian forms, they take an Indo-European perspective.

My contribution to this volume will take a slightly different approach and attempt to investigate what developments were taking place within the supposed 'outcome' categories at the earliest attested periods of Old Indo-Aryan and in the most recent prehistoric period that may be reconstructed by comparing the earliest Vedic with the Old Iranian forms. It will examine the evidence from three synchronic stages: reconstructed Indo-Iranian, the hieratic language of the early *Ṛgveda*, and the 'popular' *Ṛgveda* (maṇḍala 10) + the *Atharvaveda*, with the aim of showing which types of form were productive, which are moribund and thus likely to represent archaisms, and which are likely to represent artificial/nonce creations of the Vedic poets.[2] It will also consider

[1] In historical Greek, the *nomen agentis* compounds of the type *-*τομός* have the accent on the penultimate syllable, unless that syllable is heavy, but this accentuation must be secondary and due to Wheeler's Law (cf. Probert 2006: 93–4).

[2] This paper can only scratch the surface of the latter question. Full philological discussions of some *Ṛgveda* and *Atharvaveda* passages are required, and the whole question of the distribution of compound *nomina agentis* forms in *RV* verse demands further investigation from a metrical point of view.

closely the function of the forms in the texts because this is not always immediately apparent from formal shape and accentuation. A synchronic study has to distinguish a number of categories for nominal stems built on the root with only the thematic vowel, and the most important fact to be emphasized at the outset is that from an Indo-Iranian perspective it is not a question of a simple binary opposition as seen in *τόμος/*-τομός*, but a question of interplay between several formal and functional types. In particular the productivity of prefixed verbal nouns (*RV saṃnayá-* 'leader', *saṃvādá-* 'conversation') appears to have played a major role in the development of the Indo-Iranian categories. As a result of these parameters this paper will present much more Indo-Iranian data than has been considered in previous treatments of the subject, and within the confines of a paper of this length there can only be a brief discussion.

14.2 The early *Ṛgveda*

I. Simple *nomina actionis*: root-accented (type *bhára-* 'act of carrying')[3]
Short *-á-*:[4]

kṣáya- m. 'dwelling' (×62)	*kṣay-*, *kṣéti* 'dwell'
gáya- m. 'homestead' (×14)	*gay*^{i}-, *jī́vati* 'live'
grábha- 'seizing': only infinitival *grábhāya* (7. 4. 8)	*grabh*^{i}- 'seize'
jána- m. 'person' (×278)	*jan*^{i}- 'be born'
jára- 'wasting': only infinitival *járāya* (1. 164. 11, 2. 34. 10)	*jar*^{i}- 'waste'
tára- 'overcoming': only infinitival *tárāya* (2. 13. 12, 8. 96. 1)	*tar*^{i}- 'overcome'
dábha- m. 'harm' (5. 19. 4, 5. 44. 2, 7. 91. 2, 9. 73. 8)	*dabh-* 'harm, deceive'
náma- m. 'pasture' (3. 39. 6)	cf. Gr. *νέμω* 'pasture'
bhága- m. 'share' (×108)	*bhaj-* 'share'
bhára- m. 'act of carrying away (booty), battle, booty' (×37)	*bhar-* 'bear'
máda- m. 'exhilaration, intoxication' (×262)	*mad-* 'be exhilarated'
yáma- m. 'bridle' (×6)	*yam-* 'hold, control'
ráṇa- n. 'joy, battle' (×21)	*ran-* 'exult'

3 Roots which are reconstructed with a final laryngeal are shown as *seṭ* roots with a superscript letter *i*, and the Sanskrit grammatical terms *seṭ* and *aniṭ* will be used as shorthand respectively for 'roots with reconstructed final laryngeal' and 'roots with no final laryngeal'. When individual forms are plentifully attested only numbers of attestations for *RV* 1–9 are shown.

4 *dáma-* m. 'house' is omitted from this list because it is likely to represent a thematicization of the older root noun. For similar reasons *rása-* 'taste, juice' is omitted. Cf. Lubotsky (1997: 57).

ráva- m. 'roar' (×13)	*rav^{i}-* 'roar'
^{1}*vára-* m./n. 'wish' (×33)	*var^{i}-*, *vṛṇīté* 'choose'
^{2}*vára-* m. 'space' (1. 143. 5, 3. 23. 4, 3. 53. 11, 5. 44. 12, 8. 97. 10)	*var-*, *vṛṇóti* 'cover'
váśa- m. 'wish, will' (×18)	*vaś-* 'wish'
stáva- m. 'praise' (9. 55. 2)	*stav-* 'praise'
háva- m. 'invocation' (×103)	*hav^{i}-* 'call'
Long *-ā́-*:	
jā́na- n. 'birth' (1. 37. 9, 1. 95. 3, 5. 53. 1) (×2 *RV* 10)	*jan^{i}-* 'be born'
vā́ja- m. 'contest' (×338)	*AV vājáyati* 'arouses'
^{1}*vā́ra-* m. 'animal hair, sieve of sheep's wool' ('covering'?) (×54)	*var-*, *vṛṇóti* 'cover'
^{2}*vā́ra-* m. 'treasure' (×8)	*var^{i}-*, *vṛṇīté* 'choose'
śā́ka- m. 'power' (6. 24. 4)	*śak-* 'be able'
śā́sa- m. 'command' (1. 54. 7, 1. 68. 9)	*śās-* 'instruct'
Only in composition: *śṛtapā́ka-* m. 'cooking of boiled milk' (1. 162. 10)	*pac-* 'cook'

II. Verbal nouns with prefixed *su-* or *duṣ-*:[5] root-accented (type *subhára-* 'easy to bear')

Short *-á-*:	
durgáha- n. 'danger, dangerous place' (×6) (×2 *RV* 10)	*gāh-* 'plunge, dive'
durdhára- 'hard to hold' (1. 57. 1)	*dhar-* 'hold'
durmáda- 'having bad intoxication' (1. 32. 6, 1. 39. 5, 8. 2. 12) (*bahuvrīhi*!)	*mad-* 'be exhilarated'
duṣṭára- 'hard to overcome' (×24), *sutára-* 'easy to overcome' (6. 60. 11, 7. 97. 8) (×1 *RV* 10)	*tar^{i}-* 'overcome'
dūḍábha- 'hard to deceive' (×7)	*dabh-* 'deceive'
dūṇáśa- 'hard to reach' (3. 56. 8)	*naś-* 'reach'
duḥṣáha- 'hard to conquer' (9. 91. 5), *suṣáha-* 'easy to conquer' (6. 46. 6, 9. 29. 3, 9. 94. 5) (×1 *RV* 10)	*sah-* 'conquer'
sukára- 'easy to do' (8. 80. 6)	*kar-* 'do, make'

[5] Some forms with prefixed privative *a-* also belong to this class by reason of their accentuation: *akṣára-* m. 'syllable' (lit. 'without vanishing, flowing', *kṣar-*); *ajára-* 'without wasting' (*jar^{i}-*); *aśráma-*, *aśramá-* 'without effort' (*AV śráma-* 'effort, labour', *śram^{i}-*). Other types of *bahuvrīhis* containing root-accented *nomina actionis* mostly shift their accent in accordance with normal Vedic patterns of accentuation for such compounds; cf. Macdonell (1916: 455) concerning their accent on the final syllable when the first member is a disyllabic nominal stem in *-i* or *-u* (e.g. *divikṣayá-* 'whose dwelling is in heaven', *urukṣayá-* 'with wide dwelling'; contrast *ráthakṣaya-* 'whose dwelling is a chariot').

subhága- 'having good fortune' (×51) (*bahuvrīhi*!)	*bhaj-* 'share'
subhára- 'easy to bear' (1. 112. 2, 1. 112. 20, 2. 3. 4, 2. 3. 9, 9. 86. 41) (×1 *RV* 10)	*bhar-* 'bear'
suyáma- 'easy to drive' (×10)	*yam-* 'hold, control'
suṣáṇa- 'easy to win' (1. 42. 6)	*san-* 'win'
suṣáda- 'easy to sit on' (8. 58. 3)	*sad-* 'sit'
suhána- 'easy to kill' (4. 22. 9, 7. 25. 5) (×1 *RV* 10)	*han-* 'strike, kill'
suháva- 'easy to invoke' (×29)	*hav*^{i}*-* 'call'
Long *-ā́-*:	
dūṇā́śa- 'hard to destroy' (1. 176. 4, 6. 27. 8, 7. 18. 25, 7. 32. 7, 9. 63. 11)	*naś-* 'perish'[6]

III. Simple verbal nouns: suffix-accented (type *bhārá-* 'burden, load')[7]

Short *-a-*:	
javá- 'speed' (1. 112. 21) (×2 *RV* 10)	*jav*^{i}*-* 'speed, hasten'
[1]*savá-* m. 'impelling' (×10)	*sav*^{i}*-* 'impel'
[2]*savá-* m. 'pressing, pressed juice' (1. 126. 1, 4. 26. 7) (×1 *RV* 10)	*sav-* 'press'
Long *-ā-*:	
kārá- m. 'decisive act, battle'[8] (×7) (×1 *RV* 10)	*kar-* 'do, make'
gāhá- m. 'depth, inside' (9. 110. 8)	*gāh-* 'plunge, dive'
grābhá- m. 'handful, grasp' (8. 81. 1, 9. 106. 3)	*grabh*^{i}*-* 'seize'
tyāgá- n. 'abandonment, loss of life' (4. 24. 3)	*tyaj-* 'abandon'
nāvá- m. 'roaring, loud praising' (8. 25. 11, 9. 45. 5)	*nav*$^{(i)}$*-* 'cry, roar'
pārá- n. 'far bank, furthest end' (×21) (×6 *RV* 10)	*par-* 'bring over'
bādhá- m. 'oppression' (6. 50. 4, 9. 70. 9)	*bādh-* 'oppress'
bhāgá- m. 'fortune, share' (×41) (×19 *RV* 10)	*bhaj-* 'share'
bhārá- m. 'burden, load' (1. 31. 3, 1. 152. 3, 3. 56. 2, 4. 5. 6, 7. 37. 7)	*bhar-* 'bear'
vāká- m. 'speech' (1. 164. 24 [×3], 8. 63. 4)	*vac-* 'speak'
sādá- m. 'seat' (1. 162. 17)	*sad-* 'sit'
svāná- m. 'noise' (5. 2. 10, 5. 25. 8, 8. 7. 17)	*svan*^{i}*-* 'make a noise'
svārá- m. 'sound' (2. 11. 7)	*svar-* 'sound'

6 *dūṇā́śa-* 'hard to destroy' must be based on the transitive present *nāśáyati*: it is distinguished by its exceptional long vocalism from *dūṇáśa-* 'hard to reach'.

7 So as not to prejudge any issues, the suffix-accented type is not identified either as *nomina actionis* or *nomina agentis*, but some have clear *nomen actionis* value just like the forms in class I.

8 Cf. Renou's (1964: 103–4) discussion of this difficult *RV* word, with reference to Wackernagel. *RV* 1. 112. 1 *kārá-* may represent the cognate of OP *kāra-* m. 'army, people': cf. Mayrhofer (1986–2001: i. 340).

hvārá- m. 'snake' ('crooked motion')[9] (1. 141. 7, 1. 180. 3, 2. 2. 4)	*hvar-* 'be crooked'
Only in composition: *suyāmá-* 'having good driving, driving well'[10] (3. 7. 9)	*yam-* 'hold, control'

IV. *Nomina actionis* based on compound verbs: suffix-accented (types *saṃgamá-* 'meeting', *saṃvādá-* 'conversation')

Short *-a-*:

udayá- m. 'rising up' (8. 41. 2)	*ay-* 'go'
samará- m./n. 'hostile encounter' (6. 9. 2, 6. 47. 6) (×1 *RV* 10)	*ar-* 'go'
saṃgamá- m. 'coming together, battle' (1. 102. 3) (×4 *RV* 10)	*gam-* 'come'
upacyavá- m. 'mating' (1. 28. 3)	*cyav-* 'move'
prajavá- m. 'speed' (7. 33. 8)	*jav*^{i}- 'speed, hasten'
ādhavá- 'mixing' (1. 141. 3) (also m. 'mixer', 10. 26. 4)	*dhav*^{i}- 'shake'
vimadá- m. 'intoxication' (1. 51. 3, 1. 112. 19, 1. 116. 1, 1. 117. 20, 8. 9. 15) (×6 *RV* 10)	*mad-* 'be exhilarated'
nivará- m. 'protection' (8. 93. 15), *vivará-* m. 'hole' (1. 112. 18)	*var-*, *vṛṇóti* 'cover'
abhisvaré 'in calling distance' (3. 45. 2) (×1 *RV* 10)	*svar-* 'sound'
prasavá- m. 'impulse' (×14), *utsavá-* m. 'starting' (1. 100. 8, 1. 102. 1)	*sav*^{i}- 'impel'
saṃsravá- m. 'flowing together, confluence' (9. 113. 5)	*srav-* 'flow'
āhavá- m. 'challenge, fight' (1. 155. 6, 2. 23. 11, 6. 47. 1) (×1 *RV* 10), *vihavá-* m. 'rival invocation' (3. 8. 10) (×2 *RV* 10)	*hav*^{i}- 'call'
upahvará- m. 'circuitous course, uneven slope' (1. 62. 6, 1. 87. 2, 8. 6. 28, 8. 69. 6, 8. 96. 14)	*hvar-* 'be crooked'

Long *-ā-*:[11]

vibhāgá- m. 'distribution' (1. 109. 5, 5. 77. 4, 7. 37. 3, 7. 40. 1, 7. 56. 21)	*bhaj-* 'share'

[9] Cf. *RV ābhogá-* m. 'snake' from the root *bhuj-* 'to bend'.

[10] Debrunner (1954: 89) explains this compound as a *bahuvrīhi* containing *yāmá-*; cf. *supārá-* 'affording easy crossing', *subhāgá-* 'having a good share', containing *pārá-*, *bhāgá-*.

[11] Two *hapax legomena* in difficult passages, *ādārá-*, *atiyājá-*, have been included in this class although they have been translated variously as *nomina actionis* and *nomina agentis*. Prefixed *nomina agentis* with long *-ā-* are rare (see class VII). There are additional arguments in each case: *atiyājá-* is paralleled by two *nomina actionis* forms with long *-ā-* in *RV* 10 (*anuyājá-*, *prayājá-*); *ādārá-* is likely to represent the *nomen actionis* from which *ādārín-* 'breaker in, burglar' (*RV* 8. 45. 13) is derived.

ādārá- m. ?'act of breaking open' (1. 46. 5)	*dar-* 'attack'
atiyājá- m. ?'superior offering'[12] (6. 52. 1)	*yaj-* 'offer'
adhivāká- m. 'advocacy' (8. 16. 5), *upavāká-* m. 'address' (1. 164. 8)	*vac-* 'speak'
saṃvādá- m. 'conversation' (8. 101. 4)	*vad-* 'say'
adhīvāsá- m. 'over-dress' (1. 140. 9)	*vas-* 'wear'
pravāsá- m. 'living abroad' (8. 29. 8)	*vas-* 'stay'
pravrājá- m. 'current, stream' (7. 60. 7)	*vraj-* 'twist'
ucchvāsá- m. 'breathing out' (9. 86. 43)	*śvas-* 'blow'
abhiśrāvá- m. 'hearing, being heard' (1. 185. 10) (×1 *RV* 10)	*śrav-* 'hear'
visārá- m. 'diffusing, spreading out' (1. 79. 1)	*sar-* 'run'
āhāvá- m. 'bucket, container' (1. 34. 8, 6. 7. 2) (×2 *RV* 10)	*hav-* 'pour'

V. *Nomina actionis*, second element of determinative compound consisting of two nominal stems: suffix-accented (type *namovāká-* m. 'speech of homage')

Short *-a-*:	
indrahavá- m. 'invocation of Indra' (9. 96. 1)	*hav*^{i}*-* 'call'
Long *-ā-*:	
haskārá- m. 'the making of a noise *has-*' (1. 23. 12)[13]	*kar-* 'do, make'
jīvayājá- m. 'offering of living (animal)' (1. 31. 15)	*yaj-* 'offer'
ṛtavāká- m. 'act of speaking the truth' (9. 113. 2), *joṣavāká-* m. 'act of speaking what is pleasing' (6. 59. 4), *namovāká-* m. 'speech of homage' (8. 35. 23)[14]	*vac-* 'speak'
sahasrasāvá- m. 'pressing of a thousand, thousand(fold) Soma-pressing' (3. 53. 7 = 7. 103. 10), *prātaḥsāvá-* m. 'morning Soma-pressing' (3. 28. 1, 3. 52. 4) (×1 *RV* 10)[15]	*sav-* 'press'

12 Cf. Geldner (1951: ii. 155), 'Überopfer'.

13 Following Geldner (1951: i. 23).

14 *dhāravāká-* 5. 44. 5, although its accent is similar, appears to be an adjective with *bahuvrīhi* meaning 'having the speech of streams'.

15 Here the first member is an adverb that is not normally used as a prefix, but perhaps an extension of the prefixed type (class IV). See below for discussion of the historical interrelationship of classes IV and V.

VI. *Nomina agentis*, second element of determinative compound consisting of two nominal stems: suffix-accented (types *vājaṃbharā́-* 'bringing booty', *brahmakārā́-* 'formula-maker')

Short *-a-*:

khajaṃkarā́- 'making a battle-din' (1. 102. 6), *yataṃkarā́-* 'making constraint' (5. 34. 4)	*kar-* 'do, make', *kṛṇóti*
vṛtaṃcayā́- 'punishing the enemy' (2. 21. 3)	*cay-* 'punish', *cáyate*
kucarā́- 'going about anywhere' (1. 154. 2), *dhanvacarā́-* 'going about on the plain' (5. 36. 1)	*car-* 'go about', *cárati*
dhanaṃjayā́- 'winning wealth' (3. 42. 6 = 8. 45. 13, 6. 16. 15, 9. 46. 5, 9. 84. 5)	*jay-* 'win', *jáyati*
rathaṃtarā́- 'overcoming chariots' (1. 164. 25) (×1 *RV* 10), *druhaṃtarā́-* 'overcoming falsehood' (1. 127. 3 [×2])	*tar^i-* 'overcome', *tárati*
puraṃdarā́- 'attacking fortresses' (×11)	*dar-* 'attack', *daráyati*
puṣṭiṃbharā́- 'bringing prosperity' (4. 3. 7), *vājaṃbharā́-* 'bringing booty' (1. 60. 5, 4. 11. 4) (×1 *RV* 10), *sahasraṃbharā́-* 'bringing a thousand(fold)' (2. 9. 1), *sutaṃbharā́-* 'bringing the pressed drink' (5. 44. 13)	*bhar-* 'bear', *bhárati*
dhārāvarā́- 'loving streams' (2. 34. 1)	*var^i-* 'choose', *vṛṇīté*
tadvaśā́- 'wanting that' (2. 14. 2, 2. 37. 1)	*vaś-* 'wish', *váṣṭi*
cakramāsajā́- 'dragging its wheel' (5. 34. 6)	*sañj-* 'hang', *sájati*
janaṃsahā́- 'conquering people' (2. 21. 3)	*sah-* 'conquer', *sáhate*
aśvahayā́- 'driving horses' (9. 96. 2) (×1 *RV* 10)	*hay-* 'incite, drive', *hinóti*, ptcpl. *háyantā* (*RV* 1. 11. 18)

Long *-ā-*:

brahmakārā́- 'making a sacred formula' (6. 29. 4)	*kar-* 'do, make', *kṛṇóti*
vṛtrakhādā́- 'injuring Vṛtra' (3. 45. 2, 3. 51. 9) (×1 *RV* 10)	*khād-* 'tear at, consume', *khā́dhati*
udagrābhā́- 'holding water' (9. 97. 15), *grāvagrābhā́-* 'holding the pressing stones' (1. 162. 5), *tuvigrābhā́-* 'seizing strongly' (6. 22. 5)	*grabh^i-* 'seize', *gṛbhāyáti*, *gṛbhṇā́ti*
nakṣaddābhā́- 'harming the one who approaches' (6. 22. 2)	*dabh-* 'deceive', *dabhnóti*
kṣīrapākā́- 'cooked in milk' (8. 77. 10)	*pac-* 'cook', *pácati*
hiraṇyapāvā́- ?'purifying gold' (9. 86. 43)	*pav^i-* 'purify', *pūṇā́ti*, *pávate*
tuvibādhā́- 'oppressing strongly' (1. 36. 6)	*bādh-* 'oppress', *bā́dhate*

udavāhá- 'conveying water' (1. 38. 9, 5. 58. 3), *yūpavāhá-* 'conveying the sacrificial post' (1. 162. 6)	*vah-* 'convey', *váhati*
sarvaśāsá- 'ruling all' (5. 44. 4)	*śās-* 'instruct', *śā́sti*
vrātasāhá- 'conquering troops' (6. 75. 9)	*sah-* 'conquer', *sáhate*

VII. *Nomina agentis* prefixed with preverb (i.e. based on compound verb) or prefixed with adverb: suffix-accented (types *saṃnayá-* 'leader', *prakhādá-* 'injuring')

Short *-a-*:

araṃgamá- 'coming fittingly' (6. 42. 1, 8. 46. 17), *makṣuṃgamá-* 'coming quickly' (8. 22. 16)	*gam-* 'come', *gácchati*
satrākará- 'altogether active' (1. 178. 4)	*kar-* 'do, make', *kr̥ṇóti*
ākará- 'scattering, conferring' (3. 51. 3, 5. 34. 4, 8. 33. 5)	*kar*^{i}- 'scatter', *kiráti*[16]
ātapá- 'burning' (1. 55. 1)	*tap-* 'heat', *tápati*
vinayá- 'leading apart', *saṃnayá-* 'leading together' (2. 24. 9)	*nay*^{i}- 'lead', *náyati*
antarābhará- 'bringing into the middle' (8. 32. 12)	*bhar-* 'bear', *bhárati*
prabhavá- 'pre-eminent, mighty' (2. 38. 5)	*bhav*^{i}- 'become', *bhávati*
evāvadá- 'speaking so, speaking the truth' (5. 44. 10)	*vad-* 'say', *vádati*
paraśará- 'smasher, anihilator' (7. 18. 21, 7. 104. 21)	*śar*^{i}- 'smash', *śr̥ṇā́ti*
punaḥsará- 'running back' (7. 55. 3)	*sar-* 'run', *siṣárti*

Long *-ā-*:

prakhādá- 'injuring, consuming' (1. 178. 4)	*khād-* 'tear at', *khā́dati*
vigāhá- 'plunging in' (3. 3. 5)	*gāh-* 'plunge, dive', *gā́hate*
upanāyá- m. ?'supreme leader' (9. 91. 4)	*nay*^{i}- 'lead', *náyati*
upaśāká- 'very strong' (1. 33. 4) (cf. *śāká-*, *śākín-* 'strong')	*śak-* 'be able', *śaknóti*
āsāva- m ?'Soma-presser' (8. 103. 10) (unaccented voc.)	*sav-* 'press', *sunóti*
satrāsāhá- 'conquering completely' (2. 21. 3)	*sah-* 'conquer', *sáhate*

[16] Kuryłowicz (1956: 327) is clearly correct in attributing this prefixed *nomen agentis* to the verb 'to scatter', as this derivation is supported by *RV* collocations such as *vásva ākaráḥ* (5. 34. 4) beside *vásūnām... carkr̥ṣe* (10. 74. 1). But none of the other *nomen agentis* forms in *-kará-* can be connected with this *seṭ* root.

VIII. Simple *nomina agentis*: suffix-accented (types *ghaná-* 'club', *vāhá-* m. 'draught animal')

Short-*a*-:	
ajá- m. 'driver' (3. 45. 2)	*aj-* 'drive', *ájati*
ará- m. 'spoke of wheel' (×7)	*ar-* 'go', *íyarti*
kará- 'making' (1. 116. 13) (m. 'hand', 10. 67. 6)	*kar-* 'do, make', *kr̥ṇóti*
ghaná- m. 'murderer, club' (×10)	*han-* 'strike, kill', *hánti*
tradá- m. 'piercer, opener' (8. 45. 28) (cf. *AV tardá-* 'borer')	*tard-* 'bore through', *tr̥ṇátti*
dravá- 'running' (4. 40. 2)	*drav-* 'run', *drávati*
dhvajá- m. 'flag, banner' ('flutterer') (7. 85. 2) (×1 *RV* 10)	cf. YAv. pres. *duuaža* 'flutter'
nadá- m. 'bull' (1. 32. 8, 1. 179. 4, 2. 34. 3, 8. 69. 2 [×2]) (×2 *RV* 10)	*nad-* 'resound', *nadáyati*
plavá- m. 'boat' (1. 182. 5)	*plav-* 'swim, float', *plávate*
bhramá- m. 'flickering flame' ('wanderer') (4. 4. 2, 6. 6. 4, 9. 22. 2)	*bhram-* 'wander', *bhrámati* (*ŚB*)
vadhá- m. 'weapon' ('striker') (×35)	*vadh-* 'strike'
vará- m. 'suitor' (1. 83. 2, 5. 60. 4, 9. 101. 14) (×4 *RV* 10)	*var*^{i}- 'choose', *vr̥ṇīté*
valá- m. 'cave' (×16)	*l*-form of *var-* 'cover', *vr̥ṇóti*
Long -*ā*-:	
nāyá- m. 'leader' (6. 24. 10, 6. 46. 11)	*nay*^{i}- 'lead', *náyati*
pārá- 'making cross' (5. 31. 8)	*par-* 'bring over', *pārá-yati* 'makes cross'
vāśá- 'noisy' ('bellower') (8. 19. 31)	*vāś-* 'bellow', *vā́śati*
vāhá- m. 'draught animal' ('conveyor') (4. 57. 4, 4. 57. 8)	*vah-* 'convey', *váhati*
śākā́- 'having power, being able' (4. 17. 11, 5. 30. 10, 5. 15. 2, 6. 19. 4) (×1 *RV* 10)	*śak-* 'be able', *śaknóti*
śāsá- m. 'commander' (3. 47. 5) (×1 *RV* 10)	*śās-* 'instruct', *śā́sti*
śrāyá- 'leaning on' (5. 53. 4)	*śray-* 'lean on', *śráyate*
sāhá- 'overcoming' (8. 20. 2)	*sah-* 'conquer', *sáhate*
svāná- 'noisy' (5. 10. 5, 9. 10. 1) (also m. 'noise')	*svan*^{i}- 'make a noise', *svanáyati*

Even though this chronological stage has been the subject of several previous discussions (see especially Kuryłowicz 1956: 325–35, Lubotsky 1988: 60–72, Hajnal 1994), it is necessary to consider it again as a basis for comparison of the Old Iranian evidence and the slightly later Vedic stage.

As has frequently been noted, the uncompounded *nomina actionis* (NActs), which are traditionally considered to continue the Indo-European type **b^hóro-* (class I, *bhára-*) mostly show short *-á-* as their root vocalism, and there are only a few with *-ā́-*, the outcome that would be expected according to Brugmann's Law for all inherited roots that did not end in a laryngeal.[17] From a synchronic point of view the forms with *-á-* constitute part of a wider class of deverbative *RV nomina actionis* whose accent falls on the full-grade root: cf. type *yóga-* n. 'yoking' (*yuj-*), *póṣa-* m. 'prosperity' (*puṣ-*), *véda-* m. 'knowledge' (*vid-*), *kéta-* m. 'intention' (*cit-*), *sárga-* m. 'releasing' (*sr̥j-*), *śáṃsa-* m. 'praise' (*śáṃs-*). In addition there is a closely related class of compounds of the type *subhára-* 'easy to bear' (?, cf. Gr. type δύσφορο-), which contain formally similar root-accented verbal nouns with regular short *-á-* (cf. Debrunner 1954: 86–9). Two formations, *durgáha-, suśáka-* (*RV* 10), appear to show shortening of long *-ā-* (as attested in other early Old Indo-Aryan forms from the same roots) and such forms suggest that shortenings of the root vowel for morphological reasons could have occurred in these two classes at a prehistoric date.

Contrasting with these two types, there is another class of uncompounded verbal nouns where the accent falls on the thematic vowel, and long *-ā-* predominates as the root vocalism. There is also a contrast in meaning in several cases: *grábha-* 'action of seizing' vs. *grābhá-* 'what is seized, handful, grasp', *bhára-* 'action of bearing (away booty)' vs. *bhārá-* 'what is borne, burden, load', *bhága-* 'action of sharing/allotting' (also personified as god Bhaga) vs. *bhāgá-* 'what is shared/allotted, fortune'. Because of their distinctive meaning Lubotsky (1988: 67–72) describes the latter group as 'concrete nouns',[18] and Hajnal (1994: 199) as '*Nomina actionis* bzw. *rei actae*'.

The accent also falls on the thematic vowel in the NActs derived from compound verbs (class IV), as is regular in Old Indo-Aryan for this type of prefixed verbal noun (cf. *abhidrohá-* 'injury' (*druh-*), *niveśá-* m. 'dwelling place' (*viś-*), *visargá-* m. 'releasing' (*sr̥j-*), *saṃkalpá-* m. 'plan' (*kl̥p-*), etc.). In the early *R̥gveda* the class is almost equally divided between forms with long and short vocalism: types *saṃgamá-* 'meeting', *saṃvādá-* 'conversation'. The minimal

[17] As some of the forms with long vocalism are from roots which did end in a laryngeal (*jā́na-* 'birth', [2]*vā́ra-* 'treasure') even this sub-group cannot automatically be identified as relics.

[18] Lubotsky (1988: 68–9) classifies them together with other forms that have similar accentuation but short *-a-* in the root, which have been traditionally classified (and are classified here) as uncompounded *nomina agentis*.

pair *āhavá-* 'challenge' (root *hav^i-/hū-*) and *āhāvá-* 'bucket' (root *hav-/hu-*) has often been quoted in connection with Brugmann's Law, but apart from *prajavá-* 'speed' and probably *ādhavá-* 'mixing', all the other formations with short *-a-* are from *aniṭ* roots. However, none of the forms with long *-ā-* are from *seṭ* roots, and forms with velars from the same synchronic category such as *praketá-* 'light' (root *cit-* 'be visible') also point to an Indo-European *o*-grade formation. The category will be discussed again in connection with the *RV* 10/*AV* evidence.

A further class of suffix-accented NActs consists of determinative compounds made of two nominal stems (class V, *namovākā́-* m. 'speech of homage'). From a functional point of view this small group cannot directly reflect the *τόμος*/**-τομός* pattern, since according to the reconstructed Indo-European pattern the verbal nouns as second elements should possess *nomen agentis* value. But *namovākā́-*, *sahasrasāvá-*, etc. represent a normal Old Indo-Aryan type of determinative (*tatpuruṣa*) compounds (cf. e.g. *udameghá-* m. 'shower of water' (*RV* 1. 116. 3), *sahasrapoṣá-* m. 'prospering of a thousand, thousandfold prosperity' (*RV* 2. 32. 5)).

Compounds of two nominal stems where the second functions as a *nomen agentis* (NAg) or adjective (class VI, *vājaṃbhará-*) show the expected accent on the thematic vowel, but forms in short *-a-* are slightly more numerous than those in long *-ā-*, and all attempted explanations of the vocalic length leave a great number of exceptions. This is the class which is traditionally considered to reflect PIE **-b^horó-* and it will be discussed further in the following paragraphs. NAgs with a verbal prefix or prefixed adverb (class VII, *saṃnayá-* 'who leads together') normally show short *-a-*, unless they are derived from a root with invariable long vocalism (*prakhādá-*, *vigāhá-*) or derived from a simple nominal stem by means of an intensifying prefix (*upaśākā́-* : *śākā́-* and probably *upanāyá-* : *nāyá-*[19]). On the other hand, simple unprefixed NAgs (class VIII) with long *-ā-* are almost as frequent as those with short *-a-* and the distribution of the quantities in these uncompounded forms is likewise puzzling: for instance, why *ghaná-* with short *-a-* when the root *han-* is *aniṭ* and the initial velar points to an Indo-European *o*-grade, but *nāyá-* when the root *nī-* is *seṭ*? The roots involved are mostly different from those that supply NAg second elements for compounds of two nominal stems (only *kará-*, *vará-*, *vāhá-*, *śāsá-*, and *sāhá-* appear in both classes), and not many of class VIII can be explained in straightforward fashion as back-formations from attested compounds.

[19] *saṃnayá-*, *vinayá-* with short *-a-* represent regular NAgs in the early *Ṛgveda*; hence *upanāyá-* is more likely to be connected with simple *nāyá-*. Within the same category derivatives from the same root do not normally vary in vocalism.

In the list of forms for the NAg classes the present stem of the verb has been indicated, because it is notable that the NAgs in composition (classes VI *vājaṃbharā-*, and VII *saṃnayá-*) frequently correspond to a thematic present with identical root vocalism (*bhárati*, *náyati*). Hence many possess a synchronic deverbative character similar to that of the second members of recent compounds such as *valaṃrujá-* 'breaking the cave' (*ruj-*, *rujáti*), *agnimindhá-* 'kindling the sacred fire' (*idh-*, *indháte*), *viśvaminvá-* 'moving everything' (*inv-*, *ínvati*), *dhiyaṃjinvá-* 'enlivening thought' (*jinv-*, *jínvati*).[20] *viśvaminvá-* etc. were probably based on the *vājaṃbharā-* type, but the existence of the former indicates that the latter were analysable as noun + NAg derived from a present stem. Moreover, the two elements of some frequently occurring compounds are reflected elsewhere in the *Ṛgveda* by collocations of finite verb + object:

- *vājaṃbharā-*: *vā́jam bharati* 'brings booty' (4. 16. 16, 4. 17. 9), etc.
- *sahasraṃbharā-*: *indra sahásram ā́ bhara* 'O Indra, bring a thousand' (8. 78. 1), etc.
- *dhanaṃjayá-*: *jayati sáṃ dhánāni* 'he wins riches' (4. 50. 9), etc.

Derivation from the present stem of the verb cannot account for the vocalism of every form belonging to this class: for instance, the NAg second elements *-kará-*, *-vará-* are not paralleled by a thematic present and the long vocalism of *-vāhá-* is at odds with *váhati*. But the high degree of parallelism does raise a chronological question: can we be sure in every case that we are really dealing with an ancient NAg form or could some have been created recently on the basis of the verb's present stem according to a productive pattern? Many are *hapax legomena* in the *Ṛgveda* and never occur again. Furthermore the nonce-creation *atipārayá-* 'making cross beyond' (*RV* 6. 47. 7) can only be based on the present *pāráyati* 'makes cross' and appears to confirm the reality of a synchronic process of derivation.

Hajnal (1994: 208–10) proposed that the NAg compounds conform to a number of rhythmical patterns and the appearance of short or long vocalism depends on the quantities of the whole word. The accusative inflection frequently shown by the first member (a trait shared by the *viśvaminvá*-type compounds) serves the purpose of creating a heavy syllable and it makes the whole compound fit the metrical scheme of a *jagatī* cadence (*khajaṃkará-*, *yataṃkará-*, *janaṃsahá-*) or makes it usable as first word of any verse-line, where without the accusative inflection there would be a succession of four

[20] In the last three cases their recent origin is clear because the NAg second member is formed from a secondary verb stem that is known to have originated via an *einzelsprachlich* process of thematicization (*inóti*, *inváti*).

light syllables (e.g. first word in a *triṣṭubh* line: *vṛtaṃcayá-*, *dhanaṃjayá-*, *sutaṃbhará-*). According to Hajnal's account, in cases where an accusative inflection in *-m* is not possible for the first member, the NAg second elements with a long radical vowel (*udagrābhá-*, *brahmakārá-*) serve a similar purpose by avoiding a succession of short syllables. But it is not clear that either metrical licence or an Old Indo-Aryan rhythmical law can explain everything. A large number of rhythmical patterns have to be postulated, and even then there are exceptions (for instance, why *aśvahayá-* 'driving horses', if *brahmakārá-* 'making a sacred formula' demands vowel lengthening?). We will see below that a rhythmical explanation for the vocalism appears to be ruled out by a large body of *RV* 10/*AV* examples where there are no alternations of quantity at all (e.g. *vṛṣabhará-* 'bearing men', *ajagará-* 'goat-swallower', *medhākārá-* 'making wisdom', *jyotiṣkāra-* 'making light'). The whole question of metrical constraints on the distribution of these compounds (and others) is very interesting and deserves more detailed study, but it is unlikely to provide a full solution to the problems of vowel length.

14.3 Old Iranian

The Old Iranian evidence is classified below using the same categories as were used for the early *RV* evidence, insofar as is possible given that there is no direct evidence for accentuation.[21]

I. Simple *nomina actionis*

Short *-a-*:

gaiia- m. 'life' (OAv., YAv.)	*jī-* 'live'
jaiia- m. 'victory' (OAv.)	*ji-* 'win'
taka- m. 'running, course' (YAv.)	*tac-* 'run'
baga-, *baγa-* m. 'portion, fortune' (OAv. (meaning?), YAv.); *baga-* m. 'god' (OP)	*baj-* 'shar'
mada-, *maδa-* m. 'exhilaration, intoxication' (OAv., YAv.)	*mad-* 'be intoxicated'
sauua- m./n. 'benefit' (OAv.)	*sū-* 'swell'
snaθa- m. 'blow, weapon' (YAv.)	*snaθ*^{i}*-* 'strike'
-zana- (OP, in *bahuvrīhis: paruzana-* 'having many peoples', *vispazana-* 'having all peoples')	*zan*^{i}*-* 'be born'
zauua- m. 'invocation' (OAv.: *Yasna* 28. 3, 29. 3)	*zū-* 'invoke'

[21] Roots generally cited according to Kellens (1995).

	x^vara- m. 'wound' (YAv.)	**huar-* 'be sore'
	Long *-ā-*:[22]	
	vāra- n. 'will, wish' (OAv.)[23]	*varⁱ-* 'choose'
	rə̄na- n. 'battle' (YAv.)[24]	**ran-* 'exult'
II.	Verbal nouns with prefix **su-*	
	hušə̄na- 'having good gain' or ?'easy to win' (OAv.: *Yasna* 53. 5)[25]	*san-* 'win'
	huuāzāra- (*hu-* + **āzāra-* 'offence') 'easily offended' (YAv.)	*ā-zarⁱ-* 'enrage'
III.	Verbal nouns of the same type as OIA *bhārá-*, *bhāgá-*, *pārá-*?	
	bāga- n. 'share' (OAv.)	*baj-* 'share'
	Only in composition: *dūraēpāra-* 'whose boundaries are far off' (YAv.)	*par-* 'cross'
	Only in composition: *xšuuiβi.vāza-* 'whose flight ("conveyance") is swift'[26] (YAv.)	*vaz-* 'convey'
	Only in composition: *ucāra-* 'well made, successful' (OP)	*kar-* 'make'
	asabāra- 'horse-borne' (OP)	*bar-* 'bear'
IV.	*Nomina actionis* based on compound verbs	
	Short *-a-*:	
	aipiiaiia- m. 'undertaking' (YAv.)	*i-* 'go'
	avakana- m. 'grave' (YAv.)	*kan-* 'dig'
	pairi.kara- m. 'furrow' (YAv.)	*karⁱ-* 'plough'
	patikara- m. 'representation, image' (OP)	*kar-* 'make'
	paiti.vaŋha- m. 'item of clothing' (YAv.)	*vah-* 'wear'

[22] Two late Young Avestan compounds, both attested at *Vidēvdāt* 14. 7, may also contain nouns that belong to this class, but their analysis is quite uncertain: *tižī.dāra-* 'with sharp tusks' ('whose piercing is sharp'?) (*dar-* 'pierce'), *tižī.bāra-* 'with sharp blades' ('whose cutting is sharp'?) (*brī-* 'shear, cut'). The form of the second element in *tižī.bāra-* must be modelled on that of *tižī.dāra-*, and Bartholomae (1904: 653) translated both 'mit scharfer Schneide'.

[23] It is disputed whether this is a cognate of *RV* ²*vā́ra-* m. 'treasure'; it may mean 'what is wished for, what is willed' (by Ahura Mazda, *Yasna* 33. 2, 46. 18, 51. 6) and belong to the same class as OAv. *bāga-* (*RV* class III, *bhārá-*).

[24] See the discussion by de Vaan (2003: 473–4).

[25] From **hušana-*: *-ə̄n-* continues **-an-* in Old Avestan, but **-ān-* in Young Avestan (cf. de Vaan 2003: 468).

[26] Usually translated 'flying swiftly', but an old NAg *-vāza-* in the second part of a nominal compound should mean 'conveying' (cf. *RV udavāhá-* 'conveying water'). The fact that *xšuuiβi-* is a Caland *i*-stem corresponding to *xšuuiβra-* 'swift' (cf. *xšuuiβi.išu-* 'with swift arrow') points to a *bahuvrīhi*/possessive compound 'with swift flight'. Since its second element appears to have an intransitive/passive meaning, it may be possible to reconstruct a verbal noun of the **bhārá-* type, Av. **vāzá-* 'conveyance, flight'.

<u>Long *-ā-*:</u>	
paitiiāra- m. 'adversity' (YAv.)	*ar-* 'move'
aiβigāma- m. 'year, winter' (YAv.)	*gam-* 'come'
apaγžāra- m. 'outlet'	*γžar-* 'flow'
vītāra- m. 'crossing' (YAv.)	*tar*^{i}*-* 'overcome, go over'
pairi.frāsa- m. 'questioning around' (YAv.)	*fras-* 'ask'
fravāka- n. 'speech, proclamation' (YAv.)	*vac-* 'speak'
vīvāpa- m. 'destruction' (YAv.)	*vap-* 'lay waste'
pairi.vāra- m. 'protection around', *fravāra-* m. 'protection in front', *vī.vāra-* n. 'covering on all sides (with rain)' (YAv.)	*var-* 'cover'
frauuāza- m. 'conveyance forward' (YAv.: *Vidēvdāt* 3. 31)	*vaz-* 'convey'

VI. *Nomina agentis*, second element of determinative compound consisting of two nominal stems

<u>Short *-a-*:</u>	
frašō.kara- 'making wonderful', *maēγō.kara-* 'making clouds', *raθakara-* 'forming a chariot', *raēθβiš.kara-* m. 'priest who makes mixture of Haoma and milk', etc. (meaning of other forms uncertain) (YAv.); *dāraniyakara-* 'gold-worker', *hamaranakara-* m. 'battle-maker', *zurakara-* m. 'evil-doer' (OP)	*kar-* 'make'
t̰baēšō.tara- 'overcoming enmity' (YAv.)	*tar*^{i}*-* 'over come, go over'
zaoθrō.bara- 'libation-bearer', *nəmō.bara-* 'bearing homage', *gaδauuara-* (**-uuara-* < *-βara-*) 'club-bearing', *gaošāuuara-* 'wearing earrings', *sruuara-* (< *srūβara-*) 'horn-bearing' (YAv.); *arštibara-* 'spear-bearer', *vaçabara-* 'mace-bearer', *takabara-* 'wearing the petasos' (OP)	*bar-* 'bear'
drujim.vana- 'conquering the Lie' (YAv.)	*van-* 'conquer'
mašiiō.vaŋha- 'clothing men' (YAv.)	*vah-* 'wear'
mazdā.vara- 'choosing Mazda' (OAv.)	*var*^{i}*-* 'choose'
<u>Long *-ā-*:</u>	
nauuāza- 'boatman', *gauuāza-* 'cow-goad' (YAv.)	*az-* 'drive'

	aṣanāsa- 'attaining truth', *ahu.nāsa-* 'attaining life', *vahišta.nāsa-* 'attaining the best' (YAv.)[27]	*nas-* 'attain'
	nasupāka- 'cooking dead matter',[28] *uruzdi.pāka-* 'cooking liquids' (YAv.)	*pac-* 'cook'
VII.	*Nomina agentis* prefixed with preverb	
	aipicara- 'moving behind', *fracara-* 'moving in front' (YAv.: *Yašt* 15. 45)	*car-* 'go about'
	vīkaya- m. 'witness' (YAv.: *Frahang-ī-ōim* 8. 27)	*ci-* 'punish'
	paiti.daiia- m. 'overseer' (YAv.: *Yašt* 8. 44)	*dī-* 'see'
	haθra.vana- 'conquering at once' (YAv.)	*van-* 'conquer'
VIII.	Simple *nomina agentis*	
	vaδa-/vada- m. 'weapon' ('slayer') (YAv.)	**vad^i-* 'slay'
	snaθa- 'striking' (also m. 'blow, weapon') (YAv.)	*snaθ^i-* 'strike'
	vāza- m. 'draught-animal' (OAv.)	*vaz-* 'convey'
	hāra- 'watching' (OAv.: *Yasna* 31. 13, 44. 2)	*har-* 'watch'

It is immediately apparent that the types of formation in Old Iranian and their morphology are exactly parallel to the early *RV* classes, except in two respects. Firstly, the existence of forms corresponding to the *subhára-* type (*RV* class II) is doubtful, but this may be because the Old Iranian evidence is less plentiful. Secondly, there is no evidence at all for compounds of two nominal stems the second of which has NAct value (*RV* class V, *namovākā́-*). Without the evidence of accentuation, the assignment of OAv. *bāga-*, *pāra-* to the suffix-accented class of NAct (class III, *bhārá-*) is hypothetical but it is based on the likely assumption that *RV bhāgá-* and OAv. *bāga-*, *RV pārá-* and YAv. *(dūraē)-pāra-* are cognates.

Hence it appears that a class of NActs with short vocalism must have existed already in prehistoric Indo-Iranian: Av. *baga-*, *baγa-* 'share', OP 'god' : *RV bhága-* and Av. *mada-*, *maδa-* 'intoxication' : *RV máda-* are exact cognates, and Old Iranian has other forms with short *-a-* from inherited *aniṭ* roots, e.g. *taka-* m. 'running, course'. There also appears to have been a class of NActs derived from compound verbs which showed both short and long quantity in their root syllables: Av. *avakana-* m. 'grave', *vīvāpa-* m. 'destruction', cf. *RV* class IV, types *saṃgamá-* 'meeting', *saṃvādá-* 'conversation'.

[27] The vowel quantity shown by *-nāsa-* may not be original because long vocalism has spread throughout forms of the corresponding verb; cf. de Vaan (2003: 100, 181).

[28] Once-attested abl. sg. *nasupakāt̰* shows secondary shortening according to de Vaan (2003: 137, 159).

Correspondences between second-element NAgs make it possible to reconstruct IIran. **-kará-*, **-cará-*, **-tarHá-*, **-bhará-*, **-varHá-*, all with short radical *-a-*; also **-ājá-*, **-pāká-* with long *-ā-*, by comparing *nauuāza-* with *nāvājá-* 'boatman' (*ŚB*),[29] and *nasupāka-* with *odanapāká-* 'cooking rice' (*AV*). Among the uncompounded NAgs, Av. *vaδa-*, *vada-* 'weapon' appears to be the exact cognate of *RV vadhá-* and *vāza-* 'draught animal' of *vāhá-*.

The compounded NAgs are almost all based on roots in resonants. At first sight the Old Iranian data appears to support the theory[30] that **-Cārá-* < PIE **-Coró-* was remodelled to **-Cará-* on the analogy of **-Cará-* < **-CarHá-* < PIE **-CorHó-*, after the post-consonantal laryngeal was lost. However, the much greater frequency of compounds in **-kará-* and **-bhará-*, particularly in Old Iranian, casts some doubt on such an analogical explanation as it might be expected that this pair would have served as the model for the roots which once ended in a laryngeal rather than vice versa. Parallel thematic presents only occur beside three of the Old Iranian NAgs (*-cara-*, *-bara-*, *-tara-*), and so it cannot be demonstrated that synchronic correspondences with the verb helped to reshape this class of verbal nouns in the Indo-Iranian prehistoric period.[31]

It seems necessary to accept that, for reasons which can only be a matter of speculation, short *-a-* vocalism had become regular in both the supposed reflexes of the simple *b^h*óro*-type NActs and in the compounded -b^h*oró*-type NAgs[32] during the ancestral Indo-Iranian period.[33] A very few forms may have escaped this development because their meaning had changed at an early date, and these show the expected Brugmann's Law reflex (e.g. *vāza-/vāhá-* < *u̯oĝ^h*ó-*); but because of the limitations of the Old Iranian evidence they are difficult to identify securely, and, as we will see below, their identification

[29] *-āza-* < **-*h_2*oĝo-* could show compositional lengthening of its vowel.

[30] Hajnal (1994: 208, 218–19); cf. Kuryłowicz (1956: 330).

[31] It appears more likely that, on the basis of a few inherited cases where the formal shape of the verb's present stem coincided with that of the NAg, Old Indo-Aryan productively extended this pattern by the time of the *R̥gveda*.

[32] Just as in Old Indo-Aryan, the appearance of velar stops rather than palatals in one or two forms (Av., OP *-kara-* like OIA *-kará-*: contrast OP *cartanaiy*, Av. *-carətar-* from 'to make'; possibly Av. *vi.kaya-* from *ci-* 'to punish') provides some slight evidence that at the source of the Iranian classes there really were *o*-grade forms, but either the operation of Brugmann's Law was obstructed for morphological reasons, or it did operate and the vocalism of such regular formations was later remodelled. Otherwise the close correspondences that are observable between Old Indo-Aryan and Old Iranian would raise the possibility that the reconstruction of the Indo-European ancestral pattern may be incorrect, or that we are dealing entirely with patterns of word formation that originated and spread productively only in the Indo-Iranian branch. For instance, it is suggested by Lubotsky (1988: 70) that the τόμος/*-τομός distribution was not a law of Proto-Indo-European but merely a tendency that was developed in some branches but not others.

[33] Unless there have been large-scale parallel developments in Old Iranian and Old Indo-Aryan, which is less likely.

depends crucially on whether they can or cannot be explained as Old Indo-Aryan innovations.

14.4 New formations in *RV* 10 and the *Atharvaveda*

The *Atharvaveda* evidence presented in this section is gathered from Whitney (1881) for the Śaunaka recension (*AVŚ*), and from the books of the Paippalāda recension (*AVP*) that have been recently edited on the basis of both the Orissa and Kashmiri manuscripts (Zehnder 1999, Lubotsky 2002, Griffiths 2009).[34]

I. Simple *nomina actionis*: root-accented

kráma- 'step' (*AVŚ* 8. 9. 10, 10. 5. 25–35) (attested in early *RV bahuvrīhis*)	*kram*^{i}- 'step'
yábha- 'sexual intercourse' (*AVŚ* 20. 136. 11–13)	*yabh-* 'have sex'
yáva- 'repulsion' (*AVŚ* 9. 2. 13) (word-play on derivatives from *yu-* 'separate')	
váha- m. 'action of conveying, part of draught animal (*vāhá-*)' (*AVŚ* 4. 11. 7–8, 9. 7. 3)	*vah-* 'convey'
śráma- m. 'toil, labour' (*RV* 10. 114. 10, *AVŚ* ×8) (in early *RV bahuvrīhis*)	*śram-* 'toil'
hása- m. 'laughter' (*RV* 10. 18. 3 (infinitival *hásāya*), *AVŚ* 15. 2. 3)	*has-* 'laugh'

II. Verbal nouns with prefixed *su-/duṣ-*: root-accented

durṇáśa- 'hard to reach' (*AVŚ* 5. 11. 6) (= *RV dūṇáśa-*)	*naś-* 'reach'
suśáka- 'easily performed' (*RV* 10. 30. 15)	*śak-* 'be able'

III. Simple verbal nouns: suffix-accented

khādá- m. 'morsel, bite' (*AVŚ* 9. 6. 12)	*khād-* 'tear at, consume'
ghāsá- m. 'fodder' (*AVŚ* 4. 38. 7, 8. 7. 8, 11. 5. 18, 18. 2. 26 [×2])	*ghas-* 'feed'
nāthá- n. 'refuge, help' (*AVŚ* 4. 20. 9, 9. 2. 7, 18. 1. 13)	*nāth-* 'seek aid'
nādá- m. 'resounding, roaring' (*RV* 10. 11. 2)	*nad-* 'resound'
sāvá- m. 'impulse' (*RV* 10. 49. 7)[35]	*sav*^{i}- 'impel'

[34] Some forms attested in other parts of *AVP* have been identified by searching the text of *AVP* 1–15 published by Dipak Bhattacharya (1997), and from my own editorial work on *AVP* 11. However, the *AVP* evidence should not yet be regarded as 100% complete.

[35] Following Geldner's translation.

IV. *Nomina actionis* based on compound verbs: suffix-accented

Short *-a-*:	
vikramá- m. 'stepping' (*AVŚ* 9. 6. 29)	*kram-* 'step'
vikrayá- m. 'sale' (*AVŚ* 3. 15. 4)	*kray*^{i}*-* 'buy'
saṃgará- m. 'agreement, promise' (*AVŚ* 6. 119. 2–3)	?*gar*^{i}*-* 'welcome'
?*vighasá-* m. 'feeding' (*AVŚ* 11. 2. 2)	*ghas-* 'feed'
vijayá- m. 'victory' (*RV* 10. 84. 4, *AVŚ* 4. 31. 4, 10. 2. 6), *akṣaparājayá-* n. 'defeat at dice' (*AVŚ* 4. 17. 7)	*jay-* 'win'
pramará- m. 'dying' (*RV* 10. 27. 20)	*mar-* 'die'
viravá- m. 'roar' (*RV* 10. 68. 8)	*rav*^{i}*-* 'roar'
apaśrayá- m. ?'support' (*AVŚ* 15. 3. 7)	*śray-* 'lean on'
prastará- m. 'spreading out' (*AVŚ* 16. 2. 6, 18. 1. 60)	*star*^{i}*-* 'spread'
anuhavá- m. 'calling from behind', *parihavá-* m. 'calling from both sides' (*AVŚ* 19. 8. 4)	*hav*^{i}*-* 'call'
Long *-ā-*:	
pratīkāśá- m. 'appearance' (*AVŚ* 9. 8. 6), *saṃkāśá-* 'form' (*AVŚ* 7. 114. 1, *AVP* 11. 10. 5)	*kāś-* 'appear'
abhicārá- m. 'sorcery' ('moving against') (*AVŚ* 8. 2. 26, 10. 3. 7, 11. 1. 22, 19. 9. 9), *abhyācārá-* m. 'sorcery' (*AVŚ* 10. 4. 2), *sahacārá-* m. 'companionship' (*AVŚ* 2. 26. 1, *AVP* 2. 12. 1)	*car-* 'go about'
saṃtāpa- m. 'burning' (*AVP* 7. 15. 3)	*tap-* 'heat'
pratrāsá- m. 'alarm' (*AVŚ* 5. 21. 2–3)	*tras-* 'fear'
nirdāhá- m. 'burning out' (*AVŚ* 16. 1. 3)	*dah-* 'burn'
pramārá- m. 'dying' (*AVŚ* 11. 8. 33)	*mar-* 'die'
ālāpá-, *pralāpá-*, *abhilāpá-* (*AVŚ* 11. 8. 25) (word-play on derivatives from *lap-* 'chatter')	
sambhārá- m. 'bringing together, preparation' (*AVŚ* 9. 6. 1, 11. 8. 13)	*bhar-* 'bear'
prayājá- m. 'preliminary offering', *anuyājá-* m. 'following offering' (*RV* 10. 51. 8–9, 10. 182. 2)	*yaj-* 'offer'
vyāyāmé 'in the struggle, in battle' (*AVŚ* 2. 4. 4, *AVP* 2. 11. 4)	*yam-* 'hold, control'
upavāká- m. 'address' (*AVŚ* 9. 9. 8), *anuvāká-* m. 'benediction', *parāvāká-* m. 'malediction' (*AVŚ* 6. 13. 2)	*vac-* 'speak'
parivādá- m. 'gossip' (*AVŚ* 19. 8. 4)	*vad-* 'say'
abhihvāré ?'in detriment' (*AVŚ* 6. 76. 3)	*hvar-* 'be crooked'

parivāla- m. 'protection' (*AVP* 11. 5. 10)	*l*-form of *var-* 'cover'
nivāśá- m. 'groaning noise' (*AVŚ* 11. 9. 11)	*vāś-* 'bellow'
apavāsá- 'fading out' (*AVŚ* 3. 7. 7)	*vas-* 'be light'
vivāhá- m. 'wedding' ('conveying away') (*AVŚ* 12. 1. 24, 12. 5. 44, 14. 2. 65–6)	*vah-* 'convey'
āśārá- m. 'refuge, shelter' (*AVŚ* 4. 15. 6)	**śar-* 'cover'[36]
avaśvāsá- m. 'down-blowing' (*AVŚ* 4. 37. 3)	*śvas-* 'blow'
āsādá- m. 'seat' (*AVŚ* 15. 3. 7)	*sad-* 'sit'
āsrāvá- m. 'flux' (*AVŚ* 1. 2. 4, 2. 3. 3–5), *saṃsrāvá-* m. 'confluence' (*AVŚ* 1. 15. 3, 1. 15. 4)	*srav-* 'flow'
pratīhārá- m. 'response' (*AVŚ* 11. 7. 12)	*(b)har-* 'bring'

V. *Nomina actionis*, second element of compound: suffix-accented

namaskārá- m. 'performance of obeisance' (*AVŚ* 4. 39. 9), *ailabakārá-* m. 'making of *ailaba-* (howling)' (*AVŚ* 11. 2. 30), *vaṣaṭkārá-* m. 'performance (of the ritual) call *vaṣaṭ*' (*AVŚ* 11. 7. 9, 13. 1. 15, 13. 4. 26), *sruk-kārá-* 'making of a swallowing noise' (*AVŚ* 9. 6. 22), *svadhākārá-* 'performance of (the ritual call) *svadhā*' (*AVŚ* 12. 4. 32, 15. 14. 7), *svāhākārá-* 'performance of *svāhā*' (*AVŚ* 15. 14. 8), *hiṃkārá-* 'making of the sound *hin*' (*AVŚ* 11. 7. 5)	*kar-* 'do, make'
nāmagrāhá- m. 'seizing of the name' (*AVŚ* 10. 1. 12, *AVP* 7. 8. 6, 16. 36. 2)	*grabh^{i}-* 'seize'
sūktavāká- m. 'recitation of a hymn' (*RV* 10. 88. 7, 10. 88. 8)	*vac-* 'speak'
pāpavādá- m. 'evil speech' (*AVŚ* 10. 3. 6)	*vad-* 'say'
kṣudhāmārá- m. 'death by hunger', *tṛṣṇāmārá-* m. 'death by thirst' (*AVŚ* 4. 17. 6, 4. 17. 7)	*mar-* 'die'

VI. *Nomina agentis*, second element of compound: suffix-accented

Short *-a-*:

abhayaṃkará- 'making freedom from fear' (*RV* 10. 152. 2, *AVP* 2. 88. 4), *kācitkará-* 'performing everything' (*RV* 10. 86. 13), *divākará-* 'day-maker, the sun' (*AVŚ* 4. 10. 5, 13. 2. 34), *kiṃkará-* 'attendant' (*AVŚ* 8. 8. 22)	*kar-* 'do, make'

36 Cf. *śárman*: Mayrhofer (1986–2001: ii. 620).

yudhiṃgamá- 'going to battle' (*AVŚ* 20. 128. 11)	*gam-* 'come'
ajagará- 'python' ('goat-swallower') (*AVŚ* 4. 15. 7, 4. 15. 9, 11. 2. 25, *AVP* 5. 7. 6)	*gar*^{i}*-/gṛ-* 'swallow'
araṃgará- ?'singing fitly' (*AVŚ* 20. 135. 13)	*gar*^{i}*-/gṛ-* 'praise, sing'
bhuvanacyavá- 'setting the world in motion' (*RV* 10. 103. 9)	*cyav-* 'move'
vṛṣabhará- 'bearing men' (*RV* 10. 63. 3), *hariṃbhará-* 'bearing the golden one' (*RV* 10. 96. 4), *viśvaṃbhará-* 'bearing everything' (*AVŚ* 2. 16. 5, 12. 1. 6), *śakaṃbhará-* ?'dung-carrier' (*AVŚ* 5. 22. 4)	*bhar-* 'bear'
Long *-ā-*:	
medhākārá- 'making wisdom' (*RV* 10. 91. 8), *yutkārá-* 'making battle' (*RV* 10. 103. 2), *rathakārá-* 'chariot-maker' (*AVŚ* 3. 5. 6), *jyotiṣkāra-* 'making light' (*AVP* 1. 86. 1), *sphātikāra-* 'making prosperity', *bahukāra-* 'making plenty' (*AVP* 8. 18. 9)	*kar-* 'do, make'
amitrakhādá- 'injuring enemies' (*RV* 10. 152. 1)	*khād-* 'tear at, consume'
hastagrābhá- 'taking the hand' (*RV* 10. 18. 8, *AVŚ* 18. 3. 12), *urugrābhá-* 'broad-gripping' (*AVŚ* 11. 9. 12), *śūrpagrāhī́-* 'holding the winnowing-fan' (*AVŚ* 11. 3. 4), *kūṭagrāha-* 'holding the plough-end' (*AVP* 11. 15. 1), *hanugrābha-* 'seizing the jaw' (*AVP* 11. 2. 9)	*grabh*^{i}*-* 'seize'
odanapāka- 'cooking rice, cooker of rice' (*AVP* 5. 13. 3)	*pac-* 'cook'
ripravāhá- 'carrying (away) impurity' (*RV* 10. 16. 9), *vipathavāhá-* 'drawer of a wagon' (*AVŚ* 15. 2. 1–4), *śatavāhī́-* 'conveying a hundred' (*AVŚ* 5. 17. 12), *havyavāhá-* 'conveying the oblation' (*AVŚ* 18. 4. 1)	*vah-* 'convey'
abhimātiṣāhá- 'conquering opponents' (*RV* 10. 83. 4, *AVŚ* 20. 2. 1), *amitrasāhá-* 'conquering enemies' (*AVŚ* 1. 20. 4)	*sah-* 'conquer'
balihārá- 'bringing tribute' (*AVŚ* 11. 1. 20), *aghahārá-* 'evil-bringer' (*AVŚ* 6. 66. 1), *rasahārī-* 'carrying (away) sap', *sphātihārī-* 'carrying (away) prosperity' (*AVP* 2. 91. 4)	*(b)har-* 'bring'

VII. Prefixed *nomina agentis*: suffix-accented

Short *-a-*:	
āgamá- m. 'comer' (*AVŚ* 6. 81. 2)	*gam-* 'come'
saṃjayá- 'victorious' (*RV* 10. 159. 3)	*jay-* 'win'
atitara- 'overcoming' (*AVP* 2. 89. 1, 2. 89. 3, 2. 89. 5)	*tar*^{i}- 'overcome'
paridrava- 'running around' (*AVP* 6. 14. 9)	*drav-* 'run'
ādhavá- m. 'mixer' (*RV* 10. 26. 4)	*dhav*^{i}- 'shake'
anuplava- 'floating along' (*AVP* 7. 7. 4)	*plav-* 'swim, float'
pravadá- m. 'herald' (*AVŚ* 5. 20. 9)	*vad-* 'say'
udvahá- 'up-carrier' (*AVŚ* 19. 25. 1) (followed by *udúhya* 'having carried up')	*vah-* 'convey'
upaśvasá- ?'blower' (*AVŚ* 11. 1. 12)	*śvas-* 'blow'
atisará- 'out-runner' (*AVŚ* 5. 8. 2, 5. 8. 4, 5. 8. 7, *AVP* 7. 8. 2, 7. 8. 4, 7. 8. 5), *pratisará-* 'running back' (*AVŚ* 2. 11. 2, 4. 40. 1–8, 8. 5. 1, 8. 5. 4, 8. 5. 5, 8. 5. 6, *AVP* 1. 57. 2, 2. 64. 3)	*sar-* 'run'
Long *-ā-*:	
vibādhá- m. 'oppressor' (*RV* 10. 133. 4)	*bādh-* 'oppress'

VIII. Simple *nomina agentis*: suffix-accented

Short *-a-*:	
kṣamá- 'patient' (*AVŚ* 12. 1. 29) (of *kṣam-* 'earth')	*kṣam*^{i}- 'endure'
javá- 'swift' (*AVŚ* 19. 7. 1)	*jav*^{i}- 'speed, hasten'
hasá- 'laughing' (*AVŚ* 11. 8. 24)	*has-* 'laugh'
Long *-ā-*:	
grāhá- 'seizer' (*AVŚ* 14. 1. 38, *AVP* 9. 10. 9, 17. 37. 8), *grābhá-* (*AVP* 18. 4. 7)	*grabh*^{i}- 'seize'
bhrājá- 'shining' (*RV* 10. 170. 3)	*bhrāj-* 'shine'

This later Old Indo-Aryan evidence reveals that all the categories that are productive are accented on the thematic vowel. Although simple root-accented NActs remained in use, this type was moribund, and the inherited distinction between NActs with root accent and NAgs with suffix accent was in the process of being eliminated. It is against this background that developments at this stage should be viewed.

14.4.1 Prefixed nomina actionis

The productive type of NActs is the type with preverb and accent on the thematic vowel (*saṃgamá-*, *saṃvādá-*, class IV).[37] Out of the two formal subvarieties of NActs based on compound verbs, the type with radical long *-ā-* (*saṃvādá-*) has become much more numerous vis-à-vis this subclass in the early *Ṛgveda*. There are two attested cases where a form with long vocalism replaces one with short *-a-*: *RV pramará-*, *saṃsravá-*, but *AV pramārá-*, *saṃsrāvá-*. More often, there is a contrast with the short vocalism of a prefixed NAg based on the same root:

RV evāvadá- 'who speaks so'	*RV saṃvādá-* 'conversation'
AV pravadá- 'herald'	*AV parivādá-* 'gossip'
RV sambhará- 'who brings together'	*AV sambhārá-* 'bringing together, preparation'
RV kucará- 'who roams anywhere'	*AV sahacārá-* 'companionship'
AV kiṃcará- 'servant'	*AV abhicārá-* 'sorcery'
AV udvahá- 'who conveys up'	*AV vivāhá-* 'conveying away, wedding'

Hence the 'success' of the *saṃvādá*-type could be because its long *-ā-* served to distinguish NAct function from that of NAg in classes that otherwise would have been formally identical. Several new prefixed NAgs with short *-a-*, e.g. *anuplavá-* 'floating along' (class VII), occur for the first time, whereas the only new form of this type with long *-ā-* is from the root *bādh-*, which has invariable long vocalism. It may be observed in passing that the prefixed NActs whose root vowel is short (*saṃgamá-*) are frequently redetermined with the additional suffix *-na-* in the *RV* (e.g. *saṃgamá-* m./*saṃgámana-* n. 'going together', *udayá-* m./ *udáyana-* n. 'rising up', *āhavá-*/*āhávana-* 'calling on'). This seems to have been an earlier morphological means of differentiating the NAct function from NAgs: *sambháraṇa-* n. '(the action of) bringing together' (7. 25. 2) contrasts with *sambhará-* 'one who brings together' (4. 17. 11) just as *AV sambhārá-* does.

The distributional and chronological evidence[38] indicates that the prefixed NActs are the source of a new Old Indo-Aryan category, namely the determina-

[37] The productivity of the prefixed type is probably associated with the increasing use of compound verbs and the gradual shift towards univerbation in the Old Indo-Aryan verb system.

[38] Compounds of two nominal stems, the second with NAct value, are unparalleled in Old Iranian. On the other hand, the correspondences between Av. *frauuāka-* and the Old Indo-Aryan forms with prefixed *-vāká-*, Av. *pairi.vāra-* and *AVP parivālá-* indicate that such prefixed NActs must have existed in prehistoric Indo-Iranian.

tive compounds of two nominal stems where the second has NAct value (class V). All but one of this recent category show long vocalism:

RV āhavá-, vihavá-	*indrahavá-* 'invocation of Indra'
RV adhivāká-, upavāká-	*ṛtavāká-* 'speech of truth', *joṣavāká-* 'speech of pleasure', *namovāká-* 'speech of homage'
RV atiyājá- (?), *anuyājá-, prayājá-*	*jīvayājá-* m. 'offering of living (animal)'
RV saṃvādá-	*AV pāpavādá-* 'evil speech'
AV pramārá-	*AV kṣudhāmārá-* 'death by hunger', *tṛṣṇāmārá-* 'death by thirst'

It is striking that at both stages of Old Indo-Aryan that have been distinguished in this paper the prefixed NAct forms with long *-ā-* (type *saṃvādá-*) are without exception from *aniṭ* roots. The converse is not true since those with short *-a-* belong to both *seṭ* and *aniṭ* roots, at least in the early *RV* (e.g. *ā-/vi-havá-* from *hav^{i}-/hū-*, *saṃgamá-* from *gam-*). If two doubtful forms and *pramará-* 'death' (which is replaced by *pramārá-*) are excluded from the *RV* 10/*AV* evidence, the remaining six forms with short vocalism are all from *seṭ* roots. How should this situation be explained? The short *-a-* vocalism of the early *RV* forms from *aniṭ* roots might be analogical on the vocalism of the corresponding simple root-accented NActs (cf. *vimadá-/máda-*, *nivará-/vára-*).[39] Once the simple root-accented formation was no longer productive, its influence on the corresponding prefixed category may have declined. Yet one cannot seriously claim that all the *RV* 10/*AV* prefixed forms with *-ā-* are relics, particularly when this category appears so productive. For instance, should an Indo-European parentage really be attributed to *AV pralāpá-* 'chattering'? It seems, however, that at the origin of both the Old Indo-Aryan and Old Iranian classes[40] there must have been forms whose vocalism did conform to the pattern expected via Brugmann's Law, but that there have been subsequent factors which have interfered and disturbed it.

[39] The prefixed short *-a-* forms from *aniṭ* roots cluster in *RV* 1 and 8, which might be significant.

[40] In two cases where the early *Ṛgveda* shows short vocalism for derivatives from *aniṭ* roots (*samará-* m./n. 'hostile encounter' from *ar/ṛ-* 'go', *saṃgamá-* m. 'coming together, battle' from *gam-* 'come') Avestan answers with formations with different preverbs but long vocalism (*paitiiāra-* m. 'adversity', *aiβigāma-* m. 'year, winter'). On the other hand, Av. *vītāra-* m. 'crossing' from *tar^{i}-* is out of step with all the rest of the Indo-Iranian evidence, and might be dismissed as a false spelling (in the *Frahang-ī-ōim*) were it not for the existence of OIA *ávitāriṇī-* 'lasting, not transient' (*RV* 8. 5. 6) which also points to **vitārá-*. As their sense does not exactly match, they could both be new creations (in the case of the *Ṛgveda* a nonce-form?).

14.4.2 Nomina agentis

For NAgs, with the exception of the prefixed type (*RV* class VII), the proportion of forms with long radical *-ā-* is likewise increased: *-hārá-* (< *-bhārá-*), *-kārá-*, *-grābhá-*, *-vāhá-*, and to a lesser extent *-sāhá-* become very productive in forming new compounds. Can these forms, none of which are paralleled in Old Iranian, represent very archaic survivals, or are they creations of Old Indo-Aryan?

I will start with *-vāhá-* and *-sāhá-*, which should probably be explained differently from the others. The traditional explanation as cognates of Greek **-ϝοχός* and **-οχός* appears at first sight to be supported by the fact that *udavāhá-*, *yūpavāhá-* are found in *RV* 1, whereas formations such as *udvahá-* 'one who conveys upward', which could be based on present *váhati*, are first attested in the *Atharvaveda*. *RV vrātasāhá-*, *satrāsāhá-* could be older than *janaṃsahá-* (cf. *sáhate*), although all three are found in the *RV* Family Books. But the internal Old Indo-Aryan evidence indicates that the productivity of *-vāhá-* and *-sāhá-* results from the thematicization of the NAg root nouns *-vāh* and *-sāh* which formed numerous compounds at an early Old Indo-Aryan stage; on the latter see Scarlata (1999: 473–80, 599–613). For instance, the early *Ṛgveda* only has *havyavā́h-* 'conveying the oblation' and *abhimātiṣā́h-* 'conquering opponents', but the *Atharvaveda* has *havyavāhá-* and *abhimātiṣāhá-*. Once-occurring *RV satrāsāhá-* stands beside more frequent *satrāsā́h-* (Scarlata 1999: 611–12). Hence it is not out of the question that the only direct trace of PIE **u̯oĝʰó-* is to be found in the simplex NAg *vāhá-* 'draught-animal', OAv. *vāza-*, and all cases of *-vāhá-* and *-sāhá-* in composition arose via thematicization of root nouns. This group of formations illustrates the dangers of invoking Brugmann's Law and an Indo-European reconstruction for every individual Vedic form where it might seem plausible from a phonological point of view without examining its synchronic situation.

-hārá- 'bringing, who brings' does not appear before the *Atharvaveda*. Although a NAg *-bhārá-* is often cited for the purposes of Indo-European reconstruction, it must be emphasized that the *RV* compounds containing *-bhāra-* are *bahuvrīhis*, as their accentuation shows: *bhū́ribhāra-* means 'having a large load, much burdened' (*RV* 1. 164. 13, cf. *RV bhū́rivāra-* 'having much treasure') and *muṣkábhāra-* (*RV* 10. 102. 4) means 'having a load of testicles' (description of Indra). How then does *-hārá-* appear as a NAg in the *Atharvaveda*? Two possible solutions need to be considered.

Firstly, *-bhārá-* as a second element of a NAg compound may simply be unattested by chance in the early *Ṛgveda*, since we have *-kārá-*, *-grābhá-*, *-dābhá-*, *-pāvá-*. The metrical usefulness of forms such as *vājaṃbhará-* in particular metrical slots could have led to the exclusion of compounds in *-bhārá-*, even though they existed in earliest Old Indo-Aryan. Or, given the apparent productivity of second-element NAgs with *-ā-* at the *RV* 10/*AV* stage, such forms could have belonged to the more 'popular' registers of Old Indo-Aryan or different geographical dialects. In other words, there could be good reasons why an archaic form *-bhārá-* < **-b^h^oró-* is missing from the early *RV* record.[41]

However, it seems more likely that *-hārá-/-hārī́-* is indeed a late formation, as its phonology suggests, and that it should be explained via developments within Old Indo-Aryan. It is instructive to compare NAg *-grābhá-* from *grabh^i^-* 'seize, hold', a clear example of an innovation as it cannot directly continue an Indo-European *o*-grade formation if it is accepted that lengthening did not occur in a syllable closed by a laryngeal. By the late Saṃhitā period the element *grābhá-* appears in a range of the productive categories:

- *grābhá-* (*RV*) 'handful, grasp'
- *grāvagrābhá-* (*RV*) 'who holds the pressing stones'
- *nāmagrā(b)há-* (*AV*) 'action of seizing the name'
- *grā(b)há-* (*AV*) 'who seizes'
- *udgrābhá-* (*Vājasaneyisaṃhitā, Taittirīyasaṃhitā*) 'action of holding upwards'

The source of compositional *-grābhá-* is most likely to be the simple verbal noun meaning 'handful, grasp', which on account of its accentuation came to be employed as the second member of compounds with either NAg or NAct value. Just as *bhārá-* 'load' appears in *RV bahuvrīhis*, so two of the attested compounds in *-grābhá-*, *RV tuvigrābhá-* and *AV urugrābhá-*, may represent old *bahuvrīhis* containing the simple noun *grābhá-*. In the early *Ṛgveda* when the first element of a *bahuvrīhi* is a disyllabic nominal stem in *-i* or *-u* the second element is accented (cf. *RV tuvidyumná-* 'whose splendour is strong'). But in the later Saṃhitās this accentuation is replaced by the normal *bahuvrīhi*-type accentuation on the first element (Wackernagel 1905: 296). Because of its accent an original *bahuvrīhi tuvigrābhá-* 'whose grasp is strong' could also have been interpreted as a determinative compound 'grasping strongly'. The latter interpretation would have prevailed following the change in accent for *bahuvrīhis* with first element *tuvi-*, *uru-*, *puru-*, etc. Thus compounds such as *tuvigrābhá-*, *urugrābhá-* could have supplied the starting point for the extension of second element *-grābhá-* with active NAg value. Then the numerous new NAgs in *-grā(b)há-*, e.g. *AV hanugrābha-* 'seizing the jaw' (of an illness like

[41] Old Iranian *-bāra-* is attested once in OP *asabāra-* 'horse-borne' (cf. MP *aswār* 'horse-rider'). The passive value of **-b^h^oró-* in such Iranian compounds may be inherited: see the following discussion.

tetanus), led to the back-formation of a new simple noun with NAg value, *AV+ grā(b)há-* 'seizer' (in the *Atharvaveda* a demon of illness but 'crocodile' by the *Mānavadharmasmṛti*).

A similar reinterpretation of *bahuvrīhis* might be envisaged as the starting point for the post-*RV* spread of *-(b)hārá-*.[42] Alternatively a compound such as *AV balihārá-* 'one who brings tribute' could have arisen beside an unattested NAct **balihārá-* 'act of bringing tribute', whose second element *-hārá-* had been created on the analogy of prefixed NAct *pratīhārá-* 'response' ('act of bringing back') following the pattern of *namovāká-* beside *adhivāká-*, *jīvayājá-* beside *prayājá-*, etc. The ease with which a second-element NAct could have been extended to NAg function and vice versa is illustrated by the case of *haskārá-*: *haskārā́d vidyútas pari* (*RV* I. 23. 12) is ambiguous and may be translated 'from the *has*-noise making of the lightning' (NAct) or 'from the *has*-noise-making lightning' (NAg).[43]

It seems likely that systems of forms such as that shown above for *grābhá-* developed in the case of a number of roots, and within such systems new formations could be freely created on the analogy of others. Since simple nouns of the *bhārá*-type and prefixed NActs with long vocalism are often involved in such systems they can help to explain how new second elements of compounds with long vocalism arose.[44] A few of the uncompounded NAgs with long vocalism (class VIII, *vāhá-*) can be explained as back-formations from NAg compounds that were in existence at an early date: *RV sāhá-* 'conqueror' from *vrātasāhá-*, *śāsá-* 'commander' from *sarvaśāsá-*, *pārá-* 'making cross' from *supārá-*. Possibly inherited *vāhá-/váhati* and more recent *sāhá-/sáhati* then supplied the model for deriving *nāyá-* 'leader' from *náyati*.[45]

NAg second element *-kārá-*, whose chronological distribution in Old Indo-Aryan is parallel to that of *-grābhá-* and which shares with *-grābhá-* the

[42] The basis of the reinterpretation could have been the attested *RV* compound *bhū́ribhāra-*, which (like other *RV bahuvrīhis* with first element *bhū́ri-*) does not show the accentuation on the second element that is expected at an early date when the first element is a disyllabic stem in *-i* or *-u*. It may once have been **bhūribhārá-* which could have been reinterpreted as 'bearing much'.

[43] The ambiguity in cases such as this appears to have led to a further development, namely the creation of a new class of secondary derivatives in *-ín* based on the NAct compounds, which functioned as more clearly marked NAgs. One or two are attested early: *RV bhadravādín-* 'with auspicious speech, speaking auspiciously' and *AV priyavādín-* 'with pleasing speech, speaking pleasingly', which must be derived from NAct **bhadravādá-* and **priyavādá-* (cf. *AV pāpavādá-*).

[44] However, there are some nonce-forms in the *Ṛgveda* whose vocalism never occurs in any other form from the same root. For example, hapax *hiraṇyapāvá-* probably follows the analogy of all other *RV* compounds with first element *hiraṇya-*: they invariably have a second element whose first syllable is heavy.

[45] In the case of *śāká-* 'able, powerful' beside *śaknóti* it is merely possible to observe that unexplained lengthening occurs in other derivatives from the root *śak-* (cf. *RV śāktá-*, *śā́kman-*, *śā́ka-*).

property that it can function as the second element of either a NAg or NAct nominal compound, is a difficult case as the evidence points in two directions. Simple *kārá-* 'decisive act, battle' is probably to be linked with *kr̥-* 'do, make' but it has developed in meaning.[46] The earlier meaning 'thing done, action' could have been preserved in *bahuvrīhis* such as **purukārá-* 'whose deeds are many' (cf. *AV bahukārá-*) and this could have been reinterpreted as 'doing much'. But it is clearly more difficult to rule out a survival of *-kārá-* < **kʷoró-* as this NAg makes its first appearance in the *R̥gveda*[47] and it occurs in ritual terms such as *rathakārá-* (*AV+*), which could be archaic (cf. the case of *-pāká-* in ritual terminology mentioned below).

The above discussion has indicated that members of the *bhārá-* class, especially non-inherited forms such as *grābhá-*, may have played an important role in spreading long vocalism in the NAg categories during the Old Indo-Aryan early historical period, thereby reversing the development of the Indo-Iranian stage which had regularised short *-a-* vocalism. Hence the question must now be raised: what is the origin of the *bhārá-* type itself?

It must be borne in mind that the *bhārá-* class itself was productively extended in Old Indo-Aryan. Firstly, there are signs of extension in one or two limited semantic fields, e.g. *RV nāvá-* m. 'shouting, loud praising', *svāná-* m. 'noise', *svārá-* m. 'sound', and only in *RV* 10 *nādá-* m. 'roaring'. Secondly, as noted by Debrunner (1954: 101), some simple verbal nouns with accented thematic vowel appear to be back-formations from prefixed NActs, e.g. *vāká-* from *adhivāká-*, *upavāká-*, *savá-* from *prasavá-*, *utsavá-*, *javá-* from *prajavá-*. However, such an origin seems doubtful in the case of *bhāgá-* where the simple noun is much more frequently attested in the early *R̥gveda* than *vibhāgá-* and it has an exact cognate in OAv. *bāga-*. There appears to be an old kernel of forms which show a passive/intransitive value of the root, two of which, *bhāgá-*, *pārá-*, have cognates in Old Iranian. Uncompounded *bhārá-* has been marginalized in most diachronic discussions because of emphasis on the *τόμος*/**-τομός* pattern, but it might be suggested that such forms represent a direct continuation of the

[46] Cf. Mayrhofer (1986–2001: i. 340). There is the further complication that a homonymous noun meaning 'thing sung, song' has often been postulated (cf. *RV kārín-* 'singer'), and it is not out of the question that this could be the second element of *RV brahmakārá-* (which occurs at *RV* 6. 29. 4 in a context about singing/reciting praise), and also of the numerous *Atharvaveda* and *Yajurveda* compounds where the first element is a ritual call (*vaṣatkārá-*, 'the calling out of *vaṣat*', etc.).

[47] Although **-kāra-* is not found in Old Iranian, compounds in *-kār-/-gār-* are frequent in Middle Persian. But here it is not impossible that this morpheme originated in compounds containing the frequent Middle Persian noun *kār* 'deed'. A detailed study of the Middle Iranian evidence is needed to settle the question whether a NAg **-kāra-* may have existed at an early date or not.

same Indo-European *o*-grade type as the Greek adjective λοιπός 'left over, remaining', or the noun ὁλκός 'furrow, what is drawn'. These have a NAg accent and show a passive/intransitive meaning of the root. They also illustrate from a different branch of Indo-European how such *o*-grade forms could develop a 'concrete' meaning (cf. τὸ λοιπόν 'the rest, the future').[48] If PIE **bʰoró-*, **bʰogó-*, **poró-* were directly continued as IIran. **bhārá-*, **bhāgá-*, **pārá-* it seems possible that their long vocalism and suffix accentuation became associated with a passive/intransitive sense of the root (in contrast to the short vocalism of the NActs with active meaning) and that forms such as *grābhá-* 'handful, grasp' were created on their model early within Old Indo-Aryan.[49]

However, ὁλκός displays an active sense 'machine for dragging (boats)' as well as its more frequent sense 'furrow', suggesting that both active and passive value were possible for one and the same *o*-grade NAg form. This is exactly the sort of double value that there is evidence for in composition in the case of OIA *-pāká-*: *kṣīrapāká-* 'cooked in milk' (*RV* 8. 77. 10), *odanapāka-* 'who cooks rice' (*AVP* 5. 13. 3). We may wonder whether the second element of these compounded ritual terms somehow escaped remodelling and preserves a direct reflex of PIE *-pokʷó-* (cf. Mycenaean *a-to-po-qo* 'baker', Gr. (metathesized) ἀρτοκόπος). The relative lateness of the Vedic forms casts some doubt but the NAg with active value in *odanapāka-* is paralleled by that of YAv. *nasupāka-*, *uruzdi.pāka-*. Since there is also Vedic evidence for NAct *-pā́ka-* (attested in a compound, *śṛtapā́ka-* 'cooking of boiled milk', *RV* 1. 162. 10), this may be a unique case where a pair of unremodelled forms *-pā́ka-* and *-pāká-* < PIE **-pókʷo-/-pokʷó-* reflects the τόμος/*-τομός pattern.

14.5 Conclusion

This presentation of material and discussion has identified two Indo-Iranian categories where the direct effect of Brugmann's Law may be observed, although ancient forms are surrounded by new creations in both. Firstly the

[48] The diachronic explanation suggested here is in line with the observation made by Lubotsky (1988: 68) that such thematic nouns with a 'concrete' meaning can be either NAg or NAct in origin.

[49] The one piece of evidence that does not easily fit with this explanation is OP *ucāra-* 'successful, with good performance'. Yet it looks as if Old Persian had a noun **cāra-* 'thing done, performance', which must be associated with the root *kar-* 'make' because of the contexts in which it occurs (e.g. DB 4. 76 as object of 3sg. ipv. *kunautuv*). Taken at face value, its initial *c-* points to a lengthened *e*-grade formation. However there could have been a false association with *kar-* triggered by forms such as the Old Persian inf. *cartanaiy*, and *ucāra-* may really be from the root *car-* 'move about'. Or **kāra-* 'thing done, performance', the cognate of OIA *kārá-*, could have been remodelled to **cāra-* because it was a homonym of OP *kāra-* 'army, people'.

NActs from compound verbs (prefixed NActs) do not preserve the accentuation of the PIE *b^h*óro-* type (as in Vedic they have adopted the accentuation that is normal for determinative compounds), but they do to some extent preserve the contrast in vocalism between forms from roots which ended in a laryngeal vs. roots which had no final laryngeal. Hence this study has confirmed that the example *āhavá-* 'challenge' from *hav*^{i}*-/hū-* 'call' vs. *āhāvá-* 'bucket' from *hav-/hu* 'pour' first cited by Kuryłowicz (1927) is valid evidence for Brugmann's Law. Secondly, the most direct formal reflex of the Indo-European *b^h*oró*-type NAgs is not to be found in the second elements of compounds, but in the class of simple thematic verbal nouns represented by *bhārá-* 'load, burden', which often show a passive/intransitive meaning of the root and have developed a concrete sense. Their long vocalism results from the fact that the small group of inherited forms are all from roots with open syllables where Brugmann's Law operated.

It has not been possible to shed any further light on the developments which in the remote Indo-Iranian prehistoric period spread short vocalism across the simple root-accented NAct class (*bhára-*) and the compounded NAgs (*vājaṃbhará-*), but it has been suggested that many forms belonging to the latter class in the *Ṛgveda* may not be very old. It has also been argued that Old Indo-Aryan compounded and simple NAgs with long *-ā-* vocalism should not automatically be explained as relics, since most could be innovations created within new productive Old Indo-Aryan systems.

15

Kiparsky's Rule, thematic nasal presents, and athematic *verba vocalia* in Greek

ANDREAS WILLI

15.1 Kiparsky's Rule

The thematic 2sg. and 3sg. pres. endings of the Greek type φέρεις, φέρει 'carry' strikingly diverge from the corresponding endings in e.g. Skt *bhárasi*, *bhárati*. The latter descend from Proto-Indo-European thematic 2sg. *-*esi*, 3sg. *-*eti*, as confirmed by other languages (cf. e.g. Lat. 3sg. *legit* 'reads' < **leĝeti*). The awkward Greek material has therefore been explained either through unlikely analogical processes (e.g. Brugmann and Thumb 1913: 397–8, Kuryłowicz 1967: 166, Hoenigswald 1986 and 1997: 93–5, with pivotal 2sg. and/or secondary endings) or by assuming an independent origin in an old stative/middle ending *-*Ø* (+ thematic vowel + primary *-*i*) (e.g. Watkins 1969: 121–3). Nothing in the function and use of the Greek thematic verbs commends these views, and if there were a way of deriving Gr. -εις, -ει from PIE *-*esi*, *-*eti*, it should be amply preferred. Kiparsky (1967: 112) therefore proposed 'that an early sound change took place in Greek whose effect was to invert word-final *i* with preceding dental consonants (which were presumably palatalized in this position)':[1] hence 2sg.

[1] Kiparsky (1967: 113 n. 2) mentions as forerunners Bopp (1837: 649–50, 652–3, 660) and Curtius (1873: 201–5); cf. Cowgill (2006: 537 n. 3), who adds Ahrens (1839: 92). Nothing is gained with Mańczak's (1992: 72) irregular (frequency-conditioned) loss of -*t*- in *-*eti*.

b^heresi > *p^hereis* (φέρεις) and 3sg. **b^hereti* > **p^hereit* with subsequent loss of final *-t* (φέρει). In the same way, Kiparsky suggests, certain other forms may also be accounted for. In the 2sg./3sg. subj. **b^herēsi, *b^herēti* would yield *p^herēis, *p^herēit* > *p^herēi* (φέρῃς, φέρῃ), and 3sg. subj. φέρῃ in turn would lead to forms such as φέρη in dialects which monophthongize word-final long diphthongs. Meanwhile, the Homeric 3sg. subj. type φέρῃσι, which must be old because its ending -σι is hard to motivate in an innovation and because it acted as a model for 1sg. -ωμι (cf. Mulvany 1896 and Wackernagel 1897: 50–1), is argued to show 'that -ι, rather than being obligatorily dropped by this rule, was optionally retained' (Kiparsky 1967: 115).

By making his rule precede Osthoff's Law, the shortening of tautosyllabic long diphthongs, Kiparsky further explains some oddities in the inflection of athematic verbs. From 3sg. **tit^{h}ēti* 'puts' and **didōti* 'gives', one would reach—via **tit^{h}ēit, *didōit* > **tit^{h}eit, *didoit* (Osthoff)—an outcome τίθει, *δίδοι (and similarly 2sg. *δίδοις). These forms are attested, virtually unchanged, in Homer. The accent of *δίδοι and *δίδοις has been altered to make them seemingly thematic (*Il.* 9. 519, *Od.* 4. 237, 17. 350 διδοῖ, *Il.* 9. 164 διδοῖς), but for τίθει (*Il.* 13. 732 with scholion; contrast *Od.* 1. 192 παρτιθεῖ) even the old accentuation was known to Aristophanes or Aristarchus (cf. also 2sg. ἀν-/μεθίεις/-ιεῖς, 3sg. μεθ-/προίει/προιεῖ 'let forth': *Il.* 2. 752, 5. 880, 6. 523, 10. 121, *Od.* 4. 372). That Osthoff shortening did not take place in the subjunctives mentioned before is no counter-evidence because here 'vowel length served as the sole mark of the mood' and was therefore analogically retained (Kiparsky 1967: 116–17).

Outside the verbal system Kiparsky (1967: 122) points to the *ā*-stem dative plural, where **-āsi* would have produced **-āis* > -αις without analogical influence from the *o*-stems; and since he believes that final -ι was not *always* lost (cf. above), and that Osthoff's Law was sometimes prevented, he also postulates both **-āsi* > **-āisi* > -αισι and **-āsi* > **-āisi* > Homeric -ῃσι. Furthermore, after positing that 'original Indo-European final short diphthongs count as one mora in Greek', whereas 'all others count as two moras', he points to an apparent exception, the loc. sg. in -οι of e.g. οἴκοι 'at home'. If this went back exclusively to PIE **-oi*, the generalization would not hold, but if it (at least partly) reflected an ending involving **-d^{h}i* > -θι (cf. οἴκοθι 'at home'), everything would be fine (**woikot^{h}i* > **woikoi[t^h]* > οἴκοι). That οἴκοθι and the like are found alongside οἴκοι would be due to the 'ambiguous syntactic status of -θι, which, like -θεν and -φι, is susceptible to interpretation as either a suffix such as -σι or an enclitic such as -δε': the metathesis rule would not have operated in the latter case (Kiparsky 1967: 126–7). In addition, allowance is made for a few other exceptions: (1) all cases where the dental followed a syllabic liquid or nasal, which 'had not yet been vocalized when [the metathesis rule] applied'

(Kiparsky 1967: 129, cf. **wīkm̥ti* > Dor. Ϝίκατι 'twenty'), (2) the dat. sg. of dental stems (e.g. χάριτι 'grace'), where analogical prevention may be invoked, and (3) 'a number of adverbs, prepositions and conjunctions, e.g. ἔτι "yet", ἐγκυτί "skin deep", ἀμογητί "effortlessly", ἕκητι "by virtue of, for the sake of", πέρυσι "last year"' (Kiparsky 1967: 131). Other representatives of this last group do however show the rule. Of particular interest is the conjunction καί 'and', which cannot be separated from κασι- in κασίγνητος 'brother' (the one 'born together with') and Hitt. *katti* 'with' on the one hand, and from Arcado-Cyprian κάς 'and' on the other. Here, 'the option to apply [the metathesis rule] appears to have been exercised in some dialects but not in others' because Arcado-Cyprian κάς may come from apocopated **kasi* < **kati*, whereas καί points to **kait* < **kati* (Kiparsky 1967: 132–3).

15.2 'Neogrammarian' objections and Cowgill's restrictions

Notwithstanding these restrictions the explanatory power of Kiparsky's Rule is impressive. Its boldness, however, has impeded universal acceptance. Of the major handbooks of Greek historical phonology and morphology, Lejeune (1972) and Sihler (1995) ignore it altogether. Rix (1992) fails to mention it in the phonology part, but implicitly refers to it in the morphology section dealing with verbal endings (p. 251, 'gr. *-ei̯*..., wohl < **-ei̯t*... durch Metathese < idg. **-e-ti*').[2] The reason for this widespread neglect must be that not less than three features are 'optional':

(1) whether the rule (a) is or (b) is not applied to any particular item in a given dialect of Greek (cf. Kiparsky 1967: 132)

(2) when the rule does operate, whether final -ι (a) is or (b) is not maintained (and note that, when it is maintained, there is no longer a 'simple' metathesis) (cf. Kiparsky 1967: 115)

(3) when the rule does operate, whether Osthoff's Law (a) does or (b) does not occur (cf. Kiparsky 1967: 117, 122).

In other words, with an input of e.g. Proto-Greek **-ēti*, Attic-Ionic -ησι (1b), -εισι (1a/2a/3a), -ηισι (1a/2a/3b), -ει (1a/2b/3a), and -ηι (1a/2b/3b) would all be phonologically legitimate outputs. And since no attempt is made to specify the

[2] In his review of the first edition of Rix (1992), the dedicatee of the present volume explicitly recorded his reservations on this point (Penney 1978: 291); but knowing his colleague's penchant for 'adventurous' views he may forgive, perhaps even enjoy, the following bold but grateful attempt to convince him otherwise.

conditions under which any of these 'options' obtains, or consistently to account for them through analogy rather than sound change, Cowgill (1985*a*: 100) justifiably diagnoses a 'violation of the neogrammarian canon of Ausnahmslosigkeit der Lautgesetze', as laid down by Osthoff and Brugman (1878: XIII):

Erstens. Aller lautwandel, so weit er mechanisch vor sich geht, vollzieht sich nach ausnahmslosen gesetzen, d. h. die richtung der lautbewegung ist bei allen angehörigen einer sprachgenossenschaft, ausser dem fall, dass dialektspaltung eintritt, stets dieselbe, und alle wörter, in denen der der lautbewegung unterworfene laut unter gleichen verhältnissen erscheint, werden ohne ausnahme von der änderung ergriffen.

Do we then have to abandon Kiparsky's Rule, despite its potential usefulness? Even a staunch neogrammarian should not think so. It is perfectly possible that we simply have not understood its exact conditioning. A more conservative formulation might help to avoid the optionality trap. This is what Cowgill (1985*a*: 100–1) offers:[3]

My proposed rule is that voiceless ... dental stops, aspirated or not, preceded by a short, unaccented, non-high, non-nasal vowel and followed by word-final *-i* disappeared in the prehistory of all Greek dialects early enough that the resulting hiatuses had contracted already by Mycenaean times. What the intermediate stages, if any, leading to that loss were, I do not know. Maybe there was metathesis, maybe not.... [T]he change I am proposing would be located in time after the Greek generalization of recessive accent on finite verbs; and, if it is correct that the loss affects only **t* and **th* from PIE "**dh*" but not **d*, after the Greek alignment of the PIE "voiced aspirates" as voiceless sounds. And of course it would be anterior to the South Greek change of *t(h)i* to *si* in certain categories.

A number of unproblematic modifications of Kiparsky's views result from these restrictions:

- The φέρησι-type subjunctive is again (with Mulvany 1896 and Wackernagel 1897: 50–1) thought to be an adjustment, whether orthographic or real, of *φέρησι,[4] from **b^{h}erēti* (no loss/metathesis of **-t-* after long vowel: cf. δίδωσι, φησί, etc.); the type φέρῃ has analogical lengthening after 3sg. ind. φέρει.
- The 2sg. forms (e.g. φέρεις) are analogically differentiated from the 3sg. ones, adding secondary **-s* to regular **-esi* > **-ehi* > **-ei* (no loss/metathesis of **-s-*).

[3] For a fuller version, see now Cowgill (2006: 537–45), unfinished at the time of Cowgill's death but agreeing with Cowgill (1985*a*) on all the essential points.

[4] Cf. 3sg. aor. subj. πίε̄σι 'drinks' in *CEG* 454 ('Nestor's Cup'): Watkins (1976: 26), Peters (1998), Cowgill (2006: 539).

- Datives in -αις, -αισι, -ῃσι are again analogically remade after their *o*-stem counterparts (no loss/metathesis of **-s-*).

On the plus side Cowgill (1985*a*: 102) adds the Pindaric and Boeotian/ Corinthian ipv. δίδοι 'give' to Kiparsky's dossier, deriving it from **dídot^{h}i*.[5] In the aorist imperatives δός 'give', θές 'put', ἕς 'let' (from **dót^{h}i*, **t^{h}ét^{h}i*, **hét^{h}i*), **-t^{h}i* would be unaffected because of the preceding accented vowel (though **-i* was subsequently lost through 'imperative truncation'). Imperatives like τέτλαθι 'endure', ἕσταθι 'stand' would be analogically refashioned 'long after the occurrence of *t(h)*-loss'.

Finally, just as no loss/metathesis occurred after the vocalic nasals according to both Kiparsky and Cowgill (e.g. ϝίκατι), so Kiparsky's 'exceptions' ἔτι, ἕκητι, πέρυσι, etc. are no longer problematic for Cowgill: here too the dental followed an accented vowel, a long vowel, or a high vowel, all of which are exempt.

15.3 Objecting to the objections

Cowgill's restrictions come at a price. Firstly, if Kiparsky's derivation of καί is accepted,[6] we must abandon the attractive etymology of Hitt. *katti* 'with' as **km̥ti*, i.e. zero-grade **km̥-* + *-ti* (cf. Lat. *cum* 'with' < **kom*, OIr. *cét* 'with' < **km̥ta*; Melchert 1994: 126, Kloekhorst 2008: 462, s.v. *katta*). It is true that independent doubts have been raised about interconsonantal **-m̥-* > *-a-* in Hittite (cf. Kimball 1999: 252), but cases like *šamnanzi* 'they pass in review, disappear' < **sm̥n-enti* are weak counterevidence; no one would deny Greek **-m̥-* > *-a-* because of δάμνημι 'tame' < **dm̥neh$_2$-mi* and the like.

Secondly, and more seriously, while Kiparsky's explanation of 3sg. -ει would stand, the other *pièce de résistance* of his theory, Homeric διδοῖ, τίθει, etc. would fall away because a long vowel preceded **-ti*. Of course these forms are commonly regarded as recent thematizations (cf. Hackstein 2002: 99–102, 107–10), but such a view is only superficially plausible. Even disregarding the unexpected accent of Homeric forms like τίθει, προίει, etc., not all of which can easily be interpreted as imperfects (cf. Eust. 957. 51–2 on *Il.* 13. 732), it does not identify a convincing trigger for the thematization. With some goodwill 3pl.

[5] Pind. *Ol.* 1. 85, 6. 104, 7. 89, 13. 115, *DGE* 538; cf. Cowgill (2006: 541), against Wackernagel (1895: 25–35) and Strunk (1960: 121–3). Hackstein (2002: 108–10) further adds Cretan πρεῖγυς ~ Att. πρέσβυς 'representative' (**preti-g^{w}h$_2$ú-*, with **preti- > prei-*).

[6] Lüttel's (1981) alternative explanation of καί (borrowed from West Greek **κατι τ-* with dental dissimilation) is hard to maintain: cf. Willi (2003) and Cowgill (2006: 543).

διδοῦσι (for *δίδουσι < athematic *$dido$-nti) might justify διδοῖ (Chantraine 1961: 210)—although a plural → singular analogy is never straightforward—but the corresponding 3pl. τιθεῖσι (for *τίθεισι < *tit^he-nti) does not look thematic at all. Moreover, if the thematization theory were correct, it would be curious that, while 3sg./2sg. διδοῖ/διδοῖς, τιθεῖ, and ἱεῖ are well attested also in later Ionic poetry and prose (cf. Hackstein 2002: 100–1), not a single instance of 1sg. *τιθῶ, *διδῶ, or *ἱῶ is found. In Herodotus, attestations for δίδωμι and τίθημι are distributed as shown in Table 15.1 (compounds included).

Table 15.1 Distribution of singular forms of δίδωμι and τίθημι in Herodotus

	δίδωμι		τίθημι	
	athematic	'thematic'	athematic	'thematic'
1sg.	7 δίδωμι	0 *διδῶ	4 τίθημι	0 *τιθῶ
2sg.	0 δίδως	2 διδοῖς	0 τίθης	0 τιθεῖς
3sg.	3–4 δίδωσι	71–2 διδοῖ	0–1 τίθησι	4–5 τιθεῖ

The pattern is not what one might expect: when verbs in -νῡμι are thematized in later Greek, we find both 1sg. -νύω and 3sg. -νύει (cf. already Homeric ἀνύω 'to accomplish').

Thirdly, it remains difficult to understand why certain types of vowels (nasal, high, long) should be exempt from the rule. For the long vowels, Cowgill (1985*a*: 103) thinks of 'a kind of Sievers' Law, by which prevocalic *$ph\acute{e}reti$ became *$ph\acute{e}ret\underset{\frown}{i}$ while prevocalic *$ph\acute{e}r\bar{e}ti$ remained unchanged; then *-$t\underset{\frown}{i}$ became *-t', and, when final stops were lost, the palatal feature remained as -$\underset{\frown}{i}$ (and, of course, at some point the prevocalic variants were generalized)'. However, given words like θῆσσα 'servant-girl' (< *$t^h\bar{e}t$-$\underset{\frown}{i}a$, cf. θής 'serf') or γλῶσσα 'tongue' (< *$gl\bar{o}k^h$-$\underset{\frown}{i}a$), such a Sievers-type conditioning in prehistoric Greek is at least not obvious; and in any case, the short nasal and high vowels would still not be covered. Furthermore, there is a methodological point. Is it really in the neogrammarian spirit to narrow down a putative sound law so much that we ultimately set up special rules for almost individual cases (as with Cowgill's high-vowel exemption, which basically rests on πέρυσι)? To be fair, Cowgill himself acknowledged this when he wrote that 'I have considerable qualms about my sound law here, both because of its complex, rather arbitrary-seeming conditioning, and because Greek does not ordinarily lose intervocalic stops' (1985*a*: 103).

15.4 A sandhi perspective

So what can be done? On the following pages I will advocate an alternative way of looking at the issue, which should not offend any neogrammarian while still doing justice to Kiparsky's main evidence. Unlike Kiparsky, however, I will suspend judgement on the inclusion of dental sibilants (original **-si*) in addition to dental stops. In my view conventional analogical explanations are satisfactory for both the dat. pl. of *ā*-stems and the 2sg. in -εις next to 3sg. -ει, and we do not have any decisive evidence (such as a Mycenaean thematic 2sg. in either *-e* or *-e-i*, the second of which would inconvenience Kiparsky's account).[7]

The discussion so far has been hampered by an undue bias in favour of the 'word'. This may have its roots—but no justification—in formulations like the one in Osthoff and Brugman's manifesto ('alle *wörter*, in denen der der lautbewegung unterworfene laut unter gleichen verhältnissen erscheint, werden ohne ausnahme von der änderung ergriffen'; italics added). For obvious reasons Kiparsky and Cowgill formulate their rules only for word-final sequences of dental + **-i*: anything like, say, †δοίς < †*doits* < **dotis* 'gift' (cf. δόσις) is out of the question. But if the rule is valid only at word-end, we must not forget that 'words' are parts of larger sequences where sandhi may come into play. Kiparsky himself hinted at this in a footnote or two: 'I expect that deeper study of Greek historical phonology will show that the process in question is related to other sound changes of Greek, specifically perhaps the rule that causes metathesis in such cases as *μορуα > μοῖρα, *βανуω > βαίνω, and the rule that turns word-final *i* into *y* before an initial vowel in the next word' (1967: 113 n. 2).[8]

Once this possibility is thought through, the whole problem appears in a new light. Following Cowgill (1985*a*: 103), we may posit that prevocalic **-ti̯* became **-t^j^*, 'and, when final stops were lost, the palatal feature remained as *-i̯*'. The palatalization of word-final **-ti̯* before the initial vowel of a following word is identical to the palatalization of word-internal **-ti̯-*. The only difference is that the latter eventually becomes a sibilant (e.g. Myc. *to-so* 'so much' = /tos(s)on/ < **toti̯om*), whereas word-finally the chain **ti̯* > **t^j^* > *s(s)* was bled at the

[7] Along the lines suggested below for the 3sg., one might obtain 2sg. **-ei* already in pre-Mycenaean times (**-esi V-* → **-esi̯ V-* > **-ei̯i̯ V-* = **-ei V-* → spread to preconsonantal **-ei C-* → **-ei-s* with analogical *-s*). The absence of disyllabic -εις in Homer is interesting, but not decisive (Cowgill 2006: 539).

[8] Cf. also Kiparsky (1967: 115 n. 7) on the thematic subjunctive: 'If the idea . . . that the metathesis was conditional on *i* becoming *y* before an initial vowel in the next word is correct, we would have as alternants *legēti* # *C* but *legēit* # *V* (< *legēty* # *V*). *legēiti* could then be a contamination of *legēti* and *legēit*, and there would be no need for this option [sc. the retention of final -ι] in [the metathesis rule]'. Later on, however, Kiparsky explicitly refers to the dat. pl. in '-ᾳσι' (i.e. Homeric -ησι) as a non-analogical outcome of his rule (p. 122).

intermediate stage by the loss of final dentals. Obviously this loss would not have been automatic before a vowel, since e.g. thematic 3sg. **-et^{j} V- > *-es(s) V-* would have been phonologically possible. Hence the spread of prevocalic **-et^{j}* at least to pausa, if not already preconsonantal, positions must have preceded the loss of final dentals (**-et^{j}# > *-e^{j}#*). One advantage of generalizing **-et^{j}* was that it introduced 'paradigmatic iconicity' (Matthews 1991: 234–44): the semantically unmarked 3sg. was no longer morphologically heavier, with its disyllabic ending, than the marked 1sg. in **-ō*. The resulting **-e^{j}* ~ *-ei* (= -ει) in turn superseded any potentially feasible instances of prevocalic **-et^{j}* because the retention of a single ending is generally preferred over allomorphic variation and no phonetic difficulties arose by using *-ei* also before word-initial vowels. For the thematic 3sg. we thus obtain the stages shown in Table 15.2.

Table 15.2 Stages in the development of thematic 3sg. **-eti* in Greek

	(1)	(2)	(3)	(4)	(5)
(a)	**-eti C-*	**-eti C-*	**-eti C-* (or **-et^{j} C-*)	**-eti C-* (or **-e^{j} C-*)	**-e^{j} C-* = -ει
(b)	**-eti#*	**-eti#*	**-et^{j}#*	**-e^{j}#*	**-e^{j}#* = -ει
(c)	**-eti̯ V-*	**-et^{j} V-*	**-et^{j} V-*	**-et^{j} V-*	**-e^{j} V-* = -ει

A similar table could be produced for other vowels preceding the dental, whatever their quantity or quality. Because of the intervention of Osthoff's Law in cases like τίθει (but not the subjunctive φέρῃ, where the mood's characteristic vowel length was analogically retained), it is possible that the pre-dental vowel was palatalized already before the loss of the final dental (i.e. in stages (2c) and (3b/c), where **-et^{j}*—or **-ēt^{j}*—could then be rewritten as **-e^{j}t^{j}/*-ē^{j}t^{j}*, realized as **-eit^{j}/*-ēit^{j}*). As pointed out by Kiparsky, this would make the phenomenon parallel to the vowel palatalization (> diphthongization) in βαίνω or μοῖρα (cf. elsewhere e.g. OIr. *deich* 'ten' < **dech^{j}* < **deḱm̥*, Av. 3sg. *-a^{i}tī* < **-eti*). But since Osthoff's Law may also have intervened only at the preconsonantal stage (5a), with the result spreading from there to (5b) and (5c), this assumption is far from certain. In any case both τίθει and τίθησι are 'legitimate' descendants of **tit^{h}ēti*, as they represent the original prevocalic and preconsonantal forms respectively.[9] Similarly the Homeric subjunctive type φέρῃσι, contaminated from originally preconsonantal *φέρησι and originally prevocalic φέρῃ, is unobjectionable. And as for Ϝίκατι, πέρυσι, etc., we no longer need to discard them as exceptions

[9] Cf. also νεῖ 'spins' (< **sneh₁-ti*) in Hes. *Op.* 777, where the paradosis must not be changed to νῇ (*pace* West 1978: 354).

(Kiparsky) or restrict the rule's validity (Cowgill): here the preconsonantal variant has been generalized, just as in the thematic 3sg. indicative (and, at least in post-Homeric Greek, in the corresponding subjunctive) the prevocalic variant prevailed. That only one of the two outcomes survived is no more surprising than that different dialects should make different choices. In fact, the matter must have been settled at a fairly late stage, as shown by the paradigms of *δίδωμι*, *τίθημι*, and *ἵημι*, where Attic selected 'preconsonantal' *δίδωσι*, *τίθησι*, *ἵησι*, whereas its sister dialect Ionic went for 'prevocalic' **δίδοι*, *τίθει*, *ἵει* (with or without accentual modification to *διδοῖ*, *τιθεῖ*, *ἱεῖ*).[10] Finally, *καί* derives from prevocalic **km̥ti* > **kati*, whereas the preconsonantal alternative is preserved in *κασι-* of *κασίγνητος*. Arcado-Cyprian *κάς* is slightly more difficult to pin down since it can either descend from preconsonantal **kati* > **kasi* > (apocopated) *κάς* or from prevocalic **kat*^{j} (positions (2c)–(4c) in Table 15.2) which, still in prevocalic sentence sandhi, failed to lose its final stop so that **-t*^{j} went further to *-s*.[11]

Admittedly, Kiparsky's Rule in its new dress still presents more than one possible outcome and thus retains a degree of unpredictability. But this is no longer the sort of unpredictability criticized by the neogrammarians. The actual 'sound law' involved—the palatalization of a dental before **i̯*—operated *more* blindly and mechanically if we accept the rule. For if we do not, we have to posit that dentals followed by **i̯* were exempt from the palatalization if this **i̯* resulted from word-final **-i* before vowel. Everything else—the spread of one conditioned outcome or another—is purely analogical and therefore in line with neogrammarian doctrine (Osthoff and Brugman 1878: XIII–XIV):

> Zweitens. Da sich klar herausstellt, dass die formassociation, d. h. die neubildung von sprachformen auf dem wege der analogie, im leben der neueren sprachen eine sehr bedeutende rolle spielt, so ist diese art von sprachneuerung unbedenklich auch für die älteren und ältesten perioden anzuerkennen, und nicht nur überhaupt hier anzuerkennen, sondern es ist dieses erklärungsprincip auch in derselben weise zu verwerten, wie zur erklärung von spracherscheinungen späterer perioden, und es darf nicht im mindesten auffallen, wenn analogiebildungen in den älteren und ältesten sprachperioden in demselben umfange oder gar in noch grösserem umfange uns entgegentreten wie in der jüngeren und jüngsten.

[10] *τίθει/ἵει* and *τίθησι/ἵησι* may have coexisted for some time: the *σχῆμα Ἰβύκειον* (thematic 3sg. ind. *-ησι*: e.g. *ἔχησι* 'holds'), whether typical of Rhegine Ionic (Eust. *Od.* 7. 198; cf. Peters 1998: 585–6 n. 3) or purely artificial (cf. Thumb and Kieckers 1932: 218–19), is best explained through a proportion *τίθει* : *τίθησι* = *ἔχει* : X → X = *ἔχησι*.

[11] One could also obtain ipv. *δός*, *θές*, *ἕς* from **dót*^{h}*i*, **t*^{h}*ét*^{h}*i*, **hét*^{h}*i* in this way (Bammesberger 1992). *If* the assibilation **t*$^{(h)}$*i* > **si* was restricted to South Greek, Doric attestations of such forms might decide the matter; but see now Thompson (2008). For Pindar's *δίδοι*, Cowgill's explanation is fine and Att.-Ion. *δίδου* must be remade (whereas ipv. *τίθει* may continue **tit*^{h}*et*^{h}*i*).

The situation is no different from what we find, for example, with word-final **-ns* in Greek. Everybody agrees that **-Vns C-* resulted in **-Vs C-*, whereas **-Vns V-* yielded **-V:s V-* (with compensatory lengthening). Individual dialects then generalized one outcome at the expense of the other, showing considerable disagreement in their selection (cf. Buck 1955: 68–9). In Attic we generally find εἰς 'into' < **ens* and acc. pl. -ους < **-ons* and -ᾱς < **-ans*. In Ionic we also have -ους/-ᾱς, but normally ἐς. Further afield, Syracusan appears to have used εἰς and -ους, but -ᾰς in the *ā*-stem acc. pl. (Willi 2008: 129). No one would conclude from this that our views on word-final **-ns* in Greek are offensive to a neogrammarian. The preceding pages may therefore also serve as a more general plea against forgetting sandhi phenomena in historical phonology.

15.5 Missing nasal presents

As always, the proof of the pudding lies in the eating. However hard it may be without Kiparsky's Rule to account for the thematic 3sg. in -ει, Homeric τίθει, or the 'semi-thematic' inflection of δίδωμι and τίθημι in Ionic, any further evidence for its validity will be welcome. Such evidence, I will now argue, may be found in two other seemingly irregular features of the Greek verbal system. Since both of them centre around forms in which **-ti* followed a long vowel, they also support the case against Cowgill's restrictions.

The first point concerns the fate of the Indo-European nasal-infixed presents in Greek. It is widely accepted that the prototypical suffix-cum-ending combination 1sg. **-néC-mi* survives fairly well with roots whose final consonant was **-u̯-* or **-h_2-*: 1sg. **-néu-mi*, **-néh_2-mi* ~ 1pl. **-nu-més*, **-nh_2-més* gave rise to -νῡμι/-νῠμεν and -νᾱμι/-νᾰμεν (> Att.-Ion. -νημι/-νᾰμεν) respectively. The former pattern may have become productive already in Proto-Indo-European: it certainly is in Greek, where it is no longer confined to roots in **-u̯-* (cf. below). The latter is gradually disappearing, but in Homeric Greek forms such as 3sg. act. δάμνησι 'tames' < **dm̥néh_2-ti* or 3sg. mid. μάρναται 'fights' < **mr̥nh_2-toi* are still alive (cf. Schwyzer 1939: 693). It is therefore odd that not even Homeric Greek shows any traces of (a) a type in *-νωμι/-νομεν and (b) a type in *-νημι/-νεμεν, to represent 1sg. **-néh_3-mi*, **-néh_1-mi* ~ 1pl. **-nh_3-més*, **-nh_1-més* (cf. Strunk 1967: 56–9, responding to Meillet 1925).

The absence of (a) has been explained in another influential article by Cowgill, where 'Cowgill's Law' was established (Cowgill 1965: 157, '*no* to νυ... before labial and labiovelar consonants'; cf. now Vine 1999). Thus, 1pl. στόρνυμεν 'we spread out', 1sg. mid. στόρνυμαι, mid. ptcpl. στορνύμενος (all with analogical στορ- for *σταρ- < **str̥-*) would have arisen from *στάρνομεν,

**στάρνομαι*, **σταρνόμενος*; and because the *-νῡμι/-νῠμεν* type was flourishing, they pulled the entire **-neh₃-mi* paradigm into it. But the question arises whether the cited forms were systemically central enough to have such an effect. Normally, unmarked categories such as third person, singular, or active analogically influence more marked ones (other persons, plural, mediopassive; cf. e.g. Kuryłowicz 1964: *passim*). Moreover, all of Cowgill's trigger forms would have looked like thematic formations: so why did they not rather pull in that direction, given the overall frequency of thematic verbs? Conversely one must ask why not a single thematic verb in *-νω* adopted *-νῡμι*-type forms because of its 1pl. *-νομεν*, 1sg. mid. *-νομαι*, mid. ptcpl. *-νόμενος*.

So the solution may be different: still to be sought in Cowgill's Law, but at a much earlier stage (and Cowgill himself stressed that his law operated early, as it produced pan-Greek *νύξ* 'night', (*)*ὄνυμα* 'name', *ὄνυξ* 'nail'). That the third laryngeal was the laryngeal 'corresponding' to the labiovelar series among the dorsal stops is an old idea (cf. Mayrhofer 1986: 121 n. 101, with literature). If it is correct, despite the cautioning remarks by Penney (1988*c*: 366–9), the labial element of **h₃* (or 'x^w' with e.g. Cowgill 1979: 29 n. 12), just like that of the labiovelar in e.g. *νύξ* < **nokʷt-s*, would have triggered the change of **-noh₃-* (i.e. **-neh₃-* with laryngeal colouring) into **-nuh₃-* > **-nū-* throughout the active singular, where one should like to find the analogical base form.[12] This possibility has some interesting ramifications. For one thing, in the 'normal' *-νῡμι* type the alleged replacement of **-neu-* by *-nū-* is not unproblematic either because it presupposes a proportional analogy *-νᾰ-* : *-νᾱ-* = *-νῠ-* : $X \rightarrow X$ = *-νῡ-* (Schwyzer 1939: 695), in which again paradigmatically marginal forms (plural, middle) prevail over central ones (singular, active). For another, Greek does not preserve a single verb in *-νῡμι* from a root that certainly contained final **-u̯-* (like Ved. *śr̥ṇóti* 'hears' < **k̂l̥-né-u-ti*).[13] By contrast there are at least three relevant verbs from roots in **-h₃-*, two of which are common:[14] *ὄμνῡμι* 'to swear' (**h₂/₃emh₃-*), *στόρνῡμι* (**sterh₃-*; cf. above), and *θάρνυμαι/θόρνυμαι* 'to mount' (**dʰerh₃-*). Hence the productivity of Greek *-νῡμι* may be due mainly to these verbs in **-neh₃-*, not to an imaginary set of inherited verbs in **-neu-*, and within the type it may not be *-νῡ-* (< **-nuh₃-* < **-noh₃-*) which is analogical, but *-νῠ-* for **-νο-* in some (not all!) plural/middle forms.

12 Apparent counter-examples, as in the paradigm of **ĝneh₃-* (e.g. *ἔγνων* 'I recognized' < **-gnoh₃-m*) may be explained through analogy (cf. e.g. *γιγνώσκω* 'to recognize' < **gi-gn̥h₃-ske/o-* without **-noh₃-*).

13 *LIV* 184, s.v., lists a root **geh₂u̯-* for *γάνυμαι* 'rejoice', but *γηθέω* 'rejoice' from **geh₂-dʰ-* speaks against **-u̯-* forming part of the root.

14 Cf. *LIV* 146–7, 265–6, 599–600, s.vv. **dʰerh₃-*, **h₂emh₃-*, **sterh₃-*. The reconstruction **gʷl̥-né-h₃-* for *βούλομαι* 'to want' (*LIV* 208, s.v. ?**gʷelh₃-*) is doubtful and a suffix **-se/o-* more likely (cf. Frisk 1960–72: i. 259, Chantraine 1968–80: i. 190, s.v. *βούλομαι*).

Whether one accepts this or Cowgill's account for the absence of (a) *-νωμι/-νομεν, this group of nasal-infixed presents from laryngeal roots is taken care of. But what about (b), the missing *-νημι/-νεμεν type? Numbers are quite substantial here. Following *LIV* (s.vv.), we may include at least the following verbs:[15]

- βάλλω 'to throw, hit' ~ *gʷl̥-né-h$_1$- (*gʷelh$_1$-)
- θάλλω 'to flourish' ~ *dʰl̥-né-h$_1$- (*dʰalh$_1$-)
- πάλλω 'to sway' ~ *pl̥-né-h$_1$- (*pelh$_1$-)
- σκέλλομαι 'to dry out' ~ *skl̥-né-h$_1$- (*skelh$_1$-)
- τέλλομαι 'to turn' ~ *kʷl̥-né-h$_1$- (*kʷelh$_1$-)
- τέμνω 'to cut' ~ tm̥-né-h$_1$- (*temh$_1$-)

It is doubtful whether a 2sg./3sg. mid. in *-nh$_1$-soi/-toi, whence *-νεαι/-νεται, let alone a 2pl. in *-nh$_1$-te > -νετε, could have brought about the wholesale switch into the thematic class. But if we remember the tendency for the third person singular to trigger intraparadigmatic analogy, the lack of, say, 3sg. *τάμνησι < *tm̥-né-h$_1$-ti or *βάλλησι < *βάλνησι < *gʷl̥-né-h$_1$-ti to parallel 3sg. δάμνησι < *δάμνᾱσι < *dm̥-né-h$_2$-ti finds an explanation. Just as prevocalic 3sg. *titʰēti developed into Homeric/Ionic τίθει (τιθεῖ), so prevocalic *tamnēti (< *tm̥-né-h$_1$-ti) and *gʷalnēti became τάμνει (→ τέμνει) and βάλλει. And since these 3sg. active forms looked exactly like the newly generalized 3sg. active forms of the frequent thematic verbs, with -ει < *-eti, the thematization of the *-νημι/-νεμεν presents proceeded quickly and without residue.

Meanwhile, there was no high-frequency class into which the verbs in -νᾱμι/-ναμεν or -νῡμι/-νυμεν could be drawn with equal ease because of their 3sg. act. in *-ναι and *-νυι (< *-nāi[tʲ], *-nūi[tʲ]). Their preconsonantal variants therefore survived, just like τίθησι, δίδωσι outside Ionic. Even so, we may wonder whether such by-forms in *-ναι/*-νυι were not also responsible for the partial thematization of these two classes into the types κάμνω 'to toil' (*k̂emh$_2$-, hence *k̂m̥-né-h$_2$-) and τίνω 'to pay' (*kʷei-, hence *kʷi-néu-). In the absence of other classes with 3sg. *-ναι/*-νυι, they may have been remodelled into -νει (virtual *-na͡ei) and *-νϝει (*-nu͡ei) respectively. Homeric 3sg. pres. δαμνᾷ 'overcomes' (*Od.* 11. 221; cf. Hes. *Op.* 510 πιλνᾷ 'brings close'), by contrast, can hardly stand for *δάμνᾱ with

[15] Gr. ὄλλυμι 'to destroy' instead of *ὄλλω ~ *h$_3$l̥-né-h$_1$- is exceptional; cf. *LIV* 298, s.v. *h$_3$elh$_1$-, and Harđarson (1993: 222–3, 'nach ... ἐστόρεσα : στόρνῡμι vorgenommene Rückbildung zum *s*-Aorist ὤλεσα'). Should we posit, also because of ὀλοός 'destructive' < *Holh$_3$-u͡ós, metathesized *h$_3$elh$_1$- (cf. Hitt. ḫallanniye- 'to destroy', with ḫ-) → *h$_1$elh$_3$-, whence regular *-neh$_3$-mi > *-νῡμι (with *o*-vocalism after aor. ὀλεσ- < *ἐλοσ-: cf. στορεσ- < *στεροσ-, Sihler 1995: 225)? Other thematized nasal verbs may contain roots in *-h$_1$-, but the nature of the laryngeal is uncertain (*LIV* 129–30, 277, 305–6, s.vv. *du͡eH-, *h$_2$le͡iH-, *h$_3$re͡iH-, for δύνω 'to plunge', ἀλίνω 'to anoint', ὀρίνω 'to stir'; cf. also *LIV* 366–7, s.v. *kreh$_1$(i̯)-, for κρίνω 'to discern' and *LIV* 576, s.v. 1. *(s)pelH-, for a putative nasal present behind ἀπειλή 'boast').

the secondary ending **-t* (thus Wackernagel 1914: 103 n. 2, Schwyzer 1939: 659; cf. Chantraine 1958: 301–2), but easily for either *δάμνᾱι (pre-Osthoff) or *δάμναι, with the same reaccentuation as in τιθεῖ for τίθει. Similarly 3sg. pres. δείκνῡ 'shows' (with an unmetrical variant δεικνύει) in Hes. *Op.* 526 no doubt conceals *δείκνῡι or *δείκνυι, not **-nūt* with secondary ending (*pace* West 1978: 291).

15.6 *Verba vocalia* in Aeolic

The last-mentioned forms bring us to the second phenomenon which loses its mystery once we accept Kiparsky's Rule. Those who explain them by implausibly positing a secondary ending **-t* within a present paradigm justify their opinion by reference to Aeolic. According to an ancient grammatical tradition (Hdn. ii. 832. 37 Lentz, from Choerob. *in Theod.* ii. 332. 3–4 Hilgard; cf. Lentz 1867: cxii), τίθη 'puts', δίδω 'gives', and ζεύγνῡ 'yokes' are Aeolic 3sg. pres. forms. What we find in the Lesbian poets, however, is not only 3sg. προίει 'sends forth' (Alc. 74. 7) next to τίθησιν (Alc. 58. 23),[16] or 2sg. τίθεις (Alc. 338. 5), which presupposes 3sg. *τίθει as in Ionic, next to τίθησθα (Alc. 58. 28), but also regularly[17] a 3sg. in -ει of *verba vocalia* (or 'contract verbs'), which inflect athematically in Lesbian (Sapph. 1. 23 φίλει 'loves', 31. 14 ἄγρει 'seizes', 43. 5 κλόνει 'confounds', 164 κάλει 'calls', Alc. 5. 11 γάμει 'marries', 48. 9 and 124 κατάγρει 'destroys', 117b. 29 ὀμίλλει 'mingles', 347a. 3–4 ἄχει 'resounds', ἄνθει 'flourishes'; contrast e.g. 1sg. κάλημ⟨μ⟩ι in Sapph. 1. 16, 60. 4, φίλημμ(ι) in 58. 25). Similarly, 2sg. forms in -αις, -οις of otherwise athematic *verba vocalia* (Sapph. 38 ὄπταις 'roast' (?), 63. 2 φοίταις 'walk', Alc. 58. 21 ὀνάρταις 'fasten', 359 χαύνοις 'fill'; cf. Alc. 340 φαῖς 'say' (coni. Egenolff)) imply 3sg. forms in *-αι, *-οι just as much as occasional 3sg. forms in -αισ(ι) are best accounted for through contamination of *-αι and *-ᾱσι (Alc. 347a. 2 δίψαισ(ι) 'thirsts'; cf. Alc. 349b φαῖσι 'says' for *φᾶσι) (cf. Hamm 1957: 161–2).[18] All this is in line

[16] Cf. also Alc. 364 (conjectural) δάμναι for transmitted, but unmetrical, δάμνησι.

[17] The only exception is Sapph. 1. 20 ἀδικήει 'wrongs', possibly concealing ἀδίκησι (Meillet 1931: 200). Some coexistence of originally preconsonantal -ησι with originally prevocalic -ει in Sappho's Lesbian is not more problematic than in Homer's and Herodotus' Ionic (cf. sections 15.1, 15.3). Sapph. 36 ποθήω 'desire' (from *EM* 485. 43, also with Aeol. καλήω 'call') is more puzzling (unless subjunctive: cf. Thessalian 3pl. subj. κατοικείουνθι 'they inhabit' in *IG* IX/2 514. 3): if correct, it would support ἀδικήει, which might then be (artificially?) contaminated from *ἀδίκει and *ἀδίκη (cf. below and Theoc. 29. 29 φόρη 'carries', 30. 12 ὄρη 'sees', Blümel 1982: 169 with n. 161).

[18] Similarly, Sapph. 3. 4 λύπηις 'vex' and Alc. 313 σάωις 'save' (?) (2sg.; cf. Sapph. 129 φίλη(ι)σθα) may be remodelled from *λύπεις (∼ 3sg. -ει) and *σάοις (∼ 3sg. -οι) through analogical (re-)introduction of the long vowel found in 1sg. -ημ(μ)ι, -ωμι; and the irregular diphthong of Alc. 50. 6 φαῖσθ(α) (2sg.; cf. 1sg. φαῖμ(ι) in Sapph. 88a. 17 and 147) must be due to 3sg. *φαῖ → 2sg. (*)φαῖς (on which cf. above).

not only with the doctrine of another ancient source that gives πόημι, πόεις, πόε[ι] 'make' as the Aeolic paradigm (*P Bouriant* 8, iv. 21–2, Lobel 1932: 1; cf. Schwyzer 1939: 729 n. 4), but, more importantly, also with the inscriptional evidence of Thessalian (?, cf. *DGE* 617. 2 ἐρουτᾶι 'asks' with Blümel 1982: 177 n. 188) and Lesbian (*IG* XII/2, 645a. 44 τίμαι 'honours', *passim* στεφάνοι 'crowns'; cf. Buck 1955: 123, Thumb and Scherer 1959: 69 and 103, Blümel 1982: 172–5, Hodot 1990: 193).

These inflectional peculiarities are conventionally explained as remnants which escaped the large-scale athematization of deverbal and denominal *verba vocalia* in Lesbian (cf. Hamm 1957: 172, Hodot 1990: 194). It is not clear, however, why such an athematization should have happened at all if it did not affect the most frequent form in the paradigm (3sg.).[19] By contrast, if originally athematic verbs such as τίθημι obtained a 3sg. **tit*^{h}*ēi[t*^{j}*]* > (*)τίθει next to a 1sg. τίθημι by regular sound change, it is easy to see how originally thematic verbs in **-e̯ie/o-* (~ Att.-Ion. -έω) could be athematized given their 3sg. in -ει (e.g. 3sg. φίλει with barytonesis from φιλεῖ → 1sg. φίλημ(μ)ι). In other words, Kiparsky's Rule not only justifies the Aeolic 3sg. forms of athematic verbs and *verba vocalia* as such, as first seen by Blümel (1982: 167–82), it also explains why the frequent *verba vocalia* in -έω, -άω, -όω became verbs in -ημι, -ᾱμι, -ωμι, not just in Lesbian or Aeolic more widely (esp. Thessalian), but also in Arcado-Cyprian (Buck 1955: 123). Diachronically, Lesbian φίλει, γάμει, etc. are indeed thematic forms, but synchronically they are just as 'athematic' as, for example, φίλημμι. Herodian's τίθη, δίδω, ζεύγνῡ in turn are mere regularizations of expected *τίθει, *δίδοι, *ζεύγνυι—though regularizations whose real existence in Lesbian need not be doubted (cf. below).

Looking closely at the matter, we understand, moreover, why a similar athematization could not occur as readily in Attic or Ionic. The creation of a 1sg. such as φίλημ(μ)ι should have happened when a model like 3sg. **tit*^{h}*ēi[t*^{j}*]* still existed in its pre-Osthoff shape (either because the long vowel in **tit*^{h}*ēi[t*^{j}*]* was analogically retained or because Osthoff's Law began to operate only later); for otherwise normal thematic verbs might also have been affected by the athematization (following a proportion 3sg. τίθει : 1sg. τίθημι = 3sg. φέρει : X → X = †φέρημι[20]). Instead, the analogical proportion we need looks as follows: 3sg. **tit*^{h}*ēi[t*^{j}*]* : 1sg. **tit*^{h}*ēmi* = 3sg. **-ēi[t*^{j}*]* : 1sg. X → X = *-ēmi*. But 3sg. **-ēi[t*^{j}*]* <

[19] Denominative -ᾱμι is hardly inherited (*pace* Schwyzer 1939: 729), and Schmid's (1986) semi-thematic theory oddly starts from a thematic 1sg. and an athematic 3sg. (with secondary ending). Forms such as φίλητε, ἐφίλης, ἐφίλη with -η- < -εε- are unlikely starting-points for intraparadigmatic analogy (*pace* Hamm 1957: 172).

[20] Cf. n. 10 on the σχῆμα Ἰβύκειον.

-e̯i̯ei[t^j] (< **-é̯i̯e-ti*) had the same long vowel as 3sg. **tit^{h}ēi[t^j]* only in those dialects in which **-e̯i̯e-* > **-ee-* contracted into open /ɛ:/, i.e. Aeolic and Arcado-Cyprian, but not Attic-Ionic with its closed /e:/ (cf. Buck 1955: 28–9).[21] At the same time, the outcome of this contraction is an additional argument against the traditional 'thematic' interpretation of Lesbian φίλει etc., for without our combination of Kiparsky's Rule and Osthoff's Law **p^{h}iléi̯ei* should have yielded *φιλῆι > barytone *φίληι > later †φίλη in that dialect.

15.7 Conclusion

Summing up, we may propose a relative chronology of the phenomena discussed:

1. According to Kiparsky's Rule, which need not be restricted with Cowgill but which must be reformulated with reference to sandhi, pre-vocalic final **-Vti* was palatalized, either with the supra-segmental palatalization feature affecting the preceding vowel immediately (i.e. **-V^{j}t^j*, realized as **-Vit^j*) or with the preceding vowel acquiring the feature when the original seat of the feature was lost (i.e. **-Vt^j* > **-V^j*, realized as **-Vi*). The prevocalic outcome was generalized in the paradigm of thematic verbs. In the paradigm of athematic verbs (δίδωμι, τίθημι, etc.) the prevocalic and the preconsonantal variants continued to coexist for some time. Given their pan-Greek character and given Mycenaean forms like 3sg. *pe-re* 'brings' = /p^{h}erei/ (φέρει), these developments were pre-Mycenaean.
2. Due to Osthoff's Law, and presumably still in pre-Mycenaean times, though not necessarily before the loss of final dentals,[22] the nasal presents from roots in **-h_1-* regularly acquired a 3sg. in (eventual) -νει (< **-nēi[t^j]*). Because this paradigmatically central form was identical to its counterpart in the

[21] Since for the verbs in -άω < **-āi̯e/o-*, Aeolic and Arcado-Cyprian would not have enjoyed a similar advantage over (Proto-)Attic-Ionic, dialectal accentuation may also have played a role. A dialect with barytonesis could more easily equate a type **tít^{h}ēi[t^j]* with a type **p^{h}ílēi[t^j]* < **p^{h}iléi̯ei[t^j]*. Unfortunately, we know relatively little about the early accentuation of non-Lesbian Aeolic, let alone Arcado-Cyprian (cf. Probert 2006: 70–4).

[22] As pointed out in section 15.4, Osthoff's Law may also have intervened when **-V:i* came to stand before *C-*, *after* the loss of the final dental. 3sg. -(ν)ει < **-neh$_1$-ti* would then represent the generalized preconsonantal variant of a pair **-(n)ēi V-* ~ **-(n)ei C-* (cf. dialectal datives in -οι/-αι, for -ωι/-ᾱι, which need not reflect old locatives; Buck 1955: 86, 88). Both elements of this pair would descend from the generalized prevocalic variant of **-(n)ēti̯ V-* ~ **-(n)ēti C-*. Because of the numerous thematic presents with 3sg. -ει, preference being given to **-(n)ei* over **-(n)ēi* would be unsurprising. Moreover, the survival of *τίθηι/*δίδωι next to τίθει/(*)δίδοι (cf. below) would no longer presuppose intraparadigmatic analogy.

thematic verbs, these nasal presents (< *-*neh*$_1$-) were fully thematized, unlike those in -νᾱμι (<*-*neh*$_2$-) and -νῡμι (< *-*neh*$_3$-).

3. Similarly, Osthoff's Law regularly produced forms like 3sg. τίθει, (*)δίδοι, etc. (which would still coexist with τίθησι, δίδωσι, while giving rise to 2sg. (*)τίθεις, (*)δίδοις, etc. by analogy). Because the radical element θη-, δω- was commonly found also outside the (singular) active present, notably in the aorist system, the situation was somewhat different from the one in the nasal presents, and long-vowel variants such as 3sg. *τίθηι, *δίδωι may have been more resistant here, just as they were analogically resistant in the thematic subjunctive. For verbs like τίθημι and δίδωμι there was thus indeed a 'choice' between 3sg. τίθησι/δίδωσι, *τίθηι/*δίδωι, and τίθει/(*)δίδοι. Some of this competition continued into the historical period (as shown by the texts of Herodotus and the Lesbian poets), but each epichoric dialect tended to generalize one or another of the variants: Attic went for τίθησι/δίδωσι, Ionic for τίθει/(*)δίδοι (> τιθεῖ/διδοῖ), and Lesbian (Aeolic?) for *τίθηι/*δίδωι (whence Herodian's τίθη/δίδω by Lesbian monophthongization of final long diphthongs: cf. Thumb and Scherer 1959: 92, and, with epigraphic [ἀ]ντιδίδω, Hodot 1990: 169).
4. Wherever *τίθηι/*δίδωι was retained in such a way *and* denominal/deverbal *-*e͡ie*- contracted into /ɛ:/ in early post-Mycenaean times, the parallelism of old athematic 3sg. *τίθηι = /tit^{h}ɛ:i/ with newly contracted 3sg. *φίληι = /p^{h}ilɛ:i/ < *p^h*ile͡iei*[t^j] quite naturally triggered the transformation of *verba vocalia* in (Att.-Ion.) -έω < *-*e͡ie*/*o*- into athematic verbs in -ημι, as in Aeolic and Arcado-Cyprian. Similarly, the model of 3sg. *ἵσται could cause the transfer of the less common verbs in (Att.-Ion.) -άω < *-*ā͡ie*/*o*- into the athematic class in -ᾱμι. And just as both *τίθηι (> Herodian's τίθη) and Osthoff-shortened *τίθει (→ Alcaeus' 2sg. τίθεις) eventually surfaced in historical Lesbian, so *φίληι would straightforwardly be matched by shortened φίλει, the pseudo-thematic form that is amply attested in Sappho and Alcaeus.

Kiparsky's Rule—whether or not it deserves this label, being just the first half of the *$t\underset{\frown}{i}$ > *t^j > *s(s)* evolution recorded by every textbook—thus turns out to be far more than an elegant, but *ad hoc*, metathesis designed primarily to explain the thematic 3sg. in -ει. To accept the rule, without unnecessary limitations, is not merely compatible with neogrammarian methodology. It is also the best, if not the only, way of accounting for a number of otherwise unexplained features in Greek historical morphology and dialect grammar: the 'partial thematization' of athematic presents in Ionic, the 'partial athematization' of *verba vocalia* in Aeolic and Arcado-Cyprian, and the disappearance of nasal presents in **-νημι/-νεμεν* throughout the Greek world. The case perfectly illustrates how 'chaque langue forme un système où tout se tient' (Meillet 1903*a*: 407), where words do not occur in isolation, where phonology and morphology interact, and where variation is part of life, not a threat to philological rigour.[23]

[23] Just as the page proofs of this book were about to be sent back to the Press, Brent Vine kindly drew my attention to, and provided me with the page proofs of, Ellsworth (2011); it is encouraging to see that Ellsworth's main ideas are similar to those presented here in Section 15.4.

Part VI

Synchronic laws and rules in syntax and sociolinguistics

16

praetor urbanus – urbanus praetor: some aspects of attributive adjective placement in Latin

DAVID LANGSLOW

16.1 Introduction

My purpose here is to present a case study against the background of attempts to explain with reference to rules (or regularities, or strong tendencies), if not laws, the placement of the attributive adjectival modifier of the noun in Latin.[1] I am acutely aware of the smallness of the endeavour, but no less convinced of the utility of detailed and explicit case studies.[2] Like the 'supplements' on word order to my chapter on phrasal terms and other common collocations in medical Latin (Langslow 2000: 253–68), this essay is corpus-based. It considers a more narrowly defined set of noun phrases, but it draws material from many more Latin prose works, and refers to more recent general and theoretical

[1] I am very grateful especially to Jim Adams and Harm Pinkster for detailed criticism, also to John Briscoe, Adam Ledgeway, Jesse Lundquist, Rebekka Ott, Nigel Vincent, and the editors for numerous helpful comments and suggestions, and to Olga Spevak for kindly letting me see Spevak (2010*b*) before its publication. The present paper in effect expands on her observation (p. 27) that *urbanus praetor* 'n'est guère attesté et est à bannir des grammaires et des manuels du latin'. (Translations of Latin examples are based in most cases on the Loeb edition, with modifications of my own.)

[2] These are exemplified most recently, on a much larger scale, in the excellent study by de Melo (2010) of possessive pronouns in Plautus.

approaches to the question. Almost inevitably, one's starting points for reflections on this topic are Marouzeau's formulations (1922, 1953) and his famous example, which provides the title for this essay.[3] As a small experiment, on what I hoped would be an appropriate scale, I compiled a new corpus of instances of attributive *urbanus* in Latin prose from Varro to Suetonius.[4] In sections 16.3 and 16.4 below, aspects of traditional and more recent accounts of the normal and abnormal placement of an attributive adjective in Latin (A[djective]N[oun] or N[oun]A[djective]) are illustrated and assessed against this corpus of contexts. The findings are summarized and discussed briefly in section 16.5. Let us begin, however, by considering the corpus.

16.2 General remarks on the corpus of occurrences

16.2.1 Nouns attested with attributive urbanus

Table 16.1 sets out the seven nouns over which authors differ on the placement of *urbanus*, and the sixteen nouns occurring before and after *urbanus* in one and the same author. It also lists the nine nouns which always follow *urbanus* in two or more contexts (in one or more authors), and the one noun attested more than once always before *urbanus*. Even excluding those attested just once with *urbanus*,[5] a wide range of types of noun is found in the corpus, denoting human beings as individuals (*homo*, *praetor*, *quaestor*) and in groups, especially military or political (*cohors*, *legio*, *miles*, *multitudo*, *tribus*), various objects (e.g. *edictum*, *opus*, *praedium*, *res*), nominalized states (e.g. *libertas*, *otium*, *seruitus*), actions (e.g. *insidiae*, *motus*, *seditio*), etc. The meaning of *urbanus* in its literal, 'relational' use[6] varies slightly from context to context, reflecting

[3] Not only because *praetor urbanus–urbanus praetor* has proved so memorable, but rather because it is, I hope, not unfitting for the purpose of this volume: I mean of course with *urbanus* in its non-literal sense, since in my profoundly respectful, grateful, and affectionate experience of them over more than thirty years, John's *iurisdictio* and *prouincia* and, in all the best senses, his *officia* know no bounds.

[4] The original plan was to study Cicero and Livy, chosen because they each offer about 100 examples of attributive *urbanus*. To them, however, I have added a small republican corpus (Varro, Caesar, Sallust) and a slightly larger early imperial corpus, mainly of the first century (Seneca the Elder, Valerius Maximus, Seneca the Younger; Pliny the Elder, Columella; Tacitus, Pliny the Younger, Suetonius). I began to analyse also the (much larger) set of contexts of *praetor* with an attributive modifier in the same corpus of texts, but soon realised that that would have to be for another essay.

[5] Of these (not taken into account in Table 16.1, but considered in the analysis below), thirty-six are AN, twenty-one NA.

[6] It is relational in standing for a prepositional phrase ('in/from/for the city'). On 'relational', 'absolute' ('intersective'), and 'synthetic' uses of attributive adjectives, see Radatz (2001: 65–77). Cf. also nn. 19–22 below.

different senses of underlying *urbs*: any city, or Rome in particular, as the locus of civil as opposed to military affairs and activities; any city, or again Rome, as opposed to the countryside, or, in the case of Rome, as opposed to Italy or Greece or the provinces. In the sense 'cultured, polite, urbane', the notion of the city is of course more distant (this metaphorical use of attributive *urbanus* is surprising, to me at least, by its rarity in the corpus: see section 16.4.2.1 below).

Table 16.1 The placement of attributive *urbanus* in the corpus, by head noun, author, and number of occurrences

urbanus	AN/AxN	NA/NxA	Total no. of occurrences
[Corpus total (91 different nouns)			310]
praetor	Sen. Y. 1	Cic. 15, Var. 2, Caes. 1, Liv. 29, Sen. E. 1, Val. Max. 4, Plin. E. 1, Tac. 3, Suet. 1	57
praedium	Cic. 2, Suet. 1	Var. 1	4
tribus	Cic. 1, Liv. 2	Suet. 1	4
negotium	Plin. Y.	Sall., Liv.	3
homo	Sen. E.	Cic.	2
opes	Cic.	Liv.	2
seruitus	Tac.	Sen. Y.	2
7 different nouns			75
res	**Cic.** 8, Var. 1, Caes. 2, Liv. 1, Sen. E. 1, Col. 1, **Suet.** 1	**Cic.** 14, Liv. 2, Tac. 2, Plin. Y. 2, **Suet.** 1	36
legio	**Liv.** 17	**Liv.** 12	29
quaestor	**Liv.** 1	Cic. 8, **Liv.** 5, Val. Max. 1, Suet. 1	16
pleb(e)s	**Cic.** 2, Sall. 1, Sen. E. 1, Tac. 2	**Cic.** 2, Liv. 2, Plin. E. 3, Suet. 1	14
iurisdictio	Cic. 2, **Liv.** 5	**Liv.** 4	11
cohors	**Tac.** 7	**Tac.** 1, Suet. 2	10
exercitus	**Liv.** 3	Var. 1, **Liv.** 2	6
miles	**Tac.** 4	**Tac.** 2	6
officium	Cic. 2, Sen. Y. 1, **Suet.** 1	**Suet.** 1	5
opus	Cic., Liv., **Plin. Y.**	**Plin. Y.**	4
otium	Sall., **Liv.**	Cic., **Liv.**	4
contio	**Liv.**	**Liv.**	2
edictum	**Cic.**	**Cic.**	2
seditio	**Liv.**	**Liv.**	2
sermo	**Cic.**	**Cic.**	2
sors	**Liv.**	**Liv.**	2
16 different nouns			151

(*continued*)

Table 16.1 Continued

urbanus	AN/AxN	NA/NxA	Total no. of occurrences
militia	Cic. 1, Tac. 3		4
motus	Caes. 1, Liv. 3		4
prouincia	Cic. 1, Liv. 3		4
ars	Liv., Col.		2
coniuratio	Plin. Y., Suet.		2
insidiae	Cic., Tac.		2
libertas	Liv., Val. Max.		2
multitudo	Liv.		2
uita	Cic., Col.		2
9 different nouns			**24**
praetura		Cic. 2, Suet. 1	3
1 noun			3

Note: Authors without a figure against their abbreviated name share equally among themselves the number of occurrences of *urbanus* with the given noun.

Clearly, some combinations of noun + *urbanus* have become standard, conventional technical terms in political and military contexts. Such phrasal terms vary in the extent to which their sense reflects a semantic specialization of the noun or the adjective or both. For example, the sense of *tribus urbanae* (the tribes in or of the city of Rome), like, say, *otium urbanum/uita urbana* (leisure/life in the city, or in Rome), is close to what one would predict from understanding the noun *tribus* and the adjective *urbanus* (the latter with special reference to Rome); *praetor urbanus*, on the other hand, and the related terms *iurisdictio/prouincia/sors urbana*, have acquired a specialized reference, unpredictable—at any rate, not fully predictable—from their constituent nouns and adjective.

As for the raw figures in Table 16.1 recording the placement of *urbanus*, we see at once how variable this is. Of the thirty-three nouns attested more than once with attributive *urbanus* (in a total of 253 contexts), only ten (twenty-seven occurrences) show consistently AN or NA placement, and sixteen of them (accounting for 151 occurrences, 48.5% of the total) show variation within a single author (in bold type in Table 16.1).[7] With reference to the corpus of *urbanus* phrases, it would be accurate to say that Sallust writes *urbana plebs*

[7] The summary is distorted by recognizing variation in *praetor urbanus* itself on the strength of a single, remarkable instance out of fifty-seven. Table 16.1 is rough and ready also in that I have counted together contiguous (AN, NA) and non-contiguous (AxN, NxA) instances. The latter are considered separately in section 16.4.4 below.

and Suetonius *plebs urbana*, that Varro and Caesar put *urbana* before *res*, while Tacitus and Pliny the Younger place it after. On the other hand—lest one infer from these two cases hints of a diachronic shift from AN to NA—Tacitus says *urbana plebs*, while Livy says *plebs urbana*, Suetonius has *urbanum praedium*, Varro *praedium urbanum*. Such statements as these, however, refer nearly always to just one or two occurrences in each author, and, as the figures in Table 16.1 show, there is much more prominent variation *within* a given author, so that it is a fairer immediate reflection of these very crude data to say, Cicero has both *urbana plebs* and *plebs urbana*, or Livy sometimes says *urbana legio* and sometimes *legio urbana*, Tacitus varies between *urbanus miles* and *miles urbanus*—and we are back to square one.[8]

16.2.2 The prose authors attesting attributive urbanus

Table 16.1 suggests, and Table 16.2 shows more specifically, that the placement of *urbanus* varies not only from noun to noun but also from author to author.

Table 16.2 Placement of attributive *urbanus* by author

urbanus	AN	AxN	NA	NxA	Different head nouns (occurrences)	
					in total	with variation AN~NA
Varro	(1)	2(2)	4(5), (1)MM		8(9)	0
Cicero	14(21), 10(11)MM	4(4), (1)MM	15(47), 5(5)MM	3(3), 3(3)MM	44(95)	4(30)
Caesar	3(3)	(1)	(1)		4(5)	0
Sallust	3(3)		2(2)		5(5)	0
Livy	12(23), 9(19)MM	4(4), 3(3)MM	13(50), 3(10)MM	(1)MM	26(110)	10(63)
Seneca E.	1(1), 2(2)MM		(1)		4(4)	0
Val. Max.	3(3)	(1)	2(5)		6(9)	0
Seneca Y.	(1), (1)MM		2(2)MM		4(4)	0
Pliny E.	(1), (1)MM		2(3), (1)MM		4(6)	0
Columella	6(6)	2(2)MM	(1)		9(9)	0

(continued)

[8] Cf. Pinkster (1995: 553) on word order in a Late Latin text: 'as soon as we go into more detail, such a purely quantitative approach turns out to be unsatisfactory, and more interesting, though difficult, observations can be made... Obviously, there is no syntactic rule saying that objects have to go this or that way. It clearly depends.'

Table 16.2 Continued

urbanus	AN	AxN	NA	NxA	Different head nouns (occurrences)	
					in total	with variation AN~NA
Tacitus	9(16), 2(4)MM	(1)	5(8), 1(1)MM		12(30)	2(14)
Pliny Y.	3(3), (1)MM		2(2), 2(2)MM		6(8)	1(2)
Suetonius	4(4), (1)MM	(1)	6(7), 2(2)MM	(1)	13(16)	2(4)

Note: AxN and NxA refer to pre-modifier and post-modifier hyperbaton; figures indicate *different head nouns (occurrences)*; MM = *urbanus* is one of multiple modifiers.

Table 16.2 is to be read as follows: Livy attests 110 occurrences of attributive *urbanus*, with altogether twenty-six different head nouns, ten of which nouns (accounting for sixty-three occurrences of *urbanus*) sometimes precede and sometimes follow *urbanus*; he attests only one instance of *urbanus* following its noun in hyperbaton and in that instance *urbanus* is one of multiple modifiers of the noun. Of the thirteen authors in the corpus, five show with one and the same noun both preposed and postposed *urbanus*, and it is on these cases of variation that we shall concentrate in what follows. The absence of such variation in the other eight authors need reflect no more than the fact that they hardly ever use *urbanus* more than once with the same noun.[9] Nevertheless, their uses of attributive *urbanus* yield some good examples of general principles. Let me say here, while we are comparing authors in Table 16.2, that the *prima facie* reasonable inference from the figures that *as a basic order* Varro, for example, prefers NA while Columella strongly favours AN would be, I think, quite misleading. Having studied all 310 contexts, I am struck by the consistency with which, in all thirteen authors, preposed *urbanus* may be easily and plausibly read as being in focus or contrast (syntagmatic or paradigmatic),[10] and—no less importantly—by the converse, in both senses:

[9] Apart from *praetor urbanus*, which—with the sole exception of its single occurrence in Seneca the Younger (see section 16.4.3 below)—is resolutely NA in all authors and contexts, opportunity for variation is limited to *urbanae res* twice in Caesar, and *pleb(e)s urbana* three times in Pliny the Elder.

[10] I follow Powell (2010: 164) in my use of 'focus' (and 'topic') and in preferring 'focus' to 'emphasis'. A word or phrase in focus is salient or prominent, either intrinsically in virtue of its meaning or considered within the logical structure of its context. The word/phrase in focus may

when *urbanus* follows its noun, unequivocal focus is relatively rare, and when *urbanus* precedes as sole modifier, focus is *absent* only under special circumstances.[11]

Among the five authors showing AN~NA variation, Livy stands out—indeed, he towers over all the rest—by using both AN and NA placement of *urbanus* with ten of the fifteen nouns occurring twice or more with *urbanus* (above all with *legiones*). In comparison, variation in Cicero (with four of the ten recurring head nouns) seems positively restrained. More like Livy, in fact, is Tacitus, who attests AN and NA placement with only two of his six recurring heads, *cohors* and *miles* (cf. Livy's *legiones*), but so generates fourteen of his thirty attributive *urbanus* contexts.

16.3 Attributive adjective placement in Latin

On a prominent, if controversial, traditional typological view, Latin is held to have shifted in early or prehistoric times from AN to NA as part of the more general shift from 'head-last' to 'head-first' word order between Indo-European and Romance.[12] Some scholars, however, believe that Latin is neither AN nor NA, rather that adjective placement depends on the type of adjective and the pragmatics of the particular context,[13] or even that Latin has 'free' (at most, pragmatically determined) word order, including a free use of hyperbaton (disjunction, discontinuous structures).[14] It is generally and rightly doubted

give new, strongly stated, or perhaps surprising information (e.g. he was an *extremely witty* man), or—as most frequently in the contexts considered in this paper—it may be set in contrast (e.g. not only Italy but also *Rome*; like the country, so *the city*; wartime achievements are great, those of *peacetime* greater). By syntagmatic contrast, I mean with respect to a word or meaning present in the context, by paradigmatic, I mean with respect to complementary or antonymous words or meanings absent from, but implicit in, the context; cf. Langslow (2000: 249). On focus and other pragmatic functions, especially in the tradition of Dik (1978) and the 'Amsterdam School', see further Pinkster (1990: 4, 176–9) and Spevak (2010*a*: ch. 2).

[11] See Löfstedt (1961: 21–4) on the importance of the failure of the converse.

[12] This is supposed most importantly for the movement of the verb from after to before its direct object (O[bject]V[erb], AN [PIE, early Latin] → VO, NA [later Latin, Romance]). The classic piece within this framework for Latin is Adams (1976); cf. Pinkster (1990: 187–8) and Spevak (2010*b*: 25–6), both with further references. The correlation between AN/NA and OV/VO was challenged by Dryer (1988) on the basis of generalizations about a large number of languages.

[13] So, for example, Devine and Stephens (2006: 403): '[S]ome adjectives are mostly premodifiers (AN) and others mostly postmodifiers (NA), and others more evenly distributed between the two; but the precise factors that condition this variation are not immediately obvious.' For a recent review of classifications of adjectives in this sense and their placement, see Spevak (2010*b*: 26–34).

[14] Cf. the question, in more recent typological work, whether Latin is a 'non-configurational' language (i.e. without any fixed positions for syntactic constituents such as subject, verb, object,

whether Latin word order is genuinely free,[15] and whether hyperbaton is unconstrained and meaningless. However, whether one believes in a basic order for all adjectives,[16] or a basic NA order for some and a basic AN order for others,[17] the existence for a given adjective of both NA and AN structures, with and without hyperbaton, (again, from the earliest Latin and still in Romance) has obliged those researching this aspect of Latin word order to concentrate (a) on the meaning or function or type of A in NA and AN, and (b) on factors accounting for the occurrence of AN, NA, or alternation between them (whether for a given adjective or a given noun, or in a given period or author).

A familiar and influential systematic attempt to distinguish between prenominal and postnominal adjective placement is semantic, and goes back to Marouzeau (1922: 14–15, 1953: 1), whose work, in spite of criticism in some quarters of his approach and conclusions, still furnishes a clear and convenient starting point on this topic.[18] According to Marouzeau (and many since, with a

attributive adjective), against the criteria set out in Hale (1983). On this, see Ledgeway (2011: esp. 391, and forthcoming: esp. chs 3–5), advancing a non-configurational view of Latin.

[15] Cf. already Marouzeau (1922: 1): 'generally two different orders are not synonymous'. See especially Adams (1976: 99) and Vincent (1988: 60). Of course, if word order is pragmatically rather than grammatically determined, 'free' remains a thoroughly inappropriate label.

[16] For a basic NA order already in early Latin, see more recently (e.g.) Pinkster (1990: 185), Bauer (1995: 65–7), Clackson and Horrocks (2007: 28), and Spevak (2010*a*: 225), and, for Romance, Radatz (2001: 82) and Vincent (2007: especially 66–7), all with further references. On the other hand, Gildersleeve and Lodge (1895: 431) state that in early Latin the basic order is still AN, but by the classical period NA is more usual; for Kühner and Stegmann (1912–14: ii. 605) AN is the basic order still in classical Latin. In recent and current generative analyses, AN is the underlying order and N may or may not be 'raised' to the left in response to the meaning of A or N, or the pragmatics of the context; for a recent clear statement, see Giusti and Oniga (2006), including a good history of the question. I owe this observation and reference to Adam Ledgeway.

[17] An important recent example of this post-Marouzeau'ian approach is de Sutter (1986), who shows that in Cato's *On Agriculture* the placement of an adjective before or after its noun appears to depend on the semantic category of the adjective. Adjectives denoting the purpose or destination of the noun are almost invariably postposed, while those denoting an evaluation or dimension of the noun show a (weaker, NB!) tendency to precede.

[18] Among prominent critics of Marouzeau is Neubourg (1977, 1978), who replaces Marouzeau's 'rules' operating on 'categories' of adjective with a working hypothesis of 'a fundamental freedom' in the placement of the adjective, which is then determined in individual cases by analogy with pre-existing noun phrases. This is not the place to review Neubourg's criticisms and proposals, but it is pertinent here to observe the common ground that even he admits with Marouzeau in 'l'importance du moment déterminatif dans la signification d'un adjectif tel que *Romanus* pour expliquer sa place normale après le substantif, et l'importance de la mise en relief pour en expliquer l'inversion occasionnelle' (1977: 401). Among important recent studies, Marouzeau is taken, albeit with criticism and qualification, as a convenient point of departure by Lisón Huguet (2001: ch. 2), Giusti and Oniga (2006), Vincent (2007: 64), and Spevak (2010*a*: 224). The influence of Marouzeau, even in the work of those fundamentally critical of him, emerges clearly in the lucid review of the scholarship of the last thirty years by Spevak (2010*b*: 28, 31, 32).

bewildering variety of terminology[19] among them), an attributive adjective after its noun serves a determining or 'distinguishing' function ('discriminatif'), while an adjective in 'qualifying' function ('qualificatif') regularly precedes.[20] This is where the example in the title enters the scholarship. The urban praetor, whose lot (*sors*) or province (*prouincia*) or jurisdiction (*iurisdictio*) is the administration of the law in Rome in cases between Roman citizens, is regularly *praetor urbanus*, the adjective following since it has the determining function of denoting one of the praetors in particular. The adjective is an essential part of the designation of this magistrate. It is objective, in that its correctness is not a matter of opinion (John either is or is not the urban praetor).[21] By contrast, an urbane, cultivated, witty praetor is held, by Marouzeau's rule, to be regularly *urbanus praetor*. Here the adjective is said to precede since it expresses a descriptive, evaluative qualification of the praetor. It is not part of the praetor's designation. It is in a sense an optional comment, and a subjective one, and the adjective is scalar, in that opinions concerning the praetor's urbanity may differ; he may be thought quite urbane or very urbane (*urbanior praetor*, *urbanissimus praetor*).[22]

A subsidiary, morphosyntactic regularity commonly stated for Latin is that a participle in attributive adjectival function follows its noun.[23] This is held to apply even in qualifying function, i.e. not only to e.g. *praetor designatus* 'the praetor elect (for the coming year)', where we expect *designatus* to follow anyway as objective determiner of *praetor*, but also to e.g. *praetor doctus* 'a learned praetor' in a context where *doctus* expresses a subjective evaluation and by Marouzeau's rule above would be expected, or at least licensed, to precede. Similarly, AN ordering is said to be blocked in Latin by the prosodic rule that

[19] And, it must be said, a certain amount of confusion. So (e.g.) Lehmann's (1991: 223) characterization of prenominal position as being for 'inherent or essential' specification makes it sound dangerously close to many characterizations of the postnominal position. For the various terms used to characterize prenominal and postnominal adjectives, see the admirable table, covering both Romance and Latin philology, from Gröber's *Grundriß* to Devine and Stephens (2006), in Vincent (2007: 58).

[20] 'Objektiv bestimmende (intellektuell-sachliche) Adj. stehen habituell nach (*ius civile* wie *ius civium*, *populus Romanus*, *navis longa*), qualifizierende (affektische) treten unter der Wirkung der Betonung voran (Qualitätsadj. wie *bonus*, *pulcher*, Intensitätsbezeichnungen wie *magnus*, *summus*, *ingens* u. ä.)' (Hofmann and Szantyr 1965: 406). More recently, in different terminology: 'the different modes of semantic composition correlate in Latin with different linear orders. Extensional modification prefers the postnominal adjective; intensional, relational and descriptive modification prefers the prenominal adjective' (Devine and Stephens 2006: 481–2).

[21] In Bolinger's (1967: 14–20) terms, it is 'reference-modifying'. Further, it is fixed, rather than scalar, in that the praetor cannot be more or less *urbanus* in this sense.

[22] In Bolinger's (1967: 20–3) terms, it is 'referent-modifying'. Strictly, it is ambiguous between the intersective (or absolute) interpretation (John is an urbane man and a praetor) and the synthetic interpretation (John qua praetor is urbane).

[23] Cf. (e.g.) Marouzeau (1922: 119–23), de Sutter (1986: 165–6).

with a monosyllabic noun the adjective will follow, again whether its semantic function is qualifying or determining. Hence, *res* 'affairs' is held to precede its adjective not only in *res urbanae* 'city affairs, matters in Rome' (where *urbanae* is objective, determining) but also in *res horrificae* '(some) horrific things' (where the adjective is subjectively describing rather than objectively identifying the things).[24]

Given these ground rules for interpreting AN and NA structures and, conversely, for predicting the regular placement of an attributive adjective in a given semantic function, instances of irregular, unexpected placement (AN for NA, and NA for AN) may be explained with reference to pragmatic or syntactic features of the context.[25] In the first place, and most frequently by far, focus on a determining adjective is held to cause it to be preposed.[26] In (1), for example, *urbanis* 'civil' precedes *rebus* as it is in immediate opposition (as very often: cf. section 16.4.2.2 below) with a word meaning 'military'. This, then, is an instance of a pragmatic determinant of word order.

(1) sunt . . . qui **urbanis rebus** <u>bellicas</u> anteponant. (Cic. *Off.* 1. 82)
'There are those . . . who put military affairs before civil.'

Secondly, for an example of a supposed syntactic factor at work, the less usual placement is held to be common if either the head or its modifier is not simple but comprises two or more elements. So, for example, an attribute comprising two coordinated adjectives is held normally to follow its head,[27] as in the sarcastic apposition in (2), where *urbanus* has the subjective, evaluative meaning 'civilized, cultured, witty' which is held by Marouzeau to license its anteposition, at any rate when it is the sole modifier.

[24] 'Einsilbige Subst. sind zu lautschwach, um einen vollen Schluß zu bilden; daher steht in solchen Fällen das Adj. auch gegen die Regel nach, z.B. *vis nefaria, di immortales, vir peritissimus*' (Hofmann and Szantyr 1965: 406); cf. already Kühner and Stegmann (1912–14: ii. 605). On the variable placement of monosyllables, however, see Pinkster (1990: 185, 285 n. 37). Devine and Stephens (2006: 416) speak of 'nouns with impoverished semantics' rather than of monosyllables, which is, of course, quite a different matter. The question is beyond the scope of this essay, but, at least with *urbanus*, *res* in both disyllabic and monosyllabic forms appears to behave like any other head (cf. (13), (20c), (21a), and section 16.5 below).

[25] This is not at all to question the value of studies which set out the evidence with statistics and state tendencies rather than attempting to explain departures from a basic order. A recent example, distinguished by the comprehensiveness and clarity of its presentation of *all* relevant examples, is de Melo (2010).

[26] 'So tritt das determinierende Adj. regelmäßig voran, wenn es betont ist . . . ; doch ist zu beachten, daß gewisse bestimmende Adj. in guter Prosa überhaupt nicht . . . oder nur in veränderter Bedeutung (*urbanus praetor* "der geistreiche Praetor") vorangestellt werden können' (Hofmann and Szantyr 1965: 406, with (silent) reference to Marouzeau 1922: 14).

[27] 'Ferner wird ein mehrgliedriges Attribut meist nachgestellt; erst in nachklass. Zeit ist Voranstellung des erweiterten Attributes nicht selten' (Hofmann and Szantyr 1965: 406–7).

(2) ...cum iste atque istius amici, **homines** lauti et **urbani**, sermones eius modi dissipassent,... (Cic. *Verr.* 2. 1. 17)
'...when he and his friends, fellows of taste and sophistication, had spread stories of this kind,...'

Thirdly, hyperbaton (discontinuity, disjunction) may complicate the picture, often in tandem with explicit pragmatic focus or contrast, or with the syntactic context of a complex modifier/head, or with both. In (3), the NA order of *otium urbanum* is preserved, but both *quidem* and *et... et* signal focus on, respectively, the experiencer of the loss of confidence (*ego*) and the things he fears for, the city and leisure within it. The hyperbaton (over *diffiderem*) appears to set in focus the *otium* of *otium urbanum*, in conjunction with *urbs*, and perhaps in contrast with *illud malum urbanum*, the cause of the despondency.

(3) manabat enim illud malum urbanum et ita corroborabatur cottidie ut ego quidem **et urbi et otio** diffiderem **urbano.** (Cic. *Fam.* 12. 1. 1)
'For that mischief in the city was spreading and strengthening every day so that I for my part was starting to despair for the city and for public order within it.'

In (4), on the other hand, *res* has two modifiers (*multae... urbanae*), there is an explicit contrast in the context (comparative + *quam*), and the hyperbaton (over *exstiterunt*) appears to highlight not merely the antithesis between *urbanae* and *bellicae* but the whole phrase *multae res urbanae* as standing in contrast with (*res*) *bellicae*.[28]

(4) uere autem si uolumus iudicare, **multae res** exstiterunt **urbanae** maiores clarioresque quam bellicae. (Cic. *Off.* 1. 74)
'But if we are willing to judge truly, there have been many instances of civic achievements greater and more famous than those in war.'

16.4 The placement of attributive *urbanus* in the corpus

16.4.1 The placement after the noun

How far and how plausibly do the 'rules' sketched in the preceding section account for the 310 instances of attributive *urbanus* in the corpus? Marouzeau's hypothesis that the basic, regular placement for the adjective in determining function is after its noun predicts that we shall find many instances of N *urbanus* in its literal meaning, especially when it is without focus or when *urbanus* is one

[28] Cf., four lines earlier, *multi enim bella saepe quaesiuerunt* 'for many men have often sought war'.

of multiple modifiers, but in principle, if NA is the default order, even under one or both of the latter conditions.

Some figures are summarized in Table 16.3. At this stage, I am considering only contiguous NA phrases in which *urbanus* is the sole modifier (cf. the NA column in Table 16.2, without MM.)[29] Table 16.3 reports both types (i.e. different head nouns) and number of occurrences of *urbanus*.

Table 16.3 Attributive *urbanus* postposed (*head nouns* (*occurrences*)): without focus, in the neighbourhood of focus, and bearing focus

urbanus after its noun (NA)	NA without focus	Focus elsewhere in context	NA with focus
Varro	2 (3)	(1)	–
Cicero	9 (30)	1 (2)	9 (14)
Caesar	–	–	(1)
Sallust	(1)	–	(1)
Livy	5 (30)	2 (5)	8 (15)
Seneca E.	–	–	(1)
Valerius Max.	2 (5)	–	–
(Seneca Y.)	–	–	–
Pliny E.	2 (2)	(1)	–
(Columella)	–	–	–
Tacitus	3 (5)	(1)	1 (2)
Pliny Y.	–	–	2 (2)
Suetonius	6 (6)	–	(1)

The absolute figures are dominated, of course, by Cicero (46/95)[30] and Livy (50/110),[31] but these two hold their own also in percentage terms (each about

[29] I am also omitting for the moment the few contexts where the text is in doubt (Var. *Ling.* 5. 143, Liv. 9. 46. 11, Col. 5. 1. 6).

[30] No focus: *res*: *Fam.* 2. 12. 1, 3. 8. 9, 8. 2. 2, 10. 28. 3, 12. 23. 2; *praetor*: *Verr.* 1. 1. 39, 2. 1. 127, 2. 5. 34, *Clu.* 91, 121, *Agr.* 2. 93, *Dom.* 137, *Balb.* 55, *Phil.* 10. 7, 14. 37, *De or.* 1. 168, *Fam.* 10. 12. 3, *Q Fr.* 2. 1. 2; *quaestor*: *Verr.* 2. 1. 11, *Lig.* 35, *Phil.* 9. 16, 14. 38, *Fam.* 2. 17. 4, *Att.* 2. 6. 2; *plebes*: *Att.* 7. 7. 6; *plebecula*: *Att.* 16. 8. 2; *edictum*: *Att.* 6. 1. 15; *praetura*: *Verr.* 1. 1. 12; *acta*: *Att.* 6. 2. 6; *populus*: *Att.* 7. 13a. 3. Focus elsewhere: *res*: *Fam.* 8. 11. 4, 11. 10. 2. With focus: *res*: *Phil.* 12. 24, *Off.* 1. 84, *Fam.* 2. 17. 1, 7. 32. 3, *Att.* 6. 1. 24; *praetor*: *Cat.* 1. 32; *quaestor*: *Verr.* 2. 3. 123, *Off.* 2. 29; *quaestura*: *Verr.* 2. 1. 34; *commoratio*: *Fam.* 9. 15. 3; *consilium*: *Off.* 1. 76; *familia*: *Fam.* 14. 7. 3; *ius*: *Verr.* 1. 1. 2; *uectigalia*: *Off.* 2. 89.

[31] No focus: *legiones*: 6. 9. 5, 23. 25. 10, 34. 56. 9; *praetor*: 25. 7. 5, 26. 3. 10, 26. 10. 2, 27. 4. 4, 27. 22. 12, 27. 23. 7, 27. 33. 8, 28. 46. 6, 31. 4. 2, 32. 26. 8, 32. 31. 6, 34. 53. 2, 34. 57. 3, 35. 24. 8, 38. 42. 7, 39. 18. 8, 39. 23. 4, 40. 29. 9, 42. 4. 4, 43. 16. 11; *quaestor*: 33. 42. 2, 38. 58. 2, 39. 7. 5, 39. 19. 4, 42. 6. 11; *exercitus*: 27. 3. 9; *seditio*: 4. 35. 2. Focus elsewhere: *praetor*: 27. 23. 5; *iurisdictio*: 25. 41. 13, 27. 36. 11, 30. 1. 9, 40. 1. 1. With focus: *praetor*: 22. 33. 8, 23. 32. 18, 24. 44. 2, 34. 53. 5, 38. 54. 4, 40. 28. 10, 42. 6. 11; *exercitus*: 27. 43. 9; *res*: 3. 60. 1; *otium*: 44. 22. 14; *plebs*: 45. 35. 9, 45. 38. 1; *sors*: 30. 40. 5; *frequentia*: 5. 11. 9; *negotia*: 1. 55. 1.

50%—and their figures in each column are remarkably similar). For the other authors, the numbers are small, but only Valerius Maximus exceeds 50% (5/9);[32] Varro has 4/9,[33] Suetonius 7/16,[34] Tacitus 8/30.[35] NA *urbanus* is absent from Seneca the Younger and Columella, and occurs no more than three times in Caesar, Sallust, Seneca the Elder, Pliny the Elder, and Pliny the Younger.[36] I give all the references, even at the cost of some forbidding footnotes, so that my judgements of individual contexts may be checked. The middle and right-hand columns are of more interest than the first, which simply reports those contexts where I detect no plausible focus on the NA phrase. The presence of contrast elsewhere in the context is well illustrated in the example from Varro in (5).

(5) ...alia de causa hic magistratus non potest **exercitum urbanum** conuocare; censor, consul, dictator, interrex potest,... (Var. *Ling.* 6. 93)
'...for any other reason this magistrate (*i.e. the praetor*) cannot call together the city army; the censor, the consul, the dictator, the interrex can,...'

Clearly, the main contrast (leaving aside *alia*) is between *hic magistratus* (i.e. the praetor) *non potest* and *censor, consul, dictator, interrex potest*, and the city army appears in the predicted default NA order, *exercitus urbanus*. More tentatively, I suggest this interpretation of those four of the ten sentences in Livy (as in (6), for example) detailing the provinces of the praetors in which the city jurisdiction (i.e. that of the urban praetor) is NA *iurisdictio urbana*, and the focus seems to be on the magistrates rather than their assignments. In other cases, the name of the praetor comes first as topical (given) information, before the provinces including *urbana iurisdictio*, with, I suggest, contrastively preposed *urbana* (section 16.4.2.2 below). In (6), the provinces constitute the topic, and the focus is on the praetors, the new incumbents. It is notable that NA *iurisdictio urbana* precedes the praetor's name only twice (in (6) and at 30. 1. 9), both times at the start of a book, the elections having been reported some paragraphs before, at the end of the preceding book (29. 38. 4, 39. 56. 5).[37]

[32] No focus: *praetor*: 1. 1. 12, 3. 5. 2, 7. 7. 7, 9. 7. 4; *quaestor*: 2. 8. 1.

[33] No focus: *praetor*: *Ling.* 6. 54, *Vita populi Romani* 3. 94 Riposati; *praedium*: *Ling.* 5. 27. 2. Focus elsewhere: *exercitus*: *Ling.* 6. 93.

[34] No focus: *res*: *Iul.* 76. 2; *quaestor*: *Aug.* 36. 1; *cohors*: *Claud.* 10. 3; *tribus*: *Ner.* 44. 1; *praetura*: *Dom.* 1. 3; *adulescens*: *Gram.* 25. With focus: *cohors*: *Aug.* 101. 2.

[35] No focus: *praetor*: *Hist.* 1. 47, *Hist.* 4. 39, *Ann.* 6. 12; *miles*: *Hist.* 1. 5; *uulgus*: *Hist.* 3. 80. Focus elsewhere: *cohors*: *Hist.* 3. 64. With focus: *res*: *Hist.* 1. 90, *Ann.* 1. 16.

[36] No focus: *seruitium*: Sall. *Cat.* 24. 4; *praetor*: Plin. *HN* 10. 41; *plebs*: Plin. *HN* 6. 122. Focus elsewhere: *plebs*: Plin. *HN* 19. 59. With focus: *praetor*: Caes. *B Civ.* 3. 20. 1, Sen. *Controv.* 3. pr. 17; *negotium*: Sall. *Hist.* 2. 2. 3; *res*: Plin. *Ep.* 2. 11. 25; *opus*: Plin. *Ep.* 5. 6. 35.

[37] Everywhere else (and in the synonymous phrases with *prouincia* and *sors*) the praetor's name comes first, followed on the first two occurrences (25. 41. 13, 27. 36. 11) by NA *iurisdictio urbana*

(6) ...consules praetoresque sortiti prouincias sunt.... **iurisdictio urbana** M. Ogulnio Gallo, inter peregrinos M. Valerio euenit; Hispaniarum Q. Fuluio Flacco citerior, P. Manlio ulterior,... (Liv. 40. 1. 1)
'...the consuls and the praetors drew lots for their provinces.... The city jurisdiction fell to M. Ogulnius Gallus, that between citizens and aliens to M. Valerius; of the Spains, Q. Fulvius Flaccus drew Hither, P. Manlius Further,...'

Alternatively (but, I think, less probably), *iurisdictio urbana* in (6) and the other passages like it may be in emphatic contrast and belong in the right-hand column of Table 16.2 with the (to my mind) clear examples of NA phrases in focus or antithesis, to which I now turn.

Perhaps unsurprisingly, *urbanus* remains resolutely after (e.g.) *praetura, praetor, exercitus, ius* even in strongly contrastive contexts such as (7)–(10).

(7) ...in quaestura et legatione Asiatica et **praetura urbana** et praetura Siciliensi. (Cic. *Verr.* 2. 1. 34)
'...in the quaestorship, and the legateship in Asia, and the urban praetorship, and the praetorship in Sicily.'

(8a) ...M. Caelius Rufus praetor causa debitorum suscepta initio magistratus tribunal suum iuxta C. Treboni **praetoris urbani** sellam conlocauit... (Caes. *B Civ.* 3. 20. 1)
'...the praetor M. Caelius Rufus took up the cause of the debtors and at the start of his magistracy placed his tribunal next to the chair of C. Trebonius, the urban praetor...'

(8b) M. Aemilius praetor cuius peregrina sors erat, iurisdictione M. Atilio collegae **praetori urbano** mandata, Luceriam prouinciam haberet... (Liv. 24. 44. 2)
'M. Aemilius, the praetor allotted responsibility for cases involving aliens, was to assign his judicial function to his colleague M. Atilius, the urban praetor, and to have Luceria as his province...'

(8c) deinde ad alterum praetorem eduxi et ingrati postulaui. iam apud **praetorem urbanum** curatorem ei petebam. (Sen. *Controv.* 3. pr. 17)
'Next I haled him off to a second praetor and accused him of ingratitude. Finally, before the urban praetor, I requested a guardian for him.'

---

and subsequently (5×) by AN *urbana iurisdictio*. On 40. 1. 1 *sortiti... sunt* and *Hispaniarum... citerior*, see Briscoe (2008: 412–13).

(9) ... ut cum in Umbria se occursurum Hasdrubal fratri scribat legionem a Capua Romam arcessant, dilectum Romae habeant, **exercitum urbanum** ad Narniam hosti opponant. (Liv. 27. 43. 9)
'... that, since Hasdrubal was writing to his brother that he would meet him in Umbria, they should summon a legion from Capua to Rome, conduct a levy in Rome, and confront the enemy at Narnia with the city army.'

(10) ... depeculatorem aerari, uexatorem Asiae atque Pamphyliae, praedonem **iuris urbani**, labem atque perniciem prouinciae Siciliae. (Cic. *Verr.* 1. 1. 2).
'... plunderer of the treasury, ravager of Asia and Pamphylia, pirate in his city jurisdiction, a ruin and pestilence in his province of Sicily.'

In other cases, such as (11), a deliberate parallelism, morphological in (11a) (*-iónis -ánae ... -iónis -ánae*), syntactic in (11b) (FARM-ARPINUM ... STAFF-ROME), may tend against the preposing of *urbanus*.

(11a) ... altera epistula purgas te non dissuasorem mihi emptionis Neapolitanae fuisse sed auctorem **commorationis urbanae**, ... (Cic. *Fam.* 9. 15. 3)
'... in your second letter, you excuse yourself. You say you were not dissuading me from buying in Naples but prompting me to spend time in the city, ...'

(11b) deinde, si tibi [Terentia] uidebitur, uillis iis utere quae longissime aberunt a militibus. fundo Arpinati bene poteris uti cum **familia urbana** si annona carior fuerit. (Cic. *Fam.* 14. 7. 3)
'Secondly, if you agree, please use the country houses which will be furthest from military units. You can conveniently occupy the farm at Arpinum with the servants we have in the city, if food prices go up.'

Sometimes, however, as in (12), a semantic contrast often associated (cf. section 16.4.2.2 below) with preposed *urbanus*—here, civil vs. military—is conveyed in an NA phrase, even one that is not a lexicalized technical term.

(12a) sed tamen id ipsum est gestum **consilio urbano** sine exercitu.[38] (Cic. *Off.* 1. 76)
'But it was, for all that, executed as a political measure without the help of an army.'

(12b) sed inter labores militiae interque proelia uictorias imperium statui admonendum te de **negotiis urbanis**. (Sall. *Hist.* 2. 2 [Letter to Caesar])
'But in the midst of the toils of war and amid the battles, victories, and military command, I have decided that you should be reminded of business in the city.'

[38] Or should *consilio urbano sine exercitu* be regarded as a single noun phrase with multiple modification?

(12c) si quem id facere piget <et> **otium urbanum** militiae laboribus praeoptat, e terra ne gubernauerit. (Liv. 44. 22. 14)
'If anyone is reluctant to do this and prefers the leisure of the city to the toils of campaigning, let him not take passage.'

Similarly, in (13a), in spite of standing in clear contrast (strengthened by *etiam*) with military affairs, *urbanae* follows *res* in Cicero, as it does in Tacitus (13b) in contrast with, respectively, *militiae* and *Pannonica*, and in Pliny (13c) in contrast with *rustica*; only in the last, however, is it monosyllabic (cf. sections 16.3 above and 16.4.2.2 below).

(13a) Cleombrotus . . . temere cum Epaminonda conflixit . . . quod genus peccandi uitandum est etiam **in rebus urbanis**. (Cic. *Off.* 1. 84)
'Cleombrotus went recklessly into battle against Epaminondas . . . This sort of offence is to be avoided also in civil affairs.'

(13b) . . . quando, ut in consiliis militiae Suetonio Paulino et Mario Celso, ita in **rebus urbanis** Galeri Trachali ingenio Othonem uti credebatur; (Tac. *Hist.* 1. 90)
'. . . when it was believed that, just as he used Suetonius Paulinus and Marius Celsus in military planning, so Otho used the ability of Galerius Trachalus in civil matters;'

hic **rerum urbanarum** status erat, cum Pannonicas legiones seditio incessit, nullis nouis causis. (Tac. *Ann.* 1. 16)
'This was the state of affairs in the city when mutiny broke out in the Pannonian legions, with no new causes.'

(13c) habes **res urbanas**; inuicem rusticas scribe. (Plin. *Ep.* 2. 11. 25)
'You have the state of affairs in the city; in return, write of those in the country.'

On five (possibly six) occasions, the focus of an NA phrase is amplified by hyperbaton (cf. (3) and (4) above, and (43) in section 16.4.4 below). And finally, in three passages the text is in doubt. All three, if sound,[39] show *urbanus* after the noun, and one of them has *urbanus* in focus, in the explicit urban vs. rural contrast (cf. section 16.4.2.2 below).[40]

[39] At Var. *Ling.* 5. 143 *auspicia urbana*, if sound, is not in focus. At Liv. 9. 46. 11, where I incline to accept the arguments in defence of the tradition by Oakley (2005: 631–4), *opes urbanas* is more topic than focus.

[40] Col. 5. 1. 6: *at Galli candetum appellant in* ***areis urbanis*** *spatium centum pedum, in agrestibus autem pedum CL, quod aratores candetum nominant.* 'But the Gauls use the term *candetum* in urban districts for areas of 100 feet (square), in rural districts for areas of 150 feet (square), which is what ploughmen call a *candetum*.'

16.4.2 *Preposed* urbanus

16.4.2.1 *urbanus* 'urbane, cultivated, witty'

I turn now to instances of *urbanus* before its noun, beginning with the metaphorical sense 'urbane, cultivated, witty', in which anteposition of the adjective is traditionally held to be normal and expected. The shaking thing here, I think (cf. section 16.1.1 above), is that preposed attributive *urbanus* meaning 'urbane' is so very rare in this prose corpus. I have noted only seven secure examples, and all seven have *urbanus* in focus.[41] Two of the seven contexts, (14)–(15), show just the sort of contrast that is so commonly associated with preposed *urbanus* in its relational, non-metaphorical senses (section 16.4.2.2 below), and in the others focus and contrast or parallelism are highlighted by other means, including discontinuity as in (16) (see section 16.4.4 below).[42]

(14) genus est perelegans et cum grauitate salsum cumque oratoriis dictionibus tum **urbanis sermonibus** accommodatum. (Cic. *De or.* 2. 270)
'The style is very elegant, combining humour with austerity, and suited to both public speaking and urbane conversation.'

(15) iam illa non solum fortis, sed etiam **urbana libertas**. (Val. Max. 6. 2 ext. 2)
'Now the following liberty was not only brave but also witty.'

(16) tam **urbana** crapulae **excusatio** tamque simplex ueritatis confessio iram regis conuertit in risum. (Val. Max. 5. 1. ext. 3a)
'Such a witty excuse of intoxication and such a guileless confession of the truth turned the king's anger to laughter.'

Not only, then, is Marouzeau's type *urbanus praetor* in the sense 'urbane praetor' very rare and always emphatic, at least in prose down to Suetonius: as we are about to see, even in its technical, out-and-out determining senses *urbanus* is frequently preposed.

[41] Cic. *Verr.* 2. 1. 17, *Dom.* 92, *De or.* 2. 271; Sen. *Controv.* 9. 4. 17, 9. 4. 19; Val. Max. 5. 1 ext. 3, 6. 2 ext. 2. The metaphorical meaning 'urbane' is much commoner when *urbanus* is predicative, and underlies every instance (or very nearly so) of the adverb *urbane* and the derived noun *urbanitas*. With regard to the latter point, Adam Ledgeway observes that in Romance one would expect only the literal meaning to be available in predicative use, and infers for Latin that the licensing of the meaning of *urbanus* is not determined by its placement (which is just what I conclude from my *urbanus* corpus).

[42] Note the superlative and the *ut* clause and the imminent contrast between *eloquentia* and *urbanitas* in Sen. *Controv.* 9. 4. 17 *erat autem* ***urbanissimus homo****, ut uobis saepe narraui, ut quidquid in eloquentia illi deerat urbanitate pensaret* 'But he was a very witty man, as I have often told you, and so made up by his wit for any deficiency in his eloquence.'

16.4.2.2 Preposed *urbanus* in focus or contrast

To begin with the praetors' *prouinciae*: in Livy the three cases of (pragmatically neutral?) *iurisdictio urbana* (cf. (6) above) alternate with nine contexts, as in (17), in which *urbana* in the same relational and technical sense is preposed.[43]

(17a) Tuberoni **urbana iurisdictio**, Quinctio peregrina euenit, Numisio Sicilia, Mummio Sardinia. (Liv. 41. 8. 2)
'To Tubero fell the urban jurisdiction, to Quinctius that involving aliens, to Numisius Sicily, to Mummius Sardinia.'

Philo Romae iuri dicundo **urbana sors**, Pomponio inter ciues Romanos et peregrinos euenit. (Liv. 22. 35. 5)
'For administering justice in Rome, to Philus fell the urban lot, to Pomponius that involving cases between Roman citizens and aliens.'

(17b) comitiis praetorum perfectis senatus consultum factum, ut Q. Fuluio extra ordinem **urbana prouincia** esset isque potissimum consulibus ad bellum profectis urbi praeesset. (Liv. 24. 9. 5)
'The elections of the praetors having been completed, the senate decreed that Q. Fulvius should by special designation have the duties of city praetor and that he and no one else, once the consuls had departed on campaign, should be in charge of the city.'

In (17a), the praetors' names are repeated from immediately before, so they are clearly old information, and their assignments are new and, I suggest, Tubero's and Philus' have their antithesis marked by the preposing of *urbana*. In (17b), focus is bestowed on the *prouincia* by *extra ordinem*, and there is contrast in *ad bellum* with military affairs away from the city.

Indeed, military affairs yield, above all in Livy and Tacitus, one of the two major sets of instances where *urbanus* is clearly in contrast in its context and (therefore?) preposed. Of miscellaneous examples, illustrated in (18), I have counted six in Cicero,[44] eight in Livy,[45] three in Tacitus,[46] one each in Caesar and Valerius Maximus.[47]

[43] *iurisdictio*: 33. 26. 1, 34. 43. 6, 41. 8. 2, 42. 10. 14, 42. 31. 9; *sors*: 22. 35. 5; *prouincia*: 24. 9. 5, 40. 44. 6 (discontinuous), 45. 44. 2 (MM).

[44] *Div.* 2. 77, *Off.* 1. 82, *Att.* 9. 7b. 2 (Balbus), *Fam.* 10. 17. 2 (Plancus); *Mur.* 38 (MM), *Phil.* 14. 7 (discontinuous).

[45] 3. 50. 4, 3. 51. 8, 5. 12. 7, 9. 42. 4, 24. 9. 5, 30. 37. 9, 44. 34. 1 (in the last, John Briscoe points out to me, the polyptoton adds to the contrast); 10. 9. 11 (discontinuous).

[46] *Ann.* 1. 17, 1. 46, 2. 44.

[47] Caes. *B Gall.* 7. 1. 2, Val. Max. 2. 4. 1.

(18a) ...ipse sua concessit uoluntate ne in iis castris essem...sibique satis esse dixit si togatus **urbana officia** sibi praestitissem,... (Cic. *Att.* 9. 7b. 2 [Balbus])
'...he himself has allowed me of his own goodwill not to serve in those camps...and he told me that he would be content if I performed as a civilian functions in the city for him,...'

(18b) ...ne comitiorum militarium praerogatiuam **urbana comitia** iisdem tribunis plebis creandis sequerentur,... (Liv. 3. 51. 8)
'...to prevent the civil assemblies from following the lead of the military ones in electing the same men to be tribunes of the plebs,...'

(18c) simul iuuenem **urbano luxu** lasciuientem melius in castris haberi Tiberius seque tutiorem rebatur utroque filio legiones obtinente. (Tac. *Ann.* 2. 44)
'At the same time, Tiberius thought that the young man who was running riot in city luxury was better kept in camp, and that he himself was safer if each of his sons had a legion.'

In a further thirteen contexts, illustrated in (19), six in Livy,[48] seven in Tacitus,[49] a contrast is drawn between different parts of the Roman army, in Livy involving nearly always the city legions, in Tacitus the city cohorts or the city soldiery more generally.

(19a) P. Sempronio prouincia Ariminum, Cn. Fuluio Suessula cum binis item legionibus euenerunt, ut Fuluius **urbanas legiones** duceret. (Liv. 24. 44. 3)
'To P. Sempronius fell Ariminum as his province, to Cn. Fulvius Suessula, again each with two legions, so assigned that Fulvius should take with him the city legions.'

(19b) exauctorati per eos dies tribuni, e praetorio Antonius Taurus et Antonius Naso, ex **urbanis cohortibus** Aemilius Pacensis, e uigilibus Iulius Fronto. (Tac. *Hist.* 1. 20)
'During these days, tribunes were dismissed, Antonius Taurus and Antonius Naso from the praetorian cohorts, Aemilius Pacensis from the city cohorts, Julius Fronto from the police.'

(19c) postquam in conspectu Padus et nox adpetebat, uallari castra placuit. is labor **urbano militi** insolitus contundit animos. (Tac. *Hist.* 2. 19)
'When they came within sight of the Po and night was coming on, they decided to entrench camp. This labour, unfamiliar to the city soldiery, broke their spirit.'

48 *legiones*: 23. 31. 5, 24. 44. 3, 26. 28. 13, 35. 2. 4, 36. 1. 9. *exercitus*: 27. 7. 10.
49 *cohortes*: *Hist.* 1. 20, 1. 87. *miles*: *Hist.* 1. 4, 2. 19; *Hist.* 1. 14 (discontinuous). *militia*: *Hist.* 2. 21, 2. 94.

In (19c), the contrast is clearly between soldiers based in Rome, unused to such hard physical labour, and those serving elsewhere, but the geographical context brings us to the other major antithesis associated with preposed *urbanus*, that between the city of Rome and other parts: the region around the city, the rest of Italy, and, above all, the provinces. Cicero dominates here, with sixteen examples,[50] but this type, illustrated in (20), is widespread: five instances in Livy (all but one in Book 3),[51] four in Suetonius,[52] three in Tacitus,[53] and one each in Caesar, Sallust, Seneca the Younger, and Pliny the Younger.[54]

(20a) quid ego istius in iure dicundo libidinem et scelera demonstrem? quis uestrum non in **urbana iuris dictione** cognouit? (Cic. *Verr.* 2. 2. 39)
'Need I give you any proof of the criminal way in which this man administers the law as he chooses? Who of you did not see this in his administration of it in Rome (*i.e. before he came to Sicily*)?'

...Asiaticae iuris dictioni **urbana iuris dictio** respondebit;... (Cic. *Flac.* 100)
'...the administration of justice at Rome will respond to that in Asia;...'

(20b) ea si uenerit nec illi ante in meam prouinciam transierint, unum uereor ne senatus propter **urbanarum rerum** metum Pompeium nolit dimittere. (Cic. *Att.* 5. 18. 1)
'If it (winter) comes before they invade my province, my one fear is that the Senate, through anxiety over affairs in the city, will not be willing to send Pompey.'

clausula est difficilis in tradenda prouincia; sed haec deus aliquis gubernabit. de **urbanis rebus** scilicet plura tu scis. (Cic. *Att.* 6. 3. 4)
'The final section is difficult, in the handover of the province, but some god will guide things. Of city affairs of course you know more than I.'

(20c) sic res Romana in antiquum statum rediit, secundaeque belli res extemplo **urbanos motus** excitauerunt. (Liv. 3. 9. 2)
'Thus Roman affairs returned to their former pattern, and success in war immediately stirred up trouble in the city.'

[50] *Verr.* 2. 1. 112, 2. 2. 39, *Cat.* 4. 23, *Phil.* 7. 15, *Flac.* 100, *Flac.* Milan frg., *De or.* 1. 38, *Att.* 1. 1. 2, 5. 18. 1, 6. 3. 4, 11. 10. 2; with MM: *Cat.* 2. 6, 3. 9, *Mur.* 19; discontinuous: *Deiot.* 33, *Q Fr.* 1. 1. 43.

[51] 3. 9. 2, 3. 41. 8, 3. 65. 6, 3. 72. 7; 9. 19. 2 (discontinuous).

[52] *Iul.* 9. 3, *Aug.* 46. 1, *Otho* 1. 2, *Vit.* 5. 1.

[53] *Hist.* 1. 87, *Ann.* 13. 43, 14. 57.

[54] Caes. *B Gall.* 7. 6. 1; Sall. *Iug.* 63. 3; Sen. *Ep.* 19. 8; Plin. *Pan.* 70. 9.

his rebus in Italiam Caesari nuntiatis, cum iam ille **urbanas res** uirtute Cn. Pompei commodiorem in statum peruenisse intellegeret, in Transalpinam Galliam profectus est. (Caes. *B Gall.* 7. 6. 1)
'These matters having been reported to Caesar in Italy, since he understood that, thanks to the resoluteness of Pompey, matters in Rome had improved, he set out for Transalpine Gaul.'

(20d) is **urbanae militiae** impiger, bellorum insolens, ... (Tac. *Hist.* 1. 87)
'He had been active in his military service in the city, but had no experience of war, ...'

in prouincia singularem innocentiam praestitit biennio continuato, cum succedenti fratri legatus substitisset; at in **urbano officio** dona atque ornamenta templorum subripuisse et commutasse quaedam ferebatur. (Suet. *Vit.* 5. 1)
'In the province he showed exceptional integrity for two successive years, in the second serving as deputy to his brother his successor; in his city offices, however, he was said to have taken offerings and ornaments from the temples and to have debased some of them.'

One is spoilt for choice of good examples! In (20b, c) I have deliberately used three instances of AN *urbanae res* to illustrate emphatic preposing even here, even when, as in (20c), the noun is monosyllabic (cf. sections 16.3 and 16.4.1, and example (13) above).

AN *urbanae res* is found also (21a) in the third common opposition associated with preposed *urbanus*, namely that between urban and rural. Here the historians retire, and we find instead six examples in Columella,[55] three in Pliny the Younger,[56] two in Cicero,[57] and one each in Varro, Sallust, Valerius Maximus, and Pliny the Elder.[58]

(21a) ... ut nonis tantummodo diebus **urbanae res** agerentur, reliquis administrarentur rusticae. (Col. 1. pr. 18)
'... that city business should be transacted only on one day in every eight, country affairs on the other days.'

... ut nonis modo diebus **urbanas res** usurparent, reliquis septem ut rura colerent. (Var. *Rust.* 2. pr. 1)
'... that they attended to city affairs only on one day in every eight, and looked after the countryside on the other seven.'

[55] 1. pr. 18, 1. 1. 18, 1. 7. 3, 8. 11. 1, 8. 16. 2, 12. 46. 1. The last is in a three-way contrast, at medium-range but still perfectly clear (*illi enim* ~ *nobis tamen*; *urbanas mensas* ~ *rusticae simplicitati*; *lauta conuiuia* ~ *non magna impensa*).

[56] *Ep.* 7. 30. 2, 9. 15. 3; 9. 36. 6 (MM).

[57] *Verr.* 2. 3. 199, *Q Fr.* 3. 1. 6.

[58] Var. *Rust.* 2. pr. 1; Sall. *Cat.* 37. 7; Val. Max. 4. 8 ext. 2; Plin. *HN* 23. 166.

(21b) tu consuetudinem serua, nobisque sic rusticis **urbana acta** perscribe. (Plin. *Ep.* 9. 15. 3)
'Keep up your habit of writing in full of city affairs to me, rustic as I am.'

(21c) non enim debetis hoc cogitare: habet idem (scil. agricola, arator, *in the preceding argument*) in nummis, habet in **urbanis praediis**. (Cic. *Verr.* 2. 3. 199)
'For you must not reckon thus: this same man has the sum required in cash, or in city property.'

(21d) ... iuuentus, quae in agris manuum mercede inopiam tolerauerat, priuatis atque publicis largitionibus excita **urbanum otium** ingrato labori praetulerat. (Sall. *Cat.* 37. 7)
'... the young men, who had borne a wretched existence by manual labour in the country, aroused by private and public doles, had come to prefer city idleness to hateful toil.'

et hactenus habent se medicinae **urbanarum arborum**; transeamus ad siluestres. (Plin. *HN* 23. 166)
'So much for the medicines from trees of the cities; let us turn to those of the woods.'

The three contrasts we have glanced at (civil vs. military; the city of Rome vs. Italy, the provinces; urban vs. rural) account for all but four of the contexts of preposed *urbanus*, two in Cicero, one in Caesar, one in Sallust. In the last named (22), in the wider context there is a straightforward opposition between the whole populace and the urban populace, and the focus on *urbana* is strengthened with the particles *sed* and *uero*.

(22) ... cuncta plebes ... sed **urbana plebes**, ea uero praeceps erat de multis causis. (Sall. *Cat.* 37. 1–4)
'The whole body of the commons ... But the city populace in particular acted impetuously for many reasons.'

In Caesar (23), I suggest that *aetas*, *urbs*, and *adfinitas* are each in focus as the key element in the case made by each of the three competing candidates for the vacant priesthood.

(23) ... cum Lentulus aetatis honorem ostentaret, Domitius **urbanam gratiam dignitatemque** iactaret, Scipio adfinitate Pompei confideret. (Caes. *B Civ.* 3. 83. 1)
'... as Lentulus paraded the distinction due his *seniority*, Domitius vaunted his influence and his prestige in *Rome*, while Scipio relied on his *marriage ties* to Pompey.'

In the Cicero examples (24, 25), on the other hand, I cannot see a pragmatic justification for the preposed *urbanus*.

(24) . . . sic nostri animi negotiis forensibus atque **urbano opere** defessi gestiant ac uolitare cupiant uacui cura ac labore. (Cic. *De or.* 2. 23)
'. . . in the same way, our (human) minds, wearied by the business of the courts and city work, are restless and long to take wing free of care and exertion.'

(25) et nimirum id est quod ab hoc tribuno plebis dictum est in senatu, **urbanam plebem** nimium in re publica posse; . . . (Cic. *Agr.* 2. 70)
'And indeed this is what was said by this tribune of the plebs in the senate, that the urban plebs has too much influence in the state; . . .'

In (24), there is more a conjunction than an opposition between law court and city, and in (25) there is no natural stress on the *urbana plebs* audible in the reported words of the tribune. Both may be due rather to literary artifice.[59]

16.4.3 Multiple modification

The occurrence of attributive *urbanus* with at least one other modifier is frequent in Livy,[60] not uncommon in Cicero,[61] and rare or non-existent in the other eleven authors of the corpus; it never occurs in Caesar or Sallust, and occurs once in Varro,[62] twice each in Seneca the Elder, Pliny the Elder, Columella, Pliny the Younger, and Suetonius,[63] three times in Seneca the Younger,[64]

[59] In (24), tempting as it is to explain preposed *urbanus* with reference to the explicit urban-rural contrast (2. 22 *rus ex urbe*) more than seventy words earlier, the contrast is now between labour and leisure. In (24) the anteposition of *urbanus* creates a chiasmus (NA *atque* AN) framed with the words for labour (*negotiis . . . opere*). In (25) preposed *urbanus* creates an AN phrase *urbanam plebem* which matches prosodically the object of Cicero's attack at this point, the *tribunus plebis*, whose office it is to defend the *urbana plebes*, and who has so disgracefully slandered them.

[60] QAN: 4. 43. 4, 45. 15. 1, 45. 15. 5, 45. 44. 2; 'two city legions': 23. 14. 2, 24. 44. 6, 24. 44. 7, 25. 3. 7, 27. 8. 11, 28. 46. 13, 30. 41. 9, 31. 8. 11, 35. 2. 4, 37. 2. 6; QAxN: 34. 43. 9, 42. 35. 4; PrAN: 1. 53. 5, 22. 11. 9; PrxAN: 2. 48. 4; AAN: 7. 25. 8, 25. 5. 5, 27. 8. 12, 39. 40. 4; NQA: 6. 6. 15; NQARC: 34. 56. 4; NAA: 25. 3. 5, 45. 37. 8; QNA 'two city legions': 23. 25. 9, 23. 31. 3, 30. 2. 6, 33. 36. 2, 34. 56. 5; ANA: 3. 72. 7, 22. 10. 8, 27. 35. 12.

[61] QAN: *Mur.* 22; PrAN: *Cat.* 2. 6, 3. 8, *Mur.* 19, 38; PrxAN: *Att.* 1. 1. 2; QPrAAN: *Att.* 7. 3. 5; PrAAAN: *Pis.* 64; AAN: *De or.* 3. 139, *Orat.* 141, *Att.* 1. 17. 5, *Fam.* 9. 15. 2; NAA: *Verr.* 2. 1. 17 'witty', *Dom.* 92 'witty' (*Verr.* 2. 1. 20, *Planc.* 22; NxAA: *Phil.* 5. 20); QNA: *Phil.* 11. 11, *Fam.* 8. 1. 1; PrNA: *Fam.* 12. 1. 1; QNxA: *Off.* 1. 74.

[62] Var. *Rust.* 1. 13. 7.

[63] PrAN: Plin. *Ep.* 9. 36. 6; QAAN: Sen. *Controv.* 1. pr. 19; QPrAN: Sen. *Controv.* 9. 4. 19; AAN: Plin. *HN* 22. 76, Col. 1. 1. 18, 1. 8. 1, Suet. *Ner.* 30. 2; NAA: (Plin. *HN* 17. 219), Plin. *Ep.* 4. 11. 15 (*Ep.* 6. 28. 1); QNA: Suet. *Cal.* 13. 1.

[64] AAN: *Dial.* 9. 3. 4; NAA: *Dial.* 5. 29. 1 (*Ep.* 31. 10).

and five times in Tacitus.[65] I have made a simple, three-way distinction according to the position of the noun (after, before, or in the midst of the modifiers), and an even cruder two-way distinction among the modifiers between pronominals (demonstratives) and quantifiers (*omnis*, *plerique*, numerals) on the one hand, and other attributive adjectives on the other. The latter are nearly all coordinated with *urbanus*, i.e. not hierarchically distinct from it.[66] The numbers of contexts of these types that I have observed in the corpus are set out in Table 16.4.

Table 16.4 Patterns of multiple modifiers including *urbanu*s

MM	Q/Pr A N̲	A A N̲	N̲ Q A	N̲ A A	Q/Pr N̲ A	A N̲ A
Varro	–	–	–	1 NAAA	–	–
Cicero	5 + 1 *disc.* + 1 QPrAAN 1 PrAAAN	4	–	2 (2 + 1 *disc.*)	3 + 1 *disc.*	–
(Caesar)	–	–	–	–	–	–
(Sallust)	–	–	–	–	–	–
Livy	16 + 3 *disc.*	4	1 + 1 NQARC	2	5	3
Seneca E.	1 QAAN 1 QPrAN	–	–	–	–	–
Seneca Y.	–	1	–	1 (1)	–	–
Columella	–	2	–	–	–	–
Pliny E.	–	1	–	(1)	–	–
Tacitus	2	2	–	–	1	–
Pliny Y.	1	–	–	1 (1)	–	–
Suetonius	–	1	–	–	1	–
Totals	43 + 4 *disc.*		14 + 1 *disc.*		13 + 1 *disc.*	
After Livy	12		5		2	

Note: Q = quantifier or numeral; Pr = pronominal; RC = relative clause; *disc.* = instance of discontinuity/hyperbaton. Totals count together phrases with: N last; N first; N medial.

There are two points of interest here. First, in this (admittedly small) set of examples, a complex modifier (i.e. a series of two or more modifiers) is placed more frequently before than after its noun, even in the period after Livy

---

[65] QAN: *Hist.* 2. 93, *Ann.* 4. 5; AAN: *Hist.* 1. 74, 1. 89; QNA: *Hist.* 3. 69.
[66] The only full-fledged instance of 'nesting' or 'embedding' is at Var. *Rust.* 1. 13. 7 (see (30) below). There are three further cases in Livy (25. 5. 5 *nouae urbanae legiones*, 27. 8. 12 *urbanum ueterem exercitum*, 27. 35. 12 *nouis legionibus urbanis*), although 'new' and 'old' here are close in function to demonstrative pronouns. On different classes of modifiers, and on nesting/embedding vs. coordination of multiple modifiers, see Risselada (1984), Pinkster (1990: 73–5, 83–8), and Spevak (2010a: 229–37, 2010b: 27–30).

(cf. section 16.3 and n. 27 above).[67] This is even more starkly so if one excludes from the count of column 4 the figures in parentheses, which refer to complex postmodifiers such as those in (26) from Cicero and (27) from the early Empire.

(26) ... his criminibus, **his testibus(,) et urbanis et prouincialibus(,)** sic obrutus atque oppressus est ut ... (Cic. *Verr.* 2. 1. 20)
'... by these charges, by these witnesses(,) from both the city and the province(,) he was so crushed and overwhelmed that ...'

... uicinitas ... non erudita **artificio simulationis(,) uel suburbano uel etiam urbano.** (Cic. *Planc.* 22)
'... neighbourliness ... unschooled in that studied counterfeiting of emotion characteristic of the suburbs or even the city.'

(27) ... turba seruorum lecticam tuam **per itinera(,) urbana ac peregrina(,)** portantium: ... (Sen. *Ep.* 31. 10)
'... the crowd of slaves bearing your litter on your journeys(,) in the city and further afield: ...'

aliquando et pestilentia per genera, sicut inter homines nunc seruitia, **nunc plebes(,) urbana uel rustica.** (Plin. *HN* 17. 219)
'(Trees die) sometimes even through pestilence affecting only one type or another, as in human populations disease affects sometimes slaves, sometimes the common people(,) of town or countryside.'

tantum mihi **copiarum(,) qua urbanarum qua rusticarum(,)** nomine tuo oblatum est, ... (Plin. *Ep.* 6. 28. 1)
'Such a profusion of delicacies, from both town and country, has been offered to me in your name, ...'

These, far from determining the noun they follow, add optional information almost as an afterthought, in apposition or parenthesis as it were.[68] It is not even clear that they form a single phrase with the preceding noun—hence, the bracketed commas in (26) and (27). If, as I say, one excludes these, then the preposed complex modifiers dominate over the postposed overall by 43 : 9, and in the period after Livy by 12 : 2.

Secondly, broadly speaking, the variation in the pragmatic function of attributive *urbanus*, which (as we saw in sections 16.4.1 and 16.4.2 above) accords closely with its position after or before its noun, seems to hold even in the

[67] This is in keeping with the findings of Lisón Huguet (2001: ch. 4) in his corpus drawn from Cicero, Livy, and Seneca the Younger.

[68] Cf. Cic. *Phil.* 5. 20 *Hic pecunias uestras aestimabat; **possessiones** notabat(,) **et urbanas et rusticas*** 'This man was estimating your money, recording your properties, both urban and rural.' This, without the comma, would be an instance of hyperbaton (NxAA). I am in doubt.

presence of additional modifiers, whether quantifiers/pronominals or other attributive adjectives. In particular, phrases in which *urbanus* follows and the other modifier precedes the noun (ANA) seem devoid of focus or contrast (cf. below on Livy's *duae legiones urbanae*). I note just two cases, one in Cicero,[69] one in Livy,[70] in which there is contrast *elsewhere* in the context, and one instance in Suetonius (28), an emotive passage where an antithetical parallelism is achieved by this order.[71]

(28) ...exoptatissimus princeps maximae parti prouincialium ac militum, quod infantem plerique cognouerant, sed et **uniuersae plebi urbanae** ob memoriam Germanici patris... (Suet. *Calig.* 13. 1)
'...the prince most earnestly desired by the greatest part of the provincials and soldiers, because many of them had known him as a child, but also by the whole of the city populace because of their memory of his father Germanicus...'

Equally, among the few complex modifiers following the noun (NAA), there is only one clear instance of antithesis,[72] in Seneca the Younger (29), on legitimate reasons for anger.

(29) ...si rusticum laborem recusat aut non fortiter obiit a **seruitute urbana et feriata** translatus ad durum opus! (Sen. *Dial.* 5. 29. 1)
'...if he refuses work in the countryside or does not approach it bravely on being transferred from the holiday life of slavery in the city to real hard work!'

Several of the quasi-parenthetical cases illustrated in (26) and (27) above contain an opposition within themselves (urban/rural, city/provincial), although they do not set the phrase as a whole into focus or antithesis. However, the three good republican examples do carry, if not contrast, at least significant weight and focus. In (30), from Varro, two postposed superlatives modify *uilla urbana*, which comes close to being a phrasal lexeme ('a city-villa', with *urbana*

[69] Cic. *Phil.* 11. 11 *at hic me defendente quinquiens absolutus est:* ***sexta palma urbana*** *etiam in gladiatore difficilis* 'But I defended him five times, and each time he was acquitted: to win a sixth palm in the city is difficult, even for a gladiator.'

[70] Liv. 27. 35. 12 *cui Bruttii prouincia euenisset,* ***nouis legionibus urbanis*** *scriptis utrius mallet consulum prioris anni exercitum sumeret; relictum a consule exercitum Q. Fuluius proconsul acciperet* 'The consul to whom the Bruttii should fall as his province was to enrol new city legions and to take the army of whichever he preferred of the consuls of the previous year; the army not taken by a consul was to be taken by Q. Fulvius the proconsul.'

[71] The *plebs urbana* is both Roman, as opposed to provincial (*prouincialium*), and civil, as opposed to military (*ac militum*); cf. the oppositions set out in section 16.4.2.2 above.

[72] And here, as Jim Adams points out to me, there is the additional, imponderable factor of the role of chiasmus.

'embedded'; cf. n. 66 above). It is noteworthy that both of Cicero's, in (31) and in (2) above, have *urbanus* (postposed) in the sense 'witty'; in (31), the focus is perhaps on *sermonem*, in parallel with *homo*.

(30) nunc contra, **uillam urbanam quam maximam ac politissimam** habeant dant operam... (Var. *Rust.* 1. 13. 7)
'Now, on the other hand, they take pains to have a city-villa as large and handsome as possible...'

(31) ...et homo facetus inducis etiam **sermonem urbanum ac uenustum**, me dicere solere esse me Iouem,... (Cic. *Dom.* 92)
'...and, amusing fellow that you are, you even present an elegant and charming story to the effect that I am in the habit of saying that I am Jove,...'

Conversely, of the forty-three examples reported in the first two columns of Table 16.4, thirty-nine[73] show *urbanus* in clear antithesis in one of the three main senses described in section 16.4.2 above, either explicitly within the phrase itself, as in (32a), or explicitly within the context, as in (32b, c), or, as in (33), by implication (paradigmatically).

(32a) nulla ars neque priuatae neque publicae rei gerendae ei defuit; **urbanas** rusticasque **res** pariter callebat. (Liv. 39. 40. 4)
'No art of conducting either private or public affairs was lacking to him; he was equally skilled in the business of the city and of the countryside.'

qui agrum parauit, domum uendat, ne malit **urbanum** quam rusticum **larem** colere;... (Col. 1. 1. 18)
'A man who has bought land should sell his (town) house to avoid wishing to worship more the household gods of the city rather than those of the country;...'

cercopithecum Panerotem faeneratorem et **urbanis** rusticisque **praediis** locupletatum prope regio extulit funere. (Suet. *Ner.* 30. 2)
'The monkey-faced usurer Paneros he enriched with both urban and rural estates, and had him buried with almost regal splendour.'

[73] Of the other four, two (each with four premodifiers) are in a Ciceronian impassioned crescendo (*Att.* 7. 3. 5, *Pis.* 64); of the other two, each with three premodifiers, Sen. *Controv.* 9. 4. 19 *duas eius urbanas res* (NB the postposed monosyllable *res*!) has *urbanus* in the subjective, evaluative sense 'witty'. Sen. *Controv.* 1. pr. 19 *omnem urbanam circumfusam senatui plebem* has in common with Cic. *Att.* 7. 3. 5 *omnem illam urbanam ac perditam plebem* the presence of a participle among the premodifiers (cf. section 16.3 above).

(32b) **omnes urbanae res**, omnia haec nostra praeclara studia et haec forensis laus et industria latet in tutela ac praesidio bellicae uirtutis. (Cic. *Mur.* 22)

'All the activities of this city, all this noble profession of ours, our hard work and recognition here at the Bar lurk in obscurity under the protection of prowess in war.'

sed si... **hanc urbanam suffragationem** militari anteponis,... (Cic. *Mur.* 38)

'But if... you attach more weight to the votes of civilians than to those of soldiers,...'

(32c) igitur praemoneo ne uilicum ex eo genere seruorum, qui corpore placuerunt, instituamus, ne ex eo quidem ordine, qui **urbanas ac delicatas artis** exercuerit... eligendus est rusticis operibus ab infante duratus. (Col. 1. 8. 1)

'Therefore I advise at the start not to appoint an overseer from the type of slaves who are physically attractive, and not even from the type concerned with the voluptuous occupations of the city... A man should be chosen who has been hardened by farmwork from his childhood.'

datur et colonis, ut uidetur ipsis, non satis temporis, quorum mihi agrestes querelae litteras nostras et **haec urbana opera** commendant. (Plin. *Ep.* 9. 36. 6)

'Some time is given to my tenants (not enough, they think), and their boorish complaints make me find more appealing our literary interests and these city pursuits.'

(33) nam quis unquam dubitabit quin in re publica nostra primas eloquentia tenuerit semper **urbanis pacatisque rebus**, secundas iuris scientia? (Cic. *Orat.* 141)

'Will anyone ever doubt that in our state, in peaceful civil life, eloquence has always held first place, and jurisprudence second?'

Acanthi, **topiariae et urbanae herbae**, lato longoque folio crepidines marginum adsurgentiumque puluinorum toros uestientis, duo genera sunt: (Plin. *HN* 22. 76)

'Of acanthus, an ornamental and city plant, which covers with its broad, long leaf the banks of borders and the raised portions of gardens, there are two types:'

It is worth observing that the first and third examples in (32a) are in a sense the determining counterparts to the appositional instances in (26) and (27).

The high figure of twenty reported in Table 16.4 for complex premodifiers in Livy is inflated above all by the nine occurrences (plus one with hyperbaton) of the 'two city legions' in his third and fourth decades. Each of these (QAN *duae urbanae legiones*) is in antithesis with other army units in the immediate context, as in (34). This is not the case, with one possible exception,[74] for the other common order (QNA *duae legiones urbanae*, five times) as in (35), nor for the unique NQA + relative clause (36).

(34) Q. Mucio cum uetere exercitu (duae autem legiones erant) Sardinia; C. Terentio, <cum> legione una cui iam praeerat, Picenum. scribi praeterea **duae urbanae legiones** iussae et uiginti milia sociorum. (Liv. 24. 44. 6)
'Q. Mucius with his old army (of two legions) was to have Sardinia; C. Terentius was to have Picenum with the one legion he already commanded. Further enrolment of two city legions was ordered and twenty thousand allied troops.'

(35) . . . M'. Acilius Glabrio praetor cui inter ciues peregrinosque iurisdictio obtigerat cum **una ex duabus legione urbana** est missus. (Liv. 33. 36. 2)
'. . . Manius Acilius Glabrio, the praetor who had been allotted the administration of cases between citizens and aliens, was sent with one of the two city legions.'

(36) itaque Minucius consul, cui Ligures prouincia euenerat, ex auctoritate patrum in rostra escendit et edixit ut **legiones duae urbanae quae superiore anno conscriptae essent** post diem decimum Arretii adessent. (Liv. 34. 56. 4)
'And so the consul Minucius, who had received Liguria as his province, on the authority of the Senate mounted the rostra and proclaimed that the two city legions which had been enrolled the year before were to be at Arretium in nine days.'

Comparable with the example from Livy in (34) are those from Tacitus in (37).

(37) tum legiones classesque et, quod raro alias, praetorianus **urbanusque miles** in aciem deducti, . . . (Tac. *Hist.* 1. 89)
'Then legions and fleets and, what is otherwise rare, the praetorian and urban troops, were deployed in the front line, . . . '

sedecim praetoriae, quattuor **urbanae cohortes** scribebantur, . . . (Tac. *Hist.* 2. 93)
'Sixteen praetorian and four urban cohorts were enrolled, . . . '

[74] Liv. 30. 2. 6 *tria milia militum in eam classem ex decreto patrum consules scripserunt et* ***duas legiones urbanas*** *ad incerta belli* 'The consuls by decree of the Senate enrolled three thousand troops to serve with this fleet and two city legions for wartime emergencies.'

I conclude this section by quoting (38) the unique occurrence in the corpus of AN *urbanus praetor* 'the urban praetor', which, I suggest, owes its form to syntagmatic contrast in what resembles (since the two praetors share the single head) a complex, coordinated premodifier.

(38) an ille plus praestat qui **inter peregrinos et ciues** aut **urbanus praetor** adeuntibus adsessoris uerba pronuntiat quam qui quid sit iustitia, quid pietas, quid patientia, quid fortitudo, quid mortis contemptus? (Sen. *Dial.* 9. 3. 4 [*De tranquillitate animi*])
'Or does he do more who as peregrine or urban praetor utters the words of the assessor to those who approach, than the man who (spells out) what is justice, responsibility, endurance, courage, scorn of death?'

16.4.4 *Attributive* urbanus *and hyperbaton*

I turn finally to the twenty contexts in the corpus in which attributive *urbanus* is not contiguous with its noun, using the typology of the important recent article by Powell (2010). Five of the twenty are not hyperbaton in Powell's terms, as the word between *urbanus* and its noun is part of the *urbanus* phrase. All five show *urbanus* preposed; in four of them, as in (39),[75] either *urbanus* or its phrase as a whole is in clear and explicit antithesis with another element in the context, while in the fifth (see (16) above) *urbanus* means 'witty' and its phrase is highlighted in a parallelism with *tam . . . tam*.

(39) et quoniam mihi casus **urbanam** in magistratibus **administrationem** rei publicae, tibi prouincialem dedit, . . . (Cic. *Q Fr.* 1. 1. 43)
'And since fortune has given the management of public affairs in magistracies to me in the city, to you in a province, . . . '

It is hard to resist the implication of these cases that mere disjunction, whether or not through a syntactically alien element, can convey focus on one or both of the disjoined words.

Of the remaining fifteen examples, all 'short-range' (i.e. involving a single word),[76] three are 'invisible', being caused by postpositive particles (*quoque*,

[75] The other three are: Cic. *Phil.* 14. 7 ***urbanarum*** *maledicta* ***litium****, non inustae belli interneciui notae* 'terms of abuse appropriate to a city lawsuit, not brands of deadly warfare'; Liv. 9. 19. 2 *in omni defectione sociorum Latini nominis* ***urbano*** *prope* ***dilectu*** *decem scribebantur legiones* 'in a total revolt of the allies of Latin name, it was usual to enrol ten legions in a levy almost confined to the city'; Liv. 10. 9. 11 *ipsum auctorem fuisse . . . differendi sibi consulatus in bellicosiorem annum: eo anno maiori se usui rei publicae fore* ***urbano*** *gesto* ***magistratu*** 'that he (Q. Fabius) proposed delaying his consulship to a year with more fighting: in the coming year, he said, he would be of greater benefit to the state if he held an urban magistracy'.

[76] In one case, Liv. 34. 43. 9, an infinitive with accusative subject pronoun: ***duas urbanas*** *scribere eos* ***legiones*** 'that they should enrol two city legions'.

quidem, (*ne* . . .) *quidem*), and twelve involve a stronger word, in every case a verb (including once the unstressed verb 'to be'; cf. Powell 2010: 182). Cicero has five,[77] Livy four (again dominated by the city legions),[78] Varro and Suetonius two each,[79] Caesar and Tacitus one each.[80] Together they lend eloquent support to Powell's (2010: 176) hypothesis that short-range hyperbaton is 'always a focusing device', and to his contention that, given its 'uses in both formally rhetorical and informally conversational genres of writing' hyperbaton was 'a generalised *oral* feature' of Latin (Powell 2010: 184, focus original).[81] Of the two examples in Varro, one is from a conversational turn by one of the characters of the dialogue, the other from a rhetorically more formal preface. Cicero's four examples represent his epistolary, philosophical, and oratorical styles. Caesar's comes in reported speech in his (Caesar's own) reply to Afranius, even Tacitus' approximates to reported speech (the anxious thoughts of Galba), while Suetonius' is from more straightforward, if ornate, narrative. All without exception, like the five pseudo-hyperbata considered above, clearly convey strong focus, often in explicit contrast with another element in the context. It seems that the focus may be on either the left, as in (40),[82] or the right, (41),[83] of the intervening word, or on the disjunction as a whole, (42).[84]

(40) (placuit) item eum exercitum dimitti . . . ; consulibus ambobus Italiam prouinciam esse et **duas urbanas** scribere eos **legiones**, ut, dimissis quos senatus censuisset exercitibus, octo omnino Romanae legiones essent. (Liv. 34. 43. 9)

'(It was decided that) this army, too, was to be disbanded . . . ; both consuls were to have Italy as their province and they were to enrol two city legions, so that after the disbanding of the armies decreed by the Senate there should be altogether eight Roman legions.'

77 Cicero has five if one includes *Phil.* 5. 20 (cf. n. 68 above): *Dom.* 74, *Phil.* 11. 11, *Off.* 1. 74, *Fam.* 12. 1. 1.

78 34. 43. 9, 40. 28. 9, 40. 44. 6, 42. 35. 4. At 40. 44. 6, John Briscoe suggests to me that Livy's formulaic and always continuous *sortitus prouinciam est* (or, usually, *prouinciam sortitus est*) may have favoured the hyperbaton. Here, as on (6) and in n. 37 above, I am acutely aware of passing over in silence other delicate matters.

79 Var. *Rust.* 2. pr. 2, 3. 2. 9; Suet. *Aug.* 33. 3 (two hyperbata in one sentence).

80 Caes. *B Civ.* 1. 85. 8; Tac. *Hist.* 1. 14.

81 Cf. the conclusion of de Melo (2010: 79) on the placement of possessive pronouns that 'premodifier and post-modifier hyperbaton may be rare in early prose, but in Plautus they are quite common; so common, in fact, that they are unlikely to be stylistically marked within the context of early dramatic *Kunstsprache*'.

82 So, too, Liv. 40. 44. 6 and the first part of Suet. *Aug.* 33. 3 (ex. (43) below).

83 So, too, perhaps Liv. 40. 28. 9.

84 So, too, Cic. *Off.* 1. 74 (ex. (4) above), *Fam.* 12. 1. 1.

...anxius quonam exercituum uis erumperet, ne **urbano** quidem **militi** confisus,... (Tac. *Hist.* 1. 14)
'...anxious how far through the armies trouble might spread, and confident not even in the city troops,...'

(41) praeter eos exercitus,... praetori negotium datum, ut **quattuor legiones** scriberet **urbanas,...** (Liv. 42. 35. 4)
'In addition to these armies,... the praetor was given the task of enrolling four city legions,...'

(42) quid igitur, inquit, est ista uilla, si nec **urbana** habet **ornamenta** neque rustica membra? (Var. *Rust.* 3. 2. 9)
'How then, he said, is that a villa, if it has neither city furnishings nor rustic appurtenances?'

...in se noui generis imperia constitui, ut idem ad portas **urbanis** praesideat **rebus** et duas bellicosissimas prouincias absens tot annos obtineat;... (Caes. *B Civ.* 1. 85. 8)
'Against him military commands of a new type were being set up, whereby the same man at the gates of Rome was in charge of city affairs and governed for so many years in absentia two provinces fully equipped for war.'

The last option seems to be commonest in our twenty *urbanus* instances, and is bound to apply when the disjunction is a phrasal term such as *praetor urbanus*, as in (43).

(43) quid Censorinum? qui se uerbo **praetorem** esse **urbanum** cupere dicebat, re certe noluit. (Cic. *Phil.* 11. 11)
'What of Censorinus, who claimed in what he said to desire to be urban praetor but in fact certainly did not wish to be.'

appellationes quotannis urbanorum quidem litigatorum **praetori** delegabat **urbano,** at prouincialium consularibus uiris,... (Suet. *Aug.* 33. 3)
'Each year he referred appeals of cases from city litigants to the urban praetor, but those from provincials to ex-consuls,...'

16.5 Discussion

The findings of this case study generally bear out widely held views, but they contain at least one surprise, and deserve brief summary and discussion. First and most importantly, in sections 16.4.1 and 16.4.2 we saw frequent examples of postposed relational *urbanus* 'of the city' in focus, but only two, (24) and

(25), of *pre*posed relational *urbanus* as sole modifier *not* in focus. In particular, we saw that those authors with very few or no instances of NA *urbanus* (cf. Table 16.3 above), including Columella, who has been said to show a preference for preposing attributive adjectives,[85] prepose *urbanus* in accordance with the same principles as Cicero. Perhaps most remarkably, there is not a single *un*focused instance of preposed *urbanus* as sole modifier in the sense 'witty, urbane'.

This pattern speaks strongly in favour of a basic NA order not only for relational *urbanus*, but for *urbanus* in all its senses. In other words, there is no evidence for a competing basic AN order when *urbanus* is non-literal. Marouzeau's *urbanus praetor* type owes its anteposition in Latin prose not only, if at all, to the 'metaphorical' use of the adjective,[86] but rather to contextual focus. Moreover, there is no difference detectable between the placement of literal/technical and metaphorical *urbanus* either when used with other modifiers or in hyperbaton. Apart from (24) and (25), we had only one occasion to invoke literariness to account for unexpected anteposition (Seneca's *urbanus praetor*, (38) above), and that instance is explicable with reference either to focus or to multiple modification (both of which are present), and is remarkable—perhaps jocular, deliberately surprising—chiefly in involving the otherwise almost invariant phrasal lexeme *praetor urbanus*.[87]

Spevak (2010*a*: 229) rightly observes 'different degrees of "fixedness" of lexical units' in Latin, contrasting the invariance of (e.g.) *pontifex maximus* with the variant word order and even hyperbaton found exceptionally with (e.g.) *aes alienum* and more frequently with (e.g.) *nauis oneraria*. For sure, *praetor urbanus* is at the invariant end of her informal scale, although even this phrasal term is disjoined once in Cicero (by weak *esse*) (apart from its exceptional AN ordering in Seneca). However, the phrasal expressions considered here which use the technical sense of *urbanus* derived from *praetor urbanus* may, it is true, bear focus in their basic NA order, but they show frequent preposing of the adjective when in focus or contrast, and they are clearly not impervious to hyperbaton. In our corpus of attributive *urbanus* phrases, neither participles (or participle-like forms) used as attributes, nor the monosyllable *res*

[85] Cf. Devine and Stephens (2006: 405, 412) and the corrective discussion of Vincent (2007: 66). With reference to a much later text, Pinkster (1995: 559) can conclude that the 'pragmatic motivations . . . are the same that hold for Classical Latin'.

[86] Metaphorical meaning is one of the special effects associated by Radatz (2001) with anteposition in Romance; another is literariness, which may account for Latin examples (24) and (25) (cf. n. 59 above).

[87] Similarly, Suetonius' double hyperbaton at *Aug.* 33. 3, example (43), is probably literary rather than colloquial, but each hyperbaton is in explicit antithesis, and this passage stands out by taking a liberty with *praetor urbanus*.

(cf. section 16.3 above), show systematic divergence from the regular pattern affecting other modifiers and heads.[88]

As for adjective placement in multiple modification, our findings in section 16.4.3 bear out Spevak's (2010*a*: 235–6) statements that the pattern ANA is generally rare,[89] and that in neutral, unemphatic contexts multiple modifiers follow the noun. She goes on to state that multiple modifiers before the noun are usually associated with topic function, while focus may fall on either AAN or NAA. Those including *urbanus*, however, show a clear correlation between anteposition (AAN) and focus.

And finally, all the instances of disjunction in the corpus (section 16.4.4 above), including those in which the intervening word is part of the *urbanus* noun phrase and therefore not an instance of hyperbaton proper, are short-range and serve to signal or to strengthen focus on *urbanus* or its noun or most often the phrase as a whole. In this modest case study at least, discontinuity is constrained and meaningful.

Marouzeau has been accused of superimposing French patterns on Latin word order.[90] While this is unfair as a generalization, and risks unjustly devaluing his signal contributions to the study of Latin word order, we have seen here that preposed *urbanus* in Latin prose down to Suetonius is much more likely to be literal ('urban') than metaphorical ('urbane') and to be in focus or contrast in its context. Marouzeau's *urbanus praetor* has at best a tenuous hold on reality—the only one in the corpus is in fact the *praetor urbanus*! Happily, contributors to this volume know and honour another.

[88] For preposed participles and postposed monosyllabic *res*, see nn. 23, 24, 73, and examples (20c), (21a) above.

[89] Devine and Stephens, on the other hand, state that ANA placement is 'not uncommon' (2006: 477).

[90] See, for example, Neubourg (1978: 359–60).

17

The rules of politeness and Latin request formulae

ELEANOR DICKEY

17.1 The rules of politeness: Brown and Levinson

It has been more than thirty years since Brown and Levinson's (1978, 1987) theory of positive and negative politeness was first propounded.[1] During that time the theory has been subjected to an unending barrage of criticism, from which it has not emerged unscathed; indeed nearly every part of Brown and Levinson's argument has been not only attacked but actually disproven. Nevertheless the theory remains in common use, for it offers something that none of its detractors has been able to replace: a simple template that can be used to analyse the politeness system of any language.

In essence, the theory claims that politeness can be divided into two types, positive and negative politeness. Positive politeness consists of elements that meet an addressee's need for people to be nice to him/her, such as expressions that display affection for, interest in, approval of, or solidarity with the addressee; for example affectionate forms of address, expressions of agreement, invitations to talk about oneself, and offers of non-linguistic benefits such as gifts are all elements of positive politeness. Negative politeness consists of those elements that meet an addressee's need not to be pestered or interfered with, such as expressions that phrase a request indirectly in order to make it easy to

[1] I am grateful to John Penney for being a wonderful teacher and gently helping me learn to use the Oxford libraries, to Philomen Probert for help and encouragement with this project, and to Marina Terkourafi for fruitful discussions, careful critiques, and patient corrections of my misrepresentations of her theory. Any mistakes that remain are my own.

refuse, show deference to the addressee's status, stress the addressee's right not to comply with a request, minimize or explain a transgression, or express apologies. Thus a request phrased with 'Excuse me, sir, but could you possibly let me use that book, if you're finished with it?' makes heavy use of negative politeness strategies, while 'Sweetheart, how did you like that book? Wasn't it great? But now I need it back' uses almost exclusively positive politeness strategies. Because this distinction is supposed to be universal and relies on the lexical and semantic meanings of the phrases used, it has great predictive power: when presented with a literal translation of an isolated utterance in a language about which one knows nothing, one ought in theory to be able to tell whether it is polite—and if so, why.[2]

Brown and Levinson also argued that positive and negative politeness are used in consistently different ways, so that it is possible to use a mathematical formula to predict which one will be deployed. According to their theory, the factors that influence choice of politeness strategies are the amount of intimacy or distance between speaker and addressee, the power differential between them, and the magnitude of the issue that gives rise to the need for politeness in the first place (a request, a problem requiring an apology, etc.). Negative politeness is used when there is greater distance between speaker and addressee, when the addressee has a significant amount of power over the speaker, and/or when the issue at hand is of considerable magnitude; positive politeness is used when there is greater intimacy between the parties, when the speaker is equal or superior to the addressee in power and status, and/or when the issue at hand is minor (Brown and Levinson 1987: 71–84). Thus a graduate student might use negative politeness to make a minor request of her supervisor and positive politeness to make a similar request of a close friend, but she could also use negative politeness strategies to the friend in the case of a major request. The predictive power of the theory is thus enhanced: any utterance that can be identified as positively or negatively polite can tell a researcher something about the relationship of the speaker to the addressee and/or about the weighting of the request (or other politeness-requiring act) in their culture.

This relationship between positive and negative politeness seems intuitively right for speakers of English, and it has also been successfully applied to many other languages, in the sense that invoking this framework has allowed researchers to analyse the politeness structures of numerous languages in a way

[2] Brown and Levinson did not explicitly claim such predictive power and would probably not have wanted to endorse the strong formulation presented here (they would have said, quite fairly, that of course there are always exceptions), but it is implied by their discussion and often assumed by those who apply their theory.

that seems convincing and enlightening. These two factors account for the success of Brown and Levinson's theory: it seems to work, and therefore it is useful. However, there are some difficulties about how and why it works. Brown and Levinson originally argued for the theory using data from three unrelated languages, and on this basis they claimed universality for its basic framework. They were not unaware of the existence of languages in which the vast majority of politeness falls into one or the other of their two categories (regardless of variation in distance, power, and magnitude of the politeness-requiring act) but they explained the existence of such 'positive politeness cultures' and 'negative politeness cultures' by hypothesizing that one of those variables could in such cultures be permanently set at one end of its range. Thus a positive politeness culture could result from a cultural inclination to consider requests minor, or to consider interpersonal distance small (1987: 242–53).

Ever since the appearance of this theory, it has faced considerable opposition.[3] Much of this opposition has attacked its reliance, as reflected in the terminology with which Brown and Levinson originally proposed it, on certain other theories that have since been challenged or discredited. However, as I have just demonstrated in the preceding paragraphs, the theory can be restated without any technical terminology apart from 'positive politeness' and 'negative politeness', which were invented by Brown and Levinson themselves,[4] and it still seems intuitively correct when so stated. Since the primary argument in favour of the theory has always been this appearance of obvious rightness, it cannot be disproven by attacking any theoretical basis that can be removed without changing that appearance.[5]

More serious challenges arise from the existence of cultures in which all politeness seems to be of the same type; researchers in these cultures have not on the whole been convinced by the argument that in such cultures some variable is permanently set at one end of its range, and in practical terms Brown and Levinson's theory is much less useful for studying politeness in such languages. Nevertheless, these problems do not affect the theory's usefulness for those cultures to which it does seem to apply; a framework that is not universal may nevertheless be genuinely applicable to a large number of different cultures.

There is also the difficulty that Brown and Levinson never really attempted to prove, in any methodologically rigorous fashion, the connection between either

[3] For summaries, see Watts (2003: 85–116) and Eelen (2001).

[4] Admittedly these terms were not created *ex nihilo*—they are closely linked to the concepts of positive and negative 'face'—but they can stand on their own, so acceptance or rejection of their antecedents cannot in itself be relevant to the validity of Brown and Levinson's theory.

[5] *Pace* Arundale (2008).

type of politeness and the factors on which they claim it depends; they provided plenty of examples (a number of them invented), but rather than taking a corpus and showing that the negative-politeness elements in it were consistently associated with certain factors and the positive-politeness elements consistently associated with other factors, they left the fact that the association seems intuitively obvious (to English speakers) to speak for itself. Subsequent attempts to test Brown and Levinson's theory against actual real-life data (e.g. Terkourafi 2002, 2004) have not on the whole upheld their views.

Lastly, the theory's predictive power is reduced by the existence of utterances containing both positive and negative politeness strategies, as 'Darling, could you lend me that book?', which combines a positive politeness strategy in the affectionate address with a negative politeness strategy in the indirect phrasing of the request as a question. In fact the frequency of this combination makes it very difficult to apply a distinction between positive and negative politeness to English requests, and thus to use the predictive powers of Brown and Levinson's theory, even in English.

Particularly problematic in this respect is the most common and fundamental of English polite request formulae, 'please'. Though Brown and Levinson did not explicitly so classify it, 'please' is often taken to be a marker of negative politeness, since it is a shortened form of 'if you please', a phrase that acknowledges the recipient's right not to comply with the request. Often English 'please' is indeed used in ways that match this etymological meaning: for example in 'Please pass the salt' the word 'please' turns the impolite command 'Pass the salt' into a polite request.

But in some other contexts 'please' has a different function. A request to pass the salt could be phrased with simply 'Salt, please!'; here 'please' turns the otherwise incomprehensible utterance 'Salt' into a request. And a child who wants an ice-cream cone very badly might say 'Please, please, please, Mummy, *please* gimme ice cream, please, please!'; in this request 'please' makes it harder, not easier, for the mother to refuse the child's demands. Terms with such a request-intensifying function are often described as 'urgent', and urgency in this sense is essentially the opposite of negative politeness.

What all this means is that the term 'please' cannot be consistently classified as a marker of negative politeness: it can indeed be such a marker, but it can also have other functions, including one that is diametrically opposed to negative politeness. This example demonstrates that politeness usage cannot always be safely predicted from a term's etymological meaning.

17.2 Other formulations of the rules of politeness

Naturally there have been many attempts to replace Brown and Levinson's theory with something less problematic.[6] It is not practical to discuss them all in a piece of this length, but three particularly promising ones are worth noting. Terkourafi (e.g. 2002, 2005, 2008, forthcoming) bases politeness on frequency of usage rather than lexical meaning and argues in essence that what is frequent is polite. Terkourafi's theory also allows for unusual or marked politeness but declines to provide predictive rules for the latter. Many situations in which interpersonal interaction occurs are common and frequently repeated; in these situations there is an expected sequence of formulaic politeness, and people who deviate from the expected formulae, *even in a direction that might seem to an outside observer more polite than the expected formulae*, may be perceived as behaving impolitely. For example, in a community where shopkeepers normally ask for payment with a simple statement of the amount owed (e.g. 'That'll be twelve pound forty-five, then'), if one shopkeeper were to start saying 'So sorry to trouble you, but do you suppose you could possibly pay twelve pounds and forty-five pence for that, please?', his customers would be more likely to assume that he was making fun of them, an impolite move, than that he was being polite.

On the other hand Watts (2003) has proposed a view of politeness that, while in some respects very similar to Terkourafi's, is in one important feature its opposite: for Watts only that which is *not* usual (i.e. Terkourafi's marked politeness) should be termed 'polite'. What is normal and expected in a particular context should, he argues, be termed 'politic behaviour' and distinguished from specially noticeable courtesy, or 'polite' behaviour. For example, Terkourafi and Watts agree that in a community where shopkeepers always say 'Have a nice day' to customers, and customers always use 'please' when requesting something, these expressions are not noticed or remarked on—though of course their absence would be. But Watts, unlike Terkourafi, then argues that because only the unusual courtesy is perceived as polite, only these courtesies can properly be called 'politeness' and form the subject of research on politeness. Like Terkourafi, Watts does not provide predictive generalizations for this (marked) type of politeness; each instance must, he believes, be considered on an individual basis. The result is that Watts provides no predictive generalizations about 'politeness' at all.

[6] Eelen, writing in 2001, examined nine different theories including that of Brown and Levinson, and a number of others have since been proposed.

A third theory is of special relevance for the ancient world, because it was formulated specifically for Latin politeness. Jon Hall (2009: 8–15) has adapted Brown and Levinson's classification for the Roman world, proposing three categories rather than two. His category of 'affiliative politeness' is very similar to positive politeness, and his 'redressive politeness' is essentially the same as negative politeness; to these he adds 'the politeness of respect (*verecundia*)', which aims 'to acknowledge a decisive social distance between writer and addressee' (2009: 13) and is characterized by restrained and formal language.[7]

The purpose of this paper is to test the usefulness of these four theories of politeness by applying them to a specific problem in a limited corpus: polite request formulae commonly used by Cicero.

17.3 Latin request formulae

The main work on requests and commands in Latin is that of Rodie Risselada (1993), who worked from the linguistic perspective of speech act theory rather than politeness theory. Risselada based her conclusions on a corpus that included selected plays of Plautus and Terence and extracts from the correspondence of Cicero and Pliny (1993: 20 n. 31); the number of requests taken from any one author is not enormous, but the systematic analysis of a body of data allowed her to pronounce authoritatively on the more common formulae, and her conclusions are generally respected. For example, although readers conditioned by usage in modern languages tend to assume that a Latin request expressed with a subjunctive was somehow softer and less commanding than one expressed with an imperative, Risselada demonstrated that the subjunctive was no milder than the imperative—not because the subjunctive was a particularly abrupt way of making a request, but because the imperative itself was a widely usable form, not perceived as abrupt or rude (1993: 155, 163).

This usage is of course very different from English, where imperatives not accompanied by softeners such as 'please' tend to be stigmatized as rude except in a few specific circumstances. Nevertheless classical Latin does possess a number of words that appear to have a function not dissimilar to 'please', in that they are frequently attached to polite requests; the most common of these terms are *uelim* 'I would like', *quaeso* 'I seek', *rogo* 'I ask', *peto* 'I ask', and *oro* 'I beg'. These 'please' equivalents offer a useful subject for studying Latin politeness, as there is a large amount of information available on them (together they occur 928 times in Latin literature of the first century BC, in addition to

[7] This category draws heavily on the work of Kaster (2005).

hundreds more occurrences in earlier and later texts) and their usage is well understood.[8]

Risselada, without subscribing to any particular type of politeness theory, argues that in general these terms are polite because they soften a request by making its fulfilment optional,[9] but that *oro* is not polite at all, rather urgent and emphatic (1993: 254–5). These claims can serve as a starting point for our examination.

A corpus must, of course, be chosen with care; in modern societies significant variation can be observed between different social groups, different generations, and even different individuals in their conventions of politeness. Fortunately a remarkably homogeneous corpus exists in the form of the letters of Cicero, all of which were written over the space of a few decades by a single individual.[10] Between them, the six terms under consideration occur 661 times in this corpus.[11] They cannot, however, be treated as a unit; since Risselada argues that *oro* functions differently from the other terms, it is necessary to examine it separately.

17.4 *Velim*, *quaeso*, *rogo*, and *peto* in Cicero's letters

To begin with *uelim*, *quaeso*, *rogo*, and *peto*, Watts's theory will not help us since it provides no predictive generalizations. Terkourafi's theory requires us to examine the frequency with which these terms are used in particular contexts before their politeness can be evaluated. All four are frequent with requests in Cicero's letters, though there are some distinctions in their usage: *uelim* and *quaeso* are used more often to intimates than to non-intimates, while *rogo* and *peto* have the reverse distribution, and *uelim* is most common with very minor requests, *quaeso* with slightly more onerous ones, *rogo* with major ones, and *peto* with the most burdensome and important requests.[12] Examples of typical uses of these terms are:

8 See e.g. Carney (1964), Adams (1984), Risselada (1989, 1993: 233–328), Núñez (1995), Lech (2010: 87–117), Halla-aho (2010), Dickey (2012).

9 Risselada (1993: 250–2); Roesch (2004: 145–6) makes a similar claim about *uelim.*

10 Some letters preserved as part of the Ciceronian corpus were not written by Cicero himself; these have been removed from the corpus for the purposes of this analysis. In most respects, in fact, Cicero's usage of the terms under consideration here was the same as that of his correspondents and other contemporaries, but a few differences can be detected; see Dickey (2012).

11 This figure includes only occurrences with requests; some of these terms are also used frequently with questions, but those occurrences are not relevant (unless the question is itself a direct or indirect request, but that happens not to occur with these words in our corpus).

12 See Dickey (2012) for more information and evidence; in establishing the intimates/non-intimates distinction I have controlled for the greater frequency of minor requests in letters to intimates. There are also register distinctions among these terms: *quaeso* belongs to a somewhat higher register than the others and *rogo* to a somewhat lower one.

(1) illud tamen quod scribit animadvertas uelim, de portorio circumuectionis; ait se de consili sententia rem ad senatum reiecisse. (*Att.* 2. 16. 4, to Atticus)
'Nevertheless I would like you to pay attention to what [my brother] writes about excise duty on transferred goods; he says that he referred the matter to the senate owing to the opinion of his advisers.'

(2) da igitur, quaeso, negotium Pharnaci, Antaeo, Salvio ut id nomen ex omnibus libris tollatur. (*Att.* 13. 44. 3, to Atticus)
'So, I ask you, give Pharnaces, Antaeus, and Salvius the job of deleting that name from all the copies.'

(3) ego te plane rogo, atque ita ut maiore studio, iustiore de causa, magis ex animo rogare nihil possim, ut Albanio parcas, praedia Laberiana ne attingas. (*Fam.* 13. 8. 3, to M. Rutilius)
'I ask you plainly, and in such a way that I couldn't ask anything with greater earnestness, in a juster cause, or more from my heart—I ask you to spare Albanius and not to touch the estates that belonged to Laberius.'

(4) magno opere a te peto ut operam des efficiasque ne quid mihi fiat iniuriae neue quid temporis ad meum annu<u>m munus accedat. quod si feceris, magnus ad tua pristina erga me studia cumulus accedet. (*Fam.* 15. 12. 2, to L. Paullus)
'I earnestly request from you that you try and make sure that no injury is done to me and that no time is added to my annual tour of duty. If you do that, a crowning glory will be added to your earlier efforts on my behalf.'

According to Terkourafi's theory, then, all four of these terms are polite when used with the type of request to which they are suited, not because their lexical meaning makes them softeners but simply because of the convention that they should be used with such requests.

Brown and Levinson's and Hall's theories, on the other hand, suggest that we should look at the words' lexical meanings to determine whether and how they are polite. The lexical meanings of these terms, 'I would like' and 'I ask', are not completely easy to classify, but when added to a request such a qualifier might very well convey to the addressee that it was optional, as Risselada claims. Thus in Brown and Levinson's terms these would be elements of negative politeness, and in Hall's terms they would be elements of redressive politeness.

Such a classification, however, has some further implications. If these four terms are elements of negative politeness, *uelim* ought to be more indirect than the other terms, because stating that one would like something to be done makes compliance more optional than pointing out that one is asking the speaker to do it. So one would expect *uelim* to be used for somewhat more major requests, all else being equal, than the other terms. But this is exactly the reverse of the terms' attested usage.

A second difficulty comes with the implication that all the major polite request formulae in Cicero's repertoire express negative rather than positive politeness.[13] It is often observed that Roman culture leaned more towards positive than negative politeness,[14] so this result would make the request formulae anomalous. Since in Brown and Levinson's view positive politeness is more likely to be used to intimates, equals, and inferiors, while negative politeness is more likely to be used to social superiors and to those distant from the speaker, Cicero might be expected to prefer positive politeness. More than half his extant letters were written to close friends and relatives (chiefly his close friend Atticus, his brother Quintus, and his wife Terentia, who between them account for 53% of the letters); it seems surprising to have overwhelmingly negative politeness with the requests in those letters. Moreover, Cicero's unusually high opinion of himself prevented him from considering very many correspondents to be his superiors. If the vast majority of Cicero's polite requests use negative politeness strategies, Brown and Levinson's theory would make Cicero a far more humble character than we know him to have been.

A third problem has to do with the modifiers used with *rogo*: this term is not infrequently accompanied by terms like *uehementer* 'vigorously, earnestly' and *etiam atque etiam* 'over and over again' (see examples below). Such modifiers strengthen the force of the appeal carried by *rogo*; it is difficult to reconcile their use with a fundamental meaning for *rogo* of 'you do not of course have to do this for me'.

One could conclude on the basis of this evidence that Brown and Levinson's theory (and by extension Hall's) does not work; the different elements that they claimed for negative politeness do not in fact go together. But there is also another possibility here: perhaps it is Risselada's explanation of the terms' function as markers of optionality that is the problem. A word meaning 'I ask' need not *necessarily* indicate that fulfilment of the request to which it is attached is optional; instead it might emphasize the fact of the petition itself, which creates a connection between the two people in which the asker is subordinated to the person asked, and flatters the latter. If that is the underlying logic of terms like *rogo*, they are in Brown and Levinson's terms elements of positive politeness and in Hall's terms elements of affiliative politeness.

[13] Cicero does, of course, employ some other polite request formulae, including ones such as *amabo*, *si me amas*, and *(per)gratum mihi erit* that would be examples of positive rather than negative politeness. But none of these other formulae is at all common in his letters; the four terms under discussion here are by a considerable margin his favourites, even to close family members.

[14] Cf. Dickey (2002: 94); even Risselada herself makes this point (1993: 92 n. 30).

If one takes *uelim*, *quaeso*, *rogo*, and *peto* this way, their usage fits perfectly with Brown and Levinson's framework. According to that framework positively polite terms should be used particularly to intimates and inferiors, and those are exactly the people to whom Cicero normally wrote letters—as noted above, 53% of his letters are addressed to his wife, his brother, or his closest friend, and 55% of the requests using *uelim*, *quaeso*, *rogo*, and *peto* are found in those letters. Many of the other addressees who receive these terms are clearly clients of Cicero's or in other ways his social inferiors (e.g. his freedman Tiro); the pool of correspondents who could reasonably be expected to be targets of negative politeness strategies (e.g. Caesar, Pompey) is far smaller.

But can the use of words meaning 'I ask you' be explained as a positive politeness strategy? In the context of Roman social relations, it can. The networks within which Cicero operated laid great stress on the mutual obligations of friends, patrons, and clients. A great man was known by the number of people who supported him in gratitude for favours received or in hopes of favours to come; they paid court to him because he had the power to help them, and he in turn was obliged to use that power for the good of those whom he acknowledged to be his friends and clients.[15] In such a system the recipient of a favour was genuinely obligated to the giver; he had to repay it immediately with conspicuous gratitude and later, if he had the opportunity, by favours of his own. Therefore asking for a favour was no light undertaking; the asker put himself in a position analogous to that of a client and bound himself to future obligation if the request was fulfilled.

During the period to which almost all of his letters belong, Cicero was an ex-consul and, in his sincere estimation, the most gloriously deserving of all living Roman officials. In this respect he was the ultimate patron. When someone of that stature asked a favour, it would have been an honour to be the person lucky enough to be asked; that fortunate individual would have the opportunity to put Cicero under an obligation to him, to enjoy his kind words and gratitude in the short run, and to cash in the favour for something he needed himself in the longer term. Of course, not everyone shared Cicero's estimation of himself, so the reality of the addressee's perceptions may not always have measured up to this ideal. This matters little, however, as Cicero seems often to have been blissfully unaware of this gap in perception, and it is his own view of the social relationships involved that would have governed his use of politeness terms.

Thus by using terms like *rogo* and *peto* that unambiguously stated his request for a favour, Cicero was indeed pursuing a positive politeness strategy. *Velim* was less polite precisely because it was less direct; it did not acknowledge that

[15] See e.g. Brunt (1988: 351–442), Deniaux (1993).

Cicero was putting himself in the position of a client, and therefore it was not suitable for major requests.

The conclusion has to be that Brown and Levinson's framework has been useful in understanding the usage of these four terms: its predictive powers allowed us to uncover an error in our initial assumptions and reach a better understanding of what these terms meant. On the other hand, the extent of those predictive powers turned out to be more limited than is often thought, for the lexical meanings of the terms under investigation were capable of interpretation either as positive or as negative politeness. Terkourafi's framework was also useful, and Watts's was not helpful. Hall's framework was not meaningfully distinct from Brown and Levinson's as regards this question.

17.5 *Oro* in Cicero's letters

With *oro* we have a different situation, as the first question is whether the term is polite at all. Again, Watts's framework offers no predictions for us to use; to apply Terkourafi's we need to look at how often *oro* is used with requests. The results of such a look, though less clear-cut than for the other four terms, point in the same direction: *oro* occurs reasonably frequently in Cicero's letters with requests that appear to be polite, and it is similarly used in the speeches.[16] Most of the contexts in which Cicero uses *oro* resemble ones in which he uses *rogo*, and in some passages he uses both together, making it clear that they can appear in exactly the same context:[17]

(5) te, mi Curio, pro tua incredibili in me beneuolentia meaque item in te singulari rogo atque oro ne patiare quicquam mihi ad hanc prouincialem molestiam temporis prorogari. (*Fam.* 2. 7. 4, to Curio)
'My own Curio, I ask and beg you, by your unbelievable goodwill to me and by my own outstanding goodwill towards you, not to allow any time at all to be added to my burden as provincial governor.'

[16] *Oro* is used with requests twenty-eight times in letters and fifty-one times in the whole body of Cicero's work; the least common of the other terms, *rogo*, occurs 101 times in the latter corpus.

[17] Risselada (1993: 255) argues that such passages do not show a similarity between *oro* and *rogo* because *rogo* always comes first and is followed by *oro*, so that 'what is at first presented as a (polite) optional directive is subsequently "corrected" into an urgent supplication'. While it is true that Cicero always puts *rogo* before *oro* when the two are paired, the conjunction he uses is always *atque*, which indicates coordination rather than correction, and with only three examples of the pairing, the uniformity of the order is of doubtful significance (there are examples elsewhere of the reverse order, e.g. Marcus Aurelius in Fronto's letters 77. 10; Claudius Terentianus in *PMich.* 467. 17).

(6) nunc, quoniam tuam iustitiam secutus tutissimum sibi portum prouinciam istam duxit esse, etiam atque etiam te rogo atque oro ut eum et in reliqui<i>s ueteris negotiationis colligendis iuues et ceteris rebus tegas atque tueare. (*Fam.* 13. 66. 2, to Servilius Isauricus)
'Now, since [Caecina], relying on your sense of justice, has decided that your province is his own safest harbour, I ask and beg you over and over again to help him in picking up the pieces of his old business, and to protect and look after him in other affairs.'

(7) etsi egomet, qui te consolari cupio, consolandus ipse sum, propterea quod nullam rem grauius iam diu tuli quam incommodum tuum, tamen te magno opere non hortor solum sed etiam pro amore nostro rogo atque oro te colligas uirumque praebeas et qua condicione omnes homines et quibus temporibus no<s> nati simus cogites. (*Fam.* 5. 18. 1, to T. Fadius)
'I myself, who long to comfort you, am myself in need of comfort, because for a long time I have not taken anything as hard as I take your misfortune; nevertheless I not only urge you vigorously but even ask and beg you by our love for each other to pull yourself together, show yourself a man, and remember the general condition of mankind and the times in which we were born.'

Moreover, Cicero did not operate in a vacuum: many other Romans also used *oro* for polite requests. The term was growing in popularity during his time, and by the first century AD it was very frequent with polite requests, including hundreds of electioneering graffiti at Pompeii where *oro uos faciatis*... 'I beg you to elect...' was so standard (more than 300 examples are preserved) that it was usually abbreviated *OVF.*

Terkourafi's theory would thus lead us to conclude that *oro* was probably polite when used by Cicero. Brown and Levinson's and Hall's theories, however, offer little help this time: a term meaning 'I beg' could potentially express urgency (i.e. not be polite), or express negative politeness (if it indicated that the addressee had the power to refuse the request), or express positive politeness (if it expressed the speaker's admiration for the addressee's power and his willingness to subordinate himself to him).

Risselada's conclusion that *oro* is not polite, however, was not drawn without evidence. The argument that *oro* is fundamentally different from the terms meaning 'I ask' is based on two passages in which Cicero seems to make a distinction between *oro* and *peto* (Risselada 1993: 253–5):

(8) peto igitur a te, uel, si pateris, oro, ut homines miseros et fortuna, quam uitare nemo potest, magis quam culpa calamitosos conserues incolumis uelisque per te me hoc muneris cum ipsis amicis hominibus, cum

municipio Caleno, quocum mihi magna necessitudo est, tum Leptae, quem omnibus antepono, dare. (*Fam.* 9. 13. 3, to Dolabella)

'So I ask you, or rather (if you let me) I beg you to save these people, who are unfortunate more because of fortune which no one can escape than through their own fault, and to desire me to grant through you this favour not only to my friends themselves and to the town of Cales, with which I am closely connected, but also to Lepta, whom I value above all others.'

(9) quam ob rem a te peto uel potius omnibus te precibus oro et obtestor ut in tuis maximis curis aliquid impertias temporis, huic quoque cogitationi, ut tuo beneficio bonus uir, gratus, pius denique esse in maximi benefici memoria possim. (*Att.* 9. 11a. 3, to Caesar)

'Therefore I ask you, or rather I beg and entreat you with all my prayers to give, despite all your great cares, a bit of time to this consideration too: how by your kindness I may show myself a good, a grateful, and a faithful man in memory of an enormous obligation.'

In both these passages Cicero suggests that there is a difference between *peto* and *oro*, and in (8) he indicates that the use of *oro* might somehow be unacceptable to the addressee; as it is difficult to see how a term that enhances the politeness of a request could be unacceptable, passage (8) does appear to show that in Cicero's usage *oro* might not be polite, even in a context not noticeably different from the ones quoted above.

The difficulty is that Cicero elsewhere makes a similar statement about the use of *rogo*, which everyone agrees is a polite term:

(10) itaque te uehementer etiam atque etiam rogo, magis quam a me uis aut pateris te rogari, ut hanc cogitationem toto pectore amplectare. (*Att.* 12. 35, to Atticus)

'And so I ask you earnestly over and over again, more than you want or can bear to be asked by me, to embrace this problem for consideration with your whole mind.'

If *rogo* is polite, how could Atticus not bear its use? And what does it mean not to be able to bear being asked to do something? To take the second question first, such inability could of course be displayed in many ways, many of them rude, but if a valued friend asks one insistently to do something, the only effective way to stop him from asking while maintaining the friendship is to comply with the request: the person who cannot bear to be asked repeatedly caves in quickly under pressure. It is therefore likely that what Cicero meant when he said that Atticus could not bear him to make repeated requests was that Atticus always granted them before Cicero needed to repeat them.

To return to the first question, how Atticus could fail to tolerate the use of a polite term, the answer may lie in the type of politeness conveyed by *rogo*. I have argued that *rogo* was polite because it put the asker in a position analogous to that of a client, making clear his need for the addressee's greater power and undertaking to be bound by obligations in exchange for the help he needed. In most circumstances, it was clearly pleasant for a Roman to find himself being asked in such terms by the highest men in the land. But there were limits, because part of one's duty to one's closest associates was to be at hand for them, so that they were not reduced to having to beg for favours. For example, a Roman who allowed his father to entreat him for a favour, rather than granting it promptly, would have been behaving inappropriately. Thus to say that a particular person does not allow one to ask him repeatedly for favours is to praise that person's devotion to oneself—a type of sentiment that is fully in line with Cicero's attitude to Atticus (cf. *Att.* 12. 3, 12. 5a, 12. 18, etc.), much more so than an interpretation that has Cicero complaining about Atticus' touchiness about his requests.

If indeed passage (10) praises Atticus for being such a good friend that he grants Cicero's requests before Cicero has to ask for them twice, the same interpretation would work just as well for passage (8). The addressee there, Dolabella, had been Cicero's son-in-law until shortly before the letter was written; the two were never really intimate, but they clearly got along fairly well and remained on good terms for some time after their family affiliation was ended by Dolabella's divorce from Cicero's daughter. Under these circumstances, Dolabella might well have been expected to grant Cicero's requests without making his former father-in-law beg first. Dolabella obviously did not have the opportunity to do so in the course of the letter, as he would not receive it until the whole thing had been written. But Cicero's suggestion that he might not allow himself to be entreated with *oro* gave Dolabella the opportunity to, as it were, cut in between the *peto* and the *oro* and grant the favour forthwith, thus entitling himself to the same sort of praise that Cicero was giving Atticus in passage (10).

Thus it seems likely that although there was some distinction in meaning between *peto* and *oro* in Cicero's usage, the two were not opposites but rather allied: both were polite, and probably both were polite in the same way. Once again, a politeness theory has been useful in clarifying our understanding of the Latin; though this time Brown and Levinson's framework was not helpful, Terkourafi's allowed us to investigate politeness by using factors other than lexical meaning and thus to discover an element of polite usage that had previously been misidentified.

17.6 Requests benefitting the addressee

Sometimes the primary beneficiary of the fulfilment of a request is not the speaker but the addressee; the speaker benefits only insofar as he or she derives vicarious pleasure from the addressee's well-being, and the requests are polite because they indicate that the speaker has enough affection for the addressee to get such vicarious pleasure. English expressions such as 'Take care!' (when used as an equivalent of 'goodbye') or 'Get well soon!' fall into this category. Such requests do not necessarily use the same polite modifiers as the ones that benefit the speaker; for example 'Could you get well soon?' is not a politer version of 'Get well soon!' the way 'Could you pass the salt?' is a politer version of 'Pass the salt.' The reason is that phrases making fulfilment of a request optional only add politeness when the beneficiary is the speaker; when the beneficiary is the addressee such phrases simply weaken the affectionate concern expressed by the request itself. (On the other hand 'Please get well soon!' works fine, because 'please' in this context does not make fulfilment of the request more optional.)

In Latin this use of the imperative is very common; the epistolary signing-off formulae *uale* 'fare well' and *cura ut ualeas* 'take care that you fare well' are both examples. The five 'please' equivalents we have been discussing can all be used with such addressee-benefitting requests, and when this occurs *uelim*, *quaeso*, *rogo*, and *peto* seem to follow the same hierarchy of magnitude of request as they do for genuine requests: *uelim* and *quaeso* are used for more minor requests and *rogo* and *peto* for more major ones. For example Cicero uses *uelim* to ask friends to look after themselves generally (*Fam.* 5. 21. 5) and to let him know what they would like him to do for them (*Fam.* 3. 1. 2); *quaeso* to ask Atticus to look after himself when he has a minor illness (*Att.* 16. 11. 3); and *rogo* to ask a friend to take courage in the face of serious adversity (*Fam.* 5. 18. 1). *Oro* is also used this way (*Q Fr.* 3. 1. 25). Most interesting are two passages in which Cicero uses *rogo* and *peto* to his beloved freedman Tiro to urge him to do everything he can to recover from a serious illness:

(11) illud, mi Tiro, te <u>rogo</u>, sumptu ne parcas ulla in re, quod ad ualetudinem opus sit. scripsi ad Curium quod dixisses daret. (*Fam.* 16. 4. 2)
'My own Tiro, I ask you this: don't spare expense in anything that is necessary for your health. I have written to Curio and told him to give you whatever you ask for.'

(12) audio te animo angi et medicum dicere ex eo te laborare. si me diligis, excita ex somno tuas litteras humanitatemque, propter quam mihi es carissimus. nunc opus est te animo ualere ut corpore possis. id cum tua tum mea causa facias a te <u>peto</u>. (*Fam.* 16. 14. 2)

> 'I hear that you are suffering in your soul, and that the doctor says that's why you're ill. If you care for me, arouse from its stupor your interest in literature and your cultured humanity, on account of which you are so dear to me. Now you have to get well in spirit, so that you will be able to do so in body. I ask you to do that not only for your sake but also for my own.'

It is notable that these addressee-benefitting requests generally follow the same distribution of terms to individual addressees that we have already observed; thus for example nearly all the passages of this sort in which Cicero uses *quaeso* are addressed to Atticus, Quintus, or Terentia, while *rogo* tends to be used to more distant acquaintances. Tiro, however, forms an interesting exception, in that these two examples are the only case of *rogo* and the only case of *peto* Cicero addresses to him. Cicero frequently makes requests of Tiro, but he never phrases any that are for his own benefit as strongly as the two that are on Tiro's behalf.

These addressee-benefitting requests, I believe, provide the clinching evidence for the real meaning of Cicero's 'please' equivalents. If these terms had made fulfilment of requests optional, they would have been as unsuited to requests benefitting the addressee as English 'could you' is to 'Have a nice day.' But because they were elements of positive politeness, like the addressee-benefitting requests themselves, they were perfect for making such requests particularly effective. The requests to Tiro used *rogo* and *peto* because Cicero was trying to show his freedman that he cared so much about him that he would consider himself indebted to Tiro if Tiro did him the favour of recovering. Such an interpretation fits the contexts far better than one in which Cicero by using *rogo* and *peto* gives Tiro the option of not recovering.

17.7 Conclusion

This analysis has shown that politeness theories can be helpful in understanding even very well-known Latin expressions. Despite all its drawbacks, Brown and Levinson's framework has some real advantages that allow one to attain genuine insight into particular polite usages. At the same time there are other usages for which Brown and Levinson's theory is not helpful, and another theory is genuinely useful. Since the different politeness theories contradict each other, in that in many respects they make mutually exclusive claims about how politeness works, none of them can be simply applied as a template that will tell us, without further effort on our part, how Latin politeness worked. But several different theories have particular strengths that allow them, if judiciously applied in the context of careful examination of evidence, to enhance our understanding.

References

Ačaṙyan, H. (1909). *Classification des dialectes arméniens*. Paris: Champion.

——(1971–9). *Hayeren Armatakan baṙaran* (4 vols). Erevan: Erevani Hamalsarani Hratarakč'owt'iwn.

Adams, J. N. (1976). 'A typological approach to Latin word order'. *Indogermanische Forschungen* 81: 70–99.

——(1984). 'Female speech in Latin comedy'. *Antichthon* 18: 43–77.

——(2007). *The regional diversification of Latin, 200 BC–AD 600*. Cambridge: Cambridge University Press.

Ahlqvist, A. (ed.) (1982). *The early Irish linguist. An edition of the canonical part of the Auraicept na n-Éces*. Helsinki: Societas Scientiarum Fennica.

Ahrens, H. L. (1839). *De Graecae linguae dialectis*, i: *De dialectis Aeolicis et Pseudaeolicis*. Göttingen: Vandenhoeck & Ruprecht.

——(1843). *De Graecae linguae dialectis*, ii: *De dialecto Dorica*. Göttingen: Vandenhoeck & Ruprecht.

Alladina, S. (1993). 'South Asian languages in Britain', in G. Extra and L. Verhoeven (eds), *Immigrant languages in Europe*. Clevedon: Multilingual Matters, 55–65.

Allen, W. S. (1973). *Accent and rhythm: prosodic features of Latin and Greek. A study in theory and reconstruction*. Cambridge: Cambridge University Press.

Alonso Déniz, A. (2008). *Estudios sobre la aspiración de /s/ en los dialectos griegos del I milenio* (Diss. Madrid, Universidad Complutense; cf. http://sites.google.com/site/alcoracalonsodeniz/home/Publications).

——(2009). 'Difusión de la aspiración de la /s/ intervocálica en el Peloponeso en el I milenio'. *Cuadernos de Filología Clásica* 19: 9–27.

——(2010). 'ΔΙΟΗΙΚΕΤΑ ΔΙΟΛΕΥΘΕΡΙ̣[ ] IG V.1 700'. *Emérita* 78: 103–27.

Amsterdamska, O. (1987). *Schools of thought: the development of linguistics from Bopp to Saussure*. Dordrecht, Boston, Lancaster, and Tokyo: Reidel.

Andersen, H. (1960). 'Opedalstenen'. *Norsk Tidsskrift for Sprogvidenskap* 19: 393–417.

——(1986). 'On the noun *borg* and the so-called *a*-umlaut'. *North-Western European Language Evolution* 8: 111–28.

Antonsen, E. H. (1965). 'On defining stages in prehistoric Germanic'. *Language* 41: 19–36.

——(1972). 'The Proto-Germanic syllabics (vowels)', in F. van Coetsem and H. L. Kufner (eds), *Toward a grammar of Proto-Germanic*. Tübingen: Niemeyer, 117–40.

——(2002). *Runes and Germanic linguistics*. Berlin and New York: Mouton de Gruyter.

Arbeitman, Y. (1980). 'The recovery of an IE collocation', in J. A. Greppin (ed.), *First international conference on Armenian linguistics: proceedings*. Delmar, N.Y.: Caravan Books, 225–31.

Arbuthnot, S. (ed.) (2005–7). Cóir Anmann: *A late Middle Irish treatise on personal names* (2 vols). Dublin: Irish Texts Society.

Arnold, E. V. (1905). *Vedic metre in its historical development*. Cambridge: Cambridge University Press.

Arundale, R. B. (2008). 'Against (Gricean) intentions at the heart of human interaction'. *Intercultural Pragmatics* 5: 229–58.

Atkins, S. D. (1968). 'The *RV dyaús* paradigm and the Sievers-Edgerton Law'. *Journal of the American Oriental Society* 88: 679–709.

Awetik'ean, G., Siwrmêlean, X., and Awgerean, M. (1836). *Nor bargirk' haykazean lezowi*. Venice: Mechitarist Press.

Baart, J. L. G. (2003). 'Tonal features in languages of northern Pakistan', in J. L. G. Baart and G. H. Sindhi (eds), *Pakistani languages and society: problems and prospects*. Islamabad and Horsleys Green: National Institute of Pakistan Studies, Quaid-i-Azam University, and Summer Institute of Linguistics, 132–44.

Bahl, K. C. (1957*a*). 'Tones in Panjabi'. *Indian Linguistics* 17: 139–47.

——(1957*b*). 'A note on tones in western Punjabi (Lahanda)'. *Indian Linguistics* 18: 30–4.

Ballard, R. (1994). *Desh Pardesh: the South Asian presence in Britain*. London: Hurst.

Bammesberger, A. (1992). 'Griechisch *thés*, *hés* und *dós*', in B. Brogyanyi and R. Lipp (eds), *Historical philology: Greek, Latin, and Romance. Papers in honor of Oswald Szemerényi II*. Amsterdam and Philadelphia: Benjamins, 41–5.

Bandle, O. (1973). *Die Gliederung des Nordgermanischen*. Basle and Stuttgart: Helbing & Lichtenhahn.

Barnes, J. (2006). *Strength and weakness at the interface: positional neutralization in phonetics and phonology*. Berlin: Mouton de Gruyter.

Barney, S. A., Lewis, W. J., Beach, J. A., and Berghof, O. (2006). *The etymologies of Isidore of Seville*. Cambridge: Cambridge University Press.

Barrack, C. M. (2003). 'The glottalic theory revisited: a negative reappraisal. Part II: the typological fallacy underlying the glottalic theory'. *Indogermanische Forschungen* 108: 1–16.

Bartholomae, C. (1883). *Handbuch der altiranischen Dialekte*. Leipzig: Breitkopf & Härtel.

——(1904). *Altiranisches Wörterbuch*. Strasbourg: Trübner.

Bartoněk, A. (1987). 'On the sources of juxtavocalic *s* in Mycenaean', in P. H. Ilievski and L. Crepajac (eds), *Tractata Mycenaea: proceedings of the Eighth International Colloquium on Mycenaean studies*. Skopje: Macedonian Academy of Sciences and Arts, 41–8.

——(2003). *Handbuch des mykenischen Griechisch*. Heidelberg: Winter.

Barz, R. K., and Siegel, J. (eds) (1988). *Language transplanted: the development of overseas Hindi*. Wiesbaden: Harrassowitz.

Bauer, B. (1995). *The emergence and development of SVO patterning in Latin and French: diachronic and psycholinguistic perspectives*. New York and Oxford: Oxford University Press.

Bazell, C. E. (1952). 'Phonemic and morphemic analysis'. *Word* 8: 33–8.

Bechtel, F. (1923). *Die griechischen Dialekte,* ii: *Die westgriechischen Dialekte*. Berlin: Weidmann.

Beekes, R. S. P. (2003). 'Historical phonology of Classical Armenian', in F. Kortlandt, *Armeniaca: comparative notes*. Ann Arbor: Caravan Books, 133–211.

Beeler, M. S. (1966). 'Proto-Germanic [i] and [e]: one phoneme or two?'. *Language* 42: 473–4.

Benediktsson, H. (1967). 'The Proto-Germanic vowel system', in *To honor Roman Jakobson*, i. The Hague and Paris: Mouton, 174–96.

——(1970). 'Aspects of historical phonology', in H. Benediktsson (ed.), *The Nordic languages and modern linguistics [1]*. Reykjavík: Vísindafélag Íslendinga, 87–142.

Bennett, W. H. (1952). 'The early Germanic umlauts and the Gothic migration'. *Language* 28: 339–42.

Benveniste, É. (1935). *Origines de la formation des noms en indo-européen*. Paris: Maisonneuve.

Bermúdez-Otero, R. (2006). 'Phonological change in Optimality Theory', in K. Brown (ed.), *Encyclopedia of language and linguistics* (2nd edn). Oxford: Elsevier, 9: 497–505.

Bhardwaj, M. R. (1995). *Colloquial Panjabi*. London and New York: Routledge.

Bhatia, T. K. (1975). 'The evolution of tones in Punjabi'. *Studies in the Linguistic Sciences* 5: 12–24.

——(1988). 'Trinidad Hindi: its genesis and generational profile', in Barz and Siegel (1988), 179–96.

——(1993). *Punjabi: a cognitive-descriptive grammar*. London and New York: Routledge.

Bhattacharya, D. (1997). *The Paippalāda-Saṃhitā of the Atharvaveda. Volume one, consisting of the first fifteen Kāṇḍas*. Calcutta: Asiatic Society.

Blase, H. (1896–8). 'Zur Geschichte der Futura und des Konjunktivs des Perfekts im Lateinischen'. *Archiv für lateinische Lexikographie und Grammatik* 10: 313–43.

Blümel, W. (1982). *Die aiolischen Dialekte: Phonologie und Morphologie der inschriftlichen Texte aus generativer Sicht*. Göttingen: Vandenhoeck & Ruprecht.

Bolinger, D. (1967). 'Adjectives in English: attribution and predication'. *Lingua* 18: 1–34.

Bonfante, G. (1986). 'L'Intonation syllabique grecque, baltique, slave et védique'. *Bulletin de la Société de Linguistique de Paris* 81: 374–6.

Bonnet, M. (1890). *Le Latin de Grégoire de Tours*. Paris: Hachette.

Bopp, F. (1837). *Vergleichende Grammatik des Sanskrit, Zend, Griechischen, Lateinischen, Litthauischen, Altslawischen, Gothischen und Deutschen: Dritte Abtheilung*. Berlin: Dümmler.

Braune, W., and Heidermanns, F. (2004). *Gotische Grammatik* (20th edn). Tübingen: Niemeyer.

Briscoe, J. (2008). *A commentary on Livy, Books 38–40*. Oxford: Oxford University Press.

Brixhe, C. (1992). 'Du "datif" mycénien aux protagonistes de la situation linguistique', in J.-P. Olivier (ed.), *Mykenaïka: actes du IXe Colloque international sur les textes mycéniens et égéens*. Paris: de Boccard, 129–57.

——(2006). 'Préhistoire et début de l'histoire des dialectes grecs'. *Incontri Linguistici* 29: 39–59.

Brown, P., and Levinson, S. C. (1978). 'Universals in language usage: politeness phenomena', in E. Goody (ed.), *Questions and politeness: strategies in social interaction*. Cambridge: Cambridge University Press, 56–289.

————(1987). *Politeness: some universals in language usage*. Cambridge: Cambridge University Press.

Brugman, K. (1876). 'Zur Geschichte der stammabstufenden Declinationen. Erste Abhandlung: Die Nomina auf *-ar-* und *-tar-*'. *(Curtius') Studien zur griechischen und lateinischen Grammatik* 9: 361–406.

Brugmann, K., and Thumb, A. (1913). *Griechische Grammatik: Lautlehre, Stammbildungs- und Flexionslehre, Syntax* (4th edn). Munich: Beck.

Brunner, K. (1965). *Altenglische Grammatik* (3rd edn). Tübingen: Niemeyer.

Brunt, P. A. (1988). *The fall of the Roman republic and related essays*. Oxford: Oxford University Press.

Buck, C. D. (1955). *The Greek dialects*. Chicago: University of Chicago Press.

Bugge, S. (1893). 'Beiträge zur etymologischen erläuterung der armenischen sprache'. *Zeitschrift für Vergleichende Sprachforschung* 32: 1–86.

——(1897). *Lykische Studien*, i. Christiania: Dybwad.

Burrow, T. (1975). 'A new look at Brugmann's Law'. *Bulletin of the School of Oriental and African Studies* 38: 55–80.

Calder, G. (ed.) (1917). *Auraicept na n-Éces: The scholars' primer*. Edinburgh: Grant.

Callebat, L., Bouet, P., Fleury, P., and Zuinghedau, M. (1984). *Vitruve, De architectura: concordance; documentation bibliographique, lexicale et grammaticale*, ii. Hildesheim, Zurich, and New York: Olms-Weidmann.

Campbell, A. (1962). *Old English grammar* (rev. edn). Oxford: Oxford University Press.

Carney, T. F. (1964). 'The words *sodes* and *quaeso* in Terentian usage'. *Acta Classica* 7: 57–63.

Chantraine, P. (1958). *Grammaire homérique*, i: *Phonétique et morphologie* (3rd edn). Paris: Klincksieck.

——(1961). *Morphologie historique du grec* (2nd edn). Paris: Klincksieck.

——(1968–80). *Dictionnaire étymologique de la langue grecque: histoire des mots* (2 vols). Paris: Klincksieck.

Chatfield, C., and Collins, A. J. (1980). *Introduction to multivariate analysis*. London: Chapman and Hall.

Chomsky, N., and Halle, M. (1968). *The sound pattern of English.* New York: Harper & Row.

Clackson, J. (1994). *The linguistic relationship between Armenian and Greek.* Oxford: Blackwell.

——(2007). *Indo-European linguistics: an introduction.* Cambridge: Cambridge University Press.

——and Horrocks, G. C. (2007). *The Blackwell history of the Latin language.* Oxford and Malden, Mass.: Blackwell.

Clements, G. N., and Hume, E. V. (1995). 'The internal organization of speech sounds', in J. Goldsmith (ed.), *The handbook of phonological theory.* Oxford: Blackwell, 245–306.

Collinge, N. E. (1985). *The laws of Indo-European.* Amsterdam and Philadelphia: Benjamins.

Coseriu, E. (1958). *Sincronía, diacronía e historia: el problema del cambio lingüístico.* Montevideo: University Press.

——(1974). *Synchronie, Diachronie und Geschichte: das Problem des Sprachwandels,* tr. H. Sohre (translation of Coseriu 1958). Munich: Fink.

Cowgill, W. (1959). 'The inflection of the Germanic ō-presents'. *Language* 35: 1–15.

——(1965). 'Evidence in Greek', in Winter (1965*a*), 142–80.

——(1970). 'Italic and Celtic superlatives and the dialects of Indo-European', in G. Cardona, H. M. Hoenigswald, and A. Senn (eds), *Indo-European and Indo-Europeans: papers presented at the 3rd Indo-European Conference at the University of Pennsylvania.* Philadelphia: University of Pennsylvania Press, 113–53.

——(1979). 'Anatolian *hi*-conjugation and Indo-European perfect: instalment II', in E. Neu and W. Meid (eds), *Hethitisch und Indogermanisch.* Innsbruck: Institut für Sprachwissenschaft, 25–39.

——(1985*a*). 'The personal endings of thematic verbs in Indo-European', in B. Schlerath (ed.), *Grammatische Kategorien: Funktion und Geschichte.* Wiesbaden: Reichert, 99–108.

——(1985*b*). 'PIE **duu̯o* "2" in Germanic and Celtic, and the nom.-acc. dual of non-neuter *o*-stems'. *Münchener Studien zur Sprachwissenschaft* 46: 13–28.

——(2006). 'The personal endings of thematic verbs in Indo-European' (extended version of Cowgill 1985*a*), in J. S. Klein (ed.), *The collected writings of Warren Cowgill.* Ann Arbor and New York: Beech Stave Press, 535–67.

Cruttenden, A. (1997). *Intonation* (2nd edn). Cambridge: Cambridge University Press.

Cuny, A. (1943). *Recherches sur le vocalisme, le consonantisme et la formation des racines en 'nostratique'.* Paris: Maisonneuve.

Curtius, G. (1873). *Das Verbum der griechischen Sprache seinem Baue nach dargestellt,* i. Leipzig: Hirzel.

Dal, I. (1971). *Untersuchungen zur germanischen und deutschen Sprachgeschichte.* Oslo: Universitetsforlaget.

Davis, K. (1994). 'Stop voicing in Hindi'. *Journal of Phonetics* 22: 177–93.

de Melo, W. D. C. (2010). 'Possessive pronouns in Plautus', in E. Dickey and A. Chahoud (eds), *Colloquial and literary Latin*. Cambridge: Cambridge University Press, 71–99.

de Sutter, M. (1986). 'A theory of word order within the Latin Noun Phrase, based on Cato's *De agri cultura*', in C. Deroux (ed.), *Studies in Latin literature and Roman history*, iv. Brussels: Collection Latomus, 151–83.

de Vaan, M. (2003). *The Avestan vowels*. Amsterdam and New York: Rodopi.

——(2008). *Etymological dictionary of Latin and the other Italic languages*. Leiden: Brill.

Debrunner, A. (1954). *Jacob Wackernagel: Altindische Grammatik*, ii.2. *Die Nominalsuffixe*. Göttingen: Vandenhoeck & Ruprecht.

——(1957). *Jacob Wackernagel: Altindische Grammatik. Nachträge zu Band I*. Göttingen: Vandenhoeck & Ruprecht.

Delamarre, X. (2003). *Dictionnaire de la langue gauloise* (2nd edn). Paris: Éditions Errance.

Demiraj, B. (1997). *Albanische Etymologien: Untersuchungen zum albanischen Erbwortschatz*. Amsterdam: Rodopi.

Deniaux, E. (1993). *Clientèles et pouvoir à l'époque de Cicéron*. Rome: École française de Rome.

Derksen, R. (2008). *Etymological dictionary of the Slavic inherited lexicon*. Leiden: Brill.

Devine, A. M., and Stephens, L. D. (2006). *Latin word order: structured meaning and information*. New York and Oxford: Oxford University Press.

Dickey, E. (2002). *Latin forms of address*. Oxford: Oxford University Press.

——(2012). 'How to say "please" in classical Latin'. *Classical Quarterly* 62.

Dik, S. (1978). *Functional grammar*. Amsterdam: North-Holland.

Ditrich, T. (2010). 'The variety of expressions for Heaven and Earth in the Rgveda'. *Crossroads* 5(1): 35–44.

Dobson, E. (1962). 'Middle English lengthening in open syllables'. *Transactions of the Philological Society* 61: 124–48.

——(1969). 'Notes on sound-change and phoneme theory'. *Brno Studies in English* 8: 43–8.

Dresher, B. E., and Lahiri, A. (1991). 'The Germanic foot: metrical coherence in Old English'. *Linguistic Inquiry* 22: 251–86.

Dryer, M. (1988). 'Object-verb order and adjective-noun order: dispelling a myth'. *Lingua* 74: 185–217.

Dunbar, H., and Marzullo, B. (1962). *A complete concordance to the Odyssey of Homer* (2nd edn). Hildesheim: Olms.

Durante, M. (1976). *Sulla preistoria della tradizione poetica graeca*, ii. Rome: Edizioni dell'Ateneo.

Düwel, K. (2008). *Runenkunde* (4th edn). Stuttgart and Weimar: Metzler.

Edgerton, F. (1934). 'Sievers' Law and Indo-European weak grade vocalism'. *Language* 10: 235–65.

——(1943). 'The Indo-European semivowels'. *Language* 19: 83–124.

——(1962). 'The semivowel phonemes of Indo-European: a reconsideration'. *Language* 38: 352–9.

Eelen, G. (2001). *A critique of politeness theories*. Manchester: St Jerome.

Egetmeyer, M. (2010). *Le Dialecte grec ancien de Chypre* (2 vols). Berlin and New York: de Gruyter.

Elbourne, P. (1998). 'Proto-Indo-European voiceless aspirates'. *Historische Sprachforschung* 111: 1–30.

——(2000). 'Plain voiceless stop plus laryngeal in Indo-European'. *Historische Sprachforschung* 113: 2–28.

——(2001). 'Aspiration by /s/ and devoicing of mediae aspiratae'. *Historische Sprachforschung* 114: 197–219.

——(2011). 'ἐπίρροθος'. *Glotta* 87: 37–57.

Elenbaas, N., and Kager, R. (1999). 'Ternary rhythm and the lapse constraint'. *Phonology* 16: 273–329.

Ellsworth, M. (2011). 'The first palatalization of Greek', in S. W. Jamison, H. C. Melchert, and B. Vine (eds), *Proceedings of the 22nd annual UCLA Indo-European conference*. Bremen: Hempen, 13–31.

Euler, W. (1979). *Indo-iranisch-griechische Gemeinsamkeiten der Nominalbildung und deren indogermanische Grundlagen*. Innsbruck: Institut für Sprachwissenschaft.

Exon, C. (1906). 'Medial vowel-syncope in Latin'. *Hermathena* 32: 117–43.

Ferguson, C. A. (1990). 'From ESSES to AITCHES: identifying pathways of diachronic change', in W. Croft, S. Kemmer, and K. Denning (eds), *Studies in typology and diachrony offered to Joseph Greenberg*. Amsterdam and Philadelphia: Benjamins, 59–78.

Fernandez Alvarez, M. P. (1981). *El argolico occidental y oriental en las inscripciones de los siglos VII, VI y V a. C.* Salamanca: Ediciones Universidad de Salamanca.

Fick, A. (1905). Review of R. Meister, *Dorer und Achäer* (Leipzig: Teubner, 1904). *Wochenschrift der klassischen Philologie* 22: 593–99.

Frisk, H. (1960–72). *Griechisches Etymologisches Wörterbuch* (3 vols). Heidelberg: Winter.

Fudge, E. (1977). 'Long and short [æ] in one southern British speaker's English'. *Journal of the International Phonetic Association* 7: 55–65.

Gallée, J. H. (1910). *Altsächsische Grammatik*. Halle: Niemeyer.

García Ramón, J. L. (1999). 'Griechisch Ζητήρ· Ζεὺς ἐν Κύπρῳ, vedisch *yātár-* "Rächer" und die Vertretung von **i̯-* im Griechischen', in H. Eichner and H. C. Luschützky (eds), *Compositiones Indogermanicae in memoriam Jochem Schindler*. Praha: Enigma Corporation, 77–96.

Garrett, A. (1999). 'A new model of Indo-European subgrouping and dispersal', in S. S. Chang, L. Liaw, and J. Ruppenhofer (eds), *Proceedings of the twenty-fifth annual meeting of the Berkeley Linguistics Society*. Berkeley: Berkeley Linguistics Society, 146–56.

——(2006). 'Convergence in the formation of Indo-European subgroups: phylogeny and chronology', in P. Forster and C. Renfrew (eds), *Phylogenetic methods and the prehistory of languages*. Cambridge: McDonald Institute for Archaeological Research, 139–51.

Geldner, K. F. (1951). *Der Rig-Veda* (3 vols). Cambridge, Mass.: Harvard University Press.

Gignac, F. T. (1970). 'The pronunciation of Greek stops in the papyri'. *Transactions and Proceedings of the American Philological Association* 101: 185–202.

——(1976). *A grammar of the Greek papyri of the Roman and Byzantine periods*, i: *Phonology*. Milan: Istituto Editoriale Cisalpino–La Goliardica.

Gildersleeve, B. L., and Lodge, G. (1895). *Gildersleeve's Latin grammar* (3rd edn). London: Macmillan.

Gill, H. S., and Gleason, H. A. (1963). *A reference grammar of Panjabi*. Hartford, Conn.: Department of Linguistics, Hartford Seminary Foundation.

Giusti, G., and Oniga, R. (2006). 'La struttura del sintagma nominale latino', in R. Oniga and L. Zennaro (eds), *Atti della 'Giornata di Linguistica Latina', Venezia, 7 maggio 2004*. Venice: Cafoscarina, 71–99.

Godel, R. (1975). *An introduction to the study of Classical Armenian*. Wiesbaden: Reichert.

Good, J. (ed.) (2008). *Linguistic universals and language change*. Oxford: Oxford University Press.

Gould, S. J. (2001). 'Requiem eternal', in *The lying stones of Marrakech*. London: Vintage, 227–9.

Gratwick, A. S. (1982). '*Latinitas Britannica*. Was British Latin archaic?', in N. Brookes (ed.), *Latin and the vernacular languages in early medieval Britain*. Leicester: Leicester University Press, 1–79.

Greppin, J. (1972). 'The Armenian reflexes of IE *w and *y'. *Revue des Études Arméniennes* 9: 69–78.

——(1978). 'On Greek zeta'. *Journal of Indo-European Studies* 6: 141–2.

Griffiths, A. (2009). *The Paippalādasaṃhitā of the Atharvaveda Kāṇḍas 6 & 7*. Groningen: Forsten.

Grønvik, O. (1983). *Die dialektgeographische Stellung des Krimgotischen und die krimgotische cantilena*. Oslo: Universitetsforlaget.

——(1998). *Untersuchungen zur älteren nordischen und germanischen Sprachgeschichte*. Frankfurt am Main and Berlin: Lang.

Gwynn, E. J. (ed.) (1900). *Poems from the Dindshenchas*. Dublin: Royal Irish Academy.

——(ed.) (1903–35). *The metrical Dindshenchas* (5 vols). Dublin: Royal Irish Academy.

Haag, O. (1898). *Die Latinität Fredegars*. Erlangen: Junge.

Haas, W. (1978). *Sprachwandel und Sprachgeographie: Untersuchungen zur Struktur der Dialektverschiedenheit am Beispiele der schweizerdeutschen Vokalsysteme*. Wiesbaden: Steiner.

Hackstein, O. (2000). 'Archaismus oder historischer Sprachkontakt. Zur Frage westindogermanisch-tocharischer Konvergenzen', in G. Meiser and O. Hackstein (eds), *Sprachkontakt und Sprachwandel: Akten der XI. Fachtagung der Indogermanischen Gesellschaft*. Wiesbaden: Reichert, 169–84.

——(2002). *Die Sprachform der homerischen Epen. Faktoren morphologischer Variabilität in literarischen Frühformen: Tradition, Sprachwandel, sprachliche Anachronismen.* Wiesbaden: Reichert.

Hajnal, I. (1994). 'Das Brugmannsche Gesetz in diachroner Sicht und seine Gültigkeit innerhalb der arischen *a*-Stämme'. *Historische Sprachforschung* 107: 194–221.

Hale, K. (1983). 'Warlpiri and the grammar of non-configurational languages'. *Natural Language and Linguistic Theory* 1: 5–47.

Hall, J. (2009). *Politeness and politics in Cicero's letters.* New York: Oxford University Press.

Hall, T. A. (2007). 'Segmental features', in P. de Lacy (ed.), *The Cambridge handbook of phonology.* Cambridge: Cambridge University Press, 311–34.

Halla-aho, H. (2010). 'Requesting in a letter: context, syntax, and the choice between complements in the letters of Cicero and Pliny the Younger'. *Transactions of the Philological Society* 108: 232–247.

Halle, M. (1992). 'Phonological features', in W. Bright (ed.), *International encyclopedia of linguistics*, iii. Oxford: Oxford University Press, 207–12.

——and Stevens, K. (1971). 'A note on laryngeal features'. *Quarterly Progress Reports, MIT Research Laboratory of Electronics* 101: 198–213.

——and Vergnaud, J.-R. (1987). *An essay on stress.* Cambridge, Mass.: MIT Press.

Hamm, E.-M. (1957). *Grammatik zu Sappho und Alkaios.* Berlin: Akademie-Verlag.

Hamp, E. P. (1966). 'Three Armenian etymologies. (1. Armenian *ner* "wife of husband's brother", 2. *ayr*, gen. *aṙn*, 3. Armenian *gišer*, Latin *uesper*)'. *Revue des Études Arméniennes* 3: 11–15.

Harđarson, J. A. (1993). *Studien zum urindogermanischen Wurzelaorist und dessen Vertretung im Indoiranischen und Griechischen.* Innsbruck: Institut für Sprachwissenschaft.

Harding, E. (1937–49). *Språkvetenskapliga problem i ny belysning [1–99].* Lund: Blom.

Harris, A. C., and Campbell, L. (1995). *Historical syntax in cross-linguistic perspective.* Cambridge: Cambridge University Press.

Hartel, W. (1874). 'Homerische Studien, ii'. *Sitzungsberichte der Philosophisch-Historischen Classe der Kaiserlichen Akademie der Wissenschaften (in Wien)* 76: 329–76.

Hassall, M. W. C., Wilson, D. R., and Wright, R. P. (1972). 'Roman Britain in 1971'. *Britannia* 3: 299–367.

Hastie, T., and Tibshirani, R. (1990). *Generalized additive models.* London: Chapman and Hall.

Hayden, D. A. (forthcoming). 'Natural and artificial language in *Auraicept na nÉces* revisited'.

Hayes, B. (1995). *Metrical Stress Theory: principles and case studies.* Chicago: University of Chicago Press.

Heidermanns, F. (1986). 'Zur primären Wortbildung im germanischen Adjektivsystem'. *Zeitschrift für Vergleichende Sprachforschung* 99: 278–307.

Heidermanns, F. (1993). *Etymologisches Wörterbuch der germanischen Primäradjektive.* Berlin: de Gruyter.

Hempel, C. G. (1942). 'The function of general laws in history'. *Journal of Philosophy* 39: 35–48.

——and Oppenheim, P. (1948). 'Studies in the logic of explanation'. *Philosophy of Science* 15: 135–75.

Hermann, E. (1918). 'Die böotische Betonung'. *Nachrichten von der Königlichen Gesellschaft der Wissenschaften zu Göttingen: Philologisch-historische Klasse*, 273–80.

——(1923). *Silbenbildung im Griechischen und in den andern indogermanischen Sprachen.* Göttingen: Vandenhoeck & Ruprecht.

Heselwood, B., and McChrystal, L. (1999). 'The effect of age-group and place of L1 acquisition on the realisation of Panjabi stop consonants in Bradford: an acoustic sociophonetic study'. *Leeds Working Papers in Linguistics and Phonetics* 7: 49–68.

Hill, E. (2004). 'Das germanische Verb für "tun" und die Ausgänge des germanischen schwachen Präteritums'. *Sprachwissenschaft* 29: 257–303.

Hinge, G. (2006). *Die Sprache Alkmans: Textgeschichte und Sprachgeschichte.* Wiesbaden: Reichert.

Hock, H. H. (1973). 'On the phonemic status of Germanic *e* and *i*', in B. B. Kachru et al. (eds), *Issues in linguistics: papers in honor of Henry and Renée Kahane.* Urbana: University of Illinois Press, 319–51.

——(1991). *Principles of historical linguistics* (2nd edn). Berlin, New York, and Amsterdam: Mouton de Gruyter.

——(forthcoming). 'Vedic verb accent revisited', in J. Klein and E. Tucker (eds), *Proceedings of the XIIIth World Sanskrit Conference: linguistics.* Delhi: Motilal Banarsidass.

Hockett, C. F. (1965). 'Sound change'. *Language* 41: 185–204.

Hodot, R. (1990). *Le Dialecte éolien d'Asie: la langue des inscriptions.* Paris: Éditions Recherche sur les Civilisations.

Hoenigswald, H. M. (1944). 'Internal reconstruction'. *Studies in Linguistics* 2: 78–87.

——(1960). *Language change and linguistic reconstruction.* Chicago: University of Chicago Press.

——(1978). 'The *annus mirabilis* 1876 and posterity'. *Transactions of the Philological Society*, 76: 17–35.

——(1986). 'Some considerations of relative chronology: the Greek thematic present', in A. Etter (ed.), *o-o-pe-ro-si: Festschrift für Ernst Risch zum 75. Geburtstag.* Berlin and New York: de Gruyter, 372–5.

——(1997). 'Analogy in Cyrene and elsewhere', in D. Q. Adams (ed.), *Festschrift for Eric P. Hamp*, i. Washington, D.C.: Institute for the Study of Man, 93–8.

——(1999). 'Secondary split, gap-filling, and bifurcation in historical phonology', in E. C. Polomé and C. F. Justus (eds), *Language change and typological variation: in honor of Winfred P. Lehmann on the occasion of his 83rd birthday*, i. Washington, D.C.: Institute for the Study of Man, 201–6.

Hoffmann, R. (1997). *Lateinische Verbalperiphrasen vom Typ* amans sum *und* amatus fui*: Valenz und Grammatikalisierung (Primäres Textkorpus: Ovid).* Frankfurt am Main etc.: Lang.

Hofman, R. (1993). 'The linguistic preoccupations of the glossators of the St Gall Priscian', in V. Law (ed.), *The history of linguistic thought in the early medieval ages*. Amsterdam: Benjamins, 111–26.

——(ed.) (1996). *The Sankt Gall Priscian commentary*, Part 1 (2 vols). Münster: Nodus.

Hofmann, J. B., and Szantyr, A. (1965). *Lateinische Syntax und Stilistik*. Munich: Beck.

Hollifield, P. (1980). 'The phonological development of final syllables in Germanic'. *Die Sprache* 26: 19–53, 145–78.

Holst, J. H. (1998). 'Ein bisher unentdecktes Lautgesetz im Albanischen und damit im Zusammenhang stehende Betrachtungen'. *Historische Sprachforschung* 111: 83–98.

Holtz, L. (ed.) (1977). *Grammatici Hibernici Carolini aevi*, i. Turnhout: Brepols.

——(ed.) (1981). *Donat et la tradition de l'enseignement grammatical: étude sur l'Ars Donati et sa diffusion (IVe–IXe siècle) et édition critique*. Paris: Centre National de la Recherche Scientifique.

Hombert, J.-M., Ohala, J. J., and Ewan, W. G. (1976). 'Tonogenesis: theories and queries'. *Report of the Phonology Laboratory, Berkeley* 1: 48–77.

Horowitz, F. E. (1974). *Sievers' Law and the evidence of the Rigveda*. The Hague: Mouton.

Horrocks, G. (2010). *Greek: a history of the language and its speakers* (2nd edn). Oxford: Wiley-Blackwell.

Hübschmann, H. (1883). *Armenische Studien*, i: *Grundzüge der armenischen Etymologie. Erster Theil.* Leipzig: Breitkopf & Härtel.

——(1897). *Armenische Grammatik, Erster Teil. Armenische Etymologie*. Leipzig: Breitkopf & Härtel.

——(1899). 'Hübschmann, H. Armenische Grammatik'. *Anzeiger für indogermanische Sprach- und Altertumskunde. Beiblatt zu den Indogermanischen Forschungen* 10: 41–50.

Huxley, T. H. (1866). 'On the advisableness of improving natural knowledge'. *Fortnightly Review* 3: 626–37.

——(1887). 'Science and pseudo-science'. *Popular Science Monthly* 31: 207–24.

Isaac, G. (2007). 'The reflexes of the Celtic diphthong **au*'. *Journal of Celtic Linguistics* 11: 23–47.

Issatschenko, A. V. (1973). 'Das Suffix -chen und der phonologische Status des [ç] im Deutschen'. *Deutsche Sprache* 3: 1–6.

Jackson, K. H. (1953). *Language and history in early Britain: a chronological survey of the Brittonic languages, first to twelfth century* AD. Edinburgh: Edinburgh University Press.

——(1967). *A historical phonology of Breton*. Dublin: Institute for Advanced Studies.

Jacobs, H. (2000). 'The revenge of the uneven trochee: Latin main stress, metrical constituency, stress-related phenomena and OT', in A. Lahiri (ed.), *Analogy, levelling, markedness: principles of change in phonology and morphology.* Berlin and New York: Mouton de Gruyter, 333–52.

Jacobs, H. (2003*a*). 'The emergence of quantity-sensitivity in Latin: secondary stress, iambic shortening, and theoretical implications for "mixed" stress systems', in E. Holt (ed.), *Optimality Theory and language change.* Dordrecht, Boston, and London: Kluwer, 229–47.

——(2003*b*). 'Why preantepenultimate stress in Latin requires an OT-account', in P. Fikkert and H. Jacobs (eds), *Development in prosodic systems.* Berlin and New York: Mouton de Gruyter, 395–418.

——(2004). 'Rhythmic vowel deletion in OT: syncope in Latin'. *Probus* 16(1): 63–89.

J̌ahowkyan, G. B. (1967). *Očerki po istorii dopis'mennogo perioda armjanskogo jazyka.* Erevan: Izdatel'stvo Akademii Nauk Armjanskoj SSR.

——(1982). *Sravnitel'naja grammatika armjanskogo jazyka. Hayocʻ lezvi hamematakan kʻerakanowtʻyown.* Erevan: Izdatel'stvo Akademii Nauk Armjanskoj SSR.

Jakobson, R. (1931). 'Prinzipien der historischen Phonologie'. *Travaux du Cercle Linguistique de Prague* 4: 247–67 (tr. J. Cantineau with slight revisions as 'Principes de phonologie historique', in N. S. Trubetzkoy, *Principes de phonologie*, Paris 1949, 315–36; repr. in Jakobson 1962: 202–20).

——(1937). 'Über die Beschaffenheit der prosodischen Gegensätze', in *Mélanges de linguistique et de philologie offerts à J. van Ginneken.* Paris: Klincksieck, 25–33 (repr. in Jakobson 1962: 254–61).

——(1949). 'The phonemic and grammatical aspects of language in their interrelations'. *Actes du sixième congrès international des linguistes.* Paris: Klincksieck, 5–18 (repr. in Jakobson 1971: 103–14).

——(1962). *Selected writings*, i: *Phonological studies.* The Hague: Mouton.

——(1971). *Selected writings*, ii: *Word and language.* The Hague and Paris: Mouton.

Jamison, S. W. (1983). *Function and form in the* -áya-*formations of the Rig Veda and Atharva Veda.* Göttingen: Vandenhoeck & Ruprecht.

——(1986). 'Brāhmaṇa syllable counting, Vedic *tvác* "skin", and the Sanskrit expression for the canonical creature'. *Indo-Iranian Journal* 29: 161–81.

Jasanoff, J. H. (2004). 'Acute vs. circumflex: some notes on PIE and post-PIE prosodic phonology', in A. Hyllested, A. R. Jørgensen, J. H. Larsson, and T. Olander (eds), *Per aspera ad asteriscos: studia Indogermanica in honorem Jens Elmegård Rasmussen.* Innsbruck: Institut für Sprachwissenschaft, 247–55.

——(2009). 'Notes on the internal history of the PIE optative', in K. Yoshida and B. Vine (eds), *East and West: papers in Indo-European studies.* Bremen: Hempen, 47–67.

Jaski, B. (2003). '"We are of the Greeks in our origin": new perspectives on the Irish origin legend'. *Cambrian Medieval Celtic Studies* 46: 1–53.

Joffre, M.-D. (1995). *Le Verbe latin: voix et diathèse.* Louvain and Paris: Peeters.

Joseph, B. D., and Janda, R. (eds) (2003). *The handbook of historical linguistics.* Oxford: Blackwell.

Joseph, L. S. (1982). 'The treatment of *CR̥H- and the origin of CaRa- in Celtic'. *Ériu* 33: 31–57.

Joshi, S. S. (1973). 'Pitch and related phenomena in Panjabi'. *Pakha Sanjam* 6: 1–62.
——and Gill, M. S. (eds) (1994). *Punjabi-English dictionary.* Patiala: Punjabi University.
Kaster, R. A. (2005). *Emotion, restraint, and community in ancient Rome.* Oxford: Oxford University Press.
Kellens, J. (1995). *Liste du verbe avestique.* Wiesbaden: Reichert.
Kelly, P. (1997). 'The earliest words for "horse" in the Celtic languages', in S. Davies and N. A. Jones (eds), *The horse in Celtic culture: medieval Welsh perspectives.* Cardiff: University of Wales Press, 43–63.
Kenstowicz, M. (1994). *Phonology in generative grammar.* Oxford: Blackwell.
Kimball, S. E. (1999). *Hittite historical phonology.* Innsbruck: Institut für Sprachwissenschaft.
Kiparsky, P. (1967). 'A phonological rule of Greek'. *Glotta* 44: 109–34.
——(1973*a*). 'Abstractness, opacity, and global rules', in O. Fujimura (ed.), *Three dimensions of linguistic theory.* Tokyo: TEC, 57–86.
——(1973*b*). 'On comparative linguistics: the case of Grassmann's Law', in H. M. Hoenigswald and R. E. Longacre (eds), *Diachronic, areal and typological linguistics.* The Hague and Paris: Mouton, 115–34.
Klein, J. S. (1992). *On verbal accentuation in the Rigveda.* New Haven: American Oriental Society.
——(1998). 'Rigvedic *syá-/tyá-*', in J. H. Jasanoff, H. C. Melchert, and L. Oliver (eds), *Mír Curad: studies in honor of Calvert Watkins.* Innsbruck: Institut für Sprachwissenschaft, 362–72.
Klingenschmitt, G. (1982). *Das altarmenische Verbum.* Wiesbaden: Reichert.
Kloekhorst, A. (2008). *Etymological dictionary of the Hittite inherited lexicon.* Leiden: Brill.
Kock, A. (1898). 'Der *a*-umlaut und der wechsel der endvokale *a : i (e)* in den altnordischen sprachen'. *Beiträge zur Geschichte der deutschen Sprache und Literatur* 23: 484–554.
——(1910). 'Kritiska anmärkningar til frågan om *a*-omljudet'. *Arkiv för Nordisk Filologi* 26: 97–141.
Koerner, E. F. K. (1999). 'The authors of the idea of a language as a system *où tout se tient*', in E. F. K. Koerner, *Linguistic historiography.* Amsterdam: Benjamins, 183–200.
Kölligan, D. (2006). 'Armenian *o(v)*', in D. Kölligan and R. Sen (eds), *Oxford University working papers in linguistics, philology and phonetics*, xi. Oxford: University of Oxford, 110–21.
Kortlandt, F. (1997). 'Arm. *nêr* "sister-in-law"'. *Annual of Armenian Linguistics* 18: 7–9.
——(1998). 'The development of **y* in Armenian'. *Annual of Armenian Linguistics* 19: 15–18.
Kovács, F. (1971). *Linguistic structures and linguistic laws*, tr. S. Simon. Amsterdam: Grüner.

Krause, W., and Jankuhn, H. (1966). *Die Runeninschriften im älteren Futhark* (2 vols). Göttingen: Vandenhoeck & Ruprecht.

Kretschmer, P. (1896). *Einleitung in die Geschichte der griechischen Sprache*. Göttingen: Vandenhoeck & Ruprecht.

——(1909). 'Zur Geschichte der griechischen Dialekte'. *Glotta* 1: 9–59.

——(1910). 'Sprache', in A. Gercke and E. Norden (eds), *Einleitung in die Altertumswissenschaft*, i. Leipzig and Berlin: Teubner, 129–229.

Kruszewski, N. (1885). 'Prinzipien der Sprachentwicklung (Fortsetzung)'. *(Techmers) Internationale Zeitschrift für Allgemeine Sprachwissenschaft* 2: 258–68.

Krzanowski, W. J. (1988). *Principles of multivariate analysis: a user's perspective*. Oxford: Oxford University Press.

Kühner, R., and Stegmann, C. (1912–14). *Ausführliche Grammatik der lateinischen Sprache*, ii: *Satzlehre* (2 vols) (2nd edn). Hanover: Hahn.

Kümmel, M. (2000). *Das Perfekt im Indoiranischen*. Wiesbaden: Reichert.

Kuryłowicz, J. (1927). 'Les Effets du en indo-iranien'. *Prace Filologiczne* 11: 201–43.

——(1947). 'La Nature des procès dits analogiques'. *Acta Linguistica* 5: 17–34.

——(1952*a*). *L'Accentuation des langues indo-européennes* (1st edn). Cracow: Polska Akademia Umiejętności.

——(1952*b*). 'The Germanic vowel system'. *Biuletyn Polskiego Towarzystwa Językoznawczego* 11: 50–4.

——(1956). *L'Apophonie en indo-européen*. Wrocław: Polska Akademia Nauk.

——(1964). *The inflectional categories of Indo-European*. Heidelberg: Winter.

——(1967). 'Phonologie und Morphonologie', in J. Hamm (ed.), *Phonologie der Gegenwart*. Graz, Vienna, and Cologne: Böhlau, 158–72.

——(1968). *Indogermanische Grammatik*, ii: *Akzent, Ablaut*. Heidelberg: Winter.

Labov, W. (1994). *Principles of linguistic change*, i: *Internal factors*. Oxford: Blackwell.

——(2001). *Principles of linguistic change*, ii: *Social factors*. Oxford: Blackwell.

Ladd, C. A. (1964). 'The nature of sound-change', in H. G. Lunt (ed.), *Proceedings of the ninth international congress of linguists*. The Hague: Mouton, 650–7.

——(1965). 'The status of sound-laws'. *Archivum Linguisticum* 17: 91–110.

Ladd, R. (1996). *Intonational phonology*. Cambridge: Cambridge University Press.

Lamberterie, C. de (1988/9). 'Introduction à l'arménien classique'. *LALIES: Actes des sessions de linguistique et de littérature* 10: 234–89.

Langslow, D. R. (2000). *Medical Latin in the Roman empire*. Oxford: Oxford University Press.

Lass, R. (1984). *Phonology*. Cambridge: Cambridge University Press.

Laughton, E. (1964). *The participle in Cicero*. Oxford: Oxford University Press.

Lazzeroni, R. (1967). 'Su alcune correnti dialettali nel Peloponneso antico'. *Studi e Saggi Linguistici* 7: 63–75.

Lebreton, J. (1901). *Études sur la langue et la grammaire de Cicéron*. Paris: Hachette.

Lech, P. C. (2010). *Gender, social status, and discourse in Roman comedy* (Diss. Brown University).

Ledgeway, A. (2011). 'Syntactic and morphosyntactic typology and change', in M. Maiden, J. C. Smith, and A. Ledgeway (eds), *The Cambridge history of the Romance languages*, i: *Structures*. Cambridge: Cambridge University Press, 382–471.
——(forthcoming). *From Latin to Romance: morphosyntactic typology and change*. Oxford: Oxford University Press.
Lehmann, C. (1991). 'The Latin nominal group in typological perspective', in R. G. G. Coleman (ed.), *New studies in Latin linguistics: selected papers from the 4th International Colloquium on Latin Linguistics*. Amsterdam: Benjamins, 203–32.
Lejeune, M. (1972). *Phonétique historique du mycénien et du grec ancien*. Paris: Klincksieck.
Lentz, A. (1867). *Herodiani technici reliquiae*, i. Leipzig: Teubner.
Leskien, A. (1876). *Die Declination im Slavisch-Litauischen und Germanischen*. Leipzig: Hirzel.
Leumann, M. (1921). 'Part. perf. pass. mit *fui* im späteren Latein'. *Glotta* 11: 192–4.
——(1977). *Lateinische Laut- und Formenlehre*. Munich: Beck.
Levin, J. (1988). 'Generating ternary feet'. *Texas Linguistic Forum* 29: 97–113.
Lindeman, F. W. (1965). 'La Loi de Sievers et le début du mot en indo-européen'. *Norsk Tidsskrift for Sprogvidenskap* 20: 38–108.
Lindsay, W. M. (1894). *The Latin language: an historical account of Latin sounds, stems, and flexions*. Oxford: Clarendon Press.
——(1907). *Syntax of Plautus*. Oxford: Oxford University Press.
——(ed.) (1911). *Isidori Hispalenis episcopi etymologiarum sive originum libri XX* (2 vols). Oxford: Oxford University Press.
Lisón Huguet, N. (2001). *El orden de palabras en los grupos nominales en latín*. Zaragoza: Universidad de Zaragoza.
Lloyd-Jones, J. (1931–63). *Geirfa barddoniaeth gynnar Gymraeg* (2 vols). Cardiff: Gwasg Prifysgol Cymru.
Lobel, E. (1932). 'P. Bouriant 8, περὶ αἰολίδος'. *Archiv für Papyrusforschung* 10: 1–4.
Löfstedt, B. (1961). *Studien über die Sprache der langobardischen Gesetze: Beiträge zur frühmittelalterlichen Latinität*. Stockholm: Almqvist & Wiksell.
——(ed.) (1977). *Grammatici Hibernici Carolini aevi*, ii. Turnhout: Brepols.
Lubotsky, A. (1988). *The system of nominal accentuation in Sanskrit and Proto-Indo-European*. Leiden: Brill.
——(1997). Review of Volkart (1994). *Kratylos* 42: 55–7.
——(2002). *Atharvaveda-Paippalāda, Kāṇḍa Five*. Cambridge, Mass.: Department of Sanskrit and Indian Studies, Harvard University.
Lucidi, M. (1950). 'L'origine del trisillabismo in greco'. *Ricerche Linguistiche* 1: 69–92.
Luick, K. (1914–40). *Historische Grammatik der englischen Sprache*. Leipzig: Tauchnitz.
Lüttel, V. (1981). *Κάς und καί: dialektale und chronologische Probleme im Zusammenhang mit Dissimilation und Apokope*. Göttingen: Vandenhoeck & Ruprecht.
McCarthy, J., and Prince, A. (1993). 'Generalized alignment'. *Yearbook of Morphology* 79–153.

McCone, K. (1991). *The Indo-European origins of the Old Irish nasal presents, subjunctives and futures*. Innsbruck: Institut für Sprachwissenschaft.

——(1996). *Towards a relative chronology of ancient and medieval Celtic sound change*. Maynooth: Department of Old Irish, St Patrick's College.

Macdonell, A. A. (1916). *A Vedic grammar for students*. Oxford: Clarendon Press.

Madvig, J. N. (1842). 'De locis quibusdam grammaticae Latinae admonitiones et observationes', in J. N. Madvig (ed.), *Opuscula academica altera: ab ipso collecta, emendata, aucta*, ii. Copenhagen: Gyldendal, 206–41.

Mahandru, V. (1991). 'The Panjabi speech community', in S. Alladina and V. Edwards (eds), *Multilingualism in the British Isles*. London: Longman, 115–27.

Maltby, R. (2009). 'Priscian's etymologies. Sources, function and theoretical basis: "Graeci, quibus in omnia doctrinae auctoribus utimur"', in M. Baratin, B. Colombat, and L. Holtz (eds), *Priscien: transmission et refondation de la grammaire de l'antiquité aux modernes*. Turnhout: Brepols, 239–46.

Mańczak, W. (1958). 'Tendances générales des changements analogiques'. *Lingua* 7: 298–325, 387–420.

——(1978). 'Les Lois du développement analogique'. *Linguistics* 205: 53–60.

——(1992). 'Les Désinences de grec φέρεις et φέρει', in B. Brogyanyi and R. Lipp (eds), *Historical philology: Greek, Latin, and Romance. Papers in honor of Oswald Szemerényi II*. Amsterdam and Philadelphia: Benjamins, 67–75.

Mariès, L., and Mercier, C. (1989). *Eznik de Kołb: De Deo. Traduction française, notes et tables*. Turnhout: Brepols.

Mariotti, I. (ed.) (1967). *Victorinus, Ars grammatica: introduzione, testo critico e commento*. Florence: Le Monnier.

Marouzeau, J. (1922). *L'Ordre des mots dans la phrase latine*, i: *Les Groupes nominaux*. Paris: Champion.

——(1953). *L'Ordre des mots en latin: volume complémentaire*. Paris: Les Belles Lettres.

Martirosyan, H. K. (2010). *Etymological dictionary of the Armenian inherited lexicon*. Leiden: Brill.

Matthews, P. H. (1991). *Morphology* (2nd edn). Cambridge: Cambridge University Press.

Mawet, F. (1986). 'Les Développements fonctionnels de arménien *(e)t'e*', in M. Leroy and F. Mawet (eds), *La Place de l'arménien dans les langues indo-européennes*. Leuven: Peeters, 76–89.

Mayrhofer, M. (1986). *Indogermanische Grammatik*, i/2: *Lautlehre [Segmentale Phonologie des Indogermanischen]*. Heidelberg: Winter.

——(1986–2001). *Etymologisches Wörterbuch des Altindoarischen* (3 vols). Heidelberg: Winter.

Mažiulis, V. (1988–). *Prūsų kalbos etimologijos žodynas*. Vilnius: Mokslo ir enciklopedijų leidykla.

Meier-Brügger, M. (1992). 'Relative Chronologie: Schlüsse aus dem griechischen Akzent', in R. S. P. Beekes, A. Lubotsky, and J. Weitenberg (eds), *Rekonstruktion und relative Chronologie: Akten der VIII. Fachtagung der Indogermanischen Gesellschaft*. Innsbruck: Institut für Sprachwissenschaft, 283–9.

——(2002). *Indogermanische Sprachwissenschaft* (8th edn). Berlin: de Gruyter.

Meillet, A. (1903*a*). *Introduction à l'étude comparative des langues indo-européennes*. Paris: Hachette.

——(1903*b*). *Esquisse d'une grammaire comparée de l'arménien classique* (1st edn). Vienna: Imprimerie des P. P. Mekhitharistes.

——(1920). 'Les Noms du "feu" et de l'"eau" et la question du genre'. *Mémoires de la Société de Linguistique de Paris* 21: 249–56.

——(1925). 'Des Présents grecs en *-νᾱ-/-να-*', in *Mélanges linguistiques offerts à M. J. Vendryes par ses amis et ses élèves*. Paris: Champion, 275–85.

——(1931). 'Caractère secondaire du type thématique indo-européen'. *Bulletin de la Société de Linguistique de Paris* 32: 194–203.

——(1936). *Esquisse d'une grammaire comparée de l'arménien classique* (2nd edn). Vienna: Imprimerie des P. P. Mekhitharistes.

Meiser, G. (1998). *Historische Laut- und Formenlehre der lateinischen Sprache*. Darmstadt: Wissenschaftliche Buchgesellschaft.

Melchert, H. C. (1994). *Anatolian historical phonology.* Amsterdam and Atlanta: Rodopi.

Méndez Dosuna, J. (1996). 'Can weakening processes start in initial position? The case of aspiration of /s/ and /f/', in B. Hurch and R. A. Rhodes (eds), *Natural phonology: the state of the art*. Berlin and New York: Mouton de Gruyter, 97–106.

Menge, H., Burkard, T., and Schauer, M. (2000). *Lehrbuch der lateinischen Syntax und Semantik*. Darmstadt: Wissenschaftliche Buchgesellschaft.

Mester, R. A. (1994). 'The quantitative trochee in Latin'. *Natural Language and Linguistic Theory* 12: 1–61.

Meyer, G. (1892). *Albanesische Studien*, iii: *Lautlehre der indogermanischen Bestandtheile des Albanesischen*. Vienna: Gerold.

Meyer, K. (ed.) (1912). *Sanas Cormaic*. Halle: Niemeyer (repr. with Meyer's corrections added to the text, Felinfach: Llanerch Press, 1994).

——(ed.) (1919). 'Cormacs Glossar nach der Handschrift des Buches der Uí Maine'. *Sitzungsberichte der Preussischen Akademie der Wissenschaften zu Berlin (Phil.-hist. Klasse)*, 290–321.

Miller, D. G. (1977). 'Was Grassmann's Law reordered in Greek?'. *Zeitschrift für Vergleichende Sprachforschung* 91: 131–58.

Minon, S. (2000). 'Sifflantes géminées anomales. À propos des formes éléennes ἀνταποδιδῶσσα et θεοκολέοσσα et des anthroponymes en -φῶσ(σ)α', in L. Dubois and É. Masson (eds), *Philokypros: mélanges de philologie et d'antiquités grecques et proche-orientales dédiés à la mémoire d'Olivier Masson*. Salamanca: Universidad de Salamanca, 229–43.

——(2007). *Les Inscriptions éléennes dialectales (VI*^{e} *– II*^{e} *siècle av. J.-C.)* (2 vols). Genève: Droz.

Minshall, R. (1955). '"Initial" Indo-European /y/ in Armenian'. *Language* 31: 499–503.

Moran, P. (2007). *Sacred languages and Irish glossaries: evidence for the study of Latin, Greek and Hebrew in early medieval Ireland* (Diss. NUI Galway).
——(2011). '"A living speech?" The pronunciation of Greek in early medieval Ireland'. *Ériu* 61: 29–57.
——(forthcoming). 'Greek in early medieval Ireland', in A. Mullen and P. James (eds), *Multilingualism in the Greco-Roman worlds*. Cambridge: Cambridge University Press.
Morani, M. (1981). 'In margine a una concordanza greco-armena'. *Archivio Glottologico Italiano* 66: 1–15.
Morgenstierne, G. (2003). *A new etymological vocabulary of Pashto*. Wiesbaden: Reichert.
Morpurgo Davies, A. (1988). 'Problems in Cyprian phonology and writing', in J. Karageorghis and O. Masson (eds), *The history of the Greek language in Cyprus*. Nicosia: Pierides Foundation, 99–130.
——(1992). 'Mycenaean, Arcadian, Cyprian and some questions of method in dialectology', in J. P. Olivier (ed.), *Mykenaïka: actes du IXe Colloque international sur les textes mycéniens et égéens*. Paris: de Boccard, 415–31.
——(1998). *History of linguistics*, iv: *Nineteenth-century linguistics*. London and New York: Longman.
Morris Jones, J. (1913). *A Welsh grammar: historical and comparative*. Oxford: Oxford University Press.
Moulton, W. G. (1960). 'The short vowel systems of northern Switzerland: a study in structural dialectology'. *Word* 16: 155–82.
——(1961*a*). 'Zur Geschichte des deutschen Vokalsystems'. *Beiträge zur Geschichte der deutschen Sprache und Literatur* 83: 1–35.
——(1961*b*). 'Lautwandel durch innere Kausalität: die ostschweizerische Vokalspaltung'. *Zeitschrift für Mundartforschung* 28: 227–51.
——(1967). 'Types of phonemic change', in *To honor Roman Jakobson*, ii. The Hague and Paris: Mouton, 1393–1407.
——(1970). 'Contributions of dialectology to phonological theory', in A. Graur (ed.), *Actes du dixième congrès international des linguistes*, ii. Bucharest: Éditions de l'Académie de la République Socialiste de Roumanie, 21–6.
Muller, H. F. (1924). 'The passive voice in Vulgar Latin'. *Romanic Review* 15: 68–93.
Mulvany, C. M. (1896). 'Some forms of the Homeric subjunctive'. *Classical Review* 10: 24–7.
Nagy, G. (1970). *Greek dialects and the transformation of an Indo-European process*. Cambridge, Mass.: Harvard University Press.
Neubourg, L. de (1977). 'Sur le caractère analogique de la place de l'adjectif en latin'. *Orbis* 26: 395–403.
——(1978). 'Arguments supplémentaires en faveur de l'analogie dans l'ordre des mots en latin'. *Orbis* 27: 352–72.
Niedermann, M. (1997). *Précis de phonétique historique du latin* (5th edn). Paris: Klincksieck [1st edn, 1906].

Nolan, F. (1998). 'Phonological representation and phonetic interpretation in intonation analysis'. Manuscript of conference paper presented at Laboratory Phonology VI, York.

Nooten, B. A. van, and Holland, G. B. (1994). *Rig Veda: a metrically restored text with an introduction and notes*. Cambridge, Mass. and London: Harvard University Press.

Núñez, S. (1995). 'Materiales para una sociología de la lengua latina: Terencio y los modificadores de imperativo'. *Florentia Iliberritana* 6: 347–66.

Nussbaum, A. J. (1997). 'The "Saussure Effect" in Latin and Italic', in A. Lubotsky (ed.), *Sound law and analogy: papers in honor of Robert S. P. Beekes on the occasion of his 60th birthday*. Amsterdam and Atlanta: Rodopi, 181–203.

Nyberg, H. S. (1974). *A manual of Pahlavi*, ii: *Glossary*. Wiesbaden: Harrassowitz.

Ó Néill, P. P. (2000). 'Irish observance of the three Lents and the date of the St Gall Priscian (MS 904)'. *Ériu* 51: 159–80.

O'Donovan, J., and Stokes, W. (eds) (1868). *Cormac's glossary*. Calcutta: Irish Archaeological and Celtic Society.

Oakley, S. P. (2005). *A commentary on Livy, Books VI–X*, iii: *Book IX*. Oxford: Oxford University Press.

Okasha, E. (1993). *Corpus of early inscribed stones of South-West Britain*. London and New York: Leicester University Press.

Olander, T. (2009). *Balto-Slavic accentual mobility*. Berlin and New York: Mouton de Gruyter.

Oldenberg, H. (1909–12). *Ṛgveda: textkritische und exegetische Noten* (2 vols). Berlin: Weidmann.

Olsen, B. A. (1988). *The Proto-Indo-European instrument noun suffix* *-tlom *and its variants*. Copenhagen: Munksgaard.

——(1999). *The noun in Biblical Armenian: origin and word-formation*. Berlin: Mouton de Gruyter.

Orel, V. (1998). *Albanian etymological dictionary*. Leiden: Brill.

Osthoff, H., and Brugman, K. (1878). 'Vorwort', in H. Osthoff and K. Brugman, *Morphologische Untersuchungen auf dem Gebiete der indogermanischen Sprachen: Erster Theil*. Leipzig: Hirzel, III–XX.

Paniagua Aguilar, D. (2006). *El panorama literario técnico-científico en Roma (siglos I–II D.C.): «et docere et delectare»*. Salamanca: Ediciones Universidad.

Paul, H. (1909). *Prinzipien der Sprachgeschichte* (4th edn). Halle: Niemeyer.

Pedersen, H. (1905*a*). 'Zur armenischen Sprachgeschichte'. *Zeitschrift für Vergleichende Sprachforschung* 38: 194–240.

——(1905*b*). 'Die Nasalpräsentia und der slavische Akzent'. *Zeitschrift für Vergleichende Sprachforschung* 38: 297–421.

——(1906). 'Armenisch und die Nachbarsprachen'. *Zeitschrift für Vergleichende Sprachforschung* 39: 334–485.

——(1922). 'Deux étymologies latines'. *Mémoires de la Société de Linguistique de Paris* 22: 1–12.

Penney, J. H. W. (1976/7). 'The treatment of Indo-European vowels in Tocharian'. *Transactions of the Philological Society*, 75: 66–91.

——(1977). 'Weak and strong *i*-verbs in Old Irish'. *Ériu* 28: 149–54.

——(1978). Review of H. Rix, *Historische Grammatik des Griechischen: Laut- und Formenlehre* (Darmstadt: Wissenschaftliche Buchgesellschaft, 1976). *Classical Review* 28: 290–2.

——(1988*a*). 'Cities and founders in antiquity', in J. H. W. Penney (ed.), *Journal of the Anthropological Society of Oxford, 19/2. Special issue on names and their uses to mark the retirement of Godfrey Lienhardt.* Oxford: Anthropological Society of Oxford, 170–80.

——(1988*b*). 'The languages of Italy', in J. Boardman, N. G. L. Hammond, D. M. Lewis, and M. Ostwald (eds), *The Cambridge Ancient History*, iv: *Persia, Greece and the Western Mediterranean, c. 525 to 479 BC* (2nd edn). Cambridge: Cambridge University Press, 720–38.

——(1988*c*). 'Laryngeals and the Indo-European root', in A. Bammesberger (ed.), *Die Laryngaltheorie und die Rekonstruktion des indogermanischen Laut- und Formensystems*. Heidelberg: Winter, 361–72.

——(1989). 'Preverbs and postpositions in Tocharian'. *Transactions of the Philological Society* 87: 54–74.

——(1999). 'Archaism and innovation in Latin poetic syntax', in J. N. Adams and R. G. Mayer (eds), *Aspects of the language of Latin poetry*. Oxford: Oxford University Press, 249–68.

——(2002). 'Notes on some Sabellic demonstratives', in I. J. Hartmann and A. Willi (eds), *Oxford University working papers in linguistics, philology and phonetics*, vii. Oxford: University of Oxford, 131–42.

——(2004). 'Tocharian B *päst* and its vocalism', in J. H. W. Penney (ed.), *Indo-European perspectives: studies in honour of Anna Morpurgo Davies*. Oxford: Oxford University Press, 514–22.

——(2005). 'Connections in archaic Latin prose', in T. Reinhardt, M. Lapidge, and J. N. Adams (eds), *Aspects of the language of Latin prose*. Oxford: Oxford University Press, 37–51.

——(2006). 'Writing systems', in E. Bispham, T. Harrison, and B. A. Sparkes (eds), *The Edinburgh companion to ancient Greece and Rome*. Edinburgh: Edinburgh University Press, 477–84.

——(2009). 'The Etruscan language and its Italic context', in J. Swaddling and P. Perkins (eds), *Etruscan by definition: the cultural, regional and personal identity of the Etruscans. Papers in honour of Sybille Haynes*. London: British Museum Press, 88–94.

Pert, S., and Letts, C. (2006). 'Codeswitching in Mirpuri-speaking Pakistani heritage preschool children: bilingual language acquisition'. *International Journal of Bilingualism* 10: 349–74.

Peters, M. (1987). Review of G. de Boel, *Goal accusative and object accusative in Homer: a contribution to the theory of transitivity* (Brussels: Paleis der Academiën, 1988). *Die Sprache* 33: 285–92.

——(1998). 'Homerisches und Unhomerisches bei Homer und auf dem Nestorbecher', in J. Jasanoff, H. C. Melchert, and L. Oliver (eds), *Mír curad: studies in honor of Calvert Watkins*. Innsbruck: Institut für Sprachwissenschaft, 585–602.

Petit, D. (2004). *Apophonie et catégories grammaticales dans les langues baltiques*. Leuven and Paris: Peeters.

Pinault, G.-J. (2005). 'Analyse étymologique d'un nom de parenté indo-européen', in G. Schweiger (ed.), *Indogermanica: Festschrift Gert Klingenschmitt*. Taimering: Schweiger, 465–86.

——(2007). 'A star is born: a "new" PIE *-*ter*-suffix', in A. J. Nussbaum (ed.), *Verba docenti: studies in historical and Indo-European linguistics presented to Jay H. Jasanoff by students, colleagues, and friends*. Ann Arbor, Mich.: Beech Stave Press, 271–9.

Pinkster, H. (1990). *Latin syntax and semantics*. London: Routledge.

——(1995). 'Word order in the Late Latin *Gesta conlationis Carthaginiensis*', in L. Callebat (ed.), *Latin vulgaire – latin tardif IV*. Hildesheim: Olms, 549–60.

Pisani, V. (1950). 'Studi sulla fonetica dell'armeno'. *Ricerche Linguistiche* 1: 165–93.

——(1966). 'Armenische Miszellen'. *Die Sprache* 12: 227–36.

Polivanov, E. D. (1928). 'Faktory fonetičeskoj ėvoljucii jazyka, kak trudovogo processa 1 [Factors relating to the phonetic evolution of language as a work process 1]'. *Učenye zapiski instituta jazyka i literatury rossijskoj associacii naučno-issledovatel'skich institutov obščestvennych nauk* [*Scholarly transactions of the Institute of Language and Literature of the Russian association of scientific-research institutes for the social sciences*] (Moscow) 3: 20–42.

——(1974). *Selected works: articles on general linguistics*, ed. A. A. Leont'ev et al. The Hague and Paris: Mouton.

Powell, J. G. F. (2007). 'A new text of the *Appendix Probi*'. *Classical Quarterly* 57: 687–700.

——(2010). 'Hyperbaton and register in Cicero', in E. Dickey and A. Chahoud (eds), *Colloquial and literary Latin*. Cambridge: Cambridge University Press, 163–85.

Prendergast, G. L., and Marzullo, B. (1962). *A complete concordance to the Iliad of Homer* (2nd edn). Hildesheim: Olms.

Prince, A., and Smolensky, P. (2004). *Optimality Theory: constraint interaction in generative grammar*. Malden, Mass. and Oxford: Blackwell.

Probert, P. (2006). *Ancient Greek accentuation: synchronic patterns, frequency effects, and prehistory*. Oxford: Oxford University Press.

Quirk, R. J. (2005). 'The "Appendix Probi" as a compendium of popular Latin: description and bibliography'. *Classical World* 98: 397–409.

Radatz, H.-I. (2001). *Die Semantik der Adjektivstellung: eine kognitive Studie zur Konstruktion <Adjektiv + Substantiv> im Spanischen, Französischen und Italienischen*. Tübingen: Niemeyer.

Ramat, P. (1981). *Einführung in das Germanische*. Tübingen: Niemeyer.
Rasmussen, J. E. (1989*a*). 'On the North Germanic treatment of *eww*'. *Arkiv för Nordisk Filologi* 104: 1–9.
——(1989*b*). *Studien zur Morphophonemik der indogermanischen Grundsprache*. Innsbruck: Institut für Sprachwissenschaft.
Ravnaes, E. (1991). *The chronology of sound changes from PIE to Classical Armenian* (Diss. Oslo).
Reichelt, H. (1967). *Awestisches Elementarbuch* (2nd edn). Darmstadt: Wissenschaftliche Buchgesellschaft.
Renou, L. (1957). *Jacob Wackernagel: Altindische Grammatik. Introduction générale*. Göttingen: Vandenhoeck & Ruprecht.
——(1964). *Études védiques et pāṇinéennes*, xii. Paris: de Boccard.
Reynolds, M. (1998). 'Punjabi/Urdu in Sheffield: language maintenance or shift'. Final Report to ESRC on Grant R000221740.
Rice, C. (1992). 'Binarity and ternarity in metrical theory: parametric extensions' (PhD dissertation, University of Texas at Austin).
Riemann, O. (1885). *Études sur la langue et la grammaire de Tite-Live* (2nd edn). Paris: Thorin.
Ringe, D. (2006*a*). *From Proto-Indo-European to Proto-Germanic* (*A linguistic history of English*, i). Oxford: Oxford University Press.
——(2006*b*). 'A sociolinguistically informed solution to an old historical problem: the Gothic genitive plural'. *Transactions of the Philological Society* 104: 167–206.
Risch, E. (1974). *Wortbildung der homerischen Sprache* (2nd edn). Berlin: de Gruyter.
——(1975). 'Remarques sur l'accent du grec ancien', in D. Moïnfar (ed.), *Mélanges linguistiques offerts à Émile Benveniste*. Louvain: Peeters, 471–9.
Risselada, R. (1984). 'Coordination and juxtaposition of adjectives in the Latin NP'. *Glotta* 62: 202–31.
——(1989). 'Latin illocutionary parentheticals', in M. Lavency and D. Longrée (eds), *Proceedings of the Vth Colloquium on Latin Linguistics*. Louvain-la-Neuve: Peeters, 367–78.
——(1993). *Imperatives and other directive expressions in Latin: a study in the pragmatics of a dead language*. Amsterdam: Gieben.
Rivet, A. L. F., and Smith, C. (1982). *The place names of Roman Britain*. London: Batsford.
Rix, H. (1966). 'Die lateinische Synkope als historisches und phonologisches Problem'. *Kratylos* 11: 156–65.
——(1992). *Historische Grammatik des Griechischen: Laut- und Formenlehre* (2nd edn). Darmstadt: Wissenschaftliche Buchgesellschaft.
Rodway, S. (2009). 'What language did St Patrick swear in?'. *Ériu* 59: 139–51.
Roesch, S. (2004). 'La Politesse dans la correspondance de Cicéron', in L. Nadjo and É. Gavoille (eds), *Epistulae antiquae III: actes du IIIe Colloque international 'L'Épistolaire antique et ses prolongements européens'*. Louvain: Peeters, 139–52.
Romaine, S. (1995). *Bilingualism* (2nd edn). Oxford: Blackwell.

Ross, M. (1997). 'Social networks and kinds of speech-community event', in R. Blench and M. Spriggs (eds), *Archaeology and language*, i: *Theoretical and methodological orientations*. London: Routledge, 209–61.

——(1998). 'Sequencing and dating linguistic events in Oceania: the linguistics/archaeology interface', in R. Blench and M. Spriggs (eds), *Archaeology and language*, ii: *Archaeological data and linguistic hypotheses*. London: Routledge, 141–73.

Ruijgh, C. J. (1967). *Études sur la grammaire et le vocabulaire du grec mycénien*. Amsterdam: Hakkert.

Russell, P. (1985). 'Recent work in British Latin'. *Cambridge Medieval Celtic Studies* 9: 19–29.

——(1988). 'The sounds of a silence: the growth of Cormac's glossary'. *Cambridge Medieval Celtic Studies* 15: 1–30.

——(1995). 'Brittonic words in early Irish glossaries', in J. F. Eska, R. G. Gruffydd, and N. Jacobs (eds), *Hispano-Gallo-Brittonica: essays in honour of Professor D. Ellis Evans on the occasion of his sixty-fifth birthday*. Cardiff: University of Wales Press, 166–82.

——(1996). '*Dúil Dromma Cetta* and Cormac's glossary'. *Études Celtiques* 32: 147–74.

——(2003). '*Rowynniauc, Rhufoniog*: the orthography and phonology of /μ/ in early Welsh', in P. Russell (ed.), *Yr Hen Iaith: studies in early Welsh*. Aberystwyth: Celtic Studies Publications, 25–47.

——(2005*a*). '*Quasi*: bridging the etymological gap in early Irish glossaries', in B. Smelik, R. Hofman, C. Hamans, and D. Cram (eds), *A companion in linguistics: a Festschrift for Anders Ahlqvist on the occasion of his sixtieth birthday*. Nijmegen: Draak, 49–62.

——(2005*b*). '"What was best of every language": the early history of the Irish language', in D. Ó Cróinín (ed.), *A new history of Ireland*, i. Oxford: Oxford University Press, 405–50.

——(2008). *'Read it in a glossary': glossaries and learned discourse in medieval Ireland*. Cambridge: Department of Anglo-Saxon, Norse and Celtic.

Sadanand, K., and Vijayakrishnan, K. G. (1995). 'High tone in Punjabi: a case of deaspiration and tonogenesis'. Paper presented at the Seventeenth conference of the South Asian Linguistics Association, Austin, Texas.

Saifullah Khan, V. (1977). 'The Pakistanis: Mirpuri villagers at home and in Bradford', in J. Watson (ed.), *Between two cultures: migrants and minorities in Britain*. Oxford: Blackwell, 57–89.

Salonius, A. H. (1920). *Vitae Patrum: kritische Untersuchungen über Text, Syntax und Wortschatz der spätlateinischen Vitae Patrum (B. III, V, VI, VII)*. Lund: Gleerup.

Sammon, J. W., Jr (1969). 'A nonlinear mapping for data structure analysis'. *IEEE Transactions on Computers* 18: 401–9.

Sampat, K. S. (1964). 'Tonal structure of Majhi'. *Indian Linguistics* 25: 108–10.

Samuels, M. (1972). *Linguistic evolution*. Cambridge: Cambridge University Press.

Sandhu, B. S. (1968). *The tonal system of the Panjabi language*. Patiala: Punjabi University.
Sapir, E. (1921). *Language: an introduction to the study of speech*. New York: Harcourt, Brace.
Saussure, F. de (1955). *Cours de linguistique générale* (5th edn). Paris: Payot [1st edn, Lausanne and Paris, 1916].
Scarlata, S. (1999). *Die Wurzelkomposita im Ṛg-Veda*. Wiesbaden: Reichert.
Schindler, J. (1966). 'Hethitisch *lišši-* "Leber"'. *Die Sprache* 12: 77–8.
——(1969). 'Die idg. Wörter für "Vogel" und "Ei"'. *Die Sprache* 15: 144–67.
——(1977). 'Notizen zum Sieversschen Gesetz'. *Die Sprache* 23: 56–65.
Schmid, W. P. (1986). 'Bemerkungen zur äolischen Konjugation der verba contracta', in A. Etter (ed.), *o-o-pe-ro-si: Festschrift für Ernst Risch zum 75. Geburtstag*. Berlin and New York: de Gruyter, 245–52.
Schmitt, R. (1981). *Grammatik des Klassisch-Armenischen*. Innsbruck: Institut für Sprachwissenschaft [2nd edn., 2007].
——(1996). 'Some remarks on Armenian *nêr* "sister-in-law, brother's wife"'. *Annual of Armenian Linguistics* 17: 21–4.
Schneider, G. (1973). *Zum Begriff des Lautgesetzes in der Sprachwissenschaft seit den Junggrammatikern*. Tübingen: Narr.
Schrijver, P. (1991). *The reflexes of the Proto-Indo-European laryngeals in Latin*. Amsterdam and Atlanta: Rodopi.
——(1995). *Studies in British Celtic historical phonology*. Amsterdam and Atlanta: Rodopi.
——(1998). 'The British word for "fox" and its Indo-European origin'. *Journal of Indo-European Studies* 26: 421–34.
——(2011). 'Old British', in E. Ternes (ed.), *Brythonic Celtic – Britannisches Keltisch. From Medieval British to Modern Breton*. Bremen: Hempen, 1–84.
Schrödinger, E. (1929). 'Was ist ein Naturgesetz?'. *Die Naturwissenschaften* 17: 9–11.
Schuchardt, H. (1885). *Ueber die Lautgesetze – Gegen die Junggrammatiker*. Berlin: Oppenheim.
Schumacher, S. (2004). *Die keltischen Primärverben: ein vergleichendes, etymologisches und morphologisches Lexikon*. Innsbruck: Institut für Sprachwissenschaft.
Schwyzer, E. (1939). *Griechische Grammatik*, i: *Allgemeiner Teil, Lautlehre, Wortbildung, Flexion*. Munich: Beck.
——and Debrunner, A. (1950). *Griechische Grammatik*, ii: *Syntax und syntaktische Stilistik*. Munich: Beck.
Seebold, E. (1972). *Das System der indogermanischen Halbvokale*. Heidelberg: Winter.
——(1984). *Das System der Personalpronomina in den frühgermanischen Sprachen*. Göttingen: Vandenhoeck & Ruprecht.
Selkirk, E. (1984). *Phonology and syntax: the relation between sound and structure*. Cambridge, Mass.: MIT Press.
Siegel, J. (1988). 'Introduction', in Barz and Siegel (1988), 1–19.

Sievers, E. (1878). 'Zur Accent- und Lautlehre der germanischen Sprachen'. *Beiträge zur Geschichte der deutschen Sprache und Literatur* 5: 63–163.

Sihler, A. L. (1969). 'Sievers-Edgerton phenomena and Rigvedic meter'. *Language* 45: 248–73.

——(1971). 'Word-initial semivowel alternation in the Rigveda'. *Language* 47: 53–78.

——(1995). *New comparative grammar of Greek and Latin*. New York and Oxford: Oxford University Press.

——(2006). *Edgerton's Law: the phantom evidence*. Heidelberg: Winter.

Sims-Williams, P. (2003). *The Celtic inscriptions of Britain: phonology and chronology, c. 400–1200*. Oxford and Malden, Mass.: Blackwell.

Smith, C. (1983). 'Vulgar Latin in Roman Britain: epigraphic and other evidence', in H. Temporini and W. Haase (eds), *Aufstieg und Niedergang der römischen Welt: Geschichte und Kultur Roms im Spiegel der neueren Forschung*, pt 2, vol. 29.2. Berlin and New York: de Gruyter, 893–948.

Solmsen, F. (1907). 'Vordorisches in Lakonien'. *Rheinisches Museum* 62: 329–38.

Solta, G. R. (1960). *Die Stellung des Armenischen im Kreise der indogermanischen Sprachen*. Vienna: Mechitharisten-Buchdruckerei.

——(1963). 'Die armenische Sprache', in G. Deeters, G. R. Solta, V. Inglisian, and B. Spuler (eds), *Handbuch der Orientalistik, Erste Abteilung: Der Nahe und der Mittlere Osten*, vii: *Armenisch und kaukasische Sprachen*. Leiden: Brill, 80–128.

Sommer, F. (1948). *Handbuch der lateinischen Laut- und Formenlehre: eine Einführung in das sprachwissenschaftliche Studium des Lateins* (2nd edn). Heidelberg: Winter.

——and Pfister, R. (1977). *Handbuch der lateinischen Laut- und Formenlehre: eine Einführung in das sprachwissenschaftliche Studium des Lateins* (4th edn). Heidelberg: Winter.

Sommerstein, A. H. (1973). *The sound pattern of Ancient Greek*. Oxford: Blackwell.

Southern, M. R. (2002[2006]). 'Grain, the staff of life: Indo-European **(h$_2$)yew-os*'. *Münchener Studien zur Sprachwissenschaft* 62: 173–217.

Spevak, O. (2010*a*). *Constituent order in classical Latin prose*. Amsterdam and Philadelphia: Benjamins.

——(2010*b*). 'Le Syntagme nominal en latin: les travaux des trente dernières années', in O. Spevak (ed.), *Le Syntagme nominal en latin: nouvelles contributions*. Paris: L'Harmattan, 23–40.

Stearns, M., Jr (1978). *Crimean Gothic: analysis and etymology of the corpus*. Saratoga: Anma Libri.

Stiles, P. V. (1985–6). 'The fate of the numeral "4" in Germanic'. *North-Western European Language Evolution* 6: 81–104; 7: 3–27; 8: 3–25.

Stockert, W. (1983). *T. Maccius Plautus: Aulularia*. Stuttgart: Teubner.

Stokes, W. (ed.) (1862). *Three Irish glossaries*. London: Williams and Norgate.

——(ed.) (1892). 'The Bodleian Dindshenchas'. *Folklore* 3: 467–516.

——(ed.) (1893). 'The Edinburgh Dindshenchas'. *Folklore* 4: 471–97.

——(ed.) (1894–5). 'The prose tales in the Rennes Dindshenchas'. *Revue Celtique* 15: 272–336, 418–84; 16: 31–83, 135–67, 269–312.

Stokes, W. (ed.) (1900). 'O'Mulconry's Glossary'. *Archiv für Celtische Lexikographie* 1: 232–324.
——and Strachan, J. (eds) (1901–3). *Thesaurus Palaeohibernicus: a collection of Old-Irish glosses, scholia, prose, and verse* (2 vols). Cambridge: Cambridge University Press.
Strunk, K. (1960). 'Der böotische Imperativ δίδοι'. *Glotta* 39: 114–23.
——(1967). *Nasalpräsentien und Aoriste: ein Beitrag zur Morphologie des Verbums im Indo-Iranischen und Griechischen*. Heidelberg: Winter.
Stuart-Smith, J. (2004). *Phonetics and philology: sound change in Italic*. Oxford: Oxford University Press.
Svennung, J. (1935). *Untersuchungen zu Palladius und zur lateinischen Fach- und Volkssprache*. Uppsala: Almqvist & Wiksell.
Szemerényi, O. J. L. (1968). 'The development *s* > *h* in Indo-European languages'. *Die Sprache* 14: 161–3.
——(1996). *Introduction to Indo-European linguistics*. Oxford: Oxford University Press.
Teodorsson, S.-T. (1977). *The phonology of Ptolemaic koine*. Gothenburg: Acta Universitatis Gothoburgensis.
Terkourafi, M. (2002). 'Politeness and formulaicity'. *Journal of Greek Linguistics* 3: 179–201.
——(2004). 'Testing Brown and Levinson's theory in a corpus of spontaneous conversational data from Cypriot Greek'. *International Journal of the Sociology of Language* 168: 119–34.
——(2005). 'An argument for a frame-based approach to politeness: evidence from the use of the imperative in Cypriot Greek', in R. Lakoff and I. Sachiko (eds), *Broadening the horizon of linguistic politeness*. Amsterdam: Benjamins, 99–116.
——(2008). 'Toward a unified theory of politeness, impoliteness, and rudeness', in D. Bousfield and M. Locher (eds), *Impoliteness in language: studies on its interplay with power in theory and practice*. Berlin: Mouton de Gruyter, 45–74.
——(forthcoming). *From politeness to impoliteness: the frame-based approach*. Cambridge: Cambridge University Press.
Thompson, R. J. E. (2008). 'Mycenaean non-assibilation and its significance for the prehistory of the Greek dialects', in A. Sacconi, M. Del Freo, L. Godart, and M. Negri (eds), *Colloquium Romanum: atti del XII Colloquio internazionale di micenologia*, ii. Pisa and Rome: Serra, 753–65.
Thumb, A., and Kieckers, E. (1932). *Handbuch der griechischen Dialekte: erster Teil* (2nd edn). Heidelberg: Winter.
——and Scherer, A. (1959). *Handbuch der griechischen Dialekte: zweiter Teil* (2nd edn). Heidelberg: Winter.
Tobler, L. (1879). 'Über die Anwendung des Begriffs von Gesetzen auf die Sprache'. *Vierteljahrsschrift für Wissenschaftliche Philosophie* 3: 30–52.
Tremblay, X. (2003). *La Déclinaison des noms de parenté indo-européens en* -ter-. Innsbruck: Institut für Sprachwissenschaft.

Trnka, B. (1982). *Selected papers in structural linguistics.* Berlin, New York, and Amsterdam: Mouton.

Trudgill, P. (1983). *On dialect: social and geographical perspectives.* Oxford: Blackwell.

——(2003). 'Linguistic changes in pan-world English', in C. Tschichold (ed.), *English core linguistics: essays in honour of David Allerton.* Berne: Lang, 55–68.

——and Gordon, E. (2006). 'Predicting the past. Dialect archaeology and Australian English rhoticity'. *English World-Wide* 27: 235–46.

————Lewis, G., and Maclagan, M. (2000). 'The role of drift in the formation of native-speaker southern hemisphere Englishes: some New Zealand evidence'. *Diachronica* 17: 111–38.

Uhlich, J. (1995). 'On the fate of intervocalic **-u̯-* in Old Irish, especially between neutral vowels'. *Ériu* 46: 11–48.

Väänänen, V. (1981). *Introduction au latin vulgaire* (3rd edn). Paris: Klincksieck.

Venables, W. N., and Ripley, B. D. (1992). *Modern applied statistics with S-Plus.* New York: Springer.

Verma, M. (1995). 'Ethnic minority languages in Scotland: a sociolinguistic appraisal'. *Scottish Language* 14/15: 118–33.

Vincent, N. (1988). 'Latin', in M. Harris and N. Vincent (eds), *The Romance languages.* London: Routledge, 26–78.

——(2007). 'Learned vs popular syntax: adjective placement in early Italian vernaculars', in A. L. Lepschy and A. Tosi (eds), *Languages of Italy: histories and dictionaries.* Ravenna: Longo, 55–75.

Vine, B. (1999). 'On "Cowgill's Law" in Greek', in H. C. Luschützky and H. Eichner (eds), *Compositiones Indogermanicae in memoriam Jochem Schindler.* Prague: Enigma, 555–600.

——(2006). 'On "Thurneysen-Havet's Law" in Latin and Italic'. *Historische Sprachforschung* 119: 211–49.

Volkart, M. (1994). *Zu Brugmanns Gesetz im Altindischen.* Berne: Institut für Sprachwissenschaft der Universität Bern.

Vollgraff, W. (1909). 'Inscriptions d'Argos'. *Bulletin de Correspondance Hellénique* 33: 171–200.

Von der Muehll, P. (ed.) (1962). *Homeri Odyssea.* Stuttgart: Teubner.

Wackernagel, J. (1877). 'Der griechische Verbalaccent'. *Zeitschrift für Vergleichende Sprachforschung* 23: 457–70.

——(1895). 'Miszellen zur griechischen Grammatik'. *Zeitschrift für Vergleichende Sprachforschung* 33: 1–62.

——(1896). *Altindische Grammatik*, i: *Lautlehre.* Göttingen: Vandenhoeck & Ruprecht.

——(1897). 'Vermischte Beiträge zur griechischen Sprachkunde'. *Programm zur Rektoratsfeier der Universität Basel*, 3–62.

——(1905). *Altindische Grammatik*, ii.1: *Einleitung zur Wortlehre, Nominalkomposition.* Göttingen: Vandenhoeck & Ruprecht.

Wackernagel, J. (1914). 'Akzentstudien III: Zum homerischen Akzent'. *Nachrichten von der Königlichen Gesellschaft der Wissenschaften zu Göttingen*, 97–130.

——(1926). *Vorlesungen über Syntax mit besonderer Berücksichtigung von Griechisch, Lateinisch und Deutsch*, i (2nd edn). Basle: Birkhäuser.

Watkins, C. (1969). *Indogermanische Grammatik*, iii: *Formenlehre, Erster Teil: Geschichte der indogermanischen Verbalflexion*. Heidelberg: Winter.

——(1976). 'Observations on the "Nestor's Cup" inscription'. *Harvard Studies in Classical Philology* 80: 25–40.

——(1992). 'The comparison of formulaic sequences', in E. C. Polomé and W. Winter (eds), *Reconstructing languages and cultures*. Berlin and New York: de Gruyter, 391–418.

Watts, R. J. (2003). *Politeness*. Cambridge: Cambridge University Press.

Weinreich, U., Labov, W., and Herzog, M. I. (1968). 'Empirical foundations of a theory of language change', in W. P. Lehmann and Y. Malkiel (eds), *Directions for historical linguistics*. Austin: University of Texas Press, 95–195.

Weitenberg, J. J. (1986). 'Additional *h*-, initial *y*- and Indo-European **y*- in Armenian', in M. Leroy and F. Mawet (eds), *La Place de l'arménien dans les langues indo-européennes*. Leuven: Peeters, 90–101.

——(1997). 'The prepositional group *i y*- and the orthography of gospel manuscript M (Matenadaran 6200)'. *Annual of Armenian Linguistics* 18: 39–50.

Wells, C., and Roach, P. (1980). 'An experimental investigation of some aspects of tone in Panjabi'. *Journal of Phonetics* 8: 85–9.

Wells, J. C. (1982). *Accents of English*, ii: *The British Isles*. Cambridge: Cambridge University Press.

West, M. L. (1978). *Hesiod: Works and Days*. Oxford: Oxford University Press.

——(ed.) (1998–2000). *Homeri Ilias* (2 vols). Stuttgart: Teubner (vol. i), Munich and Leipzig: Saur (vol. ii).

——(2007). *Indo-European poetry and myth*. Oxford: Oxford University Press.

Whitney, W. D. (1881). *Index verborum to the published text of the Atharva-Veda*. New Haven: American Oriental Society.

Wijk, N. van (1939). 'L'Étude diachronique des phénomènes phonologiques et extra-phonologiques'. *Travaux du Cercle Linguistique de Prague* 8: 297–318.

Willi, A. (2003). '*καί* – mykenisch oder nachmykenisch?'. *Glotta* 79: 224–48.

——(2008). *Sikelismos: Sprache, Literatur und Gesellschaft im griechischen Sizilien (8.–5. Jh. v. Chr.)*. Basle: Schwabe.

Winter, W. (ed.) (1965*a*). *Evidence for laryngeals*. London, The Hague, and Paris: Mouton.

——(1965*b*). 'Armenian evidence', in Winter (1965*a*), 100–15.

——(1965*c*). 'Tocharian evidence', in Winter (1965*a*), 190–212.

——(1999). 'Consonant harmony in Armenian', in E. C. Polomé and C. F. Justus (eds), *Language change and typological variation: in honor of Winfred P. Lehmann on the occasion of his 83rd birthday*. Washington, D.C.: Institute for the Study of Man, 313–19.

Winters, M. E. (1984). 'Steps toward the Romance passive inferrable from the *Itinerarium Egeriae*'. *Romance Philology* 37: 445–54.

——(1997). 'Kuryłowicz, analogical change, and cognitive grammar'. *Cognitive Linguistics* 8: 359–86.

Wodtko, D. S., Irslinger, B., and Schneider, C. (2008). *Nomina im indogermanischen Lexikon*. Heidelberg: Winter.

Zehnder, T. (1999). *Atharvaveda-Paippalāda, Buch 2: Text, Übersetzung, Kommentar.* Idstein: Schulz-Kirschner.

Zilsel, E. (1941). 'Physics and the problem of historico-sociological laws'. *Philosophy of Science* 8: 567–79.

——(1942). 'The genesis of the concept of physical law'. *Philosophical Review* 51: 245–79.

Zubatý, J. (1892). 'Die ursprachliche tenuis aspirata dentalis im ārischen, griechischen und latein'. *Zeitschrift für Vergleichende Sprachforschung* 31: 1–9.

General index

ablaut 143, 229, 230
accent 9, 147–60, 163–81, 205–26, 231, 232, 239, 240, 245, 251, 252, 255, 256 n. 42, 259, 274
  acute 164, 167, 173, 177, 178
  circumflex 164, 167, 173, 177, 178
  see also stress
Achaean, *see* Greek
Achilles 54
Aeolic, *see* Greek
affricates 113, 114, 140
Alcaeus 275
Alcman 113 n. 20, 115 n. 24
Alemannic 38, 39
alignment 210–12, 217, 221
allomorphs 159
allophones 4, 45–60
  perceived/significant 55, 58
alphabet 119
America 120
analogy 2, 3–4, 7, 13, 47, 49, 51, 58, 59, 101, 106, 107, 115, 127, 136, 143, 146, 208, 256, 260, 262–8, 270, 271
anaptyxis 207
anteriority 83–6, 91–4, 97, 100
aorists, sigmatic 110, 111, 115, 171, 178
apocope 154, 158
apophony, *see* ablaut
Appendix Probi 207
Arcadia 117
Arcadian, *see* Greek
Arcado-Cypriot, *see* Greek
archaisms 182, 230
  see also formulaic language
Argolic, *see* Greek
Argolis 110, 118, 119, 129
Aristarchus 261
Aristophanes 113 n. 20, 261
Armenian 7, 103, 134–46
  Muš 145
  Šatax 145
Armeno-Greek 135
aspiration 110, 111, 112, 114, 118, 121, 127–33
assimilation 140
Assyrian 114 n. 22, 116
Atharvaveda 230, 247–58
athematization 273
Attic, *see* Greek
Attic-Ionic, *see* Greek
attributive adjectives 11, 279–312
Augustan period 84, 87, 95, 101
Augustus 224
Auraicept na n-Éces 18, 22 n. 15, 24, 29 n. 29
Australia 120
autosegmental phonology 80
Avestan 129, 253 n. 40

back-formations 137, 160
bahuvrīhis, *see* compounds
Baltic 136
Boeotia 119
Boeotian, *see* Greek
Boethius 98
Bohairic 130
borrowing 2, 21, 24, 26, 30, 57, 59, 146
  see also loanwords
Brāhmaṇas 202–3
break 185, 190
breathy-voiced release 62, 70, 74–8
Breton 148, 151, 153, 155, 156, 157, 158
bridge forms 20
Britain 64, 120

British, *see* Celtic
Brittonic 155
Brugmann's Law 9–10, 229–59
Byelorussian 58
Byzantine period 130 n. 7

cadence 185, 187, 190, 198
Caesar 283, 284 n. 9, 291, 296, 298, 300, 301, 309
Caesarius of Arles 84, 99 n. 8
caesura 185, 190, 199, 200
Cato 286 n. 17
Celtiberian 148
Celtic 62, 147–60
  British Celtic 7, 19, 20, 22, 24, 147–60
  Proto-British 149, 150, 153, 156, 157
  Proto-Celtic 7, 147, 148, 149, 156
chiasmus 304 n. 72
Chronicle of Fredegar 100, 101
Cicero 11, 86, 97, 283, 285, 290, 294, 296, 298–301, 303–5, 309, 311, 318–28
citation forms 57
cladistics 4, 33–42
clitics 208, 216, 217
  see also enclitics; proclitics
code-switching 56, 64
Cóir Anmann 20
collectives 138
Columella 284, 291, 299, 301, 311
comparative method 34
compensatory lengthening 166, 269
complementary distribution 47, 53, 60, 188, 193–4, 200
compounds 173 n. 16, 229, 232, 234, 237, 240–3, 245, 246, 248, 249, 252, 254–7
  bahuvrīhi 173 n. 23, 233, 234 n. 10, 243, 255
  determinative 235–6, 240, 244, 259
  verbal governing 173 n. 16, 173 n. 18
constraints 10, 12, 207, 210, 212
continuants 128
contraction 274
contrast 304
Coptic 130
copula 83, 84, 86, 88, 89, 94, 101
Corinthian, *see* Greek
Cormac mac Cuilennáin 17
Cormac's Glossary, *see Sanas Cormaic*
Cornish 148, 149, 151, 153, 155, 156, 158
Cornwall 153, 155
coronals 129, 133
correspondences 18, 23, 26, 27, 126
corruption 20
courtesy 317
Cowgill's Law 269–70
creaky phonation 72, 77, 81
cretic shortening 226
cyclicity 211
Cypriot, *see* Greek
Cypriot syllabary 113 n. 21, 119
Cyprus 110, 112, 116, 117, 118

Danish 49
Dark Ages 104
De agricultura (*On Agriculture*) 286 n. 17
De architectura (*On Architecture*) 84, 95
De astronomia (*On Astronomy*) 84, 95
deaspiration 125, 128–9, 130, 132–3
definite article 11
dental stops 12
deponents 87, 88, 90, 91–4, 95, 100
descriptive linguistics 2
dialect 33, 40, 41, 49, 64, 80, 111–13, 115, 118–20, 255, 262, 268, 269, 274, 275
  borrowing 57
  maps 119
diffusion 5, 102–4, 118, 121
digamma 25–9, 116
diglossia 98
Dindshenchas Érenn 20
diphthongs 163, 165, 174–8, 179–81
discontinuity 285, 289, 312
dissimilation 142 n. 49, 156, 158

Doabi 63, 64, 67, 77, 78, 80
Donatus 19, 28
Doric, *see* Greek
drift 5, 102, 120–1
Dutch 58

Egeria 99–101
Egypt 129–30
Elean, *see* Greek
Elis 110, 118, 119
enclitics 173
Endlicher's Glossary 156
English 55 n. 17, 57, 59, 67, 72, 93
  American English 120
  Australian English 120
  Canadian English 120
  Middle English 59
  New Zealand English 120
  Old English 19, 36, 37, 38, 39, 52, 54, 56
  Welsh English 120
  World English 120
epenthesis 150, 182
Etymologiae 19, 20
etymology 2, 19, 20, 21, 30, 135–46, 157, 226, 264, 316
euphony 29
exegesis 19
Exon's Law 205–26
extrametricality 208–9, 211

face 315 n. 4
Faroese 49
focus 284, 285, 289, 291, 294, 296–301, 304, 308, 309, 310–12
foot structure 208
formulaic language 182, 183, 198, 200–1, 204, 313, 318
French 59, 85
fricatives 140
  fricative weakening 111
Funen 49
Futhark 43
future:
  active (Latin) 85
  passive (Latin) 85
  perfect (Latin) 87, 88, 90–4, 96–8, 100

Garawa 210, 211 n. 6
Gaulish 148, 152, 156, 157, 158, 159–60
gemination 36, 113, 114
generalization 3, 6, 10, 21, 22
Generalized Alignment 210
generative grammar 12
generative phonology 111
German 12, 55 n. 17, 57
  Old High German 35–6, 37, 38, 39, 40, 49, 56
  Swiss German 58
Germanic 43, 50, 62, 136
  East Germanic 43
  North Germanic 43, 46, 49, 59–60
  North-West Germanic 4, 43–60
  Proto-Germanic 34, 35, 38, 44, 45, 46, 50, 59, 60 n. 20
  Proto-West Germanic 4, 33, 35, 38, 40, 41
  West Germanic 4, 33, 34, 36, 37, 39, 40, 41, 43, 46, 49, 50
glossary 17–30
glottal pulsing 70
Gothic 37, 38 n. 6, 44 n. 2, 50, 53
  Crimean Gothic 44 n. 2
Gotland 49
Graeco-Aryan 131–3
grammaticalization 89
Grassmann's Law 102–3, 115 n. 23
Greek 118, 135
  Achaean 116–17
  Aeolic 26–9, 117, 164, 166, 272–6
  ancient 4, 5, 6, 9, 10, 12, 19, 20, 25, 27, 62, 102–21, 125–33, 141, 159, 163–81, 214, 230, 254, 258, 260–76
  Arcadian 107, 108, 116, 117, 121
  Arcado-Cypriot 107, 262, 268, 273–6
  Argolic 108, 110, 111, 112, 114, 116, 117, 118, 121

Greek (*cont.*)
  Attic 28, 105, 107, 108, 111 n. 15, 164, 165, 166, 268, 269, 273, 275
  Attic-Ionic 107, 164, 166, 178, 274
  Boeotian 107, 117, 164–5, 264
  Corinthian 264
  Cypriot 108, 109, 110, 111, 112, 114, 116, 117, 118, 120, 121
  Doric 28, 116, 117, 164–5, 166, 176, 178, 268 n. 11
  Egyptian 129–30
  Elean 105, 108, 109, 110, 111, 112, 117, 118, 119, 121, 129
  Homeric 156, 172, 173, 176 n. 29, 179, 268, 269
  Ionic 105, 265, 268, 269, 272, 273
  Laconian 108, 110, 111, 113, 114, 115, 116, 117, 118, 119, 121
  Lesbian 107, 272–5
  Locrian 129
  modern 4, 6, 12
  Mycenaean 8, 103–7, 112, 113, 156, 176, 266, 274, 275
  Phocian 129
  South 268 n. 11
  Syracusan 269
  Thessalian 107, 117, 164, 273
  West 107
Gregory of Tours 84, 98, 100–1
Grimm's Law 6
Gurmukhi 63

harmony 10
Hebrew 19, 20, 22, 27, 28
Hebrew Names 19
Hellenistic period 129
Herodian 272, 273, 275
Herodotus 265, 272 n. 17, 275
heuristic principles 7–8
hexameter 180
Hindi 63, 64, 70, 78–9
'Hirt-Saussure' effect 138 n. 26, 156, 157
historical linguistics 5, 8, 11, 58
historical phonology 134
Homer 164, 165 n. 4, 168 n. 9, 172, 176–7, 179–81, 261, 264, 265, 266 n. 7, 267, 272 n. 17
Homeric Greek, *see* Greek
Horace 207
Hyginus, C. Iulius 84, 87, 95–8, 99, 100
hyperbaton 285, 286, 289, 294, 303 n. 68, 307, 308–12

Iambic shortening 209, 226
Icelandic 49
Iliad 172, 180–1
In Donati Artem Maiorem 28
India 64, 79
Indic 102, 144 n. 53
Indo-Aryan 62
  Middle 195, 203
  Modern 62, 63
  Old 61, 62, 76, 77, 80, 81, 229, 239, 242, 246 nn. 31–3, 247, 251–9
Indo-European languages 62, 82, 105, 131, 155
  see also Proto-Indo-European
Indo-Iranian 9, 129, 131–3, 229–59
infectum-stem (Latin) 83–5, 87, 89, 90, 95
infixation 211
innovations 33, 34
Institutiones Grammaticae 3, 19, 25
interpersonal distance 315
interrogative pronoun (Armenian) 142
Ionic, *see* Greek
Iranian 103, 129, 146 n. 61, 255 n. 41
  Middle 257 n. 47
  Old 230, 239, 242–7, 252 n. 38, 253, 254, 255 n. 41, 257
Irish 148, 155, 157, 158
  medieval 3, 17–30
  Middle 22
  Old 19, 22, 24, 27
Isidor 38
Isidore 19, 20, 28
isoglosses 119

Italian 84, 85, 213
Italic 93, 136
  Proto-Italic 158

Jerome 19, 28
Joseph's Law 156
Jutlandic 49

Kepler's second law of planetary motion 1–2
Kiparsky's Rule 10, 260–76
koine 112, 164, 165
koineization 64
Kuryłowicz's laws of analogy 3–5, 12–13, 83–4, 100–1

labiality 156
labiovelars 35, 103–4, 270
Laconia 110, 118, 119
Laconian, *see* Greek
language contact 79, 102
laryngeals 10, 125 n. 1, 131–3, 135, 138 n. 26, 143, 199, 230, 231 n. 3, 239, 246, 255, 259, 270, 271
Latin 2, 5, 6, 9, 10, 11, 18, 19, 20, 22, 24–30, 83–7, 128, 153–5, 156, 159, 163, 205–26, 279–312, 313–28
  British Latin 24, 153
  Late Latin 98–100, 283 n. 8
Latinisms 154
laws 1, 5–7, 9–13, 82, 102, 133, 279
law of limitation 9, 163–81
Łazar P'arpec'i 141
learner errors 39
lectal linkages 42 n. 8
lenition 22, 24 n. 18
Lepontic 148
Lesbian, *see* Greek
levelling 38, 51, 53, 58, 60, 208
Lex Agraria 217
lexical diffusion 118
lexical tone 61, 62, 65, 77, 79, 82
lexicalization 221 n. 17
lexicon 103
Lindeman's Law 9, 182–204
Linear B 103, 106, 112, 113, 117, 119
  see also Greek
linguists 1, 24
Lithuanian 136
Livy 86, 98 n. 7, 283–5, 290, 291, 296, 297, 298, 301–4, 307, 309
loanwords 24, 59, 144 n. 53, 145, 153–5, 214
  see also borrowing
Locrian, *see* Greek
Logudorese 85
lowering 45, 50
Lucretius 207
Luwian 102
Lycian A 103
Lysistrata 113 n. 20

Mānavadharmasmṛti 256
Mańczak's tendencies of analogy 4, 13
medieval linguistic thought 17–30
merger 46, 48, 51, 58, 61, 62, 82, 120
metathesis 143, 261, 263, 264, 266, 275
metre 183–204, 242
Middle English, *see* English
Middle Persian, *see* Persian
mimicry 56
minimal pairs 11, 55 n. 17, 63, 66
modifiers 302, 304, 312
monophthongization 261
moras 164, 166, 167, 209
moraic trochees 208–9
morphological change 83
morphologization 221 n. 17
morphology 83–101, 103, 276
morphophonemic genesis 58
morphosyntactic change 83
Murethach 28
Mycenaean, *see* Greek

'Narten' paradigms 171
nasals 128

nasal presents 137, 260, 269–72, 276
nasalized vowels 38
natural laws 1
natural sciences 13 n. 20
near merger 5, 61, 78, 82
neogrammarians 7, 24, 126, 262, 263, 265, 266, 268, 269, 275
Nepos 94 n. 6
New Zealand 120
Newfoundland 120
Newton's second law of motion 2
noise offset 70, 73–6, 78
nomina actionis 9, 231–5, 239–40, 242–3, 247–9, 251–3, 256, 259
nomina agentis 9, 230, 233 n. 7, 234 n. 11, 236–46, 249–51, 254–6, 258, 259
nominalization 89, 280
non-configurational languages 285 n. 14
non-syllabic resonants 182
nonce-formations 230, 256 n. 44
Norfolk 120
Norse 19, 37
  Old 36, 38
  Runic 37
Norwegian 49

odd numbers 1
Odyssey 180–1
Ogam 153
Old English, *see* English
Old Frisian 37, 39
Old Gutnish 49
Old High German, *see* German
Old Irish, *see* Irish
Old Persian, *see* Persian
Old Prussian 136
Older Runic, *see* Runic
Onasagos, King 114 n. 22, 116
opening 185, 192, 199
Optimality Theory 10, 209–26
Osthoff's Law 167 n. 8, 261, 262, 267, 273, 274, 275
Pakistan 64, 78 n. 8, 79
palatals 246 n. 32
palatalization 37, 54, 58, 260, 266, 267, 268, 274
Palladius 87
Panjabi 5, 61–82
  Doabi 63, 64, 67, 77, 78, 80
  Majhi 63, 64, 67, 78, 80
  Mirpuri 64
  Patiali 63, 77, 78
  Powadhi 67, 80
parameters 10
participles 83–6, 87, 88, 89, 93, 94, 100, 173 n. 17, 311
Pashto 144
passive (Latin) 5, 83–101
Peloponnese 110, 112, 113, 115 n. 23, 116, 117, 118
Penultimate Law (Latin) 163, 209, 224
Peregrinatio Egeriae 84, 99
perfect passive participle (Latin) 85, 88
perfectum-stem (Latin) 83, 84–7, 89, 95, 98, 100
periphrasis 83–101
Persian 138
  Middle 257 n. 47
  Old 258 n. 49
Phocian, *see* Greek
Phoenician 114
phonemes 8, 46, 48, 51, 53, 54, 55, 58, 59
  phoneme inventory 57
  potential/marginal/full 55
phonemic contrast 34
phonemicization 47, 49, 50, 51, 53, 56, 57
phonetics 61–82
phonologization 4, 44, 47, 48, 49, 51, 56, 59
phonology 30, 43–60, 64, 103, 182–204, 205–26, 276
  autosegmental 80
  generative 111
  lexical 222 n. 18
  post-lexical 221 n. 17, 222 n. 18
Pictish 19

Pindar 264, 268 n. 11
pitch 63, 67, 71, 77, 79, 82
  contour 63, 77, 78
  curve 69
  index 68, 69, 71–3, 75
  mean 68, 71–3, 75
  movement 62, 65, 68, 69, 71, 74, 76, 77, 80
  slope 68, 69, 71–3, 75
  track 68
planetary motion 1
Plautus 84, 86 n. 1, 89–92, 99, 100, 207, 223–4, 225, 279 n. 2, 318
Pliny the Elder 284 n. 9, 291, 299, 301
Pliny the Younger 283, 291, 294, 298, 299, 301, 318
pluperfect (Latin) 83, 86–7, 90–4, 96, 98, 100–1
Polish 210, 211 n. 6
politeness 11, 313–28
Polivanov's Law 4, 8, 43, 46, 48, 53, 58
Pompeii 154
Portuguese 85
pragmatics 10
prakritisms 195 n. 30
premodifiers 307
preverbs 237
primary split 46
prime numbers 1
principles 6, 12, 82
Priscian 3, 19, 24–9, 88 n. 4
proclitics 173
Proto-Indo-European 5, 6, 7, 8, 9, 11, 61, 62, 82, 103, 105, 106, 111, 113, 115, 125, 126, 127, 131–3, 134, 141, 144, 146, 151, 156, 164, 171–2, 179, 182, 183, 184 n. 5, 190 n. 20, 203, 204, 229, 230, 239, 240, 246, 253, 254, 255, 258, 259, 260, 261, 269, 285
proto-languages 7

quantitative metathesis 164
Quintilian 224

raising 45
reaccentuation 272
reanalysis 10, 174
regular correspondences 21
regularity 279
  principle 3, 7–8
relative chronology 33, 103
relative pronoun (Armenian) 142
relexicalization 48 n. 9
replacement operations 12
request formulae 313–28
retroflex articulation 36 n. 2, 65, 66
reversion 56
Ṛgveda 9, 168 n. 9, 182–204, 230–42, 246, 247–59
rhotacism 111, 208, 219, 222
rhoticity 120
Romance 5, 10, 84, 85–6, 92, 101, 136 n. 11, 154, 285, 286, 287 n. 19, 295 n. 41, 312
Rome 281
ruki 128
rules 1, 5–7, 9–13, 30, 206, 279, 286 n. 18
Rumanian 85
Runic 4, 43, 47, 48
  see also Norse
Russian 57

Sallust 282, 291, 298, 299, 300, 301
Sanas Cormaic 17–30
sandhi 175 n. 28, 177 n. 31, 266–9, 274
Sanskrit 126, 127, 129, 131–3
  Vedic 9, 168, 171, 172, 173 nn. 16–17, 173 n. 21, 179, 182–204, 230–42, 247–59
Sappho 272, 275
Saussure's effect, *see* 'Hirt-Saussure' effect
Saxon:
  Old 38 n. 5
  West 52
Scanian 49
Scholar's Primer, *see Auraicept na n-Éces*
Schwebeablaut 137

secondary split 46, 51, 58
semi-deponents (Latin) 89
Semitic 113
semivowels 182–204
Seneca the Elder 291, 301
Seneca the Younger 284 n. 9, 291, 298, 301, 303, 304, 311
Serbo-Croatian 63
seventeenth century 1 n. 2
sibilants 102–21
Sievers' Law 183–4, 198, 265
sigmatic aorist, *see* aorists, sigmatic
simultaneity 83
Skåne 49
sociolinguistics 10, 46, 121
sound:
  change 8, 35, 38, 47 n. 5, 48, 58, 60, 61, 117, 125, 130, 134, 143, 206, 221 n. 17, 222, 229, 263, 273
  law 2, 3, 5, 6, 7, 12, 62, 82, 125, 128, 142, 265, 268
  system 10
Spanish 85, 118
speech act theory 318
speech community 40, 41
spelling pronunciation 78
split 46 n. 3, 48, 56, 58
Stammbaum 41
stress 63, 205–26
  see also accent
Strict Layer Hypothesis 209
strong preterite (Germanic) 41
structural predisposition 120–1
structuralism 46, 56
subordinate clauses 96
sub-phonemic variation 46, 50, 54
substratum influence 102, 111, 116–17, 166
Suetonius 11, 280, 283, 291, 295, 298, 301, 304, 309, 311 n. 87
surface change 10
Swedish 49, 63
syllabary 119
syllabic liquids 216 n. 9
syllabicity 203
syllables 63, 205–25
synchronic grammar 10–11, 12, 211, 279–312, 313–28
syncope 9, 205–26
syntax 10, 103, 279–312
Syracusan, *see* Greek
system balance 52–3, 58
σωτῆρα rule 164–5, 166, 178

Tacitus 283, 285, 291, 294, 296, 297, 298, 302, 307, 309
tendencies 4, 11, 12–13, 279
Terence 84, 89–92, 99, 100, 318
thematic nouns 9, 229, 230
thematic presents 172, 178, 260
thematic vowel 172
thematization 10, 254, 264–5, 271, 275
Thessalian, *see* Greek
Thurneysen-Havet's Law 158
Tolstoj 54
tonal consonants 61–82
tone 5, 61–82
tonogenesis 62, 77, 80
topic 284 n. 10, 291, 312
Tower of Babel 18
trimeter (Vedic) 184–202, 204
typology 285, 308

umlaut 34, 43–60
uniformitarianism 41
universals 10–11, 315
unrounding 40
Upaniṣads 202

Valerius Maximus 291, 296, 299
Vannetais 148–51, 154, 156–8, 160
variation 41, 284
Varro 11, 280, 283, 284, 291, 299, 301, 304, 309
Vedic, *see* Sanskrit

velars 8 n. 16, 36–7, 66, 67–8, 246 n. 32
verbal governing compounds, *see* compounds
verbal nouns 233, 243, 247, 257
Verner's Law 6
Virgil 28
Vitruvius 84, 87, 95–8, 99, 100
vocal fold vibration 71
vocalic nasals 264
vocalism 229–59
voice onset time 67, 70–3, 78, 81
voiced aspirates 5, 61–3, 65, 76, 77, 78, 80–2, 127 n. 4
voiceless aspirates 6, 125–33
vowel length 68
vowel reduction 212, 214
vṛddhi-formations 141 n. 39

Wackernagel's Law 12
War and Peace 54
weak preterite (Germanic) 37–40
Welsh 20, 24, 29 n. 29, 147–58, 160
  Proto-Welsh 151
West Greek, *see* Greek
Wheeler's Law 230 n. 1
Wilcoxon-Mann-Whitney test 70
Wulfila 43

Yajurveda 257 n. 46

Zeno's paradoxes 54

Index of words

Albanian

zog 141 n.42

Armenian

ayl 145
ayci 138
aysôr 146
ayr 145
(y)ašt 143, 146 n.60
(Y)aštišat 143
aṙaǰ 139 n.33
asem 135 n.5
ban 137
banam 137
bolor 145
boyl 145
dow 139–40
dowstr 141
dowkʿ 139–40
es 139 n.32
erb 142 n.49
erbemn 142 n.49
erbêk 142 n.49
zna 141 n.38
êg, igi 135, 145
êš 145
tʿoyl 145
žoyž 140
(z-)i 142 n.49
inj 139
inčʿ 142 n.49, 146 n.61
lanǰ 136 n.11
leard 136
łeli 136 n.11
lowc 134, 136
lowcanem 136
kogi 141 n.44
kov 141n.44
havkit (ModEA) 141 n.43
howr 137 n.18
jag 141
jez 134, 135
paradigm 139–40
jow 135, 139, 140–1
jowkn 140
mari 138
makʿi 138
mez 139
mêǰ 137 n.18, 145
neard 136 n.11
nêr/ner 134, 135, 142–4, 146
nor 138
o(v) 135, 142
ozni 141 n.38
ołǰ 139 n.33
o/aṙoganem 138
or 135
ors 135, 144
ortʿ 127
owm (dialectal forms) 145, 146 n.60
owst (dialectal forms) 145, 146 n.60
owstr 141
owr (dialectal forms) 145, 146 n.60
čanačʿem 140
caneay (aor.) 140
čʿogay 138
ǰan 137, 146 n.61
ǰanam 135 n.2, 136, 137
ǰov 136, 138
ǰovanal 138 n.22
ǰori 136, 138
ǰowr 134, 135, 136–7

sxalem, *sxalim* 126
sterǰ 137 n.18
tal 141 n.45
taygr 141 n.45
têr 143
tikin 143
-woy 138
k'an 142
k'ani 142
k'ez 139
k'o 139

Assyrian
ú-na-sa-gu-su 114 n.22, 116

Avestan
-aⁱtī (3sg.) 267
aipiiaiia- 243
aipicara- 245
aiβigāma- 244, 253 n.40
apaγžāra- 244
avakana- 243, 245
aṣ̌anāsa- 245
ahu.nāsa- 245
uruzdi.pāka- 245, 258
gaošāuuara- 244
gaiia- 242
gauuāza- 244
gaδauuara- 244
xšuuiβi.išu- 243 n.26
xšuuiβi.vāza- 243
xšuuiβra- 243 n.26
-cara- 246
-carətar- 246 n.32
jaiia- 242
taka- 242, 245
-tara- 246
tiži.dāra- 243 n.22
tiži.bāra- 243 n.22
t̰baēšō.tara- 244
duuaža 238
dūraēpāra- 243
drujim.vana- 244
paēman- 145
paitiiāra- 244, 253 n.40
paiti.daiia- 245
paiti.vaŋha- 243
pairi.kara- 243
pairi.frāsa- 244
pairi.vāra- 244, 252 n.38
pantå 129
pāra- 245
baga-, *baγa-* 242, 243 n.23, 245, 257
-bara- 246
bāga- 243, 245
-bāra- 255 n.41
brī- 243 n.22
frauuāka- 252 n.38
frauuāza- 244
fracara- 245
fravāka- 244
fravāra- 244
frašō.kara- 244
nauuāza- 244, 246
nasupāka- 245, 246, 258
  nasupakāt̰ 245 n.28
nəmō.bara- 244
maēγō.kara- 244
mada-, *maδa-* 242, 245
mazdā.vara- 244
mašiiō.vaŋha- 244
yāna- 146 n.61
yāsaiti 137
vaδa-/vada- 245, 246
vahišta.nāsa- 245
vāra- 243
vāza- 245, 246, 254
vi.kaya- 246 n.32
vīkaya- 245
vītāra- 244, 253 n.40
vīvāpa- 244, 245
vī.vāra- 244
raēθβiš.kara- 244
raθakara- 244
rāna- 243
sauua- 242
stā- 129

Avestan (*cont.*)
snaθa- 242, 245
sruuara- 244
zaoθrō.bara- 244
zauua- 242
haθra.vana- 245
hāra- 245
huuāzāra- 243
hušəna- 243
x^vara- 243
x^vəng 151

Breton

Old Breton
cauel 152
cnou 153
couann 149
couatou 149
dou, dau 149, 153
petguar 150

Middle Breton
auel, avel 152
breuzr 156
cauell 152
clou 156
couhat 149, 155–6
couhenn, caoüen 149
d(a)ou 149, 153
iaou 149 n.6
kanou, cnou 153
leuyaff 149
louazr 156
louen 149, 152, 158
-*(a)ou* (nom. pl.) 149, 153
youanc 151, 158, 159

Modern Breton
avel 152
daou 149, 153
he- 159
kavell 152
Kernev 149 n.6
kerluz 157
keureug 157
kaouad 149
kaouenn 149
kraoñ 153
laouer 156
leviañ 149
-*où* (nom. pl.) 149, 153
taran 155 n.18
yaou 149 n.6
yaouank 151

Vannetais Breton
cohann 151
deu 149, 153
-*eu* (nom. pl.) 149, 153
iouank 150–1, 152, 158
kohad 149, 153, 155–6
kohann 149, 150, 152
leùen 149, 152, 155, 158, 160
leùenan 160
leùénus 160
louer 156
queneu (Haut Vann.) 153

Byelorussian
/rvú/ (1sg.) 58
/rv'oš/ (2sg.) 58
/tkú/ (1sg.) 58
/tk'oš/ (2sg.) 58
/vrú/ (1sg.) 58
/vr'oš/ (2sg.) 58

Cornish

Old Cornish
auhel 152
couat 149
leu 149
iouenc 151

Middle Cornish
awel 152
cowas 149, 155–6
crow 153
dow, dew 149, 153
he-, hy- 159

Kernow 149 n.6
lowen 149, 152, 158
lower 152
luf 156
-*ow* (nom. pl.) 149, 153
peswar 149
yow 149 n.6
yowynk 151, 158

Late Cornish
knufan 153
lew 149

English

Old English
burg 50
caru 37
ċeare (obl. cases) 37
cwicu/*cwic* 35
-*de* (weak past ind.1sg., 3sg.) 38, 40
-*des* (weak past ind.2sg.) 38
éar 136
ēowic, ēow 139
faemne 145
faran 52
fare (subj. pres.) 52
fēower 34, 39
fredde 34
fæder 40
fær 52
fære (dat. sg.) 52
færþ 51
ġeat 37
gatu (pl.) 37
ġesætte 34
ġeolu, ġeolw- 35
ġiefe 40
giest 56
giestas (pl.) 56
heorte 40
here, herġ- 35
hwone 40
īow 34
īower 34
lēaþor 156
lette 34
lūcan 136
mann 56
menn (pl.) 56
mec, mē 139
mettas 36
scūr 155
sette 34
singan 37
tunge 40
ūsic, ūs 139
wæter 39
wulf 49
þec, þē 139
þicce 36, 37
þone 40

Modern English
bad 55 n.17
bade 55 n.17
badge 55 n.17
badger 55 n.17
bag 55 n.17
bat 55 n.17
brandy 55 n.17
cadge 55 n.17
candid 55 n.17
candied 55 n.17
car 120
drench 57
female 136 n.10
get well soon! 327
hear 57
mad 55 n.17
mag 55 n.17
male 136 n.10
near 120
please 316
prestige 59
sad 55 n.17
shandy 55 n.17

English (*cont.*)

smart 120
square 120
take care! 327
visible 59
vision 59
visual 59

Finnish

rengas 45

French

boue 159 n.20
femelle 136 n.10
janvier 154

Galatian

Καυαρος 157

Gaulish

Bouus, *Bouo-*, *Βουι-* 159
Cauarius, *Cauarillus* 157
Cauannus, *Cauanos* 159–60
Κνουιλλα 159
Iouincus 159
Iuuantus (paradigm) 159–60
Iouantu- 159
Lauenus 148, 152, 159
lautro 156
Louernios, *Λουερνιος* 159 n.20
Lugoues 148, 159
Oimenus 159
-*oues* (nom. pl.) 153, 159
Ouiorix 159
secoui 159 n.20
su- 159
Suagrus 159
Suausia 159

German

Old High German

beti 36
brutta 34
burg 50
-*dēs* (weak past ind.2sg.) 38
dick(i) 36
dih 139
fater 40
fior 34
gast 56
gesti (pl.) 56
geba 40
gelo, *gelaw-* 35
heri, *heri-* 35
herza 40
hūwo 151
igil 141 n.38
iu 34
iuwerēr 34
iuwih 139
lazta 34
man 56
mih 139
quatta 34
quek/*queh* 35, 36
sazta 34
scutita 34
scutta 34
singan 37
snora, *snur(a)* 49
stehhal(a) 49
stihhil(a) 49
suht 50
-*ta* (weak past ind.1sg.) 38, 40
-*ta* (weak past ind.3sg.) 38, 40
-*tōs* (weak past ind.2sg.) 38
tratta 34
-*tus* (weak past ind.2sg.) 38
unsih 139
waȥȥar 39
wolf 49
zuht 50
zunga 40

Modern German

hören 57
Schnur 49
Stachel 49
tränken 57

Gothic

-*da* (weak past ind.1sg.) 37, 40
-*da* (weak past ind.3sg.) 37
-*des* (weak past ind.2sg.) 37
fidwor 39
gibos (gen. sg.) 40
giba (acc. sg.) 40
harjis 35
haírto 40
ƕana 40
ƕanoh 40
izwar 34
izwis 34
juggs 148
jus 135, 139
mats 36
satida 34
Schuos (Crimean) 44 n.2
siggwan 37
skaþis 127
skūra 155
stikls 49
tuggo 40
wato 39
þana 40

Greek

Mycenaean Greek
a-pe-a-sa 113 n.21
a_2-te-ro 106
a-sa-mi-to 106, 113
a-to-po-qo 258
de-ka-sa-to 113
do-se 115
do-so-mo 113
e-qe-si-jo 112 n.17
e-qe-ta 112 n.17
e-re-u-te-ro-se 106, 115
ka-ke-u-si 106
ko-no-so 113 n.21
ku-pa-ri-so 113 n.21
ku-ru-so 106, 113
me-zo-a_2 106
-*o-i* (dat.-loc. pl.) 107, 115–16
pa-sa 107
pa-si 106, 107
pa-we-a_2 106
pa-we-si 107
pe-i 107 n.7, 115
pe-re 274
pi-we-ri-si 113
qa-si-re-u-si 115
ra-wa-ke-si-jo 112 n.7
ra-wa-ke-ta 112 n.7
re-wo-to-ro- 156
sa-sa-ma 106, 113
se-ri-no 106
su-qo-ta 106
ti-ri-si 115
to-so 106, 113 n.21, 266
we-te-i-we-te-i 106
ze-u-ke-si 113 n.21

Ancient Greek

-ᾱ́ (nom. sg.) 177
-ᾱ́ (nom./acc. du.) 177
-ᾷ (dat. sg.) 177
Ἄβιος 173 n.20
Ἀγεhίπολις (Lac.) 108
ἀγχέμαχος 173 n.18
ἄγρει (Sappho, 3sg.) 272
ἀδεαλτώhαιε (Elean) 109
ἀδικήει (Sappho) 272 n.17
ἄελλα 152
ἀθάνατος 173 n.23, 174
-αι (nom./voc. pl.) 180
-αι (2sg.) 175, 180
-αι (inf.) 180

Greek (*cont.*)

-αῖν (gen./dat. du.) 177
-αις (dat. pl.) 261, 264
  -αῖς 177
  -αισι 261, 264
  -ησι 261, 264, 266 n.8
-αις (Lesbian, 2sg.) 272
-αισ(ι) (Lesbian, 3sg.) 272
a-la-si-o-ta-i (Cypr.) 109, 114
ἀλίνω 271 n.15
ἀμογητί 262
ἀμπώτε(ραι) (*P Ryl*) 130
-ᾱ́ν (acc. sg.) 177
ἄνθει (Alcaeus, 3sg.) 272
ἄνθρωπος (paradigm) 165–7
  ἀνθρώπων (gen. pl.) 173 n.22, 174
ἀνίεις/-ιεῖς 261
[ἀ]ντιδίδω (Aeol.) 275
ἀνύω 265
ἀπειλή 271 n.15
ἀπελτῖν (*P Teb*) 130
  ἀπελτοῦσα (*BGU*) 130
ἀπολαύω 152
ἀπορρηhίαν (Lac.) 108
ἀ]ποτειάτω (Elean) 109
ἀρτοκόπος 258
-ᾱς (acc. pl.) 269
  -ᾱ́ς 177
  -ᾰς (Syracusan) 269
-ᾶς (gen. sg.) 177
ἀσάμινθος 106
ἀσκηθής 127
ἀστήρ 138
ἄστρον 138
a-pa-i-re-i (Cypr.) 109
ἄχει (Alcaeus, 3sg.) 272
βαίνω 266–7
βάλλω 271
  βάλλει 271
βασιλεῦσι 115
  βαΐλέος (Lac.) 108
βούλευσαι 176
  βουλεῦσαι 176
βούλομαι 165, 270 n.14
  βούλωμαι 165
βοῦς 159
γάμει (Alcaeus, 3sg.) 272–3
γάνυμαι 270 n.13
γλακτοφάγων 173 n.19
γάλως 141 n.45
γένεσι 107
γηθέω 270 n.14
γιγνώσκω 270 n.12
  ἔγνων 270 n.12
γλῶσσα 265
δάμνημι 264
  δάμνησι 269, 271
  δαμνᾷ (Hom.) 271
  δάμναι (Alcaeus) 272 n.16
δαμόσιος (Att. δημόσιος) 112
  δαμόhιος (Western Argolic) 108, 112
δαμότης 112
-δε 261
δείκνῡ 272
  δεικνύει 272
δεξαμενή 173 n.17
δίδωμι (paradigm) 265, 268, 269, 274–5
  δίδωσι 113, 263, 268, 271, 275
  δίδου 268 n.10
  δώσει 115
  δός 264, 268 n.10
  διδοῖ (Hom., Ion.) 261, 264–5, 268, 275
  διδοῖς (Hom., Ion.) 261, 265
  διδοῦσι (Hom., Ion.) 265
  δίδω (Aeol.3sg. pres.) 272–3, 275
  δίδοι (Pindar, Boeotian/Corinthian, ipv.) 264, 268 n.10
δίζημαι 137
δίψαισ(ι) (Alcaeus) 272
Δ[μ]αίππίδαι (Western Argolic) 108
δορκάς 144
δόρξ 144
δόρυ 229

δόσις 266
δραμείται 178
δρυίδης (Gallo-Gr.) 148, 159
δῡ́νω 271 n.15
δύσφορο- 239
δῶρον 166
ἐάω 172 n.13
ἐγκυτί 262
ἐέλπετο (Hom.) 172–3
-ει (3sg. pres.) 260–1, 262, 266–7, 269, 271, 275
-ησι (*σχῆμα Ἰβύκειον*) 268 n.10
εἰαμενή 173 n.17
εἰμί 118
εἰνατέρες 142
-εις (2sg. pres.) 260–1, 266
εἷς 269
  ἑς (Ion.) 269
ἕκητι 262, 264
εἰσπορά (*P London*) 130
ἐλευθερόω 106
Ἐλευhύνια (Lac.) 108
ἕλυε 102
ἐνίκαhε (Lac.) 108
ἐπίρροθος 126
e-pi-si-ta-i-se (Cypr.) 109
ἑπόμενος 94
ἑρκοθηρικός 144
ἕρκος 144
ἐρουτâι (Thessalian?) 273
ἕ]*σσονται* (Lac.) 115 n.24
ἐστόρεσα 156
ἕτερος 106
ἔτι 262, 264
ἔτος 106
ἐϋ- 151
ἔχων 115 n.23
  σκῶσιν (*P Oxy*) 130
  ἔχησι 268 n.10
ἐψήφισα 107
-έω, -άω, -όω (Att.-Ion., verb classes) 273–4, 275
Ϝhεδιέστας (Argolic) 116
Ϝίκατι (Dor.) 262, 264, 267
Ϝορθαία (Lac.) 108 n.9
**-Ϝοχός* 254
ζειαί 138
ζεύγνῡ (Aeol. 3sg. pres.) 272–3
ζῆλος 135 n.2, 137
ζητέω 137
Ζητήρ 137
ζόρξ 144
ἠέλιος 151
ἠλευθέρωσε 115
-ημι, -ᾱμι, -ωμι (Aeol., Arcado-Cyprian, verb classes) 272–4, 275
-θα (2sg. perfect) 127, 129
θάλλω 271
θάρνυμαι/θόρνυμαι 270
-θεν 261
θηάυρόν (Western Argolic) 108
-θης (2sg. aor. passive) 127, 129
θής 265
θῆσσα 265
-θι 261
θνᾱ- 129
ἵησι (paradigm) 268
  ἵησι 268
  ἕς 264, 268 n.10
  ἵει, ἱεῖ (Hom., Ion.) 268
ἱπποπόλων 173 n.16
ἵστημι (paradigm) 171
  ἵστημι 127
  στῆν (1sg. aor.) 172 n.10
  ἕσταθι 264
-ιστος (superlative) 127
καί 262, 264, 268
κάλημ⟨μ⟩ι (Sappho, 1sg.) 272
  καλήω (Alcaeus) 272 n.17
  κάλει (Sappho, 3sg.) 272
κάμνω 271
κάς (Arcado-Cyprian) 262, 268
  ka-a-ti (Cypr.) 109
  ka-u-ke-ro-ne (Cypr.) 109
κασι- 262, 268
κασίγνητος 262, 268

Greek (*cont.*)

κατάγρει (Alcaeus, 3sg.) 272
καταχραἄστω (Elean) 109
κατοικείουνθι (Thessalian) 272 n.17
καύᾱξ 151
κεῖμαι (paradigm) 175
κελεύοι 177 n.31
  κελεύοις 177 n.31
κλόνει (Sappho, 3sg.) 272
Κνοhίαν (Western Argolic) 108
κόγχος 126
κρῑ́νω 271 n.15
ku-me-re-na-i (Cypr.) 109
λέγομεν 167
  λέγητον 166
  λέγοντα 166
λείπει 177 n.31
  λείπεται 177 n.31
λιπαρός 136
λοετρόν 156
λοιπός 258
λύπηις (Sappho, 2sg.) 272 n.18
Λύhιππον (Lac.) 108
-μαι (1sg.) 175, 180
ma-na-se-se (Cypr.) 109, 114
μάρναται 269
μαρτύρεται 178
Μεγαροῖ 165
μεθίεις 261
  μεθίει/-ιεῖ 261
μείζων 106
-μεναι (inf.) 180
-μενο- (ptcpl.) 173 n.17, 174
Μναhίμαχος 115 n.23
μοῖρα 266–7
Μῶσα (Alcman), Μῶα
    (Aristophanes) 113 n.20
νᾱ(ϝ)ός 118
-νᾱμι (Att.-Ion. -νημι, 1sg.) 269, 271, 275
  -νᾰμεν (1pl.) 269
νεῖ 267 n.9
νέμω 231
νεοσσεύω 141 n.43
νεοσσός 141 n.43
νεῦρον 136 n.11
Νικαhαρίστα (Western Argolic) 108
νικάάς (Lac.) 108
Νικαhικλῆς (Lac.) 108
-νται (3pl.) 175, 180
-νῡμι (verb class) 265, 269–72, 275
  -νῡμι (1sg.) 269–70
  -νύω (1sg.) 265
  -νύει (3sg.) 265
  -νῠμεν (1pl.) 269–70
νύξ 270
-νω (verb class) 270
  -νει (3sg.) 274
  -νομεν (1pl.) 270
  -νετε (2pl.) 271
  -νομαι (1sg. mid.) 270
  -νεται (3sg. mid.) 271
  -νόμενος (mid. ptcpl.) 270
νωλεμές 172 n.14
νωλεμέως 172
ξηραντῖσαν (*P Oxy*) 130
hο (Argolic) 116
  hοιζ (Argolic) 116
-οι (nom./voc. pl.) 167 n.8, 180
-οι (opt.) 180
οἴκοθι 261
(ϝ)οῖκος (paradigm) 168, 175
  οἴκοι (loc. sg.) 180, 261
  οἶκοι (nom. pl.) 165
-οῖν (gen./dat. du.) 177
-οις (dat. pl.) 116, 167 n.8
  -οῖς (dat. pl.) 178
  -οισι (dat. pl.) 107, 116
-οις (Lesbian, 2sg.) 272
οἶσθα 127, 129
ὁλκός 258
ὄλλυμι 271 n.15
  ὤλεσα 271 n.15
ὀλοός 271 n.15
ὀμίλλει (Alcaeus, 3sg.) 272
ὄμνῡμι 270

ὀνάρταις (Sappho) 272
Ὀνασίτιμος 109
o-na-i-ti-mo (Cypr.) 109
Ὀνησαγόρας, Ὀνηαγόρας 109
o-na-a-ko-ra-se, *o-na-sa-ko-ra-se* (Cypr.) 109
(*)ὄνυμα 270
ὄνυξ 270
ὄπταις (Sappho) 272
ὄρη (Theocritus, 3sg.) 272 n.17
ὀρῑ́νω 271 n.15
ὀρκάνη 144
ὅρκος 144
Ὀρχομενός 173 n.17
ὀστέον 127
-ους (acc. pl.) 269
-ούς 164, 177
ὄφρα 142 n.49
παιδεύοι 165
παίδευσαι 165
παιδεῦσαι 165
πάλλω 271
παρτιθεῖ (Hom.) 261
πᾶσα 107, 118
πατήρ 40
πάτος 127, 129
πέλασσεν (Hom.) 172 n.12
περίσταίν (Western Argolic) 108, 110
πέρυσι 262, 264, 265, 267
πίειρα 145
πίε̄σι (CEG 454) 263 n.4
πιλνᾷ 271
πίων 145
πλατύς 127, 129, 132
πόᾱ 145
ποθήω (Sappho) 272 n.17
ποιήσασθαι 109
ποιήσηται 109
πόημι (Aeolic, paradigm) 273
ποήάσσαι (Elean) 109
ποιήάται (Elean) 109
ἐποίεhε (Lac.) 108
ἐποίϝεhε (Western Argolic) 108
πόλεμος (paradigm) 166
πόληος, πόλεως (Att.-Ion.) 164
πολυπῖδαξ 164
πόντος 127, 132
πόρκος 144
πόρτις 127
Ποhοιδαῖα (Lac.) 108
Ποhοιδᾶνος, Ποhοιδᾶνι (Lac.) 108
ποτί 229
πρέσβυς 264 n.5
πρεῖγυς (Cretan) 264 n.5
προίει/-ιεῖ 261, 264, 272
πρός 229
-σαι (opt.) 180
-σαι (ipv.) 180
σάωις (Alcaeus, 2sg.) 272 n.18
σήσαμα 106
σέλινον 106
-σθαι (inf.) 175, 178
-σι 261
σκέλλομαι 271
σοφός (paradigm) 164
-σσαι (Elean, inf.) 119 n.25
στᾱ- (root) 129
στέγω 127
στεφάνοι (Lesbian, 3sg. ind.) 273
Στησαμενός 173 n.17
στόρνῡμι 270, 271 n.15
στόρνυμεν 269
στόρνυμαι 269
στορνύμενος 269
ἐστόρεσα 271 n.15
συβώτης 106
συκωτόν (ἧπαρ) 136 n.11
σφεις, σφεσιν (Arcadian, dat. pl.) 107 n.7
σφάλλομαι 126
σφηλός 126
Σῴζομενός 173 n.17
Σωΐβιος (Western Argolic) 109
σωτῆρα 164
-ται (3sg.) 175, 178, 180
ta-u-ke-ro-ne (Cypr.) 109

Greek (*cont.*)

-*τατο*- (superlative) 173 n.21, 174
Τεισαμενός 173 n.17
τέλλομαι 271
τέμνω 271
  τάμνει, τέμνει 271
τέτλαθι 264
τέτταρες 150
τίθημι (paradigm) 265, 268, 269, 274–5
  τίθημι (1sg.) 273
  τίθησι 268, 271, 272, 275
  τίθει (ipv.) 268 n.10
  θές 264, 268 n.10
  τίθει (Hom.) 261, 264, 267–8, 269, 271–2, 273, 274 n.22, 275
  τιθεῖ (Ion.) 265, 268, 271–2, 275
  τιθεῖσι (Hom.) 265
  τίθη (Aeol. 3sg. pres.) 272–3, 275
  τίθεις (Alcaeus, 2sg.) 272, 275
  τίθησθα (Alcaeus, 2sg.) 272
  τιθέστωι (*P Teb*) 130
τίμαι (Lesbian, 3sg.) 273
τίνω 271
τομός/τόμος 229–31, 240, 246 n.32, 257–8
to-po-e-ko-me-no-ne (Cypr.) 109
τόσσος (Hom.), *τόσος* (Att.) 106, 113, 115
τρέπω (paradigm) 168–71, 174, 175–6
  τρέπεν (Hom.) 172
τρισί 115
Τυλισôι 108
υἱύς 141
Φαμενός 173 n.17
φâρος 106
φέρεις 260–1, 263
  φέρει 260–1, 263, 273, 274
  φέρῃς 261
  φέρῃ 261, 263, 267
  φέρουσα 166
  φέρη (dial.) 261
  φέρῃσι (Hom.) 261, 263, 267
φησί 106, 263
  φαῖμ(ι) (Sappho, 1sg.) 272 n.18
  φαῖς (Sappho, 2sg.) 272
  φαῖσθ(α) (Alcaeus, 2sg.) 272 n.18
  φαῖσι (Alcaeus, 3sg.) 272
φθείρω 137 n.18
-*φι* 261
φιλεῖ 273
  φίλημ(μ)ι (Sappho, 1sg.) 272–3
  φίλη(ι)σθα (Sappho, 2sg.) 272 n.18
  φίλει (Sappho, 3sg.) 272–4, 275
φοίταις (Sappho) 272
φόρη (Theocritus, 3sg.) 272 n.17
Φραhιαρίδας (Western Argolic) 108, 115 n.23
po-ro-ne-o-i (Cypr.) 109
φυγαδευάντι (Elean) 109
χαλκεύς 106
χάριτι 262
χαύνοις (Sappho) 272
χθές 141 n.38
χρυσός 106
-*ώ* (nom./acc. du.) 177
-*ῳ̂* (dat. sg.) 177
-*ωμι* (Hom., 1sg. subj.) 261
-*ῶν* (gen. pl.) 164, 177

Modern Greek
συκώτι 136 n.11

Hittite
  eu̯a(n)- 138 n.26
  ḫallanniye- 271 n.15
  i̯anzi 138 n.26
  katti 262, 264
  liššī- 136
  šamnanzi 264

Irish

Old Irish
  boí 148
  briathor 27

cét 264
cnú 153
coär 157
crú 153
-cúalae 153
deich 267
fér 23
fescer 23
figell 23
fín 23
fír 23, 137
gabar 29 n.29
mebuir 155
loäthar, lóthar 157
loor, lour 152
oäc 148, 151, 158
roar 152
ro·fera 152
súil 151
taí 153
tiug 36
úath 157
uile 139 n.33

Italian
amare (paradigm) 84
febbraio 154
occhio 207
quagliare 154
rovina 154

Latin
acta 290 n.30
adulescens 291 n.34
aes alienum 311
allatae fuerunt 97
alumnus 94
ambulare 207
amo (paradigm) 83–7, 92, 94, 99, 100–1, 207, 209
  amans 94
  amabo, si me amas 321 n.13
amatio (paradigm) 207
ampulla 207, 219
ancipitem 218–19
anculus 212
antae 214 n.8
apricus 217
aprilis 207, 216–17
ardere 220
ardor (paradigm) 208, 220 n.15
aridus 220, 225
ars 282
asp(e)ris 225
attuli 208, 219
audacter 206, 216, 220
audere 89, 217
audire 214
  auditus sit 100
auidus 217
auspex 214
auspicia 294 n.39
bal(i)neum 214, 221, 223–5
beatus 88
bellus 213
beo 88
bonus 287 n.20
bruma 212
caldarius 208
cal(i)dus 208, 224–5
candetum 294 n.40
capitis 223
cauannum (Gallo-Lat.) 159
**cauellus* (British Latin) 152
caurus 155
cauitum 217
cautus 217
cenatus 93
cette 217
circumuectus sum 90
citra 216
ciuilis 287 n.20
cohors 280–1, 285, 291 n.34, 291 n.35, 297 n.49
columen 214
colurnus 222
commoratio 290 n.30

Latin (*cont.*)
conficio 209, 212
confectus 209
confisi fuerunt 97
coniuratio 282
consilium 290 n.30
contio 281
contra 216
corolla 219
culminis 213–14
cum 264
cunctari 215–16, 217
cuncti 220
designatus 287
dexter 212, 219
dictum 89
disciplina 217
doctus 213, 215, 287
druides (Gallo-Lat.) 159
duo 149, 153
edictum 280–1, 290 n.30
etiam atque etiam 321
exclusissimus 88
exercitus 281, 290 n.31, 291, 292, 297 n.48, 302 n.66
exteri 220
extra 216, 219
extremus 219–20
extrinsecus 217
facere 89
factum esse 89
facilius 210
facultatem 216 n.9
Falernus 222
familia 290 n.30
fauentia 214
faustus 214
Febrarius (Appendix Probi) 154
febrarias (Pompeii) 154
femina 94
fe(n)(e)stra(m) 214
ficatum (iecur) 136 n.11
fieri 89
fiere 89 n.5
fitur 89 n.5
fitum est 89 n.5
forcipes 218–19
frequentia 290 n.31
fundere 140
gaudere 211, 217
gemellus 214, 222
glos 141 n.45
(per)gratum mihi erit 321 n.13
heluos 35
heri 141 n.38
homo 280–1
horrificae 288
hospitem 219
ianitrices 142
igenuus (inscr. Cirencester) 154
imperium 221 n.17, 222
indutus sum 92
infra 216
insidiae 280, 282
instructissimus 88 n.4
in-/exterior 219
intra 216, 219
inuocatus 89
iug(e)ra 225
iumentum 138
iuniores 205 n.2, 216
iurare (paradigm) 217
iuratus fui 92
iurgium 219–20
iurigare 220
iurisdictio 281, 282, 287, 290 n.31, 291–2, 296
ius 287 n.20, 290 n.30, 292
iustus (paradigm) 213–14
iouestod (inscr.) 214
iuuencus 148
iuuentas 213
lar(i)dum 225
latrina 156

legio 280–1, 283, 285, 290 n.31, 297 n.48, 302 n.66, 304, 307
legit 260
  legunt 209
libertas 280, 282
lubere 89
  lubitum erit 90
  lubitum fuerit 91
magist(e)ra 225
magisterium 216, 219
magistratus 216–17
magnus 287 n.20
mihi 139
miles 280–1, 285, 291 n.35, 297 n.49
militia 282, 297 n.49
misertus 224–5
monitus 214 n.8
monstrum 213
mortus (Pompeii) 154
motus 214, 280, 282
mulierem 224
multitudo 280, 282
municipium 219 n.13
nauis
  longa 287 n.20
  oneraria 311
negotium 281, 290 n.31, 291 n.36
nonus 217
nuncupare 217–18
nundinae 217
nux 153
obiurig- 220
oculus 207
officina 219, 221
officium 205, 219, 221, 281
omnis 302
operatum fuisse 99
opes 281, 294 n.39
opifex 214, 222
optimus 221, 223
opus 280–1, 291 n.36
ordinare 217 n.10
ornare 217
ornus 214 n.7
oro 318, 323–6
otium 280–1, 282, 289, 290 n.31
ouis 159
participium 219
Penates 144
penes 144
penitus 144
penus, -oris 144
penus, -us 144
per-/porgere 219
peto 318, 319–23, 324–6, 327
plebs 281, 282–3, 290 n.30, 290 n.31, 291 n.36, 301, 304 n.71, 305 n.73
plerique 302
pocillum 216 n.9
Pomptinae 217
ponere 213
pontifex maximus 311
populnus 219
populus 287 n.20, 290 n.30
porcus 144
postridie 216–17
praeconem 217
praedium 280–1, 283, 291 n.33
praetor 279–312
praetura 282, 290 n.30, 291 n.34, 292
primus 219
princeps 206, 219–20
profectus fueras 91
promissus fuerat 91
propter 216, 219
prouidere 217 n.11
prouincia 282, 287, 291 n.36, 296, 309 n.78
prudentem 217 n.11
puer(i)tia 221–5
puerpera 219, 221
pulcher 287 n.20
quaeso 318, 319–23, 327
quaestor 280–1, 290 n.30, 290 n.31, 291 n.32, 291 n.34

Latin (*cont.*)
quaestura 290 n.30
quam 142
quarticipem 219
quattuor 150
querneus 219, 220
quindecim 206, 219
ratus 94 n.6
raucus 213
reccidi 213
repperi 213
reppuli 213
res 280–1, 283, 288–9, 290 n.30, 290 n.31, 291 n.34, 291 n.35, 291 n.36, 294, 299, 305 n.73, 312 n.88
retro 216
rettuli 213
rogo 318, 319–23, 325–6, 327
Romanus 286 n.18, 287 n.20
rota 126
rursus 213–14, 217 n.11
sacerdotem 216 n.9
sectus 213
seditio 280–1, 290 n.31
sepultus 206, 222
sequens 94
sermo 281, 305
seruitium 291 n.36
seruitus 280–1
sinist(e)ra 225
sol(i)dus 224–5
sors 281, 282, 287, 290 n.31, 291 n.36, 296 n.43
stab(u)larius 225
sumere 213
summus 287 n.20
superus 208
supra 208, 216–17
supremus 219–20
surgere 219 n.14
surripuit 207
  surpuit 207, 219
tigillum 216 n.9
tribus 280–1, 282, 291 n.34
uale 327
  cura ut ualeas 327
uaqua (Appendix Probi) 154
uectigalia 290 n.30
uehere 89
  uectus sum 90
  uectus fui 90
uehementer 321
uelim 318, 319–23, 327
uerens 94 n.6
  ueritus 93, 94 n.6
uet(e)ranus 225–6
uilla 304
uillum 220
uinctum fuisse 97
uindemia 217
uir 45
uir(i)dis 225
uirtutem 217
uisus fuero 97
uita 282
ullus 220
ulna 220
ultra 216
ultus fuero 90
urbanitas 295 n.41
urbanus 279–312
  urbanior 287
  urbanissimus 287
  urbane 295 n.41
urina 136–7
usurpare 206, 216, 218, 219 n.14
uulgus 291 n.35
uulneris 213–14

Latvian

piẽva 145

Lithuanian

ežỹs 141 n.38
jáura 136
jáutis 138
jávas 138
jū́ra 136–7
jū́rės (pl.) 134, 135, 136
jū́ros (pl.) 136
kóvas 151
píeva 145
pýti 145

Luwian

warša- 137

Norse

Runic Norse
-*de* (weak past ind. 3sg.) 37
-*do* (weak past ind. 1sg.) 37, 40
dohtriR 47–8, 49 n.11, 50, 60
gudija 47 n.7, 49 n.11
holtijaR 47–8, 49 n.11, 50, 60
horna 47, 49 n.11
-*kurne* 47 n.7, 49 n.11
satido 34
talgidai 37 n.4
tawide 37 n.4
worahto 47, 49 n.11, 50
wurte 47 n.7, 49 n.11

Old Norse
bøn 137
dǿtr 54
faðir 40
feima 145
gjafar (gen. sg.) 40
gjóta (*hrǫgnum*) 140
goði 47 n.7
herr 35
hjarta 40
kvikr 35
lauðr 156
syngva 37
traddi 34
tunga 40
úr 136–7
þjokkr/þykkr 36
-*ða* (weak past ind.1sg.) 37
-*ði* (weak past ind.3sg.) 37
-*ðir* (weak past ind.2sg.) 37

Old Church Slavonic

jaje 135
jatry (RussCSl.) 142
sěverъ 155
za 141 n.38
zъlъva 141 n.45

Old English, *see* **English**

Old Frisian
-*de* (weak past ind.1sg., 3sg.) 40
feder 40
fiuwer 34, 39
hwane 40
iu 34
siunga 37
thene 40
thiukke 36, 37
weter 39

Old Gutnish

dōtur 49
dȳtrum (dat. pl.) 49, 50

Old High German, *see* **German**

Old Irish, *see* **Irish**

Old Norse, *see* **Norse**

Old Persian, *see* **Persian**

Old Prussian

iūrin 136–7
wurs 136–7

Old Saxon

-*da* (weak past ind.1sg., 3sg.) 40
fader, *fadar* 40
fēmea 145
fiuwar 34, 39
geƀa 40
gisetta 34
heri, *heri-* 35
iu 34
herta 40
hwena 40
latta 34
lettun 34
quik 35
satta 34
singan 37
thana 40
thikki 36
tunga 40
watar 39

Panjabi

/bag/ 66
/bág/ 66
/ˈdʒəngi/ 66
/ˈdʒə́ngi/ 66
/kàl/ 63, 66
/kal/ 63, 66
/kál/ 63
/kì/ 66, 72
/ki/ 66
/kùk/ 66
/kuk/ 66
/nɪˈkàr/ 80
/ˈsənga/ 66
/ˈsə́nga/ 66
/ˈsəngi/ 66
/ˈsə́ngi/ 66, 80
/sing/ 66
/síng/ 66

Pashto

ndror 144

Persian

Old Persian
arštibara- 244
asabāra- 255 n.41
ucāra- 243, 258 n.49
-*kara-* 246 n.32
kāra- 233 n.8, 258 n.49
kunautuv 258 n.49
cartanaiy 246 n.32, 258 n.49
takabara- 244
dāraniyakara- 244
patiy 229
patikara- 243
paruzana- 242
baga- 242
yāna- 146 n.61
vaçabara- 244
vispazana- 242
zurakara- 244
hamaranakara- 244

Middle Persian
aswār 255 n.41
duxt (paradigm) 141 n.45
ǰaw 138
-*kar-*/-*gār-* 257 n.47
kār 257 n.47
pidar 141 n.45
pisar 141 n.45
pusar, *pus* 141 n.45

Neo-Persian
ǰaw 138
ǰawin 138
xāya 135
zāq 141 n.42

Phoenician

lhyts 109, 114

mnḥm 109, 114

Polish

jak 135, 142

Proto-Germanic, see also **Proto-West Germanic**

*-dē (weak past ind.3sg.) 37
*-dēz (weak past ind.2sg.) 37
*-dǭ (weak past ind.1sg.) 37, 40
*fadēr 40
*fedwōr 34, 39
*gebōz (gen. sg.) 40
*gebǭ (acc. sg.) 40
*gelwaz 35
*harjaz 35
*hertǭ 40
*hrengaz 45
*h^wanǭ 40
*izweraz 34
*izwiz 34
*kurna 45
*k^wik^waz 35
*latidē 34
*matiz (inflected forms) 36
*sagjaz (inflected forms) 36
*satidē 34
*singwaną 37
*snuzō- 45
*tradidē 34
*tungǭ 40
*watōr 39
*wiraz 45
*þanǭ 40
*þekuz (inflected forms) 36

Proto-Indo-European

*b^hogó- 258
*b^hóro-/-b^horó- 230, 239, 240, 246, 258–9
*deḱm̥ 267
*du̯eH- 271 n.15
*d^halh$_1$- 271
*d^heh$_1$(i̯)- 137 n.18
*d^herh$_3$- 270
*-esi (2sg.) 260–1, 263
*-eti (3sg.) 260–1, 262, 267
*-eu̯es 149, 153
*geh$_2$u̯- 270 n.13
*ĝelH- 141 n.45
*ĝneh$_3$- 270 n.12
$\hat{g}^h$ag^hu-/$\hat{g}^h$u̯aG$^{(w)}$- 141 n.42
*$\hat{g}^h$-di̯es 141 n.38
*-$\hat{g}^h$i 139
*$\hat{g}^h$o/e- 141 n.38
*g^welh$_1$- 270 n.14, 271
*$g^w\hat{g}^h$er- 137 n.18
*g^wou̯- 141 n.44, 159
*(H)i̯enh$_2$ter- 134, 135, 142–3
*(H)i̯o- 142
*h$_1$eḱu̯o- 145
*h$_1$su- 151
*h$_{2/3}$emh$_3$- 270
*h$_2$i̯u-h$_3$n̥-ḱo- 148
*h$_2$lei̯H- 271 n.15
*h$_2$nēr 145
*h$_2$ōu̯i̯o- 141 n.39
*h$_3$elh$_1$- 271 n.15
*h$_3$rei̯H- 271 n.15
*i̯aḱ- 135 n.5
*i̯eh$_2$- 137
*i̯ek^{w}r̥t 136
*i̯eu̯- 138
*i̯eu̯g- 138
*i̯eu̯H-r- 136–7
*i̯eu̯o- 138
*i̯ugom 136
*kreh$_1$(i̯)- 271 n.15
*ḱemh$_2$- 271
*k^wei- 271
*k^welh$_1$- 271
*k^wetu̯ores 150
*k^wo- 142
*leh$_2$u̯- 152
*lei̯k^w- 136 n.11

Proto-Indo-European (*cont.*)

**lei̯p-* 136
**lei̯s-* 136
**leu̯h_3-tro-* 156
**med^{h}i̯o-* 137 n.18, 145
**-m$h_1$no-* 173 n.17
**-neh_3-mi*, **-neh_1-mi* (1sg.) 269, 274–5
  **-nh_3-mes*, **-nh_1-mes* (1pl.) 269
**-oi* (loc. sg.) 261
**ō(u̯)i̯om*, **ō-h_2u̯i̯-o-* 140
**pei̯H-* 145
**(s)pelH-* 271 n.15
**pelh_1-* 271
**-pók^{w}o-/-pok^{w}ó-* 258
**poró-* 258
**skelh_1-* 271
**sterh_3-* 156, 270
**su-i̯u-* 141
**temh_1-* 271
**teu̯e* 153

Proto-West Germanic

**-dē* (weak past ind.2sg.) 39
**-dē* (weak past ind.3sg.) 39
**-dǭ* (weak past ind.1sg.) 39, 40
**fader* 40
**fewwar* 34, 39
**gat* 37
  **gatu* (pl.) 37
**gebā* 40
**gelu*, **gelwa-* 35
**hari*, **harja-* 35
**hertā* 40
**h^{w}anā* 40
**iwwar* 34
**iwwi* 34
**karu* 37
  **karā* (obl. cases) 37
**kwiku*, **kwik(k)wa-* 35
**lattē* 34
**mati* (inflected forms) 36
**sagi* (inflected forms) 36
**sattē* 34
**singwan* 37
**traddē* 34
**tungā* 40
**watar* 39
**wurdī* 41
**þanā* 40
**þikkwī* 36

Russian

bank 57
kak 135, 142

Sanskrit

akṣaparājayá- 248
akṣára- 232 n.5
agnimindhá- 241
aghahārá- 250
ajá- 238
ajagará- 242, 250
ajára- 232 n.5
ájati 238
atitara- 251
atipārayá- 241
atiyājá- 234 n.11, 235, 253
atisará- 251
adhivāká- 235, 253, 256, 257
adhīvāsá- 235
anuplava- 251, 252
anuyājá- 234 n.11, 248, 253
anuvāká- 248
anuhavá- 248
antarābhará- 237
apavāsá- 249
apaśrayá- 248
abhayaṃkará- 249
abhicārá- 248, 252
abhidrohá- 239
abhimātiṣā́h- 254
  abhimātiṣāhá- 250, 254
abhilāpá- 248
abhihvāré 248

abhiśrāvá- 235
abhisvaré 234
abhyācārá- 248
amitrakhādá- 250
amitrasāhá- 250
ará- 238
araṃgamá- 237
araṃgará- 250
avaśvāsá- 249
ávitāriṇī- 253 n.40
ávya- 184
aśráma-, *aśramá-* 232 n.5
aśvahayá- 236
asthi 127
ā 140
ākará- 237
āgamá- 251
ātapá- 237
ādārá- 234 n.11, 235
ādārín- 234 n.11
ādhavá- 234, 240, 251
-āná- (ptcpl.) 173 n.17
ābhogá- 234 n.9
-ām (gen.) 199
ālāpá- 248
āśārá- 249
āsādá- 249
āsāva- 237
āsrāvá- 249
āhavá- 234, 240, 253, 259
āhávana- 252
āhāvá- 235, 240, 259
inóti 241 n.20
  inváti 241 n.20
indrahavá- 235, 253
indháte 241
ínvati 241
íyarti 238
-iṣṭha- (superlative) 127
ucchvāsá- 235
utsavá- 234, 257
udagrābhá- 236, 242
udameghá- 240
udayá- 234
udáyana- 252
udavāhá- 237, 243 n.26, 254
udúhya 251
udgrābhá- 255
udvahá- 251, 252, 254
upacyavá- 234
upanāyá- 237, 240
upavāká- 235, 248, 253, 257
upaśāká- 237, 240
upaśvasá- 251
upahvará- 234
uru- 255
urukṣayá- 232 n.5
urugrābhá- 250, 255
ṛtavāká- 235, 253
evāvadá- 230, 237, 252
ailabakārá- 249
odanapāká- 246, 250, 258
kará- 238, 240
-kará- 230, 237 n.16, 241, 246 n.32
kācitkará- 249
kārá- 233, 257, 258 n.49
-kārá- 229–30, 254, 256–7
kiṃkará- 249
kiṃcará- 252
kiṃcid 142 n.49
kiráti 237
kucará- 236, 252
kūṭagrāha- 250
kṛ- 257
kṛṇóti 236, 237, 238
kéta- 239
kráma- 247
kṣamá- 251
kṣáya- 231
kṣárati 137 n.18
kṣā́ḥ (nom. sg.) 190 n.17, 199 n.35, 199 n.36
  kṣā́m (acc. sg.) 189, 190 n.15, 190 n.18
kṣīrapāká- 236, 258
kṣudhāmārá- 249, 253

Proto-West Germanic (*cont.*)

khajaṃkará- 236, 241
khādá- 247
khā́dhati 236, 237
gácchati 237
gáya- 231
gā́m (acc. sg.) 189, 190 n.15, 190 n.16
gā́ḥ (acc. pl.) 190 n.15
gā́s 189
gāhá- 233
gā́hate 237
gṛbhāyáti 236
gṛbhṇā́ti 236
gnā́m (acc. sg.) 190 n.15
gnā́ḥ (nom. pl.) 190 n.15
grábhāya 231, 239
grā(b)há- 233, 239, 251, 255–6, 258
-grābhá- 254–5, 256
grāvagrābhá- 236, 255
ghaná- 238, 240
ghāsá- 247
cakā́ra 229
cakramāsajá- 236
cáyate 236
cárati 236
jána- 230, 231
janaṃsahá- 236, 241, 254
jáyati 236
járāya 231
javá- 233, 251, 257
jā́na- 230, 232, 239 n.17
jínvati 241
jiyā́- 197
jīvayājá- 235, 253, 256
joṣavāká- 235, 253
j(i)yók 195–6
jyotiṣkāra- 242, 250
tadvaśá- 236
tápati 237
-tama- (superlative) 173 n.21
tárati 236
tárāya 231
tardá- 238
táva 153
t(u)va- 198
t(u)vā 198
t(u)vát 191–2, 198
t(u)vā́m 190–1, 193, 202
t(u)vé 192–3
tuvi- 255
tuvigrābhá- 236, 255
tuvidyumná- 255
tuvibādhá- 236
tṛṇátti 238
tṛṣṇāmārá- 249, 253
tyāgá- 233
tradá- 238
tvác 203
-tha (2sg. perfect) 127
-thāḥ (2sg. aor. mid.) 127
dadhi- 137 n.18
dábha- 231
dabhnóti 236
dáma- 231 n.4
daráyati 236
-dābhá- 254
dām (1sg.) 190 n.18
dāt (3sg.) 190 n.18
dā́ru- 229
divākará- 249
divikṣayá- 232 n.5
durgáha- 232, 239
durṇáśa- 247
durmáda- 232
duṣṭára- 232
duḥṣáha- 232
dūḍábha- 232
dūṇáśa- 232, 233 n.6, 247
dūṇā́śa- 233
d(i)yaús (paradigm) 183–4, 186–9, 190–1, 192–3, 195, 198, 199–201, 203–4
dyā́vāpṛthivī́ 200, 204
dravá- 238
drávati 238

druhaṃtará- 236
d(u)vā́- 184, 193–4, 198
d(u)vís 197
dhanaṃjayá- 236, 241, 242
dhanvacará- 236
dháyati 137 n.18
dhāravāká- 235 n.14
dhārāvará- 236
dhā́ḥ 190 n.15
dhiyaṃjinvá- 241
dhvajá- 238
nakṣaddābhá- 236
nadá- 238
nadáyati 238
nanā 144
nánāndar- 144
náma- 231
namaskārá- 249
namovāká- 235, 240, 245, 253, 256
náyati 237, 238, 241, 256
nāthá- 247
nādá- 247, 257
nāmagrā(b)há- 249, 255
nāyá- 230, 238, 240, 256
nāvá- 233, 257
nāvājá- 246
nāśáyati 233 n.6
niyut- 138
nirdāhá- 248
nivará- 234, 253
nivāśá- 249
niveśá- 239
pácati 236
panthā́ḥ 127, 129
payas- 145
paraśará- 237
parāvāká- 248
paridrava- 251
parivādá- 248, 252
parivālá- 249, 252 n.38
parihavá- 248
pávate 236
-pākā- 257–8
-pā́ka- 258
pā́t 190 n.15
pāpavādá- 249, 253, 256 n.43
pārá- 233, 234 n.10, 238, 245, 256–7
pāráyati 238, 241
-pāvá- 254
pā́ḥ 190 n.15
pítaḥ 200
pīvan-, *pīvarī-* 145
punaḥsará- 237
puraṃdará- 236
purā́ 188
puru- 255
puṣṭiṃbhará 236
pūṇā́ti 236
pū́ḥ 190 n.15
pṛthivī́ 199–200
pṛthu- 127
pṛthuka- 127
póṣa- 239
praketá- 240
prakhādá- 237, 240
prajavá- 234, 240, 257
práti- 229
pratisará- 251
pratīkāśá- 248
pratīhārá- 249, 256
pratrāsá- 248
prabhavá- 237
pramará- 248, 252, 253
pramārá- 252, 253
prayājá- 234 n.11, 248, 253, 256
pralāpá- 248, 253
pravadá- 251, 252
pravāsá- 235
pravrājá- 235
prasavá- 234, 257
prastará- 248
prātaḥsāvá- 235
priyavādín- 256 n.43
plavá- 238
plávate 238
balihārá- 250, 256

Proto-West Germanic (*cont.*)

bahukārá- 250, 257
bādh- 252
bādhá- 233
bā́dhate 236
brahmakārá- 236, 242, 257 n.46
bhága- 231, 239, 245
bhadravādín- 256 n.43
bhára-/-bhará- 230, 231, 239, 259
bhárasi 260
  bhárati 236, 237, 241, 260
bhávati 237
bhāgá- 233, 234 n.10, 239, 245, 257
bhārá- 233, 239, 243 n.23, 245, 255, 257, 259
-(b)hārá- 254–6
bhuj- 234 n.9
bhuvanacyavá- 250
bhūma- 199 n.35, 199 n.36
bhūmi- 199 n.35
bhū́ribhāra- 254, 256 n.42
bhū́rivāra- 254
bhū́ḥ (2sg.) 190 n.16
  bhū́t (3sg.) 190 n.16
bhramá- 238
bhrámati 238
bhrājá- 251
makṣuṃgamá- 237
máda- 231, 245, 253
mártiya- 183
mahyam 139
mā́ta 200
mā́m 190 n.15
muṣkábhāra- 254
medhākārá- 242, 250
yataṃkará- 236, 241
yábha- 247
yáma- 231
yáva- 138, 247
yávasa- 138
yaśas 135 n.5
yātar- 137, 142–4
yāmá- 234 n.10
yāmi (1sg.) 137
  īmahe (1pl.) 137
yugam 134
yutkārá- 250
yudhiṃgamá- 250
yuváti 138
yuvaśáḥ 148
yūpavāhá- 237, 254
yūyam 134, 135, 139
yóga- 239
yoṣā- 145
yoṣit- 145
ráṇa 231
rátha- 126
rathakārá- 250, 257
ráthakṣaya- 232 n.5
rathaṃtará 236
ráva- 232
rása- 231 n.4
rasahārī- 250
ripravāhá- 250
rujáti 136, 241
vádati 237
vadhá- 238, 246
vára- ('wish') 232, 253
vára- ('space') 232, 253
vará- 238, 240
-vará- 241
valá- 238
valaṃrujá- 241
váśa- 232
vaṣatkārá- 249, 257 n.46
váṣṭi 236
váha- 247
váhati 237, 238, 241, 254, 256
vāká- 233, 257
-vāká- 252 n.38
vā́ja- 232
vājaṃbhará- 236, 240, 241, 254, 259
vājáyati 232
vām 190 n.16
vār, vāri 136–7

vā́ḥ 190 n.15
vā́ra- ('animal hair') 232
vā́ra- ('treasure') 232, 239 n.17, 243 n.23
vāśá- 238
vā́śati 238
vāhá- 238, 240, 246, 247, 254, 256
-vāhá- 241, 254
vikramá- 248
vikrayá- 248
vigāhá- 237, 240
vighasá- 248
vijayá- 248
vinayá- 237, 240 n.19
vipathavāhá- 250
vibādhá- 251
vibhāgá- 234, 257
vimadá- 234, 253
viravá- 248
vivará- 234
vivāhá- 249, 252
viśvaminvá- 241
viśvaṃbhará- 250
visargá- 239
visārá- 235
vihavá- 234, 253
vīríya- 184
vṛṇīté 232, 236, 238
vṛṇóti 232, 234, 238
vṛtaṃcayá- 236, 242
vṛtrakhādá- 236
vṛṣabhará- 242, 250
vettha 127
véda- 239
véśa- 168
vyāyāmé 248
vrātasāhá- 237, 254, 256
śakaṃbhará- 250
śaknóti 237, 238, 256 n.45
śaṅkhá- 126
śatavāhī́- 250
śáṃsa- 239
śárman 249 n.36
śávīra- 157
śā́ka- 232, 256 n.45
śākā́- 237, 238, 240, 256 n.45
śākín- 237
śāktá- 256 n.45
śā́kman- 256 n.45
śā́sa- 232
śāsá- 238, 240, 256
śā́sti 237, 238
śūrpagrāhī́- 250
śṛṇā́ti 237
śṛṇóti 270
śṛtapā́ka- 232, 258
śráma- 232 n.5, 247
śráyate 238
śrāyá- 238
ś(u)van- 198
śvás 197
sájati 236
satrākará- 237
satrāsā́h- 254
  satrāsāhá- 237, 254
samará- 234, 253 n.40
saṃkalpá- 239
saṃkāśá- 248
saṃgamá- 234, 239, 245, 252, 253
saṃgámana- 252
saṃgará- 248
saṃjayá- 251
saṃtāpa- 248
saṃnayá- 230–1, 237, 240, 241
sambhará- 252
sambháraṇa- 252
sambhārá- 248, 252
saṃvādá- 230–1, 234–5, 239, 245, 252, 253
saṃsravá- 234, 252
saṃsrāvá- 249, 252
sárga- 239
sarvaśāsá- 237, 256
savá- ('impelling') 233, 257
savá- ('pressing') 233, 257
sahacārá- 248, 252
sáhate 236, 237, 238, 254

Proto-West Germanic (*cont.*)

sáhati 256
sahasrapoṣá- 240
sahasrambharā- 236, 241
sahasrasāvá- 235, 240
sādá- 233
sāvá- 247
sāhá- 238, 240, 256
-sāhá- 254
siyā́m (1sg. opt.) 197
siyā́t (3sg. opt.) 198
siṣárti 237
sukára- 232
sutambharā- 236, 242
sutára- 232
sunóti 237
supārá- 234 n.10, 256
subhága- 233
subhára- 233, 239, 245
subhāgá- 234 n.10
suyáma- 233
suyāmá- 234
suśáka- 239, 247
suṣáda- 233
suṣána- 233
suṣáha- 232
suhána- 233
suháva- 233
sūktavāká- 249
sū́r(i)yam 196 n.31
skhálate 126
stáva- 232
sthag- 127
sthā- 127, 129
snā́van- 136 n.11
sphātikāra- 250
sphātihārī- 250
sphārá 126
s(i)yá-/t(i)yá- 194–5, 201–2
srukkārá- 249
s(u)vá- (paradigm) 196–7, 198
svadhākārá- 249
svanáyati 238
svāná- 233, 238, 257
svārá- 233, 257
svāhākārá- 249
hanugrābha- 250, 255
hánti 238
harimbharā- 250
háva- 232
havyavā́h- 254
havyavāhá- 250, 254
hása- 247, 251
hásāya 247
haskārá- 235, 256
hastagrābhá- 250
-hārá- 254–5
-hārī́- 255
hinóti 236
háyantā (ptcpl.) 236
hiṃkārá- 249
hiraṇyapāvá- 236, 256 n.44
h(i)yaḥ 141 n.38, 197
hvārá- 234

Serbian

jaje 140

Spanish

higado 136 n.11
juvizio 154

Tocharian

kupre(ne) (A), *kwri* (B) 142 n.49
yāṣtär (B) 137
wär (A), *war* (B) 137
se (A), *soy* (B) 141

Welsh

Old Welsh
dou 149, 153
-ou (nom. pl.) 149, 153

Middle Welsh

baw 159 n.20
brawd 156
caur 157
cawad 149–50, 152, 153, 155–7
  cafod 149 n.7, 155 n.17
  cawod 155 n.17, 156
cigleu 153
clo 156
cneu 148 n.3, 159
cneuen 148 n.3
creu 153
cuan 149, 150, 155 n.18, 159
deu 149, 153
dryw 149, 159
-eu (nom. pl.) 149, 153
golud 152
hu- 150–2, 159
huynys 151, 152 n.12
huyscein 152
hy- 151–2
hyys 151–2
huan 147, 149, 150–1, 155, 157
ieu 149 n.6
ieuanc 151
  i(e)fanc 149 n.7
ieuhaf 151 n.10
iwrch 144
kneu 153
llawen 149, 152, 157, 159
llawer 147, 152
llyw 149
pedwar 150, 156
  pedwor 156
teu 147, 153

Modern Welsh

-au (nom. pl.) 149, 153
cawr 157
Cernyw 149 n.6
cnau 153
crau 153
cuan 149, 150
cystrawen 153–4
dau 149, 153
huan 149, 150–1
Iau 149 n.6
odi 155 n.17
rhewin 153–4
tau 153

Printed and bound by CPI Group (UK) Ltd, Croydon, CR0 4YY